The Later

EGO

James Agate

The Later
EGO

CONSISTING OF EGO 8 AND EGO 9

INTRODUCTION AND NOTES BY

JACQUES BARZUN

Crown Publishers, Inc. · *New York*

CONTENTS

AGATE AND HIS NINE EGOS

"WHO IS James Agate?" asked the eminent critic Sir Edmund Gosse some twenty years ago. Given the circumstances, the question was inexcusable—it was just one of Gosse's ways of being eminent—for at that time both men were on the staff of the London *Sunday Times*, Gosse as chief book reviewer, Agate as chief drama critic.

But American readers today may be pardoned for asking the same question, since the fame of dramatic critics, especially the recently dead, does not carry across the ocean. Students of the theater everywhere are no doubt familiar with Agate's biography of Rachel the actress, and with the collections he made of his own and other critics' writings. He himself was well known to his American colleagues, notably George Jean Nathan and John Mason Brown, but with the exception of a few articles here and there—in newspapers and anthologies—he may be said to have remained, for our insular purposes, unpublished and unread.

In time his best writing is bound to emerge, for he was a superior craftsman and dealt with subjects of perennial interest, but there would be small reason to discuss him now if during the last fifteen years of his life, that is to say from 1932 to 1947, he had not produced an extraordinary piece of work, unique in form, though not in kind, which is a storehouse of varied pleasures for the general educated reader. It has won him thousands of devotees throughout what used to be conveniently known as the British Empire, and it is sure to carry his name—exactly as he hoped—to whatever posterity the world may yet enjoy. Of the work I refer to, Agate's autobiographical diary in nine volumes called *Ego*, the reader has the two concluding installments before him.

Do not throw up your hands in feigned horror: nine volumes! Life is short, I know, and one's own life demonstrably shorter than Agate's seems to be. But in the lively chronicle which follows you will not hear the drone of a single voice; you will not exclusively retrace the fortunes of one man nor live by proxy within a limited circle of contemporary Englishmen. Far from it. You will not even keep to one set of subjects, all intellectual, but will range freely through space and time and human activity. Food and the footlights and the screen take their turn with golf and motorcars and music. Literature and choice gossip alternate with bilingual puns and portraits of celebrities—live, dead, dying. The recorder joints these with his own changing vision of himself to form the mosaic of each year-long chapter. Dip in anywhere:

> Sacheverell Sitwell has written a book about Mozart in which he said silly things about Wagner. Ernest Newman ripped the bowels out of Sacheverell, who wrote of Wagner's "vulgar, tweed-clad tunes." Osbert tried to defend his brother, and I had not the courage of my true conviction, which is that both brothers are artists who enjoy pretending to be asses. Osbert talked all the time and I never got a word in edgeways. I don't dislike him, though I understand why some people may. There is something self-satisfied and having-to-do-with-the-Bourbons about him which is annoying, though there is also something of the crowned-head consciousness which is disarming.

Or if you prefer dialogue:

> Am afraid I was rude to H. G. Wells last night. It was at the Cafe Royal and Wells, sitting at a nearby table, shouted in his loudest whisper that he had just come from *The Devil's Disciple,* and how much better it was than any film.
>
> J. A.: I don't agree. *Northwest Passage* isn't a work of art. But it brings your heart into your mouth and keeps it there.
>
> H. G.: Ah, well, I don't know what a work of art is.
>
> J. A.: Oh, yes, you do. But never mind that. Why praise one kind of good thing at the expense of another kind of good thing?
>
> H. G.: I stand corrected.

And again there is correspondence, almost never one-sided and often pleasantly extravagant, as the letters of warm friends should be:

> Dear Cardus:—*Re* your *Ten Composers.* Have corrected your spelling. Also your Italian, German, French, and occasionally your English. Have put your French accents right. Have emended your quotations. . . . Titivated your titles. In places made the clumsy felicitous. Verified your keys. Rationalized your punctuation. . . . Have elected for "Newman" *tout court,* as I can't make out whether it's the Cardinal or the critic of the *Sunday Times* who "often quotes Coleridge with affection and point." In short, I have put this entrancing book right in all matters of fact and left only its errors of taste and judgment.

No collection of samples will exhaust the variety of genres and moods which Agate makes use of. One can only say that nine volumes of this ideal bedside reading are none too many. Nor does the series as a whole leave an impression of feckless meandering. A design has been traced; inspired by the *Journals* of Arnold Bennett, those of Agate easily surpass them in richness and sense of form. Together they span fifty years of English civilization, but *Ego* is the more animated portrait of an era; it is in fact a kind of vast *roman à clef* of which the key is not hidden.

In the midst of his populous circle sits James Agate, a watchful host, or rather an unceremonious master of ceremonies, who takes care not to bore his reader-guest by too long a course of any one subject. A seasoned journalist, who worked for at least three grades of subscribers, he is adept at making every topic he touches attract every type of duffer. To me, for example, cricket and golf spell only my invincible ignorance, yet I can read with at least a primitive pleasure what Agate says of his favorite sports. He also loved to breed and show hackney horses, and he makes us share his devotion to the stables as if we were all Houyhnhnms together.

When it comes to literature and the arts, Agate invariably displays the passion of the true critic with its attendant zest for intellectual debate: he always knows what the other side is saying. He knows, moreover, how to temper insistence by a masterly use of quotation. We hear him repeatedly on *Macbeth*, about which he is truly admirable, but Hazlitt follows as prop or amendment. Agate propounds the greatness of Bernhardt and Irving, but the opposition speaks through Shaw or Max Beerbohm. At other times he peppers his pot with the adverse judgments of others upon his own opinions and character, and then defends himself with toughness and vehemence. It is a fine spectacle in these tedious days of superficial fraternity. We cheer his hits as much as we envy his poise, and the result, contrary to the French maxim, is that the Ego is not hateful but lovable.

In time we come to know the diarist as nearly as possible *au naturel*, for his rule, Never to Embellish, he observed even to his detriment. Outwardly a self-made man like Shaw, he was as fully aware as Shaw of what had gone into the making. James Evershed Agate (which, by the way, is pronounced Ay' git) was born in Lancashire in 1877, an unwilling heir to the calico trade. His father was a mill owner and James, the eldest of six children, stuck to the business for a good many years. But it was honestly that he came by his other aspirations: Manchester in the eighties was a center not solely of cotton spinning but also of art, especially music, and Agate's father took him to the Hallé Orchestra from the age of seven. Agate's mother, who had been reared in Heidelberg and Paris and had learned music on a piano once owned by Chopin, taught her son the instrument and made him a master of French.

This childhood acquirement explains Agate's feeling of freedom in quoting from Balzac and other French writers in the original: the diarist is not showing off. The reader who cannot follow him will skip—and may swear—but must not feel snubbed.

All the Agate children developed artistic interests, and we are lucky to have five of them on show in the pages of James's book. The one sister, May, became an actress and wrote from firsthand knowledge an excellent book on Sarah Bernhardt. The brothers Gustave ("Brother Mycroft"), Edward and Harry have each his special branch and tone of voice, Edward predominating as savant, satirist and composer—a proudly impecunious foil to the worldly James.

Though he was over forty when his career took shape, James was the only one to achieve real power—by which I mean not merely the power of recognized authority, but that of habitual command over his medium. Both kinds he undoubtedly owes to a trait that some may be inclined to call vulgarity. If this is correct, it is a vulgarity devoutly to be wished. In an age when many intellectuals think they owe it to themselves to be delicate, tentative and easily bruised, Agate is content to be downright, full of knowledge and underidable. His apparent complacency is simply strength. He likes Shakespeare with the same fervor and the same acute organs with which he likes wine and horses; he is at home in life and lets you know that the best of life is meant for him. Nor does his love of literature serve him as protection against a low opinion of himself, for he did not have to climb into the possession of cultivated tastes; he has no philistine memories to palliate with "sensitivity."

As late as 1920 he was keeping a shop in London, but his early acquaintance with genuine artists gave him the familiarity that breeds contempt of make-believe. Indeed, Agate carries this impatience to the point of being unjust to Bloomsbury and its intellectual mulch. He is temperamentally an anti-modernist. But for the same reason he is also free from the guilty modern wish to foist "high" tastes upon others. Although he was the first English critic to take the movies seriously (in an article of 1921 on Charlie Chaplin), he rejects the common excuse for distorting great novels and plays on the screen: "Is it to popularize Shakespeare? But with me he is already popular." Agate steadily fights the high-brow attempts to ram culture down the throats of the people; he knows it can only bastardize culture and the people, too. Yet in this he is just the reverse of snobbish: he respects the ordinary man's desire for better pubs and cheaper boxing and vaudeville, and he recognizes their priority over a National Shakespeare Theater. Not so the welfare state, which tends to be tyrannical; wherefore during the second World War Agate had to campaign so that the troops on leave might be given gay musicals instead of *Oedipus Rex* played by the Old Vic.

But make no mistake: as the stir of this humane endeavor dies down you hear Agate inveighing against a great many things generally deemed democratic and popular, such as slovenly manners and the sham education that produces commonness. Of a young woman bred on modern literacy, movies and crooners he says with certitude: "Explore her mind to its inmost crannies and you will find nothing there but curiosity about the latest hair dye."

Agate knows how much effort and steadiness are needed to develop even a marked bent toward intellectual occupations. Despite his early advantages he found he must subject himself to the stiffest discipline in order to make and keep his place as a critic. By dint of hard work after business hours he forged a technique and style that he could rely on, besides learning the history of the theater, of actors and acting, and of British and French dramatic criticism. It is from experience that he draws his definition of a professional: "A man who can do his job when he doesn't feel like it."

Agate served seven years' apprenticeship on the *Manchester Guardian*, then after army duty in France until 1918 tackled London without influence and persuaded the *Saturday Review* to let him write its drama column. Two years later he had a call to the *Sunday Times*, and afterwards subdued *The Tatler* into accepting him as film critic and *The Daily Express* as book reviewer. For virtuosity's sake he took on the job of broadcasting theatrical comments for the BBC, and he wound up as literary consultant for British M-G-M.

As if this were not enough, we soon see Agate becoming a popular lecturer, in especial demand as an after-dinner speaker. He next assumes the role of universal godfather to the ambitious young in acting, writing and making music; and he finally blossoms out as autobiographer and diarist. The writing of a few novels and the preparation of some two dozen anthologies helped fill in the leisure not taken up by golf and horses. One wonders when he found time to attend the theater.

Like Balzac and Trollope, Agate was justly proud of his powers of work. He measures and reports his annual output like an industrial nation. But he does not write in order to break records and he does not scamp. To him writing must exhaust meaning while invigorating the reader, a task which is doubly difficult when one wants to introduce uncommon facts or ideas into the rigidly guarded mind of the newspaper addict.

This never came easy. Agate might exclaim, "What fun words are!" but every play notice cost him blood. He goes at it four or five times, leaves the copy with his editor; then in the middle of dinner thinks of a better beginning or ending, rushes back to retrieve the proof—only to find that the editor (who boasts of being able, if required, to cut the Lord's Prayer) wants three hundred words taken out. *Ego* reproduces several dozen of these short articles. They are without exception terse, free from stumbles in sense, and original in a way that one comes to think of as Agatian. The writer's style is of that excellent kind which sounds like a man speaking. We are sure that its simplicity is genuine when we compare the play reviews and the letters. Here, for example, is Agate answering a friend who had asked about Olivier's *King Lear*:

> I thought Olivier began extraordinarily well, with just the right amount of testiness. A magnificent head, and everything royal about him. The whole subsequent performance brilliantly imagined and achieved. Mind working all the time and making one see things one had not previously noticed. For example, in the "loop'd and window'd raggedness" speech, at the line "O I have ta' en too little care of this!" one sensed an unclouding of the mind and a return to the responsibilities of kingship. Yes, any amount of subtlety and intellectual appeal. But was I moved? Not so much as I ought to have been. Was it because of the echoes of the same actor's Justice Shallow? And shouldn't Olivier, knowing he was going to tackle the big thing, have let the lesser one alone?
>
> . . . The actor chipped off every bit of the character—but took me out of my critical self not more than three times—in the "Terrors of the earth" speech, in the second half of the mad scene, and from the entrance with the body of Cordelia to the end. . . . Do you want it in a nutshell? Wolfit's Lear is a ruined piece of nature; Olivier's is a picture of ruins most cunningly presented.

Supply a couple of verbs in the opening sentences and this might be part of Agate's first-night report in the *Sunday Times*. His critical prose is perhaps not capable of conveying the highest originality or fineness of perception. It lacks the poetic contraction of Hazlitt, the sinewy embrace of Shaw; but like Hazlitt and Shaw it has tactical vigor and consecutiveness—none of your newspaperish maunderings which leave the reader in doubt whether any two paragraphs are really by the same man or alternately by Philip drunk and Philip sober. Agate's criticism has all the businesslike qualities which are so rare in businessmen, and of which Walter Bagehot deplored the absence in writers generally: "So few people that can write know anything . . . an author has always lived in a room, has read books

. . . but he is out of the way of employing his own eyes and ears."
Agate at his best was all eyes and ears, and he never forgot that he was
paid not simply to express but to *make up* his mind.

Besides the discovery of a formidable character, the reward of
reading the three thousand pages of *Ego* is the acquisition of a new
set of friends, inexpensive to maintain and not likely to be troublesome.
They are mostly actors, playwrights, painters, musicians and journalists, but there is also a sprinkling of semilunatics and peers of the
realm. And unlike the tight-lipped visions in Arnold Bennett's
Journal, Agate's friends talk.

There is Mrs. Patrick Campbell, for instance, listening to a bore
in full spate about the marvelous social organization of the ants—
their police force and their army. Mrs. Campbell leans forward and
with grave voice and mien interrupts: "No navy, I suppose?" Another
time, Agate compliments the charming, elderly Lady Tree on her
beautiful hair, and she gaily acknowledges: "How perfectly sweet of
you to call it mine!" Or again, he is in a restaurant with an aging
beauty, and as she reads the menu at arm's length, a catty friend
suggests that she should really reconcile herself to wearing glasses.
The retort flashes back: "There's nothing wrong with my eyes; it's
just that my arm isn't long enough!"

The conversation is often by letter, pursued for many months on
topics certain to outlast the writers. Thus Agate argues with J. B.
Priestley about immortality, with Charles Morgan about the mystical
experience, with John Gielgud about *King Lear*, and with all his
friends about his diary. All of them want something put in or left
out. It is a lesson in criticism and in human vanity to see what incurable whittlers intelligent people are. Still, this helps us to measure
Agate's mind through its inclusiveness. His brother Edward says of
him, in a sweeping untruth: "His income and his intestines fill his
whole life," but that very quotation makes it clear that somewhere
between income and intestines brother James finds a place for enshrin-
ing Edward's rare quality of mind.

Similarly we find full delineations—often self-portraits—of the
inimitable Scotsman, Alan Dent, text editor of the *Henry V* and
Hamlet films and dramatic critic of the *News-Chronicle*; of Leo Pavia,
a cantankerous musician and wit; of George Lyttelton, an Eton
scholar; of Montague Shearman, traveler, jurist and sportsman. And
more than once we meet—among many others—Noel Coward and
Cedric Hardwicke, Margot Asquith, Rebecca West, Mark Hambourg,
Sybil Thorndike, Alfred Douglas, Constant Lambert, Charles Laugh-

ton, Christopher Fry, Vivien Leigh, Laurence Olivier, George Moore, Maurice Baring and Bernard Shaw.

Before we tire of the moderns we are transported backward into the company of Lamb and Dickens, Balzac and Shakespeare. Through Agate's early acquaintance with the far-flung García family, we draw on a whole century of bygone music and theater; our diarist's delving into obscure corners of literature supplies the rest: he makes Kean, whom he never saw, as actual as Irving, whom he did see. He has a passion for saving from oblivion all that is curious or great, and he does this with a scholarly skill free from antiquarianism. A taster of prose, he is full of the poets and even exhibits himself in light verse.

More, he rescues the casual human document on its way from the mailbag to the wastebasket, and for good measure gives us an occasional fiction—sometimes a series of plots in the manner of Villiers de l'Isle Adam. At other times, he prints his friend Pavia's letters from a group of imaginary German artists in London—a little masterpiece of parody, of which the unfortunate sequel, "Sacharissa," in the present volumes, gives no idea whatever.

As these figures on different planes of existence enter, return, marry, become successful or die, and as Agate moves from one milieu' to another, one is forcibly reminded of Johnson and his circle. Agate Boswellized quite consciously. That is why *Ego* is so full of verbatim conversations, of luncheons, trips and evenings at the Club. But although he takes both roles, Agate is more a Johnson than a Boswell. He and the great Doctor are linked by their unfaltering common sense, and distinguished from their entourage by the speed and force with which they utter it. That common sense is uncommon is a platitude without ceasing to be a paradox. Agate's talk and behavior help us to solve the paradox by suggesting that common sense is chiefly integrity plus energy; it is the ability and the will to sort out the relevant from the muck of the plausible which convention automatically piles up around all things. Sticking to the point like Agate will make you fadproof like him. But it may prove dull business for others unless you also cut and thrust like him:

It was a dire day for the pictures when Hitchcock or somebody discovered that a woman screaming emits the same sound as a train entering a tunnel. Fusion became the rage, what began as woman ended as tunnel, and why she was screaming or who was in the train ceased to matter. It is this kind of thing which makes our highbrow critics hail *King's Row* as a masterpiece.

Again, in the more difficult situation of justifying himself and his work, see him clear his friends' minds of cant; they had vainly expected in 1940 that in the face of the "emergency" he would discontinue *Ego:* " 'It means that you regard your Diary as more important than the war?' I said: 'Well, isn't it? The war is vital, not important. . . . Because I am suddenly stricken with cancer, must cancer become my whole world? . . . Cancer has become vital to me, but not important; except in so far as I am a coward, it does not fill my mind.' "

There was, of course, no question of Agate's enlisting—age and bad health alike made him useless, except that with his usual buoyancy he gave speeches to entertain the troops, corresponded with strangers in the forces, and provided them with free books. But friends are a tenacious tribe, and the suggestion was made that *Ego* should record public instead of private events. Agate retorts by illustrating the inanity of setting down rumors and uninformed speculations which a few more days will render absurd. He concludes:

> In a hundred years, when my great toe began to ache and when it stopped aching will be of more interest to anybody coming fresh to this Diary than the peace terms. It will be news; they will be merely history.

Needless to say, *Ego* tells us nothing of Agate's toes. We are given just enough about his health and spirits to feel a living body behind the sentences and to recognize other grounds of likeness to Johnson. Agate, burdened with asthma, loathed death, was subject to sudden causeless fears, and shared the neurotic compulsion to touch or count objects in a certain order. But apart from this, what sanity and good humor! His favorite phrase is "Let's face it!" The words introduce no truisms but either a listing of his own shortcomings or else propositions one would not expect from so British a bloke. For instance, he reads anthropology and learns that man's brain has remained unchanged in 250,000 years: "Nonsense! I do not believe that prehistoric man was the colossal idiot that his successor has demonstrably become."

For in spite of the champagne and the wit and the love of life, Agate faces the truth of his own time and class. As Rebecca West rightly said in reviewing one of the *Egos*, "The sense of doom beats behind the frivolity like a majestic theme in the bass." It is perhaps symbolic that Agate was a lavish spender who died insolvent. Certainly his handling of the theme of money, like Balzac's, captivates the imagination. He catches up with his debts just long enough to note down the miracle, and off we are again with the hounds of income tax at heel. This imparts an element of chase and suspense we had really no right to expect from one methodical enough to keep a diary.

Like all good historians, Agate understood his time because he also lived by another clock. He belonged in heart to the high nineteenth century from which he so aptly quoted, and it is by having a foot in each era that his stature as diarist transcends the accepted standard of the genre. To me he outranks Pepys—a fair parallel, even to the presence of a Great Fire of London at the center of each recorder's work. Agate himself would not have it so:

Total Stranger: Do you hold yourself to be a first-rate diarist?
James Agate: I most emphatically do.
T. S.: To be ranked with Pepys?
J. A.: To take my place beside Pepys.

The judicious reader will no doubt reserve judgment, and at this point neither agree with Agate nor side with me nor defy us both. For one thing, he will want to read *Ego* entire before comparing it with Pepys's great work. But even now a prediction can safely be made, which is that by the end of this first sample, the reader will have ceased to hold, as regards Agate, the unenviable position of Total Stranger.

New York, March 1, 1951   JACQUES BARZUN

Jan. 1   My American friend, Sergeant Thomas Quinn Curtiss,
Monday.   saw the New Year in with me.   After which we called on
            Elliot Mason, who lives above.   Jolly party, *and nothing
said about the theatre.*

My mail :

Card from Brother Mycroft.   This is a reproduction of the
seventeenth-century painter Bloemaert's " St John Preaching."   Can
the twentieth-century artist do as movingly *in his period* ?   I don't
believe it.   I am thinking of Stanley Spencer's picture of a doll-like
Hitler, with a moustache which has obviously come off one of the
spectators' dresses, separating a couple of fighting swans.

New Year cards from George Robey, Gillie Potter, Sid Field,
Tod Slaughter, Frances Day, Naughton and Gold.

Diatribe from Spalding, beginning :

MY DEAR JAMES AGATE,
I have read many articles by you on books, films, and plays.   I
cannot remember one substantial thing you have ever said, but I
can recall many instances when you were guilty of writing the
greatest nonsense.   I have disliked you fairly intensely for about
twelve years—for your well-fed complacency and jangling wit, for
the utterly mercenary way in which you have maintained your
reputation as a critic, and for your medieval conception of butchers
and plumbers concentrating exclusively on plumbing and butcher-
ing, and not taking it upon themselves to practise as poets and
playwrights.   I recently returned from Burma, to find your articles
still prominently featured in the *Express*—damn' great headlines
vulgar as hell, and nasty little Agatean elves pottering up and down
the columns. . . .

A great deal of abuse follows, and suddenly I read :

Why do you and I love horses ?   Because their necks are
" clothed with thunder," and because the hindquarters of a good-
class Hackney are as noble a work of art as anything you will find
in the animal or vegetable kingdoms.

Letter from Kensington : " In this war, as in the last, many a
man carried Shakespeare in the pocket of his tunic, others perhaps
the Bible, and I heard of a case where a man was found in a rubber

dinghy with a copy of *Ego* 5. Unfortunately he was dead when found. . . ." Am pondering the implications of this when Jock walks in with a paper-bound, unrevised proof of *Specimens of English Dramatic Criticism : XVIIth–XXth Centuries,* presently to be published by the Oxford University Press in the World's Classics series. He points out that on pages 304 and 306 my article on Edith Evans in *The Way of the World* is attributed to Hubert Griffith ! I am getting het-up about this when he tells me he 'phoned the publishers, and was in time.

My one and only New Year resolution : to cultivate equanimity. Rupert Brooke's " And that unhoped serene that men call age " is one thing. Unhoped excitability is a very different thing. I know all about nerves-cum-wind. Nerves-minus-wind is something I don't understand and don't like. To ask the chemist for minestrone when I mean riddobron ; to be furious because the horse in Sir George White's statue in Portland Place is looking to his left instead of to his front ; to want my own way about everything, and when I don't get it yell like a baby—all this argues either brain-fag or the approach of second childhood. Here, then, is my New Year resolution : TO DO THE WORK OF TWO MEN INSTEAD OF THREE. (Leo insists on typing " the work of two men instead of *one* " !) I am determined that my equableness shall have an active as well as a passive side. Recently I read Cecil Day Lewis's *Poetry for You,* written to explain poetry to boys and girls. In the course of this he praises some lines by Spender :

> More beautiful and soft than any moth
> With burring furred antennæ feeling its huge path
> Through dusk, the air-liner with shut-off engines
> Glides over suburbs . . .

I am determined to go about the flat murmuring this, and to believe that modern youth gets the same thrill that I did when, as a fourteen-year-old, I read how the lover in *Maud*

> . . . arose, and all by myself in my own dark garden ground,
> Listening now to the tide in its broad-flung shipwrecking roar,
> Now to the scream of a madden'd beach dragg'd down by the wave,
> Walk'd in a wintry wind by a ghastly glimmer, and found
> The shining daffodil dead, and Orion low in his grave.

To equanimity and equableness I am resolved to add whatever may be the opposite of umbrage, and to be unpeeved because Richard Church in his broadcast review of the books of 1944 makes no mention of *Ego* 6. Pavia says, " Cheer up, James. Do you suppose that in 1865 Wagner would have heard one word about *Tristan* ? Not on your life. Auber, Gounod, Verdi, yes, but . . ."

In the meantime here is No. 1 of my new series, to be entitled *Cocasseries*. (**Cocasse**, *adj.*, *pop.* : Plaisant, ridicule.)

Conversation at the Café Royal :

YOUNG BLOOMSBURYITE. To tell you the truth, I'm blaze about the theatre.
J. A. Come, that's interesting. One of our intellectuals on fire about the theatre. My dear fellow, that's very, very reassuring.
Y. B. (*coldly*). You don't get it. I'm *blaze* about the theatre. Fed-up. French, you know.

Jan. 2   Anatole France used to write in ladies' albums : " What
Tuesday.   is the good of your forgetting me, dear lady, since I shall
            ever remember you ? " How, even if I want, shall I
forget Sarah, others ever and ever reminding me ? Esmé Percy sends
me a *carte postale* of S. as Phèdre addressing a human bundle. On
the reverse side I find in Esmé's best French :

Qui est celle à genoux ? Est-ce Seylor ? Non ! Est-ce
Dufrène ? Non ! Non ! C'est le théâtre entier à genoux.

ESMÉ

My own view is that it is Œnone, Phèdre's " nourrice et confidente," having the famous " C'est toi qui l'as nommé ! " hurled at her.
By the same post arrives this from Maurice Baring :

Beaufort Castle
Beauly
Inverness

29.12.44

DEAR J. A.,
It took me a year to get *Ego* 6, and a little more than a day to read it. It Oliver Twisted me.
P. 125. I am puzzled about *Le Sphinx*. I thought it was one of the plays included in the repertory of the Comédie Française, which the management of the Gaiety Theatre announced in a little pamphlet before the season opened in London in 1879. I possess or used to possess this pamphlet ; I think it escaped blitzing and is stored. Some of the " fixtures " were cancelled or altered owing to the furore which Sarah aroused and the temperamental tantrums in which she indulged. But I thought *Le Sphinx* (a play which I never saw, but which I afterwards read) was a drawing-room drama by Octave Feuillet, with some poison in it, in which S. was cast for second fiddle to Croizette and as usual made the second fiddle more important than the first. But I may be mixing it up with another play. I also have a vague recollection of reading that one of the two, S. or C., made a sensation by turning green under the effects of

poison in the death scene. This was in Paris. If I am right and the play is by Feuillet it would be frightfully interesting to get hold of the 1882 cast and see which fiddle Sarah chose when she was free of the trammels of the Comédie.

Happy New Year. Good Luck to *Ego* 7.

Yours,
M. BARING

Am replying :

Le Sphinx is by Octave Feuillet, and all I know about it is that the third act takes place in a clearing in a forest. Here is Sarah on another piece by Feuillet produced the previous year. This was called *Dalila*.

" Perrin fit la plus cocasse des distributions : il me donna le rôle de Dalila, la méchante brune et féroce princesse, et donna à Sophie Croizette la blonde et idéale jeune fille mourante.

" La pièce culbuta sous cette étrange distribution. Je forçai ma nature pour paraître l'altière et voluptueuse sirène ; je bourrai mon corsage d'ouate et les hanches de ma jupe avec du crin ; mais je gardai mon petit facies maigre et douloureux.

" Croizette fut obligée de comprimer les avantages de son buste, sous la pression de bandes qui l'oppressaient et l'étouffaient ; mais elle garda sa jolie figure pleine aux jolies fossettes.

" Je fus obligée de grossir ma voix, elle d'éteindre la sienne. Enfin c'était absurde."

Sarah goes on to say how two clans quickly formed themselves— the Croizettistes and the Bernhardtistes. The first was composed of " banquiers et tous les congestionnés." As for the second, S. writes : " J'avais pour moi tous les artistes, les étudiants, les mourants, et les ratés." I don't think S. has ever been given enough credit for her sense of humour.

Jan. 3
Wednesday.

From a letter :

I am stationed in Uttoxeter. How applicable is the G.I.'s description of Bedford—a cemetery with traffic lights. Except that there are no traffic lights in Uttoxeter ! . . . Your various *Ego's* remind me of a woman I was friendly with some years ago. If I had agreed with her for five consecutive minutes, or if she had done anything expected of her, I should have been bored.

Jan. 4
Thursday.

Dipping into Emil Ludwig's *Beethoven : the Life of a Conqueror*, I find this on the G major Piano Concerto :

At the beginning the piano emerges gently from dreams ; this is truly Beethoven improvising. Two romantic themes, renuncia- tion and hope, are gradually developed. When, after an orchestral

10

interlude, the piano is heard again solo, it is as if a butterfly rose ecstatically from its cocoon. There are no fortissimos here, and when the call to new adventures sounds, the butterfly sinks back, dreaming. The whole thing is wrapped in dark-red velvet. . . .

And about the C minor Concerto, that it begins with

stormy scale passages three octaves long, like a roaring lion appearing suddenly with threatening mien in the midst of the orchestra.

I have nothing with all this stuff about cocoons, red velvet, and roaring lions. Presently I read, " Beethoven dedicated his adagios to women." And I say that the man who can read sex into the slow movements of the Hammerklavier Sonata and the Ninth Symphony would believe that Wagner's Venusberg music is a Hymn to Chastity ! Next I read that in the F major Rasoumowsky Quartet " the 'cello continues to exude platonic wisdom." Feeling that this amateur has exuded enough nonsense, I open the window and neatly drop his book on to a passing lorry's tarpaulin'd top.

Jan. 5   In a letter from George Lyttelton :
Friday.

I am glad to see you are or have been in *Martin Chuzzlewit*—my favourite of the whole lot. How the Yanks ever forgave it I can't imagine. " When our people's frills is out they're starched up pretty stiff." But I shudder to think what the effect will be " on what we call our feelings " or rather your feelings, when with the most tedious pedantry I take my pen and change " Toopit " in your letter to " Toppit " !

Whereupon I drop everything to write :

Queen Alexandra Mansions, W.C.2
January 5th, 1945

DEAR GEORGE LYTTELTON,
Have we started something ? You elect for " Toppit." In this you are in agreement with the *Dickens Encyclopædia*. Also with the Everyman edition. On the other hand, the Memorial edition published by Chapman and Hall prefers an extra " t " so that the name becomes " Toppitt." As against these the Imperial Edition published by the Gresham Publishing Company has " Toopit." I am inclined to agree with the last. Miss Codger was the lady who wore on her forehead " a massive cameo, in size and shape like the raspberry tart which is ordinarily sold for a penny, representing on its front the Capitol at Washington." It was Miss Toopit who held that " Mind and matter glide swift into the vortex of immensity." About this lady we are told only that she " wore a brown wig of uncommon size." Isn't it reasonable to suppose a connection

11

between " Toopit " and " toupet " ?   Dickens is full of evocative names — Barnacle, Cheeryble, Mutanhed, Snuphanuph, Turvey-drop, Veneering, Verisopht.   No, if " Toopit " is a printer's error I shall maintain that for once the printer erred on the right side. You might let me know your views.

No more for now.

Ever,

JAMES AGATE

Jan. 6   A lady has sent me four volumes of *The London Stage*,
Saturday.   published in 1824–27 and containing close on two hundred " of the most reputed Tragedies, Comedies, Operas, Melo-Dramas, Farces and Interludes, as performed at the Theatres Royal."   A wonderful mine which I have spent most of the day skimming—and that is as good English as some of these old playwrights use.   They seem to have had no sense of bathos.   Thus, in Arthur Murphy's tragedy, *The Orphan of China*, Etan, entering from the tomb, says :

> Each step I move,
> A deeper horror sits on all the tombs ;
> The shrines look pale around ;   each altar shakes,
> *Conscious of some important crisis.*

Infelicities abound, as when, in Southerne's play, Oroonoko says :

> I marry'd her :   and, though my country's custom
> Indulg'd the privilege of many wives,
> I swore myself never to know but her.
> O, my Imoinda !   *But it could not last.*

Plagiarism, it seems, was rife, even Congreve stooping to it.   Almeria, in *The Mourning Bride*, mistaking the body of Zara, who has drunk poison, for that of Alphonso, alias Osmyn, says :

> Oh !   noble thirst !   yet greedy, to drink all.

Congreve, of all people, must have known that he was filching Juliet's

> O churl !   drunk all, and left no friendly drop
> To help me after ?

and ruining it.

Continuing to dip, I discover the original of the two lines quoted by John Thurtell in his speech in his own defence at the end of his trial for the murder of William Weare.   *The Newgate Calendar* gives the lines as

> The flesh will quiver where the pincers tear,
> The blood will follow where the knife is driven.

They are from Edward Young's *The Revenge*, and Thurtell in his agitation got them in the wrong order.

Again to G. L. :

Queen Alexandra Mansions, W.C.2

January 7th, 1945

DEAR GEORGE LYTTELTON,

Your last letter and a mishap in to-day's *S.T.* have combined to tell me that I am the first sufferer from Agate's disease, or proof-reader's eye. The *S.T.* ? Simply that I am made to say : " The real reason I want to see this play [*Venice Preserved*] for myself is that I want to decide whether it is or is not nonsense." You realise that " for myself " should come after the word " decide." The trouble is my old friend Leo, who has developed Pavia's disease, or transpositional mania.

Going back to my own trouble, I sat up late last night reading George Moore's *Impressions and Opinions*. But it teems with errors, apart from the appalling French ! I can understand Poor Jo calling Mr Snagsby " Mr Sangsby." But why must Poor George, in a note on Ibsen's *Ghosts*, call Mrs Alving " Mrs Avling " throughout ?

To change the subject. Here is a little thing submitted to me last week by a commencing poet :

> When lovely morning lifts her head,
> And laughing flashes on the light,
> We see her rising from the bed
> Of that old blackguard, Night.

My father-in-law used to say, or perhaps quote, about somebody, " Sa rime n'est pas millionnaire," and the same goes for this young man's scansion. But I think the metaphor is fun. It may be that I am prejudiced in his favour since he pays *Ego* 6 the compliment of comparing it to a well-made haystack.

Talking of haystacks, let's have no more beating about the bush. Are you, or are you not, going to let me dedicate *Ego* 8 to you ?

Ever,

JAMES AGATE

Lunch with Hamish Hamilton at the Ivy, the other guests being Malcolm Sargent and Horace Horsnell. What was the best play written since the last war ? The talk went something like this :

SARGENT. *St Joan*, of course.

J. A. There's no " of course " about it. We're trying to find the best *play*, and *St Joan* isn't a play, whatever else it may be.

HAMILTON. Well, what do *you* say is the best play, James ?

J. A. *Juno and the Paycock.* Shaw's play second.

HORSNELL (*sepulchrally*). Third.

SARGENT. Why third ?

13

HORSNELL. Well, if you put *Juno* first you must put *The Plough and the Stars* second; you can't separate the two.

J. A. I agree.

HAMILTON. What do you say to that, Malcolm?

J. A. (*before Malcolm can answer*). What is the most perfect opera you've ever heard?

SARGENT. *Carmen.*

HORSNELL. Attaboy!

J. A. And the second?

SARGENT. I suppose it would have to be *Meistersinger.* But there's always Mozart, you know!

J. A. (*cold-shouldering Mozart*). Would you consider putting *Rosenkavalier* third?

SARGENT (*humouring him*). I might consider it.

J. A. Suppose that these are not operas but show-horses, and the class as it stands is headed by *Carmen, Meistersinger,* and *Rosenkavalier.* Now tell me. What do you do with that great, hulking, forceful brute now coming into the ring—whose name, by the way, is *The Ring*?

SARGENT. Well, I've no choice—I should have to put it either first or fourth. Or perhaps not even fourth. There's still Mozart.

J. A. Mozart be blowed!

HORSNELL. Anyhow, Malcolm, you've made James's point and mine. Shaw's play is either first or third; it can't be second.

SARGENT. What do you say, Hamish?

HAMILTON. I think we ought to leave it to the dramatic critics.

HORSNELL. It's up to you, James.

J. A. Well, if you want my serious opinion, I should put *Juno* first, *St Joan* second, and *The Plough and the Stars* third.

(*There is a general outcry at this, and a chorus of* " But you agreed . . .")

J. A. I know what I agreed. But I've told *St Joan* to move down to third place, *and she won't budge!*

Jan. 9 At supper to-night was introduced to a Trade Union
Tuesday. representative and his sailor nephew, a well-spoken boy
with one of those homely British ' pans ' that break into an unexpected, heart-warming smile. Very anxious to improve himself, and wanted to know the origin of pantomime, having just come from the Coliseum. Name of Ivan Plowright, an odd combination of Russian and Saxon. Indeed, the boy was so obviously anxious to learn that I was put in mind of my favourite passage in Boswell. He and Johnson had taken a sculler at the Temple Stairs and set out for Greenwich.

" And yet," said I, " people go through the world very well, and carry on the business of life to good advantage, without learning." JOHNSON. " Why, Sir, that may be true in cases

14

where learning cannot possibly be of any use; for instance, this boy rows us as well without learning, as if he could sing the song of Orpheus to the Argonauts, who were the first sailors." He then called to the boy, " What would you give, my lad, to know about the Argonauts ? " " Sir," said the boy, " I would give what I have."

Plowright took part in the North African landings, and has got a new ship, which he joins on Friday. Thinks he will be away a year or more, whereupon I undertake to look after his reading. Which means that I spend most of this morning scouring the shops for some Dickens, and find copies of *Pickwick, Bleak House, Martin Chuzzlewit,* and *A Tale of Two Cities.* To these I add my own *Lorna Doone,* Palgrave's *Golden Treasury,* and Ingpen's abridged *Boswell.*

No. 2 of my *Cocasseries :*

> I'll be thinking of you Easter Sunday
> In every hymn and every prayer.
> The choir will sing, the bells will ring,
> While the scent of Easter lilies fills the air.

Heard on the wireless last night to a maudlin tune subtly combining the atmospheres of cathedral and palais-de-danse.

Jan. 11
Thursday.

The new edition of *Blessed Are the Rich* was published last week, and *Gemel in London* is out this morning.

Jan. 12
Friday.

Letter from Jock :

E5 Ward
R.N. Hospital
Haslar, Hants
11th January, 1945

DEAR JAMIE,
 I have been very peculiarly ill.

Misérable, et je vis !

Write to me soon.

JOCK

To which I have replied :

*Queen Alexandra Mansions, W.C.*2
January 12th, 1945

MY DEAR JOCK,
 Tut-tut ! I am miserable, but only at the thought that some day I shan't " vis." In plain English, I have been making my will. Nothing to leave, of course, except gold watch, cuff-links, walking-sticks, etc., but I rather want these to go to the right persons. Even so, there's always income tax, as Van Druten would put it. However, Stanley Rubinstein has insured me for £2000 against loss by

15

V1 or V2 of life, one or both eyes, and various members. But not against permanent total disablement, as I am sixty-seven and the insurance company's view seems to be that at that age one must expect total disablement from natural causes, never mind Hitler. A cheerful business. Just as I was in full testamentary spate I looked out of window and saw a " corpidge " with four horses. (Do you remember the sailor who always felt jolly whenever he saw what he called a corpidge ? " I'm jolly because it isn't me in the corpidge.") Then to lunch with George Harrap, who gave me three plates by Stephen Gooden—worth £25, it seems—the first of which is entitled " The Rider on the Pale Horse " ! ! But what of it ? We cross our fingers and defy augury.

To hand, this morning, a new highbrow magazine called *Fulcrum*, and promised another called *Dint*. The first is French, and begins with a " Goujaterie Moraliste " whose first word is " Merde." Have also received *Troisième Front*, No. 1 of a series of recent French poetry. The last item in this is a " Petit Poème en Prose," which ends :

> Derrière un arbrisseau, au versant opposé de la
> montagne, un enfant est assis sur un petit pot et
> semble souffrir. Personne ne l'aperçoit, à part moi.
> Je suis saisi d'une immense compassion.

Third, *Message from Nowhere*, with a poem of which the last three lines are

> Et dans ses yeux bataviques
> Brille la provocante splendeur mirabelle plomb fondu
> Des sacrificielles latrines ogivales bombardées.

Last, *Idolatry and Confusion*, a pamphlet with a single illustration. This is a water-closet with a lid shaped like a lyre. Why this universal, ubiquitous interest in coprology ?

No further news, except that I propose to bore you on Saturday in the *D.E.* and dazzle you on Sunday in the *S.T.*

Ever,
JAMIE

Jan. 13   Jolly meeting at the Ivy with John Sutro, Oliver Messel,
Saturday.   and Peter Glenville. This gave me my *Cocasserie*
No. 3, Peter telling me that one of his scenes in *The Madonna of the Seven Moons*, the scene in which the wicked Sandro attempts to rape the chaste Angela, had to be shot six times because at the first five shootings he forgot that the Board of Censors will not pass any seduction scene unless the seducer has one foot on the floor.

Cocasseries are coming on apace. Here is No. 4, from the most unexpected source : Lord Dunsany's *Donnellan Lectures* delivered at Trinity College, Dublin, the subjects being prose, poetry, and drama. These contain some exquisite stuff, in the course of which the lecturer quotes Macbeth's " Sleep that knits up the ravelled sleeve [*sic*] of care." Then I read :

> I think I feel sure enough of that simile to say that it must have been written after Shakespeare was married. You see, a simile is merely placing one picture beside another, taking one picture down off the wall and holding it by another one to compare with it. And one asks where was the other picture ; how far did the man have to go to get it ? Sleep of course cures care, but how did a sleeve come into it ? Why a torn sleeve ? It seems to me simple enough : Shakespeare had been having a night out, perhaps with some of those good friends who, because he was such a good fellow, decided that there ought to be some memorial to him and luckily hit on the idea of printing his plays. Well, it had been rather a rowdy night—in fact, very rowdy indeed, so rowdy that he had got his sleeve torn. He remembered that. But the wonderful thing was that when he woke up in the morning the sleeve had been all mended. If that happened the two pictures are side by side and the simile naturally suggests itself. But if it did not happen, then the sleeve seems a very odd thing to have been brought into it, and is in fact inexplicable.

Inexplicable, dear Lord Dunsany ? Only if you confuse " sleeve," that part of the garment which covers the arm, with " sleave," which is the knotted or entangled part of a skein of yarn or thread. And this was said to students ! *Quis custodiet*, etc. But these howlers are easily made. I had been a critic of Shakespeare's acted drama for nearly twenty years before I realised that " When roasted crabs hiss in the bowl " was a reference to crab-apples and not crustaceans.

No. 5 is culled from Paul Tabori's *Two Forests*. The hero of this is a fiddler who, to entice a young girl, goes through the cycles of Schubert's *Die Schöne Müllerin* and *Die Winterreise*, having previously made transcriptions of them for unaccompanied violin. And then the door opens and the girl, who must have been listening for a couple of hours or more, enters. Whereupon the fiddler plays Schubert's *Die Forelle, Gretchen am Spinnrad, Am Meer, An die Musik,* and *Ständchen,* followed by Schumann's *Kinderscenen* and " some of the pieces " in the *Album für die Jugend,* all arranged for unaccompanied violin. We are then told that both performer and listener " forgot everything until Robert knocked at the door and announced that luncheon was waiting." Presuming that the young woman's appetite for food was comparable to her appetite for music, she must have eaten an ox !

No. 6 is from to-day's *News Chronicle,* and is about Michael Tippett's oratorio *A Child of our Time.* Of this the writer remarks :

17

" It seemed to me to avoid the Scylla and Charybdis of music *about* events. That is, it kept clear both of over-specific literary narrative and of bulbously emotive symbolism."

Jan. 15   George Lyttelton writes to say that my suggestion that I
Monday.   should dedicate my next *Ego* to him

> was so delicate that I did not like, so to speak, to grab at it. I should be *very* proud indeed to be the dedicatee and go down to. fame on your shoulders—feeling rather like Leigh Hunt when he wrote about Jenny. The last book dedicated to one of my name was *Tom Jones*. My ancestor was Squire Allworthy, a kindly old fellow, but I suspect a dullish one. He was Chancellor of the Exchequer though, according to Warburton, he never could learn that two and two made four.

Jan. 16   In to-day's *Times* Lord Esher and Lord Elton tell me
Tuesday.   that my " Toopit " theory is " ingenious " and " too
           ingenious." Both possess the original monthly parts of
Martin Chuzzlewit, in which the name is spelt " Toppit."

Jan. 17   Judging by *The Unquiet Grave*, " Palinurus " would
Wednesday.   seem to be, at least in part, Gilbert's Bunthorne.

> Angst descends : I wake up in anxiety ; like a fog it overlays all I do, and my days are muffled with anguish. Somewhere in the mind are crossed the wires of fear and lust and all day long nature's burglar-alarm shrills out in confusion. I dread the bell, the post, the telephone, the sight of an acquaintance. Anguish, anxiety, remorse and guilt : TOUT EST DÉGOÛT ET MISÈRE.

And :

> In the small hours when the acrid stench of existence rises like sewer gas from everything created, the emptiness of life seems more terrible than its misery.

Also :

> Morning tears return ; spirits at their lowest ebb. . . . Approaching forty, I am about to heave my carcass of vanity, boredom, guilt and remorse into another decade.

If I knew " Palinurus " I should offer him choice of three remedies. *One.* A box of Bunthorne's colocynth and calomel pills. *Two.* Mrs Crupp's prescription : " You are a young gentleman, Mr Copperfull, and my adwice to you is, to cheer up, sir, to keep a good heart, and to know your own walue. If you was to take to something, sir—if you **was** to take to skittles, now, which is healthy—you might find it divert your mind, and do you good." *Three.* To stop thinking about "Palinurus," and go and read to blind soldiers, or wheel crippled airmen round the Park. The trouble with these super-clever high-brows—there is some exquisite writing in the book, notably the long passage about lemurs—is that they have no vestige of humour. If "Palinurus" knew what humour is or may be he could not have presented me with *Cocasserie* No. 7 :

> In the jungles of South America grows a trumpet flower fourteen inches deep, and there also is found a moth with a proboscis of the same length, the only creature able to penetrate to the honey and so procure the plant's fertilisation. I, Palinurus, am such an orchid, growing daily more untempting as I await the Visitor who never comes.

Jan. 18
Thursday.
The capture of Warsaw and the advance of the Russians have put me in mind of something which I am sending to the *S.T.* for its "Famous Retorts" series. This concerns one Népomucène Lemercier, the friend of Legouvé, the part-author of *Adrienne Lecouvreur.* According to Talleyrand, Lemercier was a brilliant chatterbox ; when he was not chattering he exuded tragedies with names like *Agamemnon.* It was Lemercier who, at Malmaison, taught Napoleon the history of France. Later on the two quarrelled, and when Napoleon sent his old friend one of the first Crosses of the Legion of Honour it was returned. In revenge the Emperor forbade the performance of Lemercier's plays ; Népomucène said nothing. Driven from his house, he took refuge in a garret and stopped both chattering and playwriting. And then one day, at the Tuileries, the Emperor perceived his old crony in a corner with other members of the Institute. Waving the crowd aside, Napoleon went up to him and said, " *Eh bien,* Lemercier, when are you going to write a new tragedy ? " " *I am waiting, Sire !* " replied the poet. Surely a magnificent remark to make in 1812 on the eve of the Russian campaign !

Letter from Kandy, in Ceylon, telling me that, as far as the writer can see, " the Bookshops as Bookshops, in this city, is Null an' Void." At the same time he sends me a delightful essay on Amanda Ros by J. O. Bartley, an Ulsterman in Public Relations in New Delhi. This quotes from Amanda's epitaph on an honest critic :

> My ! What a bubbly vapoury box of vanity !
> A litter of worms, a relic of humanity—

" lines which," says the essayist, " in a different context, would not surprise from some of our most esteemed contemporaries." Surely not " contemporaries " but " Elizabethans "—I hate the pernickety

" Jacobeans "—should be the word. I confess I see very little to choose between the quotation from Amanda and Bosola's

> Thou art a box of worm-seed, at best but a salvatory of green mummy. What's this flesh ? A little crudded milk, fantastical puff-paste.

But then Amanda had genius. Consider her verses on visiting Westminster Abbey :

> Holy Moses ! Have a look !
> Flesh decayed in every nook !
> Some rare bits of brain lie here,
> Mortal loads of beef and beer. . .

Nobody but a genius could have written " Some rare bits of brain lie here."

Jan. 19   Letter from Jock :
Friday.

E5 *Ward*
R.N.H.

18th *January*, 1945

MY DEAR JAMIE,
    Thinking on your end you are no more tragic than Falstaff : hoots awa' and havers ! You were making one of your wills away back in October 1926 when I first traversed your doorstep (with Gemel's careful alacrity !).
    And I don't seem to remember, then, that you had either a gold watch or cuff-links to leave ! Whence came the watch ? The links I can believe in, because every year the oldest actress still able to hobble on to the stage with two legs and a bad-tempered walking-stick sweetly gives you a pair of elegant cuff-links at the Ivy and promptly dies thereafter. You will receive dozens more of such coy peeping adornments—and rush home each time to write some one's graceful obituary.
    Another great man who has been dying these years and years— my dear old James Bone—told me last time I saw him at the Press Club that he used to have a friend who was the prize obituarist of *The Times*, specialising in Church dignitaries. I can't remember his name—let's call him Martin Spade-Prelate. Well, James was telling me how he used to lunch with Spade-Prelate at the Athenæum, and how much he enjoyed his coffee in the smoke-room afterwards because as each pink bishop doddered in with a post-prandial smile he would turn pale to the gills and the gaiter-buttons as soon as he caught sight of Spade-Prelate, knowing his vocation. James chuckled in his Caledonian way at the recollection. And I interrupted his chuckle by saying, " And I'll bet you another whiskey that in due time you wrote Spade-Prelate's obit, yourself ? " " Oh-oh ! " says James. " So I did ! So I did ! "

So you see why I am not unduly grave with sympathy over your wills and testaments (by no means last), your insurances, your omens that come to naught, and your glimpses of Gampish corpidges through glum lawyers' windows. I ache to be back at my job and to be in my dear little *mansarde* again with its balcony, that I used to call a loggia, and something that Sairey somewhere calls " a Parapidge with chimbley-pots to walk on in case of fire." If I were, I'd come round and cheer you up rather more than this scribbled note can do.

Your
JOCK

Jan. 20   *The Times* devotes its fourth leader to the question of
Saturday.   Miss Toppit. Am sending the Editor the following :

SIR,
    Miss Toopit retires and leaves the field to Miss Toppit.
    I hope you will not think me unduly quarrelsome if I dissent from your dictum in the matter of the evocative case : " Shakespeare, Sheridan, Scott, Dickens, Thackeray, Trollope, du Maurier (who created Sir Gorgius Midas)—they have all done it, all save the ladies, who, following Miss Austen, have refused to demean themselves to these sometimes felicitous antics." But, sir, the ladies have not refused to demean themselves. If we are to hark back to the dramatists Shakespeare and Sheridan we are entitled to go back to the pre-Austen women-playwrights. To Mrs Aphra Behn, who in *The City Heiress* has Sir Timothy Treatall, Dresswell and Foppington, and among the women Mrs Clacket (" a City Bawd and Puritan "), Mrs Closet, and Mrs Sensure. To Mrs Centlivre, whose *A Bold Stroke for a Wife* has characters called Colonel Feignwell, Sir Philip Modelove, Tradelove, Obadiah Prim, and Simon Pure. To Mrs Cowley, with her Lord Sparkle and Lady Bell Bloomer, and Mrs Inchbald, with her Mr Twineall and Mr Meanright.
    Again, I find it difficult to accept your leader-writer's statement that in comparison with Thackeray all other practitioners in the evocative are " mere blunderers." *All* others ? Did Jonson blunder with Sir Epicure Mammon, Vanbrugh with Sir John Brute, Congreve with Lady Wishfort ? If your defence is that your reference is post-Austen, how came you to forget Peacock ? Or even Surtees ? " Whether in the straightforward Sharp or Newcome, ideal for their respective purposes, or in such a pleasant whimsy as the firm from which Clive bought his paints, Messrs Soap and Isaac, Thackeray was flawless." Even so, where is the flaw in Surtees's smooth toady, Mr Soapey Sponge ?

Yours, etc.,
JAMES AGATE

Holborn, W.C.2
January 20

Jan. 21
Sunday.
On my telling my doctor, Norman Newman, yesterday, that I thought a course of something would do me good, he replied, " My dear boy, what you want is a course of nothing." Resolved, therefore, to have a day or two of loafing. Spent it re-conning, or, to be perfectly honest, making acquaintance with the plays of Aphra Behn and Mrs Centlivre. And coming to the conclusion that Aphra was a dull lady-dog and Mrs C. a very considerable wit whose quality still persists. The play of Mrs C. that I chose was *A Bold Stroke for a Wife.* It begins with Freeman telling Colonel Feignwell that Anne Lovely " is the talk and pity of the whole town ; and it is the opinion of the learned, that she must die a maid." Whereupon the Colonel remarks, " That's somewhat odd, in this charitable city." And there is Sir Philip Modelove, who, on being told by the Colonel that a person of his figure would be a vast addition to a coronet, replies, " I must own I had the offer of a barony about five years ago ; but I abhorred the fatigue which must have attended it." In the course of the imbroglio Colonel Feignwell pretends to come from the funeral of his old master. " Pray, sir," says Periwinkle, " what office bore you ? " The Colonel says he was Sir Toby's steward. Periwinkle asks his name, and the Colonel answers, " Pillage, sir." Mrs C. appears to have had fun as well as wit. Feignwell, posing as an Egyptian, produces something which he says " is called poluflosboio." Says Periwinkle, " It has a rumbling sound." To which the Colonel replies, " Right, sir ; it proceeds from a rumbling nature. This water was part of the waves which bore Cleopatra's vessel when she sailed to meet Antony." Yes, I must read more of Mrs C.

Jan. 22
Monday.
Loafing continues. A nostalgic loafing caused by coming across a phrase in William Gaunt's *The Æsthetic Adventure* —Gautier's definition of himself as " A man for whom the visible world exists." This sent me to my bookshelves and my copy of *Mademoiselle de Maupin*, which I would have said I bought when I was seventeen. But the facts are against me ; I see from the date of the edition that I must have been at least twenty-seven. It is with some confusion, then, that I recall the *Schwärmerei*, excusable in youth, which with me lasted into the thirties. It was on a bicycle ride with one of my younger brothers that I first opened Gautier's book, and I remember the Derbyshire hillside, and the summer's day, and how whichever it was of my brothers went off at my bidding with orders to pick me up in the late afternoon. And how I read for six blessed hours. Later I had the copy bound in an expensive red morocco which has admirably withstood forty years and many moves.

I see that on the first page I pencilled : " For Edward. To mark the beautiful passages is to mark the whole book—he will understand." Nevertheless, I did mark some passages, including one which, slightly shortened, I sometimes feel I should like to print at the top of my *S.T.* articles :

> Many things are boring : it is boring to pay back borrowed money ; it is boring to make love to the woman one kissed yesterday ; it is boring to write a novel and more boring to read one ; it is boring to be a porter; it is boring to be an emperor ; but what is more boring than anything on earth, in hell or in heaven, is a tragedy—unless it is a drama or a comedy.

Jan. 23   " *Du Glückstier !* " cries Leo this morning, bursting into
Tuesday.   my bedroom and upsetting my fourth, say ten-thirty-ish, cup of tea. " No sooner does one door shut for you than another opens. Exeunt your Swiss Cottage friends ; enter Mr Hatch. Look at this ! " And hands me the following letter, with the postmark " Chiswick W.4 " :

> *London*
> *January 22nd, 1945*

DEAR MR AGATE,
    I am twenty-six years of age. I am of independent means, that is to say I have an annuity of £3 17*s.* 10*d.* per week, which enables me to live in a quiet, if not luxurious, fashion. I have not taken any active part in the present war for the reason that my health did and does not permit of my exerting myself in other than intellectual ways. I have many certificates to this effect. Harley Street testifies to a chronic lesion of the cavorta ; Wimpole Street is witness to the syphonic degeneration of my bladder ; Welbeck Street pronounces my liver to be statomichic, my kidneys katomichic, and my spleen to be in that rare state known as hypertricomastia. So much for my health, which, however, has permitted me to contribute three articles to *Offing* and *The Young Politician* under the pseudonym of Tintin Nabulate.
    As you see, I give no address. The reason for this is the following :
    I am writing a novel, to be called *The Trials of Saccharissa.* This is a protest against the vapidity of latter-day fiction. A novel dealing with contemporary life and thought. A novel by an intellectual, about intellectuals, for intellectuals. A novel of massive ideas, complex emotions, superb talk.
    The matter is what the unintelligentsia would call " clean." You know as well as I do that all that scabrous rubbish of the early forties, dealing with such ephemera as socratism, lesbianism, sadism, masochism, coprophilism, necrophilism and all the other " isms," are not only *vieux jeu* but, from a cultural standpoint, as dead as the Æsthetic Movement itself. If they are alluded to it is

only to point a moral or moralise a point. My novel avoids such *non sequiturs.*

I have written the first chapters, of which I shall shortly send you some extracts. You will see from these, which are intended merely to whet your appetite, that my book is a work of genius replete with every quality that I have always admired in my favourite authors. Amongst these I give first place to George Meredith. At the age of eight I was enthralled by his later novels, and at my preparatory school would take my fellow-pupils on long walks. Then, in the middle of some ploughed field, I would read them the opening chapters of *One of Our Conquerors,* that master-piece among masterpieces. *Eheu! fugaces* . . . Yes, dear Mr Agate, the classical side of my education has not been neglected.

This morning I decided to dedicate my book to the memory of that great epigrammatist whose wit was ever translucency's self. I do not believe that you have forgotten " The figure with the helmet of the Owl-Goddess and the trident of the Earth-shaker, seated on a wheel, at the back of the penny-pieces ; in whom you see neither the beauty of nakedness nor the charm of drapery ; not the helmet's dignity or the trident's power ; but she has patently that which stops the wheel ; and posing for representative of an imperial nation, she helps to pass a penny." Or that you do not recite in your bath : " Mr Durance said that a blow now and then was wholesome for us all. He recommended a monthly private whipping for old gentlemen who decline the use of the gloves, to disperse their humours ; not excluding judges and magistrates. He said, that old gentlemen were bottled vapours, and it was good for them to uncork them periodically. He said, they should be excused half the strokes if they danced nightly—they resented motion." Who except the Master could have presented so succinctly the case against sparing the rod and spoiling the old gentleman ? Finally, I am teaching my landlady's little daughter to lisp, " The remainder of life is in the activity of my diseases." The dedication will run :

TO

COLNEY DURANCE

ARISTOPHANIC CREATION

OF

THE GREATEST OF MODERN NOVELISTS

THIS EPIGONIC TRIBUTE

You will ask why I give no address. The reason is to prevent your writing to me and saying you do not wish to receive further letters from me. I shall write no further letters. I shall send you a synopsis of each half-dozen chapters as I finish them, together with extracts from the chapters themselves. Don't make the point that my plot is not my own, that I have gone to the most familiar sources. Of course I have. Deliberately. I regard plot merely as a peg for the book's decorations, an easel on which to place my canvas.

I shall go on sending you these extracts until you are completely captivated. Mr Agate, I intend to be ONE OF YOUR CONQUERORS!
For the time being, I use a name not my own.

DURANCE HATCH

Jan. 24   Letter from Jock:
Wednesday.

*Staff Quarters
R.N. Hospital
Haslar, Hants*
21st January, 1945

DEAR JAMIE,
Strictly I ought to send you a serious letter *in re* The Richardson Nose. You and Ivor cannot *both* be right this morning. Your article seems to me a superb and characteristic expression of a quite crassly idiosyncratic point of view. It is just untrue to say (if you don't say it you imply it) that this actor cannot move us because he has a funny round nose. He moved lots of people (certainly including *me* and, I seem to remember, *you*) in, amongst other things, Maugham's *For Services Rendered* (as an axed naval officer who was driven to suicide) and Priestley's *Cornelius* (as the eponymous business-man who couldn't make good at the end of the last war). You are on very much firmer ground if you make out that his nose prevents him from excelling in romantic or classical serious parts as distinct from modern ditto ditto. (Surely he'd make an admirable Helmer, Dr Stockmann, or even Solness?) The Nose, I do agree with you, was a considerable handicap in the matter of his Othello, his Iago, his Henry V, and that silly Silent Knight of Humbert Wolfe's. But his very bluntness *helped* to make his Kent, his Enobarbus, and his Faulconbridge. I saw the last, but don't think that you did, or know that he had played it. Clever of you, therefore, to mention its possibility this morning. It is one of the six best Shakespearean performances I have ever witnessed. The other five, by the way, were John Gielgud's present exquisite Hamlet, Henry Ainley's Benedick (in 1926), Laurence Olivier's Coriolanus, Leon Quartermaine's Banquo, and Robert Atkins's Caliban.

Ever thy,
JOCK

My reply:

Queen Alexandra Mansions, W.C.2
January 24th, 1945

DEAR JOCK,
I am surprised that you should quote any practising dramatic critic against me. How many more times must I tell you that not

25

one of you has ever seen a great actor or actress, with the possible exception of Mrs Pat *en décadence* ? Not one of you ever saw Irving, or Forbes-Robertson, or Charles Hawtrey, or Ellen Terry, or Mrs Kendal, or Janet Achurch. Not one of you ever saw Coquelin, the elder Guitry, Baron, Brasseur, Galipaux, Sarah, Bartet, Réjane, or Granier. And very few of you, even if you had seen them, would have understood a word they said. Ivor is an easy prey to anybody who sits in a corner and mopes : he calls this " quietism." You fall for some nice, sturdy, straightforward player who obviously isn't going to make off with the night's takings. You call that a " natural " actor, and I say : Yes, he is natural. But according to whose nature ? You insist that I admire Richardson's Kent and Enobarbus : I have paid tribute to both performances in the *Sunday Times* and in book form. But don't you realise that both parts are serving-men and can be played *without elevation*, which is why R. was so good as Bottom, an Athenian working man ? You ask me whether he was not moving as Cornelius. But if I remember aright, C. was a broker who went broke, and about this play's ending I find that I dictated and you took down : " Mr Richardson is too genial and too chubby to make a purely philosophical exit, and too English and phlegmatic to make a theatrical one." About R.'s performance in *For Services Rendered* I remember that he played the part of an ex-Commander turned garage-proprietor who issued dud cheques and then committed suicide ; I thought him excellent as a stupid fellow as much at sea in a garage as anywhere else. And now, me bucko, as Mrs Madigan would say, let me remind you of R.'s performance in *Too True to be Good*. Again I dictated, and you took down :

" The piece was run away with, in vulgar parlance, by Mr Ralph Richardson, who spoke the long speech of the sergeant with a medieval forthrightness and a controlled passion beyond all praise ; the actor, taking his time from Bunyan, affected us like a soldier coming into church from the open field."

Does the word Bunyan suggest nothing to you ? You with your quick brain will say at once : What, is there no elevation in Bunyan ? And I say : Yes, but not the kind of elevation I am talking about. You ask me whether R. would not be admirable as Helmer, Stockmann, or Solness. I give you that dull fellow Stockmann, astonished that the shareholders in the Baths aren't delighted to be told the water stinks. But not Helmer, who is an exquisite in his way, as you would know if you had seen Courtenay Thorpe play the part. And certainly not Solness, who is as mad as a hatter, whereas R. is as sane as all the hatters in London put together. To be quite frank, Richardson has never moved me *as an actor* ; he could play Charles I and have his head chopped off in sixteen different positions without beginning to worry me. Whereas Irving. . . . But then you never saw Irving, and therefore cannot know what pathos is. On the other hand, let's give R.

the quality of his defects. He would be my first choice for Mr Valiant-for-Truth—one would believe in those trumpets. He would be my last choice for Antony; riot just doesn't go with that sturdy British countenance and that smug, self-satisfied vocal intonation. I feel about R. exactly what Lewes felt about Charles Kean:

"He has the power of coarse painting, of impressive representation when the image to be presented is a simple one; but he has no subtlety of sympathy, no nicety of observation, no variety of expression. He is peculiarly rigid—this is his force and his weakness: 'he moveth altogether if he move at all.' His face is utterly without physiognomical play; one stolid expression, immovable as an ancient mask, is worn throughout a scene which demands fluctuating variety."

I said all I have to say about R. when he played the Apprentice in *The Knight of the Burning Pestle*:

"But surely Mr Richardson is miscast? His stolid, inexpressive mien, altogether admirable in Bottom and in all delineations of the downright, and his general suggestion of the tongue-tied do not belong to the volatile, mercurial Apprentice who has been an amateur actor and spills the loquacity of which he is full. Histrionics should tumble out of Ralph because he cannot help it, and to invite Mr Richardson to do this is like asking a stonewaller to play one of Macartney's innings."

The trouble is that R. has neither vivacity nor melancholy. If he must play Tchehov let it be Lopakhin in *The Cherry Orchard*; as that highly unimaginative if speculative builder and ex-serf he would be excellent. No, Ralph is an admirable actor as long as he keeps within his limitations, which, of course, applies to all actors. Irving? I can think of only three instances in which the Old Man miscast himself—Romeo, which he couldn't look; Lear, which he couldn't speak; and the mesmerist and lion-tamer, to give him Shaw's title, in *The Medicine Man*. (This was the play which brought Shaw to bed; his Saturday article on it appeared on May 7, 1898, followed by "G. B. S. Vivisected" on May 14, and "Valedictory" on May 21.) On all other occasions there was a facet of H. I. to correspond with the part, and since he played rôles as different as Lesurques and Dubosc, Charles I and Louis XI, Dr Primrose and Cardinal Wolsey, there must have been an immense number of facets. (D'you remember Max's "multi-radiant"?) But Ralph has only one facet, something between Joe Gargery and Joe Bagstock, a solid, impermeable compound of *bonhomie* and *Gemütlichkeit*. (Why can't I learn to write English? I asked Leo about the spelling of the German word. He said they don't use the old " th " nowadays, and I said I didn't think they had any further use for the word!) To go back to R., I think he is an excellent actor in his vein, and that Vanya is outside it.

Yours ever,

JAMIE

Jan. 25　　A plague on these revivals of the *Dream* with Somebody
Thursday.　　Else's music ! With the exception of Shaw, dramatic
　　　　　　　critics have been a notoriously unmusical lot. I don't
believe that either Archer or Walkley would have known the Overture
to this play from the Overture to *Ruy Blas*, the Nocturne from " O
Rest in the Lord," and the Scherzo from the last movement of the
Violin Concerto. But has the fact that a dramatic critic cannot distinguish between the Trio in *Rosenkavalier* and " Three Little Maids
from School " ever prevented him from having views on what music
should or should not be used for Shakespeare's fairy play ? No. He
will hold that one should use " the music of the period," by which he
generally means Purcell, ignoring the fact that that composer is first
heard of in Pepys's *Diary* some forty-five years after Shakespeare's
death. To those who are not tone-deaf the argument that music
vaguely of the period *must* express that period is unsound. Unsound
because we are not listening with the ears of that period. I hold that
Richard Strauss gives to modern ears a better notion of the daughter
of Clytemnestra and Agamemnon than any concatenation of conch,
ram's horn, harp, pipe, lute, theorbo, shawm, sackbut, psaltery,
tabor, and cymbals that Euripides could have heard.

Jan. 26　　" Must a man sit esurient at his own table ? " asked
Friday.　　Lamb. Must I keep silent about my latest *Cocasserie*
　　　　　　　because I play a leading part in it ? At the Café Royal
to-night Dicky Holmes, whom I used to meet at Monty Shearman's,
leans across from the next table and says, " May I introduce Mrs
Procter ? You probably know the name." Whereupon J. A., who
is all in after four days of loafing but remembers E. V. Lucas's dictum
that a gent never shows he is tired, capers into the conversation like
some sprightly elephant. No, he doesn't what you might call *know*
the name. He remembers being at school with a jolly boy called
Proctor—all smile and freckles ? At any rate, he spelt his name with
an " o." He knows a bore of that name, and will ask the bore the
next time he meets the bore which boring vowel he affects. Then
wasn't there once an Adelaide Anne P. who wrote *The Lost Chord*
and other of what Millamant would have called filthy verses ? And
that's all the Procters he knows ; except, vaguely, something about
a Mrs Dod P. who used to paint nudes made of pewter lying on beds
made of zinc. Whereupon the lady smiles and says, " I gave up
painting like that twelve years ago." At this J. A. makes a lumbering
attempt at recovery and says he thinks women should give up all
forms of painting except perhaps a little dabbling in water-colour.
The lady says she gave that up even earlier, having found it too

difficult. Has Mr Agate any other interesting views about painting ?
J. A. " Only that the art stopped with Renoir." The lady then asks
J. A. what, since he is so fond of horses, are his views on Munnings ?
J. A. " He doesn't paint them as well as Stubbs." THE LADY. " Oh,
but Munnings gives them such beautiful, glossy coats. Which is
naughty of me, because I'm very fond of Munnings. Besides, he's a
very good painter." J. A. " Madam, Whistler was a very good
painter, and the polish on his piano is perfect." And so the game
goes on for half an hour with Dicky sitting there, umpiring as it were.
Presently they get up to go, and J. A. finds himself telling D. P. that
she is a very witty and charming woman. Yes, I think my *gaffe* is
entitled to rank as No. 8 in my *Cocasseries*.

Jan. 27   An unknown friend from Bristol sends me what I take
Saturday.   to be an exquisite little poem :

SNOW ON MY SEVEN DAYS

English snow from a heavy English sky,
Quietly greeting me, drifting incessantly, slow.
Strange I should find it enchanting—I who have cursed,
Stumbling blinded and chilled, hating the snow.

Snow on my seven days' leave. How they will laugh !
How to explain the peace and the silence it brings ?
Mine to recall it, swirling and dancing a welcome ;
Laughing it smothers me, laughing it settles and clings.

Home and the faces, rosy with happiness, waiting ;
The kiss and the long, long gaze into eyes that burn . . .
And the friendly snow crowning the blessed moment ;
Mine to remember, to live on when I return.

                                        E.P.B.

Jan. 30   Propinquity ! I spent the first hour of to-night's play,
Tuesday.   Daphne du Maurier's *The Years Between*, wondering
            what service Humpty Dumpty would have imposed on
that word. The drama now unfolding was all about Diana, an English
war widow (Nora Swinburne) whose husband, Colonel Wentworth,
M.P. (Clive Brook), had crashed off the coast of Greece. But I had
just come from a film about an American war widow whose husband
had been reported missing in the Philippines, and I found myself
asking whether to tackle the make-believe of the theatre so soon after
the actualities of the film was quite fair. Some years ago I was told
by a chauffeur that he preferred the pictures to the theatre " because
they are so much more real." Was the young man setting up a case
for celluloid as more life-like than flesh-and-blood ? No, what he was
stressing without knowing it was the difference between a photograph

of, say, an express train speeding through steam and rain and Turner's painting of the same thing. At the cinema I am, like that chauffeur, completely illuded. I had no doubt this morning that the American film company had paid some world-famous star a hundred thousand dollars to be unseen as the husband and do a thinking part away from the set. Indeed, I shouldn't have been surprised to hear that they had given him another hundred thousand dollars to go to the Philippines, crawl about, and pretend to be missing. I *felt* that the fellow was alive somewhere, tucked away, out of sight. I believed in him though I never saw him. But then I utterly believe in the cinema unless, of course, it is behaving cinematographically. When some highbrow director shows me a guttering candle and tells me it is Colonel Newcome rehearsing his " Adsum " I just say, " No, it isn't ; it's a guttering candle." And when he shows me a view of a beach at low water and claims that it is Barkis going out with the tide I say, " No, it isn't ; it's a bit of Ilfracombe." But otherwise I am completely deceived. As a filmgoer I have not been taught to pretend ; whoever alludes to a rogue elephant or to a volcano in eruption must show it to me, and will. Whereas the whole art of playgoing is concerned with pretence. And alas, I cannot believe in to-night's colonel, in spite of the fact that he is tremendously in evidence.

The author doesn't help by starting off with a whopper. Or rather, three whoppers. First, we are to believe that Colonel Wentworth didn't really crash but only pretended to, so that nobody would suspect him of being chief organiser of the underground movement in Europe. Second, we are to believe that Diana is not allowed to know any of this because she is Ibsen's Nora all over again, a tweeting song-bird who is to chirrup all over the house except when her lord and master is at his desk writing his books and speeches. Third, we are to believe that, his mission concluded and the war ended, the Colonel returns to find the canary turned bird of wisdom and representing the constituency in his stead ! Well, I don't think the du Maurier can have it all three ways any more than I believe that a heroine wearing three rows of whacking great pearls cares twopence whether working-class houses are provided with baths or not. The truest thing in the play is the Colonel's insistence that the soldier doesn't want to come back to an unrecognisable world, a world with hot and cold laid on everywhere, a world in which chamber music and poetry readings in saloon bars interfere with the proper business of drinking. (Has the Colonel been reading *Ego* 7, pages 178, 179 ?) He wants the world he knew, improved, if you must, but *along his lines* and not what the Pardiggles think ought to be his lines. A world of better and stronger beer ; of higher wages and shorter hours ; of more dependable horses and more reliable greyhounds; of larger and more palatial dance-halls. A world in which a wife stops at home and wipes her kiddies' noses instead of gadding about Westminster trying to catch the Speaker's eye. Right or wrong, this new argument, very forcefully put by the Colonel, seems to me to be of greater interest than that stale romantic stuff about the lover who goes out of a woman's life. But then I had spent the morning weeping over one abnegatory fellow, and two in one day is too much. Propinquity again.

Feb. 1
Thursday.
Until this morning I thought I knew most of the minor annoyances of existence. But I must go back a little.

For some months, and in order to give me a modicum of time in which to attend to my own work, Leo has had instructions to write to the senders of MSS. telling them that my fee for an opinion is ten pounds, payable in advance. Alas, one or two tenners started coming in, which meant that I had to put up the price to twenty pounds. Arrives, the other day, from South Wales, the MS. of a 150,000-word novel. The usual letter is dispatched, back comes the reply saying the author can't afford twenty pounds, whereupon I spend half an hour making a neat parcel of his unshapely mess, taking it to the post in the midst of a snowstorm, and standing in a queue to register it to the address on the MS. and his two letters. All this was over a week ago. This morning the parcel comes back marked "Not Known"!!

Feb. 3
Saturday.
Letter from the gentleman in South Wales, saying that unless he receives his MS. by return he will put the matter in the hands of his solicitors.

Feb. 4
Sunday.
To a lady:

Queen Alexandra Mansions, W.C.2
February 4th, 1945

MADAM,
You are worried because nobody will take a short story about a charming girl who adores Siamese cats and cold-bloodedly destroys them in turn as the first kitten is born, because kittens are more attractive. I can only suggest that you haven't hit on the right ending. Why not give the girl a fiancé who keeps putting off the wedding-day, and when reproached for not coming up to the scratch, replies, "Look here, sweetheart, I have a complex too. Only in my case it's babies instead of kittens!"

Yours sincerely,
JAMES AGATE

Feb. 5
Monday.   In a letter from New Zealand :

I have a cobber who says you are all wrong about Rachel and Sarah. Their biographical notes (he says) should be : Sisters. Born Kansas City. Worked in Hiram P. Sloshky's dry-goods and drug store. Joined Warner Bros. as crooners, tap-dancers, and hot mommas. At present working on the film *The Private Lives of James Agate.*

Cocasseries, No. 9 :

Shakespeare's play, *The Tempest,* is a " musical," according to the U.S. Federation of Musicians, whose ruling compels sponsors of the current Broadway production of the classic to employ sixteen rather than the scheduled twelve-piece orchestra and pay the musicians £7 a week more each. In reply to the producer's contention that it is Shakespeare's play with incidental music, not a musical with book and lyrics by Shakespeare, Mr Jack Rosenberg, chief of the Federation, said, " We don't care if it's by William Shakespeare or Joe Doakes. If the producers don't abide by our ruling we'll close the show."—*Reuter.*

Evening paper

Feb. 6
Tuesday.   Hatch is as good as his word. To-day I receive this :

THE TRIALS OF SACCHARISSA

CHAPTERS 1–6

(With apologies to Goldsmith's Olivia)

Synopsis

Saccharissa, beautiful daughter of the vicar of Daydream, is pursued by a handsome country gentleman of loose morals. In due course Squire Maybrow lures the unsuspecting girl from the paternal roof and seduces her. Abandoned in the middle of Virginia Water, she hails a friendly Spitfire and returns to the forgiving arms of her father, Dr Daffodil.

Extracts

Chloe thought the two would come to blows. Hypius glared at Sapor, Sapor clenched his fists as if to strike his friend. Chloe had one of her inspirations. " *Escuchar, mis amigos !* " she cried. " Matteo Grigoroso may or may not be a master of cloristic rhythm —but this is the point—every one, every painter who is also a critic and vice versa, admits that Florio da Melacrino was the greater virtuoso in sheer *line.* This isn't merely my idea ; ask

Pierre." Pierre Langouste, true son of the South, who was sketching an apple-tree growing in the lake, turned round and said, " *Mais oui. Je comprends. C'est la vie !* " After Elfrida had translated this to the others peace was restored.

.   .   .   .

Millamant Foss, sprucer than ever in her soya stockings, is the first to turn on him. " So," she cries, but not without a slight grating of the œsophagus, " you come here, Valentine, just to tell us that, in your view, Leonardo could paint. But *could* he ? He could draw. He could design. He could invent. But *paint* ? Not what *we* call paint. Not as the Cerisians, or the Neo-Cobaltists, or even the Ultra-Gambogists paint—and they are the only authorities on the really modern use of colour. Painting, *qua* painting, must be three-dimensional, ilistic, biometrical if necessary—every child learns that at school. It must be peristeal as well ; or, if you are so pedantic, the more vernacular peristheal." " Enough ! " cries Valentine, protecting himself with his parasol. " I am converted. Let us call painting a peristheal symbosis. Does that satisfy you ? " Millamant, good-natured as ever, smiles : " For the moment, yes. But later we'll ask St John Pushcart—he's more authentically definitional."

.   .   .   .

Cleverly reaching the summit of Gwrngwrn, Hilda stopped and said in her most thrilling tones, " Philosophical pictures should never be in a major key. Enharmonics, yes. But plastic planes cannot enter into the sphere of chromatic energism. There is always a tinge of the pseudo-heterogeneous, a whiff of what dear old Beagle Blossom used to call spiritual Woggery." Hilary Ellis interrupted to lead them to his studio, situated plumb in the middle of Salisbury Plain, and measuring 120 yards by 90. They were all struck by the new sketches in gouache, a little derivative, Julia thought, of post-Eleutheristic symbolism. Lady Carstairs sniffed audibly. " Really, Mr Ellis," she protested. " I find these figures a little sub-dimensional ! Think of Mantegna." " Madam," returned the painter, " you should remember the old tag—*Tempora mutantur, et nos mutamur in Ellis* ! " Hilary realised that it was the quip of his life.

.   .   .   .

Raoul Figtree was reading part of his essay on the Geometrics of Design. He ended : " Is this a lacheitis, or merely the old, old *bépouperie* ? Not for me to answer. Thousands have asked the same question. Sailors huddled in their fo'c'sles, soldiers bumping in their tanks, airmen nonchalant in the midst of flak. The best I can do is to quote my favourite author, Teneber Mastix : ' Lacheitic can never be lacheitistic. A rhombus can never be a rhomboid.' In other words, the manubial can never be the manubrial." Looking round, Raoul was surprised to find Messalina Oldcock in tears.

33

Feb. 7   **Depressed at the thought of having to sit through**
Wednesday.   ***Emma*, at the St James's to-night. Jane's " two inches**
of ivory " has never deceived me. She was a whale for
length. It would take a hoarding twelve feet by six to hold the four
hundred and forty-four small-print pages of my edition of *Emma*; no
Janeite would find it extraordinary that the public should be driven
into the roadway to enable him to peruse, without interruption, on
step-ladders and through magnifying glasses, this opuscule in all but
length, having for a centre a work-basket and for circumference the
wall of a gentleman's park. To the Janeite there is no world outside
Jane, and he insists that you swallow her whole. Now there is no
" balzacien déterminé," in Paul Bourget's phrase, who will not grant
out of the two thousand five hundred characters in the *Comédie
Humaine* at least two hundred unreadables, whereas the Janeite
enragé insists upon perfection everywhere. Leo tells me he heard
E. V. Lucas maintain that the three sentences in which Emma
accepts Mr Knightley's proposal are among the greatest in the English
language ! Walkley endorsed Miss Thackeray's statement that
" Jane's very bores are enchanting." I disagree. I hold that Miss
Bates is as boring to read about as to live with.

" Indeed they are very delightful apples, and Mrs Wallace does
them full justice, only we do not have them baked more than twice,
and Mr Woodhouse made us promise to have them done three
times. . . . The apples themselves are the very finest sort for
baking, beyond a doubt ; all from Donwell—some of Mr Knightley's
most liberal supply. He sends us a sack every year ; and certainly
there never was such a keeping apple anywhere. . . ."

Is this anything except wildly dull ? Compare :

" In Italy is she really with the grapes and figs growing everywhere and lava necklaces and bracelets too that land of poetry with
burning mountains picturesque beyond belief though if the organ-
boys come away from the neighbourhood not to be scorched nobody
can wonder being so young and bringing their white mice with them
most humane. . . . Venice Preserved too I think you have been
there is it well or ill preserved for people differ so . . . you are
acquainted Arthur I believe with Mantua what *has* it got to do
with Mantua-making for I never have been able to conceive."

Thus Flora Finching. The truth is, I suppose, that Dickens's
gusto and Jane's fastidiousness are as oil and vinegar—the difference
between a gormandiser and a governess. Walkley went on to
splutter : " The fact is, people who are bored by Jane Austen's
bores are probably bored by Jane herself." But that cock won't

fight. I am not bored by Jane's bores *en masse*. I dote, for example, on Mr Collins. But then Collins is a bore of relish, whereas Miss Bates is a bore of realism.

Feb. 8
Thursday.

" Why, Sir, if you were to read Richardson for the story, your impatience would be so much fretted that you would hang yourself." *Emma* was even more tedious than I expected. If the evening was saved at all it was saved by Miss Bates, turned by Gillian Lind into Miss Tox with the addition of St Vitus's dance plus a turban straight out of *Chu Chin Chow*. Good support by Ambrosine Phillpotts, who, as Mrs Elton, stormed that drawing-room at Hartfield House very much as Miss Snevellicci might have stormed the Dedlocks' drawing-room at Chesney Wold. (Yes, I know I am telescoping two books.) The walking, stalking, talking gentlemen walked and stalked and talked, and Neagle's Emma wanted the camera. And, of course, it was unending. Why did Gordon Glennon, who adapted, keep us in the theatre long after all pretence at interest had evaporated ? Was he fired by recollection of that Henry James story of which Chesterton said that " the excite-ment becomes tense, thrilling, and almost intolerable in all the half-hours during which nothing is said or done " ? As we came out I heard Flora Finching whisper over my shoulder, " Macaroni if they really eat it like the conjurers James why don't they cut it shorter ? "

Feb. 9
Friday.

Sat up late to-night reading Lord Moran's *Anatomy of Courage.* " Courage is a moral quality ; it is not a chance gift of nature like an aptitude for games. It is a cold choice between two alternatives, the fixed resolve not to quit ; an act of renunciation which must be made not once but many times by the power of the will. Courage is will power." But courage and cowardice are relative to the things about which a man is afraid. During the last war I had no compunction in walking down the dubious back streets of Marseilles at two in the morning. Whereas I would not, and could not at any time, walk a mile of English country road at midnight, any more than I could spend a night alone in a haunted house. (I don't believe in ghosts, but I'm afraid of them !) Last week a friend of mine who wears the ribbons of the D.F.M. and the D.S.C. was spending an evening at my flat. I asked him to fetch a syphon from the kitchen, and he at once refused. " I couldn't," he said : " there's a cat in there." I said, " I think you'll manage it," and went on smoking. He did manage it, but it took him twenty minutes !

Feb. 10
Saturday.
" May I ask whether these pleasing attentions proceed from the impulse of the moment, or are the result of previous study ? " said Mr Bennet. Change a word, and the same might be asked of my outpourings. Take this week's article on *Emma*. I made a first draft of this on Wednesday night after seeing the play—say, three hours. Spent the whole of Thursday licking it into shape—say, a further eight hours. Should have continued longer except that George Blake, an old friend of mine and a captain in the Merchant Service, blew in. It seems that one night during the January gales his ship's anchors wouldn't hold, the engines refused to work, and he was washed overboard, but, seeing that nobody paid any attention, he climbed back again. Burly people never look under the weather, but I thought he could do with cheering up, and hauled him off to see *Three's a Family*. Vera Pearce was in magnificent form, and the only remark George made was to ask whether she was married. No, I don't think that as a novel *Three's a Family* would bear comparison with *Emma*, but I found it ten times more amusing than Wednesday night's play. Spent all yesterday, Friday, revising my notice of *Emma*, sent it down to the *S.T.*, and received the proof at five-thirty the same night. Worked on it till eight-thirty, or thereabouts, handed it in, then to cinema and supper, in the middle of which I realise that to talk about " railings " to a gentleman's park is pure Cockney and that the word should be " wall." Finish supper hastily, get a car, and retrieve proof. And once having started tinkering, tinker till 3 A.M.—another five hours. By this time my brain is in a whirl, and to quieten it I absorb quantities of whiskey, sleeping tablets, and Chesterton on Dickens. Bed about four. All told, I must have worked some twenty-two hours on this notice, and even now I think that " deceived " should be " hoodwinked." But since this is getting brainsickly, I decide to-day, Saturday, to go to the concert at the Albert Hall, for which Ernest Helme has sent me two seats. Somebody is going to conduct the *Symphonie Fantastique*, and I have arranged with George Mathew to come and drag me to it. As I write, the telephone rings. It is the *S.T.* printers, to tell me that my title of " Miss Austen's Thin Gruel " won't fit, being a letter too long. Do I mind if they change " Miss Austen " to " Jane " ? No, I don't mind. Leo says the above should be called " Symphonie Typographique: Épisode de la Vie d'un Journaliste."

Alas, we didn't get to the concert after all. On the way I called in Fleet Street for a final glance at my proof, and found that somebody, possibly I myself, had miscalculated, and will I cut sixteen lines, please ? Now I know how a painter feels when the frame-maker says, "This canvas won't fit—will you cut two inches off the fore-ground, please? Unless, of course, you prefer the sky?" Messing with the stuff takes me an hour, which means either concert and no lunch, or lunch and no concert. Choose the second. After which to Grape Street, and savagely tear 14,000 words, say forty pages, out of *Ego* 7!

Feb. 11   The *Observer* prints this exquisite poem. It was written
Sunday.   in the spring of 1944; the author died of wounds in
            Normandy last June, aged twenty-two.

A WISH

Let me not see old age: let me not hear
The proffered help, the mumbled sympathy,
The well-meant tactful sophistries that mock
Pathetic husks, who once were strong and free,
And in youth's fickle triumph laughed and sang,
Loved, and were foolish: and at the close have seen
The fruits of folly garnered, and that love,
Tamed and encaged, stale into grey routine.
Let me not see old age: I am content
With my few crowded years: laughter and strength
And song have lit the beacon of my life,
Let me not see it fade, but when the long
September shadows steal across the square,
Grant me this wish: they may not find me there.

                                    D. R. GERAINT JONES

Feb. 12   The surgeon who removes a carcinoma on Wednesday has
Monday.   lost interest in Tuesday's appendicectomy and forgotten
            all about Monday's vesical calculus. The layman can
never understand this. Similarly he can never understand that when
a dramatic critic has dotted the last " i " and crossed the last " t " in
his notice he has had enough of both notice and subject. This morning
I am deluged with letters about Mendelssohn and the *Dream*, the
writers not realising that I put paid to that a fortnight ago. Since
then I have finished with *Emma*, and am now tangled up in Wolfit's
Macbeth, with which I shall be wholly preoccupied until, on Sunday
morning, the notice goes into my cutting-book. After which, just as
the surgeon is going to forget Thursday's gall-stones in Friday's short-
circuit, so next week I shall have forgotten *Macbeth* in some other play.

Feb. 13   Sup with Tom Curtiss, who has unexpectedly returned
Tuesday. from Paris. He tells me that while there is plenty to
            drink in that once gay but now embittered city, there is
nothing to eat—" eating is virtually against the law." The French are
bitter because they have not been invited to the Crimea conference.
France has been liberated, it seems, by the French themselves;

at least, the Americans and the English are never mentioned. Tom brought me a bottle of cognac, a new book about the Goncourts by Pierre Descaves, and a copy of *Le Figaro*, a small single sheet sixteen inches by eleven. It appears that the theatres are full and offer a programme which should make us blush, the plays ranging from *Antigone* to *Volpone*, and, amongst the moderns, Barrie, D'Annunzio, and Armand Salacrou. The Comédie Française has had to close owing to lack of heating facilities, Wolfit had a great success in two of Shakespeare's comedies, but Katherine Cornell in *The Barretts of Wimpole Street* just didn't go.

Feb. 14
Wednesday.
The new Deanna Durbin film at the Leicester Square is entitled *Can't Help Singing*. By my calculation she has seven songs. Allowing three minutes for each makes a total of twenty-one minutes, and the film runs for ninety. Subtract twenty-one from ninety, and the result is sixty-nine minutes of the most appalling, flat twaddle I have ever endured. All round me this morning were a number of Negro airmen, who, being children of the South, and therefore easily entertained, should surely have responded. They were not amused. On the other hand, the whites laughed a great deal, and it cannot be assumed that they were all nursemaids and pantry-boys. There was a time when D. D. used to keep still while singing ; now she wanders through bog, through bush, through brake, through briar—indeed, she falls into the first of these—down staircases, behind columns and fountains spouting some nauseating cherry-coloured liquid. And she sings and she sings, always with the same vocal intonation. Always, too, with the same facial inexpressiveness, rendered by Technicolor in terms of lightly baked gingerbread. And, of course, always the same melodic line meandering level, whatever Macaulay may say, with Jerome Kern's commonplace fount. In my view D. D. would be well advised to stop trafficking with Red Indians in the neighbourhood of the Grand Canyon and get back to that story of the Voice which, discovered one fine afternoon by a millionaire connoisseur, appears on the following evening at the Metropolitan Opera House as the Queen of Night, exercising such magic upon her audience that she is able to marry the second flautist.

Feb. 15
Thursday.
The fact that Wolfit cannot play Macbeth is neither here nor there, since many great actors have failed in the part. If Lear is often regarded as unactable it is because it is held that an actor's momentum *in a single direction* cannot be as great as Shakespeare's. If Macbeth is unactable it is on the more reasonable supposition that it is not given to a player to be

in the maximum degree and simultaneously extrovert and introvert. (I have seen one first-class Macbeth and one only—Benson. Benson was a superb Henry V and an exquisite Richard II, and his Thane was the result of adding the two together.) Wolfit's Macbeth fails because the character doesn't lie in the actor's personality. Because no actor can be Macbeth who deprives him of his poetry, introspection, vacillation, remorse. " Be bloody, bold, and resolute ! " enjoins the Apparition. But then Wolfit is already bloody, bold, and resolute, and has been so from the beginning. The character goes wrong from the start, from the words: "Duncan comes here to-night," followed by Lady Macbeth's " And when goes hence ? " This is the first in a long time (" What beast was't *then*," etc.) that murder has been mentioned between them, and now the impetus comes from the lady, who in her immediately preceding speech has already settled the business in her own mind. (" Papa is in the study praying for guidance ; Mamma is upstairs packing.") Murder is as yet only at the back of Macbeth's mind (" My thought, whose murder yet is but fantastical "), which means that there should be no more than the glimmer of an idea behind the words : " To-morrow, *as he purposes*." But this is not D. W.'s notion. At his wife's question he disengages himself, steps back a pace, goes through prodigies of winking and nodding, and ruins Lady Macbeth's " O, never shall sun that morrow see ! " To reduce this from the instigatory to the corroborative is to trump the actress's best trick. In the scene which immediately follows—the colloquy between Lady M. and Duncan—I can find no justification for Macbeth being present, veiling his face with his arm. The Thane of Cawdor is a First Murderer, not a Second ! In short, D. W. turns the whole play into a ranting, roaring, Saturday-night melodrama, full of very capable sound and fury but signifying nothing of the play's pity and melancholy. G. H. Lewes said of Macready's Macbeth that he " stole into the sleeping-chamber of Duncan like a man going to purloin a purse, not like a warrior going to snatch a crown." Wolfit's Macbeth comes out of that chamber like a furniture remover weighed down by an invisible wardrobe ! Only the most complete insensitivity could condone that jolly little march-tune which heralds the fatal entrance of Duncan under the battlements, and suggests that the play to follow is something about *Merrie Scotland* !

Feb. 16   Bored by *Laura*, at the St Martin's to-night. Does a
Friday.   would-be murderer shoot somebody without making sure
            that he has got hold of the right person ? Does a young
woman whose fiancé has a mistress lend her apartment to her rival

and then disappear ? Does a " womanthrope," to use Miss Prism's convenient neologism, commit murder because one of the sex to which he is allergic won't have him ? Do American detectives investigate a crime by making love to the suspected criminal over her coffee and cookies ? As a plain dramatic critic I just wouldn't know the answers. What I do know is that it was a pity to omit some of the original novel's dialogue. " The magnificence of my skeleton is hidden by the weight of my flesh." " I leaped like a mother leopard." " Aunt Susan once sang in musical comedy. Then she became a widow. The hyphen of marriage is best forgotten." The acting was probably very good. Raymond Lovell, trying hard to believe in his rôle, scattered tenth-rate epigrams with gusto. As the incredible Laura, a writer of advertising slogans with a passion for hot jazz and a knack equal to Helen's for turning men's heads, Sonia Dresdel swept the stage in blood-red négligés and the eager vivacity of a leading actress " resting." But then, this is the theatre whose audiences expect acting, and not the cinema where to look on catastrophe sympathetically, glamorously, and with the sweet simplicity of a boiled haddock is the most that is demanded by Streatham, Finchley, and what is known as " practically Ealing." Later I take up the paper and I read about Miss Baba la Bilbo, or some such name, that she is " the greatest screen find of the war, and a national sensation in the U.S.A. She's twenty years of age, and was an usherette and cover girl. She is like slow electricity and has the smoky and disillusioned voice of Garbo, her mystery and care-less grace, but her personality and torrid magnetism are all her own. London will have to wait till the summer to see her." Madam, I can wait.

Feb. 17
Saturday.

There is nothing like finishing a job properly. Having proof-read Cardus's *Ten Composers*, the next thing was to review it. But how ? *Express* readers are not supposed to be interested in classical music. But where there's a will there's a way, and I think I get round it with the following :

 I am emboldened to put Mr Neville Cardus's *Ten Composers* at the top of my column this week because of Dr Malcolm Sargent's story of the labourer who said after a recent symphony concert, " 'Itler's done one thing—turned me inter a blinkin' 'ighbrow ! "
 Now the labourer in question might well have heard a symphony by Schubert, Brahms, Sibelius, or he might have heard the Elgar *Enigma* Variations, or even that superb picture of London life called *Cockaigne*.
 The concert might have opened with the Prelude to Wagner's *The Mastersingers*, marvellous tribute to that sanity and generosity

of mind which Nazi Germany has discarded. This music-lover has certainly, like Delius, heard a cuckoo in spring, and probably, like Debussy, thrown his full length upon the grass and dreamed. If Dr Sargent's friend was listening to his radio set last Sunday he must have heard Richard Strauss's *Don Juan,* and would have known that to the musically-minded there is an intenser thrill than anything imparted by Clark Gable or Gary Cooper to the nitwit screen-gazer. Those are eight of Mr Cardus's composers. The other two are Mahler and César Franck, and if our friend thinks these composers are trying him a bit high I shan't quarrel.

Cardus is that rare thing among musical critics : he is a critic who is musical and who likes music. And then there is another matter. Cardus is not one-sided. I like to know that an art critic understands something about boxing and a dramatic critic something about pedigree cattle. I mistrust the musical critic who is bounded by oboe and clarinet, piccolo and bassoon, and outside that windy frame knows nothing of the world.

One of the reasons that Cardus is one of the best living musical critics is that he is the best writer on cricket. This book will tell Dr Sargent's friend all about ten famous wickets and what those were like who batted on them.

Feb. 18 Yesterday Jock, on leave, took me out to lunch, and I was
Sunday. delighted to find him in much better form and almost his old self. Told me that to criticise *Emma,* or anything else that Jane wrote and which will, could, or might be adapted from her books, is to behave like a navvy who, offered a glass of vintage claret, spits, throws it on the floor, and says, " B—— this muck; let's 'ave some bloody wallop ! " As I was turning this over Jock told me that he had made the acquaintance of a French-Canadian called—Jock swore he hadn't invented it—Fidèle Galant. I told him that this must be a character straight out of Maurice Hewlett. Anyhow, the name was so beautiful that on the strength of it I proposed to buy Jock some brandy, at which he demurred. I said, " I have more money than you have." He said darkly, " That's as may be." Now I had often wondered how he could retain his flat in King Street on the pay of an ordinary seaman, and it suddenly dawned on me that he must have made a small fortune out of the *Henry V* film. Mollified by the brandy, Jock conceded that if he were on a desert island and given the choice of one author it would not be either Jane or Proust, but Charles Dickens. I said, " If it comes to that, any sane castaway would rather have a hogshead of wallop than a bottle of Mouton Rothschild." After this went home and worked. Then to supper with Tom Curtiss. Tiny club at the top of five or six flights of stairs, lift into which four people can squeeze, and in the corner of the men's lavatory a door with a wee notice : " Fire Exit." There may be

other exits and notices. I didn't see them. Extremely good food, excellent drink, a dance-floor some twelve feet square, and a band with a loud-speaker! This rendered all talk impossible, and finally I made my apologies, and went and sat in blessed silence in the street until the car arrived.

To bed early and sleep well, with no nightmare to speak of. Spend the morning in bed, perusing the Sunday papers with, as Amanda Ros would have said, my accustomed grace. Ernest Newman very good on the vanity of conductors, though he will never better the reply of my friend Alec Whittaker (the oboe-player) to my question about who had conducted that afternoon's concert: " Sorry, James, I forgot to look." Spend four or five hours correcting the proofs of *Ego* 7, which have just started coming in. Then ponder my reply to a communication received during the week from two young ladies in Birmingham calling themselves Barbara Siggs and Hazel Young. Here is part of an enchanting letter:

> Is Mr Pavia still helping you? If not, here is a list of things we can't do:
>
> (1) Our typing is slightly hesitant (British genius for under-statement).
> (2) We don't know shorthand. (Jock couldn't do shorthand, could he?)
>
> On the other hand:
>
> (3) We don't wear jewellery, and we can both manage without hairpins.
> (4) We do *not* use scent.
> (5) We would endure draughts gladly.
> (6) We would be prepared to cope with allusions to almost anything from Herodotus to Popocatepetl.
> (7) We're awfully good at looking happily vacant!
> (8) We will dress exclusively in brown velvet (in fact, it would suit us)—or has your taste changed?

In reply sent this duplicate letter:

DEAR BARBARA AND HAZEL,
Normally—and I think that perhaps I allude to this somewhere in my *Ego* books—I answer letters like yours with something Pooh-Bah says in *The Mikado*: " Go away, little girls. Can't talk to little girls like you. Go away, there's dears." The difficulty is that I find I somehow can't bring myself to say this to you.

So let me tell you a true story. Years ago there lived somebody called Horace Walpole, who was one of the nicest, nastiest, wittiest, and spitefullest old gentlemen the world has ever seen. He flourished—and what an epistolary flourish, seeing he was the best of letter-writers !—when George III was King, in a delightful house near Twickenham called Strawberry Hill. He knew every one, including Kitty Clive, the great actress and friend of Garrick, and died a few years after the French Revolution.

Now one day, when he had become an extremely old and highly curmudgeonly old gentleman, Horace met two young women called Mary and Agnes Berry, who were about the age of his great-nieces. They had come to live with their widowed father near Strawberry Hill, and presently Walpole invited them to view his private printing-press. Although he was fifty years older than they were, the two girls conceived an affection for him which lasted until his death. After which they " cherished and embellished " his memory until they died, both in 1852.

But there is this difference between Walpole and me. In his will he left the young ladies £4000 apiece : I shall not be able to leave you anything. I should require more cherishing and embellishing than he did. He wanted to marry Mary Berry; I don't want to marry either of you.

However, I am persuaded that you are charming children. Write to me from time to time (but not too often), and I promise to read your letters, even if it is Mr Pavia who answers them. The present admirable example of the epistolary art is, however, entirely authentic, put together without any help from anybody.

Now run along, there's dears.

Your sincere friend,
POOH-BAH AGATE

Feb. 19   Tom Curtiss left for Paris last night, this time more or
Monday.   less for good.

Lunch with Eunice Frost, a bright, intelligent creature and London representative of Penguin Books, to whom I sell the first thing I ever published, my war book, *L. of C.* We are going to drop this title and call it *Lines of Communication.* Am told that owing to the paper restrictions they cannot promise an initial printing of more than 60,000 copies. Since there is no money to speak of in it, in view of tax, etc., why reprint the old book ? Because I hold that all wars are the same, and that there is no difference, except in inessentials, between Agincourt and Waterloo or between the First and Second World War. Unless I very much mistake, to-day's civilian turned soldier must be feeling very much what I felt in 1915, and might like to see his feelings put into words.

Feb. 20   It was really very naughty of Studio One to put *L'Homme*
Tuesday.   *Qui Cherche la Vérité* in the same programme as the
revival of *The Man in Grey*, one of those pieces of Regency twaddle in which the British film shows itself at its worst. Male

film stars in this country are film stars not because they can act but because they have nice long noses or sleek foreheads or something of the sort. There are one or two exceptions, of course. But the fact remains that if a young man has a good photogenic profile one picture will make him a star even if he hasn't enough acting talent to carry in the tea-things in a play at Kew. As for the young women —always with one or two exceptions—the British director seems to have taken as his slogan :

> So dumb but so beautiful,
> So dumb that it hurts,
> And I don't care how dumb you are,
> So long as you're beautiful. . . .

I didn't believe to-night in a single thing that any man, woman, child, horse, or dog did or thought or said or neighed or barked in the absurd Regency story. Whereas I passionately believed in all the actors in the French film. Think of the principals : Raimu, Alerme, Gabrielle Dorziat, Jacqueline Delubac. But then one expects these people to act. Raimu, for example, is a great comedian in the country which gave the world Coquelin. Also, it's the smaller fry who are such good actors. Are they supposed to be cashiers, or croupiers, or cab-drivers ? Very well, they *are* cashiers and croupiers and cab-drivers. You accept them. They are so good that you never dream of thinking how good they are. Whereas about your English film actor you say to yourself, " Isn't that Monty Mumble—such a clever young man. Let me see now, what did I see him in last ? Was it *Topsy Turns Turtle* or *Bob's Your Uncle* ? I remember he was awfully good as a ship's steward—I had no idea he could play a reception-clerk." The mere fact that you notice how good an actor is is clear proof that he's no good at all *in the French sense.*

The film itself is a charming little piece of malice about an elderly banker who, by the simple device of pretending to be deaf, discovers that his employees detest him, that his family loathes him, and that his mistress is deceiving him with his godson. The only flaw in an otherwise perfect little picture is that the banker appears never to have seen a play with the elder Guitry in it, because if he had he must have known that every elderly Frenchman expects his mistress to deceive him and counts himself lucky if the young man is as respectable as a banker's godson is likely to be. In fact, I remember a comedy in which Guitry insisted that he should approve his mistress's choice. But then the whole matter was thoroughly explored long before Guitry—actually by Balzac, who divulged to the world the name given by mistress and her young man to any elderly protector : *le singe.* Apart from this wee flaw the picture is witty and delightful.

44

And no wonder, seeing that it is by that witty and delightful writer, Pierre Wolff.

Feb. 21 Jock calls and tells me that the entire cast of the film
Wednesday. of *Cæsar and Cleopatra* is going to Egypt for three months, except, of course, Cleopatra ! And I tell him about a well-known actor who, taking the drama to the troops in France, said as the curtain fell on Christmas Eve, " And I look forward to being with you all again next Christmas " ! Jock spends the next three hours or so over the proofs of *Ego* 7, and then says, " Man, do ye no' wish you had a wee bit genius instead of a' this talent ! "

Cocasseries, No. 10 :

When Collette Lyons stuck two fingers in her mouth and whistled for a cab in front of a Los Angeles theatre she whistled herself into a film career. . . . Her labial dexterity was not the only factor that opened the Hollywood gates to her.

GENERAL FILM DISTRIBUTORS LTD., *Film News*

Feb. 22 Not even Gorky at his gloomiest ever made me believe
Thursday. that all Russians are miserable all of the time. And no English novelist is going to persuade me that the whole of the East End is vicious. In *It Always Rains on Sunday* I read :

Blissfully unaware that a police car had just pulled up outside his house, Mr Sandigate was in the public bar of " The Two Compasses," getting slowly but surely intoxicated. His daughter Vi was sitting on a divan bedstead three floors above Lisle Street. Slopey Collins was clinging to the railing of Coronet Grove, Tommy Swann was running breathlessly down an alleyway that led to Coronet Square. Whitey Williams chewed the damp end of a Woodbine as he came out of " The Duke of Teck," a raw whiskey burning pleasantly inside him as he went forth to " do " Mr Caleb Beasley—to " do him good and proper." Morry Higham was driving down to Brighton. His wife, Sadie, sat on a bedside trying to console her youngest baby.

The implication is that all fathers of East End families get fuddled every Sunday evening, that one daughter in each family is a prostitute, that anybody in a hurry is an escaped convict, that whoever is seen idling is waiting for a chance to bash somebody, and that all flash-looking young men are faithless husbands totally indifferent to their offspring. The blurb to this book says, " This is the real East End—flashy, lusty, and full of unconquerable vitality. You can forget the war when you read this book, for here described is the life that goes on in war and peace." This is just not true. This is NOT the real East End. This is NOT the life that goes on in war and peace. It is a lie to suggest that if in peace-time you take six houses in a row you will find them occupied by six different kinds of criminal. As for war-time, will the author maintain that all the East End lads who have joined Army, Navy, Merchant Navy, and Air Force are actual or potential criminals ? The author, who is a Mr La Bern, should go and have a look at the East End, and at the same time get somebody to explain to him the difference between rule and exception.

Feb. 24
Saturday. A great struggle to get into fewer than nine hundred words all I want to say about the nature of comedy and farce, and also tell readers what the new Drayton-Hare play is about, and how it is acted, and whether they should book seats for it. The last is the first and only thing looked for in a dramatic critic's notice by 999 out of 1000 people, blast them ! Here is part of what I ultimately evolved :

Farce is not comedy produced to absurdity in the Euclidean sense, any more than man is an extension of monkey in what the layman takes to be the Darwinian sense. As I understand it, both humans and simians stem out from the same tree but on different sides of it, and possibly the first is a little higher up the trunk than the second. Wherefore production, while it may mean sillier and sillier men and wiser and wiser monkeys, can never fuse the two. The same with comedy and farce. May I say that I have invented a rule which works for me, though I can find no authority for it and claim none ? Set down in simple terms, the rule is : Comedy treats of unreal persons in real situations ; farce deals with real persons in unreal situations. Never was any real-life old gentleman so testy as Sir Peter Teazle, uncle so benevolent as Sir Oliver, scapegrace so heart-warming as Charles Surface, hypocrite so plausible as Joseph. Immerse these in a plot, and the enjoyment of the spectator comes from the deployment of character. In farce it works the other way. The finest example in the English language —and but for Wilde's literary snobbery, according with his astrakhan collar and that ubiquitous silk hat without which he was never photographed, this masterpiece would have been labelled a farce instead of a comedy—is *The Importance of Being Earnest*, which shows how perfectly normal people behave when confronted with handbags stuffed with babies. Wherefore two things follow. The richer the comedy the more flamboyant the playing can afford to be ; the richer the farce the more solemn must be its enacting. Every character in Sheridan's masterpiece must abound in its sense of itself, revel in its own gusto, and show that it is revelling ; let Lady Bracknell betray consciousness of her absurdity by so much

46

as the flutter of an eyelid, and that gorgeous vessel founders. There are, of course, an enormous number of so-called farces having to do with the behaviour of unreal persons in unreal situations. These, being mere concatenations of buffoonery and conglomerations of horse-play, are not matter for critical consideration.

Feb. 25 Spent the greater part of last night and the whole of to-
Sunday. day looking through the proofs of May's *Madame Sarah*.
To my great astonishment I found the chapters on the " mute e " as exciting as a detective story. May has succeeded, by some means which I cannot identify, in putting the whole thing back in time so that we see Sarah through May's eyes as a young girl—a feat which Henry James and Proust would have done consciously, but which with her must have been subconscious. I was particularly interested in this passage :

> The most versatile member of Madame Sarah's company was Madame Boulanger, to whom fell all the character and comic women—a lovely Prudence in *La Dame*—a face like a cockatoo and very stout. A brilliant natural actress with no traditional nonsense about her, but whose Œnone in *Phèdre* was a really fine performance. Her features could assume a tragic cast, and she was a master of make-up. Barbara Gott always recalled her to my mind.

This confirms Maurice Baring's view, and mine, that the photograph of Sarah sent me by Esmé Percy shows her saying to Œnone: " C'est toi qui l'as nommé ! "

Feb. 26 A film parable. There was once a talent-spotter who was
Monday. paid £10,000 a year to spot talent. For eleven months
he kept his eyes open without encountering so much as a ha'p'orth of aptitude. At the beginning of the twelfth month he decided that what couldn't be spotted must be invented. So he hied him to a suburb full of ordinary-looking girls, stationed himself opposite a fish queue, and watched the young women file past. Presently he noticed one of the queue-ers whose eyes had the dreamy look of a codfish. She had no hair to speak of, her complexion was muddy, her back humped, and when she asked for a pound of plaice her voice reeked of commonness. Questioned, she said she had acted quite a bit ; once as an Indian maiden in *Hiawatha* at the Albert Hall, and once as a banana-seller in an amateur production of *Chu Chin Chow*. Whereupon she was carted off to the studio at Greensleeves on the Medway and given the once-over by a casting director in receipt of £20,000 a year, but who had yet to cast somebody. " O.K.," said this gentleman. The human codfish was then put in a crate and despatched to one of the more celluloid reaches of the Thames, where

she was kept in plaster of Paris for six months to straighten her back, during which time the manes of horses were grafted on to her head, and interior and exterior decorators messed about with her complexion. Her throat was hourly sprayed with a mixture of coal-tar and fish-glue, after which cohorts of camera-men shoved her about, and out of some thousands of shots enough were selected to make a two-minute sequence. This being shown, the Biggest Noise of All said, "Hell, bung that lollipop back where she came from!" Is there any more to this story? Yes. The talent-spotter's salary was doubled, the casting director's trebled, and the B. N. of A. gave himself a bonus of £100,000 for Having Made a Decision. End of parable.

Feb. 27   Two ways of saying the same thing :
Tuesday.

> I am dying, Egypt, dying ; only
> I here importune death awhile, until
> Of many thousand kisses the poor last
> I lay upon thy lips.
> > SHAKESPEARE, *Antony and Cleopatra*

Jean Gabin as the deserter in *Quai des Brumes* shot by bandits and saying to his sweetheart : "Embrasse-moi. Vite. On est pressé!"

Feb. 28   James Bridie has a genius for going off at a tangent,
Wednesday. but his inconsequences, like the boomerang, mostly
              come home to roost. His fun is the reverse of Bunthorne's, for the reason that there is more calculated malice in it than the casual spectator might imagine. In short, this descendant of Puck and Queen Mab is a joy. But why, in his new book of essays, *Tedious and Brief*, does he make the statement : "The animating motive of most critics is to make the artist look like a fool"? Surely this is to confuse criticism with fault-finding? My dictionary has the following :

CRITICISM. 1. The art of judging with knowledge and propriety of the beauties and faults of a literary performance, or of a production in the fine arts ; as, *dramatic criticism*. 2. Animadversion, censure.

Every serious critic takes this order for granted ; whoever reverses it is none.

March 1   I first saw *Les Trois Valses* as a film and was enchanted.
Thursday. Because of that French genius for making something
             out of nothing, an entrée out of a potato-peeling, a confection out of a handful of rags. Because of the lightness of touch.

Because of the charm. I next saw the film as a musical play at the Marigny Theatre with those exquisite players, Pierre Fresnay and Yvonne Printemps, and I remember thinking that of light comedy the same thing might be said that the French philosopher held about pleasure in general : " Le plaisir est comme la glace ; n'appuyez-pas, glissez toujours." This skimming quality was entirely lost in to-night's transfer to London and Daly's Theatre in the days of George Edwardes. Everybody worked hard, perhaps too hard. When Printemps warbled she piped but as the linnets sing, whereas with Evelyn Laye vocalising is a very strenuous and highly organised affair. " If I had learnt music," said Lady Catherine de Bourgh, " I should have been a great proficient." Now Laye has learnt music, and her desire to exhibit proficiency is wholly laudable. It is not, however, linnet-like. Her acting ? I remember an American critic writing of an American film star that " while she's having a soul, she's also got a mass of draperies ; watching them sort of hypnotises people, and keeps their minds off the spiritual things she says." Laye in this piece wears a great many elaborate frocks, and wears them so naturally and prettily that one is absolved from paying attention to the conflict of art and heart. Esmond Knight plays the three lovers, and it is not his fault that Latin sentiment doesn't go, in the arith-metical sense, into English forthrightness and pluck. The settings ? Mostly less than enchanting. Oscar Straus's music ? " Hélas," as the French critic wrote of Beethoven's share in the Paris production of *Egmont*, " pourquoi y en a-t-il si peu ? "

March 2   Three letters. The first is from my old and still unknown
Friday.   friend. The school at Broadstairs was, of course, a girls'
             school.

Tuesday 27.2.45

MISTER AYE-GATE, SIR,

A LARGE piece of paper as you will see, because it's no use using a weeny piece to you, knowing how I shall ramble on and on. Isn't my writing shaky ? Am very tired. I shall die in one of these tirednesses, and not a bad way either.

First of all and oh boy, oh boy—I have—yesterday (before I knew it)—eaten a piece of pudding made with raisins sent from America by guess whom ? Lloyd Osbourne !

I spent 22s. on Mr Wolfit, not counting coffees and programmes. Took two six-shilling tickets for *Macbeth* for a nice little woman I work with and her Wren daughter who " wants to go on the stage " ! This woman is a descendant, of some kind, of Mrs Siddons. A nice original mind, very bright dark eyes though she looks seventy, and nice eye-sockets. Her son is a fighter pilot in Holland and was a test pilot until lately. He has a wonderful Highland name that I can never remember so cannot tell you. This old-looking lady thinks nothing of going to Inverness for two days, the last time in the middle of that awful blizzard.

Your " Word to Mr Wolfit " was fine. I went to see his *Much Ado*, it is such a merry little play (I always don't really notice Hero, and wait for her to finish) and liked it, he's a lovable creature (per Willyam S.)—hope he doesn't get any heavier in his mannerisms. What a *nice* person Benedick is. One treat about Mr W. is that I hear every syllable of everything he says. Hope I never see *Lear* again, I cannot stand the blinding of Gloucester ; and Lear's making *such* a fuss—even a beautiful fuss—over his hundred knights when an immeasurable tragedy is riding out invisibly overhead. Last year when I saw *Lear* bombers were streaming over the theatre, heavy laden ; this year they streamed over still, over the Winter Garden. What is all Shakespeare's Lear compared with that throb of a bomber procession ? The curtain speech wasn't bad, for once, though intoned. Didn't drop any bricks much. The first act is always unearthly familiar to me, I was cast for Lear when I was ten at Broadstairs.

And this :

438 *Belchers Lane*   10 *Longmore Street*
Little Bromwich   *Balsall Heath*
Birmingham   *Birmingham* 12
                                        March 1st, 1945

OUR ECSTATICALLY DEAR JAMES AGATE,
! !

Our usually so fluent pens are frozen by your so great kindness that we can only say, simply and very sincerely, " Thank you."

Our reactions to your letter were varied. Barbara rushed from room to room in a state of wild excitement (comparable only to the Polovtsian Dances from *Prince Igor*). Hazel, who received her letter in the early morning and was thus still in bed, bounced up and down so much that she broke a spring (comparable only to Donald Wolfit in *Volpone*).

We are prepared to " cherish and embellish " you as and when required. Perhaps, by riveting, when we are thirty-five (" the ideal age for a woman ") we will have amassed about £4000 apiece and we will be able to start a fund for " The Cherishing and Embellishing of the Works and Person of Mr James Agate."

We had had the temerity to think of adopting you as an honorary uncle—or great-uncle (shade of our now-even-more-beloved Horace Walpole !). May we now have that very great honour ? (N.B. This should be read in a very deep voice—like the Rev. Chasuble—and if this reads like Stephen Leacock we can't help it.) We hope that you will excuse our " forwardness," and may we as dutiful " great-nieces " inquire solicitously about your health ? We have been wanting to do this before, but we did not know whether it was " quite nice." We fear that we might have committed a breach of etiquette in referring to Mr Pavia as " Leo Pavia," but having referred to him as " Leo Pavia " for so long between ourselves we can't lose the habit !—and anyhow the mere thought of calling Jock " Mr Dent " reduces us to helpless laughter ! (If ever we did meet Jock would he expect us to call him " Mr Dent " ? Actually if we did meet any of you great people we would probably stand gaping and tongue-tied, looking like soulful plaice !)

By the way, it was a great effort to restrain ourselves from writing to you straight away, but you did say " not too often," and your slightest wish is our command.

We think that's all for now.

Au revoir,

Your affectionate " great-nieces "

(by adoption—on our part, anyhow),

BARBARA SIGGS

and HAZEL YOUNG

P.S. Riveting is one of our proposed methods of obtaining a lot of money quickly. If we start riveting when we're eighteen, by the time we're twenty-six, by spending money only on bare necessities, and receiving £6 per week, we will have saved £3200 between us. *Q.E.F.* Other proposed methods of getting money are : being chauffeuses, being shop assistants ; being theatre-cleaners or programme-sellers (this is pleasure as well !) ; usherettes ; factory hands, etc. B. S. & H. Y.

P.P.S. It *was* sweet of you to remember to send us a letter each. Thank you. B. S. & H. Y.

P.P.P.S. { Pray send our kind regards to Mr Dent. }
{ Give our love to Jock. }

B. S. & H. Y.

Also this :

Kildarroch
Milner Road
Heswall
Cheshire
26 *Feb*. 1945

DEAR SIR,

I don't want the following incident to die with me, so I pass it on to you. It shows that in the Carlyle family Thomas was not the only " thrawn " member.

About forty years ago an old watchmaker told me that he was sent out from Ecclefechan to the farm of a brother of Thomas Carlyle, as a boy, to bring back a clock to be repaired. (I was told the Christian name of the brother, but I forget it.) The farmer was away for the day, and the men on the farm, having finished their tasks, came to the farmer's wife to know what they should do.

There were some palings in the yard, and she knew where her husband wanted them to be erected, so she told the men to put them up. My friend was there when Thomas Carlyle's brother came home. When he saw the erected fence, and his wife had explained what she had done, he turned to the men and said, " Pull them all down, I'll be ruled by no woman." And they were pulled down.

Yours sincerely,

R. J. WALLACE

March 4   Took an hour off in the middle of the afternoon to listen
Sunday.   in with Leo and a friend to the Henry Wood Memorial Concert. Ida Haendel had not played two bars of the Mendelssohn Violin Concerto before three voices sang out : " Too fast ! " The nostalgic second subject might have been from *Merrie England*, while the last movement was a scramble. By which I don't mean that Haendel couldn't play the notes, or that the orchestra couldn't keep up with her, but that the pace turned the thing into a frolic in which the gunpowder ran out at the heels of everybody's boots, including the conductor's.

March 5   Letter from Jock :
Monday.

Staff Quarters
R.N. Hospital
Haslar

4th March, 1945

DEAR JAMIE,

I wait and wait and wait to hear about my destiny—impatiently.

Meanwhile I take what is, I hope, a final survey of my fellow S.B.A.'s. " I wish I liked the human race : I wish I liked its silly face ! " said Professor Raleigh. It's not its silly face so much as its mindlessness that I find so mislikeable—when the war obliges me to mix with it, gregariously.

I can perfectly understand my colleagues finding difficulty with the Group Quizzes (a form of my own invention—example enclosed) with which I daily bombard them. This I do (*a*) out of sheer intellectual snobbery, and (*b*) to keep up my reputation, which—at least among the younger sort—is that of a mixture of Joad, Datas, and God.

But when, yesterday, I set an intelligence test of what you must grant to be absolutely general knowledge, I must say that I (even I who expect so little) was rather shaken by the extensiveness and peculiarity of the universal ignorance. Who was Mrs Siddons ? How far away is the moon ? Who is Somerset Maugham ? Who was Lord Lister ? What instrument does Artie Shaw play ? And Benny Goodman ? Who was Plato ? And who is James Agate ?

For Sarah I got a series of " Don't knows," and three of them called her " a murderess " ! (Probably associative idea with Seddon the murderer.) The distance of the moon, which as every schoolboy should know is only 240,000 miles away, varied between " several billions of miles," " millions and millions of miles," and " two light-years." Most of them, oddly enough, knew Maugham as a " writer " ; and all of them, maddeningly enough, knew you ! Lister, whom they *ought* to know as S.B.A.'s, drew an almost complete blank, though one said he invented chloroform and another got near enough by saying " he discovered sterility under Queen Victoria " ! A mildly witty chap said of Plato that he " invented an unexciting form of love," but none of the rest knew that he was either a Greek or a philosopher ; one, mistaking the name for " Pluto," called him " that screen dog." Can you crown it ?

As ever,
JOCK

March 6   Hundreds of thousands of young men and women all
Tuesday.   over the country are trying to write poetry without having grasped anything at all about scansion or rhyme. Hundreds of thousands of young people who would see nothing wrong in :

> Mary had a little lamb,
> Its fleece was whiter than snow ;
> And wherever Mary ran
> Her pet lamb was sure to follow.

Every day, by every post, some of their efforts arrive. Half-sheets of creased and dirty notepaper with scrubby little poems on them. Will I tell the authors what I think ? What I am beginning to think is that all elementary schools should have a poetry class in which some notion of the rudimentary principles of verse, including punctuation, should be got into the child-brain. Here are extracts from two poems received this morning. The first is called " The Tramp " :

> Maybe, he is, a forgotten hero of Mons
> Just like the rest, of, our English sons
> Maybe he fought, for, that freedom, you got
> But, now, to be a tramp, is his lot.

The second is from something in the nature of an " Ode to Winston " :

> We quote all England's battles, from Hastings to the Marne,
> Saying, in these wonderful events, the English stood by, calm.

My invariable answer is to tell these poor devils that their stuff is not poetry, and to advise them to go on writing it if writing gives them any solace. And then I cross out " solace," and put " comfort." Wonder 'tis how little mirth, or poetry, or doggerel, or anything else " keeps the bones of man from lying On the bed of earth."

March 7 **Again two ways of saying the same thing :**
Wednesday.

> For myself I confess to have the smallest possible pleasure in a French actor when he is " profond et rêveur."
>
> G. H. LEWES, *On Actors and the Art of Acting*

> Furthermore, the guy seems to be improving right along, and gets so he can box fairly well and punch the bag, and all this and that, but he always has that far-away look in his eyes, and personally I do not care for fighters with far-away looks.
>
> DAMON RUNYON, *Bred for Battle*

March 8 I cannot any longer disguise the fact that I am
Thursday. almost completely allergic to Shaw as playwright. Not entirely, but almost, since I can always see the whole of *The Devil's Disciple* and *Androcles and the Lion* and four-fifths of *The Doctor's Dilemma*. The rest of the time the plays either bore or antagonise me. To have to sit through *Man and Superman, Pygmalion, Heartbreak House, Back to Methuselah*, and even that masterpiece, *St Joan*, is to me the very ecstasy of theatrical boredom. I am prepared to admit that Shaw is the greatest brain the theatre has known since Shakespeare, but it is a brain put not, so to speak, to the service of the theatre, but using the theatre for its own purposes. Add that Shaw's world is one I don't want to live in, a joyless, arid world in which sex is merely an instrument of the Life Force to be brought into play at the bidding of the Female. In his preface to *The Six of Calais* Shaw is scornful of Congreve, who thought that " cuckoldry and concupiscent old women are things to be laughed at." Well, aren't they ? I shall stop laughing at Lady Wishfort the moment one of Shaw's hard-bitten females makes me smile. And then I don't trust Shaw. I feel he will pull a fast one on me if he can. Take his anti-vaccination remarks in the preface to *The Simpleton of the Unexpected Isles*, in which he talks about the " overwhelming evidence that vaccination has killed thousands of children in a quite horrible way, whereas no child has ever been a penny the worse for baptism since John the Baptist recommended it." The implication is that deaths from vaccination are still going on. If this is not the implication, then the statement is like arguing that because on battlefields and warships men have lost their lives through having their arms and legs cut off by hurried and ill-equipped surgeons, amputation under modern conditions should not be allowed. I imagine that what is at the back of Shaw's mind runs like this, though he may not know it : Slums are an evil. Overcrowding

encourages smallpox. Vaccination discourages smallpox. But doing away with smallpox removes one of the incentives for doing away with slums. Therefore let us have epidemics of smallpox, which will frighten the wealthy classes into bettering the conditions of the poor. Away, therefore, with vaccination. I go to a Shaw play, then, knowing that I must for three hours be in contact with a way of thinking with which I am not in sympathy, nine-tenths of it expressed in a footling idiom which Shaw thinks is wit, and I find exasperating. And knowing, too, that at any moment he is likely to break out with something which might be Isaiah or Blake, so that I dare not go to sleep. The concernancy of all this ? Simply that I spent the whole of yesterday reading *The Simpleton*, extracting and getting on to paper what it is essentially about. In the evening I went to the play knowing that I should hate every moment of it—which I did. Then home and re-wrote my article in the light of the piece as acted. Bed at three and up again soon after eight, when I tackled the thing for the third time. Worked all day, and finally turned in the article on my way to *Gay Rosalinda*, at the Palace. This turned out to be a Gargantuanised version of *Fledermaus*. Reinhardt plus Korngold. Three and a half hours. Bandbox into pantechnicon. Cohorts of flunkeys immersing bevies of sylphides in Blue Danube. Cast rather less Viennese than Oxford Street.

March 10   Again from Jock :
Saturday.

9*th March*, 1945

Postscript. My point—and writing in a hurry I forgot to make it—is that almost every one of these likeable ignoramuses knew that the instrument bewhored and bestrumpeted by Artie Shaw and Benny Goodman is the clarinet.

And then there's another thing. The whole mess (when I brought the morning papers in this breakfast-time) was far more interested in the reprieve of Mrs Jones (of " Cleft Chin " murder fame) than in the capture of Cologne. I suppose you'll call this healthy and right-minded and just as it should be ? Or do you ?

JOCK

Am replying :

Queen Alexandra Mansions, W.C.2

March 10*th*, 1945

DEAR JOCK,

I respectfully submit that you've got the wrong angle on culture and the working classes. One of the questions in the Group Quiz which you sent me asks : What is common to *Macbeth, Hero's Life, Don Quixote, Till Eulenspiegel, Thus Spake Zarathustra* ? But do you really think that a man makes a better sailor through knowing

55

about Richard Strauss ? Ropes and knots are his job, not strings and chords. I don't expect a taxi-driver to know his way about the Restoration dramatists ; what I want him to know is his way about London. Why should I complain because a bricklayer doesn't know about Mrs Siddons ? I can't build a wall ! Would you trust an engine-driver with his head in Shelley's clouds ? Seeing that until you told me I had no notion what instrument is associated with Artie Shaw, why should I expect these boys to know what Goossens plays ? I am not in the least surprised that they were more interested in the reprieve of Mrs Jones than in the capture of Cologne. Come now. Putting aside the question of the bringing nearer of your release from the Navy, would not you be more excited by the discovery of, say, a last movement to the Unfinished Symphony than by the fall of Berlin ?

No time for more, the last galleys of *Ego* 7 having arrived.

Ever,
JAMIE

March 13   Hatch again :
Tuesday.

THE TRIALS OF SACCHARISSA

CHAPTERS 7–12

(With apologies to Becky Sharp)

SYNOPSIS

Saccharissa answers an advertisement for a governess in a baronet's family at Wapping. There she meets Croydon Rawley of the Pinks, to whom she becomes affianced. Seduced by the wealthy Lord Pavilion, she is surprised by her fiancé as she is playing a Sibelius symphony to the old rake. Rawley strikes the nobleman and wounds him in the forehead. Saccharissa pleads misunderstanding, but the flower of the regiment stalks away after returning the gold cigarette-lighter which was Saccharissa's engagement gift.

EXTRACT

Whether it was the lure of Camille's excellent coffee or just because of the news that Roddy Rankin's book of verse had been accepted by Plummer and Pish, the whole gang appeared after lunch. The Spanish girl flourished her latest nosegay, Gilbert Flossey produced a sheaf of MSS., the others bulged at every angle. Camille, though just as excited as others, held up her hand for silence. " Children," she cried. " One at a time. Yesterday four of you read your poems all speaking together—I couldn't get the proper hang of any of them. I shall stage-manage this afternoon. First the Narcissans. Who speaks first ? " Walt Willow held up two tobacco-stained fingers. After much fumbling he found what he was looking for. " This poem is horizontal," he explained, " Any fool can do the perpendicular stuff." Camille, fearing that this might be a hit at Roddy, quickly interposed : " Read it to us, darling." Walt intoned :

Succour

"The mirror of your gaze reflects,
  Avows itself that not
  Where vine asserts and swells to grape
  Such Be that ruminates the all-abating plot."

Opinions differed. Roddy, pontifical, was heard to grunt through the haze of his hookah : " Not altogether bad, but too limpidic. Not opaque enough." Camille raised a different point, asking, " Isn't it a little *artificial* ? I mean, those tropes sound a bit *redundant*." But Gilbert would have none of this. " As clear as day," he insisted. " Too clear, if anything." Walt smirked at such unwonted praise and lurched over to the decanter. But others had been before him. All this time Gilbert had been lying in wait, and when Camille said, " And now for the Post-Prillians," he began to chant his

Lines for a Child

" Drooping aphasically
  the pheasant dreams
  of the lilyness of skies
  in the vast, euphorionistic
  camel-trace. Now can
  he flint, glint, mint
  the solid æons of his turbid peace. . . ."

Every one liked this, and Noble Newpin, *gauche* as always, said, " A hint of Keats somewhere, don't you think ? " Gilbert was livid. " You lumber-headed son of a keg ! " he shouted. " D'you compare *me* with that demoded little Cockney chemist ! " Camille, tactful as ever, smoothed matters over by saying, " What Noble means, Gilbert darling, is that if Keats had had *your* genius. . . ." " Which he decidedly hadn't," simpered Barbara. The discussion was interrupted by Lucifer Lux saying, " All my poems consist of one word. But it is for me to decide whether it is to be a long word or a short one. Sometimes I stretch the word to two lines, in a few cases even to three. It all depends on the mood. I call this the egocentric approach—Anatole Lessonier, you know." Whereat Netta kissed him. " Marvellous ! " she gurgled. " Darling," laughed Camille, seeing them so close together, " yours is the *real* egocentric approach, my sweet ! "

March 17   Letter from Clifford Bax :
Saturday.
                                            D2 *Albany*
                                            *London, W.*1
                                        March the 16th, 1945

AMIABLE AND PEACEFUL JAMES,
    Don't you think that we might begin the most amusing of post-war parlour-games, to be called " Obituaries " ? What fun if you and I were to exchange obituary notices of one another. . . . Yes ?

After all, everybody grieves that he will never see his obituaries : and I, certainly, would like to see what you will write about me. Have you no curiosity at all to read what *I* shall send to *The Times* when you have wings and a harp ?

Yours goutily,
CLIFFORD BAX

Am replying :

Queen Alexandra Mansions, W.C.2
March 17th, 1945

DEAR CLIFFORD,

" Do not speak like a death's head ; do not bid me remember mine end." Besides, I shouldn't know what to say about you except that you had been a man composed in equal parts of wit, charm, and genius ; that you looked like Shakespeare, Charles I, and Beecham ; that you wrote an exquisite fist ; and that at the age of ninety or so you crept, not into Abraham's bosom, but into Buddha's navel.

Ever,
JAMES AGATE

March 20   Advance copies of *Immoment Toys* arrive. To take a leaf
Tuesday.   out of Swift : " Good God ! What a genius I had when
              I wrote those early articles ! "

March 22   There is one talent for writing and another for proof-
Thursday.   correcting. Judging from *Close of an Era*, Percy Colson
              is woefully lacking in the second. Queen Charlotte was
the consort of George III, not of George IV. The author of *History of Sir Richard Calmady* was Lucas Malet and not Mrs Humphry Ward. H. W. spelt her hero's name " Elsmere " and not " Ellsmere." There is no English poet called Grey. Oscar Wilde did not say, " I feel like a lion in a den of Daniels." There would have been no point in it. The quip belongs to the disfrocked (after a libel action) Horne Tooke. Nobody ever called Henry Irving " Harry." The book is peppered with wrong French accents, and in one place bad punctuation makes Sudermann's Magda a character out of Stephen Phillips's *Paolo and Francesca*. It is news to me that Congreve and Sheridan only wrote one first-rate play, and I don't think that Shaw would relish being told that his *St Joan* is likely to rank with *The Importance of Being Earnest*. To say that *The Second Mrs Tanqueray* was " a rather silly melodramatic play " is adding insult to the injury of misquoting Paula. But the book warms my mind because I am a Victorian. Everybody of my generation must know the remark in the old melodrama : " O God, put back Thy universe, and give me yesterday ! "

(Borrowed from Shakespeare's " O, call back yesterday, bid time return.") I know none of my age who would not willingly put back the clock, and this Colson does very vividly. I like his " If Queen Victoria had ruled in Florence in the fifteenth century she would have nipped the Renaissance in the bud." And I will forgive all this book's slipshoddery for the delightful remark of Professor Jowett, who, on hearing that a junior play-producing don had cut some lines about the Athenian code of morals, sent for him and said, " I hear you have been making cuts in a Greek play. Aristophanes wrote it. Who are you ? "

Cocasseries, No. 11:

At an evening party. YOUNG LADY (*rushing up to pianist*). " Roger darling, do be a lamb and play that exquisite little thing by Delius. It isn't Delius really—the thing I mean is Delius, arranged Chopin."

March 23 Some time last autumn I reviewed John O'Hara's
Friday. *Appointment in Samarra* on its re-issue in Penguin Books.
I said :

O'Hara's novel is an exemplification of the old truth : that those who live by the sword shall perish by the sword. Except that, in the case of Julian English, for " sword " we must read " materialistic outlook and commonness of mind." There is nothing whatever to distinguish Julian from the beasts of the field except that his appetites are more complicated. His outlook is entirely dominated by high-powered motor-cars, highballs, light women, and dance bands. That there can be such things in the world as intellectual interest, art, sociology, or anything except that which satisfies his immediate physical needs never occurs to him. . . .

Within two days dozens of mothers of fifteen-year-old daughters bombarded the editor with letters calling his attention to a passage in the book in which Julian's wife, anxious to make up a quarrel, starts fiddling with his braces and suggests that they should go to bed. Now this makes reviewing very difficult. To-day Leo begs me to review a book by a young friend of his, saying, " You'll probably hate it, but it's your duty to review it." So I read it. It turns out to be a study of the day-and-night dreams of a boy of fifteen, and the pleasure he gets when a refined seventeen-year-old ties him up and whips him. And I say, " Yes, Leo, I agree that it's very well done. But what about mothers proposing to send their kids to a public school ? "

March 24
Saturday.
Fairly large and highly attentive and appreciative audience at to-day's meeting of the Henry Wood Proms Circle. The routine is as follows. Lunch with Stanley Rubinstein, then repair to Columbia Studios in the Abbey Road, where some two hundred people are gathered together to listen for three hours to the chairman and a gramophone. $33\frac{1}{3}$ Mercury and $66\frac{2}{3}$ Apollo. I think I was mercurial enough to-day.

" Let me say straight away that I have one piece of good news for you. This is that throughout the afternoon you will not hear a single note of British music. Speaking strictly as a layman, I permit myself to say that there are only three British composers of whom I ever wish to hear another note. These are Purcell—I include him merely to save my face, since with the exception of an odd song or two he bores me stiff—Sullivan, and Elgar. Do I hear somebody say Delius ? My dear friends, Delius is not a composer ; he is a monodist, a meanderer ! You will remember how Macaulay, in his analysis of Robert Montgomery's poem, quotes the couplet :

" The soul, aspiring, pants its source to mount,
    As streams meander level with their fount.

And how he goes on to say, ' We take this to be, on the whole, the worst similitude in the world. No stream meanders, or can possibly meander, level with its fount.' But then Macaulay had never heard any of Delius's music, or he would have known of one fount which never does anything else."

On the subject of British music generally I quoted something a distinguished conductor said to me when I told him what I was proposing to say this afternoon : " The reason modern British composers don't write tunes is not that they can't but that they won't. Tunes are no longer their concern ; what they're after is something that will look well on paper. You won't be very far wrong in saying there hasn't been anything to hum since Elgar. I conduct a lot of the modern stuff, and I know."

The usual practice is to play eight or nine short records in the first half and a big work in the second. Here is what I gave them :

HANDEL. *The Origin of Design* : Musette, Battle, and Finale.
GIORDANO. *Caro Mio Ben.* (Marian Anderson.)
WOLF-FERRARI. Overture, *The Secret of Susannah.*
VERDI-LISZT. Rigoletto Paraphrase. (Alexis Kligerman.)
DUPARC. *Phydilé.* (Maggie Teyte.)
SCHUMANN. Symphony No. 2 : Adagio.
STRAVINSKY. *Baiser de la Fée.*
MAHLER. Symphony No. 5 : Adagietto.
MACEBEN. Strauss-Parodie.

In the second half I played Richard Strauss's *Also Sprach Zarathustra*, preluding this by saying :

" Let me draw your attention to the fact that musical sound has nothing to do with non-musical sense. You all know that a great actor reciting the multiplication table is more moving than a bad actor messing about with Shakespeare. The sun shines equally on the just and the unjust, and great music is indifferent whether it transfigures sense or nonsense. The fact that Nietzsche was an ass—an ass of brain but an ass—detracts nothing from the fire and passion of Strauss's music. Don't listen to this music with your eyes ; use your ears. Don't worry what sort of pattern it makes in black and white. Strauss didn't ; why should you ? "

March 25   Musical comedy is something I do not wish any part of
Sunday.   in any manner, way, shape, or form. To-day's article
       has to be about the revival of *Irene*, and this is the way
I get out of it :

IREEN AND MELPOMEEN

Henry James recounts how at a dinner-party he heard Tennyson say to a young lady, " Miss de Sade ? The name sounds familiar. Ought I not to know something about an uncle of yours ? " The answer is that he ought, and then again that he ought not ; since even for Poets Laureate a little learning is a dangerous thing. Certainly it was a snag in the path of that promising author who in a recent novel quoted " Gilles de Rais' well-known account of the Marquis de Sade " ! The centuries may " kiss and commingle," but hardly to the extent of three of them.

Considering the programme at His Majesty's and reading " Book by James Montgomery," I caught myself wondering whether I didn't ought to know. . . . Yes, reader, I have descended to the idiom of " Ireen " and her friends. And what fun one could have with this idiom ! Little rhymes about

Calling Persephone
On the telephone. . . .

Now where was I ? Oh yes, that other and earlier Montgomery (Robert). He was the author of

And thou, vast Ocean, on whose awful face
Time's iron feet can print no ruin-trace.

Which couplet, said Macaulay, was an unabashed theft from Byron's

Time writes no wrinkle on thine azure brow.

What, then, had Time done to Ireen and her friends ? Nothing. One cannot injure nothing. Since the play inflicted on me what the poet Cowper calls " the indolent vacuity of thought," I took refuge in my own reflections. I contemplated a letter to the Muse of Tragedy based on the story of the minister at the Dissenting chapel who prayed, " O Lord, Thou knowest that we are gathered together for worship in an edifice known for its architectural qualities throughout the whole of the North of England." I would write, " O Melpomeen, art thou or art thou not aware that in the noblest modern theatre in the South of England we are gathered together to-night in admiration of a piece of witlessness hankered after for twenty-five years to the point of revival ? " And I went on to construct the lady's reply. (Note that she ignores the affront to her own name.) " Hail, Agathon ! Not I, but my sister Thalia—whom I beg you not to rhyme with dahlia—is in charge of the risibilities. She would probably remind you of a line in the prologue to a better-bred play :

" Unmov'd tho' witlings sneer and rivals rail ;

and go on to tell you that Montgomery the Younger would be justified in remaining unmov'd by aught you may say or write in your Sunday paper. That he has been

" Studious to please, yet not ashamed to fail.

And that in her opinion he has not failed. Agathon, farewell ! "
    That, dear Melpomeen, is O.K. by me. I declare the intrigue in this old musical comedy to be more subtle than anything Meilhac and Halévy contrived. The fun to be more sparkling than Beaumarchais, Hoffmannsthal, and Gilbert. The music to be wittier than Offenbach, Johann Strauss, and Sullivan. Nay, reader, do not think I flatter. Or if I do, it is only because criticism in this field must, if it is to satisfy the cultivators thereof, be in the nature of a dedication. And what is that nature ? Johnson, in his Hebridean small-talk, tells us. " The known style of a dedication is flattery. It professes to flatter. There is the same difference between what a man says in a dedication and a history, as between a lawyer pleading a cause and reporting it." Let this critic plead the triumph of Mr Arthur Riscoe and Miss Pat Taylor over wretched material rather than report upon the wretchedness of that material.

March 26   Wilfred Rouse tells me that a night or two ago his sister,
Monday.   who had 'flu, was drinking a jorum of hot whiskey and
            water out of a large balloon glass when a bomb exploded
overhead. Not a window was broken, and neither she nor her husband experienced the slightest shock. But the glass in his sister's hand disintegrated into thousands of tiny splinters.

THE TRIALS OF SACCHARISSA

CHAPTERS 13–18

(With apologies to the Master's Diana)

SYNOPSIS

Saccharissa is now a dance-hostess at the Plaza Hotel in Curzon Street, where she meets and falls in love with the Hon. Hotspur Dossier, a rising politician on the Conservative side. On the verge of Cabinet rank, he is forced to resign in consequence of Saccharissa having left a particularly secret blueprint of the new battleship mixed up with her shopping-list on the counter of the Army and Navy Stores, where it is picked up by the London Correspondent of the " Brighouse Evening Sentinel," a Liberal organ of great weight. Dossier goes over to the Communist party. But before doing so he seduces and abandons Saccharissa, who stays in bed for six weeks without food or drink, comforted only by her toy pom, Crap.

EXTRACT

It was getting cold, so Bertram, with characteristic *grandezza*, threw on the fire a few novels by Bertha Bobbins and Clorisse Cluck to promote what turned out to be a brilliant, if only temporary, blaze. The menial task accomplished, he continued, " What I mean, Cyril, is that I don't *write* that sort of play. I don't care two hoots about a story, or a plot, or who sleeps with whom. Ten years ago when I was sixteen, I fell in with Russ Kalinka, over from Prag after finishing his book on *The Tonalities of Dramatic Progression*. Russ said to me—I shall never forget his words— ' Always keep your dramatic theses laterally hypomastic.' What I aim at, nowadays, is breadth of axis. You follow me, Cyril ? Help yourself to the beer." " Thanks, I finished it hours ago," said Cyril. " But about this ideology of yours," Cyril went on, " it isn't new. Sven Hamsen did it years ago. What I should prefer you to aim at is something I do in my novels—the setting of the visual ellipsis against the aural elision. In my last novel, which, you remember, had no title, the characters had no names, nobody knew what anybody looked like, and there wasn't a word of dialogue. Yes, I know—the old Japanese stuff, Kokokuri and so forth—but wait. I haven't lived eight years in India for nothing. In my new book, *A Passage to Burma*, I make a concession. My hero speaks throughout in Bodo. The same when my chief woman character goes to Finland, when everybody talks Finnish. Keeps the verisimilitude upright, as it were." " Y-yes," agreed Bertram, rather half-heartedly. " But I can't do that sort of thing in my plays—you know what our actors are. The fact that most of them can't speak English hardly encourages one to entrust them with

63

say, Afrikaans or Urdu. And then the audiences are so hopeless. Marian Bottom was telling me the other day that when they accepted that play of hers about the death of Hjaltabakki the manager of the Chute Theatre insisted on all the Icelandic scenes being turned into English. Monstrous ! " " Did I show you that article in the *Cerebral Monitor* ? " asked Cyril. " All about what we've been discussing. It posed the question : ' Is our latter-day drama catalyptic or just hyperconcatenous ? ' It made the point that Molière started out by being funistic, became cerative later, and in his last plays adopted a technique which the writer called ' the leaning-on-and-towards *netio*, the old *engaña* of Campoamor.' In a word, altro-deceptive idea-mechanisation." " I don't quite agree," said Bertram. " But let's ask Pettifog—he's a dramatic critic, he should know. Pettifog," he called to a young man who was dangling half on and half off a sofa, looking at an engraving through a pair of miniature opera-glasses, " would you call Molière a synthetist or a disthetist ? " Pettifog said, " Who the hell's Molière ? "

March 28   At supper on Friday Bertie van Thal asked me to do
Wednesday.   a book about films for his firm. On the lines of *Immoment Toys*. I tackled this on Sunday afternoon at five o'clock, " this " meaning reading through and, in Jock's phrase, creaming somewhere between nine hundred and a thousand articles, tearing them out of my scrap-books, preparing a list of contents, and writing a Preface to explain what the book is and what it isn't. Title : *Around Cinemas*, based, of course, on Max's *Around Theatres*. Delivered the whole thing to Bertie at five o'clock this afternoon.

My obsession about misprints continues. Looking casually into the H.M.V. catalogue, I find seven mistakes on one page. The piece I played to Henry Wood fifty-four years ago was Mendelssohn's Rondo Capriccioso, not Rondo " Capriccio." Raff's piece is called *La Fileuse*, not *La Filieuse*. And so on. It is all very well for Pope to write :

> Whoever thinks a faultless piece to see,
> Thinks what ne'er was, nor is, nor e'er shall be.

But that is no reason why one should not try for perfection. Even so, one is brought up against Hazlitt's dictum that a work needs defects to show up its qualities. Which brings me up against the metaphysical proposition that man, attaining perfection, ceases to be of interest. Be these things as they may, and we can be sure that they will, I am delighted to note that in *Immoment Toys* I have come across no more than two misprints. I have, however, noted over sixty inelegances which will have to be smoothed away in the next edition. What sort of inelegances ? Take for example the sente nce

" This is satire at its best, in which kind the crueller the better."
" Kind " should be " sort," thus avoiding the unintended play on
the words " kind " and " cruel."

March 29   The *débâcle* in Germany suggests that Hitler is probably
Thursday.   saying to Himmler what Lambert Simnel said to Perkin
              Warbeck in a one-act drama written by ten-year-old
Master Michael Cowlen and included in A. P. Herbert's old *Riverside
Nights* : " Do you not think our followers may turn on us after they
have been sticking up for us for some time ? "

Good Friday. That Lloyd George should be laid to rest near the
              stream he knew when he was a boy reminds me of some
lines in an American poem, by Stephen Vincent Benét, on American
names.   This ends :

> I shall not rest quiet in Montparnasse.
> I shall not lie easy at Winchelsea.
> You may bury my body in Sussex grass,
> You may bury my tongue at Champmédy.
> I shall not be there.   I shall rise and pass.
> Bury my heart at Wounded Knee.

Easter Sunday.   Here is

ANOTHER LETTER TO MELPOMEEN

DEAR MELPOMEEN,

I regret I cannot find quite the adjective to describe your
treatment of Cedric Hardwicke.   " Scurvy " is hardly the word one
would use in connection with a mythological lady of your eminence.
Would our earthly goddess, Millamant, be acceptable to you ?   In
which case I will describe your behaviour as " vastly filthy."   Do
I hear you protesting that you have not behaved at all ?   It is this
of which I complain.   You have allowed this very fine actor to
turn his back on Hollywood and return to the fold and domain of
the theatre without making suitable provision for him in the way
of a part or parts.   You have permitted him to make his *rentrée*
(at the Westminster) in his old part in *Yellow Sands.*   You know
the sort of thing—the middle-aged ne'er-do-well, to the material
eye disreputable and down-at-heel, but to the inner vision still a
man of parts.   As a rôle this is a good rôle—but it is not good
enough for the man or the occasion.   Suppose great Irving to have
returned from Hollywood—may Jove's thunderbolts strike me if I
think that all the millions of Pactolus Projections would have lured
him there—imagine H. I. returning after some six or seven years to
fob us off with Corporal Brewster !

Perhaps your sister Thalia is in part blameworthy ?   Very well,
then, let me ask both of you ladies what you have in store for an

actor whose successes include Webster's Flaminco, the Shavian Cæsar, He-Ancient, Lickcheese, King Magnus, and Captain Shot-over, Besier's Edward Moulton Barrett, and Carroll's Canon Skerritt. Those who saw *Shadow and Substance*, and were not impressed by it over here, are always told that they did not see Hardwicke's performance. Well, now is the chance to let us see it. Have I any suggestions ? Yes. I suggest that this accoladed actor might like to give us a Sunday-afternoon taste of his qualities. Why not *Rosmersholm* ? I want to find out whether this rare Ibsenite bird is goose or swan. Swan, I think, albeit rather a muddled one. And since nothing could be wrong with the choice of Sonia Dresdel for Rebecca, I look to see this pair make us accept this play's ending. Can they rise to those heights at which " tragedy burns up the lamp that holds it, and flames like a star, uncon-ditioned and absolute " ? Let Hardwicke and Dresdel prove that this play is the masterpiece G. B. S. quintessentially declared it to be.

And then, of course, there is Borkman. Dear Melpomeen and dear Thalia, unite with me in inviting this brilliant player to blow John Gabriel's horn.

Your earthbound
AGATHON

Easter Monday. Jock writes from Scotland to say that his father is dying. I am not to attempt condolences, he says.

" Some glory in their birth, some in their skill. . . ." Osbert Sitwell glories in the fact that his family tree contains a duke, a marquis, an earl, and innumerable baronets. But then, we all dote on something. I dote on the fact that my tree includes David Cox the painter, Edward Shuter the comedian and original Mr Hardcastle in *She Stoops to Conquer,* and innumerable clowns and dancing masters. *Left Hand, Right Hand!* tells us that the author was christened by a bishop, and that his father's manners were " exquisite and elaborate, about the time of Charles II, but with a touch, too, of the Meredithian baronet, Sir Willoughby Patterne or Sir Austin Feverel, clinging to them." Pure Thackeray, this. I conceive it difficult for Osbert to realise that the interest of the average chuckle-headed reader begins with his activities and not with those of Chaucerian progenitors. On the other hand, this exquisite book though not exciting or arresting, presents a picture of the England now passing away which will be of the utmost value to the social historian of the future. This first instalment of what promises to be a four-volume Life is the history of a great house and a great family rather than an " indiwidgle." (Why drag in Mrs Gamp ? Reaction from the book's near-pomposity.) There is some admirable writing; Osbert is particularly good about the painter Sargent. For example:

> Sargent matched the Edwardian Age to a nicety; he was entirely occupied with outward and superficial effects. Money, one would hazard, bore for this painter the identical Edwardian sanctity that it possessed for the City magnates, sporting peers, and old-clothes and furniture dealers whose likenesses and those of their wives he was obliged to perpetuate. Yet the fact that he was so plainly more interested in the appurtenances of the sitters and in the appointments of their rooms than their faces, from which he sought refuge in the tilted top-hats, with their sombre but water-light reflections, the cravats and fur coats of the men, or in the tiaras, flashing, stiff but uneasy, above the heads of the women, or in the brocades and velvets they were wearing, in no way detracted from his popularity with them.

Many people will like John Piper's pictures of the ancestral home at Renishaw, complete with what Sairey Gamp somewhere calls " a parapidge with chimbley pots to walk on in case of fire." But I am not convinced. I just do not believe in a gloomy pile lit exteriorly by a glare from burning stables. The illustrations have the air of a cross between Flaminck—one suspects a colour scheme of gamboge and crimson lake—and the last shot in the film of Daphne du Maurier's *Rebecca*. Stevenson says about a great novel by Dumas : " A proportion of readers stumble at the threshold. In so vast a mansion there were sure to be back stairs and kitchen offices where no one would delight to linger." I suggest that the present volume is vestibule and antechamber to a mansion which, fully entered upon, will prove a storehouse of delight. Osbert is something much rarer than an aristocrat. He is an artist, and of the most fastidious kind. His writing, as writing, is gold that has passed the " furnage."

April 3
Tuesday.
Leo hands me this letter from his and my little Irish friend (see *Ego* 7, entry for December 22, 1944):

> 18 *Park View Avenue*
> *Harold's Cross*
> *Dublin*
>
> 29.3.45

DEAR OGRE,
I'm afraid you're an ogre with a tendency to be naughty. Why? For letting J. A. waste his leisure moments in replying to

me. I know James, dear fellow that he is, can't restrain these kind but rash impulses. But you ought to have more sense. Indeed, your letters would seem far too skittish, to some people. However, I enjoy people of advanced years with a youthful sense of humour. As Elia says, " I hate people who meet Time half-way ; I am for no compromise with that inevitable spoiler." You see, I suppose, that I'm writing this letter simply for the sake of getting a reply. A letter from you now and again would keep me alive. I'm bored to death. There is nothing so boring as a conventional childhood for one who knows that there is such a thing as an unconventional childhood. People in my circle don't read anything worth while, don't say anything witty, and for a young prig like me that's unbearable. I'm in the mood at this point for giving a highly emotional outburst, but I know what effect that would have on a hardened old cynic like you. But I'm boring you now, and I'd hate to think that. Spare a few moments and reply, like a nice kind ogre.

All the best
From your clever child,
J. E. JORDAN

And I weigh in with :

*Queen Alexandra Mansions, W.C.*2
April 3rd, 1945

DEAR CHILD,
    I have read your letter to Leo. Don't waste too much of your cleverness on the desert air of Grape Street. We spend most of our time discouraging talentless little brats. Now we think that you may have the knack of writing. Keep on at it. Read your best Irish authors. Study Swift, the poetry of W. B. Yeats, and the plays of J. M. Synge. Visit the Abbey and Gate Theatres as often as you can. Go and hear good music. Write to me once a month, and Leo will answer.

Yours sincerely,
JAMES AGATE

And then this comes from Clifford Bax :

*D*2 *Albany*
*London, W.*1
April 3rd, 1945

MY DEAR JAMES,
    I find that I did not thank you enough for the exceedingly lively book which you so unexpectedly gave to me. For Easter I, the world's record stay-at-home, was carried off in a car to a so-called Manor in Surrey. It was really four Tudor cottages knocked into one. There was no water-supply to the bath, though a trickle flowed into the privy ; there were countless electric-light switches

which ignited nothing, and the power-plugs were powerless. The rooms were so low that I hit my Tudor head countless times against those Tudor beams and, in fact, had to go into the garden if I wanted to stand up to my heroic height of six feet one inch.

So your book was a delightful companion. For one thing, only Shelley preferred to read while standing, and so, engrossed by your chapters, I kept to my chair, which was embroidered with a scene —Harold being crowned by Bishop Somebody—from the Bayeux tapestries. Yes, dear James, your fine old play discourses were balm to a much-bumped cranium. . . . Heroines are safely permitted to Draw Themselves Up to Their Full Height before Sweeping Out : but Authors should be lowly. Have you not told many a dramatist that simple truth ?

No ! I see now that, unloved as you may be, you are the least loathsome of your tribe or species. . . . Of course, you know about those HUGE ants who terrify humanity in Central America when they advance in phalanx ? When I read about them I always think of Critics at a First Night.

Well, now, your esteemed colleague Howard Spring says that the only persons who might conceivably enjoy my works are those who refuse water unless it has been filtered—did he say thrice-filtered ? So I envy you your robust enjoyment of Nellie Wallace, Robey, and the rest of them. It all goes, I expect, with a relish for Dickens ? Music-hall humour has always been, for me, as amusing as the noise of a child who keeps on slate-scratching. You yourself have granted me a pinch of wit in my composition, and I therefore suspect that these clownish players offend my sense of beauty and of human dignity. I could never see why, on the halls, women— as a rule—were allowed their beauty while men had to make themselves vulgar and grotesque ; nor could I see why the word " beer " should elicit " a safe laugh " or guffaw ; nor have I ever felt that sex union is either indecent or comic. To me it appears as a physical attempt to reproduce the greatest of all spiritual experiences, but perhaps you will smile at my Buddhism. However, to take " sex " seriously is to find most of the music-hall jokes just dreary. Suppose music-hall comedians continuously joked about " roses " or " Brahms "—you would find them simply tiresome. So I have not seen most of the people whom at the end of the book you have so adroitly outlined. . . .

But if you meet Mr Spring will you, dear James, assure him that on one occasion, put in first by a speculative captain, I scored eighteen runs from the first three balls of the match ? I suppose he conceives of me as a lily-dandling pseudo-æsthete !

Yours admiringly,
CLIFFORD BAX

P.S. Admiringly ? Yes, the notices are strewn with flourishes of wit and phrase which no other Dramatic Ant could have achieved.

Am replying :

DEAR C. B.,

But you didn't ought to write me that sort of letter. I don't mean the trowel stuff—I can take praise with anybody. It's the sex question which worries me ; it arouses a passion for amateur metaphysics which I hoped I had laid. Sex, or rather fecundity, is the one thing in the universe I feel sure of, in the sense that I feel that the First Cause intended it. Did the F. C., when it created oxygen and hydrogen, contemplate water ? Or did it give O and H the sex urge in the sense that two parts of H desired O to the point of creating water ? I can conceive that man is a fluke and that his highest aspirations are self-invented embroideries with which the F. C., like Barrie's schoolmistress, is not concerned. But fecundity, or burgeoning, or whatever you call it, is the concern of the tree outside my bedroom window. (Yes, trees grow in Holborn as well as in Brooklyn.) That amiable vegetable obeys its own natural law without any of man's sentimental refinements. I think every tree is right, and every monk and nun wrong. What should we think of a laburnum which was too virtuous to blossom ? And what am I to think of the silly woman I saw eating an ice at the Café Royal to-day ? She had on a veil which hung two inches below her chin. Every time she took a spoonful she raised her veil, and then lowered it again. I think it was the same woman that I saw the other evening at the theatre looking at *Macbeth* through a spotted cowl. I could have brained her. Far, far sooner would I cohabit with a blubber-chewing she-Eskimo or unwashed Hottentot than this veiled idiocy. How the man with her, presumably her husband, had not thrashed this nonsense out of her I fail to understand. I have improved upon Goldsmith's Mr Hardcastle. I like old manners, old books, old wine, and old women. And old friends like you.

EVER,
JAMES

April 4   Times change, but some of us don't change with them.
Wednesday.   Forty years ago Montague could write about an absurd melodrama : " The badinage ranges among such lawful topics as the corpulence of one's father's guests." Modern taste in jesting appears to regard a dead wife as a lawful topic. I am afraid I am old-fashioned in this matter. I don't think Dickens would have considered the materialisation—to use the spiritualistic word—of Dora to David Copperfield and Agnes as a theme for farce. I confess on the first night of Noel's *Blithe Spirit*, now getting on for four years ago, to being genuinely shocked at this play's second wife's remark : " Elvira was of the earth, earthy," and the husband's reply : " Well, she is now, anyway." Am I then offended by jokes about

heaven and hell ? It depends upon the joker. I am not offended, for example, by Hector Crémieux's libretto to Offenbach's *Orphée aux Enfers*. Nor by Halévy's little story, *Le Rêve*. The scene is Paradise, and Gaston and Raoul lay claim to the wife they have had on earth, a priest having made each this promise, one at the Church of Sainte-Clotilde and the other at La Madeleine. Raoul holds his claim to be the stronger because the priest in his case was a bishop. The Père Éternel, protesting that His earthly agents are sometimes in the habit of promising more than they can perform, tells the widow that she may choose between her husbands. To which she replies, " Si vous étiez infiniment bon, Seigneur, vous me permettriez de m'arranger avec Monsieur de Séricourt qui est là-bas dans ce petit nuage à gauche et qui me fait des signes depuis un quart d'heure." This always seems to me to be an admirable story. How comes it, then, that I can't laugh at *Blithe Spirit* ? Because it is *common* ! The film, which I saw this morning, is commoner still. Rex Harrison, Constance Cummings, and Kay Hammond do well enough in the Selfridge-cum-Harrod's glove-counter school of banter imposed on them by their material. But for me both the play and the film centre in Margaret Rutherford. I warn her that when, æons hence, she arrives in the Upper Regions, she will find me in my little cloud winking prodigiously.

P.S. I am wrong to attribute commonness to Noel. This is uncritical. The proper thing to say is that the age is common, and that Noel's plays mirror the age.

April 5   In my mail was a parcel from South Africa, in the
Thursday.   wrappings of which I found this :

DECLARATION OF INDEPENDENCE BY FOUR-YEAR-OLD SON

He will just do nothing at all.
He will just sit there in the sun,
And when they speak to him, he will not answer them,
Because he does not care to.
He will stick them with spears and put them in the dustbin.
When they tell him to eat his dinner, he will just laugh at them.
And he will not take his nap, because he does not care to.
He will just sit there in the sun.
He will go away and play with the Panda,
And when they come to look for him
He will put spikes in their eyes and put them in the dustbin,
And put the cover on.
He will not go out in the fresh air or eat his vegetables
Or make wee-wee for them, and he will get as thin as a marble,
He will just do nothing at all.
He will just sit there in the sun.

438 *Belchers Lane*
Little Bromwich
Birmingham
10 *Longmore Street*
Birmingham 12
April 5, 1946

OUR DEAR JAMES AGATE,

It has been very difficult to restrain ourselves from writing as we have just discovered your novels (*i.e.*, we have only recently been able to get them from the library). We are fascinated. We started off with *Blessed are the Rich*, and it's unlike any other novel we've ever read—and that's not meant in any nasty sense. As Mark (*Gemel in London*) Rubicon says in reply to Gemel's

" Is it a good novel ? "
" It's good everything else ! "

So are yours, and what a lot of everything else there is ! That chapter of social criticism, for example, we feel has never been excelled for lucidity, forcefulness, and truth. (Would you like us to write your " blurb " for you ? We could do it with clear consciences because we really mean it.)

In the course of re-reading Caryl Brahms's *Robert Helpmann* we came across a passage of criticism from the *Manchester Guardian* on Helpmann's ballet *Hamlet*. Was it written by Jock ? Certain passages have his touch—for example : " *Hamlet* has survived modern dress, Sir Henry Irving, Ambroise Thomas, and Dr Bowdler, and if a ballet-master chooses to translate it into terms of the *Yellow Book* Shakespeare can take it with head unbowed. . . ."

Instead of riveting we are doing Inland Revenue work during our holidays. If we come across a Final Demand for you we will carefully suppress it. But we don't think there's much chance of that—by which we don't mean that we don't think there's much chance of your receiving a Final Demand, but that there's not much chance of our coming across it in Birmingham. And talking of Birmingham, have you still got ponies near Birmingham and if so would you descend to coming to Kunzle's Cafeteria to drink tea (no coffee !) and eat trifle (this is optional !) ?

By the way, would you be interested in what we look like, because here are descriptions of each other. If you're not interested, skip it ! BARBARA is medium height and slim, by which I do not mean skinny. She has the shape of face which Louise de Quérouaille should have had to justify the description " baby-faced." Her eyes are large and slate-grey set under thick dark brows. Her nose is snub. Her mouth is normal. Her crowning glory, and for once the title is justified, is red—not that harsh scarlet which one sees so often nowadays, but a gentle " commingling " of every red shade that ever was with a slight bias towards fair. In fact, in appearance she greatly resembles Sarah Churchill, first Duchess of Marlborough. In temperament she is very much like Horatio, and not a " pipe for fortune's fingers." HAZEL is medium height and build. Her face is an ordinary shape. Her eyes are hazel and fairly deep-set, and they twinkle ! Her mouth is thin-lipped and flexible. Her nose is long and straight. Her hair is light brown and curly. She is a feminine version of John Gielgud.

Did you manage to skip all that ?

Our dutiful regards.
Yours sincerely,
HAZEL YOUNG
BARBARA SIGGS

P.S. We hope you are suitably impressed by our typing. For its accomplishment we have spent many, many hours of blood, sweat, and tears. Yet we will suffer all for your sake.

April 7   In my entry for Easter Monday I purposely did not
Saturday.   give Jock's letter. As I wrote to him : The average
            reader does not understand that in the case of the artist perfect grief is compatible with the perfect expression of grief. To-day I receive this :

Staff Quarters
R.N. Hospital
Haslar
Hants

6th *April*, 1945

DEAR JAMIE,

You ask me what I " feel " about the reproduction of my last letter to you in your next *Ego*. I " feel " primarily that it is very revealing—and therefore good *Ego*. A fig for " the ordinary reader " ! Where should we arrive if we for ever kept that banal-minded ideal in mind ? Arnold Bennett rightly put " the ordinary reader " completely out of his mind when he set down the major part of his superb *Journals*. Hence that superbity. If he had thought of " the ordinary reader "—who is so idiotically squeamish and so sedulously sentimental about death and dying—he would have deleted his observing of the pattern of the counterpane on his mother's deathbed. He would have been utterly wrong so to delete—because the note is a flashlight on A. B.'s mind, and only the crassly stupid reader could call it " callous."

Very similarly, my fantasy about an actual skeletal Death being present by my dear father's deathbed—it was so strong an impression that it can hardly be called fantasy at all—could be regarded as " callous " only by readers unfamiliar with *Ego* (and therefore unfamiliar with *me* !). Other things happened which I did not mean

73

to tell even you—but your letter this morning rather drives me to it. For example, I went to look at my father in his coffin, for the last time, the day before they buried him. What I first particularly noticed, and particularly remember, was the curious texture of the shroud which I had to draw apart so as to see his face. It was like very thin white lint—or still more like the super-thin layers of cotton-wool that used to be the packing of the best-quality chocolates. (We had some at Doughty Street once—it came from Heaven knows where—and I used it to pack Szigeti's recording of the Violin Concerto of Brahms when we sent it as a present to Brother Mycroft.)

I don't know why the texture stays in my mind. (But I equally don't see why I should not record the fact that it did—somewhere or other.) Similarly I may as well tell you, while we are on the subject, that my father had on his death-white face a most singularly beautiful smile, at once satirical and serene. This was worlds away from the tossed and anxious stare he had just before he died. . . . That smile stays on my mind, and comforts me in the subtlest way. He was—as you have no real means of knowing—a very remarkable person. I am sending two rather truncated accounts of him I wrote in the Ayrshire papers. But the complete truth is still to be told.

Thank you for your sympathy, Jamie.

JOCK

Here, then, is the original letter:

At Maybole
30th March, 1945
Good Friday

DEAR JAMIE,

I am at home on long week-end " compassionate " leave for the melancholy reason that my dear old father is sinking fast, and like to die any day, or any hour. I arrived yesterday afternoon, and he has not recognised me yet. He is terribly white and emaciated, and he cannot talk, only make inarticulate groaning noises. He was in a sorry enough state in December, but is much worse now. Death, in his conventional shape, sits by the bed, and politely gives me the chair when I go into the room. Death then stands—in exceptionally polite form—at the foot of the bed, with his thin arms crossed, waiting. Death is being quite exceptionally patient. But he is most undoubtedly there.

I write to you before any other of my friends—mainly, I suppose, because you once met my father : and the interview you had with him was long enough for you to sense his natural dignity and some little of his charm and odd, self-imposed culture. I am glad he has had little pain—throughout this prolonged pernicious anæmia that now affects his brain and senses. I have always, as you know, been excessively fond of him—partly through losing my mother in infancy, of course. He is almost bound to have expired by the time you receive this. Please don't bother to attempt that impossible thing—the note of condolence. Criticise me for the enclosed Sitwell review instead—an extremely difficult and ticklish review, by the way, in *any* circumstances! I should be back at Haslar on Wednesday.

Your

JOCK

April 8   By mythological post :
Sunday.

REPLY FROM MELPOMEEN

DEAR AGATHON,

You have fallen into an error of which I should not have suspected you. Aware that the London theatre is in a highly flourishing condition, and that a playhouse cannot be got for love and hardly for money, you proceed to the deduction that the British drama flourishes also. O Agathon! You take me and my sister Thalia to task for not finding Cedric Hardwicke a job meet for his talent. How come you, of all persons, to confuse the business of entertainment with the art of drama ? Revivals of Yellow Sands and Farmers' Wives will always make a lot of money.

Let me forget about box-office returns and consider drama. Where to-day are your playwrights ? You can remember the time when Pinero, Jones, Shaw, Galsworthy, Drinkwater, Barker, Synge, Barrie, Carton, Hankin, Maugham, Lonsdale, Davies, Harwood, and others were cluttering up the stage with masterpieces or near-masterpieces. Anyhow, let us say thundering good plays. What have you to put against these authors now ? Some have gone the way of nature ; no man at all can be playwriting for ever, and we must be satisfied. Shaw has earned the right to silence ; Maugham and St John Ervine have imposed silence on themselves ; Priestley has turned sociologist ; the tragic flame which gave you *Juno and the Paycock* and *The Plough and the Stars* is now but a flicker.

What, then, have you ? Rattigan can tell a good anecdote, Bridie can string together a number of jokes, Emlyn Williams a succession of sentimentalities, and Ustinov a sequence of atmospherics, Coward still sparkles as gaily as any of these. But we skyey folk have yet to learn that five bubbles make a vat of champagne. The goddess Minerva, who knows all things, was telling me the other day about electricity, one of her points being that unless the fluid, or whatever it is, is sure of its return it will not start. Can the reverse be true of playwriting ? Can it be that playwrights, in the certainty of having their efforts returned, hesitate to send them out ? In the days of, say, Alexander, Wyndham, and Tree a competent playwright with the knack of fitting his play to his market was reasonably sure of having it accepted. Alexander, for example, was unlikely to turn down anything by Pinero, Wyndham anything by Henry Arthur Jones, and Tree anything by Stephen Phillips, Louis N. Parker, or any other pageant-monger. To-day the situation has changed. I conceive that it must be extraordinarily difficult for any young man to sit down and write a play to the address of Pantechnicon Productions Limited.

Then what is happening to your actors ? Mr G. is too often thrown away on parts unworthy of his eminence. To insist that he shall romp about for long periods in Valentine's dressing-gown and the get-up for Oberon, or wear the sober black of John Worthing and the husband in *The Circle*, is to ask too little from our first player. Olivier is in goodish, but not good enough, case. The Button Moulder and Astrov are perhaps not great parts, but they are something, and this actor's Richard III is, in the jargon of mortals, a whale of a performance. But that, in our airy opinion, is not enough, even if you throw in the celluloid Henry. Wolfit ? I confess that you English stagger me. Here is an actor who, in the last six years, has given magnificent performances of Richard III, Lear, Jonson's Volpone, and Ford's Giovanni, and quite good, and in places striking, performances of Hamlet, Macbeth, Othello, Benedick, Malvolio, and Shylock, with Ibsen's Master Builder thrown in as make-weight. To our cloudy perceptions it seems that of all your actors Wolfit has throughout the war period been most active in the cause of British drama. What is the result ? Nobody in London will lease our last remaining actor-manager a theatre. You tell me that the actor-manager system is dead. Very well, then, let it be dead. It may be coincidence, but you cannot deny that it was during the actor-manager's period that British playwriting and acting came to their best. I was asking my sister Thalia the other day what had happened to a favourite comedian of hers. She replied, " I think he passed on some little time ago. Unless, of course, he went into Coward's *Blithe Spirit* ! One loses sight of a player after three or four years." I do not think any actor-manager of the old days would have let his public lose sight of him !

A last word. The Muses help those who help themselves, and it *is* in mortals to command success. And now no more. I hear Euterpe calling. Something about a new concert hall, I think. Farewell !

MELPOMEEN

April 9   *Immoment Toys* published.
Monday.   A letter to J. B. Priestley :

Queen Alexandra Mansions, W.C.2
April 9th, 1945

DEAR JACK,

Your article in yesterday's *Observer* said about some, but not all, of the younger critics a great deal that badly wanted saying.

There was, however, one passage which disquieted me—the passage about the older men. You write :

" It has been my experience that the older dramatic critics have on the whole been too hostile to experimental work. Often they grumble (as well they might) when given the same old stuff. But too often they grumble still harder when shown something that is not the same old stuff. They are too apt to think that dramatic technique arrived at final perfection about the time when they were young, and that any further refinements or twists are merely so much arty pretentiousness. They forget that an art, if it is to remain vital and engrossing, must avoid falling into routine. Writers must be for ever making fresh efforts, and so must dramatic critics. But often I have found ordinary members of the audience far more receptive and appreciative of what was new and original in a play than experienced and (otherwise) intelligent critics."

I have been looking into my records, and I give you a few out of the hundreds of encouraging things I have written concerning plays which were in some way or degree experimental.

STRINDBERG, *The Dance of Death*. " The curtain has not been up ten minutes before we perceive that we are not dealing with falsification of the familiar, but with a different kind of truth."

ANDREYEV, *The Seven who were Hanged*. " Is a great emotional and spiritual experience. . . . I ask more than that readers should take me at my word. I ask that they shall go and judge for themselves."

JEAN-JACQUES BERNARD, *The Unquiet Spirit*. " Adequately acted, this play is one of the most beautiful that the theatre has given us in the last fifty years. I regret to have to say ungrateful things about the indifferent presentation, infinitely preferring to laud the management's perception that this is an exquisite piece which ought to be put on."

FRANCOIS MAURIAC, *The Intruder*. " Is it presuming too much to invite the playgoer who is always complaining about the mediocrity of the modern theatre to hurry up and see a piece which is head and shoulders above everything else on the London stage to-day ? "

RONALD MACKENZIE, *Musical Chairs*. " This may be nonsense, but it is unusual, plucky nonsense. If any reader sees nothing remarkable here let him attend, say, a month of London first-nights ! "

J. B. PRIESTLEY, *Time and the Conways*. " This is the place and time, and both together and one as much as the other, to say that Mr Priestley has made a play which is magnificent drama if you grasp what it is essentially about, and first-class entertainment if you don't."

J. B. PRIESTLEY, *I Have Been Here Before*. " A magnificent play. It is no argument against a sieve that it fails to hold water ; not one but fifty ideas filter through this piece."

ROBERT ARDREY, *Thunder Rock*. " I congratulate this enterprising little theatre on breaking ground with a play infinitely superior in craftsmanship, intellectual interest, pure theatre, *and entertainment value* to anything the commercial theatre can offer in these heart-searching days."

Now about this question of novelty. Surely a dramatist is a cabinet-maker who makes cabinets to hold his ideas ? (I confess I am not enthusiastic about a carpenter who invents new shapes of boxes and then goes about looking for stuff to justify the new shapes.) When I came to the *Sunday Times* in 1923 I found the theatre sufficiently " vital and engrossing " to satisfy me. But I gave careful consideration to every new form of presentation, welcoming some forms and rejecting others. Among the rejections was Expressionism, in which the spectator could not be trusted to gather that a magnate was a busy man unless he was shown twenty typists hammering away on twenty typewriters. I rejected that pretentiousness which made people use masks or speak their real thoughts in parentheses. Above all I rejected Pirandello. I remember asking one frenzied Pirandellist what he found to arouse his enthusiasm. He replied, " Well, I like the different angles from which the problem of reality is surveyed. I like the grouping. I like the stage patterns, the gestures and attitudes of the actors. I like Ernest Milton's bedroom slippers. Of course, there is no human interest, but I like the visual surface of the thing. I like it as ballet. I should like it just as well if it were in Chinese." " But it is in Chinese," I murmured.

Novelty is, in my view, permissible (1) when it is the only way of saying something new ; (2) when it is as good a way of saying something new, to which the charm of freshness is then added ; (3) when it is a better way of saying something old ; (4) when it is as good a way of saying something old, plus the charm of freshness. You know that I disliked your *They Came to a City*, and I know that I don't claim to be infallible. It is possible that I was wrong and that the play, which seemed to me to be endlessly boring, was in reality transcendently interesting. But I did not dislike the play *because of my lack of interest in town-planning*. The fact that I care nothing whether the water in Dr Stockmann's baths was clean or dirty has never prevented me from enjoying *An Enemy of the People*. I disliked *Johnson over Jordan* not because the presentation was new but because, while pretending to be new, it was, or seemed to me to be, a mish-mash of *Outward Bound* and *Liliom* done in the demoded Elmer Rice manner. Say that in your next play you give the characters sealing-wax ears, perch them on stepladders or suspend them from trapezes, and equip them with speaking-trumpets. That will be O.K. by me if you have something to say which can only be said in that manner. I shall merely remind you that the manner is not new.

Now about those ordinary members of the audience you find more receptive than the critics. I should not dream of denying this.

I realise that while *They Came to a City* would have had mighty little chance played to an audience of Walkleys and Beerbohms, it goes down immensely with young people devoid of dramatic perception but interested in the housing problem and wondering whether they should put their prefabricated homes together in Neasden or Gerrard's Cross.

I need hardly tell you that just as I would insist upon the modernity of such young critics as Alan Dent, J. C. Trewin, and Philip Hope-Wallace, so will I admit the conservatism of some of the older ones. I have been moved to write this letter because what I maintain about my own work I maintain about the work of men like Ivor Brown, Desmond MacCarthy, and Anthony Cookman, loyal servants of the theatre honourably bearing the brunt of a battle that never ends, critics who have never shut their minds to novelty justifying itself or containing the seeds of justification. Isn't it time, my dear Jack, that you learned to discriminate ?

I shall include this letter in *Ego* 8, and think it only fair to tell you this in case you find in it matter for rebuttal. I am not cadging for copy.

Yours sincerely,
JAMES AGATE

April 14 *Saturday.* I have made it a rule, when I find an author wrong in any matters that I know about, not to trust him in matters I don't know about. Julian B. Arnold, the author of *Giants in Dressing-gowns*, fails to convince me when he calls Browning's poem " The Funeral of a Grammarian." Whereupon I desist from reading Mr Arnold on Browning and turn to what he has to say about Irving. " At the height of his fame, Irving played the character of Mathias in *The Bells* before a Bradford audience. He had reached the bedchamber scene wherein the unhappy Burgher-master, confessing his guilt in the murder of the Polish Jew, dies from the terror of his own emotions—and the great actor fell back in his chair—dead ! " Irving was *not* " at the height of his fame " ; he was *en pleine décadence.* The rest, of course, is just not true. Every schoolboy knows that the last words Irving uttered on the stage were Becket's, and that he died that night at his hotel. Our fantasist goes on to tell us that Ellen Terry died saying, " No funeral gloom, my dears, when I am gone." And so on to the end of William Allingham's poem. The facts are as follows. Ellen Terry wrote the poem on the fly-leaf of her copy of *The Imitation of Christ* and added, " I should wish my children, relatives, and friends to observe this when I die. E.T." Of her actual passing Christopher St John wrote :

Edy sat by the bed constantly, holding that beautiful, still expressive right hand. The left one was powerless, motionless. The face had not been much changed by that cruel blow from Nature.

79

But the breath of life was changed. It came more and more painfully as the dawn approached. The hand, gripping Edy's, moved from finger to finger, and with a last effort the voice, not miraculously clear and loud now, but thick and indistinct, spelt out on those fingers the word " Happy," " H-a-p-p-y," over and over again.

Whereat I close Mr Arnold's book, deciding that he is not the author for me.

April 15   Priestley didn't take long to answer :
Sunday.

> *B4 Albany*
> *Piccadilly, W.*1
> *April 12th*, 1945

DEAR JIMMIE,
   Your letter of the 9th has just arrived, and I make haste to answer it.
   Certainly you have sometimes praised experimental work, though some of the plays you mention do not seem to me to come into that category. And I cannot help wondering what you would have said of *The Dance of Death* if I had written it and not Strindberg. Just as, when I saw *Peer Gynt* at the New, and remembered *Johnson over Jordan* (which held and moved the audience far more and brought a far better performance out of Richardson), I could not help wondering what some of you would have said if I had written it. People fully as intelligent and sensitive as yourself have assured me over and over again that *Johnson over Jordan*, *Music at Night*, and *They Came to a City* (which has nothing to do with housing) gave them immensely stimulating and memorable evenings in the theatre ; and I do not hesitate to say that your failure—not to praise them, but to give them careful critical attention, as being the work of a mind that is at least as good as your own—was lamentable. I have an international reputation as a dramatist, and when a senior critic like yourself just amuses himself airing his prejudices then you not only injure me but, what is more important, you strike a blow at the whole poor struggling English theatre. Furthermore, when I do a unique thing and write a serious, if discursive, play for the Army, to be played by soldiers to soldiers—namely, *Desert Highway*—you do not even condescend to notice it at all ; and this was a play that soldier-authors like Linklater and Henriques, and dramatists like Robert Sherwood, praised enthusiastically. Yet you waste your time telling your readers that I am now a sociologist, merely because I make use of themes that attract and excite audiences everywhere but do not happen to interest you.
   I stick to my point about the older critics, and to show you that I am quite able to discriminate I offer you a brief analysis of several known to both of us. If I disguise them by initials, that is simply because you propose to print this letter.

Critic A. Intelligent and knowledgeable about the theatre, but now bored and inclined to be wilful. Made deeply uneasy by certain themes, and tries to carry off this uneasiness with a high jocular hand.

Critic B. Also intelligent and experienced. But bored at heart, and though progressive-minded in many matters is deeply conservative in the arts, and makes little or no attempt to discriminate between the vaguely " arty " and genuine originality.

Critic C. A nice, intelligent fellow. but has no real feeling for or understanding of the theatre, and tries to disguise this lack by making small adverse points. Should not be doing the job.

Critic D. First-class on the kind of play that was thought daringly original about 1911. Wants carefully realistic plays chiefly about personal relationships, which he describes admirably, but is lost—and apt to be stupid—if the dramatist has other irons in the fire.

Let me make yet another point. You talk of yourself and your friends " honourably bearing the brunt of a battle that never ends." You have not borne the brunt of any battle. When Ronald Jeans and I, neither of us a rich man, subsidised the Westminster before the war, just to give London some intelligent productions at easy prices, your whole attitude was grudging and querulous. You have never, it seems to me, at any time carefully examined the theatrical situation in London. The theatre at this moment is briskly being ruined by the conditions of theatre ownership, the old bricks-and-mortar problem. More and more theatres are taken over by men who just want to put on any rubbish. I have recently withdrawn a new serious play—as exciting as *Dangerous Corner*—because after keeping actors hanging about and refusing other engagements for months, no theatre was available ; and it was not the kind of play I could send on tour first. My comedy for the overseas troops, *How are They at Home ?* was a lightweight piece, no doubt, but nevertheless it should not have been turned out of the theatre (because of a deal) at a few days' notice to make room for a tasteless little American farce that only ran a few nights. Nor, in my view, will the serious dramatist's position be any better by creating any more new theatrical enterprises run by star actors. This is merely to return to the actor-manager system (against which Shaw fought so long as a dramatic critic) ; star actors are bad judges of plays, and cannot help looking for " vehicles " ; and so I see no hope there. Some of us are trying to make plans that may give us a chance of doing good work under proper conditions. It is too early to tell you what they are, but if and when they mature I shall be most pleasantly surprised if we receive much encouragement from dramatic critics. If you think you are honourably bearing the brunt of a battle, just try being a serious dramatist for a year or two, and then you would know what a really heart-breaking campaign is like.

Forgive this hurried stuff; I'm tired and very busy. If it sounds unfriendly, forgive that too. Remember that there was many a time when I could have hit you back—and never did.

Yours sincerely,

J. B. PRIESTLEY

Whereupon I counter :

*Queen Alexandra Mansions, W.C.*2

April 15th, 1945

DEAR JACK,

Many thanks for your letter. Can I put it this way—that neither of us wants to " best " the other, as we used to say at school ? But you have raised a point which, with respect, I cannot allow you to make. This is the statement that I failed to give " careful and critical " attention to *Johnson over Jordan, Music at Night,* and *They Came to a City,* and that I merely amused myself by airing my prejudices at the expense of these plays. You are at perfect liberty to say that the line I took about them was wrong ; I don't pretend that my judgments are necessarily right. What I do say is that, right or wrong, those judgments were the result of the utmost attention, and that they were based on principles of criticism which I have in part taken from my predecessors, and in part evolved for myself during the last thirty-eight years. You are entitled to say that my judgments are insensitive, unintelligent, stupid if you like. You are not entitled to say that they are not the result of " careful critical attention." Put yourself in Emlyn Williams's place and read what Ivor Brown and I say this morning about *The Wind of Heaven.* Ivor confesses himself embarrassed, and dismisses the piece with a pun—he calls it " The Passing of the Third Floor *bach.*" Whereas I confess to having been deeply moved. Would Emlyn be justified in saying that I had been critically attentive and that Ivor had not ? You know he wouldn't.

I am going to take extracts from the articles I wrote on the first productions of your three plays and leave the reader to decide whether those articles were critical or merely the airing of prejudices.

JOHNSON OVER JORDAN

" This play shows that Mr Priestley has been thinking a great deal about his and everybody else's approaching dissolution. Unfortunately, he has not been thinking very freshly, for though I listened hard I could gather no hint of any new thought on the subject. . . . Why harp upon physical corruption, of which no man is conscious ? Even death itself ceases to exist once he who is to suffer it realises that, as the old writer said, ' either it has happened, or it is not yet.' That, as Lady Bracknell would remark, is all there is to be said about death. . . . In this, the most old-fashioned piece he has yet contrived, our author has gone back to the Expressionism of the nineteen-twenties as practised by Messrs Toller, Kaiser, Molnar, and Elmer Rice, and dead almost before it was alive. You know the kind of thing. A business magnate wants to write a letter, whereupon twenty typists appear joggling twenty imaginary typewriters while twenty office-boys lick twenty imaginary stamps. The whole of Mr Priestley's first act is a wilderness of dusty antics of this sort. It shows the soul of Johnson repairing to a spiritual clearing-house where he is put through a lot of questions. Has he gone in for regular exercise ? Has he looked after his teeth ? Did he ever take the trouble to find out what the letters T.U.C. stand for, and what is meant by Proportional Representation ? All of which is expressed in terms of ballet. Then comes a great deal of skimble-skamble stuff about Johnson's money. But by this time fog, for me, had set in, and it did not lift when an incinerator, horribly suggesting a crematorium, turned out to be the door to a night-club. Here the characters wore masks, and the point of the lugubrious orgy seemed to be the pet proposition of the asensualists, that commercialised pleasure is dull. Hereabouts one glimpsed the tremulous approach to an idea, the notion that no human being can exist to be the toy of another human being. In other words, that the meanest drab has had a mother somewhere. But even here I think that if I were put to it I could find a Victorian ditty with the same burden. . . . I do not accuse my old friend of having consciously bamboozled us ; I suggest that he has unconsciously and with complete sincerity bamboozled himself. I sat through all but the last four minutes of his play dry-eyed, unamazed, and unexcited, and as I am honest I must hold that any play, whether about death or anything else, is a failure if it does not move me emotionally, intellectually, or theatrically."

MUSIC AT NIGHT

" Mr Priestley's *Music at Night* is a play about a new violin concerto and how a number of guests are moved by it to reveal their inmost thoughts. This is uniformly depressing, because the ultimate mood of every character is a hundred per cent. black-out made up of regrets and repinings. Much has been heard of innovation with regard to this play, and it is something of a shock to find that the principal character, Lady Sybil Linchester, ' the most successful kept-woman in London,' is only Dumas's Marguerite Gautier all over again. . . . Heaven in their infancy has lain about Mr Priestley's male characters, who one by one describe how shades of the prison-house crowded upon the growing boy, whether the man he has become is a cackling imbecile of a statesman, a merchant-prince who bought his millions at the price of a secret, or a gossip-writer with a hundred-horse-power car and a hundred silk shirts. All of these tell how the vision splendid died away. . . . In the last act the company group themselves pyramidally and explain that the Greatest Common Measure of them is the Tree of Life. Whether playgoers will or will not like this piece it is not for me to say. My complaint is not that it is not a farce, but that it is not a tragedy. To dine off noble despair is one thing ; to spend the evening nibbling at a wet blanket is another. When you have heard this piece your impulse is to say of the author not ' Hey, but he's tragic ! ' but ' Hey, but he's doleful ! ' "

THEY CAME TO A CITY

" Mr Priestley divides his characters into three kinds : those who, sensing that life in the city will be like Hampstead Heath on a Bank Holiday, wish for no part in it ; those who, embracing the communal part with passion, think that life on the new lines must be bully and are therefore willing to stay ; and those who are so much enamoured of the brave new city that they feel they must go back to the shabby old one and tell the stick-in-the-muds all about it. One judged from the warmth of the applause that the audience *en masse* endorsed Mr Priestley's sentiments *en bloc*. Were there dissentients ? One thought, very few. Did one or two ill-conditioned people coming to the theatre for pure entertainment (oh, dear !) find themselves let in for a good talking-to ? If there were any such let us hope ' sitting under ' Mr Priestley did them good. . . . If anybody asks me whether *They Came to a City* is good theatre I shall be forced to say no. And proceed to add quickly that it isn't bad theatre either. That, in my view, it is magnificent sermonising. Or you might put it that Mr Priestley has built himself a first-class tub and thumps on it to superb effect. What a tympanist the theatre has gained to make up for the dramatist it has temporarily lost ! "

If in my reviews of your plays, of which the above are extracts, there is a certain levity, it is because levity seemed to me to be the best counter to ponderosity—if there is such a word. The unthinking cocking of a snook at a playwright of your " international reputation " must obviously injure my own. Do you, a Yorkshireman, really think that I, a Lancashireman, am such a fool as to fall into a trap of this sort ?

About your fourth play, *Desert Highway*. I abstained from seeing this because I felt, rightly or wrongly, that I wasn't going to like it. And since nothing would have induced me to write damagingly about a play written to be acted by soldiers to soldiers, I just didn't go. I intended no discourtesy to one who has been, and has it in his power to be again, a great writer for the stage. Why don't you have another think about the theatre ? Why must you believe yourself called upon to write dramas about the Beveridge Plan ? Consider those first-rate playwrights, Jean-Jacques Bernard and André Obey. Do they weave dramas round the de Gaulle Plan ? If you want to go into Parliament, my dear Jack, do so, and if you put up in my part of the world I promise to vote for you. But for Heaven's sake don't drag the House of Commons into Shaftesbury Avenue !

Yours sincerely,
JAMES AGATE

April 16   From Jock :
Monday.

Sunday, April 15*th,*
at Beaconsfield

Dear Jamie,
   Your article this morning on Emlyn's *The Wind of Heaven* and
headed " A Noble Play " is a noble article—and in your highest
vein.   I read it walking between New and Old Beaconsfield, and
oddly enough reached its conclusion and culmination—" It is as
though Lear had convoked his knights to prayer "—just as I passed
the house in which that great and noble person, G. K. Chesterton,
lived and died.   So good morning and thank you !

Jock

To Jock :

*Queen Alexandra Mansions, W.C.*2
April 16*th,* 1945

Dear Jock,
   Thanks for letter.   I suspect that you would have found a lot
of your Dad in Herbert Lomas's Shepherd.
   Have just come back from Chatham, where I talked to the staff
and patients of the Naval Hospital on the theme of " Good Music
is not Dull."   You can imagine the wrangling Leo and I had about
the choice of records.   The old thing wanting me to play the boys
pieces proving that good music is *duller than they thought*—things
like the second movement of the Beethoven No. 8 or the last movement of the Mozart E flat.
   You will agree, won't you, Jock, that for the purposes of a recital
like to-day's most composers are too long in getting under way?
It's the old business of the music hall ; your serious actor can
afford to play himself in, your low comedian hasn't a second to
waste.   The last movement to Tschaikowsky's No. 4 is a superb
example.   Give the boys that opening flourish, repeated twice, you
remember, and they will put up with what follows.   Take away
the flourish, and the foot-shuffling starts at once.   Anyhow, Leo
and I spent two afternoons on the job, and presently he went off
to the H.M.V. place in Oxford Street with an impeccable list of
nine records, including the *Fledermaus* Overture, the *Valse Oubliée*
of Liszt, and the Johann Strauss *Perpetuum Mobile.*   They hadn't
one of them in stock, so I had to rely on my own little collection.
Surgeon Rear-Admiral Sankey was charming, and with his permission I improvised a jury of twelve members of all ratings and
both sexes.   Here is the result, ten marks being the maximum
for any item.   You will understand that there was time only for
snippets of the longer pieces, and if you boggle at the inclusion of
the Herman Finck I must explain that it was just to give them an
" easy."

GOUNOD.	Gigli singing *Salve, dimora.*	(91 marks)
LISZT.	Hungarian Rhapsody No. 1.	(88 marks)
TSCHAIKOWSKY.	Finale to Fourth Symphony.	(87 marks)
CHOPIN.	Two Studies, op. 25, Nos. 2 and 11.	(86 marks)
CHABRIER.	*España.*	(85 marks)
FINCK.	*Melodious Memories.*	(84 marks)
HANDEL.	*The Origin of Design.*	(77 marks)
ELGAR.	*Enigma* Variations, Nos. 8 and 9.	(73 marks)
BIZET.	Adagietto from *L'Arlésienne* Suite.	(71 marks)

As there were three minutes to go, I gave them as an encore piece Gigli in *Bohème* singing, " Your tiny hand is frozen." About a hundred and fifty people present, there was no shuffling or whispering, and everybody stayed to the end. So I think the thing can be reckoned a success. After you have left Haslar—*but not before*—I'll come down and perform for your boys, if anybody thinks they would like it.

Ever,
JAMIE

April 17
Tuesday.

I see from *The Times* that my old master, R. P. Horsley, has died. He was head of the Modern side at the Manchester Grammar School, and my form-master in the Modern Sixth. A terrifying little man, and exactly like Lewis Carroll's Walrus. And I think he knew it. From him I learned that in translation it is the spirit rather than the letter that matters. I remember some wretched boy standing up in form and reeling off something about the wind making love to the trees, and Horsley rapping out, " Nonsense ! The wind doesn't make love. It woos or kisses ! " A typical incident. When Horsley was translating he had the habit of tilting back chair, putting feet on desk, holding book, jangling keys, and combing walrus moustache with long, untrimmed nails attached to tobacco-stained fingers stuck together like fins. One day, in the middle of this, the High Master (J. E. King) walked in. Horsley's sway over us hung in the balance. Continuing to jangle and comb, he assumed his most baleful glare, and when King had traversed the long room snarled, " In future, when you honour me with a visit, be good enough to shut the door ! " An extraordinary man ! After leaving the M.G.S. I went to him on Sunday mornings for private coaching in Latin. One day he said, " I don't feel like teaching this morning. I'm going for a walk." He then thrust a book into my hand—it was Ian Maclaren's *Beside the Bonny Brier Bush*—and said, " Read that till I come back, and if it hasn't made you blub I'll flog you." Years later I partnered him in a golf foursome, and I remember no stroke in which he did not hit the ball bang on

the top, mostly driving it into the ground. Before retiring to Devon-
shire he lived for many years in Disley, close to Allan Monkhouse,
and at one time proposed to engage a valet, who, however, stayed
only one day. Going to call his master, the man said, " What suit
will you be wearing, sir ? " And Horsley growled, " Bring it in ! "

April 18   Last week I wrote about some silly piece at the Play-
Wednesday.   house that it was " an unassuming, unpretentious, un-
               affected, uninteresting domestic comedy which has been
played to seventy thousand troops in France, Belgium, and Holland.
Judging from the reception by the first-night audience, it is likely to
entertain several times seventy thousand simple folk at home." And
then the pother started, the authors writing to complain that I had
not sat their nonsense out. It's the old story. Playwrights and
novelists can never understand that an experienced taster doesn't
have to swallow a whole barrel of bilge-water to know what he's
drinking. Add to this the silly fetish whereby anything happening in
a theatre is taken by newspapers more seriously than anything of the
same quality happening outside the theatre. My answer to all charges
of deserting my post is to quote G. B. S., who, in his eighth week on
the *Saturday Review*, wrote of some comedy at the Opéra Comique :
' Taking advantage of the second interval to stroll out into the
Strand for a little exercise, I unfortunately forgot all about my
business, and actually reached home before it occurred to me that I
had not seen the end of the play." In my eleven-hundred-and-second
week on the *Sunday Times* I took advantage of the Playhouse interval
to stroll out on to the Embankment and sit in the little garden admiring the rear of a statue to some Crimean general. Like Shaw, I could
plead absent-mindedness and say that, after the manner of the couple
in Stephen Phillips's *Marpessa*, Bertie van Thal and I " into the
evening green wandered away." But we didn't. We went back to
see whether the second half could be as abjectly silly as the first. It
was. So we left.

April 19   The reviews of *Immoment Toys* have been more than
Thursday.   handsome. The *Observer* started the snowball with Ivor
               Brown's gratifying " a brilliant anatomy of all that
isn't melancholy." One of the most interesting notices was in the
Tribune. The reviewer, W. P. Rilla, wrote :

    It seems to me that criticism is essentially an objective function,
and Mr Agate's criticism suffers fundamentally from an excess of
subjectivity. Often we are told more about the critic, his likes and
dislikes, his personal habits and idiosyncrasies, than about the play

or the actors he is criticising. Time and again the greater part of an article has, like the flowers that bloom in the spring, nothing to do with the case under discussion. It does always make good reading, but often it is not criticism.

May I plead that I have done my best to be objective ? For example, when I say :

Nobody who ever saw Billy Bennett is likely to forget that rubicund, unæsthetic countenance, that black, plastered quiff, that sergeant-major's moustache, that dreadful dinner-jacket, that well-used dickey and seedy collar, the too-short trousers, the hob-nailed boots, the red silk handkerchief tucked into the waistcoat, the continual perspiration which was the outward and visible sign of a mind struggling for expression.

Every critic's shelves are stocked with superb examples of objectivity. What could be better than Bournonville's account of Frédérick Lemaître in Victor Ducange's *Trente Ans, ou la Vie d'un Joueur* :

In this part he goes through all stages of the gambling mania from the victim's twentieth to his fiftieth year ; sinks down into poverty and crime, goes about begging, a ragged, crook-backed *lazzarone*, with nothing left of all he once was—except his expressive eyes. He is given a loaf, and told to cut as much off it as he wants ; the first slice he puts in his pocket with a " Pour ma famille " that sets all hearts a-quiver ; but when, later on, after committing a murder, he brings gold home to his wife, and replies to her anxious questioning with " Je l'ai trouvé," a murmur runs through the audience, as if an abyss had suddenly opened before our eyes.

And there is Gordon Craig's wonderful account of Irving, in the first act of *The Bells*, taking off his snowy boots and buckling his shoes :

We suddenly saw these fingers stop their work ; the crown of the head suddenly seemed to glitter and become frozen—and then, at the pace of the slowest and most terrified snail, the two hands, still motionless and dead, were seen to be coming up the side of the leg. The whole torso of the man, also seeming frozen, was gradually, and by an almost imperceptible movement, seen to be drawing up and back, as it would straighten a little, and to lean a little against the back of the chair on which he was seated. Once in that position—motionless—eyes fixed ahead of him and fixed on us all —there he sat for the space of ten to twelve seconds, which, I can assure you, seemed to us all like a lifetime, and then said—and said in a voice deep and overwhelmingly beautiful—" Oh, you were talking of that—were you ? " And as the last syllable was uttered, there came afar off the regular throbbing sound of sledge-bells.

But there comes the occasion when objectivity is no more than a railway time-table in comparison with the urge the critic feels to describe his sensations in the train. It is this urge which accounts for Montague's:

> Sarah Bernhardt's faults are rank ; they cry to heaven—when she is not there. Then you see her act once more, and you feel as if you were looking again at Florence from Fiesole, or at a pheasant's neck, or Leonardo's Monna Lisa, or ripe corn with poppies in it.

Sometimes, but so rarely as to be almost never, objectivity and subjectivity go together. I know one example only :

> If the Paycock and Fluther were the planets of the O'Casey plays, Joxer and the Covey were not satellites only, they were mighty in themselves, and I shall remember for ever the angular slouch, the dragging walk, and the whole apparatus of a lean yet sensual squalor which moved in the broken boots of the actor who played these parts. So surely did Sydney Morgan work himself into the essence of these crapulous corner-boys that you felt that not the boots only, but the entire creature was held together by bits of string and by such welding and cohesive power as a glass of malt can exercise upon a thing of rags and patches. Sinclair's rascal-parts were the full-blown bladders of a taproom knavery ; Morgan's were the wry starvelings of the game. They dripped no fatness and larded no gutter. They were less largely droll than Sinclair's, but more actual, more terrible in their harsh and absolute rejection of the humbug which is so theatrically picturesque as to be endearing and refreshing.

Well, Mr Rilla, there you have it. There are objective critics and there are subjective critics, and we must all do the best we can in our own vein. It is not given to everybody to combine the two as Ivor Brown did in his magnificent " Tribute to Sydney Morgan."

April 20   Sent the following letter :
Friday.

To the Editor of " The Times "

Sir,
      One day last week, at the invitation of Surgeon Rear-Admiral Sankey, I visited the Royal Naval Hospital at Chatham. The object was an hour's talk to the staff and patients on the theme " Good Music is not Dull." I took with me an album of gramophone records of works by Handel, Elgar, Chopin, Tschaikowsky, Bizet, Gounod, Chabrier, and Liszt, the idea being to give them a topical rather than a musical interest. Let the boys think of V Day in terms of the Battle and Finale from Handel's *Origin of*

Design. Let them, while listening to Elgar's " Nimrod " Variation, remember Roosevelt. Did they find, in the fire and vim of the opening to the last movement of Tschaikowsky's Fourth Symphony, an image of Russian impetus and drive ? I admit that such an approach is strictly non-musical. But that it was effective—and effectiveness was what one was after—was proved by the fact that the boys never relaxed attention, there was no whispering or shuffling of feet, nobody dozed, and nobody left. Next morning I opened my paper to read that the London Philharmonic, the Liverpool Philharmonic, the London Symphony, the Hallé, and the Scottish orchestras are not to broadcast any more, the cause being some miserable question of remuneration. Now, sir, speaking off the book and with no pretension to technical accuracy, I understand that the B.B.C. has a monopoly of the air in this country. Since we do not grant monopolies to grocers and clothiers, the only justification for granting this privilege to the B.B.C. is the understanding, the gentleman's agreement as it were, that the Corporation shall carry out its intellectual, educational, and artistic responsibilities. Surely, sir, here is a case for arbitration. As I understand the figures, the demands of the orchestras do not seem to be unreasonable, and presumably the orchestras are prepared to put the case for reasonableness to the arbitrator. Presumably, also, the B.B.C. will maintain that anything above its present rate is not good business in the sense that vast sums paid to popular buffoons are good business. But that is not the point. The Corporation must prove that the extra sum demanded is excessive to the point at which the Corporation is justified in repudiating its moral and æsthetic responsibilities.

Some means must be found whereby this repudiation is not allowed to happen. There is plenty of materialistic discord before our young people in the immediate future, and there can be nothing better than music to resolve that discord. What is the use of instilling the love of good music into our returning sailors, soldiers, and airmen if the only organisation which can give them the best performances of that music easily and familiarly is to refuse on the score of expense ? This country has recently spent thousands of millions in the arts of war ; why should it boggle at a few hundreds expended in the arts of peace ? The B.B.C. cannot plead that it is a commercial organisation. It is this country's voice on the air.

Hitherto nothing has frightened me more than the use of the ether for advertising purposes. But if the B.B.C. cannot carry out its moral obligations, then its charter should be revoked and the air given over to commercial firms forced by competition to deliver the goods, even when some of those goods are, regrettably, of the highest quality !

Yours faithfully,
JAMES AGATE

The Savage Club
April 20, '45

April 21   How far should a writer take his readers into his
Saturday.   confidence ? Shall I " lose face " if I confess that
           the *Ego* books are not the careless jottings of idle
half-hours ? That I think *Ego*, talk *Ego*, dream *Ego* ? That I
get up in the middle of the night to make a correction ? That
before the MS. of any of my *Ego's* reaches the publisher it has
been through at least a dozen revisions ? That it is only when
the galley proofs arrive that the real work begins ? I suppose that
when I had finished with the galleys of *Ego* 7 it would have been
difficult to find fifty unaltered sentences. The reason for this is
that stuff in print reads differently from the same stuff in typescript. Very well, then. The galleys have been returned to the
publishers, and one sits back and awaits the page proofs in the
vain belief that there is nothing more to do except see that
the galley corrections have been properly carried out. Actually I
made over two thousand corrections *on the page proofs* of *Ego* 7.
For the reason that stuff in page reads differently from the same
stuff in galley. There is another and more humiliating confession.
This is that anything to which I subsequently attach value always
turns out to have been an afterthought. Henry James wrote
to his agent that the only way he could write was " to *overtreat*
my subject by developments and amplifications that have, in
large part, eventually to be greatly compressed, but to the prior
operation of which the thing afterwards owes what is most durable
in its quality." With me the long-cogitated stuff, once it has
been deleted, is deleted for good, and no trace that I can discern
remains. Whereas all my best stuff goes into the margin of my
page—not even galley—proofs. I remember talking to Leo about
this. He said, " Afterthought my foot ! Don't you know that
Dickens wrote the whole of Mr Dick's ' King Charles's head '
stuff on the page proofs of *Copperfield* ? That those two marvellous octaves at the beginning of the slow movement of the
Hammerklavier Sonata were an afterthought, sent by Beethoven
to the printers ? So cheer up." Another trouble is inaccuracy,
which is my *bête noire*. My passion for correctness amounts
to a neurosis. Not only do I look up chapter and verse, but
I compare editions, telephone to libraries, consult innumerable
dictionaries and encyclopædias, ring up Embassies. And now this
morning comes a letter asking how in *Ego* 6, page 132, I can say
that Cora Pearl appeared at the Variétés in Offenbach's *La Belle
Hélène* when I have already said in *Ego* 4, page 174, that the
theatre was the Bouffes-Parisiens, and the opérette *Orphée aux
Enfers* ? ! ! ! ! ! !

April 22   Tell *S.T.* readers to-day that in the revival of *The Duchess*
Sunday.   *of Malfi* Mr G. put up a great performance in the first
half. Like a pianist pretending that Liszt's E flat
Concerto is another *Emperor.* That if in the second he dwindled it
was because Kean himself couldn't have done more with this mish-
mash of Hamlet's " antic disposition," Edgar's " Poor Tom's a-cold,"
and a subtle prevision, which I take to be Mr G.'s own, of Pirandello's
Henry IV. That Trouncer put up a grand show as Bosola, whether
or not he knew what this mixture of Enobarbus and Thersites was
up to. And that Ashcroft did teeny-weeniers, her " I am Duchess of
Malfi still ! " sounding like " I am still Little Miss Muffet ! "

April 23   *Cocasseries, No.* 12 :
Monday.   An unknown friend sends me a poem entitled *Auch-*
mountain Glen, which appeared recently in a Scottish
newspaper, apropos, I take it, of some proposal to commercialise the
Glen. My friend suggests that the sanctuary indicated in the last
four lines is " even more exotic than that from which the Walla-
walla bird surveyed its baffled pursuers."

> Auchmountain ! ravished maid, outraged, molested !
> Poor bleeding child, sunk in an early tomb ;
> Thy flow'ry, fruitful produce now arrested,
> Thy sepulchre—thy once proud pregnant womb !

April 24   Judging from his latest effusion, I must think that there
Tuesday.   is something in Leo's and my little Irish friend :

18 *Park View Avenue*
Harold's Cross
Dublin

20–4–1945

Ave DULCISSIME LEO !
    I shall attempt to deal with your charming letter in the same
logical, businesslike manner that you dealt with mine.
    Firstly, " J. E. " stands for " John Edward."
    Re my not getting an opportunity to talk, I meant that there
is no one to talk to. At least, not in an intelligent manner. You
may, Leo, go over to your desk and deliver a magnificent speech
on " Art for Art's sake." But the desk remains dumb. You can
get no satisfaction out of making your magnificent speech. . . .
    I hope you weren't expecting a witty letter bubbling over with
Noelisms, and Irish humour as typified by Our Mr Shaw. You
bemoan the fact that the English have never heard of anybody.
Well, they can't be worse than the Dubliners. Earthly bliss for
them is realised in some awful blonde showing her hideous legs in
some film, or some horrible he-man doing vulgar gyrations in a

private cop's tailor-made. *Othello*, running for ten performances, broke all records. A ham thing like *Irish Eyes are Smiling* ran for nearly a month at one of Dublin's biggest cinemas. No wonder the late Mrs Shaw left her fortune for the advancement of culture in Dublin !

You must forgive my dulness to-day. There's a heat wave here and my latest short story hasn't turned out so well. Perhaps some day in the starry future I will send James one of my efforts.

There are no existing photos of me at my present ripe old age. Any at earlier ages show me as an odiously stupid child (which is exactly what I was.) Here is a rough description of me at present :

Body. Long, thin, and awkward. Lots of leg.

Hair. Once fair, now mousey, and has distinct aversion to restraining influences.

Nose. Sir Hook and Sir Bulbous fight a bloody battle.

Eyes. In colour—blue. In quality—like the last drop of very weak tea. In expression—" Insipid with veracity," as Henry James's father said about Swedenborg.

Mouth. Thick, sensual upper lip and ordinary unremarkable lower lip.

Altogether I'm like an embarrassed horse.

Reply if you get time. Love to James.

Vale, carissime Leo !

J. E. JORDAN

Lunching at the Ivy, by a stroke of luck I fell in with Hilton Edwards, the director of the Gate Theatre, Dublin. I told him about the boy, and Edwards very graciously said that if Jordan would call he would see whether he could find something for him at the theatre. He said he badly wanted an assistant stage-manager, and I suggested his starting the lad as call-boy with a view to his learning the theatre from the beginning. Nobody can make careers for other people, but a push at the start does no harm.

April 25   Letter from J. B. Priestley :
Wednesday.

*B*4 *Albany, W*.1

April 23*rd*, 1945

DEAR JIMMIE,

Many thanks for your letter, which I would have received earlier if it had been addressed here and not care of the *Observer*.

I stick to my point, and your quotations from your notices do not unstick me. All of them seem to me too hasty and airy in their judgment. Just as you settled yourself solidly in your stall, so too you fixed yourself in your opinion of what a play should be, without really trying to understand what I was attempting or to follow my thought. I have " bamboozled myself " in a play to which I gave long earnest thought and which I re-wrote many times. Now I do not think for a moment that I succeeded here in all I tried to do ; nevertheless, your notice is simply not good enough. (I have not the time or you the patience to take all three plays, so we will look at the first, *Johnson over Jordan*.)

Your notice says, in effect, this is a play about death and has no new ideas on the subject, has indeed no ideas at all, and is merely an attempt to revive the German-American Expressionism of the 'twenties. Every statement there, to my mind, is wrong. The play is not about death but about a man's life, which is presented in a new way—as if looked at outside time (as we do in dreams often), each act representing a certain level of the mind : the first giving us all the conscious worries, responsibilities, and anxieties of a middle-class urban man ; the second giving us the unconscious drives ; the third the poetry and deep-seated affections of such a mind. In all these acts there were, in fact, plenty of ideas ; and though they may not have been wildly original (for I make no pretence of being an original thinker, and if I were I would not choose the theatre as my medium), they were ideas, and derived an emotional impact from the way they were presented. I had a lot of trouble with Act Two (the night-club) and never got it right, but to suggest, as you do, that there was only the vague ghost of an idea in it is simply not good enough. It contains, among other things, in Johnson's long soliloquy about Desire the most careful speech I ever wrote for the theatre. (Morgan singled it out, I remember.) And the third act still seems to me, as it does to many people, the most moving thing I ever wrote for the theatre. Again, it is quite wrong to say that the play is a return to Expressionism, whose object was to flatten out character, to ignore the individual and concrete instance, and to find drama in the relations of purely symbolic figures. My object was to show a real man in real relationships, but to do it outside time, to present it all, as in dreams, in a four-dimensional manner. Thus, Johnson in Act Three was reliving his past and yet standing outside the time process, again as we seem to do often in poignant vivid dreams. (Ralph suggested all this wonderfully, I thought.) It is true that some of the production, notably in Act One, did suggest the Expressionist method ; but if the play should ever be revived I should have it done in a simpler fashion. Unfortunately, I had to go to Switzerland, with a convalescent daughter, while the first two acts were being rehearsed, and it was only Act Three that was done exactly as I wanted it.

Let me make it clear again what I am complaining about. I do not expect to be praised for everything I do (though I have the usual wistful hopes), but I consider myself a serious artist in the theatre, with a good technical knowledge of its resources, and I have struggled hard to bring experiment to a theatre terribly lacking in it, and I feel entitled to claim the serious careful consideration of senior critics. Finally, I have several new plays ready for production when good casts and theatres can be found for them.

Present conditions I believe to be the worst that serious dramatists have ever been called upon to face in this country. And I suggest that instead of being funny about my sociological interests, you turn your insight and wit on these conditions, which may soon leave you without a theatre at all.

Yours ever,
J. B. P.

I have replied :

Queen Alexandra Mansions, W.C.2

April 25th, 1945

DEAR JACK,

Would all controversies were conducted in this spirit ! This is just to thank you for your share in our little bout, and to say that I await all or any of your new plays with the greatest eagerness. I shall bend up every mental as well as corporal agent to the terrible feat of giving them careful and critical attention. Delete the word " terrible."

Yours ever,
JIMMIE

April 26   " Now let it work. Mischief, thou art afoot. . . ." My
Thursday.   letter to *The Times* (see entry for April 20) appeared
                     yesterday. This morning I get a letter from St John Baptist College, Oxford, enclosing a copy of a letter addressed to the writer's City and University M.P.'s, these being the Hon. Quintin Hogg and A. P. Herbert, asking them to back me up.

The post also brings a letter from Tom Curtiss, now settled in Paris. It has taken six days to get here. He writes :

Paris is very nearly her pre-war self externally. Blue skies— chestnut blossoms—lilac—sudden showers and a surplus of G.I.'s. The food situation remains the same, and the major restaurants— Larue, La Reine Pédauque, etc.—remain closed rather than cope with the ration regulations. Drinking is a dubious business. The beer tastes like well-water aged in metal containers, the white wine is sour, the red often non-existent, the champagne usually fake, and the cognac diluted. Saw Raimu in *Le Malade Imaginaire* last night. Wonderful performance. There's a new film of Marcel Carné, who made *Quai des Brumes*. This is a story of Debureau and Lemaître, and the Paris of their day. Beautiful photography and lovely acting, but it runs for three and a half hours !

A jolly and surprise luncheon given by Hamish Hamilton, who introduces me to a bright young man intending to open a theatre. If only some one would introduce me to some one with the power to close a theatre ! The surprise turned out to be Jock, invalided, or something, out of the Navy. I gather that he has to go to Oxford or somewhere to write for a firm of University publishers a History of the English Stage. Which, bless his dear heart, he thinks he can do in three months. I once did it in three days, producing for fifty pounds a vastly filthy little book of which I have always been ashamed and which, whenever I meet it in the Charing Cross Road, I buy and destroy. To do a good job on this subject should take three years. However, I don't discourage him.

Cocasseries, No. 13 :

This is an advertisement seen in the window of a music-shop in Uxbridge :

Selection of Melodies by Chopin

From the Columbia Picture

A SONG TO REMEMBER

STARRING PAUL MUNI AND
MERLE OBERON WITH CORNEL WILDE

Arranged and Adapted for
Piano Solo by Louis Levy

CHAPPELL   3/-

April 27   The old heart-breaking subject has turned up again. A
Wednesday.   sergeant in the Buffs submits a poem, " not with a request for advice on publication, nor for suggestions of how to break into the big money, but merely for an opinion ; so as to confirm my worst fears, *i.e.*, that I am just wasting my time, or to uphold what my friends tell me, that there is merit in the effort." The letter has this postscript : " I may add, as a point of interest, that I wrote the poem whilst engaged in tank fighting in Normandy. We were standing by to go in, and it passed an hour away." The poem is valueless. I have sent the following reply :

*Queen Alexandra Mansions, W.C.*2
April 27*th,* 1945

DEAR SERGEANT,
     It seems to me—and I have thought about it a good deal—that any work of art must have two functions. If you write a book the first function is to get something off your chest ; the second is to give pleasure to the reader. The same thing applies to a painting, a bust, or a piece of music, and equally to acting, singing, playing a musical instrument, dancing.
     Your poem is valueless as regards its secondary function, which does not mean that it is valueless in its first function. I doubt if

you could have been better employed during that hour before going into action. Look at it this way. Take the following lines :

> Matthew is in his grave, yet now
> Methinks, I see him stand,
> As at that moment, with a bough
> Of wilding in his hand.

And now the following :

> He trudged along through copse and brake,
> He trudged along o'er hill and dale ;
> Nor for the moon cared he a tittle,
> And for the stars he cared as little,
> And for the murmuring river Swale.

Magic is in the first but not in the second. Yet it is quite possible that Wordsworth, getting the second off his chest, felt as much relief as he did with the first. You wanted to write those lines before that battle, and you wrote them. You got them off your chest, and you felt the better for it. That means that your poem fulfilled its first function. But it is not poetry. Are you going to ask me to define poetry ? My dear Sergeant, better men than I have spent a lifetime over this and failed. Asked for a definition, that great minor. poet A. E. Housman replied that he could no more define poetry than a terrier could define a rat, but that he thought both he and the terrier recognised the object by the symptoms which it provoked in them. These symptoms differ with the individual. The great critic Montague said that the sight or sound of a beautiful thing gave him gooseflesh. The form this emotion takes with me is a shiver at the base of the spine. I have no other criterion. Here are one or two specimens, and they all have to do with arms. First I choose Herbert Asquith's poem which begins :

> Here lies a clerk who half his life had spent
> Toiling at ledgers in a city grey,
> Thinking that so his days would drift away
> With no lance broken in life's tournament :

and ends :

> And falling thus he wants no recompense,
> Who found his battle in the last resort ;
> Nor needs he any hearse to bear him hence,
> Who goes to join the men of Agincourt.

Next a poem by Patrick Shaw-Stewart, beginning :

> I saw a man this morning
> Who did not wish to die ;
> I ask and cannot answer
> If otherwise wish I.

and ending :

> I will go back this morning
> From Imbros over the sea ;
> Stand in the trench, Achilles,
> Flame-capped, and shout for me.

Third and last you might like to know John Pudney's *For Johnny*, of which most effective use is made in the film *The Way to the Stars*. Here it is :

Do not despair
For Johnny-Head-in-Air,
He sleeps as sound
As Johnny underground.

Fetch out no shroud
For Johnny-Head-in-Cloud,
And keep your tears
For him in after years.

Better by far
For Johnny-the-Bright-Star,
To keep your head
And see his children fed.

I cannot tell you, nor can anyone tell you, why these things are poetry, and why

Can this be then the purpose of it all,
That woman shall go through the jaws of Hell
To give another victim to the call,
Of Naziism and the Fascist cult as well ?

is not. But let me stress this equally—no man should tell you, and you must not allow any man to tell you, that the effort of writing your lines wasn't worth while. There are some things of which the act of doing is the real reward.

Yours sincerely,
JAMES AGATE

I have decided, whether it is cynical or not, to have some five hundred copies of this printed for dispatch to all those soldier, sailor, Air Force, and civilian scribblers who pester me.

April 28
Saturday.

The Statement issued by the B.B.C. to *The Times*, in reply to my challenge, leads off with a piece of muddle-headedness. Have sent to *The Times* this second letter, after which the matter, as far as I am concerned, is closed :

To the Editor of " The Times "

SIR,
Let us be quite clear what we are arguing about. In its State-ment in your issue of Friday last the B.B.C. says : " This dispute has already lasted fifteen months and has not caused any decrease of serious music in that period." Sir, why should it ? The decision of the five orchestras not to broadcast takes effect only in May !
The Statement's next sentence runs : " The B.B.C. wishes to make it quite clear that the continuing of the dispute will not reduce the amount of good orchestral music available to listeners." Sir,

let us take that Statement as being issued in complete good faith, and as a guarantee that every time there would have been an outside broadcast the B.B.C. undertakes to give listeners the equivalent inside one, with soloists of equal prominence.

Even so, the public will, in my submission, not be satisfied. Some orchestras are known for the excellence of their strings, some for their wood-wind, others again for their brass. Different conductors have different qualities. I greatly admire Toscanini, but I should not want all my music to be interpreted by him to the exclusion of all other interpreters, any more than I should want all my Shakespeare to be performed by Mr Gielgud, Mr Olivier, Mr Wolfit, or any other distinguished actor to the exclusion of all other actors.

I have expressed no opinion as to whether the demands of the orchestras are reasonable or not—that will be for the arbitrator to decide. If the arbitrator holds that the demands are reasonable, then the B.B.C., in so far as it is public-spirited, must pay up. If the arbitrator holds the opposite view, then the orchestras must climb down.

Here, sir, is an issue which should be kept clear and not obscured by fog or red herrings.

Yours faithfully,
JAMES AGATE

The Savage Club
April 28, '45

April 29   A total stranger comes up to me in the Café Royal :
Sunday.

T. S. Mr Agate, why are you so ungenerous ? A generous artist admires his fellow-artists.

J. A. Rubbish ! Do you think Beethoven admired his musical contemporaries ?

T. S. Yes, he admired Schubert.

J. A. A few songs, perhaps. If the young man had brought along a work as good as one of the Rasoumowsky Quartets the old man would have shut up like a knife. Was Wagner charmed by Brahms ? Did Balzac boost George Sand ? Did Whistler crack up Sargent ? Did Melba rave over Tetrazzini ? Was Sarah crazy about Duse ? Only the second-rate artist has time for the work of others ; the first-rate artist is preoccupied with his own output, to the exclusion of any and everybody else's. I'm your first-rate artist.

T. S. Do you hold yourself to be a first-rate diarist ?

J. A. I most emphatically do.

T. S. To be ranked with Pepys ?

J. A. To take my place beside Pepys.

T. S. Perhaps you think that, like Samuel, you ought to be Secretary to the Navy ?

J. A. Go to hell !

99

April 30   I get really angry when people tell me that the dedication
Monday.   to *Noblesse Oblige*—" For and on behalf of SYD, ERN,
               CHARLEY, and their kind "—is a pose. Yesterday evening
I went down to Bethnal Green to talk and play gramophone records
to a club for kids. Small, clean, tidy room in the Friends' Hall,
Barnet Grove, and on the wall a picture of a grove of trees—more
trees than there are in the whole of Bethnal Green, that wilderness of
flatness and bricks. I had been promised an audience of fifteen ;
actually sixteen turned up. I have no illusions at all about this sort
of thing. The street outside was full of urchins who couldn't be
bribed to come in. Neither would they stop yelling. First I sent
them a polite message—no result. I then sent the biggest boy to
tell them that if they didn't stop their noise I should come down myself
and wallop their bloody arses for them. After which there wasn't a
sound. Given this material, did I start with carols by Wilbye and
Weelkes ? No. The thing was to get their interest, and after leading
off with a bit of Handel I went straight into Ponchielli's *Dance of
the Hours* and told them to look out for the circus ponies. But
what they liked best was the four sides of Herman Finck's *Melodious
Memories.* Here, putting them on their honour, I asked for a count
of the numbers they recognised. Somewhere in the eighties would
have been the best possible ; several of them were well up in the
sixties. I particularly noticed one young monkey with an astonishing
power of mimicry. He mimicked me and the various instruments in
the orchestra and was entirely irresponsible from first to last. The
Warden told me that the lad could hardly read but is the delight of
the entire school. I was so much impressed that I asked the Warden
to tell his father, who, it seems, is a brewer's drayman, to get into
communication with me when the boy leaves school, and that if he
approves I will then put the kid in touch with Lupino Lane.

May 1   Leo comes into my room this morning and says, " This
Tuesday.   is the last you'll hear of Hatch."

THE TRIALS OF SACCHARISSA

CHAPTERS 19–24
(With apologies to Tess and Jane Eyre)

SYNOPSIS

*Saccharissa, penniless, seeks employment as a Land Girl. Arrived at
Little Strangles, Essex, she makes the acquaintance of Eric Mangold,
a rich farmer who seduces her. She then encounters Seraph Cleer, a
poet with vague notions of marriage. On hearing about Seraph, Eric*

smacks Saccharissa's face, whereupon she brains him with a hoe. Subsequent legal proceedings go in Saccharissa's favour, the jury declining to convict on the grounds that her father died in Widemoor and her mother in a mental home in Wessex. Again penniless, Saccharissa accepts another post as governess, this time to the child of a rich country gentleman, Captain Gillingham, who has a mad wife. They fall in love, and just as Saccharissa, fearing seduction, is about to relinquish her job, Mrs Gillingham, excited by drinking too much red ink, throws herself into the petrol-tank and is drowned. Gillingham and Saccharissa are united in Hymen's bonds.

EXTRACTS

Just then Hilda Stumm drifted in, and Rollo asked her at once whether, in Bannerhof's book on the history of film technique, she agreed with Bratislav Brzcnv, quoted by him at such length. " Let me refresh your memory," continued Rollo, taking out the current number of the *Film Psychologist*. ' Any non-prescience of what Iwan Plutoff calls the barotic incalcation attains to a *simacrea* fluxing itself on the edge, as it were, of coincidentalism.' Do you, or do you not agree, Hilda ? " he asked anxiously. " With every syllable," answered Hilda.

    .   .   .   .   .

Hettie Spott was not, in our understanding of the word, an intellectual at all. She was just a *mouton de Panurge*, in the sense that she modelled herself on each idol before the next one dislodged it from its pedestal. So much was clearly shown on this occasion when Hjalmar Sikersen, commenting on the degeneracy of Poupoutier's direction, blurted out in his gruff Nordic way, " None of these people *understands* the true montage. The effect should realise itself along lines of endemic simultaneity, through the mental superimposition of a triasis over the conventional diaporistic visulum. Eisenstein calls this audio-visual montage. But I go further. I demand an auro-cerebral montage which shall make possible the *tandis grandis*, the super-orasticism that ever lurks in the bisymmetry of all thought-oxidisation." Here Hettie, who was spraying herself with the new perfume, " Voyou," stopped dabbing operations to murmur, " You forget, darling. Eisenstein also claims that the so-called ' double-exposed ' image is just as inherently characteristic of audio-visual montage as—as—— " " As it is for all other cinematic phenomena," completed Noel Flipp, with ready wit. To clinch the argument, René Fauchegarbe, who had not so far spoken, said, " Geometrical presentation must always be accurate—we can have no dallyings with a rutinous perspective. Just as on the ethical plane we must have a convergent horizon, so now we must pull such levers as are compatible with the world-theory of determinism." Hettie's face was aflame at this revelation ; her eyes registered unquestioning enslavement.

    .   .   .   .   .

What was quite unforgivable of Irene Hasseldon was that she included in the picnic a dreadful barbarian, one Sir Pilligo Gasper, a fat, vulgar man reputed to have made a fortune out of discarded goloshes. Just as Gwen and Lydia were in the thick of an argument about the respective merits of Konrad Blitz and Jean Castrate, this uncouth animal interrupted them to say, " I like films I can understand. I like the sort of picture where people lie about on beaches, thrumming guitars, waving multi-coloured palm-leaves, and singing South Sea Island serenades like :

> "'Jake, I'll be trew-w-w to yew-w-w,
> To yew-w-w I'll always be trew-w-w.'"

And the wretch actually sang ! Not content with this, and despite the disgusted faces all around him, he continued, " I'm low-brow, and I'm proud of it. I don't care a damn about montage. I like to see pretty girls with lovely legs and as much of everything else as they like to show. I like to see them kiss and hug. I like to see the good rewarded and the bad punished. I like happy endings. In short, I am normal, commonplace, everyday. I am what has made England what she is, and what she always will be. As for you, you sissified saps and frillified floozies. . . ." " Enough, Sir Pilligo—thank you," commanded his hostess. " You were saying, Virginius ? " But Virginius Booper, like the others, was choking with inarticulate rage. Searching for his pocket edition of Theocritus, which he found in his cigarette-case, he proceeded to read several Eclogues in the original Greek. . . .

Enclosed was this covering letter :

> *As from The Intellectual Youth Hostel*
> *798 High Street, Chiswick, W.4*
>
> *April 30th, 1945*

DEAR MR AGATE,

You have, I hope, read what is my final instalment. *Are you conquered ?* Will you now, please, find me a publisher ? And by so doing make me the corner-stone of your immortality ?

A temporary advance of twenty pounds, should you feel so inclined, can be automatically deducted from my advance royalties. But please do not cross the cheque.

No longer incognito, I now sign myself with my real name,

OLEANDER FUGGE

May 2   According to Robert Ross, Oscar Wilde "never regarded
Wednesday.   his works as an adequate expression of his extraordinary
               genius and his magnificent intellectual endowment."
And in *De Profundis* Wilde wrote :

The gods had given me almost everything. I had genius, a distinguished name, high social position, brilliancy, intellectual daring ; I made art a philosophy and philosophy an art ; I altered the minds of men, and the colours of things, . . . whatever I touched I made beautiful in a new mode of beauty. . . . I awoke the imagination of my century so that it created myth and legend around me. I summed up all systems in a phrase and all existence in an epigram.

Suppose we have a look at these extravagant claims. Genius ? Wilde was a magnificent talker and a superb wit, and perhaps one mustn't complain that the wit all came from the same fount. A Jew, on being asked whether his dinner-table could accommodate twelve persons, answered, " Yes, God forbid ! " And in the sense that all Jewish jokes are a form of this joke, so all Wilde's jokes are basically epicene. The " distinguished name " and " high social position "—neither of which Wilde possessed—were pegs for snobbery of the worst type ; the photographs show him to have been inseparable from top hat and fur coat with an unhappy leaning towards astrakhan. Of the " intellectual daring " I see no trace. He could rattle about the philosophy of art in an amateurish way, but to say that he " altered the minds of men " is just nonsense. As for " the new mode of beauty," one might say that he touched nothing that he did not chichify. " Myth and legend " ? Gilbert's Bunthorne is the answer.

The boast about being " a lord of language." Wilde was that very different thing—the fine lady of the purple passage. Apart from his wit, he was entirely bogus. The words " art " and " artist " appear on almost every page of his writings ; yet he knew very little about the arts. In the matter of pictures Whistler was constantly putting him right. In the matter of music Wilde could make one of his characters say, " And now, let me play Chopin to you, or Dvořák ? Shall I play you a fantasy by Dvořák ? He writes passionate, curiously coloured things." No person with any knowledge of music could have written this. About his own profession :

> From the point of view of literature Mr Kipling is a genius who drops his aspirates. From the point of view of life, he is a reporter who knows vulgarity better than anyone has ever known it. Dickens knew its clothes and its comedy. Mr Kipling knows its essence and its seriousness. He is our first authority on the second-rate, and has seen marvellous things through keyholes, and his backgrounds are real works of art.

The truth is that there is more knowledge of life in six pages of Dickens or Kipling than in the whole of Wilde's scented output. All the world known to O. W. was what Pinero's Cayley Drummle called " our little parish of St James's." He was a borrower, and his showpieces about jewels and such like—how he would have hated the last two words !—were lifted from the French. The atmosphere of *Salomé* was taken straight from Maeterlinck. He was a fifth-rate poet with one first-class ballad to his credit. His sonnet to Irving ends with the astounding image :

Thou trumpet set for Shakespeare's lips to blow !

Wry-necked fife, yes. Trumpet, no. The plays ? He wrote the wittiest light comedy in the language ; the other pieces are stilted, wholly insincere Society melodramas redeemed, possibly, by their wit. If it were true that Wilde altered the mentality of his age then that could have been written of him which was written of Swinburne :

He was to young men everywhere an intoxication and a passion, awakening half-formed desires, hidden longings and impulses, and secret enthusiasms, and wielding sway more imperiously over heart and sense and soul than any other man of his time did over the intellect or the reason of his disciples.

Would one have written that of Wilde ? Perhaps. But in the sense that the young men to whom he was an intoxication were of the queerest kind.

The makers of *The Picture of Dorian Gray*, which I saw this afternoon, have cut out most of the nonsense. They have forborne to present Lord Henry Wotton with his " low, musical voice, and the graceful wave of the hand that was always so characteristic of him, and that he had even in his Eton days." And they have been wise. Dickens and Kipling ? Perhaps Albert Lewin, who directed, asked himself what Trabb's boy, or Stalky, or even America's Andy Hardy would reply to a man saying to one much his junior, " You with your rose-red youth and your rose-white boyhood, you have had passions that have made you afraid, thoughts that have filled you with terror, daydreams and sleeping dreams whose mere memory might stain your cheek with shame." But all of Lord Henry couldn't be deleted ; George Sanders, condemned to present what was left, did so in a manner suggesting a bookmaker in his Ascot toggery doubled by Svengali. Dorian Gray himself ? What could any self-respecting young actor make of a character with " cool, white, flower-like hands " and the habit of " burying his face in great, cool lilac-blossoms, feverishly drinking in their perfume as if it had been wine " ? And what about that face ? " What the invention of oil-paintings was to the Venetians, the face of Antinoüs was to late Greek sculpture, and the face of Dorian will some day be to me," says the painter Basil Hallward. And his creator describes Dorian as " wonderfully handsome, with his finely curved scarlet lips, his frank blue eyes, his crisp gold hair." Some of us whistled, some of us thought of Browning's " What's become of all the gold ? " when the screen disclosed this young Hollywood actor, black of hair, sad of countenance—sad in the pastry sense—and looking generally as though he were not the master but the footman.

I shall tell *Tatler* readers that if Hurd Hatfield wants to have any success with me or any of my generation he must at once change his name, which is much too reminiscent of Mr Hardfur Huttle, " that clever writer for the American papers," whom Mr and Mrs Pooter met at dinner at Mr Franching's, and whose table-talk has been so miraculously preserved. " Happy medium, indeed. Do you know ' happy medium ' are two words which mean ' miserable mediocrity ' ? I say, go first-class or third ; marry a duchess or her kitchen-maid. The happy medium means respectability, and respectability means insipidness." And again : " We have no representative at Mr Franching's table of the unenlightened frivolous matron, who goes to a second-class dance in Bayswater and fancies she is in Society." No wonder that Mr Pooter held Mr Hardfur Huttle to be, as others held Wilde, a marvellously intellectual man " who says things which from other people would seem quite alarming." What book am I quoting from ? *The Diary of a Nobody,* of course. Wilde's tragedy was a double one. He believed in the Dorian Grays, who even if they existed were not to survive the 'nineties, and could not believe in the Lupin Pooters, who existed then, and are alive to-day and for ever.

May 3   Am tired of all these so-called soldier letters that keep
Thursday.   on appearing in the Press. Here's part of a real one
            from my old friend Flight Lieutenant Jim Parle, D.F.C.,
D.F.M., now stationed in South-east Asia:

> I suppose you have almost forgotten my existence, but I have been in the Far East for some time so it has been difficult to call on you as I used to. I am supposed to be having an operational rest at the moment—actually I have never worked so bloody hard in all my life. I am Adjutant, Armament Officer, and Mess Secretary, to mention only a few of my jobs. It isn't too bad, though, except it is all so bloody safe. My mind is incapable of gauging the full magnitude of what is happening. Perhaps I have become temporarily hardened to superlatives. There are, however, a hell of a lot of little yellow bastards to be finished off out here before there is any real peace. At this unit there is no blood and few tears, but a great deal of toil and six times our ration of sweat.

By extraordinary coincidence the post brought me this letter from a Flight Lieutenant at Streatham :

> Some individuals are so incredibly uncommunicative that it is impossible to follow their rather doubtful movements. You may or may not recall the pilot who assisted Jim Parle (Richard to us), to some small degree, in attaining such eminent heights in his flying

career. (We had a yarn in the Café Royal one night.) And now this knavish gunner of mine has scuttled off over the horizon, and the only news one has been able to cull from various unreliable sources is that he has got himself married, without the permission of his crew, and/or has disappeared mysteriously to the Orient. Perhaps, sir, you may have more precise knowledge of his inscrutable ramblings, in which case I should esteem it an honour if . . . etc., etc. . . . Dash it all, he was one of the best friends I ever had.

It gives me the greatest pleasure to forward the gunner's letter to his former pilot, and the Streatham letter to Asia.

May 4   When I was a boy I was entirely taken in and captivated
Friday.   by historical novels. I really believed that life in Pompeii
             was such as Lytton described, and in South American forests such as Kingsley pretended. That such were the exact words spoken by Ivanhoe to Rowena, by Hereward the Wake to the Last of the Barons. I believed, in a word, in the Hengist-Horsery of the entire business. Then came a time—and I think George Eliot had something to do with it—when I ceased to believe in the literal inspiration of the authors of these books, and read historical novels purely for their style. If I read Thackeray's *Esmond* to-day I should do so because of such a sentence as :

Esmond thought of the courier, now galloping on the North road to inform him, who was Earl of Arran yesterday, that he was Duke of Hamilton to-day, and of a thousand great scenes, hopes, ambitions, that were alive in the gallant heart, beating a few hours since, and now in a little dust quiescent.

I should *not* believe in Esmond saying to Mr Addison :

" I admire your art ; the murder of the campaign is done to military music, like a battle at the opera, and the virgins shriek in harmony, as our victorious grenadiers march into our villages. . . . You hew out of your polished verses a stately image of smiling victory ; I tell you 'tis an uncouth, distorted, savage idol ; hideous, bloody, and barbarous."

Then came the time when I started going to historical dramas other than Shakespeare's, and I believed in them not at all. Thackeray, when he was proposing to write *Esmond*, asked whether History was never to take off her peruke ? In the plays enacted by Fred Terry and Julia Neilson she took it off with a vengeance. Here is Montague on the subject :

Dorothy Vernon proposes to exchange clothes with Mary Queen Scots : " I, by your leave," she says, in the metre Shakespeare used, " will wear your robes awhile." " I suppose," she subjoins, with the fine prose humour of to-day, " I must wear something."

And I myself remember a drama of the Cavalier and Roundhead wars in which an elderly Countess proposed on the day after the battle to hold her ground or flee according as her side had won or lost. "How will your ladyship get to know?" somebody pertinently asked. And received the reply: "My gossip, who is to come hot-foot i' the morn, will bear the tidings." It was at that moment that I decided that the historical drama is not only what Stevenson and Henley called "tushery," but tushery for the million.

Next came the screen, and History took off much more than her peruke. And, of course, the film being a popular entertainment, designed expressly for the million, makers of historical films took care to present their subjects as their public would like them to have been. And quite reasonably. Neither your city clerk nor your Oxfordshire ploughboy wants to see a Henry VIII who is a subject for a doctor's case-book or an Anne Boleyn who is a slut. Nor are they going to believe that the issue of such a union is going to provide this country with the greatest ruler it has ever had. No film could be expected to tell the true story of Catherine of Russia, and we reflect that even the *Oxford Dictionary of Quotations* declines to give that famous line in which Byron sums up the lady in two epithets. No, most people expect to see of the carryings-on of the Empress no more than

> Merely innocent flirtation,
> Not quite adultery, but adulteration.

Let it be said that in *Czarina*, which I saw at the Odeon to-day, Lubitsch has presented the preposterous story with subtlety and wit. Who supplied this wit in the first instance I don't know, since the screen play is by Edwin Justus Mayer, adapted by Bruno Frank from a play by Lajos Biro and Melchior Lengyel. But the wit is there all right. Somebody coming to tell the Empress that he has heard whispers of a plot being hatched against her in the Ukraine or somewhere, the old Chancellor (Charles Coborn) says, "Why should your Majesty worry? Always there is plotting; one day it is the Army, next day it is the Navy. What does it matter?" "But don't you arrange to take care of these people?" asks H.M. (Tallulah Bankhead). "But of course," replies the Chancellor. "We paid General Papakoff fifty thousand roubles to take care of Admiral Mamakoff. We also paid the Admiral fifty thousand roubles to take care of the General." "So what?" asks the Empress. "Everything turned out quite satisfactory," grins the Chancellor. "I have the honour to inform your Majesty that both the General and the Admiral were buried with full honours."

The story of this film is the never-failing one which Fielding immortalised in the letter Joseph Andrews wrote to his sister : " Had my mistress not been a lady of quality, dear Pamela, I should have thought she had a mind to me." I quote from memory. The authors, or somebody, have put a great deal of fun into that scene in which Catherine plies the simpleton with glass after glass of champagne, and promotes him in the course of half an hour from lieutenant to captain, major, colonel, and finally general. At his fifth or sixth glass the boy declares he has quite overcome his shyness and is prepared to venture that for which, on entering the room, he thought he should never find the courage. In a flutter of excellently dissembled modesty Catherine sinks on to the divan. The boy thrusts his hand into his bosom and produces his report on the plot in the Ukraine !

Why, among the multiplicity of his officials, does not a producer like Lubitsch have a Director of Details ? Why does he not engage for the French Ambassador an actor who can speak French ? Or are there none such in Hollywood ? Somebody who would know that the word is " Russie " and not " Roossie " ? An actor who knows that no Frenchman pronounces the name of his country as though it rhymed with the Scotch "manse"? These may be little things, but they count. Actually this film is free-er from this kind of fault than most, and it is from start to finish a very witty frolic and one in which Tallulah gives, in my view, the best performance of her career.

May 5   *Cocasseries, No.* 14 :
Saturday.

TALENTED, DEEP FEMALE, tired of disillusionment and lycanthropic maledom, would sincerely appreciate correspondence with educated man of ideals and ideas.
New York Saturday Review of Literature.   Personal column.

May 6   A few days ago I wrote a really savage letter to a stranger
Sunday.   sending me a quotation which I used without verifying.
                 No, not carelessness. The quotation had to go in the paper that night or not at all. The poem was an obscure one, and I just hadn't time to ransack London for a copy of it. Discovering my *gaffe*, I wrote the fellow a snorter, calling him crazy. Last night's post brings me this charming apology :

Not crazy—not even mazy—merely hazy. I relied on my memory—the tired memory of a septuagenarian. I tried to verify the quotation ; but my copy had been " borrowed " by some lewd person of the highbrow sort. Very sorry.

May 7 *Monday.*	Occupied to-day putting together what Kipling's Beetle would have called a giddy par-ergon, on the subject of the

Great Actor, being moved thereto by something Ivor wrote last Sunday in the *Observer* :

Either the gods have ceased to visit us or we have ceased to accept gods. It seems odd, and even very unlikely, that Nature, after making such mighty ones as were thus sovereign upon our stage in successive dynasties, should have lost the mould. The other supposition is that, while Nature is still turning them out, we in our more critical, less emotional way are turning them down.

Here is what I propose to say on Sunday :

THE OLDEST FALLACY

Writing some years after Kean's début, Hazlitt has this : " I am not one of those who, when they see the sun breaking from behind a cloud, stop to ask others whether it is the moon. Mr Kean's appearance was the first gleam of genius breaking athwart the gloom of the stage. . . . I cannot say that my opinion has much changed since that time. Why should it ? I had the same eyes to see with that I have now, the same ears to hear with, and the same understanding to judge with. Why then should I not form the same judgment ? "

Of all theatrical fallacies the most obstinately recurring is the one which insists that the ageing critic has not the eyes, ears, and understanding he had in his youth. That to see and hear too much is to end by understanding too little. This is the fallacy which maintains that A was not, absolutely, a greater actor than B, but is so rated by the critics because they were young and impressionable in A's heyday and are exhausted and disillusioned in B's. This school holds Charles Kean to have been as great an actor as Edmund, and on the ground that when Hazlitt wrote : " For voice, eye, accent, and expression no actor has come out for many years at all equal to Edmund Kean," he, Hazlitt, was thirty-six years of age, and that when he wrote : " It appears to me that Mr Kean *jun.* will never make so great an actor as his father," he was fifty and in the clutches of senile decay. Similarly we are told that H. B. Irving was as good an actor as the Old Man, and would have been so deemed had not Archer, Walkley, and Co. been dotards shaking a few sad, last grey hairs.

A young man has written to me : " Can you adduce any instance in which an old critic has ranked a newcomer with the players of his youth ? If you cannot, then I must conclude that the falling-off is not in the actor but in the critic." I will be content with a single example, and I choose G. H. Lewes. First, I must establish Lewes's youthful enthusiasm. Very well, then. Kean died when Lewes was sixteen. Writing many years later, the by that time famous critic began his book *On Actors and the Art of*

Acting with the statement : " Edmund Kean was incomparably the greatest actor I have seen." (Note that the man placed complete reliance in the boy's judgment.) Now apply the theory of diminishing sensibility. Assuming the law (of diminishing sensibility) to hold good, we must expect Lewes, writing of Frédérick Lemaître forty-three years after the death of Kean, to dismiss the French actor as a nincompoop. But does he ? Does he temporise ? Does he hum and haw ? No. In his first sentence he places Lemaître among " the few actors of exceptional genius." Here let me notch a point on my side of the argument. To show how nicely the critical scales can still be held when the brain is softening and the arteries are hardening, consider this fossilised critic, bound to Kean for ever, writing about another actor : " In Macready I see only a man of talent, but of talent so marked and individual that it approaches very near to genius. . . . Tieck told me that Macready seemed to him a better actor than either Kean or John Kemble." Surely, if the deterioration theory held water, Lewes would have pooh-pooh'd Macready off the stage and kept silent about Tieck and his opinions. Whereas he allows Macready as near an approach to the throne of Kean as I am prepared to allow any living modern to the throne of Irving.

To push the argument home. Did Charles Laughton's Tony Perelli suffer because of Tree's Svengali ? Or Edith Evans's Millamant because of Ellen Terry's Beatrice ? Do we frown upon Sybil Thorndike because of what we remember of Madge Kendal, upon Pamela Brown and Sonia Dresdel because of Clare Eames and Mrs Pat, upon Wolfit because of Benson ? Did recollection of James Welch in *The New Clown* saying to the ring-master " You've hurt me ! " prevent the critics twenty years later—the same critics, mark you—from hailing as a world genius that wistful little droll who in the films was to be hurt by all the world ? I claim to have had my share in ' placing ' Mr X and Miss Y, and always according to their merits *and my standards*. And I claim to know the extraordinary from the accomplished as well now as when I was a boy.

It is foolish to argue that Siddons would not impress us to-day. This is to overlook the power of genius to alter its dress. To-day the Siddons would use modern gestures and intonation ; it is the genius which is constant. Irving standing motionless and silent, using none of the means which are subject to fashion, could with a look gorgonise or melt an audience. This is something no living actor can do, because no living actor has what it took to implement Irving's malignity and ruth. And will not have so long as critics maintain that to count the washing is as tragic and difficult a feat as to deliver Medea's speech to her children. The alleged " modern approach to great acting " ? Whoever has seen a great actor knows that he is not an animal to be stalked in its lair, but a tiger leaping out upon the spectator from the bush of mediocrity and the brake of competence. That if there is any approaching to be done, it is the tiger who will do it.

EIGHT EPITAPHS

MUSSOLINI

A fixed figure for the time of scorn
To point his slow unmoving finger at.

SHAKESPEARE

PÉTAIN

Mes soldats morts,
Moi vaincu ! mon empire est brisé comme verre.
Est-ce le châtiment cette fois, Dieu sévère ?—

VICTOR HUGO

LAVAL

He hears
On all sides, from innumerable tongues,
A dismal universal hiss, the sound
Of public scorn.

MILTON

RIBBENTROP

Good-bye is not worth while.

HARDY

GOEBBELS

. . . like a liar, gone to burning hell.

SHAKESPEARE

GOERING

That bolting-hutch of beastliness, that
swollen parcel of dropsies, . . . that stuffed
cloak-bag of guts.

SHAKESPEARE

HIMMLER

May his soul die, and never-dying worms
Feast on its pain for ever.

ROSSETTI

HITLER

Und wenn dir denn auch Gott verzeiht,
Auf Erden sein vermaledeit !

GOETHE

May 9
Wednesday.   Who is going to be the first to admit that to the writing man the last five and a half years have been an inestimable boon, since they provided him with material he would not otherwise have had ? That a measureless gulf separates the artist from the ordinary man or woman, the non-artist to whom the war happens as an actuality and not as something to be expressed in terms of an art ? Throughout the last five years I was never in any real danger ; I never saw a flying bomb, and nothing ever happened nearer than a hundred yards away. If a house across the street had been blown to smithereens I should have been frightened, of course. But presuming I hadn't died from heart failure, I should have been saying to myself, " This will make a good entry for *Ego* 4, 5, 6, 7, or 8." Like the whore to whom Hamlet likened himself, I should have unpacked my heart with words. We know from Grove that during the summer of 1809—the battle of Wagram took place on July 6—Beethoven, whose lodging was on the wall of Vienna, was much exposed to the firing, and used to take refuge in the cellar of his brother's house. And what was he doing in the cellarage ? Shaking with fright ? No. Worrying about the future of Austria ? No. He was writing the E flat Piano Concerto and the " Harp " Quartet, and probably doing all the better for the excitement. I know it works that way with me. I used to look forward to the sirens, and never heard a warning without experiencing what, if I must be honest, I must call a pleasurable thrill. Any night when there was no warning was just a bore. Is this insane ? Possibly. Was I aware that a warning meant hurt and death to other people ? Yes. Did I think I was going to be specially favoured ? No. The fact remains that during the time of the fly-bombs, and afterwards of the rockets, the tempo of life was faster than it can ever be again. I am as big a coward as anybody. *But I miss the warnings.*

May 10
Thursday.   Letter from Jock :

33 *King Street*
Covent Garden
*W.C.*2

8th May, 1945

DEAR JAMIE,
     I gave myself a perfect little concert for to-day's Great Occasion, and it's a pity that circumstances didn't allow me to bring the records round to play them to you in the old endeared way. I longed to.   This is all of it :

BRAHMS.	" Tragic " Overture.
MOZART.	*Figaro* Overture.
MENDELSSOHN.	*Fingal's Cave* Overture.
ELGAR.	*Cockaigne* Overture.

On the reverse of the Mozart recording was the "Dance of the Apprentices" from the *Meistersinger*—but to include this would have been in much-more-than-dubious taste. Similarly the Elgar recording concludes with *Pomp and Circumstance*, No. 4 in G. But, of course, one left that out of the scheme similarly—for opposite, obvious, and poles-apart reasons.

You were charming about dear Graham Robertson's *Time Was* in the *Express* on Saturday, and more than charming—moving, indeed—on Bertie Farjeon's death in the *Sunday Times*. As some one said of you in a letter received by me last night : " He incalculably does the nicest things."

Ever,
JOCK

Have replied :

Queen Alexandra Mansions, W.C.2
May 10, 1945

DEAR JOCK,

Merely to read about your concert gives me a pang ; I think of the days when we would play such a programme together.

But surely you and I have nothing against *Meistersinger* ? We that have free souls, the political matter touches us not. Am I right in thinking that your objection is to the perkiness of the "Dance of the Apprentices" ?

About the *Pomp and Circumstance*, No. 4. Some glory in their birth, and some in being born English. I have no objection to Teutons who have no sense of the ridiculous glorying in being born German. What I object to is that anybody should glory in being born a member of the *Herrenvolk*. Is it that you won't have the rather vulgar March after the incomparably better Overture ? Please elucidate.

> For thou art all my art, and dost advance
> As high as learning my rude ignorance.

Ever,
JAMIE

P.S. On second thoughts don't bother.

P.P.S. But of course I do the nicest things and incalculably. As some one once said about me : " Si la schizophrénie n'existait pas, il faudrait l'inventer."

May 12   *Cocasseries, No.* 15 :
Saturday.

I walked past the houses on the east side of Eaton Square, Belgravia. In 1939 those houses were alive. They had personality and spirit as well as nurseries and kitchens. Now they have been occupied by the Army. They are almost as horrible to look at as the corpses at Belsen or Buchenwald.

Feature writer in daily paper

May 13
Sunday.

I wonder whether hanging would be more congenial if the ceremony took place in the open air on some fine day in, say, Mecklenburgh Square, with windows bulging at ten guineas a seat, five to stand, and the London Philharmonic in full blast at the Funeral March from the *Eroica*, Delius's " Procession of Protracted Death " from *Hassan*, Saint-Saëns' *Danse Macabre*, and Strauss's *Till Eulenspiegel*, the programme to be so timed that the crêpe-hung car enters the Square to the grisly yet exultant strains of Berlioz's *Marche au Supplice*. My appeals for copies of Boswell's *Johnson* to be forwarded to distributing centres in Germany for the benefit of our occupational troops resulted in something like fifty sets. I am being dishonest enough to keep one for myself, a magnificently bound specimen of Croker's fifth edition in one volume. The first page at which I open this justifies Macaulay's " The editor's want of perspicacity is indeed very amusing. He is perpetually telling us that he cannot understand something in the text which is as plain as language can make it." Johnson is arguing in favour of public executions : " Sir, executions are intended to draw spectators. If they do not draw spectators, they don't answer their purpose. The old method was most satisfactory to all parties ; the public was gratified by a procession ; the criminal was supported by it. Why is all this to be swept away ? " Croker's note is : " What could Johnson mean by saying that the criminal was *supported* by the lingering torture of this cruel exhibition ? " Croker doesn't see that what would be degradation to him was glorification to the coxcombs of the Heath looking upon execution as an actor looks on an exit. The journey to Tyburn was an honoured progress, even an apotheosis. Trulls strewed flowers in the hero's path, and weeping doxies pinned a last nosegay in his ragged coat. There is a gaiety about " He went very decent to the gallows, with a clean napkin, and an orange in his hand," which modern reports lack.

May 14
Monday.

Frank Singleton (see *Ego* 7, page 230) descended on me this afternoon. Is now editor of the *Bolton Evening News*, and I gather that what that organ thinks to-night the *Manchester Guardian* is going to think to-morrow morning. I was afraid that just as beef-eating did harm to Sir Andrew's wit, so Bolton would impair the modern Sir Toby's. Not so. Within three minutes of his arrival he had recited his new poem :

COULEUR DE ROSE

He heightened all his sins,
Saw Helen in a harlot—
Even his pink gins
Were scarlet.

There is about Frank a sense of impish fun which not even Lancashire can subdue.

May 15   In a letter from the editor of a Canadian weekly :
Tuesday.

If most Canadians do not understand the speech of English actors it is not because that speech is incomprehensible, but because the Common Man in Canada is averse from understanding anybody but his immediate associates, and them only on the most superficial level. The *Diary* which I publish weekly is expressed with almost unbearable timidity, since vigorous or forthright criticism of the national intelligence is resented with almost hysterical ferocity. Canada suffers from artistic malnutrition : music is the only art which commands respect and general support. There is no theatre except in Toronto and Montreal, and very little there. Few Canadians have seen a play, and few have seen a movie which was not made in Hollywood. There is little film criticism, and what there is is addressed to an inexperienced audience. But there is an audience for good English films among the more discerning Canadians : they welcome a relief from the childishness of Hollywood, and the prurient-pure, daintily salacious Hays Office attitude towards sex. *Fanny by Gaslight* is causing some fuss here because the heroine is illegitimate : Canada, you must understand, is a very *nice* country. No, Canada does not actively dislike English films : it is just too dumb, as a usual thing, to understand anything which is not thoroughly familiar.

May 16   Another letter from our little Irish friend :
Wednesday.

> 18 *Park View Avenue*
> *Harold's Cross*
> *Dublin*
>
> *Sat. 12th May,* 1945

MY DEAR JAMES,
MY DEAR LEO,
    First let me thank you, James, for your very thoughtful introduction. I won't embarrass either you or myself with a surfeit of sugary nonsense. Suffice to say that I am immensely grateful. I expected the interview with Mr Edwards to last a quarter of a minute—after which I would be heaved out on my egotistical ear. Actually we talked from seven till a quarter to nine ! About what ? About everything concerning the theatre, from sex-appeal to sentiment. At first I informed Mr Edwards (whose affability and condescension would have won the heart of Mr Collins) that I desired to become one of that " fine body of men "—as Max Beerbohm called the critics—but I'd better not repeat what Mr Edwards said. We discussed acting, Sarah, Rachel, and other things about which

I know practically nothing. Mr Edwards invited me to come round after each show and talk with him. (Magic words, O James and O Leo !) His partner, Mr MacLiammóir, whom I used to plague with my unasked-for criticism, drifted in, pressed my hand, swore eternal friendship, and drifted out again.

And now, dear James, please forgive me if I address the rest of this bombast to Leo. Thank you, Leo, for such a charming letter. Such taste ! I'm afraid I'm like Lady Teazle at the time of her marriage—I have no taste. Well, if you really want to know: (a) my favourite dramatists are Shakespeare, Shaw, Synge, O'Casey, and Tchehov. I also burrow in Marlowe, Kyd, Jonson, Webster, Ford, and Tourneur. And if you're of my way of thinking you may throw in Eugene O'Neill with the last three ! (b) Favourite poets are Tennyson and Yeats—why, I don't know. (c) Favourite novelists Dickens, Jane Austen, Charlotte Brontë, and—my only concession to modern taste—Hugh Walpole. (d) Favourite essayists Lamb and G. K. Chesterton. (e) Favourite annoyances Wilde and Maugham !

Thine and James's for aye,
J. E. JORDAN

May 17   Supper with Jock at the Café Royal.
Thursday.

JOCK. Did you get an old *Tatler* article I sent you the other day after clearing out some drawers ?
J. A. Yes. I wondered why you sent it.
JOCK. D'you remember writing it ?
J. A. Perfectly.
JOCK. Well, you didn't. *I wrote it !* You had gone to a horse-show.

May 18   Thornton Wilder's *The Skin of our Teeth* turns out to be
Friday.   yet another example of the playwright who, with almost
             nothing new to say, dishes out the old stuff in the new-
fangled manner. Here is Wilder's recipe. Abolish Time. Pretend the Ice Age is coeval with co-eds. Have a mammoth and a dinosaur on the stage together with a telegraph boy. Bring Adam and Eve up to date. Show Cain as High School boy with football jersey and catapult. Have the alphabet, simple arithmetic, and the wheel all in the making. Show Helen, Circe, Cleopatra in the guise of Atlantic City trollops. Have Homer and Moses put in an appearance. Have scenery that moves of its own accord. Surrealism, Dali-ism, Dadaism, and Gagaism. Hotch-potch of Shaw, Pirandello, Obey, Kaiser, O'Neill. Touches of Walt Disney, the Marx Brothers, and Olsen and Johnson. Will this make a good play ? It may or it mayn't, but it'll win the Pulitzer. Will the folks walk out ? Possibly. But they'll

talk after they've walked out, which is better than staying and not talking. Actually, Wilder's nonsense did win the Pulitzer, and on the first-night in New York a lot of the audience left. In the play which I saw to-night it all boiled down to this, that the human race can survive ice, flood, pestilence, wars, depressions and all the natural shocks that flesh is heir to. Like the man in *The Silver Tassie*, I see no magnificent meanin' jumping out of that, though I suppose I shall have to find one between now and Sunday. Lovely performance by Vivien Leigh as Sabina, the hired girl. Half dabchick and half dragon-fly.

May 19
Saturday.
Shall I *never* learn ? Open my *Express* this morning and find myself telling readers, apropos of Leonard Clark's biography of Alfred Williams, the Wiltshire poet, how, while working a steam-hammer in the locomotive shop at Swindon, he rose at 4 A.M., studied till it was time to cycle to work, read during the dinner-hour, made a hasty evening meal, and pored over his books again till midnight. How he mastered Greek sufficiently to read Xenophon, Homer, Theocritus, Plutarch. How he became a useful minor poet. How—and here the devilry comes in—they, *Express* readers, can do the same thing. The truth, of course, is that they can't. Only one in ten generations of hammer-wielders has a line of poetry in him. Now say six out of the *Daily Express's* four million readers take me seriously. This means that I shall have on my conscience the ruining of six lives, or, anyhow, holding out hopes that can never be fulfilled. In other words, putting cultural ideas into the heads of half a dozen honest fellows who won't know what to do with the ideas when they've got them, and would be much better occupied in backing horses, drinking beer, and begetting children. Gregers Werle cum Samuel Smiles is written all over my column to-day, and I am ashamed of it.

May 21
Monday.
Spent the morning playing with the notion of translating Montague's *Disenchantment* into English for the common man. What are those who would best benefit by this masterpiece going to make of such a passage as :

" I planted a set of blind hopes in their minds," said Prometheus, making it out to be quite a good turn that he had done to mankind. And the Dr Relling of Ibsen, a kind of Prometheus in general practice, kept a whole medicine-chest of assorted illusions to dope his patients with. " Illusion, you know," said the sage, " is the tonic to give 'em." It may be, but even illusions cost something. The bill, as Hotspur said of the river Trent, " comes me cranking in " presently, Nature's iron law laying it down that the more superb your state of inflation the deeper shall the dumps occasioned by the puncture be.

The reader who is *au fait* with the allusions in the foregoing does not need to learn the lesson of this book, which I want read not only by soldiers and Civil Servants but by the unlettered boss of every big business left in these Socialist days. What is to be done about it ? The only thing that I can see is to translate the book into common or kitchen-garden English.

May 22   Two good days at Lord's Test Match as the guest of
Tuesday.   C. B. Fry. Highly distinguished company, including
           Arnold Bax, Clifford Bax, Edmund Blunden, Eric Gillett, Thomas Moult, and J. C. Squire. " Plum " Warner looked into the box several times, and I made fleeting acquaintance with High Commissioners and Nawabs. Fry in good form and talked well, particularly about A. C. MacLaren, who, he said, had " a superb crease-side manner."

May 23   Part of a letter referring to my recent *S.T.* article
Wednesday.   entitled " The Oldest Fallacy " :

> Given sustained interest, a man should be a more discerning critic at the age of sixty-five than he was at the age of twenty-five. But Nature does not permit the man of sixty-five to bring his more mature powers of judgment to bear upon a theatrical performance seen by him forty years previously. We remember a " large " room of our childhood days, and continue to regard it as large until revisiting it many years later. But we cannot revisit a theatrical performance of forty years ago.

I have replied :

DEAR SIR,
    A bent towards criticism implies a sense of magnitude and proportion. At the age of six I knew exactly how big my bedroom was ; I remember calculating that it would hold my cot exactly twelve times. At seven I was taken to my first classical concert, and remember thinking that Hallé's piano-playing was tame—a judgment that was afterwards ratified. (The concert took place in the Free Trade Hall, Manchester, which seemed no smaller on my last Prize-giving Day eleven years later. Nor had it shrunk when, some forty years on, I was privileged to give away the prizes.) At nine I decided that in *La Tosca* Sarah Bernhardt ranted—another judgment that Time has approved. (In melodrama she always ranted ; in classic drama never.) At ten I knew exactly how many yards it was from the wicket to the wall of the croft in which during

the holidays I used to get out to my father's artful slows. At fourteen I realised that the school ground was not as big as Old Trafford. Now reverse the picture. Yesterday I saw the Australian crack, Miller, put together the first Test Match century since the war ; that the date is 1945 has nothing to do with my conviction that, fine batsman though Miller is, his bat does not flash quite so eye-takingly as did Macartney's.

To-day an unknown friend has sent me a fifty-year-old theatre programme. The first-night of *An Artist's Model.* Think seriously and tell me whether we could to-day assemble a cast as talented as one that contained Marie Tempest, Lottie Venne, Letty Lind, Marie Studholme, Hayden Coffin, Eric Lewis, and Maurice Farkoa. Is it because I have been looking at musical shows for fifty years that the artists of to-day must use a microphone, failing which they would be inaudible ? Let me switch to something else. Is it because I first read *Pickwick* as a boy that I cannot find its equal in the lucubrations of to-day's budding geniuses ?

M. Bergeret's little dog reflected that when he approached an object he grew smaller, and that when he retreated he grew bigger. Unearth me an unpublished essay by Hazlitt entitled " On How Actors Diminish with the Years," and I shall still say that I do not increase with age. Neither do I decrease. I have a photographic memory for an actor's expression, tones, gestures; and in my estimate of the great players I pass these memories, these old negatives, through, so to speak, the sieve of experience. In other words, I do not measure Irving by what I thought of him when I was a youngster (though that turns out to have been a just estimate), but by what I think of him now, using my " negatives " as the basis of judgment. The Child is father of the Man. Meaning that one with the critical bent carries in his earliest years an old head on young shoulders, and in his later days a young head on old shoulders. Whoso fails to encompass this is never throughout his life a critic, but always an emotionalist, or, if you prefer it, a rhapsodist.

Uncompromisingly,

JAMES AGATE

May 24 In view of the promised visit of the Comédie Française.
Thursday. Some time after the last war a quiet, unsensational light, new to the English theatre, began to filter through from France. A glow lambent yet melancholy, compounded equally of dawn and dusk. I first became certain about this gentle flooding on the occasion of the 1928 Stage Society's performance of Jean-Jacques Bernard's *L'Ame en Peine* (*The Unquiet Spirit*). True that one had been faintly aware of it in *Le Printemps des Autres* (*The Springtime of Others*) two years earlier. One saw *Martine* in 1929, *Le Feu qui reprend mal* (*The Sulky Fire*) in 1934, *L'Invitation au Voyage* in 1937, and *Madeleine* last year. As one remembers certain flamboyant moments of Sarah and one or two of Duse's abnegations

and subsidences, so, in the first of these pieces, I shall never forget the way that brilliant and regretted actress Clare Eames avoided contact with the stranger to whom she was for ever after to be in thrall. Four out of those six plays were in their way little masterpieces.

Another great event was the visit of the Théâtre du Vieux-Colombier, playing in its own language. Obey's *Noé* won us over at once. Fewer people saw *Le Viol de Lucrèce*. But those few who did will never forget that chamber, empty except for the bed round which the curtains were drawn. The Reciter and Recitress had mounted pulpits on each side of the stage. Then came Tarquin, stealing along black corridors and fumbling at dark doors while the Reciter explained the emotions tearing his breast. He entered the chamber and drew aside the curtains of the bed. The thing which should restrain him now was his kingship, voiced by the Reciter crying four times, " Tarquin-roi ! Roi des Romains ! Roi ! Roi ! " But in vain. In the last act the Reciter put the whole thing back in Time. " La grande Rome est en histoire. Athènes, jadis, à ses grandes heures, fut en beauté ; Babylone, en amour ; Troie, en alarmes. Un jour, Berlin sera en guerre et Paris en révolution. Rome, aujourd'hui, est en histoire ! " Yes, that was great playgoing.

And surely that was a superb moment in *Bataille de la Marne* when the soldiers who should defend Paris retreated and again retreated. Always they had withdrawn towards the footlights, and now, in the theatre, could go no further. " En avant ! " cried France, and the spectacular right-about-turn signified that the Battle of the Marne had begun. The victorious generals were saluted by name. Manoury ! French ! Foch ! Sarrail ! Castelnau ! Joffre ! One name was singled out for its beauty of sound. " Général Franchet d'Espérey ! Vous dont le nom est beau comme une devise ! " And the good British playgoer, given a schoolboy's knowledge of French, recognised in this apostrophe all the *panache* of France.

In the way of acting I still look back gratefully to the visit paid by the Comédie in March 1939. Never again can I hope to see such a piece of comic playing as that of Fernand Ledoux as the old crock in Regnard's *Le Légataire Universel*. What crackle and atmospherics proceeded from that bosom when bronchial disturbance permitted anything to proceed at all ! Did ever legs so vacillate ? And then there was another actor, Pierre Dux, who contrived to run the entire gamut of the *cocasse* without respect to clime or time, the equivalent of that English bridge which binds Jonson's scamps to Sid Field's scallywags.

The modern theatre gave us Mauriac's *Asmodée*, Cocteau's *Les Parents Terribles*, and Giraudoux's *Amphitryon* 38. And, of course,

Sacha Guitry's *Mozart* and *Mariette*. In the second play I can still see that half-bovine, half-imperial Napoleon III sitting in his box putting his heavily kid-gloved hands portentously together. I can still hear that half-whisper : " Il faut tâcher de ne pas être ridicule ! " In the earlier play I have not forgotten, though it is twenty years ago, that people were seen to cry, and by " cry " I mean shed tears, when Music's heavenly child appeared at the top of the gilt staircase and descended it to kneel at the feet of Mme d'Épinay. I think it will be only fit and proper to remind playgoers on Sunday of the debt they owe to France.

May 25
Friday. Southend, with George Mathew. Half-way down ran into a cloudburst and thunderstorm, the worst I remember for years. Had to wait an hour at Southend Station. No taxis, so picked up our bags and started to walk. Between two and three feet of water under the railway bridge, which meant a détour. Found the Palace Hotel unchanged, even to the crack in the drawing-room mirror—an incident of the First World War. This room and the sun-lounge, were they anywhere except Southend, would be recognised as the two best, airiest, spaciousest, viewfullest public rooms in England. The painted metal vases, bigger than Ali Baba's jars, are still here, but I miss that enormous if dingy canvas, larger than anything Benjamin Haydon painted, that used to hang in the one-hundred-and-twenty-foot passage leading to the gentlemen's lavatory. Subject ? A pride of lions.

May 26
Saturday. Took a car to the golf-course, now closed. Had a look at my old bungalow. Grass obviously not been cut since I lived there. But then it wasn't cut in my time —could never be bothered with gardening. Fell asleep in lounge before lunch. Snoozed after lunch. Did a little shopping—the rain sogged down all day—and slept through two idiotic pictures. At dinner half a bottle of champagne all to myself. Nodded over some new novels. Bed early.

May 27
Sunday. Fine, but too cold to go out with any pleasure, so sat in the sun-room and diarised. " Surely it's time people agreed to listen to Wagner's music and forget the bosh it's all about ! " George had said at breakfast. I entirely agree. Newman writes in the *S.T.* to-day : " If I know anything of him [Wagner], he would have stayed away ostentatiously from the performances [of his operas under Nazi patronage] and told Hitler and his storm-troopers frankly what he thought of them." *Frankly*, Ernest ?

I think not. I just don't see that astute little monkey in the velvet jacket asking to be sent to a concentration camp.

May 28   Leigh-on-Sea presented a charming picture from the train.
Monday.   The town was busy as a hive with scores of Ham Peggottys building and mending boats. Presently the train began to fill up, and we finished seventeen in the carriage, including an eight-months-old baby which I nursed. I am a superb nurse, and as good with children as George is with cats. And for the same reason. George and I dote on cats and babies respectively, and they dote on us. George pointed out, to the mother's great gratification—for she was a woman of education—that the kid had exactly the same hands as those of an infant in a Michael Angelo reproduction in the *Listener*, which we had with us.

May 29   From George Richards :
Tuesday.

After carrying her young for 67 days Bluebell was yesterday delivered of five beautiful, vigorous, and lively kittens. One, indeed, which I have christened Marco, showed extraordinary initiative and maturity of mind and judgment even before the umbilical cord was severed. Solomon, the second born, has a very elegant and fine-pointed tail, whereas poor Omar, the next one, has a tail kinked like a lacrosse-stick. Rosina and Cortez, the fourth and third, both promise to have excellent points. The mother continued purring throughout her two hours' " labour," and the fact that everything went so smoothly and without any sort of a hitch was due, I am convinced, in no small measure to the fact that during her confinement only certain sorts of programmes were permitted on the wireless. Modern dance rhythms, for instance, were entirely taboo, and nearly all modern composers, Shostakovich and William Walton especially, were likewise banned as being the reverse of soothing to the nerves of the gestating and the pregnant. Bluebell, like all, or at any rate most, cats, is a keen and discriminating wireless listener, but during the past two months she has been quite content to let Lush Mush, leader of the Palm Court orchestra of the Hotel Plush, Great Slush, cater for her requirements in the way of *musique d'accouchement.*

What of the lying-in itself, you will be wanting to know ? I endeavoured in every detail to order things as far as possible in accordance with the practice and customs of more spacious and gracious times as these may be gleaned from a reading of that charming French seventeenth-century *ouvrage* : *Caquets de l'Accouchée.* For instance :

" Pour préparer à l'événement solennel la chambre de la gisante était tendue des étoffes et des tapisseries les plus belles ; une petite couchette, connue sous le nom de *lit de misère*, était placée auprès du grand lit nuptial ; un bon feu brûlait incessament ; des linges de toutes sortes, tirées des grands bahuts, séchaient à l'entour. On mettait devant la cheminée une petite table couverte de linge très fin, sur cette table trois coupes, un pot de vin ou d'hippocras, trois pains de fleur de farine et deux flambeaux qui restaient allumés toute la nuit. Dans la chambre de l'accouchée, le plus grand prince du monde s'y trouvât-il, nul ne peut servir vin ou épices, excepté une femme mariée."

May 30
Wednesday.

" If I had my will I would live in a ship on the sea and never come nearer humanity than that." Thus Duse.

It was obvious at the " Q " Theatre to-night that Sonia Dresdel would prefer acting, under any conditions, to hobnobbing with ice-floes or getting as far away from humanity as deserts permit. Asked whether she could live without the stage, Duse replied in a shocked voice, " I have passed three years without acting." Dresdel cannot pass three minutes without acting. (Since three minutes is a long time on the stage, better say three seconds.) She acts, overacts, and then acts a little more. In the dictionary of her playing, to ask Mr Smith to stay to dinner is like Circe enticing Ulysses ; to kiss (*vb. tran.*) is to suck forth the soul, to make immortal ; a simple move to the door is a walk to the Paradise Garden ; to speed the parting guest is a dance half-way between a galliard and a coranto. This is the more regrettable because it is entirely unnecessary. Dresdel acted superbly all through to-night's second act, which could stand up to superb acting ; she should have " thrown away " the first and third acts, which couldn't. The play itself, *Wait, my Love*, was an honest attempt to grapple with the question of conjugal fidelity, viewed from the angles of Surbiton and Cairo. The soldier-husband said, " The woman's part in war is to fight against boredom and forgetfulness ; she must keep her vows. The man's part is to undergo the danger and the strain ; what happens to his vows is immaterial." To which his wife in the A.T.S. replied, " Rubbish ! " in a speech of Medea-like proportions. Not bad stuff, and very nearly good enough for town.

May 31
Thursday.

Letter from Tom Curtiss :

Paris
May 24, 1945

DEAR JAMES,

I wrote you a " V " letter some time ago, thinking that perhaps it would reach you in quicker order than ordinary post, but instead

" V " letters to England seem to be absolutely unanswerable documents. At least, such has been my experience; I have dispatched a score of them, and one and all are barren of replies. May this bring better luck.

VE Days I and II found Paris in a happy mood, and the Opéra, the Madeleine, Place Vendôme, and Sacré Cœur were just flood-lit in pre-war, summer-time fashion. For us, of course, the war is not over, and even the duller of the G.I.'s seem to realise this, for the Parisian high jinks, street dancing and all, were predominantly civilian on Victory night.

The Paris stage has revealed no new masterpieces. *Huis Clos*, by one Jean-Paul Sartre, had the highbrows by the ears as pretty hot intellectual stuff. A sort of *Outward Bound*, it deals with three lost souls in the Hereafter—a low-life drifter and two women, one of whom is a Lesbian. Eternity is a dreary hotel room with no windows and without mirrors. A would-be metaphysical morality play about a relentless Jehovah's vengeance, it appeals only to theatre-goers who never went to the theatre to see Molnar's beautiful handling of the same theme in *Liliom* and to those who never heard the marine sergeant's line in *Rain* : " God's a good guy." I don't think you'd like *Huis Clos*, in spite of the remarkable acting.

How is *Ego* 8 ?

Give my best regards to Leo Pavia, and tell Arthur Bates to see that you don't sit up too late, work too hard, and/or drink too much whiskey.

Always,
Tom

June 1   Letter addressed to me at the *Express* :
Friday.

DEAR MR AGATE,

Are you a self-made man because I wish you could advise me how to be one too. The trouble is, I am a woman not a man, and I don't know how to ring the changes. You see a man has much more advantage than a woman, just because she is a woman. And it's a good job we don't all get what we ask for, or Heaven help those who don't ask for much, though they might get more, without asking.

AN INTERESTED READER

June 2   I remember in Ernest Milton's Hammersmith produc-
Saturday.   tion of *Macbeth* a young boy's remarkable performance
           of the Messenger who comes to tell Macbeth about
Birnam Wood. The part is of the tiniest, something under ten lines. But the boy was so good and his fear of Macbeth so real that for two

minutes he reduced Ernest to the status of a brilliant actor, while he himself remained real.   To-day I receive this letter :

12 Brocks Drive
North Cheam
Surrey
Friday June 1st '45

DEAR JAMES AGATE,

On August 6th, 1944, in the *Sunday Times* you wrote of " a brilliant performance by a boy who will be an actor some day." Such praise for my first real work on the professional stage meant more to me than even you, with your understanding, can imagine. I had done lots of amateur work—it was my alleged resemblance to Stephen Haggard when I won the 1943–44 Finchley and Hertford Drama Festival's Prize that led to my casting in *Macbeth*.

Since then I resolved to work and work to perfect myself.   I hadn't the conventional height ;   R.A.D.A.—I hadn't the money ; none of the managements would see me.   I turned down an engagement—would I have benefited as one of the eighteen " boys and girls " in *Jenny Jones* ?—and in desperation accepted Peter Miller Street's part in *Junior Miss*.   This abomination, which in a year's tour has made me wonder how to keep sane, is at last wending its way to a pathetic end via Blackburn, Bradford, Torquay, and West Hartlepool, and I shall be out of work again.

I am in London with a week out commencing next Monday. What do I do ?   How are agents and production offices to be persuaded to see me ?   I have managed to save £30.   Knowing that I have talent that needs perfecting through good dramatic work— should I accept the first footling part that comes along ?   I know I have a long way to go, but how can I get the opportunity ?

Yours truly,
PETER MIZEN

I am writing this young man to the effect that whereas anybody in the restaurant or taxicab business would keep a register of likely waiters or drivers, in the theatre this just doesn't happen.   Am advising him to go to Hull or Hereford and look upon acting as its own reward.

June 4
Monday.
Frank Singleton dined with me to-night and then, coming back to the flat, we sat up till the small hours.   I had a bit of work to finish, and gave him *Ego* 8 to look at. Apropos of the entry for May 19 he said, " One of the things I learned at Cambridge that has always remained is this.   My tutor said to me, ' You come from Manchester, a city responsible for the most pernicious doctrine with which youth has ever been misled—the doctrine that

work will do everything. It won't. Work will do a great deal, but not everything. Sometimes it happens that a Manchester lad coming up against a first-rater finds that the man of natural talent can do more than he can with all his hard work. This brings on a nervous breakdown. Every term I send back one such to Manchester.' "

June 5   In a letter from George Richards :
Tuesday.

When I *did* get up this morning I found inside the front door an obliging letter from a dramatic critic, a rather stuffy letter from a modern poet, and a deliciously vulgar postcard and a jolly letter from Jock. OUTSIDE . . . alone and palely loitering, an anæmic egg laid by a rickety and mal-nourished hen which should forthwith be placed under the auspices and come within the scope of the beneficent ministrations of U.N.R.R.A.

I have been busy this morning . . . correcting with pencil, blue chalk, ink, and brush a dozen or so large bills and posters dotted about Bournemouth, Boscombe, Poole, and Christchurch announcing that at the Pavilion, Bournemouth, next week there would be performed a play by one " Oscar Wild." But England is England and Bournemouth will be Bournemouth, and had the bill-printer really been in form he would have called the play " Lady Windermere's *Fun*."

On the back of the envelope the query : " Do you think Citizen Kane a good name for a cat ? "

June 6   To-night's play at the Piccadilly, *Jacobowsky and the*
Wednesday.   *Colonel*, started off with a fine air of novelty. And then
it began to appear that a good deal of Franz Werfel's matter, and even manner, had been dreamed of by other playwriting philosophers. For example, the deflation of grandiosity by gumption. Here the likeness to *Arms and the Man* popped up every five minutes. And what of the other four ? Well, there was André Obey. These stragglers leaving Paris with music heard in the air and Esmé Percy in a mood of soliloquy turning him into a Reciter—what were they but the very mood and mechanics of *Bataille de la Marne* ? The plot —the outwitting of the Nazis by three simpletons and a girl—could be paralleled in any one of twenty films made since the war. Perhaps there is a playwriting mind like that of certain composers. Listening to Mahler, one recognises not only subconscious echoes of Wagner, Bruckner, Schubert, Strauss, and even Beethoven, but moods and colourings which one thinks wouldn't have occurred to Mahler but

126

for Wagner and the rest. Werfel's work is full of such echoes, moods, colourings. There was a moment when it looked as if Marianne, the Polish Colonel's French fiancée, would have to choose between the officer, who could offer her nothing but his histrionics, and the little Polish Jew Jacobowsky, whose one card was his humility and heart's need. Would Marianne take a leaf out of Candida's book and say, " That's a good bid, S. L. Jacobowsky " ? And when the Gestapo man in his death agony clawed at the mechanical piano and set it going I thought at once of the same incident in *Pépé le Moko*. The truth, I suppose, is that these things are in the air. Put it this way. If in a modern novel I read of an elderly gentleman with twinkling spectacles who undertakes scientific rambles in the company of three friends and a comic servant, and later gets entangled in a breach-of-promise case, I should assume, not that the author had read *Pickwick*, *but that he hadn't*. And on the ground that it is easier to believe in coincidence than in a filching which must be detected instantly. Wherefore let it be conceded that Werfel has never seen Obey's play, or those two plays by Shaw, or that film, or the musical show known as *The Lisbon Story*.

Montague once said that the highest courtesy in an author is to treat his reader " as no blind horse but a man who has some wit of his own and can take a thing in." The present authors—the play has been adapted by S. N. Behrman—treated us to-night as if we were inmates of a blind asylum. And what was their point ? Simply that a humble little Jew full of shrewdness and resource is of more value to society than some noisy descendant of Ancient Pistol. Well, it doesn't need two playwrights from the New World to invite the post-Shavians of the Old to remark this, let alone make a note of it twenty times. And then the comedy was tragically miscast. The Colonel is a monument of humourlessness, which means that if he is to amuse he must be played by an actor bubbling over with an inner sense of the ludicrous. An Alfred Lunt, for example. I have no doubt that Michael Redgrave tried to be funny to-night—indeed, one could see him trying. What was wrong was that he insisted on dissecting absurdity instead of warming to it. The Colonel is what a schoolboy would call a gorgeous ass ; he was turned into a solemn and regrettable one, sending cold shivers down my back as though Mr Dombey had cast himself for Cyrano. The point about Jacobowsky is subservience backed by guile, and we were given Karel Stepanek, radiating distinction and charm like a Jewish Traddles enacted by Steerforth at his most dazzling. The French fiancée was, of course, pure Wimbledon. Still, the evening had compensations. Delightful scenery, charming music, and a splash of two of wit.

June 7　　　　　Here is something I hope to say in the *S.T.* on Sunday :
Thursday.

The death of Oliver Elton at the age of eighty-four takes me back to certain criticisms appearing in the *Manchester Guardian* over the initials " O. E." It was from one of these that at seventeen I learned that great actors and, particularly, great actresses either don't know the rubbish from the masterpieces or, if they do, seven times out of ten prefer the rubbish. At nineteen " O. E. " gave me the measure of Ibsen's size and importance, *The Quintessence of Ibsenism*, published four years earlier, not yet having reached my unenterprising suburb. I remember, when I was twenty-one, the Monday morning on which " O. E. " told me what to think about *Cyrano de Bergerac* and Coquelin's acting. The performance had taken place on the previous Saturday evening, with *Le Bourgeois Gentilhomme* in the afternoon. I saw both. Here are some extracts from the three notices in question :

Bernhardt
" Last year, in *La Tosca*, we could study in its simplest form the kind of play and of heroine which M. Sardou invents in order to evoke the lower gifts of Mme Bernhardt. La Tosca, through hearing the cries of her lover while the police torture him, is wrung into dishonourably revealing the refuge of a fugitive, whose blood is thus upon her hands. Her lover is the first to denounce her, and she dies. Here the joint aim of playwright and actress was simple and unlawful ; the nerves were to be violently vexed, partly by sounds in imitation of physical agony suffered by a person unseen, and partly by the sight of La Tosca's anguish, itself supposed to be created by the same cause. There was no attempt at character. Mme Bernhardt has a genius for sinking to such parts."

July 8, 1895

A Doll's House
" The repute of Ibsen, since he first created a large band of dervishes howling against him, and a smaller band who howled on his behalf at all costs against the larger, seems to have settled into something European, which can be gauged reasonably and in his own spirit, though not with his power, of severe analysis. England is one of the provinces where the dispute, so far as it has not collapsed into apathy, has remained somewhat sectarian. Those who merely mistake Ibsen's situations for trivial and his characters for grotesque, those who from an impulse of self-preservation, representing the classes he dissects, dislike the process of dissection ; those who thank Heaven that, if Norwegians are like this, they are not like Norwegians ; and those who take the stronger line of idealistic theory in art, are all still vowed in some kind of muddled alliance against others who wish to fetter Ibsen to his own characters, or to present his art as the only art of the future. Actually, Ibsen is one of the three or four living persons with a great mastery

128

of dramatic interest and form, and one of the most incisive and critical depictors of society, not specially as it is in Norway, but as it necessarily is at this moment wherever the ideas of the French Revolution are found newly acting upon a small, discontented, and hampered but awakening community."

April 13, 1897

Coquelin in " Cyrano de Bergerac "

" *Cyrano* is kept up with half-Bacchic, half-chivalrous exuberance, and depends for its success on a heroic pitch of madness in the interpretation. It is best not read in the early morning, or in an Anglo-Saxon spirit. It is a literary play, and errs in a juster extreme than the usual literary play, which is a sterile, mulish negation of the dramatic art, and has only to be seen to collapse. *Cyrano* is hardly to be read without reference to the acting. This is only to say that it is not one of the great plays of the world, which keep their life both as literature and as drama."

June 22, 1899

Come now, you lauders of present times, let's have a show-down. Prove to me that these criticisms are superlatively good only because they appeared when I was superlatively young. Produce the modern day-to-day equivalent, and then produce it four times over, since, Elton being matched, W. T. Arnold, Allan Monkhouse, and, of course, Montague dazzlingly remain. So much for the provinces. How about London and our noble, weekly selves ? Well, we are mighty fine 'fellows nowadays, but I doubt whether any of us claims to write like Archer, Shaw, Max. At this point I hear an older voice booming, " Not even Shakespeare can write well without a proper subject. It is a vain endeavour for the most skilful hand to cultivate barrenness, or to paint upon vacuity." And I invite all vaunters of the present to ask themselves whether, before the theatre can look again for great criticism, it must not first bring back great drama. How about the Great Actor ? But that is easier said than done. I understand that in music, while great concertos are rare, virtuoso pianists are ten a penny. In the theatre it is different. Any plodding fellow with a smattering of sociology plus uplift can write something that passes for a great play. Only God can make a Tree.

June 8
Friday.
Pampering is good neither for man nor for beast. A pony that finds its own food on a bare hillside will always, other things being equal, be a better pony than one kneedeep in clover. This applies to men as well as animals, and minds as well as bodies. When I was a boy—this hangs on to yesterday's entry—the sight of an unfamiliar word in the English or in any other language would send me to the dictionary. I foraged for meanings. The youth of to-day is deprived of this wholly beneficial necessity, the edict having gone forth in many popular papers that no word in

any foreign language shall be used without a translation in bracket or footnote. When, as a youngster, I came across, say, *carte blanche* or *bête noire*, I would go to the dictionary and find out what the words meant. And probably discover one or two other things at the same time. Nowadays the papers are full of this sort of thing : " In a country which has always prided itself on its *amour-propre* (self-respect) a corresponding amount of *savoir faire* (tact) must be looked for. In any case a policy of *festina lente* (hasten slowly) must be pursued if a *débâcle* (catastrophe) ending in the inevitable *sauve qui peut* (save himself who can) is to be averted." Am I suspected of exaggeration ? I read in my morning paper :

Lord Moran, Mr Churchill's doctor, said yesterday, " It is not easy for anyone to get into Stalin's mind, but as far as one can make out Stalin thinks that the Prime Minister is a broth of a boy. Stalin doesn't like a man who lives on nuts and soda water."

*** From Eric Partridge's *Dictionary of Slang* : " Broth of a boy " : Anglo-Irish expression meaning the essence of manhood as broth is the essence of meat.

June 9   A letter :   *Officers' Mess*
Saturday.   *North-West Army Signals*
                                              Rawalpindi
                                         India Command
                                        29th May '45

DEAR MR AGATE,
    You do not know me, nor have we ever met. I have been trying to write to you ever since I landed in this extraordinary country several weeks ago—but what with the heat and Beverley Nichols, it has been impossible to concentrate on matters that did not daily surround me. However, I am now on leave, 7000 feet above sea-level, in the blessed cool of a hill station.
    I had the fortune to leave England on the same ship as Donald Wolfit and his company on their way to the Middle East. Being a struggling pre-war (and, God willing, post-war) actor, I found myself with the job of Ship's Entertainment Officer. While I was in the throes of trying to organise the very assorted talent on board, Wolfit asked, almost shyly, if he and his company could be of any assistance ! Naturally, I was greatly impressed by this very generous offer. With some hectic weeks at the Winter Garden behind them, and a Middle East tour before them, Wolfit and his team had obviously been looking forward to the complete rest which is normally offered by a sea-voyage. But, confronted by a ship full of troops on their way to India, and with the knowledge that there was no theatre on board, and that all costumes and " props " were locked and sealed in the hold, there was only one thought in the great actor's mind—to do as much as possible for the troops in the time allotted.

Within what seemed a matter of hours, the ship's dining-room was packed (and I mean packed) with troops. There was a small space at one end of the room on which we had managed to focus some of the existing lights. By this time the ship had started to roll very badly ; I was excited and, at the same time, puzzled—how on earth (or at sea) could a full performance of *Much Ado About Nothing* be given in this minute space, *sans* costumes, *sans* props, *sans* scenery—in fact, *sans* everything but actors in E.N.S.A. uniform ? The answer was easy—to Wolfit. He made a brief speech to the effect that *Much Ado* would be played exactly as it had been played at the Winter Garden, and that all costumes, props, etc., would be imagined to be complete—also, that he believed that this was the first time since the seventeenth century that a full Shakespearean play had been given at sea. Within two minutes of the start of the play the mass-illusion was complete, the audience were held in pin-drop silence, the absence of props, etc., was not noticed or mentioned again—even old Neptune realised the importance of the occasion, and stopped rolling the ship. At the finish Wolfit and his company received an ovation such as only a mass of really grateful British Tommies can give.

Much Ado was done several times so that the whole ship could see it. This was followed by several performances of *The Merchant of Venice*—a memorable one being given on deck in the middle of the Mediterranean to a really vast audience, who were perched on every conceivable part of the ship—and for two and a half hours the only sound that could be heard (apart from the magnificently audible performers) was the slight throb of the engines, and the gentle swish of that amazingly blue sea as we sped through it. This courageous and unselfish hard work was completed by a grand performance of *Hamlet*. The success of the whole effort can be judged by the send-off that was given to this valiant company at their post of disembarkation. The ship had a distinct list to starboard as every soldier on board cheered and sang them down the gangway.

With best wishes,
Yours sincerely,
DAVID DODIMEAD (*Major*)

P.S. You may be interested to know that I have just purchased *Immoment Toys* and *Ego* 6 from the oddest little bookshop in the oddest Indian bazaar.

June 10   *Cocasseries, No.* 16 :
Sunday.
God made the land and filled it with His music,
Blessed it with blossom, gave it spring and fall,
Gave to it life and love, and tears and laughter,
But to the sea He gave no thought at all.
                    From a poem in a Sunday paper

I see. While the Almighty had to think about elephants, whales just happened.

June 11   In the Leslie Stuart broadcast to-night the announcer
Monday.   referred to Signor Foli, " a celebrated Italian singer."
       And subsequently Foli was made to speak in the kind of
broken English customary with stage Italians. Now Foli was an
Irish policeman of the name of Foley, and how I came to know
about it is like this. My maternal grandmother was a music teacher
in Manchester, married to a wine-merchant who spent his life on the
sofa with gout and the plays of Shakespeare. At the time when
piano lessons were twelve for a guinea, counting thirteen as twelve
my grandmother did pretty well in charging the rich Greek colony,
whose children she taught, a guinea a lesson, counting twelve lessons
strictly as twelve. She was a woman whose determination equalled
her culture. She would not take in lodgers ; but, my father being
recommended to her as an earnest young man from the South, she
consented that he should make his home with her and her two
daughters. Then one day my father brought home one Gustave
Garcia, grandson of Manuel Garcia, the great tenor for whom Rossini
wrote the part of the Count Almaviva in *The Barber of Seville*, son of
Garcia, the centenarian singing-master, and nephew of Malibran and
Pauline Viardot, the friend of Turgenev. Into this harmonious little
circle Garcia, somewhere around the year 1870, introduced Foley, a
handsome Irish policeman with a fine bass voice and billed as " Signor
Foli." All this, of course, was before I was born.

       Some twenty-five years later I was learning the business of cotton
manufacturing at my father's mill in Nelson, Lancashire, where my
parents had taken a tiny house for me and installed me with " Old
Jane " (see *Ego* 7, page 73). One week, when my mother was visiting
me, there was a grand concert in an Institute, the artists including
Albani and Foli. I called on the great bass at his hotel, told him who
I was, and said my mother had charged me to invite him to supper
after the concert. He declined, regretting that he could not remember
any of my family ; from which position he would not budge. I was
hurt on my mother's account, though the time has come when I can
understand. For what could he have expected ? At the worst he
would be asked to hear me sing or play. At the best he would have
to answer a fire of questions : What was his favourite opera, oratorio,
ballad ? His favourite composer ? What did he think of Mascagni,
Leoncavallo, the later Verdi ? What was his opinion of Santley ?
Was it true that Wagner was ruining the singer's voice ? And so on
until he could decently take his leave. Or he might have thought
that we were hard up and wanted to borrow money. I was too young
then to realise the penalty of being any kind of public figure. Years
later I realised that an artist, having worked like a horse to entertain

his public, should be led back to some stable of his own choosing and there left to enjoy his evening feed in peace.

June 13   *Cocasseries, No.* 17 :
Wednesday.

Lauren Bacall's approach on the screen to a male adopts the technique used on women by roués and ordinary everyday wolves. She plays a " wolverine " and attributes her success in this part to what she calls her " down-under look." It was natural with her a year ago. Now she practises it on unsuspecting newspapermen.

Warner Bros.   News and Feature Service

Cocasseries, No. 18 :

" If that b—— Hitler had heard music like this he might have been a better man," an old lady of St Pancras (" twice bombed-out by the b—— I was ") told Miss Eaton, after she had heard her playing Bach's Air on the G String in the quiet Surrey village to which she had been evacuated.

From a Sunday paper

June 14   To-night's public dinner to Myra Hess, in honour of
Thursday.   her services to music during the war, was a dreadful
              affair.   The first three speakers took up *an hour and a quarter*, and did not say one memorable thing between them.   And the humour !   Elephantine persiflage about the sandwiches served at the National Gallery buffet !   As the next on the list of speakers was a former Minister of Food I left, having been told by the chairman that there would be no time for my three minutes.

June 15   Cedric Hardwicke accused me to-night of hypocrisy.   Why
Friday.   did I blame him for making pictures while I myself was
              wallowing in them ?   I said, " Boy, you've got me wrong. I don't in the least mind your making pictures.   I think you make them very well.   What I object to is your coming over here and reviving old successes when you ought to be creating new ones."   He said, " Let's get everything clear.   First, I am not one of those intellectuals who, when war was declared, ran away to America.   I was in America two years before the outbreak of war, and you will remember that we met in New York in the summer of 1937.   I was officially asked to stay on in Hollywood, and I stayed.   They have given me a year's leave of absence, and that is why I am in England. At the end of the time I shall go back to Hollywood, because I am one of those odd blokes who think a contract should be adhered to.

When I return to England for good I shall try to do the kind of plays you want. But it will have to be with my own money. When you're tied to a management you commercialise yourself and can't help it [I am transcribing roughly] because you are in a way responsible to them for their money. This means that you have to put up with some silly ass of a producer, or play with some wildly unsuitable actress because she's box-office." This conversation took place on the way to Cedric's sumptuous flat in South Street. On arrival, found Lady H. awaiting us with wonderful cocktails and a really remarkable supper. Cedric was in immense form and full of stories. How a famous Hollywood star, who poses as a great art connoisseur, bought a vastly expensive fake Manet or Renoir—C. couldn't remember which. Only to find, when he got home, the original hanging on his walls! Apropos of a former English actor, now a Hollywood star, C. remarked, " God made him a good actor ; he has turned himself into a bad one." He was full of theories about himself. " I can't act. I have never acted. And I shall never act. What I can do is to suspend my audience's power of judgment till I've finished. There are good actors and there are great actors. The great actor takes care that the audience shall have eyes and ears for no one else." I was delighted to find that he has exactly my views about producers—" They just get in the way "—and even more pleased when he confessed that from the first night to the last of the New York production of Paul Vincent Carroll's *Shadow and Substance*, in which he was such a success as Canon Skerritt, he hadn't the vaguest notion what his part was all about. We discussed my ideal cast for *Hamlet*, and C. agreed, with one exception. He said he thought the best King there had ever been was Oscar Asche. " When he looked at Gertrude the corners of his lower lip hung down like mutton chops." He said that never before or since had the atmosphere of the court of Denmark been properly conveyed. " It should be gross and licentious. Nowadays the place is so prim and Claudius so proper that you wonder what the fuss is all about." The talk then switched on to broadcasting, and both C. and Lady H. animadverted against English snobbery in the matter of sponsored programmes. They assured me I couldn't imagine the magnificence and variety of American wireless ; live performances by the best orchestras, with plenty of Toscanini. " After all," said C., " what does it matter if between the movements of a Beethoven symphony you are recommended to take somebody's cure for acidity ? You get used to it, and after a time pay no more attention to advertisements you hear over the air than you do to those you see in the English *Times*. What do you care if a well-written notice of last night's play is flanked by a puff of Sal Hepatica ? " We talked till the small hours ; then these nice people sent me back in a car. Snuggled in the corner of the back seat was a bottle of whiskey.

June 16   J. A. is a believer in taking his good where he finds it.
Saturday.   In other people's correspondence, perdy ! Here is another letter to Leo from his and my little Dublin
friend :

18 *Park View Avenue*
Harold's Cross
Dublin
June 12th, '45

MON CHER PAPA PAVIA,

What has this *enfant terrible* done to offend you ? Has he said something unusually stupid ? Has his spelling been more insulting than ever ? In brief, my sweet lion, why the stony silence ? I don't mind waiting two or even three weeks for a reply, but it is exactly four weeks since I wrote to you, telling of my perilous adventures in Harcourt Terrace. Or have the wretched postal authorities mucked about with my fragrant murmurings ?

Sir, you are cruel ! Each morning for the past three weeks have I patiently awaited the postman. My heart has pounded eagerly each morning ; my dreams have been coloured by gloriously witty notes in your distinctive typewriting. But alas, I have been so very sadly disappointed. My anxiety has been such that from a Paycockish state of " chassis " I have advanced into a Pepysian condition of " with child." I am afraid, gentle beast, that you are a " prevaricator and a procrastinator." So, please, don't postpone answering this effusion. Answer it now and be doubly witty.

My blood boils at the thought of those vulgar persons who write to James reminding him that he isn't as young as he used to be ; the person whom James answered in the *Sunday Times* a week ago was the subject of much vitriolic abuse from my faithful tongue. Personally, I dislike most persons under thirty-five. This includes actors and actresses. I like my actresses to be about thirty-nine or forty. There isn't a single movie actress under thirty, with the exception of Jennifer Jones, whom I would pay to see. Among my chief aversions are woman under twenty-five who smoke. This oddity of mine has caused me much embarrassment in the past. But I shall enlarge when I am writing my memoirs. These will be very Agatian and very sentimental. Sentimentality has caused me much unhappiness in my fifteen years. My sentimentality is not that of dear Sir James Barrie and his fragrant creations, drenched with the odour of spring flowers, "dewy with Nature's teardrops." It is a sticky, sludgy, sweaty sentimentality which has drained me of moral courage and the ability to defend myself. I have received countless little injuries in the past. I have for a while nourished

" slaughterous thoughts," but soon I have forgotten, to be injured yet again.

But this is all drivel, and I must not risk offending you. Were you a brilliant mathematician in your youth ? I am quite absurd in the face of the simplest geometrical problem. Probably because I am for ever thinking of other matters. You see, I am not what the lower middle classes call a " healthy-minded boy." I often wish I were. James seems to have been aggressively healthy in mind. What about you ? Please tell me more about yourself. (Even at present I'm thinking about something totally unconnected with this letter—Lady Longford's voice. Though I have never spoken to this brilliant creature, I very often " tail " her and her husband, simply to hear their voices.)

Now please reply and be intensely witty, and earn the unlimited gratitude of

Thy,
In a state of anxiety,
Very lone,
Very lorn
J. E. GUMMIDGE-JORDAN

P.S. As usual, my best wishes to the other J. E. Does the poor lamb still suffer from asthma ?

June 17   Four years to-day since Leo joined me—an endurance test
Sunday.   for both of us. But whether two people could wrangle so
              much and at the same time get on so well together I doubt.
Concert at the Cambridge Theatre. Denis Matthews in the *Emperor* Concerto—not quite as big a performance as I should like, but very sound and musicianly—and the best rendering of the *New World* Symphony I have ever heard. Conductor, Anthony Collins. The programme also included Collins's Idyll, " This Inarticulate Hour," from the new film, *I Live in Grosvenor Square*. I should describe this as admirable Wagner-cum-Delius, *arr.* Herbert Wilcox. Matthews, his delightful wife, Alec Whittaker the oboe-player, and Tom Lishman came back to tea, after which Leo gave us a recital. He began with " part of an unpublished piano concerto by Mozart discovered by an Austrian refugee in Linz. To be exact, the refugee had only time to copy a bit of the first movement and a few bars of the slow movement, by which time the Nazis had arrived. I will play you as much as I can remember." And did so. It was the perfect pastiche. He then tackled the *Waldstein* Sonata—with frequent haltings and stumblings. " Really, Leo," I remonstrated, " you're not playing at all well." " Neither would you," he retorted, " if you were trying to play the blasted thing in D flat ! " Followed this up with another

innovation—the Chopin F sharp major Nocturne transposed into A flat! And finished with a brilliant paraphrase on the *Rosenkavalier* waltzes in the Godowsky manner, not one note of which he will remember to-morrow morning. Having goggled and giggled their fill, my guests took their leave, we started work, and I dictated an article in C major which Leo's typewriter later reproduced in D flat.

June 18 Jock dropped in just after midnight. He shared my fury
Monday. at not being allowed my three minutes at the Myra Hess jamboree. I said, " Never mind, Jock, there are more ways than one of killing a cat. I have sent what I should have said to *The Times* ! "

June 19 *The Times* prints my letter. Which is something. Perhaps
Tuesday. I am wrong to get into a paddy about this sort of thing. The English loathe making a fuss, and their way of dealing with a great occasion is to take care that nothing shall be uttered in what an earlier century would have called " an elevated style." What's all this fuss about, anyhow ? some reader may be thinking. What did Agate want to say that was so wonderful ? Nothing at all. He wanted to *read* something Montague wrote during the last war :

> Even Armageddons are only means, and the joy of such treasures as these [*Twelfth Night*] is an end ; though the nations fight for a generation, it is to these that they will turn back in hunger at last, as they will turn to hills and the sea. Whatever else falls in this season of shaken assumptions and rearranged thoughts, the hold of great art on the mind will not give ; it will last as long as the " true and virtuous soul " that, " though the whole world turns to coal, Then chiefly lives." So it was well that Miss Horniman opened her autumn's work last night with this specimen of the undefeatable, inextinguishable treasures beside which even a 42-centimetre Krupp gun is but a fashion in hats. Peace, when it comes, would be worth so much the less to the returning soldier and every one else if the artists were only to sit down now and sigh for it.

Yes, I know that this appeared in *Ego* 4 and will appear in *A Shorter Ego*. Had I twelve tongues I would recite it twelve times ! My speech—in so far as the words were J. A.'s—would have been limited to a single sentence. All I should have said was that Myra Hess is another noble woman who has not been content to sit down and sigh for peace.

> *Stud Farm*
> *Wylde Green*
> *B'ham*
> *June 18, '45*

DEAR SIR,

You will be pleased to hear your mare has foaled a most beautiful filly (Saturday night.) I think it will be a black brown. Four white socks, star, and a little snip on its nose. A most lovely sort, walks with any amount of action, especially off its hind legs. You will be delighted with it. It is by Footlight—the brown colt that won the yearling class when we showed King Neptune just before the war.

> Hoping you are keeping well,
> Yours faithfully,
> ALBERT THROUP

This brings back all the old fever. It looks as if I might now fulfil my last ambition. I wanted to sit at the top table of Bertram Mills's circus luncheon ; I sat at the top table. I wanted to be President of the Hackney Horse Society ; I am President-Elect. I wanted to win the championship at Olympia ; Ego won the championship at Dublin, but the war came before he was ready for the supreme event at home. And now Olympia will come into its own again. Unless, of course, the Socialists get into power, when I understand that every animal in a Hackney class will receive the same-coloured ribbon, and any racehorse putting his nose in front of his comrades will be shot.

In the evening to see *Chicken Every Sunday*, at the Savoy. Who first started the notion of writing a play around groups of persons living in the same place, say a block of flats ? The idea is simplicity itself. You take a railway train whose engine suddenly emits a loud shriek, causing the occupants of six compartments to stick out of window six heads which the oncoming tunnel neatly severs. After which the dramatist proves that these six heads were distressingly, conveniently, justly, inexorably, gratuitously, ironically removed. And, in the language of lady novelists, " out of the warp and woof of six divergent tragedies a texture of common significance is evolved." To the playwright taking the easy way the genre has obvious advantages. George Jean Nathan wrote of the New York production of this play : " With a boarding-house the playwright can bring on, without apology, any shape or form of human flesh, however anomalous and grotesque." The people gathered under Mrs Blachman's hospitable roof are : the husband, president of a bank, a line of street-cars, and a laundry, all of which are failing ; three children ; an idiot boy-poet and his imbecile mother ; an Irishman who has strayed in from the Abbey Theatre ; a drunken female vaudeville artist with a passion for yodelling ; a woman who imagines herself pursued by Indians ; a coloured maid ; a fantastic creature who is a combination of Mrs Skewton and Miss Flite ; a big-business man with a wife who thinks she is Mae West ; a clergyman ; a socially conscious young man from Boston ; a poultry-farmer, and a Red Indian. As Nathan puts it : " Only Leopold and Loeb are missing." Like some light wines, some American farces will not travel. Not all farces refuse, and certainly not sustained practical jokes like *Room Service* and *My Sister Eileen*, where there was action. In to-night's piece there was only oddity of character—Nathan's " shapes of human flesh "—the farce lacked the American players, and the cast was inescapably British, Rickmansworth and not Arizona being written all over it.

Afterwards to the Savoy Grill, to keep a date with Jock and Bertie van Thal, who had been to *Peter Grimes*. I asked them to tell me in five words what it was like. Jock said, " I'll tell you in four. It was like *Maritana* ! ! " Later he said, " If you seriously want to know about the opera, Jamie, it's a work of genius."

Drank a, health to the foal, which Jock said in view of her breeding —by Footlight out of Lady Viking by Viking—I ought to call Ellida. But since *The Lady from the Sea* bores me more than any other of Ibsen's plays, Duse or no Duse, I shall compromise with Hedda. On second thoughts I shall do nothing of the sort. I don't see what these Nordic beauties have to do with an English filly. Shall call her My Pretty. Home about 1 A.M. with a delightful pre-war feeling that of the £15 with which I started the evening only ten bob remained. Worked till three.

June 21 Why are the moderns afraid of standing up to the
Thursday. ancients, since we are always being told that they are
better ? People get furious when I compare to-day's writers of opérettes with yesterday's. Why do they funk reference to Offenbach, Strauss, and Sullivan, or even Planquette, Messager, and German, since they hold the theatre of the present to be better than that of the past ? I will tell them. Even they would recognise, say, *Three Little Maids from School* as Sullivan and nobody except Sullivan, if they heard it thrummed on bazookas in the Fiji Islands. But would they recognise as indubitable Leslie-Smith any extract from *Sweet Yesterday*, to-night's affair at the Adelphi, if they heard it poured out by, say, Frankie Schubert's Otiose Otaheitans in some Tyneside Palais de Danse ? I doubt it. I suggest they would vaguely attribute it to that school of composers which, between the two wars, supplied the pseudo-Viennese drama with its sound-

equivalent. I note that the programme attributes the orchestration to a Mr Ben Frankel, who has certainly seen to it that the score is lush to saturation-point. What harps and timbrels ! What wild ecstasy ! And for the bored critic what struggles to escape ! I suppose it would be naughty to ask our modern panegyrists *who did the orchestration for Offenbach and those others* ? The essence of grand opera being to fill a void with teeming nonsense, I didn't expect this grand opérette—all about spying under Napoleon—to do more sensibly. Webster Booth and Anne Ziegler in good, and oh so frequent, voice. Reginald Tate and Hugh Miller exuding nobility and acumen. Doris Hare as a Sans-Gêne born within sound of Bow Bells. Wherefore in the *S.T.* on Sunday I shall suggest deletion of the line : " Does France move against England ? " The answer could only be : " If it does, it will be civil war ! " No, I shall invite these Mossoos and Madarms to toast each other at the boofy at Booloyne without insisting on their nationality.

June 22   Coming back to the flat after lunch, I found a Mickey
Friday.   Rooney-ish young man on the doorstep. Twenty-six,
     born ten miles from me, ex-Durham Light Infantry, just back from five years in a prisoner-of-war camp in East Prussia, most of the period in a punishment camp owing to two abortive attempts to escape. Has ideas about being an actor. If he could prove he could act, would I help ? Being in one of my benignant moods, I asked him in, gave him a drink, and when he had finished it, said, " Now act ! " " What do you want ? " " What have you got ? " " I can do the Chaplain's speech from *St Joan.*" And began : " I let them do it. If I had known, I would have torn her from their hands. . . ." I stopped him and said, " Young man, you're an actor all right. Go on." And in half a minute, stone-cold in the corner of the room, with Leo and me for audience, he produced more pathos than . . . never mind who. A bit of Jones in *The Silver Box* was not so good, and the diction in a poem of Cowper's was a mess. But that the young man is a born actor there can be no doubt. He screwed an imaginary eyeglass in his eye and gave us a lightning sketch of George Arliss as good as Nelson Keys. Then, saying I might like to see how a person would dance who had no bones, he executed half a dozen steps with great comicality. Finally he turned a couple of cartwheels and departed. I don't think he's an Edmund Kean, but he might well be another Bobbie Howes. Bits of him struck me as pure monkey. I was considerably flattered when he said he had read one of my books. " Which ? " " *Buzz, Buzz !* A fellow at Bromberg lent it me." Of course he wants a lot of disciplining and

coaching, including the elimination of the Lancashire accent. And five years' manual labour hasn't helped, except to make him as strong as a horse. Anyhow, I lost no time. As soon as he had gone I rang up Elsie Fogerty, who was most helpful and at once promised to put him through his paces. And Leo says, " Saddled with another protégé, James ? "

The mid-day post brought this note from Jock :

33 *King Street*
*Covent Garden, W.C.*2
21*st June*, 1945

MY DEAR JAMIE,

Cave ! Don't go about our part of the town saying that I said that B. Britten is a new R. Strauss. I didn't. I wouldn't have said that even about R. S. after *Guntram* or whatever his first opera was called !

But I think this morning—even more than I thought last night just after the performance—that *Peter Grimes* is a very remarkable opera—full of strangeness, and beauty, and strangeness in beauty. It is packed with originality and subtlety, has neither tedium nor cacophony, and has many instances of pure genius. If genius, for example, did not go to the making of the unearthly music that accompanies and follows the death of the little apprentice at the end of Act II—scored principally for celesta and solo viola, if you please—then I'm an unmusical Dutchman !

What a charming supper ! And in what nice good quiet form we all were !

Your alacritous
JOCK

June 23   Again from our little Irish friend—this time to me :
Saturday.

You want to know about my family ? There's nothing remarkable. None of my great-aunts comforted Parnell in his hour of tribulation. Nobody gambled away the family fortune. I had a great-uncle, who was kicked out of the Navy for drinking, and I believe my grandfather also drank. But no man can be sober for ever, and we must be satisfied. My great-grandmother was killed in an earthquake somewhere. Which is all the piquancy in an incredibly prosaic family. Are my parents clever ? Dear people, of course. My mother wallows in the philosophy of life propounded by Ethel M. Dell, Ruby Ayres, Berta Ruck, and the rest of the talented ladies who fool all the female public all the time. My father reads the newspapers. Harold's Cross has gone to the dogs altogether. The place reeks of poor imitations of the Captain— O'Casey's, not Strindberg's—and old-age pensioners who spit tobacco all over the place. Gentility is confined to a few back

avenues where everybody is as snobbish as can be, and the word
" common " echoes all through the day. When I was small I wasn't
allowed to play with " common " children. You will be interested
to know that the cook and the second footman have given notice.
At the rate things are going, the mater will have to clean the
brasses herself. I asked Lady L. about lending us a butler, but she
said she had murdered the last one some time ago.

June 24   Ernest Newman, in a third article on the subject, at last
Sunday.   tells me what I want to know about *Peter Grimes* :

Complete distinctness of speech must be maintained, in a work
of this kind, not only in the episodes of quasi-recitative but in the
more specifically lyrical portions ; for if the words escape us in a
solo lyrical passage we are necessarily reduced to listening to it in
terms of melody pure and simple, and to do that is, in the present
instance, to shift it into a genre to which it does not belong. It
hardly matters to us whether *Dalla sua pace* or *Caro nome* is sung
in English, in Italian, or in Choctaw ; even if we could follow all
the words, which is not always the case, and even if they signified
anything in particular, which rarely happens in arias of this kind—
has one listener in a million, for instance, the smallest notion of
what the words of *Ombra mai fu* mean ?—the overriding consideration is the charm of the music as pure melody, and the intellect
ungrudgingly suffers the deprivation of the words because the musical
ear is satisfied.

Now let's begin at the beginning. I don't want to see any poet's
words mimed or danced. Or acted unless they were meant to be
acted. Or sung unless they are of a triviality indicating that they
were meant to be sung. I don't believe in robbing poetical Peter to
provide a living for musical Paul. I don't believe in the marriage of
perfect words to perfect music. To quote something I wrote twenty-
eight years ago :

Perfect words and perfect music mean words and music so
perfectly charged with emotion of their own kind and so perfectly
expressed in their own way that no addition of emotion is possible.
You may compare them to two perfectly full glasses, neither of
which can by any possible sleight-of-hand be emptied into the
other. The result of setting perfect words to perfect music is that
of two fine things one must inevitably be spilled or destroyed.
There is bound to be a surrender, and it is the words which give
way.

I don't believe that Beethoven at his most celestial can add anything
to Wordsworth's *Intimations* that the poem does not contain. I don't
want to hear lambs bounding to the tabor in the Pastoral Symphony

manner, or cataracts blowing trumpets *à la Leonora*. I don't want
Wordsworth's emotion plus Beethoven's, because it doesn't work out
that way ; what I should get would be Beethoven *in place of* Wordsworth. I don't believe that Debussy, in the mood of *Nocturnes*, can
add to " Now fades the glimmering landscape on the sight." Or in
the mood of *La Cathédrale Engloutie* render more expressive

> Full fathom five thy father lies ;
>   Of his bones are coral made ;
> Those are pearls that were his eyes :
>   Nothing of him that doth fade
> But doth suffer a sea-change
> Into something rich and strange.

Nothing of Shakespeare's verse but must inevitably fade into the web
woven by the composer in that job of magnificent treachery—translation. When Shakespeare wrote these words " for music " he was
too modest ; the lyrics which set best are the trivial ones which fill,
and are intended to fill, only a corner of the mind. Does any musical
ass think he can enhance the sonnet beginning " Shall I compare thee
to a summer's day ? " These things have their own music. I defy
Berlioz to do more brassily and moltenly than the verse in *Antony
and Cleopatra*, or more heart-breakingly than " I am dying, Egypt,
dying." On the other hand, you can add a tune to " See, saw,
Margery Daw," because here is only a drop at the bottom of a child's
mug that is waiting to be filled, whereas those other goblets are full
to the brim. Would anybody outside a lunatic asylum have wanted
to add soft music to any of Sarah's dyings ? Film actresses ? But
their glass isn't anywhere near full.

I know that somebody thinks to catch me with the marriage of
Pickwick and its illustrators. They came into the world together, my
dear objector. Would you have the book re-illustrated by a modern
artist, and would you believe him, however clever he was ? Would
you have Elizabeth Bennet drawn ? My dear sir, she has been drawn
and is a horror ! Or Tess ? I can draw Tess in my own mind better
than ten Augustus Johns. Would any opera-monger take Hardy's
young woman for his heroine ? Let him invent a milkmaid of his
own, and have her seduced in five sharps. The one excuse I can find
for Britten's choice of subject is that nobody remembers Crabbe's
poem except Jock, who of course has it by heart.

I don't know whether, in the higher mathematics, you can add one
to infinity. The idea seems to me to be perilously near the Higher
Nonsense—you cannot give a man toothache who is being drawn and
quartered. Great music heightens great poetry ? I see. You can
add height to all the height there is. Add Handel to Isaiah, and the

price you have to pay for the Raphaelesque quality of " He shall feed His flock " is the monstrosity, " like a She-e-e-e-ep-herd." Whereas

Angels, ever bright and fair,
Take, oh, take me to your care !
Speed to your own courts my flight
Clad in robes of virgin white !

shrieks for music, since no sane person would dream of hearing it without. Wherefore I say that the function of music is not to attempt to heighten that which cannot be heightened, but to transfigure the rubbishy and the middling. *Carmen* ? Bizet took a magnificently sordid tale and made of it a glitteringly romantic one. *Otello* ? Verdi turned Shakespeare's drama into music-drama, and I do not think Euclid would have agreed that $A+B=A$. Many years ago I went out to Ealing to see Sarah Bernhardt at a matinée. Dumas's Marguerite Gautier died that afternoon about 5.30. At eight o'clock I saw Covent Garden's curtain go up on Melba's colourless Violetta and Caruso's Puss-in-Boots Alfredo. (The curious will find an allusion to this in one of my earlier books.) From that moment I had no doubt that *Traviata* is travesty. Suppose, since I am trying to look all round the question, that some musical genius takes in hand not the topless but the exquisite—say Housman's poem beginning " Loveliest of trees, the cherry now." Here again I am jealous for Housman. The more exquisitely done the less it will be Housman— the old story of Reynaldo Hahn coming in at the door and Verlaine flying out of the window. At least it is so in the world of my logic, which is as strict as Lewis Carroll's. Let us have an example away from the arts. Suppose somebody were to take my little horse Ego and dye him dark brown, which many consider a better colour than bright bay. Would he produce the same impression on the ringsider ? He wouldn't. I am concerned, not with whether the impression would be better or worse, but with the fact that it would be different.

So far the argument has been against the raiding of poetry to make a musical beanfeast. Now let's see what happens when the raid has been accomplished. Let me take in turn the media of mime, ballet, and opera. I have no use for mime when it usurps the place of words. Why should an actor pull his face about when Nature has given him lips and a tongue to say what he means ? I feel about your pantomimist exactly what Hamlet felt about the murderer of Gonzago wasting time semaphoring his intentions. " Pox, leave thy damnable faces, and begin." Absolute mime, if there can be such a thing ? This is exhausted after ten minutes. Now about ballet. Why should I agree that a twiddle of skirts from right to left and pointing a toe in one direction mean " He loves me," while the reverse twiddle and

the toe pointed in the opposite direction mean "He loves me not " ?
Absolute ballet ? But that to me is no more than an agreeable con-
fluence of line and movement and *chichi*, and after twenty minutes of
it I have had enough. *Enfin*, opera. To be logical I must maintain
that since Isolda may not tell Tristan that she dotes by pulling faces
or spinning teetotums at him, so she mustn't do this by screaming
her head off within an inch of his nose but with one eye on the conductor. Why, then, since ten minutes of mime cloy, and twenty
minutes of ballet satiate, can I put up with four hours of opera in
which I equally disbelieve ? Because I am ravished by opera, *on
condition that I have only a vague idea of what it is about*. In this I
wholly agree with Arnold Bennett, who maintained that opera was
tolerable only when sung in a language he didn't understand. And
how wisely. " Voglio la mia colazione "—I must trust to my Café
Royal waiter—sounds romantic. " I want my breakfast " sounds and
is ridiculous. My discovery that *Ombra mai fu* was addressed to a
tree robbed it of half its charm, since the things I had pretended it
was about were infinitely more magical. I still curse the day when
some too explicit soprano let me hear the opening words of the
Liebestod :

> Softly o'er him smiles are stealing ;
> how his eyelids gently open—
> see you, friends ?
> See you not ?
> Ever brighter beams his glory.
> Crowned with stars, on high he floats !

Floats ! And as I look at some eighteen stone of supine, ridiculous
beef I think of that fairy play about India in which Oscar Asche was
wafted to Heaven ! Is it objected that Frederick Jameson's translation doesn't do the original justice ? It would take a wilderness of
German professors to convince me that

> Wie das Herz ihm muthig schwillt,
> Voll und hehr im Busen ihm quillt ?

is beautiful or even scannable verse. I don't know, and have never
known, what words Salome is babbling in that closing scene. Is
it some heavy-handed equivalent of Wilde's tarty " J'étais une
princesse, tu m'as dédaignée. J'étais une vierge, tu m'as déflorée.
J'étais chaste, tu as rempli mes veines de feu . . . ah ! Ah ! Pourquoi ne m'as-tu pas regardée, Iokanaan ? Si tu m'avais regardée tu
m'aurais aimée. Je sais bien que tu m'aurais aimée, et le mystère
de l'amour est plus grand que le mystère de la mort. Il ne faut
regarder que l'amour." Well, just as I can do better in my mind than
this medley, as somebody remarked, of Ollendorff and Maeterlinck,

so I know that my unframed ecstasy is better than whatever Gota Ljungberg is yammering in my well-worn record made with the Berlin State Orchestra shortly after the last war. *Elektra* ? My Greek drama is more than shaky. This is why, before I see Strauss's opera, I spend the previous evening with black coffee and a wet towel. But when, say, a Rose Pauly prances about the stage in that last scene putting her knee as high as Ego used to, I don't care whether Elektra is Orestes' mother, stepmother, aunt, sister, or first cousin. And, since I don't want to know what any of them is saying, I obviously wouldn't care if the whole horrible family sang in Dutch, Spanish, or Cherokee.

I suppose my three favourite songs are Giordani's *Caro Mio Ben*, Tschaikowsky's *To the Forest*, and Strauss's *Ständchen*. *It gives me no satisfaction to know what they are about.* I don't care two hoots whether the melodies of Schumann are hung on a nut-tree, the moon, or any number of Grenadiers. To sum up. You can't add Ravel to Keats. If you do, it is at the peril of making that foam into Lux.

POSTSCRIPT

Out of every thousand readers who have ploughed through to-day's entry 999 will say, " Why does he criticise what he hasn't seen ? " These 999 are loose-thinkers holding that an essay hung on a peg must be a criticism of that peg. I have amused myself to-day by writing on the general subject of words and music ; my first job to-morrow will be to ring up Sadler's Wells for seats. I may enjoy Britten's opera very much. I may want to hear it every other week for the rest of my life. I may become Britten's slave. Which won't alter the fact that when I am being ravished by music I ignore the words, and that when I am reading great poetry I am indifferent to sounding brass and tinkling cymbal. And here is a naughty thought. I have never read a line of Crabbe's poetry that made me want to read another. Suppose no bar of Britten's music makes me want to hear the next ? Would not *that* marriage be perfect ?

June 25 Sadler's Wells can do two seats on July 17.
Monday. Letter to Frank Singleton :

*Queen Alexandra Mansions, W.C.*2
June 25th, 1945

DEAR FRANK,
     Please divert your mighty intellect from the great part Bolton is going to play, and is doubtless playing, in the coming Election,

146

to help me in a little matter. Do you know the original of the little rhyme:

> Le temps est beau,
> Et bleu le ciel;
> Doucement je vais
> A mon bordel.

There are several longer versions, but the present one seems to me to say all that need be said. Nobody here knows the author. A French major whom I consulted had an idea it was Verlaine. Probably something of the sort was current in Ancient Rome.

Did you hear some learned owl on the wireless the other evening tying himself into knots trying to explain how *A Shropshire Lad* could have been written by a man who was never in love?

One thing more. Where in Boswell is that passage in which Johnson says he doesn't mind what political views a man holds so long as he votes Tory? Or isn't it in Boswell at all? For myself, I shan't vote. In my view there ought to be professional jurymen and professional voters, chosen from people competent to weigh evidence and record an opinion. The masses? Even Ruskin could tell the workman that his voice wasn't worth a rat's squeak. I should compel them to vote, of course, because of the salutary effect of voting. But I should destroy the votes, not count them.
Kind regards from
Your liberal-minded
JAMES AGATE

P.S. I feel in my bones that I've got the verse all wrong. Is there something about " La mer est belle," and taking one's hat and stick and sallying forth " au bord d'elle " ?

June 26   From the Introduction to Sacheverell Sitwell's *British*
Tuesday.   Architects and Craftsmen:

Is not the life of the individual in our large towns, near the cinema and the fried-fish shop, with the air-raid shelter opposite, hideous and shameful compared with that of any savage? Is ours to be a world only of dog-races and the Cup Final? When we consider the spiritual values in our council houses, should we not envy the Papuan and the black fellow of the Torres Straits?

Which suggests the following one-act drama:

SANKAN AND SUDAKANA
Play in One Act

SCENE : *Any native hut in Borneo. No tables and no chairs. No eating utensils. No beds. When the hut-dwellers retire for the night they lie on the floor. Filth and abomination everywhere. Odour of decaying flesh.*

SANKAN. Mummy, can I have fish and chips to-night?
SUDAKANA. Certainly not.

SANKAN. Mummy, can I go to the pictures to-morrow ?

SUDAKANA. No, you can't.

SANKAN. Mummy, can I go to the dogs Friday ?

SUDAKANA. How often have I to tell you you're not going near the dogs ?

SANKAN. Mummy, can I go to the Cup Final Saturday ?

SUDAKANA. No, you can *not*. You ought to be ashamed of yourself. You're not a nasty little English boy. You belong to a superior race.

SANKAN. Mummy, *why* can't I go to the Cup Final ?

SUDAKANA. Because, my child, Daddy's going to give you your first lesson in head-hunting. Now go to sleep.

CURTAIN

June 27
Wednesday.
Put into practice my new ultimatum to taxi-drivers refusing to wait. " I am a journalist and must please my readers. You are a taxi-driver and must please your riders. I give good tips. You must expect to wait five minutes. After five minutes I pay ten shillings per quarter of an hour or any part of it." If they reject these terms then I give them *no tip* ! A dozen or so of persons assembled in the Cromwell Road to-day to hear an altercation at the end of which the cabman, dashing his cap on the ground and saying, " You're a imbecilic—that's wot you are ! " invited me to put 'em up. No Jingle intervening, J. A. hailed another cab that by great good fortune happened to be passing. And, in the language of Tennyson's parodist, " clomb therein and sate."

June 28
Thursday.
Letter from Brother Harry, saying that he and my niece are all set for their week's visit to London. " I have the personal assurance of the L.N.E.R. that the train will not be late on Sunday." I haven't seen Ann since she was a three-year-old paddling at Llanfairfechan ; she is now eighteen. Bertie van Thal and Jock report her an enchanting little person bristling with certificates, erudition, and fun. She has passed all sorts of examinations, and is going in for the Higher Development of Women or some rubbish of the sort. Shall tell her I'm too old to be converted. Have arranged what I hope will be good entertainment in the evenings for them. Harry's letter ends :

Owing to the fact that an injection was unwise and the fear that gas might upset my tummy, I have to-day had a tooth out without any anæsthetic ! I was assured that provided I held tight to the chair, and the handles of the forceps didn't come apart, " we shall be all right." We weren't !

148

June 29   Letter saying the writer has just read *Ego* 2 and regrets
Friday.   the inclusion of one or two improper stories.   If I like to
               delete these in the next edition he will then be able to
place the volume on his bookshelf.   Wishes I had written after
another model :

> If I should be discussed some distant day
> Say there were many things I might have said
> And did not say.
> Admired by hosts of readers, I grew old
> But honoured this conceit :
> The bawdy tales that often came my way
> I'd ne'er repeat.

Ends by asking when *Ego* 3 is coming out ! !   Leo says we must keep
the existence of this and the next one from him, lest the *Contes
Scabreux* and the *Nouveaux Contes Scabreux* send him into fits !

June 30   Letter from Frank Singleton :
Saturday.
                                        8 *Hill Cot Road*
                                              Bolton
                                        June 28, 1945

DEAR JAMES,
      I can't place your little verse, but on the analogy of the divinity
student (" I don't know the answer you ask for, but I append a list
of the Kings of Judah ") I transcribe some lines that have been
haunting me to-day :

> Je m'en vais seul du monde ainsi qu'un convié
> S'en va seul du banquet de quelque marié. . . .

Ronsard, who wrote splendid poetry for fifty years, would object
to the view that Housman was a poet who had never been in love
on the grounds that, whether he was in love or not, as a poet he
had never furnished more than some agreeable samples.   You
remember the preface to the second slender volume in 1922.   " I
can no longer expect to be revisited by the continuous excitement
. . . nor indeed could I well sustain it if it came."   The Renaissance
had more appetite for production.   Lope de Vega wrote 1500 plays !
      Do you know the lines in which four hundred years later the
Comtesse de Noailles contemplated her own death ?

> J'accomplirai cet acte unique et solitaire,
> Moi qui n'ai pas dormi seule, aux jours de la terre.

      Your verse reflects a happy adjustment to life on this imperfect
planet.   Mine seems all concerned with getting off it.
      What Dr Johnson said was :   " I don't mind what a man's
politics are so long as he *behaves* like a Tory."   I can't find where.
      I am enjoying the Election in a circus-master sort of way.
Democracy would certainly be hard pressed to defend the thesis
that every one is fit to govern.   But the lesson of the dictatorships

is that certainly no one is fit to govern alone. In the words of the
motion which I proposed as retiring President of the Cambridge
Union : " This house will reluctantly continue to interest itself in
politics."   That is still my attitude to-day.

Yours as ever,

F<small>RANK</small>

July 1   From G. W. Stonier's review, in *The Windmill*, of
Sunday.   " Palinurus's " *The Unquiet Grave* :

> Nothing but praise for its short cuts, its touches of fantasy, its
> humour, its anthologising, its bilingual idiom ; the French quota-
> tions are as much a part as Latin is to the *Anatomy of Melancholy*.

To revert to an old sore. Why, when other people are allowed to
quote gracefully and naturally, am I always accused of doing it to
show off ? Do I, then, drag in my quotations ? I think, perhaps,
in the *S.T.* to-day I do. Last week's play was all about a poet who
lost his hands in an accident and had a pair belonging to a murderer
grafted on. (On the lines of the old film called *The Hands of Orlac*.)
To-day I write :

> It is natural that anybody fitted with hands which have
> belonged to some one else should be interested in learning how
> those hands have previously behaved. The sensible thing, of
> course, would be to make *no* inquiries. Imagine Hamlet's horror
> on learning his fingers have paddled in unlawful necks and pinched
> wanton on cheeks they should not.

This is too long, and reads as if it had been lugged in. What I wrote
in my first draft was : " Imagine Lear's horror on finding that the
dead man had not kept his hand out of plackets." But would the
S.T. have liked that ? No, sirree ! But I have no doubt about
" Micawber's disgust on realising that his knuckles are those he has
rapped, the knuckles of Heep, the Forger and the Cheat " !

I can lay my hand on my heart and swear that normally, when I
quote, it is because I can't help it any more than Bacon or Burton
could, and Connolly can. Dickens quotes very little. But there are
two plays of Shakespeare which are always at the back of his mind.
One is *Hamlet* ; see Hamlet's Aunt and Mr Wopsle. The other is
Macbeth. At least two references in *David Copperfield* : " The shade
of a young butcher rises, like the apparition of an armed head in
Macbeth." Steerforth saying, " ' Why, being gone, I am a man
again,' like Macbeth. And now for dinner ! If I have not (Macbeth-
like) broken up the feast with most admired disorder, Daisy." In
Dombey and Son we are told that Miss Tox's bedroom commanded a
vista of mews " where the most domestic and confidential garments

150

of coachmen and their wives usually hung, like Macbeth's banners, on the outward walls." Now was Dickens showing off, or could he just not help it ?

With me the quotation varies with the mood. The papers have been trying to scare us recently with accounts of how the Nazis were planning to destroy cities and whole countries by focusing the rays of the sun on to them. How they were going to split the atom and so destroy the world. How death and destruction in one form or other are knocking at our doors. When my nerves are not at their best my nostrum for all this is a jumble of Stevenson which runs : " A man should stop his ears against paralysing terror, and run the race that is set before him with a single mind. . . . Death may be knocking at the door ; we have something else in hand, thank God, and let him knock." When my nerves are in reasonable shape I just think of the Fat Boy and refuse to be the Deaf Old Lady.

July 2 Monday. The York train last night was some three-quarters of an hour late, its arrival coinciding with a cloudburst. Which did not damp my pleasure at seeing Brother Harry and Niece Ann. Harry's offspring, which I shall use as pet name, turns out to be exceedingly pretty—no make-up that I can detect—and I don't notice what she's wearing, which, of course, is right. Asked what she would like to see most in London, she instantly replies, " The Zoo and the Ivy." How she will laugh when she sees those hats like outsize dartboards !—though I am afraid she will find some of the frisky old girls a trifle pathetic. As a good little niece she enormously overrates my importance in the scheme of things, wherefore I had great pleasure in showing her a letter received from Watford this morning :

One day last week I went to the cinema. The title of the supporting film was *East of Piccadilly*, the story of a murder in Soho. The murder takes place in a tenement, whose inhabitants include a mysterious American, a brace of what an inspector calls " daughters of joy " (!), and a mad actor. One of the " daughters of joy " is murdered, and her body disappears. The inspector questions the haywire ham and asks him if he has any bodies lying around loose. Says the actor : " Oh, yes, I have five—five dramatic critics ! They aren't dead yet, but they won't last long." He tiptoes across to a curtain and, with a burst of ghoulish laughter, flings it back to reveal five hanging dummies. " This," he whispers, " is the *Evening Standard* critic, this the *News*, and this *The Times* —he's pretty far gone, I fear. And this is Ivor Brown of the *Observer*. This "—and here he rolled the words round his tongue with marvellous unction—" this is—James Agate ! " Alone among that large audience I laughed. No one else had heard of you.

Saw them safely to the Prince of Wales's (Sid Field) to-night, and then betook myself to the New Theatre (Comédie Française). Beaumarchais's comedy still sparkles. Why? Because of its wit and power of observation? (The young fellow was not born a watchmaker for nothing.) Because of its Leftism? But Molière was before him. My guess is Rossini. Meaning that for the music's sake—and it was running in my head all evening—one is glad to hear the old words. Pierre Dux very amusing. Took H. and O., Gwen Chenhalls, and George Mathew to supper at the Café Royal.

July 3   Realising that I should be hellishly busy with the
Tuesday.   Comédie Française all week, I had asked Leo to look
             through some old *Tatlers* and make a list of ten of the
most idiotic film plots we have seen. The Old Thing having his own way of interpreting instructions, I find on my desk this morning ten *précis*. Here is the first one :

> The rich Philadelphia couple who marry from motives of social convenience. They agree not to live as man and wife, until she explains that she is about to become the mother of twins. Her husband, piqued at first, is reassured when his wife tells him that the happy event is the result of the previous summer's visit to France and a pilgrimage to the sepulchre of St Jean-le-Canaille.

Follow nine even less printable fantasies. But none of them, be it said, as witless as the rubbish to the private view of which I took H. and Offspring to-day after lunching them at the Ivy. Imagine the following. You are a thug and have in your power and in a Bronx cellar a detective of enormous strength. But this detective is blind, wherefore he is always accompanied by Friday, an extremely powerful Alsatian wolfhound, which you let him take with him into the cellar. Presently the detective is heard saying plaintively through the door, " Friday is thirsty." He goes on, " Surely you wouldn't have a dog whine for water ? " And you, being a softie at heart, get some water and take it into the cellar, and the dog at once buries its fangs in your throat. Whereupon the blind detective takes the key of a second cellar from your pocket and liberates his personal bodyguard. The Young Things in whose honour all this has happened are then united. When it was over O. turned to me and said, " Does London really like this sort of thing ? " I said, " Yes, dear O."

Ruy Blas ? Yes and no. It is going to behove me to step warily on Sunday next lest I fall into the error of judging the masterpieces of one nation by the taste of another. We are displeased when a French critic finds Shakespeare barbarous and Ben Jonson uncouth. Whence it follows that an English critic should not be too sure that Hugo's rhetoric is mere bombast. To the French it may—indeed, it must—be something more. Better to ask whether Hugo's drama caught the new spirit stirring in the minds of Frenchmen and, if so, crystallised it in terms of poetry. Not that I shall go as far as Swinburne, who held that Hugo, functioning as poet, eclipsed Milton and recalled " the lyric inspiration of Coleridge and Shelley, the prophetic inspiration of Dante and Isaiah, the satiric inspiration of Juvenal and Dryden." After which there was nothing left for the extravagant fellow to say of Hugo as dramatist except that he was the greatest since Shakespeare. (Forgetting Goethe, as somebody forgot Goschen ?) Again, we English are not so liberal-minded as the French. We hold in our snobbish way that the lackey who aspires to his royal mistress is a lackey still; if we pretend that he isn't it is only in a semi-serious Monsieur Beaucaire-ish sort of way. And then, phlegmatists that we are, we have little liking for the hero who is alternately braggart and sob-machine. Not Teresa del Riego herself could have dried those never-ending tears in Paul Deiber's voice to-night, though in view of the actor's youth this was a very promising performance. The composer to have kept alive this, to us, stuffed dummy of a play ? Meyerbeer in his mood of Piff-Paffery. And even then I doubt, for Meyerbeer too is dead.

Good party at the Savoy afterwards. H. and O.—who had been to the Albert Hall to hear Ginette Neveu play the Brahms—Cedric and Lady Hardwicke, Gladys Cooper, Jock, Meric Dobson, and Bertie van Thal. I asked Gladys her views about filming. She said, " They give you your part, and tell you to relax while they arrange the lights. You learn your lines while you're relaxing, and then play the sequence. As far as I know I have only seen one of my films. I go to the cinema to take my daughter, and as she doesn't like the kind of film I act in, we just don't go to them." She was in wonderful spirits and more radiantly beautiful than ever. Cedric, too, was in excellent form. " The Comédie Française is the best argument against a National Theatre." (*Not* for Sunday !) I was particularly pleased with O., who sat there mistress of herself and much less overawed than Jock, Meric, and Bertie, who did nothing but gape and gasp.

July 4   A note from Jock :
Wednesday.
                              33 *King Street*
                              *Covent Garden, W.C.*2
                              1 A.M., *July 4th*, 1945

Dear Jamie,
    A mighty fine party, sir, thank you. I had an access of party-fright just beforehand in the Strand, and almost failed to turn in at the Savoy. But I am very glad I did—now.

I longed to tell you *this*, but didn't dare—I longed to come round to your side of the table to tell it to you and Miss Cooper only. 'Tis perfectly true—and it perfectly illustrates the lady's legend, which—like her beauty—is apparently continuous. Earlier in the evening I was in my local pub, " The Bird in Hand " in Long Acre, and the following brief, astonishing conversation took place between me and my old friend, the landlord, a man of sixty-odd :

A. D. " You'd never guess what beautiful woman I'm having supper with to-night."

LANDLORD (*immediately*). " Gladys Cooper, I suppose ! "

A. D. (*after a gasp*). " Right, first time. How did you know ? "

LANDLORD (*with a grin*). " You will have your little joke, Jock. What are you having ? "

And I, of course, left it at that ! Nothing more to be said or done about it.

You—and, indeed, all of us—very nicely and creditably covered up that split second of awkwardness when she came back from 'phoning to find us all with our heads together discussing her age. " Fifty-five " was the conclusion we were arriving at—" honestly and without cattiness," as Lady Hardwicke said. But I have just found on returning home—still rather dazzled with your supper combined with G. C.'s surpassing fairness—that she was born in 1888 and will be fifty-seven in December. This fact is in John Parker's *Who's Who in the Theatre*, a book which I have always found in such matters to be either admirably accurate or admirably silent. How witty and wise is she, therefore, as well as lovely ! First, in a public reference-book to have stated her unabashed age and to ensure that that age is even higher than another actress's private speculation can make it (cattily or uncattily). Second, on the Hollywood screen always to make up to the age of the characters she has played—like a sound, conscientious actress—to make herself by artificial means older even than her own age ought to look. Third, to be young in spite of years—to have the freshness of youth, with an April laugh at old Time. I don't know how 'tis done—but I was delighted with the privilege of seeing it done, so close and so wondrous.

To-morrow I shall go about vainly trying to find anyone who looks as if he or she would believe that I sat at supper to-night with Gladys Cooper. There is no one who will not look sceptical. I used to have much the same kind of experience in the Haslar days when I would let slip to some of my naval colleagues that I was going to spend the week-end with Vivien Leigh. Young sailors would throw at me whatever was handy, and tell me not to be a confounded and blankety-blank kidder, blarneyer, and liar. Such are the penalties of a lifetime of truth-telling, whole-truth-telling, and nothing-but-the-truth-telling. Wot larks !

Ever,

JOCK

Tartuffe ? This wonder of the world lives because Molière satirised not manners, which are the human animal's clothes, but the animal itself. It is a moot point whether the immortal hypocrite should be played on Shakespearean (Angelo) or Dickensian lines. I suggest that the character has that universality which permits it to be exploited at either end of the scale or at any point in between. Jean Yonnel's interpretation to-night was a masterpiece, conveyed in terms of superb miming and glorious sonority of tone. Imagine our English Charles II in one of those black depressions known to every debauchee, add a touch of Oliver Cromwell, smear the whole with Oil of Chadband, and one would have a faint idea of this grand performance. Had sent H. and O. to *To-morrow the World*, which impressed them very much. Took them afterwards to supper at the Ivy, where they met Stanley and Vera Rubinstein, Donald Wolfit, and Rosalind Iden. Wolfit was very full of his visit to Cairo. About the Egyptians he said, " There are no middle classes. About 2 per cent. of the population live in extreme luxury, and 98 per cent. in incredible squalor. One person in every five is either blind or suffering from some hideous deformity. The most hopeless thing about the Egyptians is that they appear not to be aware of their misery, and are just waiting for some master-race to come along and turn them into slaves." He told me that some ten days ago he put young Peter Mizen (see entry of June 2) under contract.

July 5   I hope H. and O.'s holiday is not tiring them as much
Thursday.   as it is tiring me. The Comédie repeating a play already
              given, I had the night off and took H. and O. to the
Ambassadors' to see *Sweeter and Lower*. Afterwards to the Savoy, where we were joined by Harry Kendall, Hermione Gingold, Norman Newman, and Alec Shanks, the stage designer.

H. gave evidence of an unsuspected talent as a *raconteur*. Here is the first of two stories he told us to-night. An old friend of his had a nervous breakdown, and his wife, who has considerable aptitude as an artist, was compelled to market her abilities at no matter what price. She was approached by a small farmer of the Dales, who suggested that she should paint his homestead, and after haggling the deal was clinched at seventeen shillings and sixpence ! The finished painting was duly delivered, and both the farmer and his wife expressed themselves as delighted. Ten days later the farmer's wife brought back the canvas and said, " You've got a little girl on the front path. She isn't one of our lot ; she's an evacuee and we dunna want her in. Tak her out." The artist obliged, and the picture was duly re-delivered. A fortnight elapsed, and again the farmer's

155

wife appeared with the painting. The man driving the cart was a hind who had been sacked by the farmer. Could her husband's face be substituted? This was done, and once more the painting returned. Within a month the farmer presented himself at the artist's house with the picture and the following command: " Tha shows me driving away from a field with the gate left oppen. I canna bide an oppen gate. SHUT IT! "

The second story was about a valuer whose experience was entirely urban. Unexpectedly called upon to value a horse, and having no notion how to go about it, he decided to cube it. H. said to him, " Yes, my dear fellow, that's all right as regards the animal's height and length; how did you manage about the thickness? " " Oh," said the valuer, " I just drove it through a door and estimated the space left on each side! "

Spent a good part of the meal explaining to Hermione, who wants to go into serious drama, that the bed she has chosen is that of revue, and that she will have to lie on it. That if she were ten times Mrs Siddons, something in her look, tone, gesture, or even walk would recall to-night's song about Colonel Hopkins and the Stirrup Pump. But I don't think she was convinced. Glad to have been able to take H. and O. at least *once* to the theatre. To-morrow is their last night, and I am looking forward to seeing how Marie Bell will negotiate that Becher's Brook for tragic actresses—Racine's Phèdre.

July 6   The Hippolyte of Jacques Dacqmine was a superb piece
Friday.   of acting; magnificent to look at, listen to, and be
              moved by. The Thésée of Jean Yonnel was the acme of noble decorum. Phèdre herself? On the revival of the film *Un Carnet de Bal*, I noted " the brilliant self-effacement of Marie Bell." But self-effacement is the last quality one looks for in whoever is to play Phèdre. Hear Lewes on Rachel:

What a picture she was as she entered! You felt that she was wasting away under the fire within, that she was standing on the verge of the grave with pallid face, hot eyes, emaciated frame—an awful, ghastly apparition. The slow, deep, mournful toning of her apostrophe to the sun, especially that close—

Soleil! je te viens voir pour la dernière fois—

produced a thrill which vibrates still in memory.

But did Marie Bell look wasted? She was as plump as a partridge! Next I think of W. T. Arnold on Sarah's performance in Manchester in the summer of 1880. Why do I not quote myself? Because of the *Manchester Guardian*'s " One thinks one is tired of Mr Agate on Bernhardt."

The great Phèdre has hitherto been that of Rachel. It is useless to dilate upon Rachel's tragic power. Her performance alike in the second and in the fourth acts is declared by all competent critics to have been all but perfection. The doubtful question is rather whether she was capable of rendering the tenderness and the infinite piteousness of the hapless woman as she rendered her transports of passion. We can conceive Rachel as having been better than Mme Bernhardt in the denunciation of Œnone ; but we should like to know how Rachel said such passages as this :

> Œnone, il peut quitter cet orgueil qui te blesse ;
> Nourri dans les forêts, il en a la rudesse.
> Hippolyte, endurci par de sauvages lois,
> Entend parler d'amour pour la première fois :
> Peut-être sa surprise a causé son silence ;
> Et nos plaintes peut-être ont trop de violence.

The inexpressible tenderness with which those lines were sighed rather than spoken was all Mme Bernhardt's own. This line again :

> Et l'espoir malgré moi s'est glissé dans mon cœur.

And this, when she has discovered the love of Hippolyte and Aricie, and contrasts their affection with her own guilty passion :

> Tous les jours se levoient clairs et sereins pour eux.

These were the passages which Mme Bernhardt marked with the most personal and enduring charm, and in these we cannot believe that she has not surpassed her forerunners.

Marie Bell to-night showed competence, but in this play competence won't do. Great line after great line went by, and we were not moved. Surely

> On ne voit point deux fois le rivage des morts,

must conjure up the image of death or it is nothing ? Surely

> Dieux ! que ne suis-je assise à l'ombre des forêts !
> Quand pourrai-je, au travers d'une noble poussière,
> Suivre de l'œil un char fuyant dans la carrière . . .

should breathe the very spirit of heart-break ? Marie Bell gave us nothing of this. Her countenance, refusing to be ravaged, brought to the sullens of Wastwater the petulance of Buttermere. The truth is that her *moyens* are not tragic, and there is no more to be said.

Small party afterwards at the Ivy for H. and O., who had been to the Coliseum. Ivor Novello told us a story about an ageing actress examining the menu at the full length of her arm, and some friend saying, " Millicent, dear, oughtn't you to get some glasses ? " The actress retorted, " Don't be silly, Virginia ! There's nothing wrong with my sight. It's just that my arm isn't long enough ! "

P.S. In Leo's typescript Phèdre is made to say :

"Soleil ! je te viens voir pour la *première* fois."

July 7 Took H. and O. to Louis Sterling's luncheon-party at
Saturday. the Savoy. This is their last function before going to spend a quiet week-end with my sister May.

July 8 In last week's hurly-burly I seem to remember :
Sunday.

1. An orgy of what George Mathew calls " collective stupidity." Meaning the General Election.

2. Letter from a Lady. " In Tangier what you say about the drama is practically gospel."

3. Discussion on beards at the Café Royal. I said that as far as I am concerned I know only four natural and legitimate beards—Shaw, Augustus John, Clifford Bax, and Beecham. That all the rest are unnatural and ridiculous, particularly those grown by pale young men at sea. Leo said, " You ought to have seen the beards of some of the Wagnerian singers of my youth. They all had them ; it was the convention. Tannhäuser's beard came down to his navel ; he had to brush it on one side when he took up his harp to sing to Venus. Tristan had a beard, and longer, if possible, than King Mark's. Indeed, in some of those German opera-houses you couldn't tell one from the other except by their voices. And fat ! They were all fat and they all had beards. Often it was difficult to pick out Isolda, who, by the end of the Liebestod, had probably grown a beard herself. Some of those German women were very hirsute."

4. Seeing that the Editor recently tore out of the paper my review of Peter Quennell's book about Gibbon, Boswell, Sterne, and Wilkes on the grounds that *Express* readers had never heard of these great men, didn't want to hear about them, and wouldn't be the better for hearing about them, I had very little hope of succeeding with a straight review of Newman's third volume about Wagner. But there are more ways of killing a cat, etc., and the result was the better part of a column. I began by saying the life would make " an admirable subject for a novel, always on one of two conditions. One. That the author knows everything about music. Two. That the author knows

nothing about music, and knows that he knows nothing." I then divided Wagner's life into four books, and I ended :

> Wagner returns from exile and builds a theatre in Bayreuth, where his *Ring* is produced. Cosima, a masterful, narrow-minded aristocrat, now rules the roost. She is a vitriolic anti-Semite and Jew-baiter. Sarah Bernhardt, being a Jewess, strikes her as " an old she-ape." Wagner dies in Venice in 1883, probably the fourth greatest composer the world has known and the first in his own line of music-drama. Well, what about it, you English Werfels and Feuchtwangers ? What better subject than this sharp-nosed little fox who wrote some of the most glorious music the spinning globe has ever heard ? And think of the money you will make when Hollywood buys your story, forgets that Minna ever existed, and transforms the horse-faced Cosima into a nitwit blonde, and Richard into a handsome uplifter of the Spencer Tracy class with a gift for writing theme-songs !

Very artful, if you ask me !

5. Death of Elsie Fogerty at the age of seventy-nine. In accordance with her promise she saw my young actor-friend—who, by the way, is called Frank Cowburn—though too ill to let him do any of his stuff ! She was sympathetic and encouraging, and said there was something about him that reminded her of her favourite pupil, Laurence Olivier.

6. Note from Cowburn, saying that he started last week in *Strike It Again*, the Sid Field revue at the Prince of Wales's.

7. Note from my little Irish friend, with his photograph, in which I trace something of the spirituality of Stephen Haggard combined with the truculence of the Irish navvy. He writes, " I am so glad you and Leo don't quarrel. There is something so poetic about two old gentlemen passing their days together in peace and harmony...."

8. Alexis Kligerman, about to give a recital, and coming to play to us thirty-two Beethoven Variations that I don't want to hear. Also that filthy Sonata, Op. 31, No. 2, that was hammered into me by old Beyschlag in Manchester, eight Chopin Études, the F minor Ballade, the A flat Polonaise, and the inevitable Liszt. It should be said that while this is going on Leo is frantically typing in one room, I am frenziedly correcting in another, with K. in a room between. I have no doubt he has made great strides. But while this maelstrom of work is on the only strides I am interested in are those *away from Alexandra Mansions*.

9. Letter from my young friends in Birmingham, saying, " Miss Ashcroft seems to have taken your ' Little Miss Muffet ' rebuke to

heart. We were in London recently, and her 'I am Duchess of Malfi still!' seemed to have graduated to the Lady Bracknell school."

10. Lunch with Meric Dobson, who was highly excited about his new novel. I gathered that while the plot is as yet non-existent and the characters are vague, he has decided on the locale. This is divided between Great Whipping and Little Whipping, both in Dorset.

11. Letter from Jack Priestley, containing the following:

> There came a cable this afternoon from Alexander Tairov, the famous director of the Kamerny Theatre in Moscow, to say that my new play *An Inspector Calls*, which, as they say, " so fascinated Moscow with its high merits," is having its première there to-night. I only sent them the script of this play, by plane, just over two months ago. Meanwhile, we have been waiting *six months* to find a theatre for it, without success, in London. So will you please remember, when you are reviewing these second-rate farces from America and the revivals that H. M. T. insist on doing (*Lady Windermere's Fan*, for instance, which wasn't a good play when it was written and is plain rubbish now), that all the time you are being deprived of seeing a good new play by me?

12. Talk over the 'phone with J. B. P., as the result of which I wrote him this:

> I have been thinking seriously about whether I ought to let myself be roped in on this question of theatres. I am a dyed-in-the-wool Tory with streaks of ultra-red. I hold that when Labour rules the world all elegance will vanish and good manners will be a thing of the past. Except, of course, *natural* good manners, which, O. W. would have told us, are the worst sort. But have you, my dear Jack, occasion to use taxis these days? If you have you will have noticed the manners of the taxi-driver now that he is on top. I dread the time when on six days of the week I shall be herded in a communal eating-shed where the food is thrown at me with the indifference that booking-office clerks use to their customers, and on the seventh must take my turn at dishing out the food. My ideal working man is a sturdy, independent creature with a dash of servility.
>
> Now for the ultra-red streak. I believe that everything *of which the supply is limited* should be nationalised—land, water, noblemen's parks, coal-mines, hospitals, lifeboat institutions. There are, however, certain things to which nationalisation would be fatal—newspapers, for example. Another is the theatre. We have one national newspaper—*The Times*, and if anybody wants *one* National Theatre I don't mind. But I would not allow commercial speculation in theatre property. I would not allow anybody who

was not in the theatre in some artistic capacity or other to own so much as a single brick of any playhouse. This probably means a return to the old actor-manager system. And why not? The theatre was at its healthiest under that system. I do not see why players like John Gielgud, Laurence Olivier, Sybil Thorndike and Lewis Casson, and others should be at the beck and call of syndicates.

And then there is another matter. Let X be a syndicate owning half the theatres in London, and let Y and Z be a young actor and actress trying to make good, and regarded by some of us as players of undoubted talent. Now if the powers that rule X do not share this view of Y and Z, the result must be that X will never cast them. But suppose the twenty theatres to be governed, not by X, but by all the letters from A to T, one letter in control of one theatre. Then I submit that Y and Z would have a reasonable chance, and that if they fail and have to betake themselves to the provinces it is just too bad! Obviously there is a similar case to be put for playwrights Y and Z. Why not a sumptuary law whereby no man shall own more than, say, two theatres, or have any interest in more than two companies of players?

But to come to the point. All this is theatre politics, and I don't see how, as a dramatic critic, I can afford to interfere in theatre politics. I know that I can disapprove of X's owning twenty theatres and like his latest production, or approve of X's owning twenty theatres and dislike his new show. I know, and you know, that I can keep each of these things in its proper compartment. But since neither X nor the general public is in a position to be aware of this, there is a danger that if I take sides in questions of this sort my criticisms will be held to be coloured by my political opinions. Now I put my critical integrity, and the reputation for it, above everything else, always, all the time. Wherefore, dear Jack, please leave me out of it. If you can prove me wrong, and prove it to my satisfaction, I will come over to you publicly. Until then, " Break, my heart, for I must hold my tongue ! "

Yours ever,
JAMES AGATE

July 9   I am a waltz fan. I grew up revelling in Johann Strauss
Monday.   the elder, delighting in Lanner, going into ecstasies over
            Johann the younger. I love them still. What I don't love is the dreary pastiche masquerading as the real thing. The vimless, pepless, tuneless rinsings in which these pseudo-Viennese films are soused. The latest, *Waltz Time*, at the Empire, is an example. Vienna, indeed ! The film should have been called *Tales from the Wimbledon Woods*. I am glad H. and O. have returned home. Bored with yet another version of the old story about the young Empress

who flirts with a young officer, goes to a masquerade, and gets herself arrested, with the usual accompaniment of ravishing Mädeln (obviously from Streatham) and dashing Kavaliere who wouldn't understand a word spoken in Swiss Cottage, I fell asleep. I had had a surfeit of three-four time, and finding myself snoring in six-eight time, I left in double-quick time ! But not before I had realised that Carol Raye tra-la-la'd very prettily, and Peter Graves swaggered about like a British subaltern between chukkas at polo. I suspect that Tauber was somehow mixed up in it all. But the person I most envied was some one I took to be Brefni O'Rourke, though as he was recumbent on his Imperial death-bed and I saw only the actor's chin and the tip of his nose I can't be certain. Anyhow, he was soon out of it. Lucky dog !

July 10   To-day I became President of the Hackney Horse Society.
Tuesday.   Enjoyed last evening more than any other since the war. Occasion : a reception given by the French Ambassador and Madame Réné Massigli to the actors of the Comédie Française—I owe my invitation to the fact that my French goes a little beyond that of the young gentleman with the lumpy forehead at Mr Podsnap's party who said " *Esker* " and then stopped. I sat in a corner for two hours with Jean Yonnel and Pierre de Rigoult. Yonnel, off the stage, looks every inch an actor ; you couldn't possibly mistake him for anything else. Wit and the grand manner, to which must be added his superb voice. Said that to put paint on one's face, learn another man's words, simulate another man's passions, and go on the stage to court the applause of an ignorant rabble must always be a despicable business unless the actor knows and holds himself to be in touch with beauty. Said his first appearance had been as Hippolyte to Sarah's Phèdre. " I have played Hippolyte to many Phèdres, and with all the others I felt that when the Queen had declared her passion there was no reason why I should stay to hear the rest of the speech except that I was paid to do so. With Sarah it was different. She hypnotised me—I couldn't move. It was only when she took her eyes off me that I recovered the use of my limbs." Said later that when he was finished as an actor he had one ambition —to be a concierge. " In that profession there is no housing problem." Presently Pierre Dux joined us and asked whether I knew any witty English comedy which would translate. Tentatively I suggested *The Importance of Being Earnest*, of which he had never heard. Delightful evening, the champagne taking second place to the elegance of the setting and the fascination of hearing great artists discuss themselves and their art. " X is exactly right as Hippolyte ; his voice is not

dark enough for Ruy Blas." " Y has the voice for R. B. but not the shoulders." And so on.

July 11   The Eskerites were in great force at the British Council's
Wednesday.   treat last night. Again a notable absence of critics.
        Perhaps they are saving themselves for Lord Bess-
borough's party on Saturday ? Got jammed in a corner with the charming but voluble gentleman who runs the principal theatre in Cairo, in which I had to simulate interest.

July 12   The only way with miracles is to make them happen.
Thursday.   When I first conceived the idea of luring Tartuffe and
        Hippolyte to Angus McBean's studio I renounced the
idea as altogether too ambitious. To ask of overworked actors that they should transport themselves and their props, make up and pose for the benefit of *Ego*, seemed to me to ask too much. And then I took my courage in both hands and went all out for it. I addressed a supplication to the Contrôleur-Général, in which I suggested that since the *Ego* books go all over the world, my account of the visit of the Comédie, embellished by such photographs as McBean pro-posed to take, would help to spread knowledge of civilisation's most precious possession—French culture. As a letter of this sort must be elegant, and as my written, as well as my spoken, French leaves something to be desired, I sent the letter to a translation bureau and received in return a screed which the French Académie could not have bettered, and far more ornate than my draft. Gaily I signed this, and sent my houseboy with it to the theatre. It was only when the messenger was beyond recall that I remembered that the envelope bore the stamp : " Berlitz School of Languages " ! On my arrival at the French Embassy that evening Yonnel came up to me and said, " J'ai grand plaisir à rencontrer l'auteur d'une prose si majestueusement belle ! " The séance at Angus's took place this morning, and succeeded beyond expectation. After which we adjourned to the Ivy, where we were joined by Pierre de Rigoult, the Contrôleur-Général. Luncheon was a trifle hurried—they were due at a matinée—but *very* gay, though I am not quite sure that I liked Angus saying, " I understand Mr Agate's French, but not anybody else's." If there is such a thing as a terrestrial paradise then I inhabited one to-day. There had been a moment in the studio when I raised Hippolyte's arm an inch. Dacqmine said, " You find it better like that ? " I said, " No, young man, worse ! " " Then why ? " " So that I can write in my diary : ' To-day, July 12, 1945, I directed the Comédie Française ! ' "

163

July 13   To-day has been hell. I told Angus McBean that I should
Friday.   call last night some time after eleven to see the negatives
         of the French players. I called, and at my first knock all
the lights in the place were turned out ! I knocked half a dozen times,
but nobody answered. This morning I began getting into touch soon
after nine o'clock. Hopeless. I tried the 'phone ; no reply, though I
could hear the ticking of the clock on the wall, which meant that
somebody had taken the receiver off. I sent messengers. No admission. Finally, I sent Leo over. Not at home. All day we got the
most conflicting reports. Angus was sick. He was lunching with a
duchess. He had gone to photograph a herd of Hereford cattle. I
was in despair until, very late at night, he turned up at Alexandra
Mansions to explain the whole thing. It seems that, twelve out of
twenty exposures being ruined owing to a faulty box of plates, he
hadn't dared to meet me until he had developed the remainder. He
then produced eight superb heads—seven of Dacqmine and only one
of Yonnel. But what a one it is !

July 14   Excellent supper at the Savoy, given by the Franco-
Saturday.   British Society to the French players. We ate *Les*
         Quenelles de Saumon Nantua (only mine was lobster),
La Volaille en Cocotte Grand'mère, and *Le Mont Blanc aux Fruits
Frais*. Asking whether I would take *vin rouge*, the waiter whispered,
". It's the same thing as red wine, sir." I demanded whiskey and
soda. The seating arrangements were, in my view, entirely right
and proper. Lord Bessborough had on his right the wife of the
French Ambassador, and on his left Phèdre, and then me. Phèdre,
who was dressed entirely in black, turned out to be of the Hamlet's
Aunt persuasion, and I got through by enlarging upon the one line
in which she had been better than Sarah—the one favourable point
in to-morrow's notice. She inclined her head and said, " Votre Lady
Macbeth n'est pas un rôle difficile." To which I replied that some of
our English actresses found it difficult enough.

No sign of the critics, who, throughout the entire stay, have put
up an extraordinarily poor show, the Critics' Circle, from which I
resigned some time ago, doing nothing whatever about our visitors,
and most of the popular papers ignoring them. Knowing that they
were feeling strongly about this, I intimated that I should like to
say a few words. What I proposed to do was to remind our French
guests of, and acquaint our English hosts with, the story of John
Philip Kemble's visit to Paris in 1800, and the dinner given to him
by the Théâtre Français. The conversation turned upon the respective merits of English and French drama. The French actors being

for Corneille, Kemble naturally countered with Shakespeare. Whereupon one Michot said, " Molière, sir—whom have you to show against Molière ? " " Oh," said Kemble, " but Molière is not a Frenchman." " What ! " said the actor. " He is an Englishman, perhaps ? " And Kemble replied, " No, sir, he is not English." And then, according to Auger, Kemble went on, " Les petites divisions de royaumes et de siècles s'effacent devant Molière. Tel ou tel pays, telle ou telle époque, n'ont pas le droit de se l'approprier. Il appartient à l'univers ; il appartient à l'éternité." Yes, I had it all nicely memorised. It would seem, however, that what I call the Agate-As-Public-Speaker Resistance Movement is making progress. Anyhow, I wasn't called upon ; and perhaps the evening was running late. Arthur Christiansen, Henry Wood, Myra Hess, the Comédie Française—I see here the nucleus of a little book on " Speeches I Have Not Been Allowed to Deliver." Recovered my equanimity on emerging from the Savoy into the biggest thunderstorm for years. Even I don't pretend to compete with the elements !

July 15   Leo arrives this morning, asking whether I heard the
Sunday.   thunderstorm last night. " Heard ! " I snapped. " It
             kept me awake all night." " Did it ? " says he. " It
sent me to sleep. I haven't slept so well since the Blitz."

The *Observer* has let the French players depart without a word. Nothing about the quality of the Tartuffe, or the Phèdre. And I turn up the little book entitled *The Manchester Stage* 1880–1900 : " The line was taken that a city such as Manchester could claim the application of the strictest standards, just as if it were London or Paris." The line I take is that a capital such as London should apply to an august company of players from the most famous theatre in the world the standard of criticism ruling in Mancester when I was a boy.

They do these things better in France. Here are some extracts from an article by Robert Kemp on the visit of the Old Vic to Paris :

La visite que la très honorable " Old Vic Theatre Company " de Londres vient de rendre à la Comédie Française a enflammé la curiosité des gens de lettres. On a applaudi à la technique précise, à la diction colorée et forte de la troupe. Laurence Olivier, Ralph Richardson, Sybil Thorndike, Joyce Redman, Margaret Leighton, nous sont devenus chers. Nous leur cherchons des " correspondants " parmi nos comédiens vivants. C'est difficile. Ils stylisent et ils fouillent le détail plus que les Français, qui visent à la spontanéité.

.   .   .   .

Richard III a été plus fécond en enseignements qu'*Arms and the Man*, de Shaw, ou que *Peer Gynt*. J'ai vu à cette inoubliable soirée.

Gide, Mauriac, Duhamel, Émile Henriot transportés d'enthousiasme, et une grande comédienne-auteur, Mme Simone, près des larmes !

.   .   .   .

Shakespeare, peu à peu, devient notre chair, notre sang. Nous l'absorbons, nous l'assimilons. Aucune comparaison avec Goethe ! Goethe, on l'admire de confiance. Sauf *Faust*, avouons que la majorité des Français ignorent son œuvre. Ils ont, naturellement, boudé *Iphigénie en Tauride*, pendant l'occupation. . . . Ils commencent juste à goûter Strindberg et Tchékov, Ibsen s'éloigne. . . . Le succès du charmant Pirandello paraît n'avoir été qu'un feu de paille. Tandis que Shakespeare, de jour en jour, gagne en autorité, et soumet plus d'âmes à ses sorcelleries. On ne l'aime pas par soumission aux dogmes, à l'enseignement des professeurs, à une tradition. On l'aime d'un amour direct, spirituel, et charnel.

Clifford Bax, unburdening his heart about the critics, recently wrote : " The fact is, though nobody has perceived it, that a professional play-critic is a monstrosity—a sow with five legs or a man with four thumbs. Nature did not intend him, and that is why we have to conceal our repulsion when he confronts us. A keen playgoer may see, perhaps, ten, fifteen, or even twenty plays a year, and it is for him that dramatists write and that managers dangle their bait. Your newspaper-critic may see a hundred productions in a year. The result is—let me put it with unmistakable simplicity—that he does not see any play as a normal citizen would see it. He is therefore as fantastic a freak as the Yorkshireman who ate half a dozen ordinary breakfasts. However, I must give you an example of my contention. Some years ago I glanced at a play-notice by X.Y.Z., whose conceit would be pathetic if it were tolerable, and in his notice he wrote, ' Then the usual quartet of lawn-tennis players came on, with the usual racquets,' and, we deduce, immediately bored X.Y.Z. Not until I had read these words did I realise, being only an average playgoer, that several playwrights must have recently used the convenient device of a tennis-party for getting their characters on and off the stage. Does not this example demonstrate in a twinkling that X.Y.Z. may black-mark a play for some effect which will seem to me and you unobjectionable and even adroit ? He sees too many plays, eats too many breakfasts, is a monster." For " play-critic " read " film-critic," and I imagine that C. B.'s complaint still holds. Far be from me to admit that my old friend, throughout a long and distinguished career, has ever been right except about three things—the compelling fascination of Henry VIII, the wit of Nell Gwyn, and his own passion for clumping indifferent bowling out of the ground for six.

Nevertheless there is something in what C. B. says. My proposed

holiday found me pegged down to London. Did I try to get away ?
Yes. Could I get anywhere to go to ? No. If I had found anywhere,
could I have got there ? No. Would any railway guarantee that its
employees, taking matters into their own hands, would not shove me
into a siding at Nuneaton or Taunton and leave me there for a fortnight ? No. This golden land of ours is blessed with more petrol than
ever Jerusalem had milk and honey. But could I get a few tea-
spoonfuls ? No. So I sat at home, twiddled my thumbs, and when I
got tired of twiddling, betook myself to the pictures. And there I
found myself in a state of enjoyment foreign to me in my critical
capacity. I enjoyed myself as much as filmgoers who had paid. And
on one occasion, it being Sunday, I did pay ! ! ! !

In an amateurish sort of way, therefore, I shall venture to opine
that *They Knew Mr Knight* is a British film good enough to be
American. It tells a credible and extremely interesting story, and it
contains that superb actor, Alfred Drayton. I have admired Drayton
ever since his Carl Peterson in *Bulldog Drummond*. His Arthur
Fenwick in *Our Betters* was a superb performance. Here, one thought,
was a great actor in the making. And then, alas for the English
theatre, Drayton fell in with " Bunny " Hare, for whom he has
stooged ever since. I use the word " stooged " advisedly. Drayton
is a grand actor who can act, whereas the British public has always
preferred a funny man who can't help being funny. I don't imply
that Hare cannot act; what I say is that the whole of him does not
act as much as Drayton's little toe, and that, to hold the scales
impartially, the whole of Drayton will probably never be as droll as
one of Hare's aghast eyebrows. Nevertheless the fact remains that
when Drayton went into farce the serious theatre lost a fine actor.
" O the pity of it, Alfred ! O Bunny, the pity of it ! " And then I
went to see *Mr Skeffington*, and rejoiced that all the film critics, with
the exception of Campbell Dixon, whom I have not read, failed to
find the one unique and pat quotation. The film, as most people
know, is all about a vain flibbertigibbet who, despite the beauty
parlours, finds herself at sixty a wrinkled, string-throated hag. I
find it almost unbelievable that no film critic should have bethought
him of Austin Dobson's

> With the coming of the crow's-feet
> Goes the backward turn of beaux' feet.

Nor was there the slightest mention of Mrs Skewton with her rose-
coloured curtains for doctors, girlish laughter, and skeleton of the
Cleopatra manner. And when Skeffington, now blind, returns to the
wreck that was once his wife and finds her as beautiful as ever, not a

line about *The Well of the Saints*! Well, well, my colleagues, who know their business, must have come to the conclusion that to-day's readers are just not interested in Dobson, Dickens, Synge.

In the meantime I continue to dote on Hollywood, which sends me this piece of information :

> Janet Blair thinks she has invented a new type of sleeping ' suit.' It is the jacket of an ordinary pyjama set, but is a foot longer than the usual pattern, and she doesn't wear trousers with it. She calls it a ' sleeper coat,' and will introduce it in a scene from *Tars and Spars*, if the Hays office lets her.

In the Café to-night. Corduroy Trousers came up to my table and asked my opinion of *Peter Grimes*. "I'm making a piano transcription of it." I said, "For the left hand, of course ?" Trousers said, "That's an idea !" And, unbidden, sat down and started drumming on the tablecloth with unwashed Bloomsbury fingers. I am not antagonistic to youth. I expect young people to come knocking at my door. But why are the knuckles they knock with invariably filthy ?

July 16
Monday.
A messy day. In the morning went to the Test Match at Lord's. In the afternoon, in the capacity of godfather, to a christening at Westminster Cathedral. The priest having some difficulty in finding the right place in his prayer-book, I very nearly asked him the question Jack Worthing put to Dr Chasuble : "I suppose you know how to christen all right ?" In the evening to *Salome—Where She Danced* at the Leicester Square, an appalling film about Generals Grant and Lee and a Viennese bubble-dancer who was lured to a mining town in California where she sang *Der Tannenbaum*, accepted the offer of a Rembrandt, and went off in a Chinese junk, the captain of which spoke with a Scots accent, having been a medical student in Edinburgh. Supper at the Café Royal, and read myself to sleep with *Dombey and Son*. Am writing this in bed at 5 A.M., fearing the repetition of a nightmare in which Paul Dombey, who appears to be me, goes straight from his christening to Lord's, where he bowls out K. R. Miller when he is one short of Hutton's record, and is promptly lassoed by a Chinese thug, hauled off the field, and hanged from the clock-tower.

July 17
Tuesday.
The other day I met a highbrow (non-musical) and played him my record of Strauss's *Also Sprach Zarathustra*. When it was over he said, "Is it a faithful interpretation of Nietzsche's philosophy ?" I said, "My dear fellow, I'm not interested. I shouldn't care if it were called *Also Sprach Spinoza* or

Also Sprach Jeremy Bentham." Since I listen to music for the sound of it and nothing but the sound, and since even Newman admits that there is nothing in *Peter Grimes* worth listening to *for its own sake* and divorced from Crabbe's situation and words, I am obviously the last person who ought to have gone to-night to see Britten's opera. Three hours of diabolically clever scoring, all of which I would willingly have exchanged for a single tune as good as *Cherry Ripe* or *Sally in our Alley*. The " Peter Grimes ! Peter Grimes ! " chorus was effective, and the monody with foghorn accompaniment suggested that Britten has only to get his brains out of the way to write something I can listen to with pleasure. The rest ? " A blank, my lord ! " I spent most of the time wondering how much longer theatres and opera houses are going to lag behind the cinema, where you get an unimpeded view of the screen. Sitting in the fourth row of stalls, I got the impression that the floor of Sadler's Wells rakes downwards and backwards. There was a large man in front of me, blotting out half the stage, so that I saw only the right and left corners ; if I wanted to know what was going on in the middle I had to lean my body at an angle of forty-five degrees, and peer round him. Since I am too old for these acrobatics, I never at any time knew what was happening. Occasionally I caught some of the words. For instance, I heard one Boles sing :

> " I have to go from pub to pub,
> Picking up parcels, standing about.
> The journey back is late at night."

And presently, looking at what I could glimpse of the Peggotty-like setting, I found myself making notes for an opera whose title should be *Barkis is Willin'*.

July 18   Leo, who hadn't the courage to come to *Peter Grimes*
Wednesday.   with me last night but weakly listened to it on the
          wireless, also seems to have been struck by the Peggotty atmosphere. He arrives this morning with something he pretends he took from the postman. I recognise the familiar typing, read, and after some titivation present the following :

999*b Acacia Road, W.*3
July 17, 45

DEAR MR AGATE,
     I am pleased about this revival movement in English opera. No doubt you have heard of the latest work in this genre, the Opera Mimetica, *David and Dora*, after C. Dickens. The composer is a young Australian, Herman Guntz. The librettist is Conchubor

Doyle, an undergraduate from Dublin University. Personally I was very much impressed, although, from what I remember of *David Copperfield*, some of the incidents seemed a little strained. Perhaps you would like to hear something about it.

Act I. Miss Trotwood's salon in Piccadilly in the year 1815. It is dawn, the birds are singing in Hyde Park (bass tuba and tenor drum), and Mr Micawber is brewing punch. The sun appears, and various people dance in from several doors, including Mrs Micawber with the twins, Traddles and his dearest Sophy bearing aloft a cake-basket, the Misses Lavinia and Clarissa Spenlow, Mr Jorkins, who later turns out to be a *basso profundo*, the Peggottys carrying a boat, and finally Mr and Miss Murdstone, who dance a fandango. So far nothing but ballet. But now David, dancing in at another door with Dora, explains in forty-eight *entrechats* that he is in love with Dora but that Agnes, who has made more sober entry (harps), has the prior claim, her father having lent him some money. Agnes, a deep contralto, seeing Dora among the dancers, commences to pray. Dora, a volatile mezzo, is always accompanied by a grey-hound, and dances most of the time; the greyhound is also an expert dancer. There is a flourish of trombones, and the Traddleses, the Peggottys, and the Murdstones dance out to meet Miss Trot-wood, leaving the stage empty except for Micawber, who brews some more punch, Dora, who sings some coloratura, Agnes, who is praying, and David reading aloud the shorthand notes he has just made of the Prime Minister's speech. This forms a very effective quartet, whereupon the stage fills again and Miss Trotwood describes in dumb-show her visit to Doctors' Commons, which the dancers illustrate balletically. The act ends in a choral fugato on the words " Janet, heat the bath ! " rising to a splendid climax of dramatic tension.

Act II. The Traddleses' garden at Deptford. Miss Trotwood explains in mime why she thinks Dora an unsuitable wife for David —she dances too much. She agrees, however, that Agnes is too much addicted to prayer. (Here the double bassoon has an eloquent solo.) Which shall it be ? (Two muted piccolos echo her thought.) Several people now dance in, including Mr Micawber, who resumes brewing punch. Now David enters with Dora and Agnes, and announces that he has just married Dora. Guitars are heard, and a boat is seen approaching, out of which step Lord Byron, Shelley, and Leigh Hunt, who echo Micawber's words : " My dear, another glass ? " and make a dancing trio of it. Dora is in tears, she has lost her dressmaker's bill ; presently we find the dog has eaten it. Agnes now suggests a game of rounders, and all join in to Bacchantic music, Micawber continuing to brew punch. A thunderstorm threatens, and Peggotty and his family get into a boat and row back to London. The act ends with a prayer by Agnes to the accompaniment of harmonium and tenor tuba, after which she is rowed away by the three poets. The dog, left alone on the stage, dances a seguidilla, holding a red parasol.

Act III. Bedroom in David's lodging in the Temple. Dora is dying; Micawber is brewing punch. The Peggotty family dances mournfully in, carrying a small skiff which Mrs Gummidge suggests will make a nice coffin. The dog, feeling that something is wrong, goes into a routine which includes a bolero. Dora, momentarily rallying, sings about her inability to open oysters without a knife. But at last she dies, after refusing a glass of punch poured out for her by the faithful Micawber, who, to conceal his emotion, drinks it himself. David executes a masterly *pas de deuil*, Miss Trotwood a *marche funèbre* in mime, and Dora's body is borne off (strings *ppp. col legno*) with Agnes pointing upward. The curtain is now dropped for a moment, and rises again to the sound of distant drums. It is the eve of the battle of Waterloo. In the moonlight Micawber steals in to finish what is left of the punch, but, finding that Mrs Gummidge has been before him, steals out again. Left alone on the stage, the dog executes a few pirouettes and falls down dead. A cat walks in, sniffs at the dog's dead body, walks contemptuously away, and settles down to sleep on the bed on which Dora has died. Curtain.

Even from this rough précis, you will realise, dear Mr Agate, that a sincere attempt has been made to weld three arts together in the service of the mistress art of Opera Mimetica.

Yours sincerely,

ADOLAR DE BUNK

July 19   Opened the second Sixth Form Conference of the
Thursday.   Schools of King Edward's Foundation at the ghastly
hour of ten-something. Audience of about three hundred. Spoke for sixty minutes, after which they—both the boys and the girls—heckled me for ninety more. Some fifty questions, of which here are the first ten.

1. *Q. What is a good play?*
A. A play which doesn't make you yawn or fidget is a good play relative to you. A play at which only a numskull would yawn or fidget is a good play absolutely.

2. *Q. Must a good play have a moral?*
A. No. *Twelfth Night* has no moral. But no play can be *great* unless it sends you out of the theatre feeling you have undergone a spiritual experience.

3. *Q. What are the rules of dramatic criticism?*
A. Only two that matter. One. Decide what the playwright was trying to do, and pronounce how well or ill he has done it. Two. Determine whether the well-done thing was worth doing at all.

4. *Q. Is radio drama feasible?*
A. If you mean: Will plays written for the stage be effective on the radio, I say yes in the sense that a blind man presumably

gets pleasure out of going to the theatre. If you mean : Is drama specially written for the radio feasible, I reply that I have heard of a new art called radio drama. Whenever I unwittingly run into an example of this I switch off. I don't pretend that this is fair or critical.

5. *Q. Is it a sign of weak intellect to like ballet ?*
A. Not if the ballet limits itself to the agile and the graceful. But to believe that six young women hauling a young man round the stage by his hair signify Retribution overtaking Lust, and that this was in Schubert's mind when he wrote the *Wanderer* Fantasie —this is pure Harpo Marx.

6. *Q. Would you stage Vanbrugh or Farquhar in modern dress ?*
A. No.

7. *Q. Did Shakespeare or Bacon write the plays ?*
A. Both. In collaboration.

8. *Q. In view of the fact that so many French and Austrian operettas are masterpieces of wit and musicianship, why is English musical comedy what it is ?*
A. Because the English like it so. As a nation we admire any playwright, composer, actor, clown, who has no talent and is modest about it.

9. *Q. Do actors need brains ?*
A. If they can act, no. If they can't, yes.

10. *Q. Must a good play have professional actors ? Or will amateurs do ?*
A. A professional is a man who can do his job when he doesn't feel like it. An amateur is a man who can't do his job when he does feel like it.

The conference may or may not turn out to be a feast of reason ; at lunch the only flow was soul ! This annoyed me so much that when K. P. Tynan, my boy-chairman, told me that the programme included a concert, a cricket match, and a performance of *Hamlet* with himself in the title-rôle, I said, " And how, pray, will visitors know which entertainment is which ? "

July 20   Letter to Hamlet (*see above*), who had asked my opinion of
Friday.   a prose poem on the subject of " L'Art pour L'Art."

Queen Alexandra Mansions, W.C.2

July 20th, 1945

MY DEAR HAMLET,
    Of course you can write. You write damned well. You write better than I have ever attempted to write. The mistake you make is the old one of trying to do too much. Why sow with the whole

sack ? Why say : " The *avant-garde* harks grimly back to the *splendours and miseries* of de Sade " ? Must you drag in Balzac ? Why, when you are in full spate of discussion about Huysmans, lug in Voltaire ? Why tell us that Mallarmé " was passing proud, and rode in sorrow through Persepolis " ? I see no connection between the French poet and the Elizabethan one.

I don't believe George Moore ever thought of Rimbaud as " a consumptive youth weaving garlands of sad flowers with pale, weak hands." Rimbaud described himself at that period as " surly of aspect, ungainly of figure, with huge red hands like a washer-woman." And I conjure you, now and for ever, to put a stop to your punning. Say, if you must, of Guillaume Apollinaire that " devout and donnish, here was Phœbus Apollinaire turned fasting friar." But to say that " Verlaine was always chasing Rimbauds " is just *common*. Like cheap scent.

My dear boy, in a prose poem of less than a newspaper column's length you undertake to tell us about Gautier, Montesquieu, Heredia (without the accents, please), de Sade, Huysmans, Moore, Verlaine, Rimbaud, Proust, Apollinaire, Mallarmé, and Flaubert. Don't you think that these are enough without dragging in Balzac, Voltaire, Meredith, and Marlowe ? If it helped I should be the last person to object. But it hinders. Read what Montague in *A Writer's Notes on his Trade* has to say about quotation, and be guided by him. It is only old cripples like me who have to use the crutches of another man's wit to get along from paragraph to paragraph. You don't need this.

One more small thing. Remember ' Saki ' : " Stephen Thorle said, 'The gratitude of these poor creatures, when I presented them with a set of table crockery apiece, the tears in their eyes and in their voices when they thanked me, would be impossible to describe.' ' Thank you all the same for describing it,' said Comus." Why talk of Proust as " indescribably leisured " and then go on to describe that leisure ? " The jaws of his memory were ponderous indeed and marble." Even so, what possible connection is there between Proust's memory and the tomb of Hamlet *père* ? This is just plain showing-off. Take my advice. Absent thee from quotation (four syllables, please) a while.

Yours sincerely,
JAMES AGATE

July 21   Wire from Birmingham :   " I shall in all my best obey
Saturday.   you, madam.   Hamlet."
          When Bertie and I were making out the list of people we thought should be asked to contribute to Home and van Thal's series of " Letters " Clifford Bax was the first person we thought of. The MS. was delivered in due course, and I took violent exception to one passage in it—about the critics he has known—which Bertie

invited him to delete. But he wouldn't. Wherefore, in to-day's *Daily Express*, I clump him for six :

> Mr Clifford Bax's view of the theatre's function is much higher than that of Shakespeare, who, turning history and legend into thumping good plays, didn't care two hoots whether his Elizabethan audience was edified or not. But there is one respect in which Mr B. is inferior to Mr S.; he has not the older dramatist's knack of popular success. Mr B.'s plays have hardly ever been *that*— indeed, his best play, *Socrates*, cannot get a hearing—and Mr S.'s plays were almost always a wow.
>
> Now this riles Mr B. exceedingly, and looking about for somebody to blame he pounces on the critics. He tells us that a critic earns his living " by selling his opinion of what ten, twenty, or thirty other persons, each of them more gifted than he, have striven to build up into an attractive evening." This is flat nonsense. Edmund Kean was more talented than Hazlitt—but only in the way of acting. Ten, twenty, or thirty of Kean's co-players, putting their heads together, could not have written one of Hazlitt's notices. Then take this passage :

"Among play critics I have known only two who were not publicly ludicrous on account of an immeasurable self-esteem. The self-esteem of the rest is so embarrassing to any normal person that I, for example, hardly know where to look when I have to converse with one of them, because it is precisely as though I had to speak, with an air of inferiority, to a ridiculous and bedizened tart."

Besides being nonsense, this is unnecessarily rude. Among the critics Mr Bax has known are Shaw, Archer, Walkley, Max Beerbohm, and Charles Morgan, and I leave it to him to decide which two out of the five are exempt from affront. I regret having to say this. Mr Bax is, besides being a witty and exceedingly elegant playwright, a very good cricketer. But it was never his habit, I think, when he saw his stumps shattered, to turn round and abuse the umpire. Why cannot he play cricket in the field of drama ? I am sorry to have to write this about a little book that is otherwise entirely admirable, and contains some excellent advice to young playwrights. I recommend this book—on condition that the purchaser obliterates pages 12 and 13. A convenient way to do this would be to gum them together.

July 22   Heard last week from Harrap's that five thousand un-
Sunday.   bound copies of *Ego* 7 are in a railway siding somewhere
              between Edinburgh and London and have been there for
some days, the railway being cluttered up with more important commodities. Remembering the time during the last war when I dispatched hay to Salonika and knew all about trucks standing in sidings, I said, " Are they well and truly *bâche'd* ? " " Are they *what* ! " said Harrap's, and I explained that *bâche* is the French for

tarpaulin. They reassured me, and said they hoped to get the sheets to the binders in a day or two. Binding will take a month, after which I shall have to wait six weeks while enough girls and string can be found to send the thing to the bookshops. Publication in October may therefore be possible. Since I handed three-quarters of the book to Harrap's last October and the balance on January 1, it seems clear that nowadays twelve months are required between delivery of a book and its issue even by the most expeditious of publishers. But of course the Labour Government which we are obviously going to get may change all that, and I can see future *Ego's* treading on each other's heels and people saying, " *Can't* the old fool keep quiet ? " The answer is : No, the old fool can't. And in any case, who grumbles now because Mozart turned out the E flat, G minor, and Jupiter symphonies in six weeks ?

July 23   Postcard from Clifford Bax :
Monday.

At your age you must try not to write rubbish. Shaw and Morgan are not celebrated for diffidence, modesty, and lack of self-esteem. Item, I do *not* know Beerbohm and never saw Walkley. Prepare a place for a new writ in the writ-drawer. Item, *The Rose* has had something like 250 performances ; *Polly*, my first success, had about 360. Wherefore, a WRIT for belittling my professional position.
Come to Fry's box for the next Test Match—if he secures one. We missed you at the last Test.
                                                                C. B.

Have replied :

All right, all right. Then which of these five practising critics are " bedizened tarts "—Ivor Brown, Anthony Cookman, Alan Dent, J. C. Trewin, Philip Hope-Wallace ? I imagine that the two you except will view your pronouncement with an auspicious, and the others with a dropping, eye.
Yes, I'll come to the Test Match with pleasure.
                                                                J. A.

Cocasseries, No. 19 :

There was a name outfit for the straight dansapation, and a Cuban combo which sold the Latin stuff.
                                ROY COHEN, *Sound of Revelry*

July 24   From Moray McLaren :
Tuesday.
                                                Gilgal Hospital
                                                    Perth, Scotland
                                                    21/7/45

MY DEAR JAMES,
I think it would amuse you to learn that, remote and lonely here (recovering from a nervous breakdown), the only person who

will cash my cheques locally is—The Undertaker. Whether this is done out of kindness of heart or to ensure possible future custom I don't know. But it's true.

I am recovering hand over fist, writing hard, and enjoying being an individual, not a cog in a machine. Do write a line and tell me that you have not forgotten one who has drunk so much champagne, both verbal and vinous, at your expense.

MORAY MCLAREN

To which I have replied :

Queen Alexandra Mansions, W.C.2

July 24th, 1945

MY DEAR MORAY,

You, of course, remember your Lord Ogleby in Colman's *The Clandestine Marriage*. How on his dressing-table were drops for the gout, waters against the palsy, and cordials against matutinal depressions. But how about me, who have for three weeks sauntered forth with smelling-salts against faintness, ampoules against my head flying off, and powders against whatever fit impends ? To-day I consulted my doctor, who happens to be in hospital after what he calls a tidying-up operation. He said with some acerbity, " You didn't come to see me yesterday as you promised. I suppose you were feeling better." I then spilled the beans, and he has put me on a diet—no work, no whiskey, a little champagne, and, if I won't go away, visits to the Zoo and the Ballet. I am different from you, my dear Moray, in this respect— I am tired of being an individual, and would welcome being a cog in a machine.

Of course I have never forgotten you. It was you who argued with me that claret was the proper thing to drink with fish, and, as evidence, produced two exquisite bottles of Pontet Canet. This was in Edinburgh some fifteen years ago. We went up the West Coast afterwards, if you remember. It was during this trip that I had my one and only psychic experience. It was eight o'clock in the evening, we were out walking, and I suddenly saw our chauffeur bob up in the middle of a field. We moved towards him, and he at once disappeared. We searched the field and found nobody ! Returning to the hotel, we questioned him, and he swore he had been indoors all the time and had never left the bar. I also remember you showing me a mountain-range some six miles long which every evening at sunset turned itself into a recumbent Highlander. If I don't dream, we also visited the Pass of Glencoe. I remember that in spite of your kilt you looked and talked throughout the trip exactly like Dr Johnson.

Since too much letter-writing falls into the category of Norman Newman's " work," I must stop. Let us meet soon, and I will produce two bottles of whatever there is to be got.

Yours ever,

JAMES AGATE

All my papers having given me a fortnight's holiday, it is up to me to stop working forthwith. There are, however, letters which have got to be written, and here is one :

To the Editor
  " The Times "

SIR,
   The author of your admirable leader, " Stubborn Illusion," says there is " still a lively conflict of evidence " as to how the heroic Richardson took his failure to break the Australian last innings defence in the Manchester Test Match of 1896. I have the best of reasons for stating that the conflict is one of opinion only, the evidence being strictly on one side.
   It all begins with a passage in Neville Cardus's *Days in the Sun* (1924) :

   " He stood at the bowling crease, dazed. *Could* the match have been lost ? his spirit protested. Could it be that the gods had looked on and permitted so much painful striving to go by unrewarded ? His body still shook from the violent motion. He stood there like some fine animal baffled at the uselessness of great strength and effort in this world. A companion led him to the pavilion, and there he fell wearily to a seat."

   Sir, my old friend, now in Australia, confessed to me when I challenged him that he never saw the match and gave me his permission to say that he never saw it. Again, it was to me, talking cricket between the acts of a dull play, that H. J. Henley boomed, " I won't have it ! After the winning hit Tom legged it to the pavilion like a stag and got down two pints before anybody else." Henley was fourteen, and may well have seen the match.
   Sir, I was nineteen. I saw every ball bowled, and for the last innings sat directly behind Lilley keeping to Richardson. I saw him miss Kelly. I saw the winning hit. Now, sir, the Old Trafford crowd in my day never invaded the playing area except at the end of an exciting match, a habit known to visitors as well as to the home team. In the mind's eye I can see two Australians and eleven Englishmen legging it to the pavilion with the tall figure of Tom Richardson leading by many yards. If a historian should tell me that Napoleon remained rooted to the field of Waterloo hours after the battle was lost I should know that he was speaking essential truth ; that he skedaddled as fast as post-horses could leg it is correctness of a lesser order. Cardus, who watched the great match at the age of seven from behind the bars of his nursery window some miles away, had the secret of the higher truth. But on the lower ground he tarradiddled.
                                                    I am, sir, yours, etc.,
Holborn, W.C.2   JAMES AGATE
   July 24th, 1945

And who could resist this from a boy in the Air Force ?

2245367 *A.C. Zakon, C.B.*
28 *S.P., c/o* 115 *Wing*
R.A.F., M.E.F.

15.7.45

DEAR MR AGATE,

With the conceited ambition so familiar to youth I have tried to foster an appreciation of sincere literature within myself over a period of the last few years. To that end I have read a little of Charles Morgan, Compton Mackenzie, D. H. Lawrence, Rabelais, Bromfield, Thackeray, and several of the other incomparable giants, as well as a welter of the rubbish that is becoming increasingly popular to-day.

Fortunately, however, my present station boasts a tiny library to which I habitually turn for mental nourishment.

Recently I discovered a book by W. J. Locke; namely, his *Morals of Marcus Ordeyne*, which you, in your infinite erudition, doubtless read long ago. I had heard of Locke as the author of *The Beloved Vagabond*, but the person who told me of him dismissed him cynically as a hopeless sentimentalist. When I had finished reading *The Morals* I was convinced that it was only a little short of genius, and certainly the most enchanting story I have ever read.

Now, Mr Agate, I am one of those mad dogs of Englishmen forced by circumstances to go out in the midday sun; also a lengthy sojourn away from home may have rendered me a little too easy to please.

In fine, I should like your opinion, as I respect your Olympian wisdom in these things, and I hope sincerely that you will spare me a little of your precious time to reply. To that end I am enclosing a stamped addressed envelope.

Yours sincerely,
C. B. ZAKON

Some cynical reader may say that not to reply was easy. Well, nerve-storm or no nerve-storm, I cannot disappoint a lad who tells me in a P.S. that his camp is situated four hundred miles south of Khartoum ! And we at home grumbling at a minor heat-wave ! So here goes :

Queen Alexandra Mansions, W.C.2
July 24th, 1945

MY DEAR BOY,

I am sorry not to see eye to eye with you in the matter of W. J. Locke. Oddly enough, the first piece of dramatic criticism I ever wrote for the *Manchester Guardian* was about the play which he made out of his novel, *The Morals of Marcus*. According to my recollection, Marcus was an ass who gave chivalrous hospitality to a young woman in circumstances which pointed to her being his mistress, and when the neighbours disapproved became werry fierce and sarcastic. .A drivelling, fatuous piece! Years later I met the author, and committed the deadly sin of contempt. I thought he had a mind like a stingless jelly-fish. He was a worse *writer* than I am, and that he was a better man is neither here nor there. Unless we hold with à Kempis :

> Au grand jour du Seigneur sera-ce un grand refuge
> D'avoir connu de tout et la cause et l'effet ?
> Et ce qu'on aura su fléchira-t-il un juge
> Qui ne regardera que ce qu'on aura fait ?

If you can't translate this write me and I will translate it for you. There's something about a 2/3000 mile correspondence that your Holborn-Paddington post-bag lacks, don't you think ?

Yours sincerely,
JAMES AGATE

Then I must acknowledge a note from my sailor-friend, Ivan Plowright (see entry for January 9), who writes from China to say he received the books, and hopes to see me in a couple of years or so.

Then there is the gentleman who writes from Leamington Spa to complain of my habit of " shoving gobs of French all over the place. Why ? Have you the presumption to suggest that the sense of this French is so exquisite that it would not be possible to translate it into the language Shakespeare used ? Might I suggest that you write your books in the language that most folk in this country understand ? "

I replied :

SIR,
Are you a potman that you should use the language of the spittle-strewn public-house bar ? Of course there are things in one language that will not go into another. Find me the French for :

> Downy windows, close
> And golden Phœbus never be beheld
> Of eyes again so royal ! Your crown's awry ;
> I'll mend it, and then play.

And then find me the English for :

> Tournant sa tête pâle entre les cheveux bruns
> Vers celui qu'enivraient d'invincibles parfums,
> Elle tendit sa bouche et ses prunelles claires ;
> Et sur elle courbé, l'ardent Imperator
> Vit dans ses larges yeux étoilés de points d'or
> Toute une mer immense où fuyaient des galères.

What goes for Shakespeare and Heredia goes for me too.

People who want to read my books must learn French. If they won't the loss is theirs, not mine.

JAMES AGATE

July 25   Just as an economy campaign always starts with more
Wednesday.   expense—for example, a calf-bound ledger in which to
        record one's economies—so any rest-cure must be pre-
ceded by straightening-up operations of vast complexity. Worked
myself to a standstill yesterday.   Then tuned in to the Proms
(*Siegfried's Rheinfahrt*) in time to catch that little twiddle in the
clarinet, taken up later by flute and violins, that haunted Wagner
from *Rienzi* to the Liebestod.   The old, old story.   Siegfried is a
preposterous, sword-brandishing (the equivalent of sabre-rattling)
Teuton in whom I have no interest.   Yet I never tire of the *Rheinfahrt*.   Peter Grimes is an Englishman in whom I am supposed to
have every interest.   But do I want to hear " Peter's Orefahrt " ?
Ten million times no.   Supper consisted of two bits of spam and a
bottle of Bollinger 1928.   (Six pounds odd, but economy works that
way.)   Came back to the flat and put on my thirty-year-old record
of *Siegfried's Journey*, followed by the Funeral March.   As the next
record in my cabinet was the Overture to *Meistersinger*, I played that
too.   Old Ludwig had the right notion.   The ideal way to listen to
music is late at night with no audience except oneself and a houseboy to put the records on, with five shillings to compensate him for
his broken slumbers.   About 2 A.M. I reached my Richard Strauss
section.   Why has nobody perceived that the jollification at the
beginning of Britten's third act is just watered-down Baron Ochs ?
Towards 3 A.M. I heard myself say, " Always remember, Arthur, that
in the theatre the clotted cream of pure sound is better than the
vinegary lees of sour intellectuality."   Arthur said, " Righto, I won't
forget.   Now what about me putting away the whiskey and you
going to bed ? "
    The afternoon post brings this from Jock :

Tuesday, July 24

DEAR JAMIE,
    These past two days I have been at my old self-appointed task
of reading the entire criticism of the *Manchester Guardian* since its
beginning in 1821.   The war impertinently interrupted this when I
had reached the middle of 1896.   The files are kept, as you know,
at the B.M. Newspaper Place, Colindale.   It is pleasant—nearly
country ; the sun shines, birds sing, and haymakers make hay
outside the windows.
    I knew all was going to go well yesterday morning because the
first thing my eyes fell on (oddly enough after our long midnight
telephone conversation about *Frou-frou* the night before) was this :
    July 1st, 1897. " Madame Sarah Bernhardt last night repeated
at the Adelphi her well-known performance of *Frou-frou*.   In all
the quieter scenes of the play she was delightful, but she has

gradually come to overact very decidedly the more violent passages, such as the scene with Louise in the third act, and with de Sartorys in the fourth."

In the following day's paper I found :

July 2nd, 1897. "At the Lyric Theatre last evening Madame Réjane appeared, for the first time in London, as Frou-frou, thus directly challenging comparison with Sarah Bernhardt, who is playing the same part at the Adelphi. It cannot be said that either ' actress is distinctly superior to the other. Madame Réjane's performance is in many ways more artistic than that of her great rival ; but Madame Bernhardt certainly gives to some of the chief scenes a greater depth and variety of colour."

So that was that. And I had a rare day's hunting.

To-day began not nearly so propitiously with my eyes falling on this (in December 1897) :

" Rarely have the lobbies of the Palais Bourbon presented so animated an appearance as to-day, when the latest developments of the Dreyfus case were discussed with passionate excitement. The opinion was expressed on all hands that the letters attributed to Major Esterhazy were monstrous, if genuine ; but there was considerable disposition to doubt their authenticity. M. le Blois denies the assertion made by the *Eclair* that he drew up a statement of the case for M. Scheurer-Kestner in collaboration with Lieutenant-Colonel Picquart."

This, of course, took me away back to another hot July of ten to twelve years ago when you locked up poor Brother Edward and me in Briar Cottage, Beaconsfield, for three days and nights so that we might sift the contents of Schwarzkoppen's wastepaper-basket, reduce the Veiled Lady's score of letters to two at most, and Scheurer-Kestnerise generally on behalf of your damned Dreyfus play—while you gallivanted in London ! (I never liked you less !)

However, after so disconcerting a start (and in spite of occasional headline interruptions like " The Dreyfus Scandal " and " The Dreyfus Uproar " and " Trial of M. Zola " and " M. Zola Mobbed " and " A New Dreyfus Sensation ") I had another morning full of events much after my own heart—visits to Manchester of Olga Nethersole, and Irving and Ellen Terry (in *Madame Sans-Gêne*), and Forbes-Robertson in *Hamlet* (first time). And finally—just when the bell was ringing for the half-dozen dusty researchers to pack up and go home—there occurred the one far-off divine catastrophe to which the whole *M.G.* creation was in those days moving. In short, in May 1898 Mr Gladstone died—and his life and death were described in how-many-d'you-think columns of that mighty paper ? THIRTY-FOUR COLUMNS AND A QUARTER ! ! !

Your exhausted

JOCK

P.S. Proust's charming M. Swann, sered, old, and gnawed by cancer, gently remarked to a sympathetic friend, "I should not like to die, you know, before seeing the end of the Dreyfus Case!" I shall still be reading something about the old business in the last paper I pick up in this life!

P.P.S. And my God! d'you see the headline of the *Express* this morning: "J'accuse: by Daladier."

I raise my eyes and see on the wall the framed issue of *L'Aurore* for Jeudi 13 Janvier 1898, which an unknown friend gave me for the first night of my "damned play."

LETTRE
A M. FÉLIX FAURE
Président de la République

Monsieur le Président,

Me permettez-vous, dans ma gratitude pour le bienveillant accueil que vous m'avez fait un jour, d'avoir le souci de votre juste gloire et de vous dire que votre étoile, si heureuse jusqu'ici, est menacée de la plus honteuse, de la plus ineffaçable des tâches?

Vous êtes sorti sain et sauf des basses calomnies, vous avez conquis les cœurs. Vous apparaissez rayonnant dans l'apothéose de cette fête patriotique que l'alliance russe a été pour la France, et vous vous préparez à présider au solennel triomphe de notre Exposition universelle, qui couronnera notre grand siècle de travail, de vérité et de liberté. Mais quelle tâche de boue sur votre nom—j'allais dire sur votre règne—que cette abominable affaire Dreyfus! Un conseil de guerre vient, par ordre, d'oser aquitter un Esterhazy, soufflet suprême à toute vérité, à toute justice. Et c'est fini, la France a sur la joue cette souillure, l'histoire écrira que c'est sous votre présidence qu'un tel crime social a pu être commis. . . .

And then the old names start—Mercier, Sandherr, Henry, du Paty de Clam, Boisdeffre, Esterhazy, Picquart, Scheurer-Kestner, Mathieu Dreyfus. . . .

Also this from "Curly":

1803621 *Sgt. Bowdery, J. C.*
341/116 *H.A.A. Battery, R.A.*
B.L.A.
17th July, '45

Dear Jimmie,

I am writing from Hamburg; a city half-razed by incredible pin-point bombing. Would that the peoples of Coventry and Bristol, Plymouth and London, and all those places so ruthlessly savaged by the Luftwaffe, could tour the ruins that are Germany to-day. Let them look closely : they will see that houses, sliced by bombs, are still inhabited. Many Germans are living in rooms which have but two walls, sleeping high up on a precarious perch dislodged easily by a powerful wind. And in those few buildings which have escaped the fury of the R.A.F. there is overcrowding on a scale difficult to picture : eight and ten and twelve existing in rooms that four would crowd. There is little food : black, puddingy bread, greasy milk, poisonous cigarettes, endless queues that even the English housewife has not experienced. What an utter, final defeat, you think. But is it ?

The Germans seem resigned to the occupation of the Fatherland. I have known no open acts of hostility directed against us, some civilians smile as you pass, bid you good-day or raise their hats. German soldiers salute, although as they get used to us and our foolish, easy-going ways these salutations decrease daily. But glimpse the look in German eyes when they are off-guard, and you will read an intense hatred. I have seen this manifestation of their true feelings too many times for my piece of mind. They don't consider us their conquerors. We are a nuisance which must be endured until the day dawns when we leave their country, out-manœuvred by a race whose clever cunning even now has not been appreciated. We are losing the peace—I'm sure of it. In trying to prove to these sadists (you've only to watch the children at play to understand the Hun) what little gentlemen we are, we're becoming laughing-stocks. The German will understand the discipline of blows and whippings and shouted commands—and no other.

Two minor disturbances have taken place during the past week, directed against the Italians, of whom two, I believe, were killed. The populace was punished by the imposition of a seven-thirty curfew for three evenings. Last night movements were heard in the garden of the house in which we are billeted. One wag in my room observed, " Don't be alarmed—no one would dare come in and kill us—they'd get a week's early curfew ! " Life as a garrison soldier in Germany is not good. I'm longing for my release, which will, I hope, come at the year's end.

You are well, I trust, and not overdoing things.

Regards to Leo.

Sincerely,

CURLY

Black Thursday. My first reaction to the Election result was to make the following entry in my Diary :

Death robbed Roosevelt of his triumph, and now the mob has stolen Churchill's glory and trampled it underfoot. " The decision of the British public has been recorded in the votes counted to-day. I have therefore laid down the charge which was placed upon me in darker times." Words which should make Englishmen blush for a thousand years.

My next reaction was to 'phone Edgar Lustgarten and tell him that I was applying for naturalisation as a Patagonian. He said, " I shouldn't if I were you—they might make you President ! " And then I pulled myself together. There is no question of scurviness towards the greatest Englishman since Queen Elizabeth. The seed of to-day's affair was contained in something Lady Oxford said at lunch at Gwen Chenhalls's a few days after Churchill became Prime Minister : " Winston is the one man who can lead this country to victory. When he has got it he will cry like a baby. He is a fighter who loves fighting ; nothing else really interests him, though he may pretend it does. He is the last man to handle the reins of peace." Many electors must have asked themselves this question : Am I to vote for Winston and abandon my principles, or should I stick to my principles at the risk of seeming ungrateful ? For once in a way Churchill seems to have lacked a sense of the stage. His proposal, turned down by the Socialists at the Blackpool Conference, that the Coalition should continue until the end of the war with Japan, when there should be an election, was a mistake. What he should have said was : " Leave me in power till we've finished off the Japs, when I will retire and not embarrass the country with any nonsense about gratitude." He should not have risked defeat. Incidentally, it is no use the Tories thinking they are going to get back in six months' time because the Socialists are going to make a mess of things. The new Government won't make a mess of things, and there is enough way on the ship to keep it going for a year or two whoever is in control on the bridge.

Having written the above, I rang up the head waiter at one of my favourite restaurants and said, "Listen to me carefully, Paul. I am quite willing that in future you address me as ' comrade ' or ' fellow-worker,' and chuck the food at me in the manner of Socialists to their kind. But that doesn't start until to-morrow morning. To-night I am bringing two friends with the intention that we may together eat our last meal as gentlemen. There will be a magnum of champagne and the best food your restaurant can provide. You, Paul, will behave with your wonted obsequiousness. The *sommelier*, the table waiter, and the *commis* waiter will smirk and cringe in the usual way. From to-morrow you will get no more tips. To-night you will all be tipped royally." The head waiter said, " Bien, m'sieu." That was at a quarter-past six. At a quarter-past nine I arrived and was escorted by bowing menials to my table, where I found the magnum standing in its bucket, and three plates each containing two small slices of spam ! Who would have thought a head waiter to have so much wit in him ?

229 *Portland Road*
Edgbaston
Birmingham 17
25.7.45

DEAR MR AGATE,

You have dealt with me very temperately. But may I (it shall be for a few moments only) have leave to quibble ? My prose poem exudes booksiness because the characters I limn in exude booksiness. Its atmosphere is their atmosphere ; and its faults are their faults. My mistake, I take it, is not that of trying to say too much, but of seeming to know too much. I have, as you must know, never read de Sade (the nearest approach to him I have made is that best of bedside books, *Psychopathia Sexualis*) ; I have only seen the glow of Balzac refracted and dimmed by upstart crows of critics ; and of Meredith I know only *The Egoist*. My prose poem is impressionism at its worst—literary impressionism. Its sufficient beauty is to conjure up by stealth from books an image of the wordy marvels that were burgeoning in France after 1850. And if I consider that a line of Marlowe may be perverted to apply to Mallarmé I unhesitatingly pervert it. The only connection between the two is : there is no connection. Just as my only rule is : there are no rules. Art laughs at locksmiths. My quid-pro-quoem is irritatingly derivative and allusive because the Symbolists were ; it is criticism in their own rarefied cloud-country.

I know what Rimbaud looked like ; I don't think George Moore did. The lines I quote, which he, impossibly, used to describe R. L. S., might easily represent his own over-idealised concept of the young jesting pirate. And as to the " ponderous and marble jaws " of Proust : when I note that Shakespeare has coupled two words which by their pompous sonority suggest weight it is a sign of my own innate breeding and modesty that I prefer using his phrase to coining one of my own.

Like Sterne, " I begin with writing the first sentence—and trusting to Almighty God for the second." But my quotation-book never leaves my side. My principal fault (and it is quite unforgivable) is expounded by Nietzsche :

" What is the characteristic of all literary decadence ? It is that life no longer resides in the whole. The word gets the upper hand and jumps out of the sentence, the sentence stretches too far and obscures the meaning of the page, the page acquires life at the expense of the whole—the whole is no longer a whole. The whole has ceased to live altogether ; it is composite, summed-up, artificial, an unnatural product."

My work is a chain of soft phrases. I can only thank my Muses that it is the writer's privilege to have his chain tested by its strongest link.

Yours sincerely,
KENNETH P. TYNAN

My reply :

July 27th, 1945

MY DEAR HAMLET,

Now and again fact draws level with fiction, and you appear to me to approximate very closely to my—or perhaps I should say our, since one Leo Pavia was the real begetter—Oleander Fugge, alias Durance Hatch. (Who this personage is you will learn from the pages of *Ego* 8.) In the meantime, my dear boy, there is this difference between us. I never go to my quotation-book except for the purpose of verification. I think you are wrong in likening yourself to Sterne. You begin by writing the first sentence, and then trust to the *Oxford Dictionary of Quotations* for the rest. In your flirtation with verbal surrealism I, as an old fogey, cannot follow you. And will not.

> Costly thy language as thy thought can buy,
> But not express'd in fancy ; rich, not gaudy :
> The style, says Buffon, oft proclaims the man.
> Farewell: my blessing season this in thee.

POLONIUS

July 28 An unknown young man writes from the Mediterranean :
Saturday.

My obeisances to the ubiquitous L. P. Could he not write a few more Strindberg studies ? I think I should like him. As *Ego* 6 is the first I have read, he appeared before me like Minerva from Jove's brow—or rather, like Gargantua rampageous from his mother's (father's ?) left ear.

Feel like writing to the young man to say that I wish L. P. would devise some means of retreat along these or any other lines. He moans that he is deaf and cannot hear what I dictate. He laments that his handwriting is illegible, and when I ask him why he doesn't make it legible, replies, " What's the good ? I'm too blind to read it anyhow ! " In addition he has the paper-saving mania, which means that his notes are taken down on the backs of old notes for old articles, fifteen words to a page. When the dictation is finished he gathers up some forty sheets and strews them, paperchase-wise, along the thirty-yards stretch between his desk and mine. Presently he retrieves and proceeds to type them in the order in which they have been picked up, without regard to sequence. Here is something he laid before me to-day :

Mr Wolfit's revival of *King Lear* finds me on tenterhooks. Tenterhooks about what ? Remember, I receive some twenty to thirty manuscripts a week which my secretary returns automatically. Your play is not in my flat, and I can only conclude that it has been returned. Tucked away in Hazlitt's lesser-known essays there is a curiously grudging account of Goldsmith's master-piece. But this actor, although most musically inclined, is not a Liszt. To me, all microphones look and sound alike. Nine years now go by.

Fuming, I ask, " What the devil is this rubbish ? " and L. P. says imperturbably, " I thought it was rubbish when I was taking it down." He is both cause and cure of my *énervement* ; nobody else has his twofold genius for annoyance and stimulation. All the same, I think it was for the best that we couldn't get into the hotel at Southend. " If you think I'm going to sit on my behind for four days," said Leo, " looking at that mud and that mob, you're mistaken. I shall take the typewriter ! "

My trouble is that I can't stop working, the most I can do in that line being to change the work. Yesterday I had arrived at the last sentence in the last of the articles I am to write for three weeks— I am comparing Irene Vanbrugh and Nancy Price with the film actresses who have to be shoved into seventeen different positions before the camera-man can take a shot that isn't ridiculous :

> When you hear those voices, watch those gestures, note the faultless timing and the virtuosity attained by the simplest means —when either of these superb war-horses takes the stage we say : She paweth in the valley and rejoiceth in her strength. She swalloweth the ground with fierceness and rage. She smelleth the battle afar off, the thunder of the leading man and the applause.

I wrote this out by hand, partly because I was pleased with it, and partly because I knew Leo would make the ground swallow the war-horse. Half an hour later I was sitting at the Embassy Theatre, looking at and very much liking Joan Temple's *No Room at the Inn*, a play about a sadistic slattern who ill-treats five children billeted on her, one of them a little boy of ten, and is murdered by them. Fine performance by Freda Jackson. When I got home I turned up my cutting-book and found something from *The Times* in the 'eighties :

> However lamentable the fact may be, there is undoubtedly a class of playgoers whose notions of dramatic art are satisfied with the reproduction upon the stage of the sordid scenes of low life they see every day around them. A coster's barrow with a load of vegetables, or a free fight carried on by roughs whose merit it is to look as if they had walked straight upon the stage from the purlieus of the Borough of St Giles, has for these people an attrac-tion which the highest efforts of literary or poetical genius would fail to exercise.

The word " Borough " struck a note, and I decided that to-night's play, under the title of *The Evacuees*, is our next English opera. Consider the last scene. The slattern, having come to the end of her vocal resources, throws herself on the bed on which she is presently to be smothered, and mutters, " Sod the little swine ! I'll teach him to ruin my new hat ! " Leo, saying, "And what you hear in the orchestra is something like this," seizes a piece of music paper and jots down half a dozen bars with which I would undertake to spoof any living conductor, not to mention the musical critics.

Lunch to-day with André Bernheim, who told me some lovely stories. About Lucien Guitry going with his mistress to his hatter's. Each hat was pronounced too big, too small, too grave, too gay. At the tenth she said, " Ah non ! Pas celui-là. Tu as l'air d'un vieux maquereau ! " With a shrug Guitry handed the offending felt to the shopman and said, " Celui-là me vieillit ! " About Galipaux, in a comedy by Sacha Guitry, drawing up his will and leaving 30,000 francs to his native town of Cherbourg, 20,000 to his wife, 40,000 to his mistress, 10,000 to an illegitimate daughter, and suddenly interrupting himself to say, " Bon Dieu de bon Dieu, où est-ce que je vais trouver tout cet argent-là ! "

Wind up my first day of rest-cure with another letter to Hamlet :

Queen Alexandra Mansions, W.C.2

July 28th, 1945

EXPECTANCY AND ROSE OF THE FAIR STATE,

I am very anxious not to mislead a clever pen like yours. What exactly is the point of " jesting pirate " ?

I have made some study of the matter, and the result of my thinking is that anything quoted must *go the same way as the author's stream*, whereas your quotations—and allusion is a form of quotation—peg the reader back. Here are passages from four great dramatic critics, showing how they used embellishment. I will begin with Shaw. He is writing about *Her Advocate*, a play by Walter Frith :

" Just as another Frith frankly said, ' I cannot do you an artistic picture like Botticelli's " Primavera " or the like, but I'll do you a railway station or a Derby Day to the life '; so the author of *Her Advocate* seems to have said, ' I cannot write you a dramatic poem, like *Twelfth Night* or *Pelléas et Mélisande*, nor do I pretend to any of the qualities of Molière or Labiche, Goldsmith or Sheridan, Ibsen or Sudermann ; but I'll do you a criminal trial that will be as delightful as the real thing.' There is a sort of greatness in this frank recognition of one's limitations. In the National Gallery it is quite possible, after breathing the finest ether of the true artistic atmosphere among the early Italian pictures for an hour, to spend a few minutes looking at ' The Derby Day ' without resenting its absolutely prosaic character any more than you do that of the fire-hose. It is the same with *Her Advocate*."

Now take Walkley on the subject of Dumas *fils* :

"How to qualify him ? A dramatist who can give Scribe and Sardou points and a beating at their own game ; a prophet who has brought down new Tables of the Law from a Sinai hard by Mont Valérien ; an apostle whose prefaces, pamphlets, articles, are so many Epistles to the Lutetians ; moralist, philosopher, mystic, dabbler in occultism, deist, socialist, conservative—to be thus prodigal of differences is to be a mere centre of perplexity, a rallying-point of the bewilderments. To Montesquieu's Persian or Goldsmith's Chinaman his whole theatre would seem one prolonged nightmare. . . ."

Here is Max on Duse :

"I have often wondered why Sydney Smith said he ' would as soon speak disrespectfully of the Equator.' After all, the Equator is a mere geographical expression. It casts no weird spell of awe over mankind. On the contrary, seafarers, when they come to it, put on false noses and play practical jokes. For ' Equator ' read ' Duse,' and then the remark has point. There never was an influence so awe-inspiring as Duse. At her coming, all the voices of the critics are hushed. Or rather, they are uplifted in unisonant dithyrambus."

And lastly Montague on Tree :

"Isidore Izard, the ' hero,' is a predatory financier on the grand modern scale, no mere maggot skulking in the cheese, but a really first-rate beast of prey, with the City for his jungle, and ranging it royally. The type, excellently conceived, is acted by Mr Tree with buoyancy, observation, and inventive ingenuity. His Izard has the fine, flamboyant, blackguard geniality of one of Lamb's ' higher race of men,' only that he does not borrow, but takes ; he gives you the right impression of rollicking invincibility at his own game ; he is the true taxer, ' who calleth up all the world to be taxed ' ; he is as ' the sea, which taketh handsomely at each man's hand.' Mr Tree acted the man's self-enjoyment to perfection in the second act—much the best scene in the play— where two lesser rogues tackle him, and he ' does ' them with a tranquil gusto almost romantic, singing bits of songs by the way, like Cyrano improvising a ballad while he pinks a less efficient swaggerer."

Well, here are four critics who were masters of all I mean by "quotation" instead of borrowers allowing quotation to be their master. Shaw, Walkley, Beerbohm, Montague—each ornament swells its author's stream and becomes part of it. No, I do not want you to write like any of those four great critics. I don't want you to write like Desmond MacCarthy. Or like Ivor Brown, Alan Dent, me. I want you to make for yourself a style—which can be done only out of your own bowels and nobody else's—that will make readers say, "That's Tynan," just as people say, "That's

Hazlitt " or " That's Lewes."   Let me assure you that poking about
in books of reference is no way of attaining the one thing that
matters in all the arts—individuality.   At the moment I see little
more in you than blown youth blasted with other people's ecstasy.
So chuck it, and start life on your own !

POLONIUS

July 29   True to form, the B.B.C. faded out Ginette Neveu last
Sunday.   night ten bars before the end of the Beethoven Violin
Concerto.   But then they would have no compunction in
fading out some reciter of verse at the line :

> At last he rose, and twitch'd his mantle blue . . . ;

though they would prefer :

> To me the meanest flower that blows can give . . .

Some day Broadcasting House will come into its own and fade out
Hamlet at :

> But I do prophesy the election lights
> On Fortinbras : he has my dying voice ;
> So tell him, with the occurrents, more and less,
> Which have solicited.   The rest is . . .

The Concerto was cut short by the news telling us that Mr Potsdam
has gone to Attlee !   Or something of the sort.   The news that our
Daniel has gone to put his head in the Russian lion's mouth may
well be more important than any concerto.   But why doesn't whoever is in charge of the Proms go into the artists' room ten minutes
before the concert and say, " You know you're being broadcast ? "
(Conductor and soloist signify that they know.)   " You know the nine
o'clock news is a MUST ? "   (Both assent.)   " You know you've got
forty-five minutes for the concerto.   How long did it take at the
rehearsal this afternoon ? "   (The conductor : " We finished dead
on time.")   Here whoever is running the concert should do a bit
of quick thinking.   He should remember something a famous conductor said to me about a famous opera-singer : " The Volga Boat-
men, hauling away with a rope, couldn't have hurried that cow up."
So my manager would say to conductor and artist, " Dead on forty-
five minutes won't do.   I must have two minutes to spare.   The
applause greeting Madame may delay the start.   Or Madame's violin
may break a string.   Or Madame may have a sneezing-fit in the
middle of the slow movement."   And if I were the Prom manager I
should turn to the soloist and say, " Look here, Madame What's-
your-name, if you don't get through that concerto in forty-three
minutes you never show your face at *my* concerts again ! "

Lunched with Jock, who said there was a Dreyfus letter for me in the post. Told me that when he took H. and O. to Rules he tried his game of ' Preferences ' on Harry, who answered every question without a second's hesitation. Here are his answers :

Favourite Words
Pink
Shandygaff
Eschscholtzia

Likes	*Dislikes*
TSCHAIKOWSKY	WAGNER
SOUSA	BRAHMS
CHOPIN	SIBELIUS
SHAKESPEARE	TENNYSON
KIPLING	BURNS
WHITTIER	WORDSWORTH
JAN VAN EYCK	TURNER
HOGARTH	HOLBEIN
COROT	GAINSBOROUGH
H. G. WELLS	MEREDITH
DICKENS	THACKERAY
RIDER HAGGARD	MY BROTHER JAMES

Favourite Line in Poetry
" Gentle Jesus, meek and mild."

July 30   The papers made a fine showing on the death of Lady
Monday.   Oxford. The best notice, *of course*, was in the *Manchester
Guardian*, which always does anything worth doing better than any other paper. This makes up for doing things that aren't worth doing worse than any other paper. To-day it prints some two thousand words which ought to go into any anthology of modern English prose. Nothing could be better than :

Margot was a wonderful hostess and a wonderful talker. She even on occasions knew when not to talk, though she always had ten thousand things to say. Many even of those who normally disliked to be silent could sit happily listening by the hour to her piquant reminiscent monologues. Her talk was never tedious for an instant, except when it concerned the subject-matter (as distinguished from the personalities) of politics. Then, indeed, it could be infinitely tedious. She rarely exhibited even a modest grasp of a political or economic problem, and so she could be as tiresome and as impervious to argument as any other echo.

Since I shut my ears to people who knew Bernhardt only in her old age, so I feel that nothing I write about this great figure and brilliant creature can have any real value. I never knew Margot, and

I never knew Mrs Asquith. My acquaintance began with the Countess of Oxford and Asquith, when, soon after her husband's elevation to the peerage, Viola Tree took me to lunch at her house somewhere in Bloomsbury. I had met her unofficially some weeks before, when I sat next to her at the Everyman Theatre on the first night of a play by her daughter, Princess Bibesco. I remember that for days afterwards my side was blue, owing to the proddings of the maternal elbow as each supposedly witty thing came along. At the Bloomsbury luncheon I remember only Asquith, sitting at the head of the table, quietly smiling while the Countess was explaining to some Russian dancer how to chalk her shoes so as to prevent slipping. And how the rest of us said nothing, and I left wondering that a man like Asquith could tie himself up for life with a tornado. Some years later she came up to me at Lord's and said, " You won't know who I am. Can you direct me to Lord Baldwin's box ? " I said, " As I don't know who Lord Baldwin is, how can I ? " She said, " If it isn't our dear, clever Mr Agate ! " I said, " If it isn't our dear, foolish Lady Oxford ! " At the same time administering a gentle slap. Whereupon her daughter said, " Mr Agate is quite right, dear ; you deserved it." Mostly we got on famously. I can be a good listener, and am all for solo performances. If there is a good talker at the table then I stay completely mum. At many of Gwen Chenhalls's luncheons à trois she and I would say nothing and listen to Lady O. laying down the law about politics, literature, art, science, Mr G.'s acting, and her parlour-maid's corns. She was a woman of extraordinary refinement of mind. You couldn't tell her a story which was in the least risqué. I made one attempt, and the reception was such as Mrs Pipchin would have accorded Master Bitherston.

And here is Jock's letter :

Colindale
Friday

DEAR JAMIE,

Your damned Dreyfus Affair interferes with my work in spite of myself ! (It must, of course, fascinate anybody with a mind— even me !) In July 1898 M. Zola declares the whole tangle to be " frightfully absurd." But on September 2nd I find a startling turn under the heading : " The Dreyfus Scandal : Colonel Henry's Suicide." And in the same issue the *Manchester Guardian* speaks up nobly in a long first leader :

" With all that one knows of the life and character of Captain Dreyfus before his trial and of the distinguished men who have championed his cause so bravely against a fanatical and foul-mouthed opposition supported by the majority of Frenchmen, one is practically forced at this stage to believe in the prisoner's

192

innocence. . . . It is equally clear, we hope, that the first step towards reorganising the War Office and re-establishing public confidence in its actions will be at once to recall Captain Dreyfus from his desert island and give him a fair open trial wherein he may demonstrate his innocence. Nothing less than an immediate revision of the scandalous trial of 1894 can repair the injury that has been done, not only to Captain Dreyfus, but to the fair fame of his country."

On September 22nd there is another short leader to say that Colonel Picquart has had a charge of forgery trumped up against him, and that these uneasy goings-on in France " awaken the suspicion that even now a powerful party at the War Office is sparing no pains to obscure the truth about the Dreyfus Case."

At the end of October there are violent anti-Dreyfus demonstrations in the streets of Paris. In the middle of November Dreyfus himself is (falsely) reported dead. In December there is a report of Picquart's trial, and renewed agitation. And at the very end of the year—where my time was up !—Captain Dreyfus was reported to have embarked for France again for the second trial.

I cover, you see, about six months a day—and this particular day has been the least exciting of the three I have spent at the job this week. And yet not so very unexciting either ! Leaving public affairs *and* the theatre and music out of it, you wouldn't—would you ?—as *Express* book critic call six months " unexciting " which gave you Kipling's *The Day's Work*, the first complete edition of Meredith, the first general printing of *A Shropshire Lad*, Henry James's *In the Cage* and *The Turn of the Screw*, Mrs Garnett's translations of Turgenev, Monkhouse's *A Deliverance*, and Hardy's *Wessex Poems*.

In the Drury Lane pantomime at the end of the year, *The Forty Thieves*, with Dan Leno, etc., there was a specially successful burlesque interlude called " The Zoological Gardens " in which many figures in the public eye were " vociferously recognised." These included Lord Salisbury and Mr Chamberlain and W. G. Grace and Tod Sloan (who was he, please ?) AND Zola and Esterhazy and Dreyfus !

Ever,
Jock

P.S. It would be pleasant, though hardly possible, to finish the mighty task by October 15th this year, which will be the *tenth* anniversary of my becoming the *M.G.*'s London dramatic critic.

July 31   Yet again, without fuss, the *Manchester Guardian* calmly
Tuesday.   manifests its superiority over every other paper in the world. It gives this morning a detail, 8 inches by 7, of a picture by a forgotten artist, H. Jamyn Brooks, in the possession of the National Portrait Gallery, showing Margot Tennant attending the private view of the Old Masters exhibition at the Royal Academy in

1888 and walking round the room with Mr Gladstone. Other figures are Lord Jersey, Holman Hunt, John Ruskin, Lord Spencer, Sir Charles Tennant, Marcus Stone, and G. F. Watts. No other newspaper, except perhaps *The Times*, would have thought of reproducing this, and *The Times* didn't think. Every other paper, even if it *had* thought, would have turned it down.

Note from Hamlet :

> 229 *Portland Road*
> *Edgbaston*
> *Birmingham* 17

DEAR MR AGATE,
    I believe in artifice for art's sake.
    I do not believe in sincerity or profundity.
    I believe in superficiality. I believe in shallowness.
    In fact, *quand même*, I believe in

> KENNETH P. TYNAN

This is immediately followed by a telegram in reply to one from me saying I hoped to spend most of next week at Sutton Coldfield and would he come to the show at which I am judging ?

> POX DEVOUR ME FOR HAVING ALREADY ARRANGED TO BE IN LONDON AUGUST 3RD TO 12TH WHAT NOW LETTER FOLLOWS—HAMLET.

The Post Office, staggered by the basic English of the first three words, repeats them to make sure.

Note from Tom Curtiss, now in Berlin :

> I visited the Führer's Reichskanzlei residence this afternoon, and found the great man out, along with the roof, the windows, and most of the walls. I managed to unearth a whole collection of medals, from the Iron Cross (first class) to the German Mother Award presented to women bearing more than five children at once, or something of the sort.

At lunch run into Pat Kirwan, film critic of the *Evening Standard*. Pat says that in spite of knowing nothing about music or cricket he greatly admires Neville Cardus. " But tell me," says Pat, " phwat does he mean by saying some pianist put his leg in front of a straight wan ? "

Modern manners. Leaving the Café Royal, J. A. hails a taxi :

TAXI-DRIVER (*hefty, bellicose and quite obviously out for trouble*). Put yer stick dahn ! Oo d'yer fink yer wavin' at ?
    J. A. Sorry. Drive me, please, to Partridge and Cooper's, the stationers in Fleet Street. (*Is driven there ; driver has altercations with two bus conductors.*)

J. A. (*descending*). I shan't be two minutes, and then perhaps you'll be good enough to take me to Grape Street.

TAXI-DRIVER. I ain't doin' no bloody waitin'.

J. A. (*patiently*). When I say two minutes I mean two minutes.

TAXI-DRIVER. I don't care wot you says and wot you means. Pay us off, will yer?

J. A. If you wait you'll get paid and well paid. If you don't wait you won't get paid at all. Here's where I live. (*Hands him an old envelope and goes into shop.*)

TAXI-DRIVER. ! ! ! ! !

J. A. (*reappearing after the stipulated two minutes*). Grape Street. (*Driver says nothing, and on the way saves the life of a jay-walker by a miracle of skill and awareness.*)

TAXI-DRIVER (*arriving at Grape Street*). There oughter be a lor agin them effin' pedestrians. Thenks, Guv'nor. No 'arm meant.

J. A. Smart bit of work! (*Taxi-driver grins and drives away.*)

Aug. 1
Wednesday. Every lifetime has its peak days, and yesterday was one of mine. At 2 A.M.—I was working at *Ego*—the telephone rang. It was Pierre de Rigoult, Contrôleur-Général of the Comédie Française, saying he was just back from Scotland, and that he and Pierre Dux, the Administrateur-Général, wanted me to dine with them that night as they had something to give me. The dinner took place at the Ambassadors, and I was presented with a scroll signed by all the members of the visiting company of the Comédie in order of seniority.

The conversation over dinner—the food was exquisite—was very animated, if sometimes a little difficult. My hosts plied me with embarrassing questions. " Is Gielgud a great actor ? " (They had seen him the night before in *The Circle*.) I got out of this by saying that the piece is not one by which they should judge Mr G., who is not a comedian. De Rigoult said, " You can't see his eyes." Next question : " Has he the scaffolding for a great actor ? " I told them that Mr G. has more poetry than any other actor of our day. " Have you any great actresses in the sense that Clairon, Rachel, and Bernhardt were great ? " I wriggled out of this by asking whether there are any of that kind in France to-day. " Who is your worst good actor ? " Ten names trembled on my lips, and I suppressed them all. (De Rigoult gave a lightning and instantly recognisable imitation of the worst of modern good French actors.) " What, M. Agate, has been your greatest moment in the theatre ? " I said, " Bernhardt as Pelléas rushing on and saying in reply to Mélisande's ' Qui est là ? ,' in a voice half-way between famished tigress and strangled dove, ' Moi, moi, et moi ! ' " " And your next greatest ? " I replied, " Any moment in all the hours I spent watching Henry

Irving." De Rigoult said, "You meant that Irving's worst was better than anybody else's best?" I said, "Je vous le jure!" They made the point that to them our English actors have no " jeu." That they do nothing with their lines *qua* actor, and are content to speak them as the author wrote them. I agree, with the exception of Seymour Hicks. Not one English playgoer in a hundred will understand what is meant here. In boxing a blow starts at the back of the heel, travels along the entire torso, and culminates at the point of contact. A French actor delivers each and every line with his whole body, from his toes to his eyebrows. Our theatre is manned by signposts ; theirs has the animation of a puppet show. On the political side I gathered that while there is a 1000 to 1 chance that Laval was aiming at circumventing the Hun by *roublardise* (I don't think they believed this), Pétain is the resolute, unforgivable traitor. As for de Gaulle, he is a *maître-gaffeur*, whose career is over.

Having arranged for a car, I enticed my hosts to the Maison McBean, where the Presentation of the Scroll was photographed. Then bundled them with Angus to Grape Street, where we toasted each other's countries in my last bottle of champagne, brought over from France by "Curly," who had charged me to drink it only on a noble occasion. And then I showed them round the Musée Sarah. Dux had not seen S. until the year after her operation, when, in Racine's *Athalie*, she was brought on in a palanquin. (He surprised me by saying that the drama of Corneille is more alive than that of Racine. About the latter : " C'est la tragédie de salon." I told him Edmund Gosse's remark about Racine's verse : " Poetry in silver chains.") De Rigoult didn't see S. until just before her death, and both were very anxious to hear my record of her in *Phèdre*, saying that, so far as they knew, nobody in France, and certainly not the Comédie, possessed it. Now I have two records of this : one very old and worn, the other, hardly used, given me by Ivor Novello. It was, of course, the latter that I presented to Dux, who formally accepted it on behalf of the Comédie. Further libations being indicated, my last bottle of whiskey but one was now requisitioned. Here I had the happy idea of ringing up Jock, telling him to jump out of bed, huddle into some clothes, and run " like the swift hare " to Grape Street. This he did, saying, on his somewhat breathless arrival, " If it's to meet anybody less than George Nathan or Pare Lorentz I'll be gey fashed wi' ye." He was, of course, enchanted, and talked to my visitors in excellent French, with not a little of his native brilliance. The party broke up about 1 A.M., Dux and de Rigoult having to be at Croydon Aerodrome at seven o'clock this morning. By the way, they took with them a certificate from me assuring the Censor that Racine never wrote anything subversive or in any way connected with current affairs ! Dux has enormous charm—but it is almost as though there were no face of Dux but merely a rallying-ground for all the scamps in Molière. De Rigoult speaks little, but to the point.

The others having departed, and the last bottle of my whiskey now handsomely in action, Jock says, " Jamie, you've ten minutes in which to write down the names of the hundred best players, male and female, of all nationalities since Roscius. And I'll do the same." We finish on time, and comparison shows eighty names common to both lists. There are gaps, of course—I forget Stanislavsky, Joanny, Mrs Oldfield, Sada Yacco, and Adrienne Lecouvreur. Jock's omissions include Macklin, " Little " Robson, De Max, Kitty Clive, Mrs Jordan, Jeanne Granier, and Duse (! !). The concernancy ? An idea Jock is going to put up to the Imperial Tobacco Company against the time when they resume their cigarette-cards. To bed about 4 A.M., entirely sober, which I attribute to the greater intoxication keeping the champagne and whiskey within bounds.

Aug. 2
Thursday.

I have this year delivered two lectures—the first to working lads, the second to a collection of earnest female school-teachers. I propose to reproduce a part of each.

OF KINGS' TREASURIES

I want to talk to you about success. And I am to tell you that it is in the power of every one of you present to achieve success in some capacity. I give the lie to Addison. It *is* in mortals to command success. With this proviso—that if your talent is for bricklaying it is no use trying to write poetry, while if you are a poetic genius you will probably be a poor hand at laying bricks. Don't misunderstand me. I don't say that Burns couldn't plough a straight furrow, or that Bunyan didn't know pot from pan. But can it be doubted that their minds were elsewhere ? And this is the point I want you to get. *The wish to be an artist is a blessing if it is coupled with the power to be one. The wish without the power is a curse.* Moreover, the power must be a lasting one. Somerset Maugham has a passage in which he lays it down that every young person possessed of any kind of sensitivity has the power to write one story, paint one picture, compose one tune. Maugham goes on to draw a tragic portrait of the young man who spends the rest of his life trying to force his brain to give something it cannot yield.

It is the practice if not the rule of the medical profession not to tell a patient that he has an incurable disease from which he cannot recover. The notion is to give the poor fellow the heart to go on living. Does this, and should this, apply outside medicine ?

Should a critic of books, plays, art, music, tell a young aspirant that he is suffering from the incurable disease known as lack of talent, and will never get better ?

The other day I received a letter from a man at Weston-super-Mare saying :

" Will you have a look at my novel ? It has been returned by sixteen publishers, but I take comfort in the fact that Jane Austen's *Pride and Prejudice* was turned down by as many. However bad you may think it, do not tell me that there is no hope of improvement. I am twenty-four, and shall go on writing until I am eighty. I do not want a wife and children or even happiness. I shall be content to write and starve. There are no sacrifices I am not prepared to make for my work, and I have the constitution of a Balzac. So please let me know what you think about my *Greyhounds in St Paul's*."

I have read this young man's book, whose real title I keep back. Or at least read as much of it as I could endure. The plot was a farrago of absurdity, the characterisation nil, the dialogue null, and the style porridge. The young man was, you see, suffering from the prevailing malady of the age—ambition without qualification. , You are anxious to know what I told this young man. I told him the truth. But I also copied out for him something written by my friend James Bridie about a third-rate artist :

" He paints dreadful daubs in a third-rate studio on a third floor. He is full of theory and spleen. He knows that his work is bad and that the world is right in despising it, but this is no comfort to him. He is an artist ; and if he is cross-eyed, colour-blind, and afflicted with the shaking palsy, he must still express the urge which is in him, even if it means insult, blows, and starvation."

I amplified this by saying that the artist to whom painting is its own reward must be satisfied with that reward and not look to have his pictures hung on the line. And therefore I say to all of you, if your daubing and scribbling gives you pleasure, or is a form of self-expression which you need as you need food and sleep, then by all means go on with your daubing and your scribbling. As Chesterton said, I think about golf, if a thing is worth doing at all it is worth doing badly.

I have before me a book entitled *The Truth about Writing*. This is by Mr Cecil Palmer and is published by Heinemann. It contains this passage :

" The point about any book since the world began has not been that the author desperately wanted to write it, but whether somebody could be induced to read it. That some young man or young woman with an itch for scribbling must get a novel out of his or her system is no reason why the poor mutt with an itch for reading should absorb that novel into his system."

Let me elaborate. The only criterion about a book is whether it is good or bad. If it is a bad book, it is of no account that the author lived for six years on bread and water in order to write it. If it is a good book, it doesn't matter that the author wrote it between bouts of drunkenness and on the backs of unpaid bills, keeping himself the while on bread snatched from the mouths of the widowed and the fatherless.

Now I come to the young man who is possessed of genuine talent. And I have to tell him that talent alone won't do. That he is under a moral and artistic obligation either to market his talent or to get somebody else to market it for him. I have no sympathy with the Schubert who could write an immortal work, throw it into a drawer, go out and get fuddled, and leave it to chance to rescue his masterpiece. And I have not the beginnings of sympathy with the theory that the world is full of undiscovered genius. If it is genius it will be discovered. And I have less than no sympathy with the view that people who have made their way in the world owe their success to luck. In what follows I am going to be egotistical, not, I assure you, in order to give rein to my vanity, but because I can speak from facts of which I have first-hand knowledge. It offends me to the very soul when I hear some one saying " Agate has had all the luck." I assure you that any success I have achieved has been striven and plotted for.

I began my writing career first as dramatic critic to the *Daily Dispatch* and then to the *Manchester Guardian*. In those days there were no repertory theatres in Manchester, and the plays were all London successes. The curtain fell at eleven o'clock, the notice had to be in by one, and I was a slow and unready writer. For seven years, and in case I should dry up, I never went to the theatre without having in my pocket an account of the plot derived from the London newspapers on the occasion of the London production. (I never used one of these " insurance " articles.) I then walked about the streets of Manchester from one o'clock in the morning till three in order to correct the proof, and I was at my business of selling calico the same morning at nine o'clock. Was I lucky in that my parents had given me a constitution which could stand this strain ? Yes. But I gave my constitution the backing it needed. I did not smoke till I was twenty-one, and had no sex experience until I was twenty-five.

After the war of 1914–18 I kept a shop in Lambeth. Learning that the post of dramatic critic of the *Saturday Review* was likely to become vacant, I asked a well-known dramatic critic whom I met at a dinner to C. P. Scott, editor of the *Manchester Guardian*, if he would introduce me to Filson Young. He said no, so I introduced myself and for twelve months contributed a weekly article over which I took three days, re-writing it as many as six and seven times. I do not think that when Leonard Rees, the editor of the *Sunday Times*, appointed me to succeed Sydney Carroll he asked for the Telephone Directory, closed his eyes, and made a dab with a pencil.

How did I become film critic to the *Tatler* ? In this manner. Learning that the post of film critic to that paper was about to become vacant, I decided to apply. But what chance had I who had no film criticism to show ? So I hatched a little plot. I was dramatic critic to *Eve* at the time, and I suggested to the editor that it would be a novelty if for one week I and the charming lady who did the film criticisms should change over. This was agreed to, and I was cute enough to choose a week in which Emil Jannings appeared in one of his great films. I put into my article everything I knew and more. Armed with this, I marched into the office of the *Tatler* and got the job.

The *Express* ? Some time in the early summer of 1931 my friend Reggie Pound, who was then the feature editor of the *Daily Express*, told me that the position of book-reviewer on that paper was likely to become vacant at any moment—would I keep in touch ? For a fortnight Reggie took no meal alone except breakfast ! About a quarter to twelve one evening at the Club of which we were both members Reggie said, " Can you come over and see Beverley Baxter ? " I said I could and would. I was shown into Baxter's office soon after midnight and came out at half-past twelve the official book-reviewer to the *D.E.* Was that luck ? But I will not weary you. When the publisher of my first *Ego* refused to take my second I found another firm. When the second publisher refused to publish the third *Ego* I found a third publisher. And if I had not found George Harrap I should have had the thing printed and bound at my own expense, and pushed it round the town on a hand-cart. In my time I have been published by eighteen publishers, each of whom I have approached and none of whom has approached me. Is that luck ? I served the B.B.C. as dramatic critic for seven and a half years, beginning with a fee of three guineas a talk and ending with a fee of nineteen guineas. I leave you to guess whether they increased the fee out of pure generosity or because I insisted on it.

To sum up. I may have some capacity as a writer. The fact is that for the last quarter-of-a-century I have worked eleven hours a day over sheer writing and not counting the time I have spent on attending theatres and seeing films and reading books for review. I entirely hold with Thomas Edison, who said, " Genius is one per cent. inspiration and ninety-nine per cent. perspiration." An American novelist has just been asking : Where would Lindbergh have been if he hadn't made Paris but had just dunked himself in the Atlantic and got himself saved and fetched back to Boston on a boat full of codfish ? The answer is that he would have had another go and made Paris. And if he hadn't he wouldn't have been Lindbergh. Wherefore I tell you this. The world is so arranged that you can all make a success of something, while a man who fails has only himself to blame. Remember, too, that while there is only one way of succeeding there are hundreds of recipes for failing—idleness, inattention, carelessness, the notion that

" this'll do," lack of initiative, want of drive, absence of tact and patience. But the list is inexhaustible. There is an old saying: Nothing succeeds like success. A great wit once altered this to: Nothing succeeds like excess. Let me tell you boys that nothing is more likely to win success than the will to succeed. Unless it be excess of the will to succeed.

OF QUEENS' GARDENS

The difficulty, my dear young ladies, is that I am the last person who ought to be addressing you to-night. Do I mean that you would have done better to invite my opposite number, Mr Ivor Brown? No. Or that brilliant young critic who will probably be my successor on the *Sunday Times*—although I haven't gone yet—whom I used to call Jock, but now, with the reverence of the master for the pupil, call Mr Dent? Certainly not. Or my revered predecessor, Mr Sydney Carroll, now amply and benevolently presiding over this meeting? No. Let me then reverse my preamble and put it that whereas I am the right person to address you, you are the wrong audience for me to address.

Do you remember that passage in *The Importance of Being Earnest* in which Lady Bracknell asks, " Is this Miss Prism a female of repellent aspect, remotely connected with education?" Dr Chasuble replies, " She is the most cultivated of ladies, and the very picture of respectability." Whereupon Lady Bracknell has her famous " It is obviously the same person." You ladies remind me of this passage, with this difference: that you have the most attractive aspect and at the same time the closest possible connection with education.

Now I have a very limited belief in education. I hold that the indiscriminate use of it does more harm than good. I believe that when Wilde wrote, " Ignorance is like a delicate exotic fruit— touch it, and the bloom is gone," he intended something more than a mere witticism. In my view nine-tenths of, I won't say the human race, but London children, are the worse for education. And for the reason that the education they are given is the wrong sort. So far as I can see, modern education leads the child out of the darkness of healthy ignorance into the denser night of soul-destroying commonness. I do not believe that instruction in my time has had any effect except to increase the number of ways in which the young people of to-day can be common. You teach a young girl to read; and she reads nothing except the film magazines. You give her music lessons; her only interest in music is the bilge spewed by crooners. You teach her to write; at twenty she can hardly spell her name. You teach her deportment; she jitterbugs. You tell her that cleanliness is next to godliness; she covers her face with messes and her nails with filth. Explore her mind to its inmost crannies and you will find nothing there except curiosity about the latest hair-dye.

You have not begun to teach the average London child how to speak its own language. So far as I can observe, no child has been taught not to say, "You was at the pictures last night, wasn't you?" And I am under the impression that "between you and I" is in more general use than it was when I was a boy. You have not even taught these young women to speak up so that they can be heard. I am a constant user of the telephone, and I am not deaf. Yet twenty times a day I have to say to the young woman at the other end, "Speak up, miss; who wants me?" You have not taught the young girl to believe that the ladder of culture is more important than ladderless stockings. She is content to be common. You have not persuaded her not to want to be common. You have not convinced her that education is a good thing.

And now I am going to leave this question of education, merely remarking that if I had my will, young girls would be taught nothing but cooking, sewing, and how to keep a house clean, and young boys no more than the trades by which they ultimately hope to support the young girls. This as to nineteen-twentieths of the youthful population. It would be left to the discretion of teachers to pick out the odd five per cent. who can be educated. For note this. Before you can educate a mind you must have a mind to educate. It is a part of democratic cant to pretend that Nature has been fair and equitable in her distribution of mind. She has not; she has been infinitely capricious. Nineteen-twentieths of the population in this country has no more mind— I am not talking of soul—than a lamp-post.

Now let me be logical. I am talking of the cultural potentialities of the mob, which has no more connection with the ultimate value of culture than the shape of the mob's nose or the size of its feet and hands. I agree that the common people, to use a convenient term, have put up, are putting up, and will put up as long as there is a man or woman of them alive, the most heroic battle in our history, on sea, on land, and in the air. That does not mean that they are susceptible to culture. I also agree that a young Bloomsbury æsthete who can quote Eliot and Joyce by the yard may be an unspeakable skunk. I say that education should aim at teaching nineteen-twentieths of the young the best way of making beds, ploughing fields, and being good citizens generally. And limit anything more complicated to the odd twentieth.

And now I realise that what I have been asked to talk about is not education but the drama. Well, what do you want to know about the drama? Must I tell you the plots of Shakespeare's plays, how many times they have been performed, and who acted in them? Or give a list of the minor Elizabethan and Jacobean playwrights? Or tell you that Wycherley came before Congreve, and not the other way round as most people think? Or how there was a long dull period in the nineteenth century in which nine-tenths of our plays were borrowed from the French, or, as Henry

Morley said, were translated, or adapted, or freely altered from the *Pomme Pourrie* of MM. Péché and Bonbon ? How, on December the 9th, 1892, the intellectual theatre was inaugurated by the first performance of Mr Shaw's *Widowers' Houses* ? How, six months later, this was followed by *The Second Mrs Tanqueray* ? How, in 1906, Galsworthy with his *Silver Box* ushered in a new era of play-writing ? And how, simultaneously, the Irish movement, headed by Lady Gregory and J. M. Synge, brought enchantment to our shores ? But all of this—indeed, any of it—would be dull talking for me, and dull hearing for you. Besides, I very much want to talk to you about something else. In a word, I want to discuss with you my own educational limitations.

Let me confess that my spiritual home is the Café Royal ; at least I sup there every night. And every night I hear the young people around me talking an art-jargon I am wholly unable to understand. What they are talking about is something which I am going to call Modernity in Art. I have always believed that an artist, whether he be poet, composer, painter, must be able to make his meaning clear to anybody of average cultural intelligence. Shakespeare and Milton and Wordsworth and Shelley made whatever they had to say perfectly clear. It is true that there have been poets—Donne and Browning, for instance—who were often highly, some have said needlessly, obscure. But in so far as they were not *trying* to be obscure, I hold that they failed in this part of their work to do their job perfectly. I doubt whether there was ever anything in Beethoven, with a few exceptions, which was not reasonably clear to the really intelligent and understanding listener of his day. Or in Wagner. Or in Berlioz or in Debussy. Or did not become so in the next generation. In the realm of painting I find comparatively little difficulty. You can always see what the old masters were getting at. You may not be enthralled by a painting of a side of beef. You may think as I do, that the Rokeby Venus shows a woman taking up an elaborate, unnecessary, and entirely unconvincing pose merely to look at herself in a mirror. Yet you have no difficulty in recognising that these two pictures represent (*a*) a side of beef, and (*b*) a woman lying on her side. Similarly, in the famous *Baptism of Christ*, by Piero della Francesca, the fifteenth-century Umbrian, you have no difficulty in recognising the figure in the background as that of a man pulling off his shirt prior to immersion, in exactly the same way that the modern footballer discards his jersey. Now there must be advancement in the arts as in everything else. We cannot stop it. And by advancement I mean not enhancement but complication, for I do not think that the world has improved one jot on the poetry of Shakespeare, the music of Bach, the painting of Michael Angelo. Young ladies, I said at the beginning of this talk that I was the last person who ought to address you. I repeat this. I live in Queen Alexandra Mansions, and should be quite content if Art had stopped short at the cultivated court of the Empress Alexandra.

To be perfectly frank, I haven't the slightest desire to read any novel later than Henry James, see any play later than Ibsen, hear a note of music after Richard Strauss, or look at any canvas after Renoir. I can only hope that the *Sunday Times* doesn't get to hear of this, since if it does it will sack me, and rightly.

Aug. 3   Picking up the telephone this morning, I overhear Leo
Friday.   on the extension talking to Norman Newman : " Really, doctor, you must prescribe for James something more than your boluses and bromides. That blasted *Ego*'s killing him. He thinks of nothing else, it robs him of his appetite, and drives him to drink. He has to take sleeping-draughts to forget it, and even then Arthur Bates tells me he hears him get up in the middle of the night and go into the study. Once he followed him and saw him fish the damn' thing out and start correcting it. He was at it for over an hour. I beg of you, doctor, make him send the stuff away, beyond reach. You will, doctor ? Thank you, thank you." There is a point at which fiddle becomes faddle. Balzac's painter, Frenhofer, dibbled and dabbled at the portrait of his mistress until nothing was left except a foot. How, since Bank Holiday looms, am I to prevent the orgy of " Frenhofering " that threatens me ? I don't forget that *Le Chef-d'œuvre inconnu* ends : " Le lendemain, Porbus, inquiet, revint voir Frenhofer, et apprit qu'il était mort dans la nuit, après avoir brûlé ses toiles." Or that Pope got himself into such a state over his translation of the *Iliad* that he wished himself hanged. J. A. hanging himself through too much *Ego* would be a charming irony.

Dine at the Savoy with André Bernheim and his wife. B. is a good-looking man in the forties, with white hair and a position in the French Ministry of Information. His pretty wife speaks French with an accent which intrigues me so much that finally I ask what it is. She says, " The purest Connemara ! " The other guest was Dorothy Dickson. She has the Victorian quality of *graciousness* which the modern beauty, pert and provocative, lacks. Reminded Dorothy how, years ago, Tibby Griffith had ranked her dancing with the frescoes of Michael Angelo, Milton's *Paradise Lost*, and Wagner's *Ring*. How I corrected Tibby, saying that the last word about D. D.'s dancing was Florizel's remark to Perdita about wishing she were " a wave o' the sea who might ever do nothing but that." Dorothy said, " Yours was the better criticism ; any woman would have preferred Tibby's." Later B. drove us to Paddington, where D. smiled her way through the crowds and somebody said, " She'll get a seat all right, even if it's in the cab with the engine-driver ! "

Then to the Bernheims' flat in Charles Street, where we drank marc of extraordinary potency. A delightful evening, at the end of which my host presented me with a photograph of Irving as Vanderdecken in *The Flying Dutchman*.

Aug. 4   Lunch with Hamlet, who says, " I would give all
Saturday. literature for one rare meal a day. I wouldn't swap the aural and visual arts, which I rate higher than the literary." Also : " The moderns are born great ; the romantics achieved greatness ; the classics have had greatness thrust upon them." And again : " My approach to the piano is to make it sound like the harpsichord." During lunch he asks for my opinion of

STONE AND FLESH
A Fragment

She-idol, plump and solemn, beetle-browed ;
Naked unendingly, awaiting Pan ;
An inhumanity of rock, unploughed
By casual engine or ungracious man ;
A bulging, lustless, super-fecund womb,
Swaying and sagging over tub-like thighs—
An acre of incarnate elbow-room—
As sexlessly insipid as pork pies.

And an amusing hour ends with the following dialogue :

HAMLET. May I introduce you to a friend who insists that the best art of the twentieth century has come out of the trumpet of a jazz-musician called Bix Beiderbecke ?
J. A. No.

Aug. 5   Hamlet won't take no for an answer. Which finds me
Sunday.   lunching at the Imperial Hotel with his three young friends. These turn out to be : Hugh Manning (twenty-five, and the Roger Livesey type), hoping to be an actor. Julian Holland (twenty, type of East in *Tom Brown's Schooldays*), admirer of Bix Beiderbecke, has a job at the B.B.C., and hopes to be a playwright. He and Hamlet at one time thought of a drama with Satan as the Creator and Christ as Fallen Angel, but dropped it. David Bench (a myopic, charming, Beetlesome child of seventeen) goes in for Yoga, spends the greater part of his time contemplating the tip of his nose which he can actually see, hopes to reduce life to a permanent blank, has written a book on *Civilisation without Activity*. Has never heard of " Palinurus," but when I quote " Others merely live ; I vegetate," is much impressed. Bring them round to Grape Street for coffee, and play them my " Strauss-Parodie " record, causing the Beiderbecke fan to say that this is white ecstasy and

therefore inferior to the Negro article. They are immensely tickled by Leo, and he takes to them at once. In spite of their nonsense they are pleasant, well-mannered, engaging creatures, and not at all conventional Bloomsbury. Even when, at lunch, I produce a large sheet of paper headed " Bêtises," *and proceed to make notes*, they are in no way disconcerted. In view of their non-resentment at my treating them as precocious babies, am considering a little book to be called *L'Art d'être Grand-Oncle*.

*Aug. 6   Letter from George Lyttelton :
Monday.*

*Finndale House
Grundisburgh
Woodbridge
Suffolk*

Aug. 5, 1945

Dear James Agate,
      It is many weeks since we have communicated, but what of that ? You, I know, are in a perpetual state of overwork, and I hesitate to write, knowing that you will answer and give yourself so much less time for adding the final touch to what a host of readers is awaiting. When my old tutor, Arthur Benson, said something to Henry James in similar circumstances, H. J. instantly replied, " My dear Arthur, my mind is so constantly and continuously bent upon you in wonder and goodwill that any change in my attitude could only be the withholding of a perpetual and settled felicitation." What is that in Agatese ? But the immediate occasion of my writing is your letter to *The Times* on Tom Richardson and your bold and welcome exaltation of artistic truth over factual. There are two very similar examples. George Hirst told me that he never said, " Wilfred, we'll get them by singles," when Rhodes joined him with 15 to get for the last wicket in the Oval Test Match 1902. And Rhodes told my nephew that Trumper never said, " For God's sake, Wilfred, give me a moment's peace," in the Sydney Test Match in 1903, though of course both these remarks *should* have been made. Must all the great " last words " go the way of Pitt's " My country," etc. !
      I see Mr Clifford Bax has been in a high state of indignation with dramatic critics. Are there many who foam at the mouth when your name is mentioned ? I expect it is all right when they meet you. " Having no good opinion of the fellow, I was resolved not to be pleased. . . . But the dog was so very comical that I was obliged to lay down my knife and fork, throw myself back upon my chair and fairly laugh it out." I won't insult you by saying where that comes from. I hope *that* was not touched up by James B.
      The Election ! Surely we haven't altered very much from Eatanswill, or is that the reaction of a mugwump ? I don't think eighty years of education have done much for the sovereign people

—judging by the arguments that they seem to think good ones. My daughter is just back from Potsdam and has brought me a piece of Hitler's own table as a souvenir !

Yours ever,

GEORGE LYTTELTON

I reply :

*Queen Alexandra Mansions, W.C.*2

August 6th, 1945

DEAR GEORGE LYTTELTON,

I take my pen in a hand which, a few hours ago, touched that of Field-Marshal Montgomery, my admiration for whom is great, though less than that of the Southampton typist who, after being presented to Robert Taylor, vowed she would never wash her right hand again.

The encounter—alas, there was no photographer to record it— took place in the passage behind C. B. Fry's box at Lord's during the Victory match against Australia. I was one of a party which included Clifford Bax, Eric Gillett, Douglas Jerrold, R. C. Robertson-Glasgow, a witty poet called Denzil Batchelor, and other great and semi-great personages, including the Duchess of Malfi from the Haymarket Theatre. As I entered, Clifford put a finger to his lips, pointed to the Duchess, and raised his eyebrows as much as to say, " What about that *gaffe* now ? " I replied, also in pantomime, " I am James Agate still ! "

If there is one thing I enjoy more than anything else it is listening to experts talking shop, always provided the shop is not cats, postage-stamps, or motor-cars. Fry said about Whitington : " I'll tell you how that fellow will get out. Every stroke should be a piece of ' swing,' which means that the poise of the body must be *forward* in sequent sympathy with the swing. Every now and again this fellow plays a forward stroke with the body poised backwards. This means that he is bound to pop one up sooner or later." C. B. had hardly finished speaking when Whitington did exactly as he had predicted, and was caught at forward short-leg.

During a patch of dull play Fry told me this about the famous Ashes match of 1882. In the 1920 edition of the Badminton *Cricket*—the original of which was largely written by your family —" Plum " Warner writes, " The true story of this match has never yet been told." Two pages of magnificent reporting follow, though even here " Plum," out of the kindness of his heart, says nothing about the essential thing—the quarrel between Spofforth and Grace. W. G., as you know, was up to every trick of the game, including one or two of his own. In the second Australian innings Murdoch played a ball to leg and ran a single, the wicket-keeper, Lyttelton—your uncle ?—going after the ball and returning it to Grace moving to the stumps from point. Jones going out of his ground to pat the pitch, Grace promptly broke the wicket and Jones was given out. Later, in the pavilion, Spofforth said to

W. G., " By God, you deserve to lose the match for that. And, by God, you shall ! " Fry said he got the story from " Plum," who had it from Murdoch. In his, Fry's, view, the umpire ought not to have given Jones out—he was not attempting a run, and was justified in thinking that the ball, being landed in the wicket-keeper's hands, was dead. And that W. G., by going to the wicket, had constituted himself wicket-keeper within the spirit of the rules.

Had a few words with " Plum." D'you remember Motley on Thackeray ? " He has the appearance of a colossal infant, smooth, shiny, a roundish face, a sweet but rather piping voice, with something of the childish treble about it." This is a perfect description of " Plum " to-day. Told me that with ten hours of sleep, a tonic, and vast quantities of milk, he manages to keep going. Actually he looks very fit and well set for his century.

I went to Lord's partly in deference to the doctor, who has ordered me three weeks' rest. The labour we delight in physics brain-fag. Meaning that I am working only on *Ego*. I would invite myself down to see you if I thought you would like it and I could get there. The difficulties in the way of the latter are insuperable ; I will not stand in trains, and I cannot get petrol. And then there is a third difficulty. Britten's opera, *Peter Grimes*, the scene of which, as you probably know, is laid in Aldeburgh (or Aldeborough), has given me a phobia about Suffolk. So much so that in future if I can't go to Norfolk except via Suffolk I shan't go to Norfolk.

I entirely agree with you about the sovereign people. Coming back from Lord's, I heard one bedizened little baggage say to another, " I ses, not a lady wouldn't do it, I ses." And you will be amused to know that I interrupted this letter to ring up the Duty Officer at the B.B.C. to ask what the hell the Corporation meant by letting some ignorant female tell their ten million listeners that Oscar Straus was " yet another member of the Strauss family " ? Thus is history written and error perpetuated.

Ever,
JAMES AGATE

Aug. 8   Again from George Lyttelton :
Wednesday.

Finndale House
Grundisburgh
Woodbridge
Suffolk

Aug. 7, 1945

DEAR JAMES AGATE,

The worst (or best ?) of writing to you is that your reply always demands another, and so it goes on. You must often be in danger of being snowed under by your correspondents, though I find it hard to imagine any storm which you would not ride !

Thank you for the Spofforth incident, which I did not know,

though I often heard my Uncle Alfred talk of that match. The story is fairly fully told in Wisden, but not, of course, Spofforth's outburst; it adds that after a lot of angry talk, " a prominent member of the Australian XI admitted that he should have done the same thing, had he been in Grace's place." The old man had a good deal in him of an earlier champion, Lord F. Beauclerk: " My lord he comes next and will make you all stare With his odd little tricks a long way from fair." How did " It isn't cricket " become the most self-consciously high-minded of all verdicts ? I never met Charles Fry till last year when " Plum " gave us lunch. He was very good company—made some very illuminating remarks on cricket, and a few strikingly wayward and heretical, though I fancy many of them were made to pull " Plum's " leg—*e.g.*, that Bardsley, Tip Foster, and Woolley were not among the twenty-five best bats of the last fifty years, that W. Gunn was better than Shrewsbury, that Tom Richardson's great bag of victims was largely composed of tail-enders (quite untrue), etc.

Thank you for Motley on " Plum." Excellent ! " P.'s " great merit is that he has never become pompous or jealous or querulous as so many great games players do. Do you realise what a fine team could be made of cricketers who committed suicide ? They don't on the whole grow old gracefully. In old days when my uncles talked of players they had known the reminiscences were always ending " died of drink."

I am sorry about your Suffolk complex, because we should much like to see you here, though like every one else we have no staff and roughish food. I suppose you think the county is entirely inhabited by " the lame, the blind, and—far the happier they !— the moping idiot and the madman gay." The original Peter Grimes was a much grimmer figure than I gather he is in the opera —a sort of male Mrs Brownrigg, who " wanted some obedient boy to stand, And bear the blows of his outrageous hand." We are about ten miles from Aldeburgh, in Fitzgerald's country rather than Crabbe's. I think I must soon take a hand in that stuffy little correspondence about the rose-tree on F.'s grave at Boulge.

Forgive all this rigmarole. Let me end with a bit of treasure trove which at any rate I know you will like if you have never seen it. Some one told it to the late John Bailey as the sort of specimen of Swinburne's humour which Gosse ought to have put in his Life and didn't—an invention of Swinburne's of Queen Victoria's con-fession to the Duchess of Kent of her one lapse from virtue, put for some Swinburnian reason into French : " Ce n'était pas un prince ; ce n'était pas un milord, ni même Sir R. Peel. C'était un misérable du peuple, un nommé Wordsworth, qui m'a récité des vers de son *Excursion* d'une sensualité si chaleureuse qu'ils m'ont ébranlée—et je suis tombée." Perhaps it was a good thing he was not made Poet Laureate.

Yours ever,
GEORGE LYTTELTON

And again from J. A. :

Queen Alexandra Mansions, W.C.2

August 8th, 1945

DEAR GEORGE LYTTELTON,

Your Queen Victoria nonsense is lovely.

I agree with Fry. Neville Cardus is responsible for most of the hocus-pocus about Woolley : " To add up the runs made by Woolley—why, it is as though you were to add up the crotchets and quavers written by Mozart." Perhaps I was unlucky with F. W., who, when I saw him, never did anything but get himself beautifully out, as Henry James would have said.

Nothing more of interest, except that at five minutes to twelve to-night I rang up the B.B.C.—this is becoming a habit—asked for the Duty Officer, and harangued him thus : " Sir, the fact that a Labour Government is in power is not a reason that your Corporation should muddy and defile the well of English language. Your announcer has just told us that ' The Government's no right ' to do something or other. And ' It's only been told to-day that Mr Churchill. . . .' Sir, would you have Lady Macbeth say, ' The raven himself's hoarse,' or Macbeth, ' This supernatural soliciting can't be ill, can't be good ' ? Would you at your Morning Service say, ' Almighty and most merciful Father ; We've erred, and strayed from thy ways like lost sheep. We've followed too much the devices and desires of our own hearts. We've offended against thy holy laws. We've left undone those things . . .' " And I slammed the receiver down without waiting to hear his excuses. Alan Dent tells me that the reason the B.B.C. won't employ me any more is that they think the miserable twopence-halfpenny they give for a talk should close the talker's mouth. Between you and me, I don't mind ; they need me far more than I need them. Wait till the centenary of, say, Madge Kendal, when they will be on their knees to me—if I am still alive—to tell the public how she acted. And I shall say, " My dear Talks Department, ask young Footle and young Tootle. I will give you one tip, however. Tell F. and T. that Madge K. was not Harry Kendall's mother. For one thing, the spelling's different."

Ever,

JAMES AGATE

Aug. 9 Again from the Sudan :
Thursday.

2245367 *A.C. Zakon, C.B.*
28 *S.P., c/o* 115 *Wing*
R.A.F., M.E.F.

1.8.45

MY DEAR MAN,

This particularly odious form of address is prompted wholly by your addressing me as your dear boy. I share the average distaste of the average male of twenty-one years (which, by the way, I attain this month—just a bit too late to do my duty for the Conservatives) at being called anyone's dear boy.

I must thank you for the expedition of your reply, a rare thing in these days, and inform you that I am suitably deflated by your completely opposite view of W. J. Locke. By the time I reach your venerable antiquity no doubt I shall have similar good taste. My chief reason for writing to you is to ask you to cast your magic over the vast public you variously entertain or annoy and ask a great favour of them. We have a painfully small library on the camp, consisting, unfortunately, mainly of detective stories. Oh yes, we also have a novel or two by the authoress Mrs Humphry Ward !

This state of affairs is not a dazzling outlook for the men on the station, and the situation is not enhanced by our long leisure hours. Owing to the intense heat most of the year round, we do not work after 1 P.M. This leaves us nine hours' spare time until lights out. We are lucky if we get one film during the week. Apart from a small native village, we are in the wide open spaces. As you will appreciate, such long periods with nothing to do are painfully boring. Imagine yourself in the situation ; not more than five decent books, which one has read at least twice, within several hundred miles. " Desert Island Discs " has nothing on us.

My request is that you put an appeal to your readers to send us some books, specifically addressed. The normal result of a Books for the Services Fund is that the big stations take the best of them and leave the small stations with nothing but almost unadulterated tripe. Mr Agate, if you did this you would ensure a hundred happy airmen praying for you every night. Such cheap salvation must surely appeal to you.

I await, with some apprehension, your reply, and meanwhile remain,

Yours sincerely,
CHARLES B. ZAKON

I answer :

*Queen Alexandra Mansions, W.C.*2
August 9th, 1945

DEAR AIRCRAFTMAN ZAKON,

I feel for you, and think of a passage in Kipling's *Soldiers Three* which runs :

" There·was the Canteen, of course, and there was the Temperance Room with the second-hand papers in it ; but a man of any profession cannot read for eight hours a day in a temperature of 96 or 98 in the shade, running up sometimes to 103 at midnight. Very few men, even though they get a pannikin of flat, stale, muddy beer and hide it under their cots, can continue drinking for six hours a day. One man tried, but he died, and nearly the whole regiment went to his funeral because it gave them something to do. It was too early for the excitement of fever or cholera. The men could only wait and wait and wait, and watch the shadow of the barrack creeping across the blinding white dust. That was a gay life."

I imagine that to you 103 degrees represents the cool of the evening !

As you say, I am old ; indeed, half-way between second childishness and oblivion. This being so, infantile games are permitted me ; for example, one I have just played. Reading your appeal, it occurred to me that it would be fun to make you and your friends a present of a little library, each book corresponding to a letter of the alphabet. Leaping—perhaps " crumbling " would be the better phrase—out of bed, I first ransacked my own shelves, this resulting in some ten or fifteen volumes. I then hied me— " creaked my way " would be better—to the Charing Cross Road. I don't pretend that what I am sending you are the twenty-six best books in the English language. If they were I shouldn't send them. Let me remind you of an incident in Dumas's great novel. Fouquet, about to give a banquet and sending his major-domo to market, discovers him at the wine-merchant's placing an order for the cheapest *vin ordinaire*. Being reproached, the major-domo answers, " Sir, this wine is for your meaner guests, who would be offended by that to which they are unaccustomed." I quote from memory. So the books I am sending you will not all be the best. Some are masterpieces and some are not.

To change the note a little. When, at some future time, you hear people say what a selfish, curmudgeonly old boor I was, say that in Aleppo once. . . . You see how my mind wanders. What you might like to say is that once, on a day in August, I devoted some six hours to lightening the boredom of a band of unknown airmen, hoping that this might discharge, say, one millionth part of the debt I and all old fogeys and stay-at-homes owe to the youth of this country.

Yours sincerely,
James Agate

P.S. A bright idea glimmers in a corner of this benumbed brain. This is to use for packing of the parcels—there will be three or four—some score or more of Penguins.[1]

[1] Months later as *Ego* 8 was going through the press I received the following :

2245367 *A.C. Zakon, C.B.*
R.A.F. Unit, Malakal
M.E.F.

Dear Methuselah Agate,
I thank you for your letter of the 9th August. The personnel of this camp and myself are overwhelmed with gratitude for the trouble you have taken in order to send us some readable literature. The appearance of a venerable wraith, muffled to the ears and probably wearing red-flannel combinations, tottering unsteadily down the Charing Cross Road as it (the wraith) battled valiantly against the mild mid-August zephyrs, must have presented an unusual and alarming sight to the casual passer-by. Have no fear, Mr Agate ; whatever your other readers may say about you, I shall always think of you as a sort of Deus ex Queen Alexandra Mansions—somewhat dilapidated, but none-the-less a kindly god.
I remain, with all good wishes,
Yours gratefully   incerely,
Charles B. Zakon

Aug. 11   **Epigram from Clifford Bax :**
Saturday.

> Thou hast conquered, O damn'd Galileo ! Hiroshima is grey with thy
>   breath.
> Now Science will atomise all things, and the arts are foredoomed to
>   their death.

Aug. 12   Taking the worst possible view of the atomic bomb, I
Sunday.   still don't believe that it can " reduce the earth to a
             scorched orb circling the sun but with no one to dis-
tinguish night from day." There still remains the Law of Diminishing
Returns. Which means that when the last bomb has been dropped
—last because there are no more technicians left to make another—
there will still be pockets of humanity in Greenland, Ecuador, Sene-
gambia, Franz Josef Land, China, and the Australian Bush. The
worst that could happen, then, would be the necessity to build
civilisation all over again. And probably build it for the better. (I
just don't believe that Eskimos, pigmies, and head-hunters could
produce an eyesore as monstrous as the Odeon Cinema in Leicester
Square.) It may be that Shakespeare's plays and Beethoven's
symphonies will be lost. This would be a pity, though I think I
might miss lesser things more. What was it that Elia resented that
death should take from him ? Not the major passions, but a trivial
catalogue ending with " innocent vanities, and jests, and *irony itself*."
I should hate to think that·fun itself goes out with life. Somebody,
somewhere, sometime, is going to re-discover that all the world's a
stage, that the quality of mercy is not strained, and that the uses of
adversity are sweet. Just as somebody, somewhere, sometime, is
going to write a play to prove that ambition, jealousy, and tyranny
don't pay in the long run. What I· should hate to lose is the irre-
coverable oddity. Say that passage in which Coventry Patmore
describes his first sight of Leigh Hunt :

> I, being at seventeen or eighteen years of age, or perhaps
> younger, an admirer of the *Indicator* and *Rimini*, set off with a
> letter from my father, an old friend of the poet, informing him of
> my ambition to see him. Arriving at his house, a very small one
> in a small square somewhere in the extreme west, after a walk of
> some five or six miles, I was informed that the poet was at home,
> and asked me to sit down until he came to me. This he did after
> I had waited in the little parlour at least two hours, when the
> door was opened and a most picturesque gentleman, with hair
> flowing nearly or quite to his shoulders, a beautiful velvet coat
> and a Vandyck collar of lace about a foot deep, appeared, rubbing
> his hands and smiling ethereally, and saying without a word of

preface or notice of my having waited so long, " This is a beautiful world, Mr Patmore ! "

To cut it short, my attitude to the atomic bomb and the hurly-burly it is going to create is entirely Skimpolean ! " I am capable of looking on and of being interested. I *do* look on, and I *am* interested. What more can I do ? "

Aug. 13   Found this human document in Shaftesbury Avenue
Monday.   to-night :

Saturday 11*th August*

DEAR NELLIE,
    I would like to thank you very much for your nice letter I was glad to see your handwriting once again. Well dear how is the world serving you these days alright I hope. Yes Nell I saw Bill but he did not mention any thing about going away. I had a letter from his mum she said that he might be home for a week end so I guess there was something going on may be Ted will meet him hope so for our sake yes Nell I do pray for them they are only kids yet I dont know what they feel like poor kids. Still Nell we will have to trust in the Lord to send them back to us. Well Nell I must tell you this there is a new lot of U.S. boys here now I am lucky I have pick up with a nice one I only wish you were here with me. This blokes name is Bob I have been out with him every night since he has been here I shall be sorry when he goes I have got to see him tonight I may be going to the dance and then I am going to the show on Tuesday so you can guess I am having a good time. Well Nell the news has just started I am waiting for them to tell us it is peace.

Cheerio,
GERT

Aug. 14   At twelve to-night it happens. To use Osbert Sitwell's
Tuesday.   phrase, " those clever, patriotic little apes of Japanese "
               have stopped " hurling themselves about." Japan has surrendered. And then the Prime Minister orates in a manner which drives home the *inartistry* of the Election. Where is the voice that launch'd a thousand ships and burnt the topless towers of Berlin, Hiroshima, and Nagasaki ? Where, in the new P.M.'s punctilious, careful accents, is the old leader's " swell of soul " ? Pathetic anti-climax—the curtain falling on a great actor, and the understudy taking the call ! One small glass of brandy, and since I find I can't sleep I go to my shelves and take down *The Return of Sherlock Holmes*.

    It was, then, in a year, and even in a decade, that shall be nameless, that upon one Tuesday morning in autumn we found two visitors of European fame within the walls of our humble room in Baker Street. The one, austere, high-nosed, eagle-eyed, and dominant, was none other than the illustrious Lord Bellinger, twice Premier of Britain. The other, dark, clear-cut, and elegant, hardly yet of middle age, and endowed with every beauty of body and of mind, was the Right Honourable Trelawney Hope, Secretary for European Affairs, and the most rising statesman in the country.

And just as I am wondering whether Messrs Attlee and Bevin would recognise their honourable selves in the foregoing, the row starts. The plebs has got out of bed, and is on its way to Piccadilly Circus to celebrate.

PEACE

1945

VJ Day.   It is twenty minutes past eleven in the morning of the
Greatest Day in History. H.M. the King has driven in
procession to Westminster to open Parliament, and on the air nothing
but antiquated musical comedies with the alternative of " X and his
Apache Band " in " Fête Tzigane." Wonderful ! Amazing !
Gigantesque ! Where, in God's name, are the L.P.O., the L.S.O., the
Hallé Orchestra, the B.B.C. Orchestra ? What has become of
Beecham, Cameron, Barbirolli, Boult ? Why weren't orchestras and
conductors standing by ? *Everybody, even Cabinet Ministers, knew it
was about to happen.* Here, I suggest, is a programme the German
wireless might have sent out if Germany had won :

DEUTSCHLAND ÜBER ALLES

DIE WACHT AM RHEIN

HITLERMARSCH

SIEGFRIED'S FUNERAL MARCH
(In Memory of the Fallen)

RIENZI : OVERTURE

EROICA SYMPHONY

EIN HELDENLEBEN

EIN FESTE BURG IST UNSER GOTT

The programme to begin at seven A.M. and continue till midnight,
with relays of live orchestras and conductors and no nonsense about
recording. People tell me the English win wars because they like
musical comedy, and the Germans lose wars because they like music.
I don't believe it. In the meantime my staff has the day off. I hate
crowds, the Café is inaccessible, and it is raining. Nothing remains
except to munch some stale bread and staler cheese, break my rule
about the day-time non-consumption of alcohol, *and work* !

Aug. 21   At the revival to-night of *Lady Windermere's Fan* I asked
Tuesday.   Lady Alexander, exquisite as ever and looking like the
lids of Juno's eyes, whether in the 'nineties peeresses at
private dances wore tiaras. She said, " They wore them at the
tea-table ! "

Aug. 22   Lunch with Bertie van Thal at the Savoy, where a
Wednesday.   really extraordinary coincidence happens. (First let me
                say that Bertie's life at the Food Office is one unbroken
sea of milk troubles. Either London is drowning in milk and there
are no bottles to put it in, or there is an avalanche of bottles and no
milk.) Now for the coincidence. At the next table is Kay Hammond
with her little boy. Gathering that he is fond of cricket, I beckon
him over and tell him how I once bowled out W. G. Grace. Whereupon John Clements leans across and says, " This is unbelievable.
In the lounge before lunch I was telling John how at a public dinner
my father heard W. G. say that on the sands at Blackpool he had
been bowled first ball by a little boy of seven whose name he never
knew ! "

Aug. 25   Geoffrey Bennett rang up late to-night to say that
Saturday.   at Wolverhampton Show this afternoon that old
                gentleman, Ego, came out of his retirement and,
exercising all his old charm, romped home in a class for private
turn-outs.

Aug. 28   Clifford Bax's dinner to C. B. Fry. Last night at
Tuesday.   the Ivy. Seating : Fry, Ernest Short, Guy Butler
                (holder of the world's 300 yards record for nine years),
R. H. Howe, Clifford, Arnold Bax, Denzil Batchelor, J. A.
Fry was in great form and as difficult as ever to tell anything to.
He is like R. L. S.'s Cockshot in the essay " Talk and Talkers "—
" Let me see. Give me a moment, I *should* have some theory for
that." C. B. doesn't need to see and he doesn't want a moment.
I told the table about my conjuring tricks, and he at once explained
them. I gathered that they have something to do with the Ivy's
electric wiring system. Said he had no regrets on retiring from
first-class cricket. " The big matches were fun, but I never want
to see Leicester and Derby again as long as I live." Went on
to tell us how he was thinking of a new career. Racing. " I
shall go to a racing stables for a year, after which I shall be
an immense success." Denzil Batchelor said quickly, " What as,
Commander ? Owner, trainer, jockey, or *horse* ? " D. B. also said,
" What a treat it would be to hear some B.B.C. announcer say,
' Ladies and gentlemen, it is now 7.55 P.M. As we have nothing
worth putting on the air we shall close down till to-morrow morning.
Good night, everybody. Good night.' "
    During dinner the question arose as to the world's funniest book.

" Most humorous " were, I think, the exact words. The voting went as follows, each diner being allowed two votes.

Alice in Wonderland	4 votes
The Diary of a Nobody	2 ,,
Vice Versa (Anstey)	1 vote
Eliza (Barry Pain)	1 ,,
Eliza's Husband (Barry Pain)	1 ,,
Don Quixote	1 ,,
Pride and Prejudice	1 ,,
Experiences of an Irish R. M.	1 ,,
Candide	1 ,,
Tartarin de Tarascon	1 ,,
Tartarin sur les Alpes	1 ,,
Berry and Co. (Dornford Yates)	1 ,,

No mention of Amanda Ros, Anita Loos, or Damon Runyon. And not a word for *Pickwick*.

Later somebody carried me off to a night-club—my first venture in this kind. From the fact that one had to go burrowing in the ground under a garage to deposit one's hat, and climb three flights of stairs, I gathered that the place was extremely smart. Lighting a deep heliotrope, reminding me of the little café in Harlem called Moon-Glow. Instead of goings-on to shock Heliogabalus a frigid propriety. Numberless and immaculate waiters. And, of course, too much band. Boring. Or would have been if a clever and rising young actor had not expounded to me, at length, his plans for starting a repertory theatre.

Aug. 30   Twelve jeweller's shops failing to produce what Old
Thursday.   Eccles called " a jewelled gaud," I have arranged with
                    the *Daily Telegraph* to insert the following in its
Personal Column :

Elderly dramatic critic requires baby's rattle.

Sept. 1   In a letter from Neville Cardus :
Saturday.

I am sick of Australia ; compared with Sydney or Melbourne, as far as culture or common sense go, Rochdale is as Athens under Pericles. I have not heard ONE witty remark from an Australian in five and a half years. *Dein bin ich, Vater !—rette mich !*

Ever,

NEVILLE

Queen Alexandra Mansions, W.C.2

September 2nd, 1945

DEAR JOCK,

If I had not passed a self-denying ordinance in the matter of work I should now be setting about a formal essay entitled " A Gossip on a Novel of Charles Dickens." However, I compromise with a letter. And naturally a letter to you, who awakened my too-long-dormant interest in *Dombey and Son*. I have read this in bed every night since your letter to me in the earlier part of this summer. What a masterpiece ! Twenty times have I had to put it down through sheer excess of admiration.

Were you at any time struck by the resemblance of Edith Granger to Hedda Gabler ? This first occurred to me when Cleopatra says, " The sword wears out the what's-its-name." And Edith says coldly, " The scabbard, perhaps." On the next page is Cleopatra's superb remark about Henry VIII : " Such a picture, too, he makes, with his dear little peepy eyes and his benevolent chin ! " You remember that Chesterton singles this out ? It is, I think, the best thing in the book, with the possible exception of Cousin Feenix's remark on the occasion of his call to apologise to Dombey for his " lovely and accomplished relative's " behaviour: " I have been in a devilish state of depression ever since ; and said indeed to Long Saxby last night—man of six foot ten, with whom my friend Dombey is probably acquainted—that it had upset me in a confounded way, and made me bilious." Do you remember G. K. C. on Cousin Feenix ?—" As consistent and as homogeneous as wood ; he is as invincible as the ancestral darkness." But I won't quarrel if you prefer the reply of Mr Toots on being told by Susan Nipper that Florence will never love him : " Thank'ee ! It's of no consequence. Good night. It's of no consequence, thank'ee ! " One of the most moving things to me in the book is the fact that Dickens does not forget the dog, Diogenes. " Autumn days are shining, and on the sea-beach there are often a young lady and a white-haired gentleman. With them, or near them, are two children—boy and girl. And an old dog is generally in their company."

The last page suggests something which will infuriate you— that there are too many pages. Arthur Bates, who looks after me, said the other evening on seeing me immersed in *D and S*, " Should I like that book ? " I at once asked him what kind of books he liked. He said any kind. Could he tell me the names of some of their authors ? After thinking for a few minutes he said—and I give you my word I'm not inventing or improving—" Shakespeare, Byron, Keats, Tennyson, Damon Runyon, Sherlock Holmes, Alan Dent." When I had recovered I read a page of *D and S* at my topmost reviewing speed and found it took me two minutes. (Nobody can beat me at reading quickly when I want to.)

Allowing Arthur three minutes—it would be nearer four—the result must be thirty-four solid hours of reading. As I don't suppose he gets more than half an hour to read each day, which includes newspapers, it follows that it would take him between three and four months to get through *D and S*. And that is too long. Do you realise that in thirty-four hours he could read a dozen crime stories ?

The point is how to get young people to read Dickens, and I suggest by cutting him. The characters I should leave out of any shorter *Dombey* would be Sol Gills, Capt. Cuttle (who is desperately unfunny), good Mrs Brown, Alice Marwood, the Toodle family (in part), John and Harriet Carker. I should reduce Walter Gay to a minimum, and cut at least half of Florence, whose value largely disappears with the death of Paul. I feel too that those interminable colloquies when Dombey, Edith, and Carker go into conference might be shortened.

Look again at chapter XX—"Mr Dombey goes upon a Journey"—and tell me whether it should not end at " He had seen upon the man's rough cap a piece of new crape, and he had assured himself, from his manner and his answers, that he wore it for his son." This is superb, worthy of Balzac at his most transcendent. Why go on ? Isn't it better to shorten masterpieces—written in an age when there was more time on hand—with a view to getting the present age to read them, than to leave them in their integrity and the certainty that they will not be read ? (There is always the full text for whoever wants it.) I know all about Tennyson and his " I wish there were a great novel in hundreds of volumes that I might go on and on." Our young bank-clerks are not Tennysons. Why, out of a too-nice regard for punctilio, should the next generation—or this—be deprived of all knowledge of Miss Tox, Mr Toots, Cleopatra, and Joey B. ?

Of course, shortening needs to be done not only with care but with a touch of genius. There would be no re-writing, and the plot would be kept together by italicised résumés. Why don't *you* do it ? You could do all the novels in something under three years. Please don't send me a MacStingerish reply. They've already cut Shakespeare's *Hamlet*, Boswell's *Johnson*, and Handel's *Messiah*. And I've just cut Agate's *Ego* !

Ever,

JAMIE

P.S. My favourite minor characters in this great book ? The Native and Mr Towlinson. The first is an enchanting combination of Man Friday and Queequeg. The second is all the devoted people who have looked after me from Freddie Webster onwards. If I am a trifle inconsequent please know that I am writing this at 3 A.M., half in and half out of bed.

P.P.S. Did you see that G. W. Stonier recently expressed his willingness to give all Dickens for three pages of Proust ?

P.P.P.S. Two remarks I came across recently. One about C. D. by that ass Emerson : " He has no insight into character." The other by Emily Eden anent *Pickwick* : " The only bit of fun in India."

P.P.P.P.S. Good night !

Sept. 9   Letter to George Lyttelton :
Sunday.

*Queen Alexandra Mansions, W.C.*2

September 9th, 1945

DEAR GEORGE LYTTELTON,

I am sixty-eight to-day. I propose to celebrate it by *writing* a birthday letter of which you shall be the recipient.

By the time you get this you should have received *Ego* 7. I think you'll agree that Harrap's have produced this beautifully. NO misprints that I can detect, though there are one or two small over-lookings on my part. For instance, on October 9, when I went to Brighton, I appear to have spent the evening both at the films and at the theatre. Actually I went to the pictures in the afternoon. On page 218, entry for October 16, the grammar is a little wonky, and on page 293 the little besom's backside doesn't want a comma after it. But there's nothing I am really worried about except the entry for July 25 on pages 156 and 157. When this left my hands Heredia had no accents, as you know he mustn't have. Authorities : the compilers of *Les Cent Meilleurs Poèmes* (*Lyriques*) *de la Langue Française*, Larousse, who even gives a picture of him without the accents, Dent's *Short Biographical Dictionary of Foreign Literature*, the *Encyclopædia Britannica*, and my brother Edward at the age of fourteen. I have spent a great part of my life keeping Heredia clear of accents. There were none in the original passage which occurs in *Their Hour upon the Stage*. There were none in the page-proofs I passed immediately before printing. And now some well-intentioned person makes me write " Hérédia " twice ! I feel exactly as though somebody had made me talk about " out-Héroding Hérod."

Have done pretty well for birthday presents. Cables from Charlie Rogers, my ex-houseboy, and Neville Cardus. From John Barrington a beautiful walking-stick in snake-wood with tortoise-shell handle and gold mounting. From Gwen Chenhalls one pair of socks, one handkerchief, and half a pound of sausages. From Coral Browne, pretty woman and good actress, a bottle of whiskey. From Leo Pavia, Adelaide Ristori's *Études et Souvenirs*. From George Harrap a pipe, and from Jock two tickets for a Beecham Concert. On the whole I think that isn't a bad lot. Anyhow, I'm satisfied. As it is my birthday I shall give myself the pleasure of copying out for you something you will recognise, but in the form in which Ristori spoke it :

" Le Thane de Fife avait une femme. Et maintenant où est-elle ?
Ne pourrai-je jamais rendre ces mains propres ? Assez, Seigneur,
assez, avec tes terreurs tu gâtes tout. Toujours cette odeur de
sang ? Hélas ! tous les parfums de l'Arabie ne pourront jamais
désinfecter cette petite main ! Oh ! oh ! oh ! Lave tes mains, va
mettre ton vêtement de nuit, ne sois pas si pâle ! Je te le répète.
Banco est enseveli et il ne peut sortir de sa tombe ! Au lit ! au lit !
On frappe à la porte, viens ! viens ! viens ici ! donne-moi la main.
Ce qui est fait est fait. Au lit ! au lit ! . . ."

This gives me an idea. I think I shall translate the whole play into
this sort of lingo and then send it to the French Benjamin Britten
to turn into an opera.

Yours ever,
JAMES AGATE

From Jock :

Spooncreel
Maybole
Ayrshire

September 7th, 1945

DEAR JAMIE,

A Very Happy Birthday !

And I'm beginning to believe at last that you *do* grow old,
because you begin to use *understatement* after years of abusing the
other thing. You say, " Don't be offended if I say that there is
beginning to be a shade of fainéantisme about you ! " *Beginning*,
indeed ! And *a shade*, forsooth ! I know all about myself——

And yes ! I *will/shall* write for Home and van Thal a " Letter
to a Godson on Serendipity—its Meaning, Use, and Abuse." My
self-knowledge, my Macbethian " strange and self abuse," will
stand me in good stead and help me to't. And I shall drive myself
—nay, flog myself—into sending them 12,000 relevant words on or
before the 7th March, 1946. That is an undertaking, a promise.

And now about this not-easily-defensible notion of your abridging Dickens—or my abridging Dickens—or anybody's abridging
Dickens. It *could* be done—I might even permit myself to go so
far even as to say it *should* be done—for schoolchildren between
twelve and sixteen (who read drastically abridged Swift and Defoe
anyhow). Even there I would insist on its being done (if it must be
done), not by any one person, but by a committee of six highly
sensible Dickensians. For a random suggestion :

(1) J. B. Priestley
(2) W. H. Salmon (editor of the *Times* weekly, with whom I
     had a wondrous Dickens pow-wow at the Press Club the
     other night)
(3) Robert Lynd
(4) Rebecca West
(5) James Bone, and
(6) either You or Me.

For adults I would not give the scheme any sanction. Any adult worth a hoot tries Dickens once and, if he finds him palatable at all, re-reads his own favourite sections *à son gré*. Here are we, Jamie, you and I, two adults ; both presumably worth several hoots in some respects, and we don't begin to agree in detail about a novel which finds us both madly enthusiastic—*Dombey and Son*.

You want to cut Captain Cuttle (who is " desperately unfunny " to you and G. K. Chesterton, but delightful in all he says and does to the rest of the world) ; the Toodle family in part (and I wholly adore it) ; half of Florence (who is to me the most tolerable and touching of all of Dickens's maidens) ; and (more understandably) good Mrs Brown and one or two minor characters.

But, look you ! some of your likes are my aversions. What do you, or we, or our committee, do about that ? I have always found Joey Bagstock exceedingly tiresome, and I skip (when I re-read) the innumerable descriptions of his incipient apoplexy—just as most people probably skip the nauseating references to James Carker's teeth. *No, no, no !* And no again—the more I think of it ! He would be a very brave man who should abridge a Dickens novel for adult readers. You try it, if you dare. It would be like trying to kidnap Master Alexander MacStinger ! (And *did* you observe, by the way, how Mrs MacS. quietened that masterful mite during her wedding to Captain Bunsby ?)

Ever thy
JOCK

P.S. Boswell's *Johnson*, Handel's *Messiah*, and *Ego* are beside the point. They are not fiction. Or are they ?

*Queen Alexandra Mansions, W.C.*2
September 10*th*, 1945

DEAR JOCK,

Ye'll dae a fine Letter, and Rubicon will be proud of his Gemel. Erudite allusion for the use of German editors later on.

Yes and no about your Dickens suggestions. I would trust Rebecca West with an abridgment of Shakespeare but not Dickens. No woman has ever laughed at C. D., and the sex is not going to start now. On the whole I think I am against a committee. My plan would be one novel, one abridger. As follows :

Pickwick	J. A. ?
David Copperfield	J. B. Priestley
Bleak House	Bernard Darwin
Great Expectations	Neville Cardus
Dombey and Son	Alan Dent
Martin Chuzzlewit	George Lyttelton
Nicholas Nickleby	Robert Lynd
Little Dorrit	Hugh Kingsmill
Our Mutual Friend	D. B. Wyndham Lewis

There was an enchanting little scene in the Café Royal last night. This was when John Barrington, the irresponsible young man about whom you will read in *Ego* 7, approached my table bearing a tray on which was a cake of his own baking with sixty-eight matches stuck in it. Which were then lit while a small choir of his friends sang "Happy Birthday to You." The C. R. has known some extraordinary scenes, [but nothing, I take it, pleasanter than this. There was champagne, and I wish you had been there.

Ever,

JAMIE

Sept. 12
Wednesday.
I am perfectly well aware that one should not lose one's temper over trifles. I lose mine *when they interfere with my work*. Wrote to the Telephone Manager in Gerrard Street yesterday to inform him that the war is now over and I am tired of wasting one hour a day owing to his blasted telephone not working. Threaten a letter to *The Times* giving an hour-by-hour account of one day's attempts to avail myself of a service for which I pay a half-yearly bill of over twenty pounds. End with the polite assurance that I don't want to make a fuss, but can something be done please? Result, the 'phone to-day has been completely dead—at any rate up to five o'clock, while all messages to engineers from outside telephone boxes have proved unavailing. If this continues I shall go over the road, dial 999, and demand the immediate presence of police, fire-engines, and ambulance.

I cannot understand why the little Carlton Theatre in the Tottenham Court Road is not full to overflowing. The custom there is to have one French film and one British one; by telephoning beforehand one can always find out when the British rubbish has exhausted itself. The French films are invariably entrancing. At least they are entrancing to me. I saw to-night a model little film called *Les Yeux Noirs*, with an exquisite performance by Simone Simon and a most moving one by Harry Baur, in my opinion as good an actor as Jannings at his best. When is the British film industry going to wake up to the fact that it hasn't got an actor who can play men of a certain age? Always with the exception of Frederick Leister, whom it doesn't use, and Alfred Drayton, whom it won't use except for farce. There is a delicious performance, too, by Jules Berry, who seduces like a gentleman, and not, as a British director would insist, like a counter-jumper in sports jacket and size eleven in tennis shoes.

Sept. 15
Saturday.

Letter from Ivor Brown :

> *In the Chilterns, pretty,*
> *little, odious country—*
> *odious, that is, if you find*
> *big country and moorland*
> *amorous. This leads to*
> *cogitation on why odious*
> *should be a passive*
> *adjective and amorous*
> *active. There is no*
> *answer, as in most queries*
> *concerning English usage.*

Sept. 14*th*

DEAR JAMES,

Thank you very much for *Ego* 7, which you ought to have called The Seven Against Ego or Septem Contra Me, the Seven being Jock, Leo, Lyttelton, Van Thal, Cardus, Shakespeare, and Amalgamated Anons. You are getting lazy—incredible—and relying too much on the stooges. Of course, you can write them (bar Shakespeare) out of the field, but the man that pays his fifteen bob merits more of you and less of other people. When *you* are writing the book it is better ' Ego ' than ever : when not, not.

Yours,

IVOR

Sept. 16
Sunday.

Went to Birmingham yesterday to judge the Harness Classes at the Show given by the Sutton Coldfield Equitation Club. Had a look at my foal, which is coming on nicely and gives every sign of living up to her name, " My Pretty."

Sept. 18
Tuesday.

It is the firm conviction of all newspapers with what Montague called " the largest circulation in the solar system " that their readers are interested only in headlines. There is a magnificent example of this in the paper to-day. Soberly the article sets forth that

The whaling season opened yesterday with the departure for the Antarctic of two of the world's biggest factory ships, the British-built *Sir James Clark Ross* and the *Empire Venture*—each manned by 300 Norwegians—and 16 whale-catchers and trawlers.

And the sub-editor says to himself rightly : Who cares ? He then remembers that increased whaling means increase of oil for all sorts of things, including cosmetics. Which gives him his headline :

IT MAY MEAN LIPSTICKS

Whereupon half the female population of these islands apprises itself of the departure for the Antarctic of, etc., etc. *C'est gigantesque !* Indeed, it's almost as gigantic as the whales. Or as Leo's typing, whereby "new era of prosperity" becomes "new ear of prosperity," "Jock" turns into "Kock," and Pinero writes a play called *His House in Cider*.

Sept. 19 In the *Daily Telegraph*'s Personal Column :
Wednesday.

Elderly critic's godson, fourteen weeks, thanks *Daily Telegraph* reader for beautiful rattle.

Sept. 21 I am no transmogrifier. I do *not* want to see *Gerontius*
Friday. danced, hear the *Eroica* arranged for string quartet, or *Das Lied von der Erde* transcribed for piano-accordion. I do *not* want to read *Tartuffe* as a novel, or see *Die Welt als Wille und Vorstellung* filmed. I just don't believe in the artistic impulse behind the transmogrification. Let's take X's best-selling novel, *Peepshow for Cyclops*. I just don't believe that one morning X's agent goes to him and says, " Say, boss, d'you reckon print's your book's best vehicle ? I see it as a play, and so do Messitup's. You'll have to change the setting from Biarritz to Blackpool. As a matter of fact, I mentioned this to Stanley Blockhead. He set to work and got it into three acts that'll amaze you." Or that a couple of years later the agent goes again to X and says, using the grammar of his kind, " Look here, between you and I, that play notion didn't quite work out. I see *Peepshow* as a film. In fact, so does Morris Dummkopf, who wants to produce it with Franz Esel as director. You'll have to turn it round. Make your British soldier an American marine, and substitute Bataan for Blackpool." I shouldn't mind these well-intentioned worsifications. But I just don't believe they happen. I believe the agent goes to X and says, " Say, Big Boy, just cut that artistic bunk, willya ? Jeezers, are you nuts ? Turn the darned thing into a play somebody can make a film of afterwards ! What, you won't ? Well, then, let Hymie Greenstuff do it. I got him to dramatise Lysol's *Fresh Woods*. *New Pastures* he called it. We sold it to Niagara Films for a packet. They made it for Harry Twitch and called it *Blue Mantle*. It cleaned up everywhere." Every moment of to-night's *A Bell for Adano* proclaimed that it was not conceived as a play. And why call the hero Joppolo ? " Melancholy trisyllable of sound, unison to Nincompoop and every name vituperative under heaven." I tried all the variations. Proppolo and Coppolo, Doppolo, Floppolo, Moppolo—fond spouse would be Mrs Moppolo—Sloppolo, Woppolo. The bell ? This merely shows the author of the original story believing that money-grubbing Sicilian peasants drool like sentimental American novelists.

DEATH OF LEO

Sept. 26
Wednesday.
   A woman friend of Leo's, who was to have taken him to hospital this morning for a rest cure, telephoned me at eleven o'clock that he had passed away. " I couldn't have wished a better end for him. It seems he went to bed very happy, grumbling at the best of landladies, and died in his sleep." He had cried wolf so often that it was not until last week that I thought about a doctor, who insisted upon a long rest. To occupy his mind I made him spend yesterday reading and reviewing a book about music. He produced an admirable, concise, logical, and faultlessly typed notice ending : " The usual misprints are happily absent. Perhaps this is because the book has been produced in America, where proof-readers seem to take more trouble than they do in this dear, slap-dash land." Dear, muddle-headed Leo ! I had asked him whether one should spell Austen with an ' e ' as a *first* name. Whereupon he threw up his hands and said, " Jane did ! " Just as I was remonstrating about this the door-bell rang, and a soldier announced a car for Greenford ; I had forgotten all about a lecture engagement made some months ago. I said, " Well, Leo, this means no silly nonsense about good-byes." I did, however, manage to get out something about his unending devotion. But he cut this short, and waved me out of the room. Even so, I had no notion that anything serious was impending. His courage in sticking to his job deceived us all.

Sept. 27
Thursday.
   At the theatre to-night Jock handed me this :

> 33 *King Street*
> *Covent Garden*
> *W.C.*2
>
> 26*th September*, 1945

DEAR JAMIE,
   I am genuinely sorry—but rather more for you than for Leo, who is already in his Jewish heaven and fussing in the library of that dubious paradise, I've no doubt !

It is all very odd this death-and-dying business. You may remember me telling you something about my queer " psychic " (I suppose it needs the inverted commas) experience at the death of our dear kind Hugh Walpole. Well, as soon as I put the tele-phone down this morning I found myself at my piano and playing without choice—if you know what I mean—the first and last movements of Schumann's *Waldscenen* suite—the *Eintritt* and the *Abschied*. My hands just picked out this particular suite, I don't know why, and put it up to be played. I have never heard Leo play it, though he has in his time played me lots of out-of-the-way Schumann. It sounded wonderfully appropriate—the questing romantic entry into the forest, and the resigned and not over-sad leaving of it. And I found myself playing with far more than my usual expressiveness—with an expressiveness I can't usually com-mand. It was, I know (though you may think me mad to say so), just dear old Leo saying Hail and Farewell to me—with a good deal of his own superb musicianship especially *telepathed* for the occasion.

He was the queerest, most exasperating, most endearing mixture of Lamb's George Dyer, and Proust's Bloch, and a wondrous spluttering, splenetic, benign character in Turgenev's *Rudin* called—as I remember—Pigasov. I am unable to imagine your Grape Street flat without him, and I shall very much miss his shuffle, his drawl, his screech, his snuffle, his laugh, his com-plaints, his compliments, his Viennese courtesies, *and* his brains, whenever I call on you again.

Sympathetically,

JOCK

Sept. 28
Friday.   *The Times* prints this :

MR I. L. PAVIA

Mr James Agate writes :

" Leo," as he was generally called, was immensely proud of having studied under Leschetizky, and even more proud of that notice which a famous musical critic gave him when he appeared as a juvenile prodigy at the St James's Hall some sixty years ago. " He went at the *Waldstein* sonata like a young avalanche, *fortissimo sempre crescendo e prestissimo sempre accelerando*, keeping his feet cleverly over the straightforward bits, staggering gamely through the syncopated passages, going head-over-heels up and down the flights of octaves, and finishing, flushed but unbeaten, after a record-breaking neck-or-nothing ' reading ' that would have made Rubinstein gasp and Mme Schumann faint." The boy was destined to be a failure in a wider field than piano-playing, but also to prove in his own person—to the everlasting credit of the law of compensation—that the lady in the Henry James story was not talking entire nonsense when she reflected that " There was some-thing a failure was, a failure in the market, that a success somehow wasn't."

Leo Pavia had a measure of genius, and all of it strictly un-marketable. He was a walking literary as well as musical reference library, and knew most of whatever there is to be known about Restoration comedy, Johnson, Jane Austen, Dickens, Thackeray, Goethe, Schiller, Ibsen. He could quote Richardson ! He trans-lated Wilde's plays into German, wrote a great deal of music that was half Johann and half Richard Strauss, and was for many years a player of professional bridge in which he combined maximum skill with fantastically poor cards. No man ever enjoyed bad luck more ! He was schizophrenic long before the thing became fashionable, half of him being entirely rational, the other half living in a world in which it was taken for granted that pigs have wings and cows jump over the moon. His piano-playing was marked by an exquisite cantabile, but he could not pick up one object without knocking over two others. He was a combination of Lamb's friend George Dyer, Tchehov's Ephikhódof, and half a dozen characters in *Alice in Wonderland*. He was a superb talker who never listened, or, listening, got whatever was said the wrong way round. He had the best sense of pure fun, plus the finest wit, of any man I have been privileged to know, with a gift for making conversational *gaffes* both natural and cultivated. Vulgarity of mind died in his presence. His death creates a void which his friends will not attempt to fill.

By preposterous coincidence the only other obituary notice in *The Times* to-day is one of the composer Leo most hated—Béla Bartók.

Sept. 29   Two pews were more than enough to hold the little
Saturday.   gathering at the Crematorium. Helen Roeder ; Betty Ricketts ; George Mathew ; my houseboy, Arthur Bates, breaking his holiday and bringing a posy; and J. A. The door of the chapel had been left open, letting in a flood of autumn sunshine and the twittering of a few late birds. From the organ the Adagio from the Sonata Pathétique, then Helen, George, and I took it in turns to read " Fear no more the heat o' the sun," after which the slow movement from the *Emperor*. Leo had always said he wanted Shakespeare and Beethoven.

Oct. 3   " Surtout, pas de génie ! " wrote Villiers de l'Isle-Adam
Wednesday.   at the head of one of his *Contes Cruels*. All about an aspiring journalist who, being asked his price, replied, " Three francs a line." The editor observing that not even Hugo or du Terrail made such extravagant demands, the young man coldly remarked, " I see that M. le Directeur fails to realise that I am *totally* unknown ! " He goes on to swear that he is possessed of an unbeatable *niaiserie* of ideas and an incomparable banality of style.

To which the editor replies, " O Youth ! O springtime of life ! Let me tell you, young man, that to be utterly without talent is to be an outstanding figure. That I have spent twenty years and half a million francs in pursuit of this unique phenomenon. That my office-boy is the author of four magnificent dramatic works which have been crowned by four academies ! Convince me, young man, of your perfect nullity, show me a manuscript full of faulty spelling, of which the French is not even approximately French, and all of it written in a handwriting that nobody can read, satisfy me that your claim to be a complete imbecile is valid, and I will pay you *six* francs a line ! "

Interviewing several aspiring secretaries, I ask each what his ruling passion is. The first says reciting Gertrude Stein. The second elects for reading Edith Sitwell in bed. The third, when asked whether he has read *Pickwick*, replies superiorly, " Yes. But in French, of course ! " I finally settle on a young man whose passion is writing essays on *Carlyle considered as Humorist*, and *Dickens as Social Reformer*. But there is this in his favour—*he is as ignorant as one can reasonably expect*, having read no line of Scott, Thackeray, or George Eliot. (It goes without saying that he can spout Gerard Manley Hopkins, D. H. Lawrence, and T. S. Eliot by the yard.) Obviously very willing, types quickly, efficiently, and intelligently, has no notion of spelling, and helps me with my English ! For example, I am told that I must not call Falstaff " the old toper, sorner, fribble." The first two words are permissible, it seems, but not fribble. And then it starts. Patiently I explain that fribble was the word used by Henry James to describe Balzac's Baron Hulot. Which means that I must then tell him who Hulot was, and throw in a kindly word about Balzac and James. In the middle of which it occurs to me that fribble was not H. J.'s word but George Moore's —which entails a lecture on G. M. ! By which time I have forgotten what I was going to say about the old toper, sorner, and whatever third appellation John Booth-Palmer would approve. However, one cannot have everything, and I have always thought that the editor in the French story demanded too much !

Oct. 6   Brother Mycroft sends me a cutting from the *Man-*
Saturday.   *chester Evening News* for October 4, '45.

The Boy with Horse-mania

Magistrates at Manchester County Court to-day heard a novel complaint. The father of a 16-year-old Stretford boy, charged with stealing a cycle, said : " I have a motor mechanic business in which I want him to help me, but he has horse-mania.

" He leaves me to go sleeping in stables, and associates with any characters so long as they have something to do with horses. He is so horse-mad that I don't know what to do with him."

The boy was remanded for a medical report. Why? Shallow, and even Silence, would have had enough wit to tell the father to put the lad among horses.

During the war the Savage Club dinners became luncheons. To-night the dinners were resumed ; I attended and presented the Club with the marble bust carved by Sarah. (See *Ego* 6, p. 195.)

Oct. 7   Cancelled my engagement at Birmingham next Sunday.
Sunday.   The train journey, two lectures at 3 and 6 P.M., the wait
on New Street station for a train which is bound to be late, to arrive at Euston and queue up for non-existent taxis, and then walk home, without a meal since breakfast—no, it isn't good enough. Have offered to go if I am motored from and to Grape Street. Doctor concurs.

Wrote 150 words for an advertisement for second-hand machinery. Also 1200 words telling Moscow why I think Edith Evans is a good actress.

Our film critics :

Shakespeare has provided Ida Lupino with the title of her book on four generations of Lupinos. She calls it *The Dusty Way*, taken from her late father Stanley's favourite quotation from *Macbeth*, " All our yesterdays have lighted fools the dusty way to death."
Sunday paper

Oct. 8   In a letter from a young highbrow :
Monday.

But what we can hardly learn, except with great difficulty and a sublime thick-skinedness [*sic*] and patience, is that other people who evince the same wrong-headedness as we ourselves did in our own time of madcap wool-gathering and flaunting egoism of youth have just as much right to despise us for having passed to that measure of understanding which is, to their minds, something near the border of indistinction and extinction as we have to despise them for being, as we think, arrested morons of the thinest [*sic*] water.

Ends by comparing me unfavourably, *very* unfavourably, with " Palinurus." " There you have a writer full of wise sores [*sic*] and really modern instances."

231

Oct. 9
Tuesday.
So, fifty years after Edmond de Goncourt's death—he
stipulated twenty—we are to have the full text of the
Journal. *The Times* is lukewarm about this, and there
is opposition in France. I quote from the seventeenth issue of the
new and admirable French weekly, *Spectateur*, principally devoted to
theatre and films.

Edmond de Goncourt collectionnait les racontars scandaleux qui,
même refroidis par le temps, gardent une odeur nauséabonde.
Évidemment les gens dont il est question là-dedans sont disparus
depuis belle lurette, et beaucoup de ces histoires sont déjà très
éventées. . . . Victor Hugo, à l'extrémité de son âge, gardait un
goût puissant pour les jeunes personnes. . . . Zola, qui avait
épousé l'amie de son impécunieuse jeunesse, fit, devenu célèbre,
deux enfants à sa femme de chambre. . . . Alphonse Daudet est
mort d'une maladie très pénible, dont périrent plusieurs rois de
France. . . . Maupassant, avant de finir chez le docteur Blanche,
dormit avec pas mal de dames grandes ou petites . . . les belles
révélations, en vérité! Et tout à fait de nature à rehausser le
prestige littéraire de la France. Paul Bourget, lorsqu'il était
étudiant, a fait ses farces. Catulle Mendès a aimé Augusta Holmès
qui . . . Mirbeau a épousé Alice Regnault qui . . . Léon Daudet
a divorcé d'avec Jeanne Hugo qui . . . Qu'est-ce-que tous ces
commérages apportent de neuf dans l'histoire de la " vie littéraire,"
pour employer la pompeuse expression de Goncourt? Cet homme
consignait religieusement de pareilles misères, sans omettre
les détails les plus crus, les particularités les moins ragoûtantes,
reniflant avec délice les sécrétions les plus faisandées de la nature
humaine. Loin d'en réduire l'importance, il en aurait volontiers
ajouté. Il y a en lui du Restif de La Bretonne, du Maxime du
Camp, et de l'Horace de Vieil-Castel. Si on publie toute sa friperie
intégralement,—qu'est-ce-qu'on dira ? On dira que les grands
hommes ont leurs faiblesses et que l'humanité ne sent pas toujours
bon. Mais on dira surtout qu'Edmond de Goncourt était un vieux
cochon, doublé d'un hypocrite, qui faisait des mamours aux confrères dont il volait les secrets pour les déshonorer devant la
postérité. Est-ce un tel résultat que cherchent les membres de
l'Académie Goncourt, chatouillés par le démon de la curiosité, et
ne vaudrait-il pas mieux

. . . qu'en un profond oubli
Cet horrible secret demeure enseveli ?

I disagree with the writer in the *Spectateur*. I want to know
everything that can be known about considerable artists. The point
—though Goncourt may not have intended it—is not that Victor
Hugo ran after little girls, but that the runner after little girls should
write imperishable masterpieces.

232

Oct. 10   Letter from Leo's and my little Irish friend :
Wednesday.

18 *Park View Avenue*
Harold's Cross
Dublin
6th October, 1945

DEAR JAMES,

I am desperately sorry.

Like Harold Skimpole I am a " mere child " and my emotions are usually false. But I am genuinely sorry. Leo was always very kind to me in his letters, and I don't think I ever fully realised that he was seventy and ill. It seems incredible that a sick man could write with such unfailing cheerfulness, but I might have known from passages such as this :

" I grow serious. And if you had had a heat-wave and then a week of freezing cold, rain, snow, sleet, *and* a cold in the head so violent that when you sneeze the houses on the other side of the road commence to wobble . . . you would be in a grave state of mind. I was so grave I thought for a whole day of nothing *but* the grave. And about the Sting. Sting, do I say ? Not at all ; at the worst, only a mighty clout on the head."

Again :

" I was a cynical child, bitter-tongued and ruthless. That I have grown so sweet and benevolent in later years, is just the mellowing of a vintage wine. Oh, John, pray that the dust and the cobwebs may not cover the bottle all too soon ! "

I've nothing more to say. I can't be flippant in the realisation that Leo won't answer me. But this is awful ! I shall shed tears in a moment. You are very lucky to have had a brother like Edward Agate and a friend like Isidore Leo Pavia.

Sincerely,
J. E. JORDAN

Oct. 11   From Raymond Mortimer :
Thursday.

As from the Reform Club
*S.W.*1
October 6, 1945

DEAR JAMES AGATE,

I recommend no one to read *Ego* 7, or for that matter any of the *Ego's*, in bed at night, as I have been doing, for one can't put the bloody book away and get to sleep. I am flattered, gratified, amused by your references to me. I hoped my style, like my person, was at least as spare as yours, and now am wondering how to amend it so that the gentle reader won't think me fat.

I want to argue with you about some words, no, not argue, you don't like argument—I want to insinuate some doubts into your blissfully assured mind.

P. 26. *Minoperative. Vive le néologisme*, but this particular example is unplausible. *Minus* isn't an adjective like *magnus*, and wouldn't usage demand *minoroperative* ? I agree that would be a vile word. But isn't yours rather vile too ? I saw a pin-table saloon the other day in the prettiest town in England—it was called The Playdium.

P. 41. " The allusion, of course, is . . ." Why " of course " ? I suspect that Quin was talking to a lady at her tea-table, with a *négrillon* in attendance. Nothing surprising about this— why drag in Hogarth ?

P. 152. I am scribbling this in the country, far from a Dumas, but are you sure that " des amis, des amis comme Prudence " shouldn't be " amies " ? They appear as " elles " in the next sentence.

P. 156. What authority have you for embellishing Heredia with acute accents ? The answer to this, I suspect, may be " Barrès." But Heredia himself never, as far as I know, used the accents. Of course, the pronunciation is as if they were there, but the name is Spanish.

P. 177. *Haphazardly*. Admissible, but is it worthy of so discriminating a word-fancier ? *Haphazard* makes a very pretty adverb with nothing added to it.

P. 251. *de Musset*. You can quote a thousand instances to support you, but is it not better usage to say either *Alfred de Musset* or just *Musset* ? Proust was once hauled over the coals by a friend for the same habit, and answered that he supposed in future he must call the painter Dyck, *tout court*. I'd like to quote Sainte-Beuve to support my view, but I can't find the reference.

P. 255. I doubt if the Duchess of Sermoneta, who is an Italian, would write *Ceracolo*, since there is no such word. But the misprint may be her printer's, not yours.

P. 258. *She looks like I do in a spoon.* I suspect that Mrs Campbell would have said " *as* I do " ?

P. 271. *Bon viveur.* I just don't believe it, though there's a club in a coign of Mayfair with this name. A *bon vivant* is an epicurean like yourself ; a *viveur* is a rake, whether or not like yourself the reader cannot easily discover from your otherwise so strip-teasing volumes. I wouldn't deny the possibility of a *viveur* being *bon*, but don't you mean *bon vivant* ?

I've not forgotten your inconceivable fireworks at the Churchill Club. You were what I once saw advertised in Liguria, a *Professore pirotecnico*. Nor have I forgotten your hospitality. I hope to persuade you soon to eat *chez moi*.

Yours ever,
RAYMOND MORTIMER

P.S. I was interested in the figures you give of the words written by Balzac and Dickens. Can you tell me where to find these ? I have long wanted to know how the great novelists compare in mere productivity. Your own record leaves me flabbergasted. . . .

> . . . and still the wonder grew
> That one small hand could set down all he knew.

I have replied :

*Queen Alexandra Mansions, W.C.*2
October 11*th*, 1945

DEAR RAYMOND MORTIMER,

How nice in a world of atom bombs, strikes, and a shortage of everything except stupidity, to discuss something that really matters.

P. 26. *Minoperative* is a poor thing, but I've created it and I'll stick to it.

P. 41. Because the book of theatre anecdotes from which I got this story went to the trouble of a footnote to make the point about the Hogarth print.

P. 152. Have looked it up and am relieved to find that " amis " is right.

P. 156. When I saw this I could have drunk hot blood ! I enclose a sheet of the page-proof finally passed by me showing the unembellished " e's." And then some clever fellow altered it behind my back.

P. 177. This only shows the danger of using English when French will do. I ought, of course, to have written " armed *à l'improviste.*"

P. 251. Isn't this rather according to the taste and fancy of the individual ? I would go to the stake rather than talk of de Balzac or de Maupassant or de Goncourt. In speaking I generally say Musset, but the balance of the sentence—" Merle Oberon is as much like George Sand as I am like de Musset "—seemed to my ear to require the " de." I'm very likely wrong.[1]

[1] I *am* wrong. As *Ego* 8 was going through the press I received a letter from Belgium containing this paragraph :

" Une seule erreur que je relève dans *Ego* 7 : l'emploi du ' de ' quand vous citez Alfred de Musset sans citer son prénom. On dit ' Alfred de Musset, Alfred de Vigny, Henry de Montherlant, le duc de Saint-Simon,' mais d'autre part ' Vigny, Musset, Montherlant, Saint-Simon,' sans la particule."

P. 255. I am quoting at two removes—Dicky Helme and the Duchess. And possibly Viardot-Garcia got it wrong. I suspect the word to be *Cenacolo*. I have no Italian dictionary and am not an authority on da Vinci.

P. 258. No, I think that's what Mrs Campbell said. I should certainly say, " He stammers like I do," though I should write, " He stammers as I do." After all, which of us, waiting on a railway platform and seeing a train draw in, has not said, " This is us " ? Do you suggest, " This is we ! " ?

P. 271. Don't think I can plead guilty ! What I mean to imply is a *bon vivant* with a dash of the *viveur*, and that is why I created *bon viveur*, knowing that it isn't French. I suppose that when one plays about with words one ought to make it clear that one is playing about.

Re Balzac and Dickens. I have no authority for the figures, which are my own assessment. But what, after all, are seven, eight, or even ten million words ? I read in to-day's *Evening News* that a Mr Charles Hamilton, the creator, under the pen-name of Frank Richards, of Billy Bunter, that perpetual schoolboy whose adventures filled the pages of *The Magnet* for years and years and years—I read that this genius estimates his total output at 60,000,000 words !

I want to thank you for taking so much trouble. This question of accuracy has become an obsession with me. In the seven volumes of *Ego* I have found fifty-three definite errors which have crept in despite a vigilance fantastic to the point of brain-sickliness. My diary may be forgotten with me, but there's a possibility that it may be reprinted, and I hate to think of error being perpetuated. I am doing all I can to prevent this. The errata are carefully copied into each volume of my specially bound set. My publishers, my literary executors, and my lawyers have copies. Thus have I tried to make assurance doubly, trebly, quadruply sure. All the same, I shouldn't be in the least surprised to find you appearing in 2045 A.D. as Mortimer Raymond ! Anyhow, bless you for the letter.

Ever,

JAMES AGATE

Oct. 12
Friday.

Our intellectuals again ! The new outbreak is called *Focus One.* I cull from a poem entitled *Broadjump* by Don Roscher :

> Day's first urine
> Finds me desperately embracing
> The anonymity that is To-morrow.

To me this is not poetry. But then, I should not consider

> Brushing with hasty steps the *dung* away

to be poetry.

Next I try the prose : *Nine Men Upsidedown* by Reginald Drake. I read :

> Outside the clangour's clash a butcher trips, gripped in the shark-maw hulk of mutton falls, head in sheep's carcase nipped at neck, his leather legs and blue-white apron sprawls.

One has only to re-set this to see that it is verse of some kind :

> Outside the clangour's clash a butcher trips,
> Gripped in the shark-maw hulk of mutton falls,
> Head in sheep's carcase nipped at neck,
> His leather legs and blue-white apron sprawls.

Again :

> Awhile the clammering rookblack gossips crane,
> And flowerstall chalkface stares with redlip pout. . . .

And so it goes on. I can see the point of microbes and black-beetles ; the highbrow defeats me. It would be interesting, by the way, to know at what date the highbrow first came into being. There were none when I was a boy ; we did not dream of calling intellectual giants like Browning highbrows. The term was not used about any of the contributors to *The Yellow Book*. I still think the best thing ever said about the genre is Basil Macdonald Hastings's " There's nothing like consulting a highbrow if you want to hear something that is funny as well as daft."

Oct. 13
Saturday.
Watching Alec Clunes's Hamlet at the Arts Theatre last night I remembered the postscript to Hazlitt's essay entitled " The Fight " : " Toms called upon me the next day, to ask me if I did not think the fight a complete thing ? I said I thought it was." It was only when I turned up the essay this morning that I realised that Hazlitt used as motto :

> . . . The *fight*, the *fight's* the thing,
> Wherein I'll catch the conscience of the king.

And remembered that the Gas-man, showing his tremendous right hand, would say, " This is *the grave-digger*." Odd ! Decided that Alec's Hamlet was complete in itself, which means that to-morrow I shall not be comparing it with any other Hamlet. I liked it very much and went round to Alec's dressing-room afterwards. For two reasons. First, to tell him how good he had been, and second, to blow him up for leaving out the jingle about " Imperious Cæsar." That Shakespeare could, wittingly or unwittingly, at this juncture, contrive something that is less than great poetry and more than doggerel, something with a hint of the nursery rhyme that *in its place* is better than grandiosity's tumbling seas—this is sheer miracle.

Oct. 17
Wednesday.
In *Ego* 4, page 147, I wrote, " How long was Robinson Crusoe on his island before he saw Man Friday's footstep ? Answer : Ten years." Where, if you please, is the flaw in that ? In the length of time ? No. Where I went wrong, and where, I suppose, ninety-nine people out of a hundred would go wrong, is in taking the footstep to be Man Friday's. It wasn't, as an unknown friend has been to a great deal of pains to point out. Here is the evidence, the pages being taken from the edition published by S. W. Partridge and Co. :

" Being now in the eleventh year of my residence, and, as I have said, my ammunition growing low, I set myself to study some art to trap and snare the goats, to see whether I could not catch some of them alive ; and particularly, I wanted a she-goat great with young. . . . It happened one day, about noon, going towards my boat, I was exceedingly surprised with the print of a man's naked foot on the shore, which was very plain to be seen on the sand " (p. 110).

R. C. reflects : " That I had lived there fifteen years now and had not met with the least shadow or figure of any people yet " (p. 122).

He sees his first trace of savages : " It was now the month of December, as I said above, in my twenty-third year ; and this, being the southern solstice (for winter I cannot call it), was the particular time of my harvests, and required me to be pretty much abroad in the fields, when, going out early in the morning, even before it was thorough daylight, I was surprised with seeing a light of some fire upon the shore, at a distance from me of about two miles, toward that part of the island where I had observed some savages had been, as before, and not on the other side—but, to my great affliction, it was on my side of the island " (p. 137).

He cannot sleep : " It was one of the nights in the rainy season in March, the four-and-twentieth year of my first setting foot in this island of solitude, I was lying in my bed or hammock, awake, very well in health, had no pain, no distemper, no uneasiness of body, nor any uneasiness of mind more than ordinary, but could by no means close my eyes, that is, so as to sleep. . . . In my reflections upon the state of my case since I came on shore on this island, I was comparing the happy posture of my affairs in the first years of my habitation here, with the life of anxiety, fear, and care which I had lived in ever since I had seen the print of a foot in the sand " (p. 148).

He meets Friday : " About a year and a half after I entertained these notions (and by long musing had, as it were, resolved them all into nothing, for want of an occasion to put them into execution) I was surprised one morning by seeing no less than five canoes all on shore together on my side of the island, and the people who belonged to them all landed and out of my sight." Then follows the famous account of Crusoe's rescue of the savage (p. 152).

And here is the K. O.: "I was now entered on the seven-and-twentieth year of my captivity in this place; though the three last years that I had this creature with me ought rather to be left out of the account" (p. 174).

My correspondent ends this letter: "From this it will appear that the footprint was not Man Friday's at all, but was seen some eleven years after Crusoe's shipwreck and thirteen years before Friday came into the picture. I trust that in some future *Ego* you will see fit to put this serious matter to rights."

Oct. 18
Thursday.
  'Sblood, but is there no more "to" a Greek tragedy than to a musical comedy? (I am writing this immediately after the Old Vic's production of *Œdipus* at the New Theatre.) It is proper that after *Pass Down the Car, Please!* the producer should be haled out of the wings to praise the wardrobe mistress and tell us who arranged the dances. Proper because musical comedy has no effect on the mind. But the whole point of Greek tragedy was to stir the Greek mind profoundly, and send it home reflecting that no man is to be counted happy until he is dead. The Greek audience was not depressed? Like Mrs Gummidge, it revelled in depression? I am using a non-Greek mentality to look into a Greek one? All this is not the point. *The old tragedy is profoundly moving even if you don't believe a word of it.* And then Michel Saint-Denis ruined it with a speech about how nice it was to be producing plays again, and even nicer to be associated with Dame Sybil. After which he meticulously and categorically thanked everybody. In the world of opera, where the sublime and the ridiculous are one, this nonsense is just not tolerated. At the end of *Tristan* no producer comes forward to thank Messrs Squills for the love-philtre, or Messrs Cordage and Wain for the new rigging. Nor do they follow *Elektra* with *The Pirates of Penzance*! Who wants to see *The Critic* after *Œdipus*? I didn't and wouldn't. And so left, declining to entertain an Œdipuff complex.

Oct. 24
Wednesday.
  Ego 7 published.
  Letter from Clifford Bax:

D2 *Albany, W.*1
23 *October*, 1945

MY DEAR JAMES,
  Only twenty-four hours ago I was writing to thank you for *Gemel*, a gift which was totally unexpected: and now here I am writing once more to Grape Street and to thank you for *Ego* 7. But, if in one sense only, I am a confirmed Egoist, and therefore

239

had already snapped up a copy at Prince's Bookshop. I have sent it to Meum Stewart.

I thoroughly agree with myself—that we are not quite good enough for *Ego*. Crabb Robinson had all the luck. Goethe really was a considerable mind. Hazlitt we agree about. And then there was Coleridge who presumably was NOT a bore ; Keats, Shelley, Byron, and Wordsworth, the old prig, and delightful Lamb. What you could have made of them. . . . Still, although you are not nearly selective enough, *Ego* is, I believe, more readable than Bennett's companionable Journals. I suspect you would be wise to let humour run in and out like an April breeze in a copse, and not to search for it quite so diligently. Nevertheless, I have not ceased telling myself that the ants have no navy.

Gemel is extremely clever—so far as I have read in it : but it doesn't progress, and you made the ruinous error of buttonholing your reader. Surely you realise that the object of a novelist or story-teller is to draw the listener into the story ? But you cannot do this if you make your book in some degree a dialogue—no, monologue—between Author and Reader. It is as though the actors in a play were every now and then to say, like Bully Bottom, " I'm not really a ferocious lion. Just imagine me with my feet on the mantelpiece," and so on. You destroy your own spell.

Going back to Dryden, do you know his exquisite lyric " When Alexis lay pressed . . . " ? I would have put it in my anthology with pride, only it would not " do " for schools.

Thank you for the books and for the spirit which sped them hither.

Yours ever,

CLIFFORD BAX

I have replied :

MY DEAR C. B.,

It is possible that the characters in *Ego* with the exception of Charles Burgess are small Fry. But one must do as one can, as Dr Johnson remarked.

I accept your criticism about the too-diligent search for comic relief and have crossed out yesterday's entry about the October gale doing its strip-trees act.

Ever,

J. A.

Oct. 30   From my little Irish friend :
Tuesday.

18 *Park View Avenue*
Harold's Cross
Dublin

27. 10. 1945

DEAR JAMES,

Many, many thanks for *Ego* 7, in which I am engrossed. You really can't realise what a pleasure it is to be able to have at least one of your books in my possession. Of the twenty-seven books of yours which I have read, *Ego* 7 is the first I have owned. The book seems to me a great deal less vulgar than *Ego's* 1 to 5 (I haven't read 6).

Page 15. I believe *Ego* will become, after some preliminary ups-and-downs, a classic. A few years after your death, people will cease to read *Ego*. Then, after a century or so, some clever young man will "discover" you. Whereupon, people will read the *Ego's*, and then write books about them. Then, essays will be written about your "circle," and enquiries will be made. . . .

Pages 160–162. I'm very interested in what you say about Oscar's plays. I myself can only bear *The Importance* and *Salome*. The others creak, and are exceedingly dull. Recently in this God-forsaken city Mr Edwards produced *An Ideal Husband*. As soon as I heard it was to be done I started a campaign against it. I besieged Mr Edwards (who, by the way, has grown tired of me ; the novelty of being told your business by a child wears off) with complaints. But it was produced, I was bored to death, and everything was a great success. Not that I object to artificiality. I adore Congreve and Sheridan. But two hundred years have not yet tarnished the gold of the characters of *The Way of the World* and *The School for Scandal*. Fifty years have sadly chipped the gilt-paint of Oscar's creations.

Page 280. George Moore. Once, when I was more priggish than I am now, I thought G. M. an odious character. Careful reading and re-reading of *Ave, Salve,* and *Vale* taught me how wrong I was. He had, I think, a singularly fresh and unspoiled mind. I, a schoolboy, take myself very seriously. I take my views on sex, religion, and politics, all very seriously. George Moore was another schoolboy who did much the same. A proof of his eager, schoolboy-eager mind is the perfect gravity with which he related his expedition with Æ on bicycles, in search of the ancient Irish gods. He was always credulous and always absurd in a manner startlingly like mine. The "sinning" of G. M. can be taken just as seriously as the "sinning" of a schoolboy. Susan Mitchell, in her very good book on George, wrote, "Mr Moore is no Rabelais, his Irish nature forbids it." And again, "Perhaps the Latins can sin gracefully, the Irish cannot." Which hits the nail on the head. G. M. was a very great literary craftsman, but he never grew out of his callowness.

In case you're interested, Dublin is getting crazier and crazier, vulgarer and vulgarer. If things continue as they are, Dublin will become the stronghold of Philistinism. The latest UNFORGIV-ABLE eccentricity has been to present *A Midsummer Night's Dream* in Persian settings and costumes. Everybody (except Sybil Thorndike's son, Christopher Casson, who played Oberon) seemed to have his mouth full of half-masticated buns.

I beg and implore you for a picture of Leo ! He himself promised me one " when I get back all the things I have given to various people to take care of."

My very best wishes, dear James,

J. E. JORDAN

Paul Howard, Leo's old friend, sends me by air-mail from Australia Leo's last letter to him. I cull:

We have a high opinion of 7, full of me as usual. He's busy with 8 now. No one ever plays Godowsky nowadays here. The pianists are always sniffy about the poor old darling, say he is too overladen and what not. Then you simply can't get a copy of any of his works either new or second-hand. I have toured London in vain. And most difficult to get in New York, I'm told. Why don't you have your copies photographed and distribute them, as Leopold used to do with his MSS.? My admiration is as great as ever, but I have nothing to feed it on except memory. And when we moved from Swiss Cottage the Symphonic Metamorphoses were lost in the transit. I hear an old gentleman in Shropshire possesses a copy of the Albeniz Tango-transcription and sits on it all day lest it gets stolen. The only copy in England, so they say. The British Museum has two pages of the Triakontameron, but it's still closed. Do ask your Governor-General whether he can't do something about it—I hear he plays the Sonata marvellously. You don't deserve this nice witty letter because yr last letter to me was a Stinker. But I'm nothing if not forgiving. You must be getting on, too, Paul. I'm turned seventy with twenty-five diseases but still do a seven-hour day seven days a week. And my piano-playing is still exquisite, and I am still the best Chopin player in Europe.

Looking through Cerfberr and Christophe to-night, I came across something which is pretty close to Leo. It occurs in the article on Schmucke (*Le Cousin Pons*):

Allemand catholique, homme d'un grand sens musical, naïf, distrait, bon, candide, simple de mœurs, doux et probe de caractère.

Add wit, and there would be the essential Leo.

Nov. 2
Friday. From Vivien Leigh:

As from 4 *Christchurch St.*
Chelsea
October 30th, '45

MY DEAR JAMES AGATE,
I am absolutely delighted to have your *Ego* 7. Whether you thought of me in my enforced purdah or whether you had quite forgotten that—for me—unhappy circumstance, it was extremely kind of you to think of it and I know it will cheer and entertain me exceedingly. Thank you so very much.
I have only glimpsed so far, but one of my glimpses tells me you are to abandon the Glohwurms. *Please* don't, they have become a greatly looked forward to family and I don't think we can do without them.
I wanted to write to you when I read the news of Leo Pavia's death but Jock said "Don't," so I didn't, but I do now send you

my sincere sympathy along with my good wishes and hopes that we shall meet in the spring, when I hope to be allowed to work again.

Yours ever,
VIVIEN LEIGH

To which I replied :

Queen Alexandra Mansions, W.C.2
November 1st, 1945

MY DEAR VIVIEN LEIGH,
Thank you very much for your letter. Hurry up and get well or people will think Larry thrives in your absence. *He is becoming a great actor*, and I was preparing to say so when Saint-Denis upset me with his speech-making.

Alas, poor Katzengebiss, Gänsebrust, and Glohwurm. Leo Pavia was their father; I was only their godfather. No, there can't be any more. They are perfect and imperishable, and I shall leave them in their perfection and imperishability.

Roll on, spring! If winter comes can Vivien be far behind ?

Ever,
JAMES AGATE

Nov. 11 The *Illustrated London News* has a photograph of the
Sunday. recent gale, with a wave dashing against a breakwater forming a magnificent picture of Ralph Richardson as I see him in the rôle of Lear. Cut this out, mounted it and sent it to Ralph, and received a charming reply.

Nov. 12 Letter from the Isle of Wight:
Monday.

Sometime ago, my husband read an article, written by you which said that whilst reading a book called *The Turn of the Screw* by Henry James, it was so thrilling that you had to stop reading it for a while, even though you were sitting on the Leas at Folkestone and surrounded by hundreds of people. This intrigued my husband, who has since tried to obtain a copy, but has never succeeded. Would you please tell me who the publishers are, or better still, where I could get a copy ?

The reply :

Queen Alexandra Mansions, W.C.2
November 12, 1945

DEAR MADAM,
Your letter being opened, Mr Agate's eyeballs turned back to front, he frothed slightly at the mouth, and fell into a fit from which, I regret to inform you, he has not yet recovered.

Yours faithfully,
JOHN BOOTH-PALMER
Secretary

Later :   My employer showing signs of consciousness, and his lips moving, I bent down and caught the words, " Out of print."

Later still : I am glad to say that Mr Agate's consciousness is now restored. His first words on coming round were, " Damn the woman ! I'd forgotten all about the book, and now she's brought it up again."

J. B.-P.

Nov. 13 *Tuesday.*   Attended the memorial service for Henry Ainley at St Martin-in-the-Fields.

About H. A.'s personal " tragedy " I have nothing to say. And can have nothing. " I am myself indifferent honest." Nor can *Ego* be concerned with his private virtues. His humility. His fortitude. His will to continue the struggle. His gentleness. His kindness. His readiness to help others. God rest him ! But in so far as *Ego* is and has been concerned with the theatre, to say nothing might be deemed a slight. Very well, then. I blame Nature for having given this near-great actor too much and not enough. For having lavished on him a combination and a form which automatically brought up Hamlet's description of his father, to which was added a voice like a cathedral organ. For having drawn back her hand and given a man physically endowed to play tragedy the instincts of the comedian. H. A. was almost the worst Hamlet, and quite the worst Macbeth I have ever seen. I dealt faithfully with both these performances at the time ; the curious will find the notices in *Brief Chronicles.* About Ainley the comedian I did not see enough to make up my mind. I never saw the play called *Quinney's.* In *The Great Adventure* he seemed to me to be admirable in the first act but too big for the rest of the play. Of his Strickland in *The Moon and Sixpence* I find that I wrote : " Let it be said that Mr Ainley always acted up to the height of his author's intentions, and sometimes soared a good deal beyond them." And again of his performance in *Iris* : " The essence of Maldonado is repellence, of Mr Ainley, attraction." Of his Hassan :

Mr Ainley did, perhaps, less than was possible with Hassan, and he was bound by his part to remain, let us say, in the middle distance. And I think his ghazal, beginning " How splendid in the morning glows the lily," was too full-throated. The lines did not hang in the air as they should. The thing is a cadenza to be caressed, and Mr Ainley proclaimed it something after the manner of battalion orders.

I missed, alas, his Benedick. Of his Prince Fazil I wrote : " Mr Ainley eludes absurdity with skill." In *The Anatomist* the play let the actor down :

> Mr Ainley prepared the way magnificently for a truly terrible picture of the a-moral scientist in action, only to find that there was no battle to be fought.

These are all of the actor's performances that I remember except two. He returned to the stage in St John Ervine's *The First Mrs Fraser*, and I wrote :

> Mr Henry Ainley received a tremendous ovation on his return after his long and serious illness. I should have welcomed him if he had appeared as Caliban, in which rôle he would, I venture to think, have been happier than in the part of the Scotch financier. For there are the beginnings of nobility in Caliban, and Mr Ainley has always been the embodiment of that commodity. His mien is still, and must ever be, noble, and his gait majestic. His voice continues to be that which an American writer has described as " the Bells of Bredon voice." On this actor the paltriest morning-coat takes on the aspect of a wedding garment. In plain English Mr Ainley is more the antique Roman than the modern Scotch man of business. Of course he acted well, but it was only in the way in which kings travelling incognito may be said to act well. Mr Ainley is cut on the grand scale and suggests less of the little scale than anybody living. I can only offer him this consolation for a failure in verisimilitude : that though Henry Irving was a great actor he could not have played pawnbroker, linen-draper, or milkman. Majesty is majesty, and there's an end on't.

The last play in which I saw him was Bridie's *Tobias and the Angel*. I wrote :

> Mr Ainley acts superbly throughout. His assumption of common humanity is very well done, and he is not afraid of diminishing his Angel by the use of irony and even fun. He looks magnificent whether in rags, golden mail, or ultimate white. When in the last scene he stands pedestalled and remote from the reunited family he seems more than life-size, in the way in which Michael Angelo could create a figure more than Man and less than God.

Ainley's tragedy as actor consisted in this, that his tragic figures were less than tragic size. " The greatest artist is he who is greatest in the highest reaches of his art." Only in the lower reaches did Ainley achieve anything that could be called greatness.

43 *Black Lion Lane*
Hammersmith, London, W.6

November 13*th,* 1945

DEAR AGATE,

I was very glad to see in the *Sunday Times* last Sunday your decided view about this modern-dress mania applied to tragedy of the past. It simply won't do. It does not modernise ; it only emphasises the gulf when players are " masked in our modern small-souled garb." The phrase is Heine's, and he has, to my thinking, hit on the real trouble. When I went years ago to two of King Edward's Garden Parties, the Orientals in their gowns were more effective to view than all the expensive fantasies of feminine fashion.

I did not see Andromache in evening dress when I was at the Lyric. She was ill, and the other woman who took her part was more reasonably attired. But I noticed her small boy in flannels as a blot on the scene. The translator, who happened to be next to me, agreed that a purple robe would have been much more suitable for a son of Hector and grandson of King Priam. As for the wrestling act which precipitates him into the arms of a soldier, it is pure farce. And Helen, pleading for her life, talks like a flippant fish-wife. However, the fine and hard-worked Hecuba makes the play worth while.

These moderns, it seems, must guy or debunk somehow any tragedy of classic repute. I don't so much object to soldiers in a bright uniform strange to us, but the Herald should have been differentiated from them—at least by a special head-dress. In the Greek drama he is a real sacrosanct swell, under the special protection of Hermes, and even Kings are shy of interfering with him when he takes to violent action. I could not see *Œdipus.* He was guilty of killing a Herald, a shocking crime, and this being so, I don't see how any scholar can regard him as innocent from the Greek point of view. As Sophocles has arranged the story, the Herald could not be the one man to escape, as he would have proclaimed the affray abroad as an outrageous wholesale murder of a sacred mission to Delphi. Euripides in his account avoids the herald-killing, which must have struck the Athenian audience as beyond any possible justification. Perhaps this flaw in the plot of Sophocles kept his play out of the first prize. Who on earth told you that the style of Sophocles was bald ? I should like to examine the gentleman's bumps. I have read thousands of books in five languages, and to my mind Sophocles has the most accomplished style the world has seen. I ought to know, as I have been studying him steadily for fifty years, and was taught by one of the great authorities on him. He can use common words and adapt common phrases with magical effect. So could Shakespeare, but he had a way of not keeping it up for more than ten lines or so. So could

Virgil with his " Sunt lacrimæ rerum," but his rhetorical variations grow tedious now and then. In the second Æneid there are four different words for Troy and the Trojans in little over a line. I must apologise for writing so much.

Yours sincerely,
V. RENDALL

My old friend makes one mistake. I have never said that Sophocles' style was bald. Having no Greek, how could I ?

Nov. 16
Friday.
I had a great fright to-day. Having treated myself to Szigeti's recording of the Mendelssohn Violin Concerto, I sat down after lunch with coffee and a cigar and had it played to me on my E.M.G. gramophone. The first three sides were admirable. Lovely tone ; Szigeti, the L.P.O., and Beecham all in great form. Settling down to the Andante, I heard the most appalling, unaccompanied rubbish. " You've changed the record ! " I shouted. " No, I haven't," said the houseboy. " Start it again ! " I said. The same vile muck. And I thought that at last " it " had come, " it " being the madness that my occasional brain-storms make me aware and afraid of. I thought of Johnson's fears. Of Lear's prayers. Of that poem in which Dowson, I think it is, claims that the insane are to be envied. I remembered that the other day, as I was sitting in the cinema, the screen faded out and all my old nightmares enacted themselves all over again. Alcohol, my doctor had said succinctly. Then I thought of Maupassant coming home one night to see himself sitting in his own arm-chair. Could there be aural as well as visual hallucination ? Why not ? Why shouldn't I be mad ? Haven't I worked hard enough to expect madness ? I had been drinking rather less than usual lately. But then my unexpected conjuring feats had been turning up more often ; yesterday a collar-stud thrown on to the piano-lid stood on its head. On Monday I had dreamed of an actor for the first time in my life, and on Tuesday morning that actor was the first person I met. Yes, I was certainly mad. And then I realised that I must take hold of myself. And did. Began by examining the record, and found on the fourth side Paganini's—it would be that devil—Caprice No. 9, *La Chasse*, with the concerto resuming on the *fifth* side, after which it remained uninterrupted. Since it runs to seven sides why didn't the makers put the Paganini stuff at the end ? Better still. Why not leave the side blank ?

Nov. 18
Sunday.
Scott Goddard, deputising for Ernest Newman, who is on holiday, writes at length about Michael Tippett's " Symphony 1945." The audience, he says, were cool. But at the beginning of the article he incautiously lets out that he heard two

rehearsals, an " illuminating lecture " by the composer, and the performance before he " felt the flesh growing over the bones." Suppose that before I could enjoy a play I had to attend two rehearsals and listen to a chat by Mr Shakespeare or Mr Ibsen ! In the next column Eric Newton says of Epstein's " Lucifer " that " for all its emotional tensity, *it isn't quite the right shape.*" Italics mine. Why didn't Scott Goddard say of Tippett's symphony that for all its emotional tensity it doesn't make quite the right sort of sound ?

Nov. 20   Letter to the Editor of the *Daily Express* :
Tuesday.

Sir,
     Here is a list, for which I vouch, of my attempts to communicate with you by telephone this morning :

11.00	Get " Telegrams."
11.02	" Telegrams " again.
11.04	Still " Telegrams."
11.06	Cleaners at a night-club.
11.08	Butt into private conversation.
11.10	P.C. continued.
11.12	" Toll."
11.14	" Telegrams."
11.16	Dialling tone, but no answer from anybody.
11.18	'Phone goes dead.
11.20	" Telegrams."
11.22	Another private conversation.
11.24	Dialling tone, but no answer from Operator, Engineers, " Trunks," " Toll," or " Tim."
11.26	" Telegrams."
11.28	" Engaged " signal before completion of dialling.
11.30	Ear-splitting noise.

Having wasted exactly thirty minutes I then send my houseboy out to some near-by telephone boxes to ask you to telephone me. Three are out of order, but he is lucky with the fourth.
     11.35   You ring me up.
     This has been going on for weeks. I manage somehow to contact the engineers twice a day. I hope they are well. I enquire after their families. Our relations are of the friendliest. Once a smooth-spoken young gentleman came round, fiddled about, and assured me that my telephone was in perfect order. " Better," he said, " than many others in the neighbourhood."
     May I suggest that the Government would do well to stop concocting plans for an ideal world in the future and set about some for making what world we have work now ?

Yours, etc.,
JAMES AGATE

At a party in Chelsea a few nights ago the guests played a new form of the old game of Consequences, each writing down what seemed to him or her the most idiotic line that could get itself printed in a magazine devoted to modern verse. The host was so much impressed with the imbecile sequence that he made a fair copy and sent it as a serious contribution to our highest-browed Bloomsbury editor. In due course he received a letter which talked of " unusual promise," and would the young poet care to submit something of greater length ?

Nov. 21   Stevenson has something in " A Gossip on Romance "
Wednesday.   which I think is extremely apt to the cinema :

> There is a vast deal in life and letters both which is not immoral, but simply non-moral ; which either does not regard the human will at all, or deals with it in obvious and healthy relations ; where the interest turns, not upon what a man shall choose to do, but on how he manages to do it ; not on the passionate slips and hesitations of the conscience, but on the problems of the body and of the practical intelligence, in clean, open-air adventure, the shock of arms or the diplomacy of life. With such material as this it is impossible to build a play, for the serious theatre exists solely on moral grounds, and is a standing proof of the dissemination of the human conscience. But it is possible to build, upon this ground, the most joyous of verses, and the most lively, beautiful, and buoyant tales.

To which I would add films. Can it be doubted that if R. L. S. had written for the screen his pictures would have dealt with ships and shipwrecks, bullyings and mutinies, skulls, cross-bones, and the ends of planks and ropes ? Or that his dialogue would have teemed with allusions to long-boats and jolly-boats ? I feel that he would have wanted all films to be boys' films. Certainly, *Captain Kidd*, at the London Pavilion last night, is a first-rate boys' film, full of the hurly-burly of the pirate seas in the days of William and Mary. Laughton is grand throughout, with a good deal of sly humour. (Why doesn't Hollywood go to the nearest bookshop—are there bookshops in Hollywood ?—dig up a copy of *Jonathan Wild* by that good scenario writer, Fielding, and present our Charles as that Truly Great Man ?) There was nothing for fourteen-year-olds in Noel Coward's *Brief Encounter*, at the New Gallery this morning. The story concerns a married woman who has the misfortune to fall in love with a married doctor. " What happens to Laura and Alec might so easily happen to you or me," says Synopsis. But what I want in the cinema is something that can't possibly happen to me.

Synopsis goes on to remark that this "makes screen entertainment which is unusually arresting and full of drama and suspense." I wonder ! Alec persuades Laura to meet him in a flat borrowed from a friend, and then—I am still quoting Synopsis—"the unexpected return of the friend prevents anything worse than a humiliating flight for Laura." Worse ? *Worse ?* But surely this postulates the world of what a man or woman should choose to do. The world of passionate slips and the hesitating conscience. The world in which some things are moral and others immoral. It was for and by this world that Stevenson held the theatre to exist. I believe that if R. L. S. had been present at the New Gallery to-day he would have protested that what he was seeing was theatre rather than film, and psychological novel rather than theatre.

Nov. 22   Emrys Jones, reviewing *Ego* 7, writes :
Thursday.

> Mr Agate gives the impression that he is always coming from Somewhere and going Somewhere. . . . Of the private Mr Agate we know little from these journals. One feels that when he gets down to writing about himself he is very much reviewing the public character that he is. Such reticence, admirable in most parts, is not the stuff of which great diaries are made.

But of course I'm always going to and from places when I can get the transport. Yesterday, for example, I had a luncheon that I couldn't get out of, a matinée that finished at five o'clock, and a play that started at half-past six. In addition, I should have attended an amusing publisher's cocktail party had it not been that in that hour-and-a-half I had to get to and from Grape Street and review five books for the *Express*. After the evening show, and out of sheer courtesy, I looked in at a stage party to celebrate the thousandth night of something or other. What time does this Mr Jones think that I have left for a private life ? And what does he want to know about how I spend the private hours that are left ? Am I to tell him that at midnight I covet my neighbour's ox, at 1 A.M. his ass, at 2 A.M. his wife, and from then till breakfast-time his sisters and his cousins and his aunts ? Hamlet could accuse himself of such things that it were better his mother had not borne him. But he did not tell Ophelia what those things were, and I doubt very much whether he confided them to his " tables." What is good enough for Hamlet is good enough for me.

My letter to the *D.E. re* the telephone service appeared yesterday morning. From which moment my 'phone has been dead.

Nov. 23 I am always delighted when anybody sends me an old
Friday. book. To-day arrives *The Gentleman's Magazine* for the
year 1768. Enchanting articles on The Identity of King
Charles's Executioner, Arguments against the Inoculation of Children
in early Infancy, A New Improvement in Fire Engines. A review of
an Essay on the Future Life of Brute Creatures contains this :

> All who have hitherto attempted to reconcile moral and natural
> evil with a first cause infinite in power, wisdom, and goodness, have
> been driven into absurdities that might well warn others, like a
> beacon, and prevent their shipwreck.

Good eighteenth-century Unitarianism ! The number for March has
a poem entitled " On hearing the Rev. Mr Dodd Preach." (Presumably one of those sermons " addressed to the passions.") This begins :

> Heard but the libertine thy pulpit lore
> Pathetic Dodd ! the wretch would sin no more ;
> No more with vice his ebbing life disgrace,
> With riot mark, or infamy debase !

And ends :

> Go on, judicious Pastor, awe the bold,
> Still, still improve the Young, reclaim the Old,
> With pleasing energy thy Saviour preach
> And virtue animate, and candour teach,
> Still make fair chastity thy darling theme,
> While Magdalens support and prize its fame ;
> Then nor till late, may Heaven reward thy care,
> And make thee angel in a brighter sphere.

Underneath is written in ink : " Since Hang'd."
Lastly, this item from the Historical Chronicle for February :

> A most horrid murder was committed at Wotton-Underidge,
> in Gloucestershire, by one Wallington, a shearman, who, about ten
> in the morning left his work, and in a cruel manner murdered his
> own father. It has since appeared that the murderer was out of
> his mind : for upon examination he said he had seen a vision, and
> that the devil had commanded him to do the murder exactly at
> ten o'clock ; and it was observed that he went out several times to
> look at the clock, and that he kept his time precisely. He then
> went to a neighbour and with seeming satisfaction told him *he had
> done it* ; and being asked what, his answer was, *he had killed his
> father.*

Nov. 25 It was to be expected that the musical critics would make
Sunday. a field-day of Purcell's bi-and-a-half centenary. I think
Martin Raymond in to-day's *Observer* provides the best
fun. At the Wigmore Hall jamboree

> the two chief figures among the performers, Benjamin Britten and
> Michael Tippet, did not merely perform music : they were evidently

out to put a case : the case for the rediscovery of a great composer of the highest importance for present-day music, still grievously crushed under " the bulwarks of music in 19th-century England."

There is, it seems, in Purcell's music,

a kind of unsentimental, impersonal objectivity, a determination, while stating all kinds of emotion in precise and sometimes extreme terms, never to be overwhelmed by any of them, a modesty of statement which, after the emotional excesses of Tschaikowsky or the late Viennese, satisfies a deep need to-day.

And then what Stalky would have called the Martiniferous Raymond begins to have his doubts.

It seems somehow impossible to build up a night's programme of Purcell's works that is not jumbled or monotonous or both. . . . The stuff doesn't add up. It never allows the mysterious and complicated atmosphere of concentrated festivity which is the secret of a concert to arise.

(Then why throw stones at Tschaikowsky and Strauss who have this "concentrated festivity" at their finger-ends ?) The article concludes:

The simple truth seems to me that Purcell cannot be fully revived so long as our musical culture remains, in the main, bound up with concert-giving and concert-going. Of course, if the great cities should disappear, and the concert-halls and the concert audiences with them, and music should again become a mainly home-made affair, a matter of families and circles of friends singing and playing together for their own enjoyment—then, I think, Purcell's day will come again. But not till then.

Which gives me the following little musical scene :

SETTING : *A drawing-room in Glossop.*

FIRST MUSIC-LOVER. Rather a pity about that bomb destroying Manchester, don't you think ? Not the city, of course, but the Hallé. They were in the middle of *Heldenleben.* I must say I think it's rather a shame.
SECOND MUSIC-LOVER. In some ways, yes. What about trying out a new Purcell I've discovered ? Sonata for dulcimer and stromento di porco ?

Jay Pomeroy invited me to his box at the Cambridge Theatre this afternoon. Myra Hess in Mozart's B flat Piano Concerto (K. 595). The shallowest water by which this melodious bird ever madrigalised. Then Tschaikowsky No. 5. Drenched with self-pity. But I like listening to it just as I like looking at a fuchsia drenched with rain.

Nov. 26   In a letter from Jock :
Monday.

I had a singular experience last week. I went to the National
Gallery and heard an excellent String Quartet—the Zorian—play
Beethoven in C minor (in the Op. 18 set) and Béla Bartók No. 4,
said to be the toughest of the six. Wasn't that plucky of me ? The
Beethoven begins divinely, continues agreeably, and concludes in a
Haydnish, busybody way. But the Bartók, the Bartók ! It's no
good saying you've never heard such noises, for *I have* heard such
noises. It's evocative music all right. The opening *Allegro* took
me straight back to childhood and gave me in turn the rusty
windlass of a well, the interlinking noises of a goods train that is
being shunted, then the belly-rumblings of a little boy acutely ill
after a raid on an orchard, and finally the singular alarmed noise
of poultry being worried to death by a Scotch terrier. The second
movement, *Prestissimo con sordino,* gave me continuously and
throughout its short length the noise of a November wind in
telegraph-wires on a lonely country road. The third, *Non troppo
lento,* began with a dog howling at midnight, proceeded to imitate
the regurgitations of the less-refined or lower-middle-class type of
water-closet cistern, modulating thence into the mass snoring and
wheezing and body-sounding of a Naval dormitory around the dawn
—and concluded inconsequently with the 'cello reproducing the
screech of an ungreased wheelbarrow. The fourth movement,
Allegretto Pizzicato, took me straight back to the noises I made
myself, on wet days indoors, at the age of six, by stretching and
plucking a piece of elastic. And the fifth, *Allegro molto,* reminded
me immediately and persistently and vividly of something I have
never thought of since the only time I heard it : the noise of a Zulu
village in the Glasgow Exhibition in the year 1911 when I was six
—a hubbub all the more singular because it had a background of
skirling Highland bagpipes. *Both* noises emerged in this final
movement of this Fourth Quartet of Béla Bartók.
    These are not worked-up impressions invented to amuse you.
I set them down on the back of my programme while listening to
this music. There was a big audience, and an enthusiastic one.
They all seemed to me to have the frozen, perfunctory smiles of the
crowd that watched the Emperor walking through the streets in
his wonderful New Clothes—just before the small child piped up :
" But the Emperor has nothing on ! " The queer thing is that I
have a conviction (all the stronger after hearing this amazing work)
that the Emperor Béla *has* something on. And I'm furious at being
unable to see quite what it is !

Nov. 27   To err is human, etc., etc. But what would Pope have
Tuesday.   thought if he had known that the *Oxford Dictionary of
            Quotations* would give his dates as " 1786 ?–1872 " !
Perhaps that interrogation mark was never happier ! In view of this

I shall not lose much sleep over a Scotch lady's rebuke that Jock should not have written, and I should not have printed, ' stravaging ' when, actually, the Scots word is ' stravaiging.'

Nov. 28   Lectured to the Royal Society of Arts. Title: " A
Wednesday. Moment in the History of the Theatre." Went off all
             right, I think. C. B. Cochran in the chair. House full,
but nobody from the commercial managements though they all had
special invitations sent them.

Nov. 29   In a letter from a lady :
Thursday.

 I saw Henry Irving twice only. The first time was in *The Bells* at Swansea. The only picture remaining in my memory of that performance is that of Irving taking off his gaiters. Before the play began, the crowd of people in the gallery, mostly young Welsh men, whiled away the waiting time by singing. Irving sent out a message from his dressing-room to say that he was sorry he could not hear well enough from that distance to appreciate the music fully, but he would be honoured if the audience in the gallery would remain after the performance and sing again for him. They did. Irving came before the curtain and listened for twenty minutes to the harmonies of *Aberystwyth*, *Cwm Rhondda*, and *Dafydd y gareg wen*. You know them. Irving then spoke his thanks and said that the evening would always live in the store-house of his memory. " I wish you all a very good night." That was Irving, the man. The second time I saw him was not long before his death. I was walking along the sea-front at Minehead, when I became conscious that the people ahead were parting to stand at the sides of the pavement. Strolling along between them, bowing slightly to right and left, came Irving. It was a royal procession of one. That was Irving, the actor.

Nov. 30   Telephone put right and letter of thanks despatched.
Friday.

Dec. 8   In Kipling's poem about the old three-volume novel
Saturday.   occurs the line :

 We never talked obstetrics when the Little Stranger came.

But Kipling is demoded, as all Bloomsbury knows ; there isn't a pair of unwashed, uncombed, long-haired corduroy trousers pretending to be a poet that hasn't complete contempt for the author of *The Seven Seas*. To-day when we sit down to write verse we are midwives to a man. I open *Voices on the Green*, a collection of New Writing about Childhood, and discover that modern genius talks obstetrics *before* the Little Stranger comes.

> " You dream," he said, " because of the child
> Asleep in the nest of your entrails. . . ."

And I think of a line from *David Copperfield* :

> "Ba-a-ah ! " said my aunt, with a perfect shake on the contemptuous interjection. And corked herself, as before.

Dec. 11   Took Jock to the Press view of *Cæsar and Cleopatra.* So
Tuesday.   bored that I didn't know where to look ! Cæsar like an
          elderly Peter Pan, and Cleopatra just out of Roedean.
Apollodorus the apple of every shopgirl's eye, and so on. Poor use
of the camera which prompted Jock to whisper, " This is the first
time I've thought of Alexandria as a rose-red city half as old as
Denham." Lunched with Donald Wolfit, after which I came back to
the flat, and read in Winifred Graham's autobiography how Father
Ignatius, who had preached about Marie Corelli's *Sorrows of Satan*
at the Portman Rooms, took for his theme the authoress's " *The
Vision at the Savoy,* a story of Christ passing through the fashionable
supper crowd in that well-known hotel off the Strand." How the
preacher had patted her and said, " Go on, my dear child, like this."
Shall ask *Express* readers whether Ignatius could have been loyaller.

Dec. 14   Sibelius is reported to have said on his eightieth birth-
Friday.   day last week, " If you want to discuss art you must
          talk to men of business. Artists only discuss money."
This is something the public refuses to understand. I started my
day's work at 9 A.M., corrected the proof of my first *Tatler* article
on the *Cæsar and Cleopatra* film, and having done this set about a
second article on the same theme, the *Tatler* requiring a double dose
in view of Christmas. Titivated to-morrow's *Express* article and
revised Sunday's stuff, by which time it was 9 P.M. Grabbed a bit
of food and took ten minutes to climb five flights of stairs somewhere
in Covent Garden to keep a long-standing, flat-warming engagement.
Had just enough breath left to say I like plenty of soda when some
earnest ass wanted to know what I thought of the Shaw film. Put
into use my special technique, which means that when total strangers
come up to me and say, " Do you mind my talking to you ? " I reply,
" Not at all, so long as you don't mention any play, film, book, or
piece of music." " But that's what I want to talk about," said a
young man two evenings ago. I asked him to excuse me, saying that
I had been working since breakfast-time and that I made it a rule not
to take part in any intelligent conversation after ten o'clock. He said,

" I am deeply sorry for you." I said, " You impertinent young hound. Go and be sorry in some other part of the Café ! " Thus is a reputation for rudeness thrust upon one ! I gently explained to to-night's bore that I had spent the day trying to do justice to a great writer, that I couldn't put ten hours' work into a sentence, and that I was too tired to try. He said, " Sorry ! I ought to have known you would have had enough of the pictures. Very tactless of me ! What do you think about a National Theatre on the other side of the river ? "

Dec. 16   Writing in 1908 about a little book which somebody had
Sunday.   put together about Sarah Bernhardt, Montague had this
               noble thing :

Like many of us the author saw the paragon in her prime, and as long as any two such persons live and can communicate, the world retains some sort of corporate sense of the nature of her greatness : after that, her death, now unfinished, will become complete—as complete as that of a Dürer might be if the paper had mouldered away under the last of all the surviving impressions and reproductions of his prints and nothing remained but the stuff written about them in books.

And now Maurice Baring has gone, Maurice who wrote about Sarah better than Montague, or Symons, or anybody.

When I have seen the parts that Sarah Bernhardt made her own performed by lesser artists I have wondered what has happened to the play. If it was classical, *Phèdre*, for instance, one wondered where all the glory that was Greece, and all the grandeur that was Versailles, and all the music that was Racine had gone to : one longed in vain for those haunting, thirsty eyes that sent an electric current through the whole theatre, for that voice that made you think the words were being spoken for the first time ; for those gestures which were too swift to analyse, for that harmony and rhythm in utterance, movement, speech and silence, crescendo and diminuendo, speed and pause and delay, that combined to produce and build something as concrete as a beautiful frieze or statue, as logical and ordered and disciplined as a great fugue, and as intangible as the gleam of sunshine on a wave or the reflection of a rainbow in the clouds.

The date of this, as far as I can gather, is 1923. Twenty years later the writer, an old man verging on seventy, semi-paralysed, was painfully, at the expense of many hours of labour, putting on to paper in his own hand letters from his retreat in Scotland to a dramatic critic whom he hardly knew. Letters about their common recollection of performances fifty years ago. Montague is dead. And now too is Maurice Baring. I must believe that a little more of that " strange russet leaf " which was Sarah Bernhardt has died with him.

Dec. 18 Speech delivered at the Gaumont-British Annual Press
Tuesday. Luncheon, J. Arthur Rank in the chair :

Mr Chairman, Ladies and Gentlemen :

There is a scene in Pinero's *Sweet Lavender* in which Mr Bulger,
a hairdresser, is about to blunder into a married lady's bedroom.
Deterred, he says, " I dare say I could have passed it off with a
pleasantry." I dare say I could pass off to-day's occasion with a
French quotation and a joke or two. Rightly or wrongly I feel
that something more serious is called for, and my defence for
taking up this attitude is based on a longer professional interest in
film criticism than anybody in this room. The article on Charlie
Chaplin entitled *Hey, but He's Doleful!* published in the *Saturday
Review* in 1921 with the sanction and encouragement of Filson
Young, and being one of my earliest contributions to that paper,
was the first criticism of the film as a serious art and the film actor
as a serious artist to appear in the Press of this country. That
fact establishes my *bona fides* to-day.

Critics are always being told that their criticism should be constructive. Very well, then. I have been graciously accorded six
minutes, and I intend to employ those minutes constructively.
Whatever may be feasible in the domain of Lewis Carroll, in the
world as we know it constructiveness is possible only *before* an
event. To say of a cathedral that it is hideous, and to say no
more, is destructive criticism ; constructive criticism will say,
" That cathedral's damned ugly. Pull it down, build it differently,
and in this different way." But why not run up the building in
the mind's eye, as it were ? Why not visualise the deed before
the attempt ? Lady Macbeth is very sound on this subject. "Things
without all remedy should be without regard." "What's done
cannot be undone." This applies not only to cathedrals but to
cinemas, and to the films exhibited in cinemas.

Mr Rank has just spent an enormous amount of time and money
and enterprise and courage. With what result ? One critic is
bored. Another critic would hate to sit through *Cæsar and
Cleopatra* again. A third talks of " a cold triumph." A fourth holds
the picture to be " hollow at heart." I can well believe that Mr
Rank is dismayed and hurt by this. (Let me tell him that he will be
much more dismayed and hurt to-morrow when the *Tatler* appears
and some whey-faced fellow tells him of an article which he wanted,
but was not allowed, to call *Cheops and Tomato Sauce.*) If Mr Rank
is disappointed in the critics it can only be because they have failed
to give him that help which he feels should be the reward of time,
money, enterprise, courage. But, I repeat, help, constructive help,
can be given only before the event. There is nothing to be done
now about this film. But how about *St Joan* ?

Let me use my mind's eye to pierce the future and say now
what will inevitably be held later about any film made from this
great play. Théodore de Banville, practising as a dramatic critic

257

nearly a century ago, laid it down that " the eye grows swiftly weary of all stationary spectacle, however spectacular, and demands motion." From which one could almost think that he foresaw the cinema, where the shots change every forty seconds. Now might not Théodore, were he living to-day, have gone on to ask how an essentially peripatetic medium can hope to interpret an essentially static play? Maurice Baring, whose death we all deplore, asked " whether it was a greater thing for a poet to have soared high into the heavens of passion, or to have dived deep into the grey seas of reason. ' Into those seas,' he said, ' Victor Hugo never dived, and into those heavens Goethe never soared.' " Taking my cue from Baring, I say that into the ocean of knees-under-the-table, hammer-and-tongs, Shavian argle-bargle Mr Pascal dives something constrainedly, while into the swift-moving firmament of the cinema's archangel Gabriel Mr Shaw never soars at all.

Not once in *St Joan* does this master-playwright " let himself go " cinematically speaking. He refuses to show us the coronation, obviously any film director's *bonne bouche*. He refuses to give us the defence of Compiègne and that unsuccessful sortie in which the Maid was taken prisoner, surely another cinematic tit-bit. He insists upon talk, magnificent talk, but still talk. Words, words, words. He proceeds from the argument in the English tent to the pow-wow in the ambulatory of the cathedral, and thence to the trial scene. For the better part of two hours nobody crosses the stage, and hardly his legs. In his preface Shaw says, " To see Joan in her proper perspective you must understand Christendom and the Catholic Church, the Holy Roman Empire and the Feudal System, as they existed and were understood in the Middle Ages." In what perspective, then, does the screen propose to show us this great figure? As a girl dressed in men's clothes and so rude that the soldiers take her for one of themselves? As a young woman in blue armour adorned with silver stars, brandishing a gold sword, and prancing about on a white charger? Shall we be given a coronation scene with specially built organ and specially trained choristers? A pitched battle between the Maid and the Duke of Burgundy? And a slap-up bonfire at the end? Since Joan talks like blazes, blazes are her appropriate end. But in the play the blazes happen off-stage. To build a picture on what Shaw deliberately left out may be a film director's idea of fun, but it will not be Shaw's play, whereas to re-create the talk word by word and syllable by syllable to the exclusion of everything extraneous may be Shaw but will not be the film public's idea of fun. The essence of cinema is to cut the cackle and come to the 'osses. Shaw in *St Joan* deliberately cuts the 'osses and sticks to the cackle.

One word more. If any picture I, as a film magnate, am to make must be a Shaw picture I should choose *Androcles and the Lion*, in which Rome could flaunt her decadence *ad lib.*, and the sound recorders be given a free hand with the clash of chariots, the groans of gladiators, the plaints of martyrs, the impatient snarls of wild beasts. On the other hand, if I were not bound to Shaw I should go to some great English novel, say Thackeray's *Esmond*, where the author's intention is not impeded but swept on by the duels, the great battles, the crowd and court scenes, the press of famous men, the onrush and array of history. I should consider Kingsley's *Westward Ho !*, or Reade's *The Cloister and the Hearth*. On one of these I should spend my million, and if I had a few pounds left over I should take a *little* studio and make a *little* picture out of Shaw's masterpiece.

Lastly, I should give a luncheon to the Press and say, " Ladies and Gentlemen. Such and such are my plans. Tell me what is wrong before I start to work on them. Tell me now." I have ventured to tell Mr Rank what must, even with genius at the helm, be wrong about *St Joan*. I hope he does not make this picture. I hope that, if he does, it will gross twenty million pounds. For that will be his only reward.

Dec. 20   Lying in bed at 4 A.M. and reading *Little Dorrit* to cheat
Thursday.   myself of feeling ill, I came across this :

> Bar said, there was a certain point of mental strain beyond which no man could go ; that the point varied with various textures of brain and peculiarities of constitution, as he had had occasion to notice in several of his learned brothers ; but the point of endurance passed by a line's breadth, depression and dyspepsia ensued. Not to intrude on the sacred mysteries of medicine, he took it, now (with the Jury droop and persuasive eye-glass), that this was Merdle's case ?

Was this, I wondered, J. A.'s case ? Bicarbonate of soda, hot water, and half a teaspoonful of sal volatile answered Yes.

Christmas Day. Jolly luncheon party at Louis Sterling's. A
lieutenant in the R.N.V.R. told me that when he was in command of a patrol yacht on the Thames he had as mate a surrealist painter whose masterpieces fascinated the engineer, a pure Cockney. " Blimey," the latter said, " I'll have a go." And proceeded to depict a pint pot, giving it half a face with one eye situated in the chin and a couple of cogwheels for ears. And proudly submitted it for criticism. " Y-e-s," said the surrealist, putting his head on one side. " It has *balance*, of course ! "

In the evening to supper with Gwen Chenhalls, the only other guest being Anthony Asquith, who, knowing he was going to meet me, brought and gave me a volume of Morley's *Miscellanies*, inscribed to Margot Asquith by the author. After which we had a hammer-and-tongs argument about the ultra-moderns. Surrealists and Atonalists. Since Puffin doesn't read Dylan Thomas and I won't listen to Bartók the fight was along Tweedledum and Tweedledee lines. For me the whole matter is summed up in Malcolm Sargent's story of how he stopped a rehearsal and asked the composer whether he meant B or B flat. And received the answer, " I knew when I wrote it, but I don't now. Play which you like ! "

Boxing Day. Worked in the morning and took Ralph Baker to lunch, after which I relaxed. Smoked Louis Sterling's Christmas cigar, drank some of Lady Hardwicke's bottle of whiskey, read Morley on Machiavelli, noting how Margot had underlined the noblest passages, and turned loose among my gramophone records Joseph Azzopardi, a young Gibraltar evacuee and friend of my houseboy in bed with toothache. Nobody rang up, and the whole a perfect afternoon except that towards the end the gramophone decided to play everything presto and couldn't be dissuaded.

Dec. 27   Wrestle for half an hour with an article by Rayner
Thursday. Heppenstall in the new highbrow miscellany, *Orion*, on
             that super-boshite Georges Bernanos, to whom, I
understand, infant Bloomsbury turns as soon as it has got through *Reading without Tears*. I cull :

> The night a new priest arrives in the village, a man is murdered. The new priest, sensitive, pale and mysteriously ill, turns out in the end to be a girl. The murdered man was the expected priest. The girl commits suicide after a confession. Lesbian practices lay at the root of her disorder. In other words, she had broken a very serious *tabu*. The priest paid the price of her guilt and unhappiness. After masquerading as a priest and thus taking his function to herself, she also must die. That is the plot of *Un Crime*.

Give it up and, deciding that I like my eroticism neat, without bogus psychological trimmings, turn to the Marquis's *Juliette*, which some kind soul has sent me as a New Year's gift.

> Le calme rétabli, les deux cadavres furent jetés dans un trou à dessein préparé au fond d'un petit jardin attenant au cabinet où cette scène venait de se passer, et l'on se rhabilla.

 I would give all the Bernanos bunk for those three words " Le calme rétabli."

Dec. 29   Attended the *M.G.* dinner to James Bone, retiring after
Saturday. forty-odd years on the staff and as a director. The
             greatest London editor the paper has ever had. Highly
distinguished gathering of sixty, and lots of people present whom one had thought dead long ago, all of them spryer than me ! The

speakers, without exception, read their bits. I had prepared and got by heart an elevated composition modelled on Hazlitt's Farewell to Mrs Siddons : " The stateliest ornament of the public mind . . . a voice to open the chambers of the human heart . . . a trumpet to awaken the sleeping and the dead." Vastly fine ! But I am very small beer at the *M.G.* nowadays and was not called on. Or at least not until some fourteen or fifteen other speakers had had their say— after which the Chairman looked at his watch and said, " Well, I think that's all, unless Mr Agate would care to say a few words." Now I hope I know when is the time for oratory and when not. So I jettisoned my speech and said a few words out of hand.

Dec. 31   From Chesterton's *Criticisms and Appreciations of the*
Monday.   Works of Charles Dickens :

All this was what Dickens stood for ; that the very people who are most irritating in small business circumstances are often the people who are most delightful in long stretches of experiences of life. It is just the man who is maddening when he is ordering a cutlet or arranging an appointment who is probably the man in whose company it is worth while to journey steadily towards the grave.

Why did I not think of this when Leo was alive ?

Jan. 1   Five New Year cards. One, anonymous, shows an
Tuesday.   opulent maiden, bare as to bosom and feet, " poring upon
              the brook that babbles by," and reading an elegant
tome. Title : " I think it's a novel by Charles Morgan." The
second is a hand-coloured drawing from and by Angna Enters
entitled " Vienna Provincial." I like to think that this is our old
friend Isolda Gänzebrust when young. The third is from Nigel Bruce,
still in Hollywood. Fourth is from Donald Wolfit : himself as Lear.
Fifth is a nostalgic photograph of Réjane, sent by her son.

Jan. 2   *Cinderella* at the Adelphi. Buttons, alas ! too old.
Wednesday. One could almost imagine this Cinderella saying to
              Flanagan, " O my dear, dear bud, welcome home ! "
Indeed, one wished she would, and even finish Margery Pinchwife's
accueil : " Why dost thou look so fropish ? Who has nangered
thee ? " " Nangered ? " I can see Bud's face as he repeats this.
" What's ' *nangered* ' ? "
       How poor the modern songs are compared with those of fifty years
ago ! Vesta Tilley made it seem natural that Robinson Crusoe should
exchange those Arctic furs appropriate to Juan Fernandez, or
wherever it was, for the West End blue serge suit, double-breasted
fancy waistcoat, straw hat, and whangee cane in which to tell the
story of Percy and Gladys—Romeo and Juliet of the warehouse and
shop—whose romance, embodied by other Percys and Gladyses, gilds
with eternal summer the dingy Margate boarding-house. In the
'nineties singers of the tender passion did not drool—remember the
lilt and riot of Marie Lloyd's " The Wedding Bells were ringing " ?—
and the Blues had not yet infected the ether with their megrims. As
I write somebody turns the knob of my radio, and I hear an oily,
scented male voice crooning :

        " . . . like asparagus in season,
          And that is the reason
          You'd be so nice to come home to."
And I think again of Vesta Tilley, and the greater charm, sophistication, and sense of her

        " Into a cookshop he goes dashing ;
          Who should bring his plate of hash in
          But the girl he had been mashing
          By the sad sea waves."

Jan. 3
Thursday.
At the Café Royal to-night I met a Bloomsburyite who started babbling about Jean-Paul Sartre and his philosophy of Existentialism. In the course of his babbling he let out that he had never heard of Fred Karno. Whereupon I told him to keep quiet while I jotted down a General Knowledge Paper for a Youth Envisaging a Literary Career. And put Mooncalf through it, with astonishing results. He thought the earth's diameter was 93,000 miles. Thought Lent was the period between Easter and Whitsun. Hadn't heard of Euclid. Couldn't multiply $a+b$ by $a+b$. Had never read a word of Milton, Tennyson, Keats. Couldn't quote any line from Gray's *Elegy*. Couldn't fill in the blanks in " From fairest — we desire increase, That thereby beauty's — might never die." Saw nothing wrong about " The expensive spirit is a waste of shame. . . ." Hadn't opened any book by Dickens or Thackeray. Had never heard of Sayers and Heenan, " W. G.," Fred Archer, John Roberts, Arthur Roberts, Harry Vardon. Didn't know what school Tom Brown went to, or who was its headmaster. Thought Henry VIII had eight wives, but could mention only Lady Jane Grey. Had never heard of the Jameson Raid. Saw nothing wrong with " hidjus," the " woom " of Time, Volterre, Gerter, Walt Whiteman. Thought Grock was a patent medicine. Had no notion which Gilbert and Sullivan character wanted to make the punishment fit the crime. " I hope not ! " said Mooncalf. And started to put the case for abolishing punishment in favour of rehabilitation through self-respect. Winding up with : " The trouble with you old men is that you confuse formative principles with factual knowledge. The object of education is to enable the individual to make original contribution to the whole. And you mix this up with spelling ! "

Jan. 4
Friday.
The following speaks for itself :

> *Amesbury Lodge*
> *George Road*
> *Guernsey*
> *Channel Isles*
> *3rd January 1946*

DEAR MR AGATE,
An austerely bound copy of Boswell's *Life of Johnson* came into my possession several months ago in the most gratifying manner possible. You announced that you had a very limited number of copies, and would present them to those members of H.M. Forces who wrote and asked nicely !
From my mud-spattered outpost of Empire in the Fen country I

wrote. When the little volume arrived I wrote again, to say thank you.

Then—well, the attached poem finishes the melancholy tale. The poet, an Australian Air Gunner, shared my love of the absurd Doctor, and often we read extracts by the light of the remote Norfolk moon.

But the poet, like my copy of the book, is gone. He was blown to pieces over Germany during the last few weeks of the war.

He was nineteen years old.

Yours very sincerely,

Penelope Philip-Smith

ON LOSING YOUR COPY
OF
" DOCTOR JOHNSON "

Once, while I kissed you,
  A little yellow book
That clever hands had made,
  And fine-set print
Endowed with august character,
  Tiring of the life it knew
(Melancholy without stint),
  Spent in the shade
Of dusty corners—drugged, by chance,
  By your new, exciting nearness,
Rebellious did race
  Along the ledge, to dance,
And topple down, in drunk distress,
  Into the brook.

Perhaps there *was* a splash !
  Protesting cry,
And clutching of a cardboard throat
  As the water, rising high,
Flowed o'er his well-thumbed coat,
  A gurgling and pedantic sigh
As he sped
  To a sanded shelf.

          But I
Then was kissing you, who, if the stars
  Had fallen in a shining heap
Along the entire, moon-lit wall,
  Would not have heard them fall yourself!
Would not have felt the pebbles start,
  For you were too close
To my head and my heart
          To see the deep-
Shaded doctor looking from his sleep
(Peruke a little twisted on his head).

Naiads used his silver-headed cane,
Reed-garlanded, for a maypole,
  On the green river-bed.
And, on a well-hosed knee,
  A pleading little fish-boy
Cried for his watch-chain.

R. A. Dowe

Jan. 5
Saturday.

A young man, twenty-four, Traddles type, calls on me to know whether he is a poet. Not having read his verses, I say confidently No. Says he thinks he may be a better musician. I say, "Play something." And he plays half of the first movement of his first sonata. Not bad. Then something for a film—mixture of Addinsell and Rachmaninoff. Then *Wood Echoes,* which he thinks is a *mélange* of Delius and Sibelius, and I tell him is Edward German edited by Norman O'Neill. When he has gone I find this on my desk :

> And you came to me late,
> Your cheeks smeared with the wet signatures of Spring,
> After a little loneliness and silken laughter
> Alone by night like a tired king.

Jan. 6
Sunday.

This week's letters :

1.

Eastbourne
2.1.46

DEAR MR AGATE,
Do you think you could stand living with a genious for long ? Of course my sister Connie may not be a genious but she acts like one which is worse. She has just writen a play and its going to be acted and she says she's going to send it to you for you to judge. If she does please tell her its tripe (it is very probably tripe in any case), then perhaps she won't be so awfull to talk to. She won't let me see her play because she says it isnt fit for little boys. (I'm 15)

In disgust
F. RUBBLE

2. Remembering my dear Rebecca's enchanting letter after Brother Mycroft had called her " odious " (*Ego* 2, p. 105), I have no hesitation in including part of the latest from my little Dublin friend, J. E. Jordan :

> Browsing in *Ego* 2, my back against the hard library shelves, my chest heaving with joy, I was delighted to see how much your nice Brother Mycroft dislikes that awful Rebecca West. The woman is intolerable. For me her one redeeming quality is her genuine love for you. God knows I'm no Virginia Woolf fan, but I infinitely prefer her " meandering " novels, which you find intolerable and unreadable, to the gibberings and mouthings of la West. I grunted in satisfaction when I saw in your Jan. 2nd *Tatler* article mention of Théodore de Banville and his foreseeing of the cinema.

265

I wondered when you were going to use that ; I was amazed that a man of your perspicacity had not noticed the startling common sense of Baring's essay on " Punch and Judy," in which he quotes Théodore. But now you have used it, and I'm glad. Baring's death shocked me. Only Shaw (ninety this year), Wells (eighty this year), Belloc (seventy-six this year), and you (sixty-nine this year) remain of my literary gods. Enough. I'm gibbering in a singularly Rebecca-ish manner.

3. From Reginald Moore, Editor of *Modern Reading* :

If you find anything odiously intellectual in this number of *Modern Reading* I promise to eat your page of the *Express*.

A challenge is a challenge, and here is how, on Saturday, I propose to take up this one :

Opening *M.R.* at an article entitled " Henry Goes Honky-Tonk," I find Henry Treece telling me :

1. That the thrill of Boogie Woogie " comes from the adventure of letting the hands ' taste ' the white and black in spontaneous rhythmic patterns."
2. That Boogie means " an America of smoke-laden below-stairs dives where a thug talks quietly out of the side of his mouth to a moll in a fur coat, and a third-rate pugilist argues in a Bowery voice with a wild-collared newspaperman whose mind is on selling more and more of the latest kind of cereal so that he can buy a faster car on a new instalment plan and so get an even snappier dame than the one in the corner in the fur coat."
3. That this below-stairs music, this tuneless row, this animal frenzy, this natural expression of garage-hand or coloured cab-washer, " states a proposition, an hypothesis, in terms almost as pure as a Bach fugue, or a Debussy Prelude. . . . That, then, is what Boogie means to me ; it can send me in a way I have never known before. No, not even from a Marlowe rant, or the first thrill of Pieter Breughel."

Bon appétit, Mr Moore !

Jan. 7   Cutting from a provincial newspaper : " The quartets
Monday. played were those of Cesar French in D major and Hugo
         Folf's Italian Serenade."

Letter from a young highbrow asking whether I am aware that I base my prose on the principle of systole and diastole. Somewhat spoils the effect of this by calling Jock and me the Caster and Pollocks of dramatic criticism. After which I am not surprised to hear that I am " a jagua wollowing in its jungle."

Jan. 8
Tuesday.

E. V. Lucas once said in praise of a man that " he never let you know if he was tired." I just can't help showing when I am whacked. In the early autumn of 1857 Dickens wrote to Forster :

> Too late to say, put the curb on, and don't rush at hills—the wrong man to say it to. I have now no relief but in action. I am become incapable of rest. I am quite confident I should rust, break, and die, if I spared myself. Much better to die, doing. What I am in that way, nature made me first, and my way of life has of late, alas ! confirmed. I must accept the drawback—since it is one—with the powers I have ; and I must hold upon the tenure prescribed to me.

Why do I quote this ? Because at the pantomime at the Cambridge last night I remember lighting a cigar as the curtain went up. And then nothing more till it came down at the end of the first half. And they told me that the Ganjou Brothers had been throwing Juanita about !

Jan. 10
Thursday.

Letter to an old friend :

Queen Alexandra Mansions
*Grape Street, W.C.*2
January 10th, 1946

DEAR GEORGE LYTTELTON,
    I sat up late last night re-reading Max's *And Even Now*. In the very first essay, " A Relic," I thought I caught Max out in the sentence: " A temper so violent as Mlle Angélique's must surely have brought its owner to the grave, long since." Could Max be right, and Fowler, after all these years, wrong ? Can ' since ' be used in the sense of ' ago ' ? Unlike Max to use a vulgarism in a book every sentence of which has been, to use Lear's phrase, " squinnied at." Three o'clock in the morning found me looking for some classic example which would justify Max. I found it in Sir Philip Sidney : " About two years since, it so fell out, that he was brought to a great lady's house."
    In the essay " Quia Imperfectum " I found a charming howler. Max, projecting a museum of uncompleted masterpieces—this to include Penelope's web and the original designs for the Tower of Babel—suggests " an early score of that one unfinished Symphony of Beethoven's—I forget the number of it, but anyhow it is my favourite." *Why don't men of letters get somebody to check them when they write of things outside their range ?*

And then I really did catch him out. This was in the essay " A Point to be Remembered," the point being that the Very Eminent, desirous of making an impression on a greenhorn, should always make an entry and never be entered upon : " Let those of them who have been playgoers cast their minds back to their experience of theatres. Can they recall a single play in which the principal actor was ' discovered ' sitting or standing on the stage when the curtain rose ? No. The actor, by the very nature of his calling, does, must, study personal effect. *No playwright would dare to dump down his principal actor at the outset of a play.*" (Italics mine.) Whereupon I began to cast about for refutation of Max's theory. *Richard III* : "Now is the winter of our discontent." *Volpone* : " Good morning to the day, and next, my gold ! " *Faustus* : " Settle thy studies, Faustus, and begin." Manly, in *The Plain Dealer* : " Tell not me, my good Lord Plausible, of your decorums, supercilious forms, and slavish ceremonies." Valentine, in *Love for Love*, telling Jeremy to clear his books away. Sir John Brute, in *The Provok'd Wife*, saying, "What cloying meat is love, when matrimony's the sauce to it ! " And what about Almeria, in Congreve's *The Mourning Bride*—that play which, d'you remember, was the first cause of our coming together ?—with her " Music has charms to soothe the savage breast " ? Peer Gynt telling his mother he's not lying ? Rebecca West telling the housekeeper to lay the table for supper ? And Alice telling Edgar, in Strindberg's *Dance of Death*, that it would be decent to keep quiet about a silver wedding ? These are all I had thought of up till 4 A.M.

Ever,

JAMES AGATE

P.S. 5 A.M. What about *Œdipus Rex* and *Le Misanthrope* ?

Jan. 13
Sunday.
Peter Brook, the stage director, has an interesting letter in to-day's *S.T.* about his recent production of *King John* at the Birmingham Repertory Theatre :

It was obvious from the first that the audience would miss the meaning, and thus the force, of the whole of the great soliloquy about " Commodity " because of the complete change of sense that this word has undergone. Yet, to substitute another word throughout would have been unpardonably irritating to those who knew the speech. Consequently we introduced an extra phrase on the first appearance of the word to ' plant ' its meaning :

> That smooth-fac'd gentleman, *Expediency,*
> *Or, as they say,* tickling Commodity,
> Commodity, the bias of the world. . . .

P. B. seems to be worried about the legitimacy of this. On the whole I am for rather than against, *when strictly necessary*. In the

Bastard's speech there is no great poetry to be interfered with, and no familiar passage. But are we to have the emendation

> Thus conscience—*meaning thereby consciousness,*
> *Awareness*—does make cowards of us all?

Or

> Season your admiration—*since you start,*
> *And all your visage cries astonishment*—
> With an attent ear, etc., etc.

I strongly suspect that when Lady Macbeth told her husband he had " broke the good meeting With most admired disorder " she was not using " admired " in the modern sense. But I should boggle at some such elucidatory rewriting as :

> LADY M. You have displaced the mirth, broke the good meeting,
> With most admired disorder—*going off*
> *The deep end at a silly, peevish ghost*
> *Strongly suggests that Scotland's majesty*
> *Should get a hold on's self.*

And I should certainly not allow any Macbeth I directed to enlarge thus-wise :

> Thou hast no speculation—*naught to do*
> *With throwing sprat to catch your mackerel,*
> *Nor yet debating if to be or not,*
> *Nor e'en that perlustration Walkley loved,*
> *But used in purest sense of optic power,*
> *The opposite of nictitation,*
> *Ablepsy, amaurosis, and the like*—
> *Let me repeat : horrible shadow, know*
> Thou hast no speculation in those eyes
> Which thou dost glare with.

But enough of babble, as Gilbert's Lady Jane remarked.

Jan. 14   From Henry Treece :
Monday.

January 12, 1946

I see you have been naughty again. Nevertheless, I commend your assiduity in smacking me. I cannot believe that you don't like Boogie. That would be like saying you won't have a telephone in your house, or cannot stand Technicolor. Anyway, I shall say a bad thing about you in my next book, *How I See Apocalypse*, as though you or I cared.

HENRY TREECE

But it is in Mrs Osa Johnson's *Bride in the Solomons* that I find the final word on Boogie-Woogie. It appears that if, in these islands, you want a native to bring you your saw you say, " You ketchum one fellah saw belong me." If the man is exceptionally stupid you have to explain to him that the saw is part of the hammer family. Wherefore you say, " You ketchum one fellah, he brother belong hammer. You push him, he go ; you pull him, he come." Boogie-Woogie bears the same relation to music that the Solomon Islander's gibberish bears to English.

Jan. 15   " Mais je vais vivre ! Ah ! que je me sens bien ! " were
Tuesday.   the last words of Dumas's heroine. Jan de Hartog's
        young woman puts it the other way round : " Let me die ! I have all I want ! " This pair had two things in common—consumption and a lover. Well, times change, as somebody remarked. One hundred—to be exact, ninety-eight—years ago union with the beloved was the be-all of existence ; to judge from Hartog's *Death of a Rat* (Lyric, Hammersmith), union to-day is the end-all. But perhaps we should look not to the time-lapse, but to the characters for the explanation of so startling a *volte-face*. Poor Marguerite was, God bless us, a thing of naught, whereas Yolan is a distillation of pure spirit. As I sat in my stall I couldn't help thinking of that Julia, spouse of Henry Wititterly, certified as " all soul " by Sir Tumley Snuffim, and for whose life that eminent physician would not give a pinch of snuff. Not that he did not do his medical best. " I believe I may venture to say," said Mr Wititterly, " that Mrs Wititterly is the first person who took the new medicine which is supposed to have destroyed a family at Kensington Gravel Pits." And Julia, in a faint voice, believed she was. If I had been one of the two doctors in de Hartog's play I should have tried the stuff on Yolan. The pretentious creature was a Bachelor of Astronomy. In addition, she was a Galtonic visualiser, or possibly a Dunne's-Theory-of-Time-ist (so clever a girl would not need to bother about a Dutch translation) who " interpreted actual reality in terms of prognostic reality." This enabled her to foretell the entry of Holland into the War three months later, and draw a picture of the elderly doctor dangling from a gibbet with blue tongue protruding between blue lips. Which brought us to the atom bomb. And finally to what every highbrow playwright with a gammonable management at his mercy wants to talk about—the ultimate meaning of life and death. " Life," said Yolan, " is expelled from matter at death, and returns as other matter at birth." (Had she never heard of Ibsen's Button-Moulder ?) Like Julia Wititterly, Yolan " formed an immense variety of opinions on an immense variety of subjects." Pamela Brown lovely, and not to be kept by boshist or flapdoodler from

pacing upon the mountains overhead, hiding her face amid authentic stars.

Jan. 16   Letter to a columnist :
Wednesday.

Queen Alexandra Mansions
Grape Street, W.C.2
January 16th, 1946

MY DEAR COLLEAGUE,
  My justification for this letter, remonstrance, or what you will is that we are colleagues and I am persuaded that we have the same feeling for the memory of a great artist. But I cannot help thinking that you have traduced a great stage figure. Unwittingly, I am sure. Let me come to facts.
  You ask, " What should we make of Sarah Bernhardt now ? Have we grown out of the particular form her genius took ? . . . Perhaps I am influenced by the horror which my only sight of her bred in me—this terrifying old woman with her crimped hair, trying to play a boy of twenty." So far I have nothing to say ; you are perfectly entitled to hold, and record, any impression you may have. What, in all courtesy, I will say to you is that you must not misrepresent facts. You say that you saw Sarah Bernhardt play L'Aiglon " just before her last illness, from a bath-chair." To which I can only say in my most Shakespearean manner,

> Columnist, as low as to thy heart,
> Through the false passage of thy throat, thou liest.

Or put it that thou misstatest and taradiddlest ! Thou didst not see Sarah play L'Aiglon from a bath-chair. In the absence of qualification this implies that Sarah had that contraption wheeled on to the field of Wagram and spouted from it. If you saw her in this piece after her operation it could only have been in the death scene, which she played on a sort of couch or camp bed. Verneuil is categorical about this :

" She adored *L'Aiglon,* and, being no longer able to perform it herself since her operation, she liked to see it come to life again in the persons of those who succeeded her."

" *L'Aiglon* . . . which she played until she was sixty-nine."

" . . . the death of L'Aiglon, a magnificent spectacle, but the epilogue of a play in six acts. When she played it alone her regrets became more poignant at having to renounce the rest of the part."

  Sarah had an intense horror of the ridiculous. After the amputation of her leg she *never* appeared in any part which necessitated movement. *Les Cathédrales*, the death scenes of Marguerite Gautier and the little Duc de Reichstadt, *Daniel*, and those portions of one or two classical rôles in which she could declaim from a palanquin or litter—these, I think, were all. To suggest that she broke this self-imposed rule is unfair to a great artist's sense of discretion.

You also tell your readers that Sarah was relatively unknown and had made no particular stir until " in one of those plays which Sardou turned out as rapidly as works our industrious Mr Rattigan " she produced *la voix d'or*.

But what are the facts ? The first piece of Sardou in which Sarah played was *Fédora* (1882). Now let us glance at her career up to that point. She had appeared at the Comédie Française in *Hernani, Phèdre, Adrienne Lecouvreur, Froufrou, La Dame aux Camélias, Le Sphinx, L'Étrangère, La Princesse Georges*. She had taken London by storm. (See *La Comédie Française à Londres*, 1871–1879, edited by Georges d'Heylli ; Ollendorff, 1880.) She had completed her seven months' tour of America, during which she gave 156 performances in 50 towns, the box-office takings amounting to 2,667,600 francs. She had been hailed by Sarcey as the possessor of " a talent of the first order." Victor Hugo had written verses to her. She had been painted by Parrot, Louise Abbéma, Bastien-Lepage, and Walter Spindler. And here is something which nails to the counter your fiction about the *voix d'or*. I quote from Sarcey's article in the issue of *Le Temps* for November 11, 1872. The great French critic was commenting on Sarah's début at the Comédie in *Mademoiselle de Belle-Isle* :

" Elle dit ses trois premiers actes avec un tremblement con-vulsif, et nous ne retrouvâmes la Sarah de *Ruy Blas* que dans deux couplets qu'elle fila de sa voix *enchanteresse* avec une grâce mer-veilleuse."

And yet you would have your readers believe that in 1882 Sarah had made no particular stir and the golden voice had not been heard.

Fie upon you, my dear colleague ! What about an inch or two of sackcloth and a sprinkling of ashes ?

Yours sincerely,
JAMES AGATE

Jan. 19
Saturday.
There was a fine gathering at the *Sunday Times* luncheon to its editor, W. W. Hadley, in honour of his eightieth birthday. Witty speeches from Desmond MacCarthy and Ernest Newman. R. C. K. Ensor very good on W. W.'s kindness, wisdom, and courage. There being nothing left

for me to say, I filled in with some nonsense about the eternal conflict between contributors and advertisers :

> I wonder often what the Papers buy
> One half so precious as the Space they sell.

Jan. 20
Sunday.
Fell in to-night with a Dr Freddy Renner, a native of Hamburg and a distant connection of my old friends there. He talked to me at length of his recent experiences in Nuremberg, where he has been watching the trial. " Most of the accused are listless and apathetic, like ghosts, or even dead men. Only Goering shows any liveliness, which he uses to curry favour with the Americans." Among the other things I gathered were :

1. The Germans are wholly preoccupied with how to get food, cigarettes, chocolate.

2. In so far as they have a mind for anything else they have no guilt-consciousness.

3. They are indifferent to what happens to the war criminals. These are the men who misled the Fuehrer and let him down.

4. The average German knew nothing about the atrocities, and neither did Hitler.

5. The only hope for Germany is in another Fuehrer.

6. The German ideology is unchanged. War is war. " The Americans are very happy in Nuremberg. Next time we shall be happy in New York."

The foregoing was given to me by Dr Renner as the essence of over a thousand conversations. Dr Renner also told me that the Grand Hotel at Nuremberg is a replica of the film *Congress Dances*, while the rest of the town is desolation.

Jan. 21
Monday.
Up at eight, make fire, warm some coffee, and burn some bread, houseboy and char being down with 'flu. Rush to imbecile film. Rush back to record imbecility. Rush to Shakespeare Memorial Luncheon an hour late. (You'd think Stratford could get *Love's Labour's Lost* right. But no ; everybody talks about " Love's *Labour* Lost.") Speech. Another imbecile film. Record imbecility. Whacked—since I don't get any lunch—to the point of cutting the *News Chronicle* Centenary Jamboree, in spite of having laid out 4*s*. 6*d*. on a set of dress studs. Half a bottle of champagne and early bed. Say 2 A.M., as there are still a few things to be done to *Around Cinemas*.

Jan. 24
Thursday. My secretary, John Booth-Palmer, asked and obtained my consent to this letter :

Queen Alexandra Mansions
Grape Street, W.C.2
January 24th, 1946

The Secretary
The Students' Union
The London School of Economics
Houghton Street
Aldwych, W.C.2

DEAR MR SECRETARY,

Please forgive Mr Agate for not replying to your letter right away. I haven't seen my employer for several days. Pressure of work unfortunately prevented him from noticing the pile of correspondence that was gradually collecting round him, and, alas ! he is now completely covered ! The housekeeper, the house-boy, and myself have been working like slaves to get the mass of letters cleared away. We work on the chain system. I type the replies as they hand up the letters. At our present rate it ought not to be long before we uncover Mr Agate, though the postman still mercilessly pours batches through the letter-box. At one time we thought of asking the Borough of Holborn to lend us a snow-plough, but we decided against it, as Mr Agate isn't very strong. An occasional flurry and a few grunts *de profundis* lead us to believe that he is still working.

If you would care to write again in a short time I am sure my employer would be pleased to lecture. Indeed, I think I heard him say so just before he went down.

Yours faithfully,
JOHN BOOTH-PALMER
Secretary

Jan. 25
Friday. Letter from Henry Treece :

55 *Ferriby Road*
Barton-upon-Humber
Lincs
January 24th, 1946

DEAR JAMES AGATE,

Your Solomon Island hammer-and-saw argot is interesting, though not very relevant. However, it seems to me that the native English has its *uses*. It carries a meaning between a brown man and a white one, which otherwise would not be possible.

Boogie does approximately the same thing, though because of

its formal restrictions that message must be a limited one, as I explained in my article. Nevertheless, it is a message that some people need, and which isn't conveyed by Handel or Scriabin or Delius or Elgar. It is almost purely physical in its appeal, and produces a certain exhilaration, a musical drunkenness, which certain folk like. Now the pleasure of this exhilaration is intense and not to be ignored; any more than one might ignore the pleasures produced by gin and bitters, a nice leg-glide, a beefsteak, or some of Tennyson. For all these pleasures are facets of that multiplicity which adds up to LIFE.

I too know about ' good ' music; but I am liberal enough to understand that there is more in music than can be got out of any one composer, or form, or period. Boogie, at its own level, supplies an emotional element of a specialised sort, which is absent in other forms of music. It is a primitive element, but an important one.

It is perhaps foolish to pursue on paper an argument which depends largely on auditory sensations—and I must admit that you were remarkably good at selecting those passages from my article which didn't come off because of that—but I would ask you to listen tolerantly to the piano records of Albert Ammons, " Lux " Lewis, and Pete Johnson some time. I don't imagine that you will ever like Boogie, but I feel sure that you will come to recognise in it a rhythmic and sometimes harmonic subtlety which puts it well above the cultural level of your Solomon Islander's jargon.

Yours sincerely,
HENRY TREECE

My reply :

Queen Alexandra Mansions
Grape Street, W.C.2
January 25th, 1946

DEAR HENRY TREECE,
But we agree ! Many years ago George Moore described the reading of sloppy novels as " an alternative form of bicycling." I am perfectly prepared to regard Boogie-Woogie as an alternative form of sexual intercourse. But I will never call it music.

Yours ever,
JAMES AGATE

Jan. 27   Granville-Barker (*Prefaces to Shakespeare, Fourth Series*)
Sunday.   doubts whether *Othello* can be ranked with the major
            tragedies.

Hamlet dies spiritually at peace ; Lear's madness has been the means to his salvation ; by interpreting his life's hell to us even Macbeth stirs us to some compassion. But what alchemy can bring the once noble Moor and the savage murderer into unity again ?

But suppose Shakespeare wasn't bothering about unity ? Suppose he happened on Cinthio's story and thought what a damned good play it would make ? Why must he always write high-minded tragedies ? Why not a full-blooded drama, if he feels like it ? The Charles Morgans won't be pleased—I remember how worried the *Times* critic was because Zola's Laurent and Thérèse hadn't the nervous system of the Macbeths—but I don't think that matters. Ivor Brown confessed on Sunday that the " chop her into messes " stuff sickened him—" one should be braced, not sickened, by tragedy." But why insist on tragedy ? *Macbeth* is a tragedy, and *Richard III* a melodrama. I put *Othello* midway between—what the French call a *drame*. No, this isn't a play for the Emersons, the Matthew Arnolds, or any critic who doesn't understand temperament. It has never been a play for English actors, always with the exception of Kean. (Macready ? Too moral, too grave, too sublime.) The rest of 'em have all tended to make Othello behave like Mr Dombey apprised by Carker that Edith is extending her favours to Major Bagstock. The Moor's spiritual home is not Portland Place, but all that temperamental zone south of Marseilles where volcanoes spout like whales and pastrycooks rip up their wives for an *œillade*.

Jan. 29   Letter from Ivor Brown :
Tuesday.

The " *Observer* "
22 *Tudor Street, E.C.*4
January 28, 1946

DEAR JAMES,
About Othello. If Shakespeare had written a play about a Sicilian pastrycook who knifed his women whenever he fancied another man's paw upon them, well, all right. A Sicilian tragedian could roll about in this mud-and-blood, and nobody would complain. But Othello starts almost as a Noble Roman : he is a rational and admirable man : then, for utterly insufficient reason, he becomes ape and tiger. I don't believe in him—and Iago isn't easy either. The result to me is *sordid* in a way that Shakespeare otherwise is not. Later on he could be (within the conditions of redeeming genius) silly, whimsical, grotesque—but not squalid ! If *Othello* is to be judged as a crime-story, then the villain should be a more natural creature than the icy, diabolonian Iago, and Iago's victim must be far less sensible at the start. If the excuse is Moorish Blood, then the vice of the blood must be manifest earlier instead of spilling over all at once.

Yours,
I. B.

Jan. 30   Note from May addressed to Kween Alexandra
Wednesday.   Mansions :

Fernhill
Lower Kingswood
Sunday

JIMKINS,
    I kommiserate with your kold. Here is a pound of koffee. Take kare of yourself.

Your krazy sister,
MAYKINS

    P.S. Have diskovered a new way of making the letter ' k.'

Jan. 31   " Oh that mine adversary had written a book ! " Oh
Thursday.   that my friends wouldn't write plays ! Three hours—
           three hours and a quarter, to be exact—at the West-
minster to-night : Clifford Bax's sentimental *The Golden Eagle.* All about Mary Queen of Scots. Clifford is obviously in love with an idealised Mary, who is about as interesting as a tapioca pudding. What I wanted to see was the Mary who looked like the flower, but was the serpent under it. Endowed with the brains of an Ugly Duchess. Resolute and remorseless schemer. Artist and virago, scholar and creature of appetite. The brilliantly clever woman who, at her trial, conducted her own defence. The defiant martyr who went to her execution in a bodice of crimson velvet and a petticoat of crimson satin. The obstreperous old girl who, on the scaffold, after the Dean of Peterborough had preached an interminable sermon at her, stood up to him in disputation and " prayed in opposition to him." But then hardly anybody ever writes the play one wants on this subject. To-night's company, headed by Claire Luce, did, I suppose, all they could with the milk-and-watery stuff. Not a glint of humour anywhere, except that every time David Horne came on I thought we were going to hear about that other Gunpowder Plot. Something to do with the hat and cloak, I suspect.

Feb. 1   Second letter to my columnist :
Friday.

Queen Alexandra Mansions
*Grape Street, W.C.*2
February 1*st,* 1946

MY DEAR COLLEAGUE,
    Your apology, recantation, or what you will has roused most of the breed of Agates ! My sister writes :
    " *Ce monsieur m'agace.* He maintains in his second article that he saw Sarah play ' only parts ' of *L'Aiglon* from a sitting position.

That again is not true. He saw her play only *one* part—the death scene. Can't you drive it into the dear fellow's head that *Sarah played no scene sitting down which before her operation she would have played standing up* ? Then why does he say that ' most of her triumphs were scored in plays not always of the first quality ' ? Her greatest triumphs were in Racine, Hugo, Musset, Meilhac and Halévy, Dumas *fils*, Rostand, and Maeterlinck. She tried her hand at Shakespeare, Molière, Voltaire, Sudermann, Coppée, Lemaître, Mirbeau, Catulle Mendès, and d'Annunzio. She played *Fédora*, *Tosca*, and the other Sardou pieces for the reason that our own Irving played *The Bells*—the financial reason. And, by the way, tell your friend from me that if he must instruct us about the French theatre, which we saw and he didn't, he might at least get his accents right."

I have discharged the task laid upon me. But I warn you, my dear colleague, that if we have any more nonsense we shall let loose our Brother Mycroft, a javelin of rebuke in comparison with whom May and I are but paper darts.

Ever,
JAMES AGATE

Feb. 2 Rummaging in a drawer to-day, I came across this.
Saturday. It seems that I had asked Leo to help me out with a *Tatler* article, and the thing is supposed to be an extract from a highbrow novel I am recommending M.-G.-M. to film :

Basil Bommery was, as usual, the last to arrive. Hot and dusty from his long journey, he eventailled himself with the *écran* painted by Boucher and given to his grandmother as a girl by Napoleon III. The circle, now complete, gathered round Professor Debuffer to hear something of his adventures in Central Africa. The Professor first produced a curious musical instrument, in shape a little like a helmet, with six strings on each side. This, he explained, was the Malanka-Cambamba, or Magic Harp of Angola, as it is called by the natives. He struck a few chords on this, chanting some verses in the Kapagongo dialect. Beckoning his audience to come nearer, the white-haired savant proceeded :

" When we arrived at Katapana we were received by six chiefs, each of whom offered us a putrescent coconut as an emblem of friendship. I produced my fiddle, Geoffrey Biddulph his viola, and together we played sonatas by Bach for two hours. This greatly excited the chiefs: they danced, and one of the chiefs' wives served us with Choroka-Choroka, a dish consisting of faded aspen-leaves braised in molasses, and a delicacy, I was afterwards informed, normally proffered only to Royalty. A chief called Ovakuangar then played some tribal songs on the Machuculumbwe, a double-flute with twenty holes. This, explained Ovakuangar, serves the dual purpose of being used as a musical instrument or a weapon in tribal disputes, since it is capable of discharging bullets at the rate of fifty per fifteen seconds. Dr Livingstone, I was told, had some difficulty in evading these missiles after reading the tribe of Chikumbalas lengthy extracts from Wordsworth's *Excursion*.

" After this Sandra Lobilla and I played on our two bassoons, at which the chiefs were much delighted. They danced again and threw spears ecstatically at some of their women, who dodged them with practised *expertise*. One of the chiefs, I regret to say, threw a spear at me which nearly lodged in my rear. I protested against this, but the chief chief explained that it would be unthinkable, according to the etiquette of his tribe, not to throw a spear at at least one guest in the course of the rejoicings. Next the chiefs ordered their soldiers to perform the Mkanyela, which is danced on one foot and one arm, each soldier balancing simultaneously a giant pineapple on his nose. The effect is enchanting, and reminds one of Gydnya Kosseloffsky in Rostopschin's delightful ballet *Night on the River Vodka*. After the dance the chiefs invited us into their tent, which was decorated with the painted skulls of relatives, and served us with their own hands a huge dish of Bambocha, a fricassee made, so I was told, of the choicest Magagora lizards.

" We also drank the native brew, Chanuhongu, distilled from the gall-bladders of baby ichneumons. On parting the chiefs presented each of us with a skull containing stewed vipers to sustain us on our journey. Altogether a delightful visit, though Sonia Bodega found some difficulty with the native flies—or barotse, I think they are called—which are sometimes as much as two feet long and so powerful that they are capable of snatching up the local babies and carrying them off to the river."

Every one was greatly impressed by the Professor's travel-story, and a nostalgic touch was added when the venerable lecturer threw himself face-downward on the thistles and murmured, in a voice choked with tears, " Karaheitei Bazizuzu Olikaka, kaka, koko." For some moments there was silence. And then, " Quelle nuit ambrosienne ! " sighed the Baronne de la Frôle-Derrière.

Feb. 5   In a delightful letter from G. B. E. Noel, of the Red
Tuesday.   House, Lewes Road, East Grinstead :

There is one man who for years went through the most exasperating experiences—not just occasionally, but at least twice nightly and at matinées. And never a word—not even a " tut "— did he utter, although subjected to the ribald laughter of the crowd. Yet he never did anything to improve his lot : whenever I saw him his clothes appeared, like those of the Divine Sarah (Gamp—not Bernhardt), to be " a shade more snuffy," his hair more frowsy, and his boots, like those of the discredited Pecksniff, more dim and villainous. The poor man's appearance would have startled anyone but a farmer. Starting from the top was—not a hat—that came second on the list—the first was a hank of hair—" if 'air you calls it "—sticking through holes in the Wreck of the *Hesperus* which was his hat. Frowsy whiskers and stubble covered his face, about a six months' growth. A football jersey and a great-tattered morning-coat that might have been made for a seven-foot-high Herbert Campbell. The tails swept the ground behind, and the ragged sleeves almost did the same to the ground in front ; trousers like Charlot's, only not so smart or well-fitting ; and the soles of his boots gaped from the uppers like the jaws of thirsty dogs.

In this very unsuitable outfit the man endeavoured to mount a bicycle which was in an even worse condition than his wardrobe. Whereas his clothes at least hung together, his machine did not ; it seemed to disintegrate before one's eyes whenever he tried to make the smallest adjustment. What struck me most about this man was his infinite patience *rebus in arduis*. If his sleeves caught once in his bicycle they caught a dozen times. They caught in the handlebars, the brake, the saddle, the pedals, the spokes, the step—everywhere ; and each time he carefully disentangled his rags—in case he tore them, I suppose—and started all over again like Carlyle. He had evidently neglected the care of his machine as much as his toilet, as no nuts were tight—in fact, when he was at last in the saddle the handlebars came out by the roots as soon as he sat back. He rode round and round on the bicycle, and each time he came round full circle there was something else missing, until at last there was nothing left but a sort of elemental cycle ; a monocycle now, just one wheel and pedals, and he was still riding it. But laugh ! What an artist !

After the show I had been invited to the Vaudeville Club, where my friend the secretary asked if I'd like a game of billiards. He then introduced me to a very dapper little man, and I thought to myself how very neat he looked and how well turned out. He was clean-shaven, with hair newly trimmed. He wore a white stiff collar with what looked like a new navy blue suit and shoes obviously finished off with a bone. " Sorry," I said to the secretary, " I did not quite get the name." " Sam Barton," answered the secretary. " You know, the Tramp Cyclist ! "

Feb. 7
Thursday. At Firth Shephard's luncheon to-day sat between Mary Jerrold and Coral Browne. Firth told us that in his new play there would be thirty-six young actresses—not chorus-girls, but actresses. What did Mr A. say to that ? Mr A. said he hadn't thought there were thirty-six actresses in the country. Harry Green, superb in accent and gesture, told a wonderful story. How, when he gives his six-year-old son a present costing a dollar, the kid immediately sells it to his young brother for two dollars. " I tink it should be because his mother is Swedish ! "

Feb. 8   Here are the first half-dozen in my new series entitled
Friday.   *Winged Words* :

No. 1 : Miss Courtneidge is our English Duse.

Dramatic critic, evening paper

No. 2 : The very title, *Œdipus Rex*, evokes the smart psychologist's waiting-room, or the shades of plump Good-time Charlies
who used to trail round the Riviera in the wake of their mammas.

Columnist in smart weekly

No. 3 : Monia Liter's music can be as sentimental as a baby's
toes.

Radio critic, Sunday paper

No. 4 : Miss X has the snubbiest nose, the trustingest eyes,
the friendliest little mug in all womanhood. She moves as though
there were little toy balloons under her feet.

Film critic, daily paper

No. 5 : Like many other musicians, Johann Strauss obtained
his first musical education in a church. One day his teacher found
him swinging a nifty polka. Like Geraldo and Jack Payne, young
Strauss had to get about a bit.

Organist at West End cinema

No. 6 : One happy afternoon when God was feeling good He sat
down and thought up a beautiful country, and He called it the
U.S.A.

From the film " Forever in Love "

Feb. 10   Noses, ears, and lips ! Likewise, goats and monkeys !
Sunday.   What is this demon of inaccuracy which pursues me even
           to my bed ? I am comfortably tucked up last night with
the second volume of *A Shorter Ego*, where I read about the War
Office apologising to me for not having been able to *race* my address.
So I fling the book into the fireplace, reach for Kingsmill's *Johnson
without Boswell*, and open it at :

> Cleanse the *full* bosom of that perilous stuff
> Which weighs upon the heart.

Why does H. K. make Johnson misquote ? Or are we to believe that
Johnson accepted Pope's wretched emendation ? This morning I
open the *Observer*, and find Ivor writing about last week's murder play
at the Embassy, " We are in no mood for watching the heart of our
blood-boltered Mr Bowling melt in the presence of a pious miss." But
Shakespeare applies his adjective to his murderee and not to his
murderer. To ' bolter ' is old provincial English, meaning to ' mat in

tufts '; and it was Banquo's hair which became matted, and not Macbeth's.

Talked about this to-night to the Sixty-three Club, which has something to do with the United Universities Club in Suffolk Street. Went on to compare the thoroughness of fifty years ago with the slipshoddery of to-day. Was terribly tired when I began, but freshened up after a bit.

Feb. 12   Speech at the Luncheon for the Reopening of the Curzon
Tuesday.   Cinema :

MR CHAIRMAN, LADIES, AND GENTLEMEN :
No young film critic has ever heard of Chadband. These clever young gentlemen will tell you all about Pudovkin's " Theoretical Postulates of Discontinuity " ! But they raise their eyebrows if you mention Joe Gargery or Harold Skimpole, and it is inconceivable that any of them should have heard of Chadband. Wherefore, for the benefit of these young intellectuals, should there be any present to-day, I shall explain that Chadband is a character in a novel by Charles Dickens. That he was a large, oily man with the idiosyncrasy, or what non-highbrows call habit, of defining things by their opposites, and generally in the form of a question. " My friends, what is peace ? Is it war ? No. Is it strife ? No."
One of the ways of describing the films at the Curzon Cinema, which has given us so many hours of delight and whose reopening we are celebrating to-day, is to say what in the past they were *not* like. I have been looking up my cutting-books to see what was being produced at other West End cinemas in the same week that the Curzon opened. I find that at the largest of them I saw one of New York's Four Hundred, dressed in the height of fashion of 1934, explaining to her husband in a crater on Mount Vesuvius that she had always been faithful to him. " I knew it," he said. This was his dying utterance, and as the curtains drew together the rose-pink sirocco carried the words away.
That was the kind of film which the Curzon did *not* present. Well, what kind did it present ? What did it lead off with ? It led off, I find, with a drama about Franz Schubert dying of mislaid spectacles and a broken heart. In a cornfield, which presently merged into a cathedral, with Martha Eggerth in full blast at the famous *Ave Maria*. Next there was a film about Beethoven, who contracted deafness through listening to the voice of Nature in a thunderstorm. However, it didn't really matter, because throughout the rest of the film that great actor Harry Baur was busy composing the " Moonlight Sonata," and a deaf man can listen to moonlight as well as one whose hearing is perfect.
I don't think the Curzon is going to make those mistakes again. I don't think it will show us Tschaikowsky hammering away at that

concerto, or our Mr Addinsell concocting that Warsaw rubbish. It is true that we are threatened with something about Berlioz and his *Symphonie Fantastique*. But I feel that the French film of to-day fantasticates better than it did. It is announced that the Curzon will give us none but French films—in my humble opinion the best in the world. This being so, think of the lovely things we are *not* going to have. No Hollywood star or starlet. No British bread-and-butter Miss explaining to James Mason or Stewart Granger in a modern West Kensington accent that she is Defoe's Moll Flanders. No cinema organist alternating Jerome Kern's " All the Things You Are " with Handel's *Largo*. No. We look forward to films as sophisticated as the one we saw this morning. On behalf of the guests here to-day I thank this utterly delightful cinema, whose reopening makes us giddy with expectation, for this morning's film. Let me assure the new management that whatever films it puts forward will receive the critics' fascinated, rapt attention.

Feb. 14
Thursday.

Wolfit will have to take comfort in the fact that a man may be a very fine actor and still not succeed as Othello. There was Irving, for example. Dutton Cook ended his notice of the 1876 performance :

Mr Irving's acting abounds in emotion and passion, with grateful intervals of desperate calm, as when Othello stands petrified and aghast at his own most miserable folly and crime, resembling, it must be confessed, as he folds round him his robe, one of the late Mr Fenimore Cooper's Mohawk braves draped in his blanket.

Shall say on Sunday what Henry Morley said about Fechter in the same rôle : " Though he wins no laurels, he loses none." After all, it was very clever of D. W. to arrange that, as the old Hungarian song so nearly said, more was not lost on Mohawk's field.

Feb. 18
Monday.

Week-end at Brighton on my disgusting doctor's orders. Find that my bedroom is on the fifth floor in an hotel without a lift. Asthma supervening, I crawl along the front at the rate of a hundred yards every quarter of an hour, having to stand in my tracks for two or three minutes at a time. As this is a bore to me and a nuisance to my friends, finally retire to hotel lounge, having slipped a lot of work in among my shirts. Wretchedly nervy the entire time, but am completely restored, or as much restored as I can expect to be, on getting into Victoria Station.

Feb. 21   On the advice of my increasingly disgusting doctor
Thursday.   see a specialist, who asks if I can go to live in South
               Africa. I say I can't and won't, whereupon he recom-
mends half a teaspoonful of bicarbonate of soda after breakfast. All
this takes up the entire morning. Which means that before I go to
bed I must write my *Sunday Times* article about last night's play,
see to-night's play, write about that, and then break the back of my
Express stuff.

Feb. 23   *Scarlet Street*, the new film at the Leicester Square
Saturday.   Theatre, has been banned in America. Presumably
               because it shows a gold-digger, her fancy boy, and an
amorous old fool for what they are. Had the first been shown as the
victim of a brutal stepfather, the second as Mr Decent-at-Heart
anxious to retrace his steps and take the right turning, and the third
as an old gentleman whose form of going gaga is being kind to little
girls all would have been well. But since they are painted for what
they are, and since the picture shows their alleged inevitable bad end,
America, which includes Chicago, in its pudicity has banned it.
A really immoral film would have shown the three in their true
colours and living together in perfect amity. Which, of course,
is what happens in real life. For myself I thought it a grand
film, and when I got home re-read that section of *Splendeurs et
Misères* which Balzac called " A combien l'Amour revient aux
Vieillards."

Feb. 24   *A Shorter Ego* was published during the week. Am
Sunday.   horrified to find that in the entry for February 8, 1942,
               I ask what Macbeth's going hence has to do with Lady M.
" Macbeth's " should be " Duncan's," of course. This figures in my
comprehensive list of *errata* made some months ago. But too late
for the short version, which was then binding. I suppose slips of the
pen—I prefer to call them slips of the mind—are unavoidable. Only
last week in the *S.T.* I alluded to " an old *Russian* song," knowing
all the time that it is *Hungarian*. On Monday morning I received
three postcards : " *Hungarian*, darling ! " " *Hungarian*, Mr Know-
all ! " " *Hungarian*, you bloody fool ! " But the slips should be
very rare. What I cannot understand is the columnist who gets
every other French accent wrong and discourses of Victorian Sardou
and Michael Arlan. Or the first-rate publisher who can pass *père de*

famille.   Or the admirable novelist who can quote from the old rhyme

> They drink the champagne she sends them,

and not hear that there is a syllable missing.   I shan't be able to sleep until I have dropped the author a postcard :

> They drink the champagne what she sends them.

Feb. 26
Tuesday.   Rest-cure not going well.   Rush to idiotic film about one of those young Americans who graduate at a university, study art in Paris, and return home with a vocabulary of words of one syllable : " She looked good to me, and she smelled good to me."   The whole thing took place in a wallow of Techni-horror, a welter of swimming-pools, and a world of arrested mental development.   Back to flat and prepare speech in honour of seventieth birthday of Harrap's Chairman.   Eat too little and drink too much, with result that speech goes well.   To flat again, where I sit down to write a thousand words about this morning's rubbish, but must break off to receive a deputation from the French Embassy, who want me to find a theatre for a young group of French players calling themselves " L'Atelier."   Get rid of deputation with maximum Agatian charm, finish article, and then in a snowstorm to Swiss Cottage, where I sit in a rotten temper through Sean O'Casey's *Red Roses for Me.*   Now I just don't believe in an Irish navvy who says, " Time's a perjured jade, an' ever he moans a man must die."   But then I have enough wit left to realise that I am not supposed to believe in an actual navvy any more than in actual Dublin slatterns chanting in unison like a Greek chorus composed of Kathleen ni Houlihans.   To cut it short, the trouble with to-night's play is that the characters talk O'Casey's poetry and not theirs.   Arrive at the Café Royal round about ten and find it closed, grab a bite somewhere else, and then home, where I sit up to some unthinkable hour struggling with a first draft for Sunday.

Feb. 27
Wednesday.   Work all day on the O'Casey stuff, then to theatre, home about midnight, and another go at the wretched article, which won't come right.

Feb. 28
Thursday.   " My sermon on the meaning of the manna in the wilderness," said Wilde's Dr Chasuble, " can be adapted to almost any occasion, joyful or, as in the present case, distressing."   At seven o'clock to-night, while still

hammering away at that difficult *S.T.* article, remember that at eight I am addressing the students of St Mary's Hospital and have got nothing ready. Booth-Palmer suggests I should use the lecture to the Sixty-three Club delivered some three weeks ago, which is all right except that neither of us can find it. Decide instead to use Tuesday's speech (Harrap's) coupled with the orations at the Curzon and Shephard luncheons. Great success ! Whaur's your Dr Chasuble noo ?

March 1   Here are the final exhibits in the Shakespeare-Bacon
Friday.   controversy :

  Exhibit A.   Letter from J. A. to his friend Edward D. Johnson :

February 4, 1946

You make me very cross. Only the most pedantic, pernickety, and even brain-sickly accuracy excuses entry into the lists of the Shakespeare-Bacon controversy. Why, then, on page twenty-four of your *The Fictitious Shakespeare Exposed* do you say :

" If Will Shaksper, the countryman, was the author of the plays, he was curiously unobservant of animated nature. Nowhere in the plays do we find any mention of a kingfisher, an otter, a water rat, a moorhen, or a heron. In all the woods in the plays there is no wood-pigeon, woodpecker, or squirrel " ?

Otter. What about the following colloquy from *Henry IV, Part I* ?

FAL. Setting thy womanhood aside, thou art a beast to say otherwise.

HOST. Say, what beast, thou knave, thou ?

FAL. What beast ! why, an otter.

PRINCE. An otter, Sir John ! why an otter ?

FAL. Why, she's neither fish nor flesh ; a man knows not where to have her.

Water rat. What about *The Merchant of Venice* ?

SHYLOCK. There be land-rats and water-rats.

Heron. I need not remind you that Hamlet's " I know a hawk from a handsaw " refers to the heron.

Squirrel. There are three references in the plays. You will find them in *The Two Gentlemen of Verona, A Midsummer Night's Dream,* and *Romeo and Juliet.* Now tell me. If I find you wrong in matters that I can check sitting at my desk how am I to trust you in matters for whose verification I must go abroad ?

The motto of all Baconians should be Polonius's

> Hath there been such a time, I'ld fain know that,
> That I have positively said " 'tis so,"
> When it proved otherwise ?

Why, then, do you say " 'tis so " when there is a hundred-to-one chance that it isn't so ? You say that "Jonson described Shaksper as ' a poet ape, an upstart, a hypocrite and a thief.' " I take it that this refers to an epigram in the collected edition of Ben Jonson's works, first published in 1616 ? Now let's be clear about this. Here is the epigram, and you will tell me if it is the one you are alluding to :

ON POET-APE

Poor Poet-Ape, that would be thought our chief,
Whose works are e'en the frippery of wit,
From brokage is become so bold a thief,
As we, the robbed, leave rage and pity it.
At first he made low shifts, would pick and glean,
Buy the reversion of old plays ; now grown
To a little wealth, and credit in the Scene,
He takes up all, makes each man's wit his own.
And, told of this, he slights it. Tut, such crimes
The sluggish gaping auditor devours ;
He marks not whose 'twas first : and aftertimes
May judge it to be his, as well as ours.
Fool, as if half eyes will not know a fleece
From locks of wool, or shreds from the whole piece ?

But where is the actual name which would put the thing beyond doubt ? I agree that the epigram points to Shakespeare and, if you like, that there is nobody else who fills the bill. But surely what you should have written is " Jonson described an assuming-bumptious dramatist—*presumably* Shakespeare, etc."

I am (a) disquieted, because now I don't know how much you have faked—or taken for granted, which amounts to faking—in your *Don Adriano's Letter* ; and (b) worried, because I am getting communications from eminent K.C.'s asking why I don't make mincemeat of you.

Exhibit B. Letter from Edward D. Johnson :

February 13, 1946

You are right in thinking that I was referring to the epigram in Ben Jonson's works published in 1616. I think it is clear that this epigram refers to Shaksper, as there is no one else who can possibly fill the bill. I agree that I should have written the paragraph as you suggest.

With regard to *Don Adriano's Letter* ; I set out the letter as it appears in the First Folio, together with a table showing all of the letters. It is impossible for this table to be faked, as anyone can check it over for himself. The signatures are clearly in the table, and cannot be the result of accident. If you care to send me the names and addresses of the eminent K.C.'s you mention I will send them a copy of *Don Adriano's Letter* and ask them what they make of it.

I do not know if you have ever studied that great book the First Folio. If some day you could spare me one half-hour of your precious time I should like to show you the First Folio, and I am quite sure that I could convince you that this was a production of Francis Bacon's.

Can you account for the fact that in the First Folio we get the following message : " F Bacon all my writings I did place in the grave at Stratford of our actor Master Will Shaksper A grave on peril of a curse I will devise In the hollow ground under earth behind a grate of iron bars there will be found my books " ? The curse on the grave was evidently placed there by F. B. to prevent the superstitious villagers from disturbing the grave for a considerable period of time. It is, of course, impossible to get the grave opened, as the Shakespeare Trust would fight tooth and nail to prevent this, as they would be afraid that if the grave was opened it would probably mean the end of Shaksper, Stratford, and the Shakespeare Trust.

Exhibit C. Second letter from J. A. to E. D. J. :

February 15, 1946

I am enormously interested in what you tell me about the First Folio. I suppose the ' message ' is one of those cryptogram things. Something of this sort ? Since ' William Shakespeare ' contains eighteen letters the solver takes the eighteenth, thirty-sixth, and fifty-fourth letters, and so on, until he gets his ' message.' If he finds that he wants a seventeenth letter instead of an eighteenth he just knocks the ' e ' off the end of ' Shakespeare.' Does he want the sixteenth letter ? Then he also deletes the ' e ' in the middle. And so on with all the various ways of spelling ' Shakespeare.' And then there's ' William,' or ' Will,' or just ' W.' Or the first name could be omitted altogether. And if the thing doesn't come right that way the solver jettisons ' William Shakespeare ' and starts again with ' Francis Bacon.' It must be great fun. Now, my dear sir. Am I doing the Baconians an injustice or not ? Could you briefly give me an idea of how this ' message ' is arrived at ?

Exhibit D. Second letter from E. D. J., shortened :

February 18, 1946

Francis Bacon inserted a number of ciphers in the First Folio of the ' Shakespeare ' Plays, one of the most interesting being what may be termed a sixth-line word cipher. He chose the sixth lines because he never missed an opportunity of showing the numerical seal or count of the name Bacon, which is 33. When planning the lay-out of the First Folio he decided that each full column should contain 66 lines, as 66 is double 33, which represents his name. Looking at the number six six, he thought it would be a good idea to insert cipher messages on the sixth line counting down and the sixth line counting up the columns, but as this would not give him sufficient scope he decided also to use the sixth lines counting up or down from the entrance or exit of a character, and also the sixth lines counting up or down from the beginning or end of a scene, and it will be found that this is the method that he adopted. He also used the reverse page numbers, and to show the reader that he is going to do this he numbered the last page in the First Folio, which should be 399, 993—the reverse of 399. He also mis-paged certain of the pages to make pages bear the same number, either true or false. This sixth-line word cipher is an extraordinary piece of work, and the way in which he inserted words in lines which bear the same number counting from certain points on pages which bear or represent the same number, and then arranged for such words when joined together and interlocked to form sentences to convey messages to the reader, and his ability to incorporate such words in the text so as to make sense with the rest of the text, is almost beyond human comprehension. But the fact remains that he did so, taking a great delight (although it may appear childish) in juggling with letters, words, and numbers, to make them do exactly what he wished. Only a man with a mathematical brain and an infinite capacity for taking pains could have carried out such an arduous task.

Johnson then gives seven lines from the First Folio, with the italicised words alleged to constitute the message :

" *Heeres the challenge, reade it, I warrant theres* "
" Must we pursue and I have found *a path to it* "
" Not stay for him to kill him, have I not at the *place I did* "
" *In all my writings.* Go with me and see "
" have the gift of a *Grave* "
" Last night I heard they lay at Stony *Stratford* "
" But beare it as *our* Roman *actors* do "

A message to the reader is at once seen formed out of the words at the *beginning* or *end* of these lines, with the exception of the last line, when the words to complete the message are found in the middle of this line, as follows : " Here's the challenge, read it—I warrant there's a path to it—I did place—all my writings in—our actor's—Stratford Grave."

Exhibit E. Third letter from J. A. to E. D. J. :

February 23, 1946

I am not surprised that the message given in your second letter doesn't quite tally with the first. I don't suppose you carry your First Folio about with you any more than I used to cart around my books on the Dreyfus case. Nor will I boggle at the assumption that " our actor " means Shakespeare ; it couldn't be anybody else. Or at the transpositions without which you would be defeated. But there is one thing I want to ask. When did F. B. place his writings in the grave ? Before, during, or after the funeral ? Is there any evidence that he was at the funeral ? Travelling in those days was a slow business. The news would have had to get from Stratford to London, and then F. B. would have to make his journey. (We know that the funeral took place within three days.) Is there any evidence as to the date at which the " Cursed be he " tablet, or whatever it is, was set up ? Did F. B., if he wasn't at the funeral, break into the grave later and then set up the warning ? He talks about " a grate of iron bars," which is a cumbersome bit of furniture. Is it supposed that F. B. did all the tinkering unbeknown to the Church authorities ? Didn't they question an old gentleman prowling around in the dead of night ? Or did F. B. declare his identity ? Then, in the spring of 1616, when Ellesmere, the Lord Chancellor, was dangerously ill, wasn't Bacon pretty busy trying to manœuvre himself into the job ? Would he, in the circumstances, be likely to be wandering about the country prising open tombs ? If it wasn't F. B., who was his deputy ? I don't expect a complete answer to these questions, since this would probably take up too much of your time. What I should like is the general line of reply. And may I ask you to put established facts in black ink, and surmises in red ?

Exhibit F. Third letter from E. D. J. :

February 26, 1946

You ask me a number of questions which I cannot possibly answer, and which I should imagine no one else can either, after a lapse of 330 years. If any writings were placed in the grave it must have been some considerable time after the funeral, probably when the slab containing the curse was placed over the grave. So far as I know the first reference to the curse is in Malone (1790). F. B. in the cipher says that he erected the statue on the church wall. He must have obtained the permission of the Church authorities to do this, but how or when we shall never know. W. S. died in April 1616.

It would take some time to produce both the curse tablet and the monument, and it seems quite likely that these were not placed in the church for several years after the death of W. S., and this would give F. B. plenty of time to collect the writings ready for interment at the time the curse tablet was placed on the grave. There are, of course, no established and proven facts, and that is the trouble. The claim that F. B. wrote the plays does not depend on this cipher, but on the evidence contained in the First Folio, and that is the reason why I want to show you a number of very interesting things in this great book, quite apart from this cipher.

February 27, 1946

I shall be delighted if next time you are in Town you will bring me the First Folio, if it's portable, when I promise you I will look at it in a " trifling, ladylike, amateur manner " that isn't going to compromise me. I think you Baconians have got something. But not everything ; I just cannot believe that all these cryptograms and ciphers are flukes. My theory is that F. B., who was a frequenter of playhouses, fell in with young Shaksper from Strat-ford, and that the two put their heads together in a trifling and gentlemanlike manner that didn't compromise either of them. What I will not believe is that Shaksper had enough knowledge of the polite world to produce the whole of the plays himself, or that the author of the essays, which read like the prospectus of an insurance company dealing in endowment policies, had an ounce of poetry in his composition. But deeper into the subject I will not delve. It has for me the same fascination as the Dreyfus case, the Mystery of the *Marie Celeste*, and the Wallace case. Or you might put it that while in respect of this question of total authorship I am a poor Shaksperite I am a hell of a bad Baconian.

I wind up with a note from my friend Arnold Taylor :

One might wish that W. S.'s dealings in malt and in his old age were otherwise, but not long ago it was discovered that the blame-less Titian, when in his nineties, indulged in some very shady speculations in timber, so William is at least in good company. I have a book *Le Mystère Shakespearien*, by Georges Counes, a Dijon professor. It sets out the theories of the various claimants to the authorship of the plays—Bacon, Oxford, Derby, and Rutland. He does not criticise them, but leaves them to contradict each other. And his witty conclusion is " Il me semble que, comme Bacon disait que, si un peu de science éloigne de Dieu, beaucoup de science y ramène, si une étude superficielle du problème Shakespearien éloigne de Shakespeare, une longue étude y ramène." To which I think we may safely say " Amen."

March 2   Quiller-Couch, Maurice Baring, Logan Pearsall Smith—
Saturday.   I have regarded these three as a preserve of my own.
            In the sense that I was always dipping into *Shake-speare's Workmanship*, *Punch and Judy*, and *On Reading Shakespeare*, and alone of the dramatic critics quoted from them. Often. And now the last of this gracious trio has gone. I never met " Q," and was on the point of writing to tell him of many years of admiration when he died ; wherefore a few weeks later I persuaded the B.B.C.

to let me give a Sunday reading from the essay on *The Tempest*. I set this down for reasons similar to those which made Pearsall Smith think it lawful to copy out De Quincey's famous passage on the knocking at the gate in *Macbeth* :

> I conclude by asseverating that were a greater than Ariel to wing down from Heaven and stand and offer me to choose which, of all the books written in the world, should be mine, I should choose—not the *Odyssey*, not the *Æneid*, not the *Divine Comedy*, not *Paradise Lost* ; not *Othello* nor *Hamlet* nor *Lear* ; but this little matter of 2000 odd lines—*The Tempest*. " What ?—rather than *Othello* or than *Lear* ? " Yes : for I can just imagine a future age of men, in which *their* characterisation has passed into a curiosity, a pale thing of antiquity ; as I can barely imagine, yet can just imagine, a world in which the murder of Desdemona, the fate of Cordelia, will be considered curiously, as brute happenings proper to a time outlived ; and again, while I reverence the artist who in *Othello* or in *Lear* purges our passion, forcing us to weep for present human woe, *The Tempest*, as I see it, forces diviner tears, tears for sheer beauty ; with a royal sense of this world and how it passes away, with a catch at the heart of what is to come. And still the sense is royal : it is the majesty of art : we *feel* that we are greater than we know. So on the surge of our emotion, as on the surges ringing Prospero's island, is blown a spray, a mist. Actually it dwells in our eyes, bedimming them : and as involuntarily we would brush it away, there rides in it a rainbow ; and its colours are wisdom and charity, with forgiveness, tender ruth for all men and women growing older, and perennial trust in young love.

Neither did I ever meet Logan Pearsall Smith, but am glad to think that I sent his *On Reading Shakespeare* to Maurice Baring, who did not know it, a few weeks before M. B. died. In the section called " The Enigmas " L. P. S., discussing the old question whether Shakespeare is better on the stage or in the study, and preferring the second, writes :

> How, I ask you, are stage-enthusiasts—I ask you, Granville-Barker, and you, too, Desmond MacCarthy, and you, Maurice Baring—going to answer Robertson, Charles Lamb, Hazlitt, Coleridge, Goethe and me ? It is really up to you to make a reply ; and such a reply to be valid should, I suggest, enumerate first of all the scenes in Shakespeare's plays which are only effective upon the stage ; and secondly a record of concrete esthetic experiences, of the rendering of Shakespearean rôles by great actors and actresses by which the imaginative impression of these rôles has been deepened and enriched.

The complete answer to this would need a book. But here, I think, is something out of the play of *Hamlet*. The Ghost has stalked away on the line " Adieu, adieu, adieu ! remember me." Whereupon Hamlet, lying on the ground, has his " O all you host of heaven ! " Of all the Hamlets I have seen Wolfit is the first to go into his swoon *lying on his back*. He recovers, and apostrophises the first thing that meets his eyes—the stars. Since, in my knowledge, no other Hamlet has thought of this I doubt whether the notion has occurred to many readers. Then take that bit in *King Lear* where the stage direction reads, " Enter Lear, fantastically dressed with wild flowers." I find an enormous increase in pathos when I have the visual sense of the benign, summer-afternoon sunshine. And I certainly do not think that the scene in *Antony and Cleopatra* where the stage direction " Music of hautboys as under the stage " leads up to " 'Tis the god Hercules, whom Antony loved, now leaves him," is as effective to read as when you hear the music and see the soldiers who recognise it as a portent. I think that Pearsall Smith perceived a divided duty in this old allegiance. At one moment he writes :

> It certainly does sound preposterous for those who love Shakespeare's drama to peer only through their spectacles at its text ; to shudder at seeing it acted, and to maintain that the fullness of its dramatic effect is thwarted and counteracted by the only means of securing that effect which ever, for a moment, occupied Shakespeare's thoughts.

At another :

> I persist in reading Shakespeare's plays with my own intelligence, and in witnessing their performance in a theatre of my own imagination, lit as it is by the light of lamps far different from those which glared before the stage.

But the book is balanced, sane, witty, and lovely everywhere. For myself I have a tripartite duty—to its author, to " Q," and to Maurice.

March 3 There is this to be said for British films, that they never
Sunday. descend to the level of Hollywood's worst. One day
last week I saw a picture in which a horse galloped up to John Wayne, who was throwing steers in a rodeo competition, to tell him that Jean Arthur wasn't going to die of pneumonia. Or perhaps it was the horse that wasn't going to die, and Jean who came cantering up with the news. Nothing as pitiful as that happened

at the British Film Festival, organised by the *Daily Mail* and held at the Leicester Square Theatre this afternoon. The occasion was mildly interesting because of the mild quality of the six films, bits of which were recited by flesh-and-blood actors into a microphone. There were three resonant speeches by Eric Portman, Anton Walbrook, and Robert Donat, but for the rest I couldn't get up any kind of interest. The music struck me as being of a hopeless mediocrity, so many attempts to improve on Elgar and doing less well than Edward German. And why did they have to trot out that resounding piece of emptiness the *Warsaw* concerto? This was all very well as background music to the film for which it was designed, since it wittily suggested that something in the concert line was going on. As I sat listening I watched my old friend Alec Whittaker tootling away as gravely as though it had been the *New World* symphony. Unless I dreamed, he kept his eyes closed throughout the entire proceedings, but opened them once to wink prodigiously in my direction. The object of the jamboree was the award of a trophy representing " a nation-wide recognition of brilliance in acting and production, based on the judgment expressed voluntarily by the great British cinema-going public." Meaning, I take it, the readers of a particular daily paper. But suppose the result of the *Daily Mail* plebiscite doesn't agree with the recent *Daily Express* plebiscite on the same subject? And suppose the *News Chronicle* and the *Daily Herald* weigh in with more plebiscites? In any case how much judgment has the great British cinema-going public? Enough to choose between Mr A's teeth and Mr B's shoulders, Miss X's ankle and Miss Y's calf. Odd, by the way, that there was no mention of two films which made some stir at the time—*Henry V* and *Cæsar and Cleopatra*!

March 4   I see by the paper that Donald Wolfit has been talking
Monday.   to the Critics' Circle. " Dramatic critics must possess the faculty of keeping young in heart." How old in heart, meaning how worn in mind, does D. W. think Shaw was when he put on the map of this country the greatest dramatist since Molière? And put him wittily on the map?

But the first act of *Rosmersholm* had hardly begun on Monday night, when I recognised, with something like excitement, the true atmosphere of this most enthralling of all Ibsen's works rising like an enchanted mist for the first time on an English stage. There were drawbacks, of course. The shabbiness of the scenery did not

trouble me; but the library of Pastor Rosmer got on my nerves
a little. What on earth did he want, for instance, with *Sell's
World's Press*?

D. W. went on to say that Shaw's criticisms had been brilliant, but
he did not think they should be imitated. I cannot think of a time
when the London stage had more need of an imitator. Finally D. W.
suggested that Clement Scott was a far better pattern for the health
of our theatre than the new freeman of Dublin. Meaning, as all
actors mean, that the function of the critic is not to dissuade people
from seeing twaddle, but to gloss over twaddle in order to pack the
people in. Before I was told to take things easy I should have
written a full-length letter to Wolfit telling him my views on what to
me is nonsense and why I hold it to be nonsense. But such a letter
would have taken me two hours, whereas this Diary entry has taken
me ten minutes. Wherefore let it be put on record that to-day I
made my first successful attempt to do less work.

March 5　　*Symphonie Fantastique*, at the Curzon, is a bad film
Tuesday.　　because the material is not there to make a good one.
　　　　　　Berlioz's life falls into three categories. His music—there
is not enough of it in this picture. His unending struggles, and the
infinite boredom of the scribbling by which he had to keep himself
alive.

　　　I return to my treadmill—journalism—once more, and oh!
the horror of it! The misery of writing to order an article on
nothing in particular—or on things that, as far as I was concerned,
simply did not exist since they excited in me no feeling of any
description whatsoever.

The film merely hints at this. Last there's the wit; this film has
none. What it does give is the marriage with Henriette Smithson,
and the tedious second marriage with Marie Recio. Of Smithson
there is very little to tell. When Charles Kean went over to Paris
to play Hamlet she was his Ophelia, and a very bad one; Hazlitt
dismisses her in a sentence : " Miss Smithson is tall ; and the French
admire tall women." About the second wife there is even less to
be said. She was a fool who, to quote Grove, " frequently imperilled
the success of her husband's work by insisting on the leading part in
its performance." To-day's film showed her as one of those lambent
imbeciles who desert an artist at his most need on the plea that it
will be good for his art. But there were compensations. The nobility

of art, the power of music, and the compulsion of work—all these were recognised. There was no suggestion of commonness. Even so, there were things in Berlioz's life which could have been done better. Paganini makes one entry after the failure of *Benvenuto Cellini*, when he comes to tell the composer that he has written a work of genius. After which he stalks away like the Ghost in *Hamlet*. How much more dramatic to have reproduced the scene from the Life. It was after a concert at which both the *Symphonie Fantastique* and *Harold in Italy* had been given :

> Paganini, with his little son, Achille, appeared at the orchestra door, gesticulating violently. Consumption of the throat, of which he afterwards died, prevented his speaking audibly, and Achille alone could interpret his wishes. He signed to the child, who climbed on a chair and put his ear close to his father's mouth, then, turning to me, he said, " Monsieur, my father orders me to tell you that never has he been so struck by music. He wishes to kneel and thank you." Confused and embarrassed, I could not speak, but Paganini seized my arm, hoarsely ejaculating, " Yes ! Yes ! " dragged me into the theatre, where several of my players still lingered—and there knelt and kissed my hand.

Next day Berlioz tells us that he received a letter from the virtuoso enclosing a note for twenty thousand francs. Who would have expected a French film to miss this ? Good performance by Jean-Louis Barrault, and nice to see that the film company includes the composer's name in its list of credits !

March 6   In a letter from George Lyttelton :
Wednesday.

> By the way, Charles Fry on W. G. as compared with Ranji. How could he judge ? He never saw W. G. before the 'nineties. My father, who often played with the old man in the 'sixties and often saw him in the 'nineties, always said the young W. G. was much better than the old one, and he was no *laudator temporis acti.* Mainly because he was far quicker, which is not surprising, as he was at least six stone lighter.

March 9   Last night's *Song of Norway*, at the Palace, was a
Saturday.   glittering horror. Sat up half the night demolishing
              it :

> Berlioz, who was punster as well as wit, wrote to Madame Ernst, " On vous demande comment vous avez passé la nuit, jamais comment vous passez l'ennui." Or one might ask, *A quoi*

rêvent les jeunes filles as their eyes and ears drink in the enthralling story of how Chopin died of George Sand, and Schubert of mislaid spectacles ? To find their answer is easy. They ask why the whole of life should not be light opera, why young ladies should not for ever clasp to their bosoms bunches of myosotis presented by blushing cavaliers. But of what do old men dream as they watch the familiar witlessness unfold itself, the critics who could tell you the plot backwards before the curtain goes up, the carpers who think that sumptuosity and glitter should clothe something more than vacuity ? Archer's recommendation was sleep. Did some of us, gazing at that handsome backcloth of alp and fiord, murmur something about " night-dews on still waters between walls of shadowy granite, in a gleaming pass," and ask ourselves whether the modern poet despises song or just can't sing ? Or did we think of that sea in terms of Ibsen ? How Ellida came from it and little Eyolf fell into it. How the " Indian Girl " sailed over it. How Peer Gynt might have been drowned in it. How Captain Alving caroused and made lewd jokes by it. How Oswald Alving braved it when he went to Paris, unless, of course, he took the overland route via St Petersburg and Pskof. Did we add up the number of times anybody in the plays is allowed to eat or drink anything ? (Mrs Borkman, who hasn't seen her sister for eight years, doesn't offer her even a cup of tea.) Did we, in the mind's eye, conjure up a vision of the Old Man glaring out of his hedge-hoggery of whisker in rapt disfavour at the I'm-to-be-Queen-of-the-May frolics and gambollings ? Did we, getting back to the matter in hand, cast about for reasons why a composer known to be third-rate—' miniaturist ' is a politer word—at the beginning of the evening should be rapidly declining to fifth-rate as the pro-ceedings drag on, and will be seventh-rate before the curtain finally falls ? Did we ask why, in the ball scene, six young women should take to dancing Solveig's Song ? Or wonder whether six old women would make six teetotums out of the dying Ase ? Or make a bet with our neighbour on how long it would be before the waiters handing round the ices lifted up their voices and gave us yet another chunk of that Piano Concerto ? And so on. . . .

March 11   The modern critical dislike of Richard Strauss is becoming
Monday.   farcical. Here is the *Times* music critic on the concert
              given yesterday by the Concertgebouw Orchestra of
Amsterdam :

Berlioz's *Symphonie Fantastique* was chosen—mercifully in pre-ference to *Ein Heldenleben*—to show the capacity of the orchestra at its full strength.

This opens up a charming field. Presently we shall be reading :

Elgar's *Cockaigne* Overture was chosen—mercifully in preference to *Till Eulenspiegel*—to show the orchestra's sense of wit.

Or :

Mozart's *The Marriage of Figaro* was chosen—mercifully in preference to *Rosenkavalier*—to show the orchestra's sense of period.

Or even :

Brahms's *Feldeinsamkeit* was chosen—mercifully in preference to *Morgen*—to show the singer's feeling for natural beauty.

March 12
Tuesday. Falstaff was the cause that wit was in other men. Nobody can take it from me that I am the cause that people write me good letters. I just don't believe that anybody in London received three better letters this morning than I did. Here they are :

From a sergeant in the Pacific :

> *NX123658*
> *Sgt. G. McIntyre*
> *Legal H.Q. Morotai Force*
> *Morotai*
> *Australian Military Forces*
> *27th February* 1946

Dear Mr Agate,

This letter is written from the tropical island of Morotai—" the Island of the Dead " to the Indonesians. At present Japanese war criminals are being tried here for offences against us and our Allies.

In a case before the court to-day the men had taken part in the execution of an airman whom they had captured on some island in the Banda Sea. There have been several similar cases, but a new element was introduced this morning.

Kateyama, the accused, has given his evidence. He had been chosen to do this solemn service (the beheading) in honour of those condemned. " In Japanese chivalry, we thought it an honour on behalf of the condemned, not to ourselves. It was my first experience to carry out that solemn but dreadful execution," was part of his plea.

Kateyama speaks English, and claims to be a Christian—a Methodist. He has an Aunt Winnie in Japan. " Aunt Winnie " is an Englishwoman, born in London, and married since 1937 to " Uncle Yamaguchi " of Tokio. When she heard that Kateyama had been arrested as a war criminal she wrote good-character references for him, expounding at length his careful upbringing and expressing belief in his innocence. She added, however, that if he had done wrong he was to be punished. Throughout his evidence he spoke of his " Aunt Winnie " or " Auntie," and much had been made of his good connections.

To-day is February 27, 1946. This morning *Ego* 7 arrived for me from Australia. Reading it before the afternoon sitting commenced, I reached the entry for 27 February 1944, the pronouncement of Austin Melford, "Close those eyes, Geoffrey—close them. Ah, yes, I've murdered him. *What will his aunt in Japan say ?*"

It was as a voice from another world, similar to those cases where guidance is sought by plunging a pin into an inspired writing, and extracting an enlightened text. I at once drew the attention of the Prosecutor (whom I am assisting) to the extraordinary circumstances. The Defending Officer was consulted, and the matter brought to the attention of the court. An exhausting discussion followed as to whether your script should be elevated to the status of an inspired pronouncement, or on the other hand, of equal significance, would it be reasonable to regard past pronouncements from inspired sources as no more than coincidental dipping into ' profane ' writing ?

Opinions were hotly expressed—sacred and profane—and it is now up to the court, in arriving at their verdict, to decide how much weight should be given to the incident—" Karma or Coincidence ? "

The implications are far-reaching. In effect, there is the possibility that may arise of a general and legal (International Law) recognition of your *Ego* attaining to and containing (in your lifetime) some mystical significance.

It is a chain of unusual events—your London story 27 February 1944, the inclusion in *Ego*, the arrival on Morotai via Sydney on 27 February 1946, the execution trial with all its emphasis on his aunt in Japan, and the reading in the atap-roofed court hut at such a moment in all time.

As a consistent and appreciative reader of the *Egos* and other books and essays by you, it gives me much pleasure to bring the facts before you.

Yours sincerely,
GRANT McINTYRE

Later P.S. The court has just announced its verdict. Kateyama has been found guilty.

G. McI.

Still later P.P.S. The court has just sentenced Kateyama to death by shooting. Congratulations and salutations, Mr Agate, and does it make you feel elevated or frighteningly responsible ?

G. McI.

From St John's Wood :

March 10th, 1946

DEAR MR AGATE,

Pursuing and enjoying yet another *Ego*, I am reminded that there once lived in this house an even greater Bernhardt-addict than yourself. She lived here most of her life, and died shortly before we came in 1914.

Miss X always dressed entirely in black, and never went out except when Sarah Bernhardt was in London. She then dressed in undiluted white and sallied forth in a carriage—often visiting the actress, who returned the visits to this house.

Miss X had a box at the theatre, and attended every performance of her goddess; she also sent her one dozen red carnations, every day of the year to whatever part of the world Bernhardt might be in, from the florist in Finchley Road, at the top of this road. The ex-owner, the late Mr Amy, once told me that this order was worth £500 a year to him.

When we came here the garden was full of busts of the Divine Sarah. We had a divine time throwing divine bricks at them, pieces of which still form indispensable parts of our somewhat-less-divine rockery. Creeping Jennie now grows over the noses you both admired so much!

With thanks for much enjoyable reading.

I remain,

Yours sincerely,

RONALD T. HORLEY

From C. B. Fry:

1. W. G. was very tall, and long and loose of limb, and when young a large-sized athlete. He was very keen and shrewd and kindly and domineering—except with squires and noblemen. He was rather sheep-faced, vacillating with females, but *very* fond of his wife.

2. In his time wickets were good on the county grounds but *lively*, and *the* danger was *fast bowling*, and there were a lot of *good* fast bowlers.

When a batsman went in (a top-notcher) he felt that if he could master the fast stuff the rest was easy, comparatively.

3. Now W. G. stood tall, and simply thumped fast bowling all over the place. He didn't *lunge*. He just stood where he was and *pressed* it or leant against it. *And* he was a very clever and safe late cutter, as he was well above even the high rising ball and cut with an almost straight bat rather like a slicing backstroke. He so outplayed all the other bats of his time *at the fast bowling* that *this alone* gave him indisputable and admired eminence.

4. He could play medium pace bowling on good wickets with a toothpick—with his huge reach, fine timing, and lambent eye.

5. Above all he was studiously correct, and he really did watch the ball—ate it up with his eyes.

6. He never liked good slow bowling as he did fast, and was rather doubtful at good leg-breaks. But he was a magnificent driver both off and on, and when young could jump out to clout the good length ball from the slower bowlers.

7. His body poise was *correct* for the main strokes, but he had

no *nicety and beauty* of poise, no facile adaptability as Ranji had ; nor had he the acrobatic quickness of Don Bradman. Ranji had, and the Don has, a much quicker and more facile power of hand (usually called wrist) that gives acceleration of the stroke just before impact.

8. W. G. was a fine hitter on wet wickets, but not a specially good back player, and he could, or did, not hook—not free enough of foot.

9. W. G. was a tremendous batsman—a giant. But he was conventional, compared with Ranji and the Don.

10. Ranji's virtues were (*a*) peculiar quickness, (*b*) lovely supple facile body-poise, (*c*) brains.

11. W. G. was Cœur-de-lion, Ranji was Saladin (*cf. The Talisman*).

12. W. G.'s fame was as the Champion All-rounder. He was the best change bowler of his time, and worth his place on this count alone in the England XI. That is usually forgotten. His vivid, giant, bearded personality was one reason he was regarded as the nonpareil.

13. The difficulty in these valuations is, in dealing with *evidence*, to distinguish scientific observation and sentiment. W. G. was a beloved national institution and his excellence sacrosanct. He was a terrific big fellow and a great sportsman.

14. By the way, he had immense *stamina*, and could go on batting at full pressure all day.

15. *N.B.* Through all his best seasons in England Ranji had asthma, and often did not sleep till 6 or 7 A.M. He was a marvel.

C. B.

March 13
Wednesday.   Twelve years ago the play made out of James Laver's *Nymph Errant* was a good entertainment. Or perhaps Cole Porter's music and a cast containing Gertrude Lawrence, Norah Howard, Bruce Winston, Morton Selten, Austin Trevor, and my sister May turned it into good entertainment. To-night's new version, which they call *Evangeline*, seemed to me vulgar tawdry, and silly beyond words. In the middle of the scene in which Evangeline (Frances Day) makes her bargain with the slave-dealer an odd thing happened. The stage disappeared, and in its place I beheld a vision, or succession of visions, constituting the new musical play to end all musical plays. First a ball in old Vienna. Brahms, minus his beard, resplendent in the uniform of the Budapest Guards, casts a countess from him, announcing that he is now all for music and the simple life. In the second act B. is wandering in the woods in search of some long-lost Hungarian dances. The third act happens in

a gipsy encampment, bounded on one side by Mohac's Field and on the other by Wardour Street, the distant spire being that of St Mohac-in-the-Fields. To the thrumming of zithers peasants madly dance. Flagons circulate gaily, and copious draughts of yohimbine, penicillin, and M. and B. are consumed. Seated on a log in the foreground is the now fully bearded composer taking it all down in full score. As the curtain falls the Four Serious Songs are being crooned, swung, jazzed, and jived through floodlit loud-speakers. The vision then faded. And as I opened my eyes the Chief Eunuch was lowering Day through a manhole into the Bosphorus.

March 14
Thursday.

Here's a how-de-do. Here's a state of things. May is naturally anxious to see a reprint of her book on Sarah, and Bertie van Thal, who would like to oblige, can't at the moment because he hasn't the paper, wherefore he seeks my moral and advisory support. The result is a letter from May to me beginning, " Dear Mr Jorkins, I rang up Mr Spenlow yesterday. . . ." To which I have replied, " Dear Agnes Wickfield, must you behave like Dora ? " If there is a moral here it is : Never come between a sister and her publisher. May is a great if sometimes masterful dear, and I shall have my revenge by publishing a picture of her at the age of two, fondling a photographer's stuffed seagull.

March 15
Friday.

Of all the reviews I have ever had of the longer or shorter *Ego* Frank Singleton, of the *Bolton Evening News*, has written the one which has given me the most pleasure :

" The English," says Mr James Agate, " instinctively admire any man who has no talent and is modest about it." He himself presents them with the contrary problem ; and though he likes to be admired he makes no concessions to achieve that end. In succeeding volumes of his diary *Ego* he has told us of his extravagances, his debts, his stepping ponies, his friends, and above all the theatre and theatre world in which he is such an outstanding figure. Now he has himself made from this exuberant record *A Shorter Ego*, of which two volumes are published. By doing so Mr Agate has achieved a book which may well fulfil for him that " insane desire," as he calls it, to perpetuate oneself. By contracting his diaries Mr Agate has achieved an improvement like Macaulay's when, after his return from India, there began to be noticeable in the unbroken stream of his conversation " flashes of silence."

It is no good criticising Mr Agate. You must take him as he so generously allows you to find him—on every page, in every paragraph, take him or leave him for other diversions and consolations in whose existence he will not believe. He offers incomparable entertainment, and it is a dull reader who cannot catch beneath the exuberance the muffled drums of life relentlessly advancing beyond laughter into the unknown. The self-professed egotist can recognise " that timidity of which every man in his heart of hearts knows something." The lover of life is conscious of death approaching. His book will live as one of the most extraordinary records of vitality in the language, and when Mr Agate is really old he can, like the Wife of Bath, be tickled to the roots of his heart to remember that he has had his world as in his day.

March 16 Last night of *Sweeter and Lower*. Sent Gingold two
Saturday. white camellias, symbolising the blamelessness of her
life and mine. Also a letter saying, " Good luck to your next show. Let's hope the first night doesn't take place on the same day as the Regent's Park Van Horse Parade, which I am judging. I should hate to confuse the two." G. wore the flowers in the last scene, and at the end produced my *billet doux* from her corsage and read it to the audience.

March 17 Reply to an unknown correspondent, telling me that he
Sunday. is the original of Comus in Saki's *The Unbearable
Bassington* :

This gives me a real thrill. Munro's masterpiece is one of my favourite bed-books. *I never tire of it.* But can you have been so enchantingly impossible ? I doubt it. And I am certain that H. H. never said when you, an officer, invited him, a corporal, to dine in your mess, " Between you and *I* now is a great gulf fixed." But then I don't believe that Abraham said to a certain rich man, " Between *we* and you there is a great gulf fixed." Saki's Comus would have found it a pleasure as well as a duty to expose this howler. The person he would most have liked to abash in public ? His potential patron, Sir Julian Jull, of course. Again, I just can't believe that you didn't die in that West African swamp. " His epitaph in the mouths of those that remembered him would be : Comus Bassington, the boy who never came back." Since no man can contradict his epitaph you must be bogus, a fake, an impostor. But an impostor I should much like to meet in the flesh. Will you lunch with me on any date you like to name at the Ivy Restaurant, 1.30 ? I'll invite the ghosts of Francesca, Ada Spelvexit, Lady Caroline Benaresque, Élaine de Frey, and Courtenay Youghal. Apart from these, all the haunt shall be ours. And, of course, Saki's. In the meantime I start to-night re-reading the book for the seventh time. Which is one more than Stevenson with *Le Vicomte de Bragelonne*.

March 18   Lunched at the Ivy with George Lyttelton and Edward D.
Monday.   Johnson. The latter told us that his seventh great-
             grandfather and Dr Johnson's grandfather were the same
person. He brought with him a facsimile of the First Folio and
staggered us. At the end of the afternoon I made him, so to speak,
a present of his ciphers, the point being that while they prove Bacon
to have had a great hand in the plays they do nothing to disprove
Shakespeare's part in them. As G. L. put it, " Nothing that anybody
can show me will make me believe that Bacon wrote ' Come unto
these yellow sands.' "

March 19   About Baconians in general I feel that if they could
Tuesday.   force on the world recognition of Bacon's authorship
             of Shakespeare's plays they wouldn't mind if the works
disappeared to-morrow. Whereas Shakespeareans love the plays
for their own sake, and take no more than an amused interest
in who wrote them. At least that is my position. And I shan't
budge.

March 20   To satisfy reviewers clamouring for a more personal
Wednesday.   *Ego* I throw them this, being a detailed account of last
                night's doings :

11.30 P.M.   Arrive home.
11.40 P.M.   Two tablets of Veganin to stop toothache, since the
                dentist wants a morning and I haven't one to spare.
11.50 P.M.   Bisodol to correct evening's indiscretions.
12.0 A.M.   Inhale Riddobron against asthma.
12.10 A.M.   Dessert-spoonful of bicarbonate of soda.
12.20 A.M.   Dose of Pulmo (lung tonic).
12.30 A.M.   Ephedrine tabloid and inhale Riddobron again.
12.40 A.M.   Capsule of Adexolin (Vitamins A and B) and tablet
                of Redoxon (Vitamin C).
12.50 A.M.   Open bottle of whiskey and box of cigars.
 1.0 A.M.   Set about first draft of *S.T.* article on last night's
                play, Paul Vincent Carroll's *The Wise Have Not
                Spoken*.
 2.0 A.M.   Two liver pills, and resume work till
 4.0 A.M.   Bed, where I take sleeping tablets and cough till 5.0.
 8.30 A.M.   Open letter from George Lyttelton beginning, " It
                was delightful to find you in such good form,
                triumphing with contemptuous ease over all the
                bodily betrayals of which Nature is so lavish as
                the years pile up."

March 21		Diarising by time-table rather appeals to me. Here
Thursday.		is my day :

9.0	A.M.	Cough till
10.0	A.M.	Pull *S.T.* article into shape and go on pulling till
1.30	P.M.	Lunch at the French Embassy.
3.0	P.M.	Preside at Council Meeting of Hackney Horse Society.
5.0	P.M.	Write entirely fresh *S.T.* article.
7.0	P.M.	Stare at revue at Duchess Theatre.
9.30	P.M.	Café Royal, where a total stranger comes up to me :

> T. S. How do you think the theatre of this war compares with the theatre of the last war ?
>
> J. A. I'm afraid that would take a lot of answering.
>
> T. S. Quite. What do you think of the American invasion of the English stage ?
>
> J. A. That too is a complicated question.
>
> T. S. Well, what do you think about a National Theatre ? You must have some views about *that*.
>
> J. A. Some other time, perhaps. I'm afraid I'm too tired to go into all that now.
>
> T. S. Of course. At your age . . .
>
> (*The young man goes back to his seat, and J. A. hears him say to his friends,* " Gosh, that's a bore ! ")

11.30	P.M.	Another go at *S.T.* article.
3.30	A.M.	Bed.

March 22
Friday.

One of the marks of greatness is the power to rise to the occasion plus the knowledge of which occasions are worth rising to.

March 23
Saturday.

Winged Words :

No. 7 : Edward Molyneux made my frock when I remarried it expressed exactly the right note of sophistication, sentimental regret for an early mistake (on my part !), and happy confidence in the future.

Paris Correspondent in smart illustrated paper

No. 8 : *Antony and Cleopatra* is not Shakespeare's greatest play, but it is perhaps the finest exemplar of his " negative capability."

Programme of the Marlowe Society, Cambridge

March 24
Sunday.

My stuff about Paul Vincent Carroll's *The Wise Have Not Spoken* reads fairly well, I think. The trouble I had with it was due to the old difficulty Walkley noted, that of writing an orderly article round a muddled play. *Shadow and*

Substance was a muddle ; the new piece is worse. Who are the wise ? And what would they say if they opened their mouths ? How will shooting at the police make a farm pay ? Will the soil benefit by an increase of spiritual awareness in the tillers ? Why are half the family lunatics, not in the metaphorical, but in the literal sense of being certified imbeciles, taken away to a madhouse ? Jock Dent was gammoned to the extent of saying the play is " much too good for the West End." (The comparison, I take it, is with the nitwit farces about American adolescence.) In my view Carroll's piece isn't good enough for any End. It is a play of ideas which have nothing to do with each other and are not related to any central theme. When Hilda Wangel waves her shawl because her idealism has killed her old architect you may think she is an interfering hussy, but you realise that she has made her point—that it is better for the old to cease to live than cease to dare. That is Ibsen's play in a nutshell, and any play of ideas which won't go into a nutshell is not a good play of ideas. Jock seems to take up the position of Shaw's parson-burglar, who liked expounding a doctrine that was beautiful and subtle and exquisitely put together. " I may feel instinctively that it is the rottenest nonsense. Still, if I can get a moving dramatic effect out of it my gift takes possession of me and obliges me to sail in and do it." I rear up when a moving and dramatic play turns out, on analysis, to be nonsense. Jock is of the opposite school. He has always hated argument outside the theatre as well as inside. Whereas I love argument, everywhere. When a man, be he schoolmaster or playwright, produces a piece of chalk and on a blackboard sets down this sum in simple addition

$$\begin{array}{r} 3 \\ 3 \\ \hline 7 \\ \hline \end{array}$$

I just say " Fudge ! " And I don't care how exquisitely the figures are made or how strikingly the board is posited on its easel.

March 25   Letter from a Scotch lassie :
Monday.

I have no priceless first edition for you, no link with Boswell, no thing of Sarah's. A random reader, an undiscriminating play-goer, and with but little music in my soul, I must seem a curious correspondent. And so I am. It isn't admiration—you're not that good. It isn't criticism—I'm not that good. And it is most certainly not a ' crush '—you look a bull-necked, bad-tempered sort of person. Since I'm not even a customer, being library-fed, how dare I push my dull pen under your busy notice ? A favour—to be sure. Please, Mr Agate, don't die for a very long time.

You see, I have just discovered you and am journeying joyfully through the *Egos*. You have become a pleasant comfort in my life—like old tweeds or a husband or a favourite chair—not exciting or important, but something to look forward to and hurry back to after the day's work. I deeply love London, and you are very much of it. I visit it periodically, *femme de province* that I am, for a whole week at a time—stay at the Club—do some shows—buy a silly hat and pretend I am somebody. I stand for a moment in Piccadilly, my eyes tight shut, and look at yesterday's glories—then spend an hour in Bond Street, the eyes wide open, looking for to-morrow's bargains (I am a compatriot of Jock's). I hover round old houses, refurnishing them with Regency ladies. I walk with Walpole, I picture Pepys, and fain would add Agate.

Too Scotchly shy to ask you to drink a dish of tea with me at my " kennel in St James's Street " when I come for my week's wallow at Easter, I shall seek out this Ivy place and maybe see you passing by. Having given you the Freedom of my special London, I am anxious to know how you look in it—but—*alive*—please !

March 26   I sat at the Thirty Club dinner to Arthur Rank between
Tuesday.   the Editors of the *Express* and the *Tatler*. The speeches
              were in the following order : Chairman, Arthur Rank, J. A., Robert Donat, Beverley Baxter, John Mills. Seized the occasion to attack combines. Asked whether the world of thought would be richer if some millionaire were able to buy up *The Times*, the *Manchester Guardian*, the *Birmingham Daily Post*, the *Yorkshire Post*, the *Scotsman*, and the *Glasgow Herald*. Enlarged on this and theatrical monopoly. Suggested that union is weakness, since it means regimentation of thought, and where you have that you cannot have freedom of opinion. Said we must compose ourselves to the Rank situation, since to that situation we had come. And I concluded :

I do not attack, and have no intention of attacking, directly or by any kind of insinuation or innuendo, the commercial cinema. The business of entertainment is one thing and the pursuit of an art is another. It would be nice if ' the pictures ' and the art of the screen were as inseparable as Abbott and Costello. But they are not. They can be separated, with honour to each. No wise man would say that an artistic picture must not be produced because it is not a money-maker. And similarly, no wise man would ban a money-making picture on the ground that it is not intellectual. Was *The Wicked Lady* designed to titillate the ears of the groundlings ? But Nature has given the groundlings ears, and they are entitled to have them titillated. I do not attack Mr Rank or his companies. Economic and political conditions doubtless demand that this country opposes to Hollywood's nincompoopery British nincompoopery of equal competence. I wish these commercial films well, and am happy that the British forces who make them are under the command of a general whose integrity, enterprise, and acumen are beyond dispute. But let Mr Rank take a tip from the publishing trade. It is a fact that every publisher of any pretensions to a name makes a point of putting out one good work a year knowing that he will lose money by it. Possibly not for love of that good work ; and certainly to maintain his imprint. But at least he does it. Let Mr Rank devote one of his many studios to pictures as good as the modern French and Russian pictures, and the German pictures in the days of Ufa. Let him devote one-fiftieth of his power and resources and floor-space to first-rate films without regard to what they gross. I shall be glad to sit on the board of any such unit, and without remuneration. I doubt whether this is more than an empty figure of speech. I do not believe that Mr Rank will listen to me. No film magnate has ever listened to me in all the twenty-five years I have been pouring out advice. As the schoolmistress says in the film of *The Corn is Green*, " I have worn my fingers to the bone knocking my brains against a stone wall." Let me go back to this question of pictures that pay and pictures that are works of art. To be quite sure that I had made no mistake about the quality of *The Wicked Lady* I went to Camden Town the other evening to have another look. I was told that the queue extended to Swiss Cottage. It was useless to go on to Swiss Cottage, where the film was also showing, since that queue extended to Camden Town. I see no harm in this. There are millions of people all over the country who will be as much moved by this film as I am by *Hamlet*. This rubbish has its place in the scheme of things, and Mr Rank is entitled to purvey it. But let him do what I ask and set one good film against forty-nine money-makers. Always in the knowledge that there is no law of Nature which says that all good films must lose money. The law is that certain kinds of bad films will always make a great deal of money. My offer, then, is plain. Let Mr Rank accept it and he is my friend for life, and the *Tatler* will fill its glossiest page with his praises. If not, he is my enemy, and has yet to learn the number of ways in which I can track him down, ambush him, and lure him to his doom.

March 28   Letter from Accident Insurance Company asking how
Thursday.   my health is in view of my age. Have replied that I can
                  still see well enough not to walk into the fire, and hear
well enough not to cross the street in front of a fire-engine. That I

have enough asthma to stop me worrying about my nerves, and sufficient bronchitis to keep my mind off my heart. That I should be disquieted by a certain puffiness suggesting dropsy were it not compensated by some promising twinges of gout.

March 29 Sean O'Casey has once again gone too far, and on Sunday
Friday.   I propose in the *S.T.* to take his trousers down and
            spank him :

In the course of an article entitled " The People and the Theatre," which appears in the first issue of *Theatre To-day,* Mr O'Casey writes :

" The critics, instead of being stout and indubitable guides to where there are swans, invariably (as far as new work is concerned) lead the people to where there is naught but a gaggle of geese. . . . Whenever has a London critic, with clamour and encouragement, furnished the English stage with a new and first-class playwright, from at home or abroad ? "

This is " piffle before the wind," and I propose to be the wind. (If my citations are taken from one newspaper it is because the *Sunday Times* is the most convenient of access.) Noel Coward, *The Vortex* (1924) : " Brains must ultimately come by their own, even in the theatre ; and Mr Coward has brains to spare." Jean-Jacques Bernard, *The Unquiet Spirit* (1931) : " One of the most beautiful plays in the last fifty years." Ronald Mackenzie, *Musical Chairs* (1932) : " I have seen this play twice, and am now ready to burn my boats about it. It is, in my view, the best first play written by any English playwright during the last forty years." J. B. Priestley, *Dangerous Corner* (1932) : " If this play does not take the town it will be the town's fault. In Mr Priestley we have an obviously first-class playwright in the making. If adequate encouragement is not forthcoming and Mr Priestley should decide not to go on with the job, the public will have only itself to blame." Rodney Ackland, *After October* (1936) : " If the playgoer has one grain of playgoing sense to rub against another he will be entranced." Clifford Odets, *Paradise Lost* (1938) : " This failure is better value for money, dramatically, emotionally, and in the scale of pure entertainment, than all of London's current successes put together." And what but the excitement of two critics on seeing the MS. of Peter Ustinov's *House of Regrets* secured a production of this first play ? Will Mr O'Casey still refuse to see " clamour and encouragement " in the foregoing, which I could multiply a hundred times ?

Now let me go back to the year 1925. At the Royalty Theatre in November of that year London had its first glimpse of a new play by a young Irishman. The critic of the *Sunday Times* began his notice with a reference to Henry Morley's discovery that " the English temper jibs at undiluted tragedy. Whether for good or ill, the English audience, says Morley, has a habit of looking out for something upon which to feed its appetite for the absurd. The orthodox writer of melodrama satisfies that hunger with a comic under-plot, and by so doing 'saves his terrors whole.' " The critic then described the plot of the new piece, which he called " the work of a master." And the notice ended, " This is a great play, in which both educated and uneducated will see any amount of that fun which Morley declared to be our heritage." Six months later the same critic was writing of this new playwright's next play, " This piece contains that greatness which is something different from the sum of small perfections. . . . Mr O'Casey has done what Balzac and Dickens did—he has created an entirely new gallery of living men and women."

In view of the foregoing does the author of *Juno and the Paycock* and *The Plough and the Stars* still complain of lack of clamour and encouragement ? He cannot, unless words do not mean to him what they mean to the rest of us. No, readers, I am not peeved. I make no moan about serpents' teeth and thankless playwrights. Ingratitude will not vanquish me. I shall go on praising plays that seem to me good, and damning those that seem to me bad. And so will the entire body of critics. Why, then, make a fuss about an obvious case of ill-temper ? Because Mr O'Casey is a great man of the theatre, and the errors and inaccuracies of great men call for refutation before the prestige of their begetters gives them a validity they do not possess.

April 2   A chink in the Shavian armour. Henry Wood once said
Tuesday.   that he never conducted any piece, however familiar,
            without running through the score an hour or two before
the performance. I should not dream of going to see an Ibsen play without having a look at what Shaw and Archer had had to say. In the case of the big Shakespeares I do much the same thing. Before to-night's Valk-Wolfit battle I looked up G. B. S. on Wilson Barrett's Othello. Magnificent, of course—I mean the criticism. But I also found in the same article a passage which shows the Great Man at his critical worst. He is writing about Janet Achurch in *Antony and Cleopatra* :

On Monday last she was sweeping about, clothed with red Rossettian hair and beauty to match ; revelling in the power of her voice and the steam pressure of her energy ; curving her wrists elegantly above Antony's head as if she were going to extract a globe of goldfish and two rabbits from behind his ear ; and generally celebrating her choice between the rare and costly art of being beautifully natural in lifelike human acting, like Duse, and the comparatively common and cheap one of being theatrically beautiful in heroic stage exhibition.

What G. B. S. *subconsciously* felt was that he preferred looking at Duse in *The Lady from the Sea* to Achurch in Shakespeare's *A. and C.* Feeling this way, his normally acute mind got itself tangled up and demanded that Janet should model her playing of Shakespeare's Queen on Duse's Ibsenite and fishy lady ! And then my mind started working. " A globe of goldfish and two rabbits." What was the echo here ? And then I remembered a " Lost Lecture " by Maurice Baring, the one entitled *Actors, Actresses, and Goldfish.* I turned this up and presently found :

It may be doubted whether the reason Duse's high dreams never came true was not that they could not come true, and whether perhaps the Roman and all other publics were not right to prefer her in Sardou and truncated Ibsen and Pinero, than if she had acted Greek plays, Shakespeare, and poetical dramas written for her by highbrow Italians. I believe myself she was not a tragedian, that she was not of the race of Mrs Siddons ; that she could not compare with Sarah Bernhardt in the interpretation of poetic drama ; when you saw her in something domestically dramatic you thought how wonderful she would be in Shakespeare, but when she did play Cleopatra the part swamped her, and you thought that she was a charming little Italian dressing up as a queen.

What do I want to prove ? That Duse was not a genius ? NO. That genius of one kind must not be compared with genius of another ? YES. Let me be quite clear about this. There are parts in which goldfish must be produced and juggled with in view of the audience, and parts in which they must be swallowed in the dressing-room one hour before the performance with an eye to that indigestion which the audience will mistake for soul. Let me insist, for the hundredth time, that Duse could no more tear down the ceiling than Sarah could sit about moping. And that it was no fault in one actress not to succeed in the manner of the other. But to go back to Janet. Why did G. B. S. blame her for not being " beautifully natural " as the serpent of Old Nile, and what would he have said if some other critic had blamed Duse for not tantrumising ?

April 4   Lunched with George Robey, his wife and her mother.
Thursday.   Asked George to settle the question of priority as
between Vesta Tilley and Marie Lloyd. He said, " I should put Marie first. She had to create it all out of herself, whereas Tilley had her wonderful masculine props to rely on. But they were both tremendous artists, and it's a very near thing." About the men of his time he said, " Dan Leno first. After him Tom Costello,

Harry Randall, Little Tich, Chirgwin, Eugene Stratton, Will Fyffe."
He was in great form, and told us how some dusky potentate had
bestowed a diamond bracelet on his wife and kissed him. " I think
he liked me best."

April 5   If Duvivier, or any good French director, had been in
Friday.   charge of *The Postman Always Rings Twice* (Empire)
              I imagine that on the first day of shooting he would have
assembled his cast, taken one look at the husband, and said, " Send
for Michel Simon ! " I have never forgotten the performance given
by this great French actor in the French version of this film. I
imagine that D. would then have turned to the wife and said, " Miss
Turner, don't you realise that you are supposed to be a little slut
who married the greasy owner of a sandwich joint because nothing
better offered ? That you have been peeling onions and scrubbing
pans for the past three years ? That your nails are ragged and
broken ? That your frocks are crumpled and dirty ? That only a
hobo would desire you ? Why, then, do you look as though you
had just won a beauty competition for bathing belles ? Get off the
set and go swimming with Johnnie Weissmuller ! " And as for John
Garfield : " You're a nice boy, and your sports shirt is highly becoming. What about scoring that try for Yale ? " I believed every
word of the book and every word of the film when it was made in
French and called *Le Dernier Tournant*. At the Empire to-night I
didn't believe anything at all. Nor, to judge by the ripples of laughter
in the audience, did anybody else believe any of it very much. Not
all the might, power, and majesty of Metro-Goldwyn-Mayer, plus
the suavity of my old friend Sam Eckman, plus the redoubtable
MacPherson eyeglass—not any of these things, taken singly or all
together, is going to make me believe that any young woman can go
through a complicated murder, including a motor-crash over a
hundred-foot cliff and a hundred-foot climb back, without getting
at least one speck of dust on a confection whose immaculacy would
make Persil blush.

April 6   Letter to George Lyttelton :
Saturday.

> *Queen Alexandra Mansions*
> *Grape Street, W.C.2*
>
> *April 6th*, 1946

DEAR GEORGE LYTTELTON,
          Prison looms ! The Income Tax people want £1057 4s. 6d. on

Tuesday morning. They won't take no deniging. I haven't got this or anything like it, and shan't have another £1057 4s. 6d. on July 1, or anything like that either. If the specialist who asked me recently if I could go to live in South Africa had said Brixton the answer would have been in the affirmative. What is worrying me is whether I shall be allowed my asthma cigarettes and " squizzer," my private name for the spray which enables me to breathe. In the winter I am helpless without this. But " sumer is icumen in," and if incarceration impends it will be during the next few months.

The first thing I see on looking at my *News Chronicle* this morning is the heading " Home Office to Train Girl for Ballet." Why, then, does not this enlightened Home Office see that your humble servant can only do his work on whiskey at £4 a bottle, cigars at 7s. 6d., and transport at 15s. a mile ? That these things are to him what coffee was to Balzac ? I have cut out champagne; the rest are my irreducible minimum. But to pretend that I am happy about all this is nonsense. Do you realise that if I were to drop down dead this minute I shouldn't have a ha'penny to leave to anybody ? Even my cuff-links would be forfeit !

Sitting chin-sunken about this at the Café Royal last night, I was violently slapped on the back by a total stranger, who said, " I understand you were a great friend of old B——. He died in my arms. How are *you* ? "

(At this point in my diarising a middle-aged Jew whom I don't know pushes past the houseboy and insists on seeing me. " My name is Baumgarten. I vork for the tailor vot repairs your suits. Vot do I vish ? I vish that you should help my wife, who shall go on the stage. . . .")

Would you like to read a short story about a form-master who made up his mind to murder his wife ? On the theory that there is safety in numbers he poisoned the lemonade of a group of parents gathered round his wife and watching the Old Boys' cricket match. Everybody died, nobody suspected anybody, the coroner was happy, and presently the form-master was promoted to head-master. The author of this, a Mr Neil Bell, says in his preface : " A novelist hardly works at all : once he has learned his trade it is the easiest and pleasantest occupation imaginable, and to pretend that it is hard and exhausting work is simply not true : and the better seller you are the less work you need do : one novel (a couple of months' pleasant occupation) a year will keep you handsomely. The rest of the year you can play. . . ." I see. Hardy wrote *Tess* in eight weeks, and spent the rest of the year folk-dancing in Wessex !

Sorry to keep on drooling, but I've got to quieten my nerves somehow, and choose you rather than drink. Did you see some-body's suggestion the other day that Tchehov's *Cherry Orchard* should be transplanted to the South of Ireland ? " Varvara would become Babs." Monstrous ! I entirely agree with George Moore's "All proper names, no matter how unpronounceable, must be rigidly adhered to ; you must never transpose versts into kilometres, or roubles into francs ; I don't know what a verst is or what a rouble is, but when I see the words I am in Russia."

(Three-quarters of an hour taken up here by film director— I had forgotten the appointment—wanting me to help him cast Paula Tanqueray in a film of the old play. I tell him to run away and not bother me with the impossible. The film public insists on a name and a face, and I insist on a woman with talent and the right sort of talent. Finally I recommend three actresses, on the understanding that all of them put together won't be worth Mrs Pat's little finger. As for our whey-faced screen ninnies, I tell the director I'd rather see a milk pudding act. And he agrees.)

I hope you didn't miss the story of the middle-aged woman who, in Lincoln Cathedral the other day, cried out in a loud voice, " I denounce Magna Carta. It is a relic, and relics are denounced in the Bible." Mr F.'s aunt all over again. And then they say that Dickens exaggerated !

And now I must shut up. I began this letter in a " Beggared Outcast " state of depression. I end it looking for a coach and a bag of walnuts. Am due to make a speech to-night at the Savage Club dinner, Mark Hambourg in the chair, and have no doubt at all but that I shall be in riotous spirits.

Yours ever,

JAMES AGATE

April 7 Sunday. On a Saturday night at the beginning of the year a young Canadian airman came up to me and asked if he might say how much he admired . . . I said no he mightn't, and what was he doing in London ? He was flying back to Canada on the following Tuesday, and had wangled week-end leave by telling his C.O. a fib. What fib ? Well, that he was in pictures, and had some business to fix up. I said, " With that face you *are* in pictures. Go away now and meet me at one o'clock to-morrow at the Café Royal, where I'll get a woman to look you over." Next day Gwen Chenhalls took one look and signalled O.K. Between us we persuaded Angus McBean to open his studio, where Gwen took him for a sitting while I went on to my concert. Over lunch the young man had told us that his parents wanted him to go into real estate, but that he was all for a film career, here in Britain and not in Hollywood. That they would let him return to London *to a job*, but not just to look for one. So I got busy. Alec Clunes, on seeing the photographs, said, " Why didn't

I have a face like that to play Hamlet with!" And went on: "If the boy does come over he can walk on at the Arts Theatre until he finds his feet." M.-G.-M. were encouraging, but said they would have no floor-space for seven months. I then decided to tackle Rank, on the theory that any man who controls millions must have imagination. I wrote a short letter and enclosed a photograph, which, I suggested, showed something of Charles Boyer with a dash of Ray Massey. I vouched for the boy's fluidity of temperament: "It's a safe bet he can either act now or be made to later on." And I ended with a demand for a contract!! Next day the telephone rang, and I was informed that a contract for six months at something above a living wage was in the post. This was on Thursday last. I cabled the boy's parents on receipt of the message, and this morning received a reply: " George sailing on the *Aquitania* on the 15th." The young man's name is George Calderwood. But we can alter that.

April 8   Three letters.
Monday.   From Neville Cardus saying he has met a fifteen-year-old
            girl in Sydney who wants to go on the stage. "She is a
Czech, and for the last few years has been interned in Java. I have
never seen her act."

   From a young woman in Cardiff. "Can you tell me of anyone
who will give sound criticism to a would-be poet for a very moderate
charge? I say 'moderate,' since I have received several estimates,
none of which is under half a guinea. . . ."

   From my brother-in-law in Surrey. "I can get three loads of
poultry manure for the loan of one of your *Egos*."

April 9   Wrote again to Arthur Rank:
Tuesday.

                              Queen Alexandra Mansions
                                  Grape Street, W.C.2
                                     April 9th, 1946

DEAR MR RANK,
   First let me thank you for your courtesy and consideration in
the matter of George Calderwood. I cabled him, and received the
reply that he sails in the *Aquitania* on the 15th of this month. He
will report to Mr Henley immediately on arrival.
   In view of our meeting on the 16th, to which I am looking
forward with great pleasure, I think perhaps it would help if I
clarified the position by telling you exactly where I stand with
regard to British films. As an income-tax payer I am obviously
delighted when films can be exported against dollars. As a critic

I hold that that is outside my province. I am not interested in what any picture grosses, or whether it is exportable. My concern is with the making of some British pictures so good that educated audiences abroad will want to have them in the way that educated audiences here want to have the best French films.

I don't suppose that there will be any time, or that you will want to discuss this, on the 16th. Nevertheless, I should like to put a few things before you in a friendly and non-controversial spirit. I don't think we can compete with Hollywood just by spending money. For the good reason that at the moment we haven't the talent to spend it on. A film director called on me the other day and asked me to help him cast Paula Tanqueray in a film of Pinero's *The Second Mrs Tanqueray*. I just had to tell him that the English screen doesn't possess a Paula, for the reason that it has no film actresses who can look forty, and convey good breeding and a sense of moving habitually in a drawing-room in contra-distinction to putting on a lot of period clothes and being photo-graphed in a studio.

Since none of our screen actresses can play anything except adolescents there is obviously not a Paula among them. Whereas in America one would cast Bette Davis, Greer Garson, and half a dozen other mature actresses. On the male side we have some good-looking young men, all of whom smack more or less of the suburban lawn-tennis club. Not a bad thing to smack of, but not the stuff of great acting. We just haven't got anybody like—taking a few names at random—Spencer Tracy, Humphrey Bogart, Edward G. Robinson, William Bendix.

But there is one kind of film which we in this country, with our less individualistic talent, can do better than anybody else. This is the semi-documentary—films like *The Way Ahead* and *The Captive Heart*. These depend not on stars, but on team-work, at which our actors are very good indeed. Actors like Mervyn Johns, Gordon Jackson, Jimmy Hanley. And there are youngsters coming on. I know of one boy-actor of genius. This is David O'Brien, who, at the age of fourteen, put up a marvellous performance in *To-morrow the World*, which ran for over a year. This child is now at Stratford, where he is to play two parts. But his life is heading for tragedy, and he knows it ; *he knows he will be worn out before he is twenty*. I have shown horses most of my life, and I know that if you show a three-year-old more than three or four times you will break his heart, and you will have no horse at six. Now I ask you to believe that this boy has at least six times the talent of Freddie Bartholomew at his best. It seems to me that it is the duty of the film industry, when it hears of something that may be genius, to have a look at that genius, and try it out, and, if it sees promise, nurse it. Arrangements should be made with young O'Brien's parents to send that kid to school, and for the next four years cut down his acting to a maximum of three months a year. For the rest of the time let him study and get fresh air and grow ! Why not look up the film *No Greater Glory* and see if a remake of this wonderful film would suit this boy ? I do not think this country is bankrupt in the way of talent. I believe it is there if it is looked for. And I believe also that we are not doing the best by the talent we have.

I hope you will absolve me from impertinence and credit me with the best motives in all this. It has seemed to me that no purpose is going to be served by two people meeting without each having some idea of the other's point of view. To put it in a sentence. I hold there is no future for British pictures if we devote all our energy to the hopeless task of beating Hollywood at its own game. But that there is a great future before the cinema industry of this country if we can convince intelligent picturegoers abroad that there are some ways in which, when we like, we can lead the world. I want to see a cinema in London for British post-war, post-documentary pictures as good as those showing at the Curzon, the Academy, Studio One, the Rialto, the Tatler in Charing Cross Road, and the Carlton in Tottenham Court Road.

Yours sincerely,
JAMES AGATE

April 10 Out of devilment I added a P.S. to Sunday's article on
Wednesday. the Valk-Wolfit set-to in *Othello*.

P.S. On the assumption that Bacon had a good deal to do with this play. How the old boy must have chuckled when he thought of this sentence in the essay " Of Suspicion "—" There is nothing makes a man suspect much, more than to know little ; and therefore men should remedy suspicion by procuring to know more, and not to keep their suspicions in smother "—and realised that it was precisely the following of this advice which led to Othello's downfall. " Be sure thou prove . . ." " Give me the ocular proof . . ." " Make me to see't . . ." " Give me a living reason . . ." But for following Bacon's advice Shakespeare's Moor could have slept on both ears content with his " I do not think but Desdemona's honest." Similarly Shakespeare's Hamlet would have dispatched his uncle and reigned in Denmark if he had not taken Bacon's tip and remembered that " boldness is a child of ignorance and baseness." What about a book going through the essays and plays and showing that Shakespearean catastrophe is invariably the result of paying attention to Bacon ? And on whose side would such a book be ?

Whereupon somebody weighs in this morning with a long argument to prove (?) that the whole of the great scene in which Iago begins to sow suspicion in Othello's mind—the scene beginning " Did Michael Cassio, when you woo'd my lady, Know of your love ? "— was based on Bacon's essay " Of Cunning."

Essay " Of Cunning " [1625]

It is a point of cunning to wait upon him with whom you speak with your eye. . . .

The *breaking off* in the midst of that one was about to say, as if he took himself up, breeds a greater appetite in him with whom you confer, to know more.

I knew another, that when he came to have speech, he would pass over that that he intended most ; and go forth and come back again, and speak of it as a thing that he had almost forgot.

" Othello " [1622]

IAGO. Wear your eye thus, not jealous, nor severe.
(*Showing him how.*)

OTH. And, for I know thou art full of love and honesty,
And weigh'st thy words before thou giv'st them breath,
Therefore, these *stops of thine* fright me the more :
For such things in a false disloyal knave
Are tricks of custom.

OTH. Leave me, Iago.
IAGO. My lord, I take my leave.
IAGO (*returning*). My lord, I would I might entreat your honour
To scan this thing no further. . . .
Note if your lady strain his entertainment
With any strong or vehement importunity ;
Much will be seen in that.

All this is admittedly taken from the learned Dr Charles Creighton's book entitled *An Allegory of " Othello "* (1912). But *Othello* was first acted in 1604, and Bacon's essay was not published till 1612. Further, *Othello* was not published till 1622. Whence we are to argue, I suppose, that Bacon in this play put into practice precepts he was not to lay down for another eight years. Alternatively that this scene was not in the spoken play, but written in after the essay came out ! ! But wait a minute. The essay itself has a curious history. " In the edition of 1625, it is four times as long as in that of 1612, but the opening paragraph of fifteen lines is exactly the same in both, and the closing paragraph is also the same, except that the last three lines of 1612 are transferred in 1625 : the whole difference is that an intermediate section of some ninety lines is omitted from the first printing, or interpolated in the second. This is the section which contains the artifices of Iago and Edmund. It consists of eighteen specific points, which are introduced as ' the small wares of cunning.'

318

Those are the illustrations of the general principles, so that the essay in its originally printed form (1612) was, in a sense, complete without them. Probably the illustrations, being so many as they are, were collected from time to time, and not completed until long after the general principles." I see. The illustrations were not complete enough for the first printing of the essay (1612), *but complete enough for the first production of the play* (1604). Fantastic ! !

April 11	A literary day. Begin by telling *Express* readers that
Thursday.	the writers of the so-called poetic drama are not going
	to gammon me :

Not having seen Miss Anne Ridler's *The Shadow Factory*, I hold it improper for me to say what I think of it as drama. Having read it, I permit myself to pass an opinion on it as poetry. An artist and the director of a factory are discussing the use of the loud-speaker. The director says :

> It isn't popular, I'll admit.
> Even the Unions opposed it at first :
> But I stood out for it ; I can't afford to lose it.
> You know the advertising maxim :
> Make your point by repetition,
> Never mind the irritation.
> I find it invaluable. Piece-work, for instance :
> That's unpopular now, you see,
> But after a month of the slogan you heard
> I shall expect a world of difference.
> But to return to our main affair :
> I'm sure we can come to a suitable agreement.

I'm sorry, but I cannot regard this as poetry. And if a play by a poet is as good as *Hamlet* and *Macbeth* put together, with *King Lear* thrown in, *and all the poetry thrown out*, I should still decline to see it. Them's my prejudices, them is.

Later am approached by distinguished dilettante, and the following conversation ensues :

D. D. I am collecting material for a book on Alfred Douglas as Poet. Would you like to contribute a chapter saying why you consider him the greatest master of the sonnet since Shakespeare ?
J. A. No.
D. D. Why ?
J. A. Because he isn't.
D. D. Would you like to amplify that ?
J. A. Certainly. Strip Milton and undress Wordsworth, set out their matter in prospectus English, and the world is still richer for a great thought. Take the clothes off Douglas, and nothing remains.

D. D. D'you think that's important ?

J. A. Very.

D. D. Don't you think that Douglas gave the 'nineties poise and significance ?

J. A. What has that to do with Shakespeare ?

Some day I must write an article about the excessive insistence on period scenery and costume both in stage plays and on the screen. Stage producers and film directors seem unable to grasp that a modern audience looking at the revival or screening of a famous play should not be more preoccupied with the settings and the costumes than the audience on the original first-night was preoccupied. *Unless, of course, the play will not stand up to revival on its own merits.* Went to-night to the Curzon to see the revival of *La Bête Humaine.* Did anybody notice that the clothes were not strictly 1890 ? That the engine was not the type that Lantier drove fifty-six years ago? That the carriages were the best the P-L-M boasted in 1937, or whenever the film was made ? No, nobody noticed these things because Zola's story still stands up as a story of to-day. Arrived home, I took down *L'Assommoir*, which I have always regarded as a masterpiece. (I can only assume that people who claim this for *The Lost Week-end* haven't any French.) Here, for the sheer pleasure of copying it out, is the ending. Gervaise has died at long last :

Mais la vérité était qu'elle s'en allait de misère, des ordures et des fatigues de sa vie gâtée. Elle creva d'avachissement, selon le mot des Lorilleux. Un matin, comme ça sentait mauvais dans le corridor, on se rappela qu'on ne l'avait pas vue depuis deux jours ; et on la découvrit déjà verte, dans sa niche.

Justement, ce fut le père Bazouge qui vint, avec la caisse des pauvres sous le bras, pour l'emballer. Il était encore joliment soûl, ce jour-là, mais bon zig tout de même, et gai comme un pinson. Quand il eut reconnu la pratique à laquelle il avait affaire, il lâcha des réflexions philosophiques, en préparant son petit ménage.

— Tout le monde y passe. . . . On n'a pas besoin de se bousculer, il y a de la place pour tout le monde. . . . Et c'est bête d'être pressé, parce qu'on arrive moins vite. . . . Moi, je ne demande pas mieux que de faire plaisir. Les uns veulent, les autres ne veulent pas. Arrangez un peu ça, pour voir . . . En v'là une qui ne voulait pas, puis elle a voulu. Alors, on l'a fait attendre . . . Enfin, ça y est, et, vrai ! elle l'a gagné ! Allons-y gaiement !

Et, lorsqu'il empoigna Gervaise dans ses grosses mains noires, il fut pris d'une tendresse, il souleva doucement cette femme qui

avait eu un si long béguin pour lui. Puis, en l'allongeant au fond
de la bière avec un soin paternel, il bégaya, entre deux hoquets :
 — Tu sais . . . écoute bien . . . c'est moi, Bibi-la-Gaieté,
dit le consolateur des dames . . . Va, t'es heureuse.
  Fais dodo, ma belle !

 " Fais dodo, ma belle ! " This moves me as much as Othello's
" O ill-starred wench ! Pale as thy smock."

April 12   Something must be done about this overwork. Here is
Friday.   the tale of yesterday's mishaps :

  1. Turned up an hour and a half late for a luncheon date with
Roger Eckersley, who, more than excusably, had thought I wasn't
coming. Traipsed from Boodle's to the Ivy, where
  2. I had forgotten a party at which I was the host.
  3. Overlooked an appointment with a very special dentist kindly
arranged for me by Blanche Robey.
  4. Failed to make use of a ten-guinea seat for a charity matinée
under Royal patronage.
  5. Forgot I was to attend the Royal Academy banquet. Spent
the greater part of to-day concocting and dispatching apologetic
lies. Nevertheless I wrote a damned good article yesterday. So
what the hell !

  Letter from a well-wisher :

  May I draw your attention to Page 187 in *A Shorter Ego*,
Vol. I, where you liken the defendants before the New York night
court to " the inmates of one of Gogol's doss-houses." Gogol,
mon pied ! You mean Gorky, and you know it !

What can I do except beat my breast ? Woke up at six o'clock
this morning, having dreamed that I had made Beaumarchais say,
" Ce qui est trop bête pour être chanté, on le dit." Calm restored
when the post brings the proof, showing I had worried for nothing.

April 13   The theatre managers are at it again, and once more
Saturday.   there is talk of barring me from first-nights. In a way
                I sympathise. Many of them have not been taught to
see beyond the box-office. They fuss because I have no patience with
rubbish. When you tell them that just as there are swing and jive
concerts at which nobody would expect Newman to look in, and
trashy novels that nobody would expect Desmond to look at, so
there are theatrical entertainments that I just can't sit through—

when you tell them this they goggle. They have spent weeks, months, in dressing, lighting, and providing a setting for something they don't recognise as inanity. Why should they ? To this type of mind nothing on which money has been expended is inane. Anyhow, the storm is on ; I may weather it, or I may not. The *Observer* once patted me on the back for having " with the minuteness of a Himalayan surveying-party charted the highlands of Ibsen." Wonderful if I am hurled to destruction because I couldn't sit through *Song of Norway* !

Winged Words :

No. 9 : We believe in this play, and we're going to fight. We shall fight, just as Mr Churchill told us, on the beaches and in the streets. Boys and girls, we are at this moment like the men at Dunkirk.

Popular actress after musical-comedy flop

No. 10 : If the troubled soul of the tragic Wilde has any contact with this world it must have been soothed by the spontaneous and delighted laughter of their Majesties and the Princesses.

Dramatic critic. Evening paper

No. 11 : This incarnation of concreteness, this apotheosis of the " too, too solid flesh," greatly perturbs the Puritan of logic. Over art's nude torso of erotic radium he hastily flings the covering garment of some safe preconception to spare his modesty.

Review of Jacques Maritain's " Art and Poetry "

April 14   Spent the morning writing an Introductory Note to
Sunday.   A. E. Wilson's *Playwrights in Aspic*. I have always
              been passionately, absurdly fond of parody and pastiche.
Some of Max's *A Christmas Garland* first came out in the *Saturday Review* in 1906, and my oldest newspaper-cutting book shows that I pasted in the ' contributions ' week by week. I was going to treasure them, whether they came out in book form or not. (This did not happen till 1912. Chatto and Windus.) I know only one other volume, or rather three other volumes, comparable to Max's in wit and actuality. These are Paul Reboux and Charles Muller's *A la Manière de*. . . . Of the sixty pieces the best seems to me to be the one on Edmond de Goncourt. Mme Loisel is to attend a ball, and we read :

Ainsi élégantisée, Mme Loisel eût tenté l'art des Latour, des Slingelandt, des Lawrence et des Rosalba Carriera ; elle possédait à la fois ce magnétisme souriant qu'exercent les adorables portraits du XVIIIᵉ siècle, et cette captivance flexible qu'on voit aux

Geishas d'Hokousaï et d'Outamaro. La princesse de M . . . disait un jour : " Nulle part la cohésion de molécules dont est fait l'être humain ne s'agrège plus harmonieusement qu'au bal."

Then comes the ball :

. . . avec ses enlacements berceurs au rythme d'un orchestre caché derrière un bosquet de gobéas, de palmiers et d'araucarias speluncas ; avec ses flirtages furtifs, ses étreintes en gants blancs ; ses passages d'une trémulation épileptoïde à un voluptueux étalement sur une causeuse capitonnée, à un badinage éventé d'une odeur d'œillet ou d'opoponax qui se mêle à l'arôme musqué de la femme ; le bal avec ses amusantes notes de clarté rose que les reflets des bougies piquent sur les épaules nues ; le bal où les teintes prismatiques des toilettes semblent décomposer la lumière en vibrances protéiformes, puis la recomposer soudain, dès que la giration des valses confond à nouveau les bleus, les jaunes, les oranges, les violets et les verts, et cela tour à tour, avec l'irisé capricieux d'un arc-en-ciel en vif argent.

This seems to me to catch, miraculously, the combination of scrupulous artist doubled with the self-conscious innovator.

April 15   From an old lady giving her address as " Jasmine
Monday.   Cottage " :

DEAR JAMES AGATE,
    It is good the way you deal with highbrow prose and poetry in *Ego* 7, and no doubt in other *Egos* too, which I have not read yet, altho' I intend to. It seems to me that the appropriate word for this sort of ' poetry ' is *masturbitic*.
                              Gratefully yours,
                              AN OLD LADY OF NINETY-THREE

April 16   E. J. Robertson, of the *Daily Express*, gave a small
Tuesday.   luncheon party in a private room at the Dorchester
              to-day for the purpose of bringing Arthur Rank and me
together. Also present Major Harold (Benny) Baker, General Manager of the Odeon circuit. No frills on Rank, who was obviously well disposed, and struck me as possessed of unusual understanding. But then I don't believe that a man can be shoved into the control of sixty-three millions of capital without having genius of some kind. I believe that he propels himself, and that it is the job of whoever comes into contact with a self-propeller to find out what his genius is. But since luncheon parties are unreliable affairs, in the sense that the interruption of a waiter may distort what one says, I decided to *read* what I had to say on the subject of British films. (I am not such a fool as to suppose that R., who is a busy man, came to the luncheon

for the sake of my *beaux yeux*.) Something R. said the last time we met suggested that he thought our film critics are prejudiced against British pictures. And I thought it was up to me to-day to disabuse his mind of this. Here is what I read :

In the matter of the film critics' alleged prejudice against British films. Here are some extracts from the notices of *Caravan* :

Caroline Lejeune (the *Observer*) :

The British *Caravan*, remotely drawn from Lady Eleanor Smith's novel, is so brazenly bad that it is almost exhilarating.

Dilys Powell (the *Sunday Times*) :

Finally a British film, *Caravan*, with Stewart Granger, Jean Kent, costume, gipsy weddings, and some moth-eaten dialogue which forces me to remark that, wherever my caravan may rest, it won't be here.

Richard Winnington (*News Chronicle*) :

Caravan is a blend of colourless glamour, sexless sex, passionless sadism, confident vulgarity, and Corner House period that Gainsborough have perfected.

Helen Fletcher (*Sunday Graphic*) :

Caravan doesn't say good-bye to any conventions. It's the sort of film that was old before it was born. There's nothing new in it, and nothing fresh. The best you can say is that at least it lacks the smut of *The Wicked Lady*. To enjoy it you need to have a mind that throbs to every sob of the novelette and a heart that throbs at every exposure of Stewart Granger's torso.

Campbell Dixon (the *Daily Telegraph*) :

If there is any ingredient left out of *Caravan*—sense, or life, for instance—you might let the producers know ; but, candidly, I think they are blameless. There just wasn't room.

The Times :

This particular caravan does not rest until it has completed the round of cinematic *clichés*. Lady Eleanor Smith at least wrote a novel, but here everything is reduced to the terms of the novelette.

The above are six responsible critics of the highest integrity, and it is manifest nonsense to suppose that the foregoing are not their genuine opinions. The writers in *The Times* and the *Sunday Graphic* use the word ' novelette,' which is the key-word to the whole situation. There is obviously a film audience for the film-novelette as there is for the novelette in fiction. Shop-boys and shop-girls are entitled to the kind of entertainment that appeals to them. The point is that the British film-novelette cannot compete with the Hollywood film-novelette for reasons with which I have already acquainted Mr Rank. But even supposing that he can sell *Caravan* against dollars it is impossible that this picture should bring kudos to, or add to the prestige of, British pictures. I do not say that pictures like *Caravan* should not be made. What I do say is that while they will undoubtedly make money in this country, and may make money abroad, they will not help to raise the status of British pictures in the esteem of intelligent people. I want to be quite clear about this. I should no more attack Gaumont-British for making *Caravan* than I should attack the dressmaker who runs up cheap frocks for housemaids. The pictures which I shall go all out to support are pictures of the quality of *Millions Like Us*, *The Way Ahead*, and *The Captive Heart*. But these are large-scale films, and the material for a large-scale film, British in outlook and implications, does not come along every day. Now the French have a genius for making beautiful small films, costing very little money, the fame of which travels all over the world. I allude to films like *Le Rosier de Madame Husson* and *La Fin du Jour*. It is absurd to say that we cannot make pictures of this quality in England, for the reason that we have not yet tried. And when we do try, as in *Brief Encounter*, the director is so nervous that he hides it behind the skirts of a full-length performance of Rachmaninoff's second Piano Concerto. In my view one single film of the quality of any of the French films I have mentioned would do more for the credit of British pictures than fifty *Caravans* and *Wicked Ladies*.

Rank listened with extreme attention and asked for a copy.

April 17   Again to George Lyttelton :
Wednesday.

Queen Alexandra Mansions
Grape Street, W.C.2
April 17, 1946

DEAR GEORGE LYTTELTON,
    I want your advice. For some time I have been wandering about the flat murmuring " worse if I continue." This is an echo of an old jingle I saw in *Punch* many years ago :

> It's very hard to versify
> If rhyming isn't in you ;
> I think it will get worse if I
> Continue.

You've got the point, of course. Do I wind up *Ego* with No. 9 ? Have done about a quarter of this, and the plan is to run it to the end of the year, in time for publication on my seventieth birthday, in September 1947.

    Here are some of the arguments for stopping. Or rather here is the only one that has weight with me. The book would be a com-

plete, rounded-off whole, and I should like to leave a work of art.
You may look on the whole thing with a semi-favourable eye like
Brother Mycroft, who wants me to give it up in favour of another
theatrical biography like my *Rachel*. (But I don't want to write
about anybody else.) Or you may think with Alan Dent that the
Diary should never have been published in my lifetime. (I can
just see the publishers rushing to secure a million words by a
defunct dramatic critic !) The point is that, in so far as *Ego* is
a work of art at all, to finish with No. 9 would make it a complete
thing. And then there's the allied question : Is my mind good
enough to run to further length ? Is the bulk getting too big for
the intellectual content ? .

I know that Pepys gave up because of his eyesight, and
Macready when he left the stage. But I am not blind yet, and
don't feel at all like Johnson's veteran. Actually I shan't be able
to stop setting down whatever seems to be worthy of remark.
(Edgar Lustgarten said yesterday that if one took Arnold Bennett
out of the *Journals* there would be nothing left, whereas if you
eliminated J. A. from *Ego* there would be a lot.) The idea, in that
case, would be a Postscript published by my literary executors
(ugh !) if they thought fit.

The alternative is to finish 9 and then bravely tackle 10, 11,
and 12 ; so spacing them that 12 would end on June 1, 1952.
This would complete the twenty years, *Ego*'s first entry being
dated June 2, 1932. I realise that there would be about this
something of Stevenson's " Who would find heart enough to begin
to live, if he dallied with the consideration of death ? " Let's take
it that after seventy " continued existence is a miracle." That is
no reason why one should hang about doing nothing except wait
for the miracle to cease. Last, I take as my cue Whitman's
" After the Supper and Talk," with the ending :

> . . . loth, O so loth to depart.
> Garrulous to the very last.

From *Sands at Seventy*, published in 1888. After which he gaily
embarked on *Good-bye, My Fancy*, published in 1891. He died in
'92. The *Works*, by the way, run to twelve volumes. Accepting
that I have enough power of self-criticism to know when I am
going gaga, and supposing that I don't, I want you to advise me,
and entirely on the artistic score. Except for the delight of reading
your fist I would enclose a postcard with two words written on it :

STOP
GO

and ask you to run your pen through one of them.

Ever,
J. A.

P.S. Perhaps " work of art " is putting the thing too high.
Let's change " art " to " contrivance." I originally planned to

end *Ego* 8 with VJ Day. And did. Then Leo died, and I realised that readers who had heard of this but who couldn't know anything about the time lag between delivery of manuscript to publisher and publication of book would wonder at my apparent heartlessness. Which meant that I decided to carry the book on to the end of the year, utilising some 30,000 words of *Ego* 9. Which, again, meant deleting some 30,000 words to keep within the prescribed length. I did the deciding and deleting in thirty-five minutes one morning round about two o'clock.

One more little thing. I talked last night for an hour or so with four young men from Sherborne, up in Town on a seven-a-side Rugby tournament. Average age sixteen and a half. I felt that the age we are moving into is theirs, not mine. Horace Walpole had the sense to disappear with the eighteenth century. Ought I not to do the same ? H. W. went out when poke bonnets came in. Ought I not to kiss my hand to a generation obviously about to plant its foot in my behind ?

April 18   The Gentle Art continued :
Thursday.

Queen Alexandra Mansions
Grape Street, W.C.2
April 18*th,* 1946

To the Art Critic of the " Evening Standard " :

SIR,
   You write of Cézanne's water-colours that they are " rather like the game of chess, in which a masterly player, after two or three moves, has foreseen the conclusion and does not need to move any more pieces."
   I see.

WHITE	BLACK
(*Dr Lasker*)	(*Capablanca*)
1. P to K 4	1. P to K 4
2. K Kt to K B 3	2. Q Kt to Q B 3
3. K B to Q B 4	3. K B to Q B 4

Then Lasker : " I say, Capablanca old boy, it's no use making any more moves. I foresee the conclusion." Sir, I have been showing harness horses for close on forty years and have the honour to be President of the Hackney Society. But you will not find in all the millions of words I have written a single illustration from the hunting-field. This because I don't know the first thing about hunting, and know that I don't know.

Your obedient servant,
JAMES AGATE

William Gaunt, Esq.

Further Essay. Letter to a reviewer of *A Shorter Ego* :

Queen Alexandra Mansions
Grape Street, W.C.2
April 18th, 1946

SIR,
You write that Shakespeare trumpeted and roared. To which category would you assign " Full fathom five " and " When that I was and a little tiny boy " ? You invite me to forget about horses and actors and read Auden and Spender and Comfort and Dyment and Treece. I am to try to comprehend the " new assonances, word-music, and thought-patterns." But I have read and I do comprehend, and I just don't like. If a poet has no word-music his thought must interest me ; if it doesn't, I care nothing for the thought-pattern. You tell me to note how, even when to-day's poets have failed, they have " opened new roads of technical development." As well ask me to approve the bouquet and body of a claret because somebody has found a way of making it out of old gum-boots !

Yours faithfully,
JAMES AGATE

Peter Baker, Esq.
c/o " Poetry Quarterly "

Easter Sunday. Horrified to find this morning that in last night's notice of the new Palladium show I made Virgil pile Pelion upon Ossa. It should, of course, have been the other way about. What was clever of me was to write the stuff in such a way that if it had to be cut it would still make sense. Actually, on receipt of the office message I cut the stuff myself, from ten inches to five, and in something under two minutes, as the taxi which was to take the copy to the *S.T.* office wouldn't wait. *I just put my pencil through every other sentence.* This meant sacrificing an elephant, a Ranee, a rainbow and a likening of Nat Jackley's marine to Kipling's " limping procrastitute " and " giddy harumfrodite." However, I managed to keep in a carthorse, a comparison between Tessie O'Shea and a battleship, a passage showing a surprising knowledge of the Yukon in 1890, and two quotations from Stevenson. A nice bit of work showing the super-professional touch. Meaning that the casual reader won't suspect the alteration of a word.

This afternoon, for the first time in my life, I was the first member of the audience to arrive at a theatre. The little Academy film theatre. The picture was *Fric-Frac*, the French comedy about crib-cracking. Directed by Maurice Lehmann, with Fernandel, Arletty, and Michel

Simon. The picture was at 3.55, the programme starting at 3.30. Realising the house would be packed, I arrived at 2.45 (!) and wheedled my way in. Spent the waiting time making comparative lists of the things France has meant to Raymond Mortimer, Charles Morgan, and J. A. *Enfin " Fric-Frac " vint.* One and three-quarter hours of superb realism, delicate irony, and exquisite wit. Three wonderful performances, and a fourth, unstarred, by a girl called Hélène Robert which would just make nonsense of anything our vaunted British film-stars could do. And then, from Fernandel as the innocent, I learned something that has always been a mystery to me—what Blackpool sees in George Formby. Fernandel begins by saying to the gangster's girl with whom he has fallen in love, " J'eusse préféré que vous vinssiez seule." And ends by understanding that in thieves' slang *scarper* means ' to clear out.' For Blackpool this would need translating. I can imagine Formby saying in the first instance, " I was 'oping, miss, you'd do me the favour of turning up alone." And ending by saying, " Git up them stairs ! "

Easter Monday. Fulfilled engagement to help judge the London Van Horse Parade. Reassembled what is left of my old horse-showing finery, determined that, whether or not the judges recognised which were the right horses, the horses should have no difficulty in picking out at least one of the judges. The day was exquisite, Regent's Park was looking lovely, the cherry-blossom was better than Housman's poem about it, and the judging was superb ! Took Gwen Chenhalls to lunch at the Savoy, and all very gay.

More of the Gentle Art :

Letter to Stephen Watts, the dramatic critic of the *Sunday Express* :

Queen Alexandra Mansions
Grape Street, W.C.2
April 22nd, 1946

DEAR STEPHEN WATTS,
    What on earth has made you suggest to your readers that the cheats and crib-crackers in *Fric-Frac* belong to the *demi-monde* ? " Il faut arriver de l'Afrique pour avoir cette idée-là ! " as Dumas's Olivier de Jalin said. Michel Simon, Arletty, and the man in gaol do not belong to the half- or even quarter-world ; they are " les bas-fonds de la société." Here is Dumas's own note on the *demi-monde*—the word, as you of course remember, which he introduced to the French language : " *Demi-monde.* Établissons donc ici,

pour les dictionnaires à venir, que le demi-monde ne représente pas, comme on le croit, comme on l'imprime, la cohue des courtisanes, mais la classe des déclassées." Paula Tanqueray and her kind. Nothing to do with burglars, who are not on the fringe of anything.

Yours sincerely,
JAMES AGATE

April 23 An exchange of letters :
Tuesday.

10 *Shepherd House*
Shepherd Street, W.1

21.4.46

DEAR MR AGATE,
The pity of it ! Leo Pavia is one of your best character studies. I felt I *knew* him from *Ego*, although some of his sallies seem to have just missed it, while your brother Edward could score nothing but bull's-eyes. I always imagined L. P. as a product of specifically German-Jewish culture (not *Kultur* !). In fact, he must have been *un Européen par excellence*. Please reassure me that he worshipped Pallenberg. He must have.
Why not publish the Collected Letters of Edward Agate ? Living and dying with his *panache* of artistic integrity unstained must make a man worthy of being remembered.
Why listen to envious critics and deprive your readers' grandchildren of the knowledge of what the food cost that went to the making of James Agate's frame ?
And all this from a man who faithfully promised to refrain from pestering you with further letters. I should hate to become a nuisance to you, and therefore hereby solemnly dissolve you from any obligation, moral or otherwise, you might feel to answer any letter of mine. If I begin to bore you, throw me away unread.
I saw you sitting in your box at the Winter Garden (like the Cardinal at the Hôtel de Bourgogne) the night Mr Valk bawled Desdemona out of her misery. I can't help feeling that his General was too Teutonic for a Moor. More Rommel than Othello. But the passion of his jealousy was Othello all right, and so were all the other emotions. Othello was all over the stage that night. Shakespeare was nowhere.
The quotation about " a man of genius who is not a man of honour " on Page 162 of *A Shorter Ego II* comes from *The Doctor's Dilemma.* You might be interested to know.
" *Was* duftet doch der Flieder " ? What, no lilac ? Some shades may haunt you for this. " *Wie* duftet doch der Flieder " ?
I was enchanted by your review of the new Priestley. I too like my Priestley this side of Jordan.

Yours sincerely,
GUY DEGHY

I counter :

Queen Alexandra Mansions
Grape Street, W.C.2

April 23rd, 1946

DEAR MR DEGHY,

Many thanks for your letter. Too busy to do more than sketch a reply.

Who is or was Pallenberg ? Even my twenty-year-old secretary, who knows everything, hasn't heard of him. I have just heard, meaning that when I see the name in the *New Statesman* I turn the page at once.

There is no more of my brother Edward that I think he would want to be published.

I don't take any notice of critics except to put them in their place. I should love you to become a witty nuisance.

Re Valk. I agree, except that he was more like Von Stroheim as Rommel. Of course the perfect Othello must have poetry as well as passion. But, if I must choose, I prefer some unmellifluous brute—and Valk is very far from that—to some unwarlike pansy.

Of course I know where the line about the man of genius who is not a man of honour comes from. But there's an art in concealing knowledge as well as displaying it. Makes the reader pat himself on the back. I knew whom I was improving when, in my Dreyfus play, I gave Esterhazy his exit line : " Monsieur Zola, do you know anything more pitiful than a man of dishonour who has not made a success of it ? "

" *Was* duftet." But for years, as soon as the lilac has been out, I have been wandering round my flat humming and saying to myself " *Wie* duftet . . ." Now I am cursed with the mania for accuracy, which makes me verify everything—even the things I'm sure about. If you will do me the honour to call on me I will show you the H.M.V. record, Catalogue Number D 1351, where " *Was* " stares me in the face printed in gold letters. Fool, fool ! I ought to have (*a*) relied on myself or (*b*) consulted a German record. My trusted Leo Pavia *m'aurait sauvé*, as Balzac in his last illness said of his own creation, *le docteur Bianchon*.

Yours sincerely,
JAMES AGATE

Winged Words. No. 12 : I have done a lot of work already at the Passacaglia. This does not seem to me like the creation of man at all, it is inspired, and that is not forgetting that I have an intimate acquaintance with all the great master works from Bach, Brahms, Beethoven, Liszt, Busoni, Medtner, and all the others— no greater monument to the memory of Schubert is possible. Of all the countless pages composed since the dawn of music, your Passacaglia and 44 Variations is the apotheosis.

Letter to the Pianist. Paul Howard
" *Midnight Thoughts on Leopold Godowsky* "

Finndale House
Grundisburgh
Suffolk

April 21, 1946

DEAR JAMES AGATE,

After giving, for nearly forty years, advice that was rarely sought and still more rarely taken, it is a new and valued honour to have it asked for ! I have pondered long over your letter, and will answer with the frankness that J. A. expects from his friends and always gives them.

I think you should certainly go on with *Ego* after No. 9. The only valid reasons, to my mind, for stopping would be that (*a*) you or (*b*) others are bored with it. Is there any sign of either ? You say that when talking to those young Sherborne lads you felt the coming age was theirs and not yours. Well, all men over fifty (earlier ?) almost always feel something of that, especially when such times as we live in have so gashed and mangled so many traditions that the young may well feel that they really have no roots in the past—that what anybody said or thought before 1914 or even 1939 has no importance for the present. All I can tell you is that, to my certain knowledge, you have many faithful readers among the young—of both sexes.

And how is your seventieth birthday an end or climax for anyone but you ? If you were seventy-conscious (like Whitman), and imparted that consciousness to your readers, it would be different, but you aren't and don't. Mentally you have nothing of the rising septuagenarian about you. If you want a time-climax, I think *Ego*'s twentieth year, or even No. 12, would be a much better one. But a diary surely needn't be *teres atque rotundus* like a poem. Pepys's stopping through his fear of blindness was wholly to be deplored. The right time for *Ego*'s end will be when you feel (shall you ever ?) a waning of that interest in men and things and of that felicity in wording it, which, if you don't mind my saying so, makes the *Egos* such enormous fun to read and re-read. That will be the moment for drawing to an artistic close, with " calm of mind, all passion spent." Or, to use your own less Miltonic but equally expressive phrase, if you don't go gaga. I am sure you should go on. After all, still later than *Sands at Seventy* Whitman wrote, " On, on the same, ye jocund twain ! My life and recitative . . ."

As to your parallel between Horace Walpole going out when poke-bonnets came in and you yielding to the *argumentum a tergo* of the rising generation—well, H. W.'s letters are still read by those who do read (it may be, of course, that in 2000 no one will), and the wearers of the poke-bonnets are stopping some bung-hole. And so will *Ego* be read when those Sherbornians' great-grandchildren are toothless nonentities, and good men will be lamenting after finishing Vol. 12, " What, is there no more ? "

Well, them's my sentiments. You may think them irrelevant, stupid, and negligible, but you must not think them anything but absolutely sincere.

Yours ever,
GEORGE LYTTELTON

I couldn't let this go unanswered.

Queen Alexandra Mansions
Grape Street, W.C.2
April 24th, 1946

DEAR GEORGE LYTTELTON,

You have lifted a great load from my mind, for I believe that I should have taken the contrary advice if you had given it. Some of my best friends think very little of *Ego*, and argue that I ought to wind up the career I make so much fuss about with a piece of major dramatic criticism. But I know that I haven't got a piece of major criticism in me—for example, I don't care two hoots about the new poetic drama—and have spent the war years trying to conceal from *Sunday Times* readers how thin the soil is. One of my friends suggests a vast theatrical biography. Another wants me to review the trend of dramatic criticism in this country since there was any, complete, I understand, with critical essays on Hazlitt, Lewes, Shaw, Archer, Walkley, Montague, Max. They don't seem to realise that even if I could do this I am too tired. And then again, *I don't want* ! The truth is that I have exhausted the Theatre. On the other hand I have not yet exhausted Life, though that old hussy has taken a lot out of me these last few months.

In the meantime here are bits out of four letters, all received since I wrote you.

From a Lieutenant-Colonel, writing from the Royal Bombay Yacht Club :

" Again many thanks, and may you long live, to annoy me with your discourse on life in general and J. A. in particular."

From a lady in Western Australia :

" Just a word of thanks to you for Septego—a word from an admirer 'way across the world in a sleepy little suburb in Western Australia—*the* deadest track of country in the world. I've been here for five years—thanks to those two odious little men Hitler and Togo, and nothing has happened to me except your *Egos*. So please don't die—for at least another year—for I'm sure I'll be here for Huitego."

From a journalist exiled in Buenos Aires :

" I have discovered the ideal way of passing the immense number of hours required to digest all the food one eats here : I subscribed for six books at a time at Harrod's library ; and took out all the *Egos*. And I have read them all again, with as much happiness as I first read them, which is saying a lot. Although I've only been away from home for a month, and shall be back in three weeks, they made me feel homesick for London, and to hell with the food and drink here."

From a Squadron-Leader in Canada :

" I am amazed at myself. I, the merest layman, have uttered a small, polite growl at the direct, lineal descendant of Hazlitt. I am horrified. I can only atone by my idolatry. At home once more in Canada, six *Egos* and four books of criticism (no more were procurable) stand on my shelves, slightly uncomfortable, perhaps, in the shadow of the Rockies, but much thumbed, much talked-over with friends, who may read them, but *only on the premises*, and who, poor souls, had never heard before of James Agate. Each morning brings the thought " to-day may be the DAY," for Harrap's are sending me the very last copy of *Ego* 7 they possess. . . . Will that make amends, especially as it is all true ? "

I have bothered you with these extracts to prove to myself that your advice is right and that I am right in taking it. Who am I to say No to India, Australia, South America, and Canada ? Wherefore I hoist myself shakily into the saddle and ride somewhat gaspingly on, trying to feel like something by Burne-Jones and looking, doubtless, like the White Knight in *Alice*.

Anyhow, thank you and bless you !

Ever,
J. A.

P.S. The rain of correction never ceases. Brother Mycroft writes me to-day :

" *A Shorter Ego*, Vol. I, Page 159. ' Hari-kari ' should be ' Hara-kiri.' (Jap., *hara*, ' belly ' ; *kiri*, ' cut.' *Chambers's Dictionary*.) "

Sackcloth, please, or rather " Hairi-shirti " !

April 25   The young man from Canada has arrived and been
Thursday.   presented to Rank, who received him with open arms.
    Everybody suitably impressed, and within half an hour we got a fashionable bootmaker to add an inch to his height. After the ordeal, which he came through very well, I took him for a drink to a little club where the wireless was discoursing *Tristan and Isolda*. This settled the question of the name, since everybody is agreed that " George Calderwood " is too long. I laid it down, and the boy agreed, that he shall be known as Tris Calder.

Last night at a Bloomsbury party into which I had been inveigled a Beard brought up a young man and said, "Mr Agate, here is somebody who would like you to talk to him." I waved them away, but the Beard insisted. Again I waved, but the Beard wasn't to be denied :

> J. A. The old gentleman will be witty by and by.
> THE BEARD. Sir, the young man can wait.

April 26   Waking early and unable to get to sleep again, I composed
Friday.   the following poem :

SALUTE TO VITAMINS

Vitamins A, B, C, and X, Y, Z,
Are indicated to correct those low
Ascorbic-acid levels leading to
Derangement of protein metabolism.
Oh, for a box to well and duly numb
Hypersensation due to this or that,
Also my woefully impaired response,
Erythropoietic it seems to me,
Which may or may not be anæmia . . .

I had got so far when the post arrived. The first letter was from Cambridge. " I am drawing a bow at a venture because I don't know whether you are still alive." Perhaps I am not. Perhaps I am losing vitality. Perhaps my ascorbic-acid levels are too low. Rang up my disgusting doctor, who ordered me away for a week, advice which I think I shall take, Brother Harry urging me to go to Bridlington to cheer his spouseless and unoffspring'd thoughts. Before I go I feel that one more Essay in the Gentle Art is called for. Hence this letter to Bertie van Thal :

> *Queen Alexandra Mansions*
> *Grape Street, W.C.*2
>
> *April 26th,* 1946

DEAR BERTIE, SWEET BERTIE, LOVELY BERTIE,
You know I dote on you. Why, then, do you behave like a mindless oyster ? Have you not over and over again shown me your blurbs for other people ? Why take it on yourself to pass the blurb to *Around Cinemas* without consulting me ? What in Bloomsbury—my new expletive—do you mean by calling my shy little essays

PERTINACIOUS ?

This word means obstinate, perversely persistent as beggars are. And my essays are not beggars. Dear Bertie, lovely Bertie, sweet Bertie, withdraw the blurb or I'll withdraw the book and publish with the insignificant Macmuddle or the paltry Poop instead of the omnipotent Home and van Thal. Then there's the jacket-photo of Gish. Don't you realise that this suggests that the book is illustrated, with resulting disappointment to the reader ? Whereas between covers she comes as a surprise. Remove her, please. " I beseech you, be ruled by your well-willer." If you aren't, by Fitzroy Square I'll revoke the dedication to my next book . . . and how will you like that ?

J.

April 28
Sunday. The train to York was one hour and twenty minutes late. No stop except Doncaster, and signals in our favour all the way. Reason for being late ? Just that the engine couldn't go fast enough. Arthur Bates and I missed the last two seats, and had to sit on our suitcases all the way. But we had the corridor all to ourselves and were really very comfortable. Found Harry physically fit but mentally tired. I agree that when a surveyor does a sum in acres, roods, and perches and gets the answer in pounds, shillings, and pence it is obvious that he has been overworking.

Spent the evening going through the family archives—*i.e.*, a dozen or so of huge newspaper-cutting books. Found all sorts of things, including a photograph of Harry at the age of four. He kept his curls—bright gold and nearly waist-length—till he was six, and I remember how my mother cried when my father insisted that they should be cut off. Also a photo of Brother Mycroft as Titania in a school performance of the *Dream*—unnecessary to say who was the Bottom on that occasion ! We borrowed Harry, whose curls—they were really ringlets—made him the ideal Peaseblossom. This is perhaps the place to recall—if I have not already done so—the rôles in which I distinguished myself as a boy actor. Bottom, Shylock, Cardinal Wolsey, Harpagon in Molière's *L'Avare*, and Don Diègue in Corneille's *Le Cid*. All that I had of the good performer was a good memory.

April 29
Monday. A three hours' tour of the beauties of York is not my notion of a rest-cure. But Harry was not to be denied, and the Castle Museum, known as the Kirk collection, is certainly a breath-taking affair. The first exhibit you see is a series of period rooms—a Victorian parlour more authentically documented than any stage-set Irene Hentschel has ever dreamed of, a Georgian room, a Yorkshire farm-kitchen, and so on. Suddenly you look out on to a street with bow-window'd shop-fronts, cobble-stones, a barouche, and an early hansom. People are walking about, and at first you don't realise that they are visitors to the Museum ;

it was only the stillness of the two horses that made me realise that the whole thing was under glass. Wonderful detail, down to the differentiation between the proud Hackney in the gentleman's carriage and the humble nag in the coach plying for hire. A remarkable collection, principally the work of one man, a country doctor, presented to the city just before the War and now housed in the old Castle.

The notion that you cannot have high wind and fog at one and the same time is false. At Scarborough, after a journey through country which Harry says is best described as ' open,' we ran into a ' sea-fret ' coupled with a marrow-freezing wind. (The two perfectly explain Sibelius !) Found a delightful boarding-house, newer than any pin, a pub with unlimited whiskey, and a hire-service driver willing to wait. Otherwise this place—Bridlington—is as though somebody had uprooted Hackney Wick and planked it down on Canvey Island. Went to the pictures and slept through *Meet Me on Broadway*. Harry says that the proper thing to do on a rest-cure is to rest. Bed before twelve.

April 30   Cold and cheerless. Nothing to do, and nothing to see
Tuesday.   except ex-repertory actresses trundling about on bicycles.
              Diarised and got chilled to the bone sitting on Flamborough Head. To the pictures (twice), after which Harry entertained us with card tricks—which he has not done for twenty years—and it was all very, very Tchehovian.

May 1   Letter from my monitor :
Wednesday.

10 *Shepherd House*
*Shepherd Street, W.*1

27.4.46

DEAR MR AGATE,
    " Samedi, aujourd'hui, deux heures après dîner, Monsieur de Bergerac est mort assassiné." Having had dinner at eight, I settled down to read the paper at ten, and was informed that *Cyrano* is to be produced in English. Which butcher will be commissioned to tear the noble alexandrine into the shreds of blank verse ? Also that Mr Olivier is to play Lear. He likes playing old men, and did very well indeed as Shallow. But Shallow is a man of human proportions and Lear isn't. He is well over life-size, and I doubt whether Olivier can fill that figure. Then those two hardy old bores *Love's Labour's Lost* and *Doctor Faustus* are to be with us again. To cap it all, another Priestley, the title of which clearly indicates that it will be what Goethe called " ein garstig' Lied, ach ein politisch Lied ! " And I had hoped that Mr Pascal's ' generosity '

had provided the costumiers with enough togas, helmets, laurel wreaths, and Roman armour to enable the Old Vic to put on *Julius Cæsar, Coriolanus,* or *Antony and Cleopatra*; perhaps another Chekhov, another Ibsen, another Shaw and—as Mr Olivier has the paraphernalia for the Grecian nose—perhaps another Greek. But the programme for the next season is hardly suitable for what will undoubtedly be Britain's National Theatre. Such a pity, because the last season was superb. I have never seen Chekhov acted as it should be, even by Russians. The Old Vic *Uncle Vanya* was to my mind perfection.

Never again consult a gramophone record for reference. But if you take a morbid delight in hunting for howlers, glance through an H.M.V. catalogue. It is full of the funniest specimens. Incidentally, this week's prize howler goes to (obviously) a typist on the *Daily Telegraph*. A musical notice dealing with the abominable Bartók refers to the Hungarian cymbalist Ady. He was a symbolist poet.

Concerning modern lyrics, one could paraphrase Beaumarchais's dictum—namely, that which is too stupid to be sung should be swung. If this gibberish is only written to accentuate or syncopate the music, I suggest a more effective and modern course—namely, to let the band-leader beat the rhythm on the crooner's head with a functional chromium blunderbuss or periodically tug at a cat's tail to punctuate the syncopes. Even the late T. E. Dunville's lines about hobnail and boat-tax made some sort of sense, and they certainly put to shame anything like this modern notion of syncopulation.

Bol-li-ka, wol-li-ka!

Guy Deghy

Motored to Scarborough, partly to renew acquaintance with Mrs Laughton, mother of Charles, and partly to show Harry the Queen's Hotel, where *Ego* was begun. Found my old friend in great fettle—Charles's name was blazoned all over the cinema across the road—and the Pavilion as charming and elegant as ever. Alas! the Queen's Hotel, where I stayed with Monty Shearman in 1932, has been badly damaged. From which it is evident that certain bricks and mortar have not outlived my powerful prose.

May 3   On Wednesday morning the page proofs of *Ego* 8 arrived.
Friday.   Put in fourteen hours of solid work on them—good rest-cure stuff !—and sent them off to my good friend Frank Dunn, to check and counter-check.

May 4   Scoured the countryside to find a cricket match. Too
Saturday.   early. Did the Lighthouse on Flamborough Head.
Or rather sat in the car and drank in the sunshine and listened to Jack Hill, its amiable driver and own brother to Joe

Gargery, tell his story of Yorkshire's Most Predatory Female. His small boys, aged three and two, had taken their seven weeks' puppy for a walk. On their return in tears and minus the puppy he gathered that they had met a little girl accompanied by her mother, that the little girl had stroked the puppy, and that her mother had said, " Pick it up and take it home."

In the evening to see Shirley Temple in *Kiss and Tell*. In London I should have thought this a horror; here it was my last defence against a touring company in *Lilac Time*. A revolting story of a chit of fifteen who, to screen a school-friend, pretends to be pregnant. (What the six-year-old little girl in front of me made of it I don't know.) One witty line uttered by the outraged father, unable to contact the doctor spending the afternoon on the links : " Obstetricians shouldn't play golf ! "

We go back to-morrow, thank Heaven !

May 6   Harold Hobson, who deputised for me on Sunday more
Monday.   than brilliantly, sends me this note :

> *Our Town*, which I saw on Tuesday, is the most exhilarating play I have yet seen, whose third act is presented in a graveyard by a cast of corpses. Have you seen Yorkshire play Lancashire at Bramall Lane on Whit Monday ? Well, *Our Town* is slower, much slower, than that. There is one pace of America making up to a pretty girl. There is another pace of America entering a war. *Our Town* is the pace of America entering a war.

And now I must settle down to serious work again. I have been grieved not to encounter in all the acres I have covered a single stroke of wit, and humiliated to find that I was not the cause of wit in other men. Shall tell *Tatler* readers that Wilde was 100 per cent. right when he said that country people, who have no means of becoming cultured or corrupt, stagnate. That I hold Yorkshire to be a mistake. That next year, as a good Lancastrian, I shall go to Morecambe, which salubrious resort combines, as the polite world knows, the wit of Paris with the elegance of pre-War Vienna, and adds to the virtues of Buda the vices of Pesth.

May 7   Letter to George Lyttelton :
Tuesday.
                          Queen Alexandra Mansions
                              *Grape Street, W.C.*2
                                   May 7th, 1946
DEAR G. L.,
    Roast me in sulphur ! Wash me in steep-down gulfs of liquid paraffin ! Have just discovered that in an early essay, " Play-

going," I attribute "You are old, Father William" to Words-worth! Also that in *Ego* 7 I make Dumas's Olivier de Jalin say, "Il faut arriver d'Afrique" instead of "de l'Afrique"! Let me keep my reason and change the subject.

Yesterday, at the London Sessions, my burglar was sent to prison for nine months. I had placed the time at three o'clock in the afternoon or shortly after, whereas Booth-Palmer swore to 3.45, and was confirmed by the local cop, who had entered 3.52 in his book. Whereupon Counsel for the defence asked the jury to regard me as a muddle-head whose testimony in other matters could not be relied on! Did I boil? I think I should have boiled over if I hadn't caught in the Judge's right eye something that might have been a wink. My idiot burglar—I thought he was distinctly feeble-minded—is an East End Jew tailor who has had and held three jobs in twenty years and has the highest refer-ences, including one from his last employer, who is willing to take him back. The police inspector very gentle and considerate. Spoke about a poor home and no money saved, but a contented wife and two well-cared-for children. These kids are going to worry me. Who's going to feed them till their father comes out? I wish now that Booth-Palmer hadn't caught the fellow red-handed. Or that we had had the sense to let him go. Is this feebly senti-mental?

And last for something more cheerful. Coming back from Yorkshire I travelled with a man who told me a lot about himself and then asked what my trade was. I said, "Dramatic critic." He said, "Ay. A ticklish job. I had a brother as used to be dramatic critic to Carl Brisson."

No more for now.

Ever,
J. A.

May 8
Wednesday.
A storm in a Wagnerian teacup blows, so to speak, a pretty gale. One such has been whistling round my head throughout the past fortnight. It began with a letter from a lady:

How dare you think of my Cobbler's "Flieder" as the lilac? Never again keep company with Hans Sachs in Kew in Lilac-time —but in Nuremberg on St John's Eve look with him for the serpent under the not-so-innocent elder-flower. It wasn't the torrents of spring, but midsummer madness, that went to every-body's head that night in Act Two. It wasn't Proserpine, but the Elder-Mother, who crazed the townsfolks' wits, and set them serenading, brawling, and eloping in the moonshine. Don't trust your memory, your dictionary, or even your botany. Trust your sense of superstition—and on St John's Eve mistrust the elder-flower as you would the serpent. *Der Flieder war's! Johannis-nacht!*

Whereupon I hied me to the nearest considerable town and consulted the reference library's up-to-datest dictionary. In the German-English section I found : " *FLIEDER*—elder ; *spanischer Flieder*—lilac." In the English-German section : " ELDER—*der* (*schwarze*) *Holunder*." Lastly I looked up *Holunder*, and found that in German lilac is *spanischer Holunder* ! Difficult enough when lexicographers differ, but when the same dictionary quarrels with itself . . . !

And all the time the storm over " *Wie* duftet " and " *Was* duftet " continued unabated. It was while inspecting the Lighthouse on Flamborough Head that I decided to apply to Ernest Newman for elucidation. He at once replied :

> In virtually every edition I know, both of score and of poem-apart-from-the-score, it's *Wie*, which is undoubtedly the correct word. But, very strangely, there's *one* exception. In the original *orchestral* score it's *Was* ! ! ! You can take this as certain : I have a copy of the original issue of 1868. A facsimile of the whole of the orchestral *manuscript* was published some years ago, but as I don't possess this I can't say whether it's *Wie* or *Was* there. If it's *Was*, I should say, offhand, that this is merely another of the many mistakes Wagner used to make in the hurry of getting his stuff on to paper : in *all* the editions of *Tristan*, for example, he makes Brangaene speak of " blue strips of land " in the *West*, when obviously he means in the *East*.

Und das ist das ! Unless, of course, some dictionary would like me to spell the last word with two s's and a curly tail to the second one like the serpent under the elder ! Query : Have we been misreading Shakespeare all this time ? Did Lady Macbeth say " Look like the innocent Flieder, but be the serpent under't " ?

May 9   In a letter from Belgium :
Thursday.

> Vous êtes, Monsieur, un homme selon mon cœur. Sauf que *A Shorter Ego* me laisse sur ma faim, je veux bien vous avouer que je n'ai plus eu de lecture plus délectable depuis le *Journal* de Jules Renard. Mais, entre nous, votre frère Édouard—à en juger par ce que vous rapportez et reproduisez de lui—était d'une autre trempe que vous ! Quelle intégrité ! Quel caractère ! Quel esprit ! Quelle plume, aussi ! Salva reverentia, vous n'arriviez pas à sa cheville ! Je vous avouerai que, parvenu à la page 115 du tome II, à la date du 22 octobre 1940, j'ai été profondément affecté par la nouvelle de sa mort—laquelle m'a laissé mélancolique pour le reste de ma lecture.

May 10   My doctor, *de plus en plus dégoûtant*, insisted on my visit-
Friday.   ing his dentist in Hackney rather than continue on a diet
          of Codein, Anadin, and Veganin.   It was the first time I
had had a tooth extracted to the accompaniment of a cornet solo in
the street immediately beneath the surgery window.

   To-night's revue at the Ambassadors, *Sweetest and Lowest*, was
immensely witty and cruel.   If ridicule could kill, the Picasso-ites,
four British film-stars, and one globe-trotting actor-author-propa-
gandist would be handing in their checks.

May 11   The Gentle Art again :
Saturday.   To Patrick Kirwan, film critic of the *Evening Standard* :

   I could forgive you believing that Meyerbeer wrote *Faust* and
Donizetti *Rosenkavalier*.   What I will not excuse is your thinking
that " I Want to Sing in Opera " was sung by George Formby *père*.
Ever heard of Wilkie Bard ?

May 12   In his introduction to the English edition of *More than*
Sunday.   *Somewhat* E. C. Bentley wrote :

   In all the Runyon stories, as published in America, I have
found only one single instance of a verb in the past tense.   It
occurs in one of those included in this book ; and you may try
to find it, if—as Runyon's guy might say—you figure there is any
percentage in doing so.   And, as that same guy might go on to say,
I will lay plenty of 6 to 5 that it is nothing but a misprint ; but I
do not think it is the proper caper for me to improve on Runyon's
prose, so I leave it.

   In *Furthermore* I found another example of the past tense :
"The Lemon Drop Kid *put* a lozenge into his mouth."   Now, in *Runyon*
à la Carte, I discover two more.   In the story called *Old Em's Kentucky*
Home I find :   " Not far from the house are the remainders of some
buildings that look as if they *burned* down a long time ago."   In *Cleo*
occurs :   " She is a brown-haired pretty who *had* a dancing background."   As this makes a total of three slips which I have detected—
three more than any other student—what about Harvard presenting
me with an honorary degree ?

May 13   Spent last Saturday morning diarising and answering
Monday.   letters.   No, I will not go down to Bristol and lecture
          for a fee of three guineas plus expenses.   No, I will not
talk to East Anglians for no fee and no expenses.   No, I do not know
why brass bands are always out of tune.   No, I cannot tell a young

man how to become a " litiry " critic. Yes, I will write an advertisement for a commercial firm, and supply a photograph, if (*a*) the stuff
they are selling is something I can reasonably be connected with,
and (*b*) they give me £100 free of tax. No, I do not know the value of
a complete set of the Waverley Novels, edition unknown. Yes, I will
lunch with the representatives of the French film industry and talk
for as long as they like in return for a glass of cognac. No, I am not
on the staff of *Punch*, and what makes the blasted idiot think I am.?
Yes, I am prepared to say which are the best twelve books in the
English language, and do so. Tell a literary society in Cheshire
that the best way to find out why Ibsen was a great dramatist is
to read his plays. Yes, I will write 1200 words at one-quarter
my usual rates for a paper published in Moscow to help its
readers to some knowledge of the English theatre. Yes, I will
talk free of charge to some East End boys and girls. Thirty-one
letters, plus two manuscripts returned, also a book on Beddoes lent
me by a Bloomsbury intellectual and which unaccountably turns out
to be the property of a public library in the Midlands. Item, a
signed photograph to please a Miss Boakes who cannot endure life
in the Mendips unless she has my picture to look at.

And then an extraordinary thing happened. Some time before
the War Clement Scott's daughter gave me her father's newspaper-
cutting book containing several thousand dramatic criticisms covering
the period 1811–33. I turned this into a little book called *These
Were Actors*. Then, during my stay at Oxford in 1940, an anonymous
donor presented me with four small volumes of theatrical press-
cuttings for the years 1885–93. Bound in shiny black stuff and
falling to pieces. To me enormously interesting, but not enough for
a volume. On Saturday morning I received an enormous parcel,
which turned out to contain one hundred and twenty large envelopes,
each holding ten and sometimes twenty cuttings about some play or
production. Period 1897–1906. In less than ten minutes I had
decided to make another little book out of these and the black books.
Unfortunately the original collector—a covering letter explained that
they had been bequeathed to the sender, who had chosen me as an
alternative to the salvage dump—had in nearly all cases cut off the
name of the paper and the date. This obviously called for a lot
of niggling work, and I had given Booth-Palmer the week-end off.
And then the doorbell rang, and a young man carrying a lot of *Egos*
presented himself. Would I sign them, please ? Now I have ε
shark's eye for anybody to get me out of a jam. " Come in. Who

and what are you ? " " John Compton. Air Force." " Hobbies ? "
" James Agate and cricket. I'm pretty good at the first and not bad
at the second." " How bad at the second ? " " Before the War
I won one of Jack Hobbs's bats. Took 8 wickets for 4 runs. Was
given a trial at the nets at Canterbury. Last week I did the hat
trick with the first three balls of the season. Also made top score."
" Going in for cricket when you get demobbed ? " " No. Not good
enough. I was better at sixteen. What I'm looking for is something
connected with the theatre." " Where are you stationed ? " " St
Athans. On leave till Monday night." " My secretary's on leave.
Care to do a locum ? Three guineas plus hotel bill." " My hotel's
fixed up and I don't want money." " Well, what do you want ? "
" To be in *Ego*."

And so the bargain was struck. We worked for the rest of Saturday, all Sunday, and all to-day till the boy had to leave. By that
time all the 1500 cuttings had been dated and arranged in their proper
order.

May 14   Last night after the young man had gone I sat on work-
Tuesday.   ing. At 4 A.M. the book was finished. Sixty thousand
            words plus forty illustrations, some from my private
collection and some as the result of rummaging in the shops on my
way back from lunch yesterday and to-day. There's always time
to do a thing if you want to do it hard enough.

May 18   The Hackney Show has come and gone. Two beautiful
Saturday.   animals. Frank Haydon's Solitude, a thirteen-year-
            old bay stallion by Buckley Courage out of Dark Vision
by St Adrian, and Nigel Colman's Black Magic of Nork by Spotlight
out of Silhouette of Nork by Mathias A. I. I could have looked at
these all day. The Luncheon was, I think, a success. Certainly a
better meal than any I have eaten in London during the past six
years. Forty guests, who got through ten of the dozen bottles of
Burgundy and eight of the dozen of champagne Eddie Tatham kindly
let me have. One of the ignominies, or perhaps I mean humiliations,
attendant upon war is that hosts watch every time a glass is lifted
in the hope that a few drops of the unprocurable stuff may be left
over ! I did quite well to-day with six whole bottles for booty. Made
a goodish, because very short, speech on the theme of You Can't
Give Old Heads New Shoulders, the idea being to welcome new
blood. Crewe is unchanged : I could write a book about its repositories

and horse sales. It was at Crewe that I met Alexander Gemmell, bought Vivianette, and sold Talke Princess and First Edition. The old desk is still in the hall of the delightful Crewe Arms Hotel, and the day and night porters have been there for forty-one and thirty-three years respectively. George Mathew went with me; Brother Mycroft, Albert Throup, and Frank Dunn turned up; and all very jolly, including that gay and gallant sportswoman Lady Daresbury, for whom I have invented the sobriquet, "Betsey Trotwood on Horseback."

May 19 Whenever I have been out of Town for a day I always
Sunday. expect to find that the world has been remade in my
absence. But it hasn't. Awaiting me last night was the first copy of *Around Cinemas*. I open this, and my eye at once falls on "It is impossible to take seriously the Andromagues [*sic*] and the Chimènes of Messrs Racine and Corneille." And what, pray, are "one's evening's [*sic*] studs and waistcoat buttons"?

Next I turn to the accounts of yesterday's heavyweight affair between the British Bruce Woodcock and the American Tami Mauriello. In this once again the Englishman rose from the canvas after the count of ten a sadder and a wiser man. Here is Woodcock talking to the New York representative of the *Sunday Express*—it seems that Tami had caught him with his head on the left side of his, Bruce's, skull above the left ear:

> This is in no sense an attempt to make an excuse, first because I have always said that no squealer deserves any sympathy in a rough game like boxing, and secondly because I know this was just one of those accidents that happen in any rough-and-tumble. It could just as easily have happened to Mauriello as to me.

But why do these mishaps invariably happen to our side? Why, since this one could just as easily have happened to the American fellow, didn't it? *It never does.* I don't know whether Montgomery is a good general or not. I know that whenever in the last war we had a victory he was around and about. I am tired of those brilliant generals who are always mixed up with defeats. And I am equally tired of the British heavyweight who does nothing except come up pluckily for more. In the meantime Mr Mauriello gives me No. 13 in my *Winged Words* series:

> I had a haircut and a shave and a manicure before the fight in honour of the Englishman. We gentlemen got to stick together.

Tami Mauriello in an interview

345

May 20   What about an essay on " The Beauties of Hazlitt " ?
Monday.   Though a master of quotation—the index gives three
         thousand five hundred and twelve—W. H. could come
to the point better than any other English writer I know. It is
this quality that I admire most in him, and it is upon Hazlitt and
not Montague that I have modelled what I am pleased to call my
style.

> The Cockney ventures through Hyde Park Corner, as a cat
> crosses a gutter. The trees pass by the coach very oddly. The
> country has a strange blank appearance. It is not lined with
> houses all the way, like London. A cow in a field, a magpie in a
> hedge, are to him very odd animals—he can't tell what to make of
> them, or how they live.

This is superb, and to me better than Lamb, who fantasticates too
much and could never have written " Mr Nollekins died the other day
at the age of eighty, and left 240,000 pounds behind him, and the
name of one of our best English sculptors." But then Charles
wouldn't have wanted to write like this ; he was all for the bypath
and not the highroad. Talking of roads, I came across this to-day in
the essay " On Old English Writers and Speakers " :

> The Rev. Job Orton was a Dissenting Minister in the middle of
> the last century, and had grown heavy and gouty by sitting long at
> dinner and at his studies. He could only get downstairs at last by
> spreading the folio volumes of Caryl's Commentaries upon Job on
> the steps and sliding down them. Surprised one day in his descent,
> he exclaimed, " You have often heard of Caryl upon Job—now you
> see Job upon Caryl ! "

Though I dote on W. H. I am not dotty about him. There are
essays in this volume, No. VII in my set of thirteen, that I think I
shall not re-read. " On Dr Spurzheim's Theory " and " On the
Systems of Hartley and Helvetius " are two of them.

May 21   Horror, horror, horror ! Looking through *Around*
Tuesday.   *Cinemas* in bed, I find a passage in which I jot down " a
         list of a dozen English classics I have not read. *Gulliver's*
Travels, Roderick Random, Heart of Midlothian, Emma, Lothair,
Wuthering Heights, A Tale of Two Cities, Middlemarch, Beauchamp's
Career, Ulysses, and *The Forsyte Saga.*" What is wrong here ? They
don't tot up to twelve !

Protests are pouring in about my use of the word ' nigger ' in last

Saturday's review of Edwin Peeples's novel about negroes, *Swing Low*. It seems I must not use the word ' nigger.' (I had quoted a few lines of my account of Harlem given in *Ego 8*.) One correspondent wrote :

> Nobody who knows and understands the negro mind would use that word publicly—that is to say, no white person would do so. Strangely, the coloured people themselves use it frequently, but they have a rooted objection to its use by the white folks. Had your review been published in an American publication you would have been inundated with letters of protest, not only from the coloured people themselves, but also from white people who know the negroes ! The word ' nigger ' is a carry-over from the days when unthinking people (*i.e.*, the vast majority) looked down on negroes as being very little if any better than animals—it was a term of contempt. It is still to be heard in the deep South, but no public man would dream of using it in public.

I have replied :

> I know all about ' negroes ' and ' niggers.' Don't you realise that there is a lilt in " Brown niggers, yellow niggers, pale niggers, black niggers " that is utterly lost if you substitute ' negroes ' ? Do you suggest that the old rhyme should be altered to " Ten little negro boys " ? And surely you should have realised that my use of the word ' nigger ' was confined to what I had the vanity to regard as a lyrical passage ? That in the rest of the article the word ' negro ' was scrupulously adhered to ?

May 22
Wednesday.

Two letters. From Dilys Powell :

14 *Albion Street*
*Hyde Park, W.*2
20.5.46

MY DEAR JIMMIE,
Your cinema book has been rapturously received in this house. Too rapturously, in fact, for instead of grinding out my usual pieces about cinematography I find myself rushing to read Agate on " Earth " and " The White Hell of Pitz Palu " (and how good I find the Old Maestro !). I need not tell you that my enjoyment is heightened from time to time by paroxysms of disagreement. And, of course, by spasms of pride when I reflect on the dedication. Well, my dear Jimmie, I thank you, I thank you, I thank you, as Bemelmans would say. I am vastly honoured.
Your flattered and devoted,
DILYS

From George Lyttelton :

Finndale House
Grundisburgh
Suffolk
May 21, 1946

MY DEAR JAMES AGATE,

Once again a red-letter day—coinciding with a change of wind to the soft south after a month of the one that Kingsley was so hearty about. Many thanks indeed. I have so far had no time to read more than page 100 (and spot the misprint that made you shudder), as my sister, who hates the cinema, has been reading it all the morning. And the answer to the question why she reads it when caring nothing for its subject is much the same as Stella's about the Dean and a broomstick. What a good page by the way No. 100 is. I agree with it all. Didn't George Moore rise, or was he dead in 1931 ?

By the way, here is a tiny gift for you, who, I know, enjoy examples of human folly. In his history of the American language Mencken writes " the *finicky* and always anti-American Samuel Johnson." I don't know how many English adjectives there are, but I am sure you know practically all of them. Can you think of a sillier one than this ?

Yours ever,
GEORGE LYTTELTON

P.S. A schoolgirl when asked the question, " In what countries are elephants found ? " answered, " Elephants are very large and intelligent animals and are seldom lost." I hope you didn't know that.

May 23
Thursday.

I once knew a murderer. He was a charming young man, of a gay and debonair manner, and a free and open-handed disposition. Excellent company. Alas ! that when funds ran short he conceived and executed the notion of insuring and setting fire to his mother. Had I been briefed for the defence I should have argued that Sidney Harry Fox was a Dickensian who had been led away by Sam Weller's, " Wery sorry to 'casion any personal inconwenience, ma'am, as the housebreaker said to the old lady when he put her on the fire." He certainly did not belong to the more revolting type of murderer, the poisoner. The point to make about these gentry—not, of course, the kind which poisons for money—is the exquisite depravity of their satisfactions. Neill Cream liked to talk about women, music, money, and poisons. Teignmouth Shore ends his account in the " Notable British Trials " :

His actions were probably governed by a mixture of sexual mania and sadism. He may have had a half-crazy delight in feeling that the lives of the wretched women whom he slew lay in his power, that he was the arbiter of their fates. Sensuality, cruelty, and lust of power urged him on. We may picture him walking at night the dreary mean streets and byways of Lambeth, seeking for his prey, on some of whom to satisfy his lust, on others to exercise his passion for cruelty ; his drug-sodden, remorseless mind exalted in a frenzy of horrible joy. Whatever exactly he was, the halter was his just reward.

This Famous Trial used to be my favourite bed-book ; there was a time when I knew the names of all his victims in chronological order—Ellen Donworth, Matilda Clover, and so on. The point about this morning's film at the Gaumont is the sexual gratification accorded to any strangler by the act of strangling. Which means that anybody who attempts to make a film on this subject is at once up against the film censor. The strangler's motive being strictly unavowable, some other must obviously be found. What about making him the son of a public hangman, whose fingers owe their peculiar habits to heredity ? That this is all my eye and the late respected Mr Billington won't trouble the one-and-nine-pennies. What might a little incommode them is that the widow of the common hangman should be living in one of Belgravia's costlier mansions. Wherefore it becomes necessary to make the strangler the grandson of a hangman, with a father (deceased) who also showed signs of " strangler's twitch " fortunately kept in control. In other words there is no harm in a film about sexual mania so long as the maniac's motive is not sex. Eric Portman very good.

May 24
Friday.
  Last night, before sending away the corrected page proofs of *The Contemporary Theatre* (1944 *and* 1945), I had one more quick look through and discovered that I had re-christened Bartók and given him the name of Bella ! This morning I receive a p.c. from George Lyttelton apropos of *Around Cinemas* and my making Johnson say, " Sheer ignorance, ma'am ! "

" Sudden fits of inadvertency will surprize vigilance, slight avocations will seduce attention, and casual eclipses of the mind will darken learning."

Not that the old man would have cared a straw and, after all, in the dictionary ' sheer ' is an exact synonym for ' pure,' and ' pure ' for ' sheer.'

May 25
Saturday.
  Gwen Chenhalls motored me and John Compton to Redhill, where I judged the harness classes at the Surrey County Horse Show ; Colman's Black Magic of Nork won the championship with lots to spare. John is a really modest young man. On Sunday evening last he left his home in

Canterbury at 1 A.M., arrived at St Athans at 6.30, and was in the field at 10.30, taking 5 wickets for 16 runs. Yesterday he took 5 wickets for 6 runs. Total since the season started : 13 wickets for 72 runs. And still doesn't think he is good enough for county cricket.

May 26
Sunday.
Decided to put my " Shorter Dickens " problem to George Lyttelton, promising myself to abide by his decision. Here it is :

Finndale House
Grundisburgh
Suffolk

May 24, 1946

MY DEAR JAMES AGATE,

This is very difficult !—because, *me judice*, you are absolutely right, and so is Alan Dent (thus proving that John Morley was right when he spoke of " the plain maxim that it is possible for the same thing to be and not to be ").

You say that half a loaf, etc. *He* says, " No, because it is currant bread, and, however you divide it, many epicures will say that the half you have thrown away contains the tastiest currants." A mean metaphor. Let us rise higher and say, Doesn't it all come to this : Are the Dickens novels to be regarded as Holy Writ, which is the argument against abridging the Bible ?—though how we should be spiritually poorer by not knowing that Huz was the brother of Buz I don't know. If you had a committee of Dickensians sitting on each novel the result would be that when they had finished (*a*) they would not be on speaking terms, and (*b*) they would have eliminated about 750 words. I agree with you too about R. West. Dickens is not for very clever women any more than Boswell is. Did, *e.g.*, Virginia Woolf ever mention either, though she had plenty to say about Defoe and Swift and Donne and Hardy ?

It is mainly the length (and the sentiment) which puts off the modern reader. Those who also say that his characters are not true to life and that his humour is long-winded wouldn't read him whether abridged or not, and in Browning's words may be " left in God's contempt apart."

So on the whole I am definitely with you in your arguments. And I should very much like to do one, *Martin Chuzzlewit* for choice if you have not earmarked him. How potent is environment ! Three miles away FitzGerald spent much time cutting down for his own amusement all the masterpieces of English poetry and prose—except Browning, whom he would not read at all.

I hope that my postcard did not make you very cross, and that you will not blast me, as you did that poor man from Berkhamsted, with some withering words about sheer (or pure) pedantry. And you will be quite right.

Yours ever,

GEORGE LYTTELTON

May 27   In the wrappings of a parcel of dried fruits sent me by an
Monday.   unknown friend in New Zealand I came across this,
           culled from I know not what paper, date March 2, 1946,
author H. McD. Vincent :

Roger Blunt, whose batting and bowling figures loom up from
the past Plunket Shield and national cricket, has one astounding
record which can never be excelled. He once hit 48 runs in an over
—eight 6's in a row—a performance duly recorded with that
compact and silent vehemence imparted by figures when in the
pages of Wisden. There have been mighty hitters in the past,
and yet none of them had ever done what Blunt, who was anything
but a great hitter, did on that occasion. Watching it was like
watching a billiards break by a champion. It seemed natural,
inevitable, each stroke coolly conceived and precisely executed.
There was no hastiness in it. A man near me said, " He's put the
blooming lot over the fence."

Blunt had been ambling along easily, never forcing the pace,
in a first-grade club match, when the significant moment came for
which (he told me later) he had been waiting. He hooked the
first ball over the boundary, did the same with the second, the
third he on-drove, the fourth went over cover point's head, the
fifth he lifted over square leg, the sixth was an on-drive which
just got there, the seventh he hooked, the eighth went beyond the
covers.

Variety ? The bowling made it so, for Ernie Caygill, a Riccarton
medium-pace change bowler, became flustered, and his deliveries
went this way and that, but the essence was that Blunt dealt
with each ball scientifically, placing himself for each shot with
an air of utter detachment from emotion. Each ball just cleared
the boundary, but I have the impression that Blunt in those
minutes of calculated endeavour knew exactly where each would
land.

When he had ended the crowd seemed to feel the whole
thing as anticlimax. It had seen a hitting record made, but it
didn't seem as if there had been any real hitting. There had
been no lurid moments, no spontaneous applause with each
hit, merely interested silence and a feeling of sureness and
inevitability.

To me the remarkable aspect about that over was that having
planned to do what had never been recorded as having been done
by any batsman before, without any excitement, Blunt set about
it as a perfectly normal task well within his powers.

He was a deceptive type. His manner on all occasions was so
unruffled as to be almost negative ; his refined and polished voice
suggested innate gentleness.

Other than his deeds, he gave no hint of an abounding confidence in himself, and of a cold determination in action. By his
deeds he is remembered.

May 28　To-day has been what I call a full day.　Up before nine
Tuesday.　and wrote 1200 words, being the script for a wireless
　　　　　debate sometime in June on " What is the Value of
Dramatic Criticism ? "　Lunch with Bertie van Thal and a Big Noise
in the book-distributing trade, to whom we put up the " Shorter
Dickens " proposition.　He said that the moment we started on it
some big publisher would rush out a complete reissue of the full text
and swamp us.　Or else some common little fellow would undersell us
with a still shorter version, cut by some hack, vilely illustrated, and
flaunting a hideous cover.　Which means that in current slang ' we've
had it.'　All I can do now is to break the news of our disappointment
to Lyttelton.　Back to flat and do so.　Rewrite the stuff about
Dramatic Criticism.　Rush down to Broadcasting House to record
my share in to-morrow's " How not to make a Historical Film."
(Nothing like a switch of subject to keep the mind active.)　Back to
flat and have a last look at proofs of *Ego* 8, which Frank Dunn has
returned with hundreds of ' marks ' !　Then to the Unity Theatre to
see revivals of the films *The Battleship* " *Potemkin* " and *Kameradschaft.*
Slight giddiness, but pull myself together with a watercress sandwich !
Take Gwen Chenhalls to supper and on to a party at Harry Kendall's,
where I meet Franklin Dyall and we talk about Irving and what
to-day's young playgoers would think if they saw the dying Louis XI
come crumbling through the curtains in sky-blue silk.

May 29　To-night's broadcast went all right, I think.　The way
Wednesday.　it came about was this.　Roy Plomley insisting that I
　　　　　should do it, and I being too busy to write it myself,
I gave him *Around Cinemas* and a pile of old *Tatlers* and told him to
pretend he was me.　Here is the result which I delivered with all
possible gusto and the minimum of titivation, Plomley grinning at
me a couple of yards away.　The debate was ushered in by a spoof-
trailer : " Glamorous Guillotine—the film in which the true story of
the French Revolution is told for the first time."　The film director
was played by Alexander Sarner.

　　　J. A. Folks, my name is Agate—James Agate.　Some of you
may have heard of me.　Among the thousands of films that I have
seen in the last twenty years there have been many in the category
of the masterpiece which you have just heard.　Perhaps the
genius who concocted that trailer let his sense of humour get the
better of him, but I don't consider that he grossly exaggerated.
Exaggerated—but not grossly.　On the whole I don't dislike these
films.　As one of our youngest, and therefore one of our most

intellectual, critics has observed : "Most intelligent people like sometimes to take an evening off and enjoy two hours of passion, blood, and elephants." It worries me very little that Helen of Troy should look and behave like a Ziegfeld Folly, wear a wrist-watch, and have a zip-fastener to her tea-gown—I don't even care if she trails a Pekingese so long as it doesn't obstruct my view of Achilles dragging the body of Hector round the battlefield. Most of these extravaganzas are really Westerns with a different costume, and doubtless they do much to amuse the children. Some grown-up children, too. They shouldn't be judged too harshly. Personally I don't wince when a silk-clad courtier, wearing his sword on the wrong side, says to his peroxide queen, " Gee, your majesty's swell! Thanks a lot ! " in the accents of the Bronx. This is O.K. by me. But——

F. D. Mr Agate, if I may interrupt here—I am a director who specialises in historical subjects, and I think that you have only tackled half the issue. You have been talking all this time about the kind of historical film which quite rightly you compare with the Western—the big highly coloured melodramatic jobs with a chase in the last reel. But there are other and more thoughtful historical pictures—biographies—careful and accurate reconstructions of famous historical events.

J. A. So your line is care and accuracy ?

F. D. It is.

J. A. Then you, sir, are one of the people I was coming to a minute ago when I said " But," and you rudely interrupted me.

F. D. I apologise.

J. A. I never, never apologise, and I never accept apologies. I was about to say that I forgive historical films on condition that I am not supposed to take them seriously. It is such as you, sir, with your pretended accuracy and your bogus authenticity, that I cannot forgive. Get your personages right and never mind their clothes.

F. D. I don't understand you. Every one of my pictures is the result of months of careful and accurate historical research. Every chair—every table—every footstool—every sofa-cushion. . . .

J. A. Yes, I know. And every antimacassar. Take that recent Wilson film. What the dickens did it matter that the furniture in this picture was an exact reproduction of the furniture in the drawing-room at the White House——

F. D. Leaving that on one side for a moment, history is seldom so obliging as to provide a ready-made film story.

J. A. Now we're coming to it.

F. D. There is no sense in making a film with a dull story. You must have a little licence to change your story around a bit, but you can ensure with care that your background is authentic.

J. A. But if your historical personages can't be as authentic as your background, then you must invent some imaginary ones. And if you are going to fantasticate the lives of real people why not go the whole hog and make the whole thing fiction ?

F. D. I think people like to see real historical personages on the screen.

J. A. Real ? I saw recently what was supposed to be a screen biography of a real person—Frédéric Chopin. Showpan, they called him. There is no possible film story in the rather colourless life of that real historical personage—so they made one up, in glorious Technihorror. It was a jumble of nonsense from beginning to end. For example, the film suggested that Chopin toured Italy, Austria, Hungary, Holland, and Denmark to help the starving Poles. Actually, being hard up, he toured Liverpool and Glasgow to help himself !

F. D. That was a musical film rather than an historical one. You can't say they messed up the music.

J. A. They showed us Chopin composing at the age of ten the D Flat Valse which is now known as Opus 64. Then I have memories of a film biography of Marie-Antoinette. All I got from this was that the Queen of France was a pretty woman who looked like Norma Shearer, lived in a large palace, had an affair with a young man, and her head cut off for some reason which was never made clear.

F. D. Very well, you've picked your example—let me pick mine. Take the British picture *Victoria the Great*. I don't think you can find fault with that on its history. It was a very successful picture, and you would be in the minority if you found fault with it.

J. A. I should find fault with it, and I should be in the minority. To be in the majority one must be wrong. But I think we'll leave the old girl out of it. Not enough time for that great figure.

F. D. I shall be interested to read your criticism of the film I'm making at the moment. It's a story of the Norman invasion. With a period as early as that, of course, most of our story has to be supposition—so you won't be able to find fault with us there. We are using 40,000 people for the battle of Hastings, and every piece of armour has been copied from examples in the British Museum.

J. A. Numbers mean nothing. Reinhardt could stage the Thirty Years War with an army of 30 people. The difference between 40,000, 4000, 400, or even 40 people is only in the way you use them. As to the rest, the proper job of a film director is to see that his story is right, shove the film stars about, tell them when to stare at the camera and when not, and explain to them what the words mean. I don't give a fig for your armour. If there was more time I would tell you the old story of the musical-comedy actress who, before she tackled some nonsense about Cleopatra, made herself personally acquainted with every mummy in the British Museum. But there isn't time. They want us to shut up. Glad to have met you.

May 30   How can I forget Sarah if other people won't let
Thursday.   me ? To-day arrives a photograph of her—enchanting,
              amusing, grotesque—sitting under a rock apparently
somewhere in Mexico. Date 1911. The covering letter is from the
British Embassy in Paris, and asks if I want any others of S. The
wrapper is a copy of *Le Charivari* for November 25, 1865. I cull :

M. Victorien Sardou—à mon humble avis un des premiers
auteurs dramatiques de ce temps—possède, peut-être à cause de
cela, un nombre incalculable d'ennemis.
Et parmi ces ennemis tous des confrères, sans en excepter un,
pas même ceux qui ont réellement du talent.
L'un d'eux même, fort dramaturge en disponibilité, à qui l'on
reprochait cette faiblesse, répondait l'autre soir :
— Dame, que voulez-vous donc que je déteste à présent,
puisque Dumas fils ne fait plus rien !

May 31   Letter to a highbrow :
Friday.

DEAR DANIEL GEORGE,
      I have been reading your " Alphabet of Literary Prejudice "
in the new *Windmill* which, incidentally, makes *Perimeter* and
Arc-en-Ciel look even sillier than they are. I say nothing about
your French accents—English printers have always regarded these
as foreign fiddle-faddle.
      The point I chiefly want to make concerns the letter **Q.** Here
you say : " Quotations, if used at all, should be used sparingly."
Where, if they had taken your advice, would Bacon and Montaigne
and Burton have been ? And Lamb ! What about the wonderful
passage in the essay, *In Praise of Chimney-sweepers*, in which Lamb
remembers that a bad sweep was once left in a stack with his brush,
to indicate which way the wind blew ? Elia goes on : " It was an
awful spectacle, certainly ; not much unlike the old stage direction
in *Macbeth*, where the ' Apparition of a child crowned, with a tree
in his hand, rises.' " When a writer can do as felicitously as that I
don't mind if he is 90 per cent. quotation ! The vulgar object to
the art because they feel they are being somehow cheated ; this is
particularly true of newspaper readers, and of the Sunday variety
truest of all. They have paid their wretched tuppences, and are
determined that their dramatic critic, or whoever it is, shall earn
the whole of that tuppence, and not ease up with filchings from
other writers. No, sir, in this matter of quotation you are not on
the side of the angels.
      Talking of angels, you quote, under the letter M, Meredith's

      I dream'd a banish'd Angel to me crept :
      My feet were nourish'd on her breasts all night.

But I have always been told that angels were purely male, and that when Walter Scott wrote his famous

> When pain and anguish wring the brow,
> A ministering angel thou !

he was taking an unpardonable liberty. And surely if there are she-angels there must be she-devils, and I have never thought that some of those red-tailed little things that in the next world are going to prod one with toasting-forks will be females. And then we must be consistent. What about she-archangels, and discovering that one of them is Mrs Humphry Ward ? I fancy that these he-shes would come into Elia's category of *male aunts*.

. By the way, under N, one living Novelist you ought to read is Hugh Edwards. Bennett or Gosse or Montague, anyhow somebody, is supposed to have said that if there were only one copy of a really good book, and it was dropped in the middle of the Sahara, it would still somehow or other contrive to be rescued from oblivion and ultimately find its public. I feel that this is true about *All Night at Mr Stanyhurst's*. Reviewing this, I said, " So far as my reading goes, this is the best long story or short novel since Conrad." Whereupon half a dozen readers wrote to say that the book had nothing in common with Conrad. But this was merely to be expected ; one has only to say that somebody has written the best long-short poem since *The Ancient Mariner* to be told that the comparison is vitiated because the new work is not about albatrosses. And that's all, except that I have been going about the house all day repeating your admirable line, " Over the cool black begonias the giraffe coughed abruptly."

To conclude. I have read your Alphabet, and indeed the whole magazine, with the greatest interest and amusement, and I don't mean this in Fluther Good's " derogatory " sense. But I forget that you don't like quotations.

Yours sincerely,
JAMES AGATE

June 1
Saturday.

In the middle of *Portrait in Black* I found myself wondering about Shakespeare's play. Did there never come a time when Lady Macbeth, who was not sleeping well, turned to her husband and said with another intonation, " What beast was't then That made you break this enterprise to me ? " Did Macbeth never remind his spouse of his resolve to proceed no further, and how she had egged him on with all that talk of cats in adages and babies' boneless gums ? Sat up late last night turning this into Sunday's article, after playing with the idea of finding a parallel in Abel Hermant's *La Fameuse Comédienne*, to which some of this play's incidents bear a superficial resemblance. " Monsieur," says the fifth-rate actress to her former lover, ex-" télégraphiste " in Montmartre,

" if ever I deceive my husband it will not be with the father of my child ! " Doubt, however, whether the chaste columns of the *S.T.* are quite the place for this. I still dote on A. H.'s book, the one and only procurable copy of which I gave to Jock some ten years ago. This, however, is now back with me, " on permanent loan," and forms part of my bedside library—the trials of Neill Cream and William Herbert Wallace, the stories of Damon Runyon and Dorothy Parker, Saki's *The Unbearable Bassington.*

Was roused by an Apparition in mink standing at my bedside. It was Gwen Chenhalls come to motor me to the Royal Windsor Horse Show. With her was Tahu Hole, a large, pleasant man, and great-nephew of Dean Hole. Lunched in the car—cold turtle soup, pâté de foie gras sandwiches, hard-boiled eggs, chocolate, and whiskey. Their Majesties present at the Show, and the championship won by Colman's Black Magic. How good a horse is he ? I put him second to Field Marshal, of whom Geoffrey Bennett wrote in his *Famous Harness Horses* : " On his day few horses that have ever lived could withstand him. His quality and conformation were almost faultless, the carriage of his lovely neck superb, and his action so high, so balanced, so natural, and so true—a real aristocrat ! " Black Magic lacks a little, but only a little, of the *elegance* of the older horse, and it is in my mind that he does not put his knee quite so high. But he takes rank with Field Marshal as one of the six best performers I have ever seen, the other four being the brown mare Charm, the gelding Black Capenor, the bay mare Modern Maid, and a certain bright bay gelding which I need not name.

Winged Words. No. 14 : In Barking there may be nowadays few windmills to tilt at ; it may be difficult to find a Sancho Panza.

Leading article. Evening paper

June 2   The Preface to *Around Cinemas* published to-morrow,
Sunday.   contains these words :

This book is not intended to be documentary, educational, didactic, comprehensive. It sets forth no æsthetic theory of the film. It is in no sense a history. . . . The principle on which I have chosen my little essays ? Not according to the importance of their subject-matter, but according to my liking for what I have written.

Which doesn't prevent the *New Statesman* from writing : " The reader will be disappointed who expects to find here a coherent per-spective of the cinema as such. Still, there's a pretty water-colour of

Lillian Gish." The reviewer ? G. W. Stonier, always so good when he is not writing about me. The *Daily Herald* (John Betjeman) is ecstatic, and Harold Hobson writes in the *Sunday Times* : " We are able to witness, through a space of nearly a quarter of a century, the æsthetic development of Mr Agate. It is a fascinating and infinitely amusing occupation." Perhaps I am best pleased by a line in Monica Dickens's review in the *Sunday Chronicle*—a line about my ungullible critical faculty. " Ungullible " is the word I have been waiting for.

In the afternoon Gwen Chenhalls, who has taken up her appointment as Chauffeuse Extraordinary to Queen Alexandra Mansions, motored me to Farnham Royal to take tea with John Clements, whose father, a delightful old gentleman with silver hair, does not see eye to eye with his son about acting. Meaning that he regards Irving as the greatest actor he has ever seen or is likely to see, while John, who never saw H. I., won't go further than that he was " a great but not a good actor." And I think of Chesterton on Dickens :

> Whatever the word ' great ' means, Dickens was what it means. Even the fastidious and unhappy, who cannot read his books without a continuous critical exasperation, would use the word of him without stopping to think. They feel that Dickens is a great writer even if he is not a good writer.

Came away with a volume of *The Theatre* for 1880, edited by Clement Scott, containing an account of Ellen Terry's first appearance as Beatrice, at Leeds, and another of Sarah Bernhardt in *Froufrou*. Also a comparative estimate of Rachel and Sarah by one who had seen both in *Adrienne Lecouvreur*. This teems with wrong accents, and there is also the statement that the lines hurled by Adrienne at her rival are from *Phèdre*. I would have wagered my right hand that they are from *Bajazet*. And now, alas ! I shall never know. Maurice Baring is dead, the play is unprocurable, and somebody has borrowed my unique copy of the now out-of-print Legouvé's *Mémoires*.

June 3 In a letter from Ivor Brown :
Monday.

> I haven't had time yet for *Around Cinemas*. It shall to my bedside. Meanwhile I thank you for the compliment to my golf, never justified and now merely a mockery. But I did beat a nice young swiper the other day who got on to every green in two and then took three putts, while I achieved the holes in four shots of equal length, a form of retort to the 300 yards' drive which ultimately destroys all resolution and self-control. But then one has to keep holing the final hundred-yarder—a strain, but I managed it.

At 2 P.M., just as I was thinking about lunch, received this wire from Jock :

Have to deliver yet unwritten lecture at Stratford Thursday morning entitled The Truth about Shakespeare. Please send me amusing and characteristic note on subject and so help me out.

Went to the Ivy, had chats with Arthur Rank and Douglas Byng, and back to the flat at 3 P.M. Dictated Note, which Booth-Palmer typed with so much comprehension and celerity that we managed to catch the 6.30 post.

NOTE FOR JOCK

So you have let yourself in for *The Truth about Shakespeare* ? A *tour de force* to accomplish which you would have to know all about (*a*) Truth and (*b*) Shakespeare. Though, like Lady Macbeth, thou'rt innocent of the knowledge, dearest Jock, I still applaud the intention. Here is a Note for you to re-deliver after what flourish your nature will.

To whom are you supposed to lecture ? Fiji Islanders ? Esquimaux ? Or the kind of wild and woolly American about whom John Clements told me this story when I had tea with him the other day at Farnham Royal ? (Has it ever struck you that though the Yanks can invent charming names like " Abe's Top Hat " for their home towns they, being poor benighted republicans, cannot call anything " Royal " ?) Having now put you on the worst of terms with your audience, let me tell you John Clements's story. The scene was a camp concert. He appeared before the curtains and announced a recitation of " Once more unto the breach, dear friends, once more." Whereupon a burly G.I. in the second row buried his face in his hands and said, " Christ ! " John recited the speech, at the end of which the same G.I. jumped to his feet, applauding wildly and crying, " Jesus ! "

Well, what are you going to tell your young friends ? I should feel inclined to say something like this :

Shakespeare was not a crashing bore like the whole of Corneille and nine-tenths of Racine.

Shakespeare is the most exciting dramatist the world has ever seen, the runner-up being Ibsen.

Of all playwrights Shakespeare is the one who most often " takes your breath away, or sends a momentary wave of coldness across your face, or elicits whatever your special bodily signal may be of your mind's amazed and sudden surrender to some stroke of passionate genius." Montague, of course. And perhaps you'd better explain who Montague was.

Still continuing with what you could say, you might remind these boys that Shakespeare wrote two plays in one of which, *Hamlet*, no actor has been known to fail, while in the other, *Macbeth*, no actor has been known to succeed. I find it very difficult to place the five major tragedies—*Hamlet, Macbeth, King Lear, Othello, Antony and Cleopatra*—in their proper order. I think perhaps the thing to say of them is what one says of Beethoven's piano concertos, that whichever you are listening to at the moment is the best. I was sitting the other night at *Macbeth*, where my senses were assaulted by that sequence beginning

> To be thus is nothing;
> But to be safely thus : our fears in Banquo
> Stick deep ;

and ending

> Light thickens, and the crow
> Makes wing to the rooky wood :
> Good things of day begin to droop and drowse,
> Whiles night's black agents to their preys do rouse.

Followed immediately by the banqueting scene, on the heels of which came the scene with the Witches and the show of Kings.

> Thou art too like the spirit of Banquo : down !
> Thy crown does sear mine eye-balls. And thy hair,
> Thou other gold-bound brow, is like the first.
> A third is like the former. Filthy hags !
> Why do you show me this ?

And I found myself wondering whether the whole range of drama has anything to show like this, including Hamlet's Advice to the Players, the Play-Scene, and the scene in Gertrude's closet. Would you like to tell your listeners what I think is the greatest or perhaps the most visually and aurally exciting line in the whole of drama ? I find this not in *Macbeth*, but in *Hamlet*. It occurs in Act I, Scene 1. Bernardo is chatting to Horatio and Marcellus on " a platform before the castle " :

> Last night of all,
> When yond same star that's westward from the pole
> Had made his course to illume that part of heaven
> Where now it burns, Marcellus and myself,
> *The bell then beating one,—*

I have put the last line in italics, and you must read it that way, for this is the line I mean. What is there so remarkable about it ? Simply that it breaks off, and the stage direction is " Enter Ghost." Imagine the effect of the first appearance of the Ghost at that first performance !

But I may be getting too serious. This may be not at all the kind of thing you are wanting to hear. Do you want me to reopen the Shakespeare-Bacon controversy ? I am as firm against this as the authorities are firm against opening the grave at Stratford. Nevertheless there is a little story which is not un-apropos :

A publican desired an artist to paint him a sign. The artist agreed, saying he had long wanted to paint a red lion. The publican preferred a white horse. The artist stood his ground, and for a time they wrangled, until finally the publican pointed out that it was he who was paying for the sign. " If you put it like that," said the artist, " you shall have a white horse. *But don't be surprised if it looks like a red lion !* "

It has always seemed to me odd, to say the least of it, that Shakespeare, if he was not Bacon, should have been at such enormous pains to make it possible for subsequent generations to think that he was. For example. Everybody now listening to you must know Cardinal Wolsey's lines in *Henry VIII* first published in the Folio of 1623 :

> O Cromwell, Cromwell !
> Had I but serv'd my God with half the zeal
> I serv'd my King, he would not in mine age
> Have left me naked to mine enemies.

Isn't it a trifle curious that shortly after Bacon fell from power in 1621 he wrote a letter to King James in which this occurs : " Cardinal Wolsey said that if he had pleased God as he had pleased the King he had not been ruined."

Again—and once more I am indebted to my friend Edward D. Johnson—I hold it queer that " in the play *Troilus and Cressida* we find the following words :

> Not much
> Unlike young men, whom Aristotle thought
> Unfit to hear moral philosophy.

The point here is that Aristotle never said any such thing, that he spoke of *political* philosophy, not *moral* philosophy. In *The Advancement of Learning* Bacon quotes Aristotle as saying, ' Young men are no fit auditors of *moral* philosophy.' " Edward D. Johnson thinks it an odd coincidence, and I agree with him, that both Shakespeare and Bacon should make the same mistake when quoting Aristotle. But there, I don't think it matters. The plays are the thing, and I don't care two hoots who wrote them. They have afforded me more delight than all the operas, all the art galleries, all the books I've read, all the rounds of golf I've played, all the ponies I've shown, all the whiskey, and all the cigars.

I end what I hope your audience will not have found dull with two quotations from a writer whom you and I cherish almost to absurdity. This is Logan Pearsall Smith. And here is the first quotation :

" Of all of Shakespeare's plays, *Macbeth* is the most Shakespearian in the more sombre meaning of the epithet, and in the word ' Macbeth ' as we evoke it, we see the splash of blood ; dreadful shapes appear and flicker, dimly, as in dim crystal-gazing ; Macbeth steals to Duncan's chamber, the inexplicable Third Murderer silently draws near the scene of murder ; Banquo's ghost sits at the feast, shaking his gory locks in silence, and Lady Macbeth moves and mutters in her sleep."

The second quotation is :

" In one of the greatest passages he wrote—and Prospero's speech has been described as the finest passage in Shakespeare, if not in all the literature in the world—I find the expression of one aspect, and to me the most essential aspect, of Shakespeare's spirit. Best of all, I love those plays, *Hamlet, As You Like It,* and *The Tempest*, which, like the *Sonnets* with their shimmering moods, are silvery-tinted with this cast of thought. To dream, to meditate, to lose ourselves in thought beyond the reaches of our souls, to love the gay appearances of the world and know them as illusions—this temper of an ironic mind, of a happy, enjoying, and yet melancholy nature, expresses itself in a secret rhythm, a cadence, a delicate and dream-like music which is, for me, the loveliest poetry of the world."

So you see, my dear Jock, that, like others, our old friend is divided against himself. He cannot decide between the blood and thunder of *Macbeth* and the, may I say, urbanity of *Hamlet*. The truth about Shakespeare is that he is a world, and that no standard exists by which to measure the smoky tumult of Vesuvius against the Mediterranean's blue serenity.

June 5   A letter :
Wednesday.

DEAR CHRISTOPHER FRY,
It is very nice to hear from you, and I have the pleasantest recollection of our meetings at Oxford. Since then you have taken to the poetic drama, which alters things. I don't believe that there has been a poet with any sense of drama since Shakespeare, and I don't believe there is any dramatist living to-day with any sense of poetry. Or any poet either. How can I lunch with, for example, a man who thinks

> Our life is urban but its core is sex
> Wherefore a city's centre is its shops,
> Its cafés, restaurants, theatres, and all places
> Where men and women touch upon this power—
> A city is, in short, life's choicest bower.

is poetry ? Suppose I were to write

> Thank you, dear Fry, for your kind invitation.
> The Carlton Grill would suit me mighty fine,
> Though, for myself, I think the Café Royal,
> Where, since they know me, I can get a table.
> Yes, I'll be right on time. That's if I'm able.

Would you think that poetry ?
I wish you hadn't turned dramatic poet. I detest, abhor, execrate, and give your kind to sixscore thousand devils, as in no instance to be excused or tolerated, but shunned as universal vipers, to be branded, proscribed, and spoken evil of. As Elia

would say, in no way can I be brought to digest you ! And why must you fellows all write plays with titles like *Turn Right for the Crematorium* ? Is there no other subject in the world except death ? I suppose that, being youngish, you still think death is great fun. I am oldish, and don't.

Ever,
JAMES AGATE

June 6
Thursday.
As though the task of reducing to critical coherence Alec Guinness's adaptation of Dostoievsky's *The Brothers Karamazov*, which I saw at the Lyric, Hammersmith, last night, were not already sufficiently difficult, the air authorities responsible for Victory Day celebrations chose Holborn and my working hours this morning for a rehearsal. Groups of aircraft flew over my roof like coveys of partridges. To drown them I put on Weber's *Euryanthe* Overture with my loudest needle. During which I settled down to make up my mind whether Valk, who played old Karamazov, is or is not a great actor. Decided in the affirmative, and if I am wrong shall attribute it to the simultaneous arrival of three men, one to cut my hair, and two to dry-clean my carpets by the noisiest process known. In the middle of it all I have occasion to refer to *Red-letter Nights* and my notice of the Quintero Brothers' play, *Fortunato*. And there, bung in the middle of the page, I find a dreadful misprint—" *dévotee* enragée." Which means that I become *enragé* without being *dévot*. Is there then no end to it ? Go out to lunch, drink a bottle of champagne to restore brain-tissue, and come back to find a perfect article. Except that I rewrite it twice more.

Winged Words. No. 15 : " Evelyn Keyes' legs are looking particularly svelte these days. She contends it is because she is wearing garters that belonged to Mistinguett."

Film gossip

June 7
Friday.
The *Daily Herald*—some of the other national papers having turned it down—prints the following little poem, a reassertion of something I wrote some years ago. Set in what is known by printers and newspaper men as a ' box,' and away from comic drawings and the like :

FOR THE FALLEN

God keep you, Jack, Harry, and Ben !
You fought for Christ's kingdom, and then—
There's no more to your story
Save the power, and the glory,
For ever and ever.—Amen.

V-Day.   Some little time ago the makers of Basildon Bond notepaper held a competition for the Best Letter Written by
a Member of the Forces during the recent war.   The Judges were
Margery Anderson, Commander Campbell, and J. A., the film-
critic of the *Tatler*.   The writer of the winning entry was the twenty-
two-year-old

> Pte. I. Rowbery 4928327
> 2nd S. Staffs Regt. (Signal Section)
> Att. 1st Airborne Division.

He was killed at Arnhem.   This letter by a Wolverhampton working
lad moves me more than some more celebrated literary efforts, and
I am grateful to the boy's mother for her permission to reproduce it,
" because it may help other parents."   There was a covering envelope
marked : " To the Best Mother in the World."

> *Blighty*
> *Some time ago*

DEAR MOM,
      Usually when I write a letter it is very much overdue, and I
make every effort to get it away quickly.   This letter, however, is
different.   It is a letter I hoped you would never receive, as it is
just a verification of that terse black-edged card which you received
some time ago, and which has caused you so much grief.   It is
because of that grief that I wrote this letter, and by the time you
have finished reading it I hope that it has done some good, and
that I have not written it in vain.
      It is very difficult to write now of future things in the past
tense, so I am returning to the present.
      To-morrow we go into action.   As yet we do not know exactly
what our job will be, but no doubt it will be a dangerous one in
which many lives will be lost—mine may be one of those lives.
      Well, Mom, I am not afraid to die.   I like this life, yes—for
the past two years I have planned and dreamed and mapped out
a perfect future for myself.   I would have liked that future to
materialise, but it is not what I will but what God wills, and if by
sacrificing all this I leave the world slightly better than I found it
I am perfectly willing to make that sacrifice.   Don't get me wrong
though, Mom ; I am no flag-waving patriot, nor have I ever
professed to be.
      England's a great little country—the best there is—but I
cannot honestly and sincerely say " that it is worth fighting for."
Nor can I fancy myself in the role of a gallant crusader fighting
for the liberation of Europe.   It would be a nice thought, but
I would only be kidding myself.   No, Mom, my little world is
centred around you, and includes Dad, every one at home, and my
friends at W'ton—*that* is worth fighting for—and if by doing so it

strengthens your security and improves your lot in any way, then it is worth dying for too.

Now this is where I come to the point of this letter. As I have already stated, I am not afraid to die, and am perfectly willing to do so, if, by my doing so, you benefit in any way whatsoever. If you do not then my sacrifice is all in vain. Have you benefited, Mom, or have you cried and worried yourself sick? I fear it is the latter. Don't you see, Mom, that it will do me no good, and that in addition you are undoing all the good work I have tried to do. Grief is hypocritical, useless, and unfair, and does neither you nor me any good.

I want no flowers, no epitaph, no tears. All I want is for you to remember me and feel proud of me; then I shall rest in peace, knowing that I have done a good job. Death is nothing final or lasting; if it were there would be no point in living; it is just a stage in every one's life. To some it comes early, to others late, but it must come to every one some time, and surely there is no better way of dying.

Besides I have probably crammed more enjoyment into my 21 years than some manage to do in 80. My only regret is that I have not done as much for you as I would have liked to do. I loved you, Mom; you were the best Mother in the World, and what I failed to do in life I am trying to make up for in death, so please don't let me down, Mom, don't worry or fret, but smile, be proud and satisfied. I never had much money, but what little I have is all yours. Please don't be silly and sentimental about it, and don't try to spend it on me. Spend it on yourself or the kiddies, it will do some good that way. Remember that where I am I am quite O.K., and providing I know that you are not grieving over me I shall be perfectly happy.

Well, Mom, that is all, and I hope I have not written it all in vain.

Good-bye, and thanks for everything.

Your unworthy son,
IVOR

Whit Sunday. Would that Hazlitt had written an essay " On the Muddleheadedness of Reviewers "! Lejeune in the *Observer* spoils a dithyrambic notice of *Around Cinemas* by saying :

> The author takes an obstinate delight in divagation, turning from Mickey Rooney to Trabb's boy, withdrawing with frank relief from a consideration of Norma Talmadge to a memory of Sarah Bernhardt, wandering from his assigned subject to random reflections on the theatre, the novel, the world of music, and the field of sport.

Random, dear Lejeune? In the dictionary sense of haphazard, without settled direction or purpose? Without knowing where I am going ? But I always know where I am going, and with what object. There is one view of St Paul's Cathedral from Ludgate Circus and another view from Blackfriars Bridge, and in any article I write on the Cathedral I am as likely as not to shift my viewpoint and, in the course of shifting, throw in a few observations on circuses and bridges. But the second viewpoint is never lost sight of, and will be established at the end, to the astonishment of the reader who hasn't perceived that all my roads lead to St Paul's. According to Lejeune I must not refer to Sarah even when the Talmadge is making nonsense of *La Dame aux Camélias*. And why does she lead with the Mickey Rooney—Trabb's boy comparison ? Doesn't she see that this is my ace of trumps ? That I do not stray into the Sarah country while discussing Mickey, or lug Trabb's boy into my adventures with the Talmadge ?

How does Trabb's boy come into my Mickey Rooney article ?

What is the reason for the extraordinary Rooney-resistance of which I have been conscious for some time ? Or, as we should say over here, this dead-set against Mickey not by the public, which to see him in *Babes on Broadway* filled the Empire to overflowing five times on Tuesday last, but on the part of the highbrow critics ? Of this young man's technical accomplishments there can be no doubt. His sense of humour is generally conceded. His over-powering pathos in *Boys' Town* and half a dozen other films must be obvious to anybody who is not blind, deaf, and dumb in the worst sense. He sings enough to eke out Miss Judy Garland whenever the director mistakenly thinks that young lady requires eking out. He plays the banjo with a virtuosity this country knows nothing about. He is a poor mimic, and his efforts in the present film to impersonate Carmen Miranda, Sir Harry Lauder, and Richard Mansfield merely show a greedy director anxious to get from a super-willing horse rather more than it can give. Yet there is no doubt to my mind that within strict limits Mickey is a great actor. He can keep still. He can listen. He can let you know what is going on in his mind without pulling faces. He has geniality. Nature and not the sound-director has put the tears into his voice. And he has the one quality by which all great actors are known—that you can't keep your eyes off him. Is he pocket-size ? Then this snub-nosed little tough is a great actor in miniature . . .

Here I want to make a point which in my view has not been sufficiently considered by our high priestesses of the fine shades. This is Rooney's power to exuberate. And to exuberate is woe-fully lacking in the acting world to-day. Here is Quintessential Boy, and perhaps the reader will care to look with me again at something G. K. Chesterton wrote on the subject :

" The scene in which Trabb's boy continually overtakes Pip in order to reel and stagger as at a first encounter is a thing quite within the real competence of such a character ; it might have been suggested by Thackeray, or George Eliot, or any realist. But the point with Dickens is that there is a rush in the boy's rushings ; the writer and the reader rush with him. They start with him, they share an inexpressible vitality in the air which emanates from this violent and capering satirist. Trabb's boy is among other things a boy ; he has a physical rapture in hurling himself like a boomerang and in bouncing to the sky like a ball."

I take it that it is the *bounce* of Trabb's boy which offends my colleagues, who appear to feel as the Misses Lavinia and Clarissa Spenlow might have felt if this amazing human combustion engine had come bouncing and boomeranging into their decorous, birdcage existence. In the present film Mr Rooney exuberates more than I have ever seen him exuberate ; he exudes more energy, more magnetism, more *life* than all the other characters in the film put together. But he should never impersonate.

Now let's get this thing straight. Does the illustration from Dickens give a reader who has never seen Rooney a better idea of him ? Does it add to what I have to say about him ? *If it does it is not divagation.*

Whit Monday. The last seventy-two hours have been a day-mare. I disentangle :

1. The arrival of John Compton in the middle of the celebrations on V-Day. Had the typescript of *Those Were the Nights* arrived, and did I want any help in titivating ? I said yes to both. Which resulted in my spending an entirely happy day instead of getting into a black (and childish) rage because of all the people in London only I want to work. This should be called Agate's Disease.

2. A good notice of *Around Cinemas* in the *Manchester Guardian*. The reviewer thinks the book wants a few footnotes : " Witty by-play with names, events, and catch-phrases which were in every reader's mind at the time of reading Mr Agate's weekly column is by now sometimes frankly incomprehensible." Meaning that people have forgotten those advertisements signed " Callisthenes."

3. Deleting a quip from my notice of Alec Guinness's production of *The Brothers Karamazov*—" Alec Guinness is good for you ! " But my win for good taste did not end here. Also deleted the remark that Ernest Milton's Father Zossima is twin brother to Hermione Gingold's King Lear.

4. Amusing notices of Michael Tippett's Symphony played by the

National Symphony Orchestra under Walter Goehr at the Central Hall :

The Times

This experiment at any rate is not convincing that two historically different manners can be brought into a modern synthesis—the result is too drab.

The *News Chronicle*

It is unusual music, of a kind that will never bring into play the emotions of any but those who are moved by manifestations of the exploring mind. As such, the symphony is an illustration of the strange power of abstract thought to convey beauty to the watchful observer. It will never be a popular work, but it will continue to touch the widespread few profoundly.

The *Daily Express*

The texture of the music (as a disciple explained in the programme) " is often polyphonic, meaning that there may be two or three lines of melody at one time." There are, indeed, moments when it suggests four different radio programmes played in four adjoining flats.

Nostalgically I bethink me of the days when William Glock, in the *Observer*, tipped us Tippett week after week. And I write a sonnet, or at least the beginning of one :

> William ! thou shouldst be Glockenspieling now :
> Tippett hath need of thee . . .

5. A letter from a W.R.N.S. officer :

With reference to *Ego* 7, Page 302 (this is the Naval formula for every sort of letter), you, for once, are wrong and Dean Inge is right. The bad man never does reach satiety : instead of sating his desire he destroys it. It's all in *Macbeth*, from the murder of Banquo onwards. I know one ought not to think of Iago outside the framework of the play, but suppose he had got away with it and tried again : he would have been caught by the law of Diminishing Returns and found that he got less and less excitement out of it all each time.

" . . . The Metaphysicals, and Milton beyond them, went even beyond Shakespeare, for they imagined hell, and whatever may be thought of the doctrine of hell theologically and morally, it is a very great poetic idea. Shakespeare's people were able—they were compelled—altogether to die. Lear, outraging nature, was outraged by nature, but he died. Macbeth, self-robbed of sleep, found a living somnambulism, but he died. They glanced at that other vision in moments—' Hell is murky.' But it is Satan whose everlasting and hopeless desire restored the full vision to English verse, the ' perishing everlastingly ' of that great ode the Athanasian Creed.

> I would be at the worst : worst is my port,
> My harbour, and my ultimate repose,

and he cannot be."

(New Book of English Verse, Introduction)

6. A second photograph of Sàrah sent by my unknown friend at the British Embassy in Paris. This time as Lorenzaccio—delicious, enchanting, and supremely silly — the pose suited to Yvonne Printemps as Mozart. But then Sarah could be adorably silly, as when, in *Les Cathédrales*, after Amiens, Bourges, and Notre-Dame de Paris had announced their booming selves, she put on her most winsome smile and said, " Je suis la Cathédrale de Strasbourg," with the purr of a delighted kitten.

7. An unknown friend in Oxford sends me in return for my " serendipitous wit " a poem entitled *The River Thames*, by John William Pitt. This describes the river from source to mouth, and my friend calls it " remarkable." This is, I feel, to do less than justice to a work showing that, in poetry as in everything else, where there's a will there's a way. I cull three stanzas :

Famed Oxford, fifty-four miles from the source of " Father Thames,"
Possesses many colleges, all architectural gems ;
The chief ones being Christ Church, Hertford, Pembroke, Jesus, Queen's,
Corpus Christi, Magdalen, all great men's boyhood scenes,
And not forgetting Worcester, Merton, Trinity, and New,
And Keble, Brasenose, Oriel, St John's, and Lincoln, too.

    .   .   .   .   .   .

Adjoining is the chapel which by Henry VIII (eighth) was built,
But which good Queen Victoria, lest memory should wilt
Of Albert, her beloved Consort, lavishly restored,
In permanent memorial of Britain's princely lord.
This is the final resting-place of Duke of Clarence, who,
As Britain's heir-presumptive, died in 1892.

    .   .   .   .   .   .

Not far below is Twickenham (upon the left-hand side),
A pleasant London suburb, which still takes especial pride
In having been the residence of several famous men,
Who earned the nation's gratitude, remembered by their pen.
When Poet Laureate, Lord Tennyson was living here,
And, eke, that Dickens, Swift, and Pope were residents is clear.

8. See an imbecile film called *Bedelia*, in which a husband will not believe that his wife, who has already disposed of three husbands for their insurance money, is proposing to murder him, until he sees the cat, which has eaten of the fish intended for supper, turn on its back and die under his nose. Spend half the evening wondering by what economic or ethical or æsthetic law I should be compelled to

waste my time. And then something clicks in my brain, I take down Wilde's *Intentions*, and I read :

> Criticism is no more to be judged by any low standard of imitation or resemblance than is the work of poet or sculptor. The critic occupies the same relation to the work of art that he criticises as the artist does to the visible world of form and colour, or the unseen world of passion and of thought. He does not even require for the perfection of his art the finest materials. Anything will suit his purpose. And just as out of the sordid and sentimental amours of the silly wife of a small country doctor in the squalid village of Yonville-l'Abbaye, near Rouen, Gustave Flaubert was able to create a classic, and make a masterpiece of style, so, from subjects of little or no importance, such as the pictures in this year's Royal Academy, or in any year's Royal Academy for that matter, Mr Lewis Morris's poems, M. Ohnet's novels, or the plays of Mr Henry Arthur Jones, the true critic can, if it be his pleasure so to direct or waste his faculty of contemplation, produce work that will be flawless in beauty and instinct with intellectual subtlety. Why not ? To an artist so creative as the critic, what does subject-matter signify ?

Had Wilde been living to-day he would doubtless have added films to the base metal which a creative critic can turn into gold.

9. May and my brother-in-law, Wilfrid Grantham, to the rescue. When Wilfrid was writing his play about Rachel he got a friend of his in Paris to refer to the MS. of Scribe and Legouvé's *Adrienne Lecouvreur* to find out what passage from the classics Adrienne had declaimed. (See entry for June 2.) He was told that it was from that drama, begun by Molière and finished by Corneille, entitled *Psyché.* Act III, Scene 3, beginning at :

Ne les détournez point, ces yeux qui m'empoisonnent.

My edition of Molière has this footnote : " L'auteur de *Cinna* fit, à l'âge de *soixante-cinq ans*, cette déclaration de Psyché à l'Amour, qui passe pour un des morceaux les plus tendres et les plus naturels qui soient au théâtre. (Voltaire.) "

But, May adds, these lines, which were good enough for Rachel, didn't satisfy Sarah when she made her own version of the play. Referring to this in *L'Illustration Théâtrale*, she finds that Sarah did, in fact, substitute a passage out of *Phèdre*—the famous

Oui, prince, je languis, je brûle pour Thésée,

from Act II, Scene 5, to which she tacked on the equally famous

Hélas ! ils se voyoient avec pleine licence,

from Act IV, Scene 6.

10. Letter from Guy Deghy reproaching me for not replying to one of his. Ends: " And after all this just a quotation from Anatole France (to remind you, for no doubt you know it): ' La vertu comme le corbeau niche dans les ruines.' "

11. Reply to Deghy:

Since May 10 I have corrected the proofs of two books; written, or rather put together, two more; turned down a project for shortening the novels of Charles Dickens (after sitting up the whole of one night cutting *Pickwick*); reviewed my own book in the *Express*; delivered one broadcast and prepared another; written an article for an American magazine (they rejected it because what they wanted was guff about the Little Theatre Movement and I wrote what I thought); written two more articles for Glasgow and West Hampstead which were accepted, not to say gobbled up; jotted down notes for a lecture Alan Dent was to give to Americans at Stratford; presided over the Hackney Society's Show at Crewe, judged at another show and attended a third; visited a sick friend at Haywards Heath and one who was not sick at Farnham Royal; entered up my Diary; made six enemies, and had a tooth out; all this in addition to my usual work. And you want me to answer letters. Go and croak yourself hoarse under your own battlements, you old raven!

12. The *Times* musical critic writes about the two Prize Symphonies—Cedric Thorpe Davie's Symphony in C major and Bernard Stevens's Symphony of Liberation: " What was lacking in both was a great tune that would have provided a true climax embodying our joy and thankfulness and resolution." *A great tune?* What does this critic expect after he and his kind have been shoving Bartók down our native composers' throats for years. *A true climax?* But when Tschaikowsky produces one it is impressed upon us that he is, like the wretched greengrocer at the Bath swarry, a low thief and an unreclaimable blaygaird.

13. Letter from a lady in Portuguese East Africa saying that " the monotony of life in this empty hole "—what about giraffes, hippopotamuses, the Portuguese ?—" is broken only by my husband's chuckles over *A Shorter Ego*. I ask to be allowed to share the fun, and am told that I shouldn't understand."

14. A delightful lunch with Christopher Fry, at which we discussed everything except the poetic drama.

15. Arrival of a large, rich plum cake, the gift of a lady in Adelaide.

June 12   Took Cedric Hardwicke to see *Beware of Pity*, in which
Wednesday.   he co-stars with Albert Lieven, Gladys Cooper, and
              Lilli Palmer. All about how an Alpine climber is under
a moral obligation to marry any girl without legs. Or something
equally silly. (I am told that Stefan Zweig's novel says the exact
opposite.) Cedric in great form at lunch. Said of a *very* eminent
American statesman that Americans, meaning New-Yorkers, look on
him as they would look on a piano-player in a brothel who did not
know what was going on upstairs.

June 13   On Tuesday at 3.15 P.M. I had the bright idea of
Thursday.   a sequel to *Around Cinemas*, started by something
              Lejeune wrote about hoping the first volume wouldn't
be the last. Eighteen years of the *Tatler* at fifty articles a year means
that I had nine hundred to choose from for the first book. Take
away ninety and there still remains eight hundred. I decided the
milk would stand another creaming. 'Phoned Bertie van Thal to
come over at once and concur. Which he did at 3.25. The book was
delivered at 4.30 P.M. to-day. Is that all I did in the forty-eight
hours ? It is not. I attended one cinema and one theatre, and wrote
articles for the *Tatler* and the *Express*.

June 14   The Gentle Art once more. Letter to the Musical Critic
Friday.   of the *News Chronicle* :

DEAR SCOTT GODDARD,
     I suggest that other things come home to roost besides chickens
and curses. For example, musical criticisms. You write in to-day's
News Chronicle :

    " Handel's *Solomon*, which contains some of the loveliest of his
choruses, is so rarely given that the elect crowd to hear any performance. They make a small crowd these days ; the Albert Hall
was miserably empty last night, an interesting illustration of the
present state of musical taste in London."

Well, what can you expect after shoving Bartók and the rest of the
cacophonous crew down the throats of our young people ? For it
is the young people who go to concerts nowadays. You are not
quite as bad as the *Times* man who, when he writes of Tschaikowsky
or Richard Strauss, gives the impression that he has been in touch
with defilement and abomination.
     I keep a pretty close eye on you, my friend. Do you remember
a day or two ago cracking up Tippett's Symphony as " a manifestation of an exploring mind," and " the strange power of abstract
thought to convey beauty to the watchful observer " ? Whereupon

I imagine the following conversation between two young persons, watchful observers of your column :

FIRST Y. P. I see they're giving Handel's *Solomon*. What about it ?

SECOND Y. P. What about what ?

FIRST Y. P. Going to hear it.

SECOND Y. P. My dear, you must be nuts. Handel's nothing but tune. No abstract thought. *His mind just doesn't explore !*

Looking forward to reading you on Toscanini when he comes.

Yours ever,
JAMES AGATE

Followed by letter to the Editor of the *Star* :

SIR,

The first question in to-night's Quiz is " In which Shakespearean play does the phrase ' What the dickens ' occur ? " And the answer given is *She Stoops to Conquer*.

I have always felt that what Juvenal wrote was " *Quiz* custodiet ipsos custodes ? " Or should I attribute this to Horace ?

Your unsleeping
JAMES AGATE

June 16   Dilys is incorrigible. " The visual detail, both of setting
Sunday.   and of behaviour, is memorable : a lamp swinging on
its flex as the boy stumbles through the dead girl's room. . . ." What I want to know is what a tobacconist's assistant is doing with a flat as big as my own, with innumerable divans, couches, armchairs, and electric lights ? And whether in Sweden young women die of drink before they reach the age of twenty ? But there are lots of things in *Frenzy*, at the Academy, in which I believe. I believe in the schoolmaster who cares nothing at all for women, but wants to paste the hides off the little beasts in front of him. And I entirely believe in the sadistic usher who distributes his favours indifferently while humming to himself *à la Floradora* :

> Yes, I must thrash some one really,
> And it might as well be you.

June 19   Here is a bit of my broadcast debate on the Value of
Wednesday.   Dramatic Criticism.

A YOUNG MAN. It would be very interesting, Mr Agate, if you would tell us your opinion of the value of dramatic criticism.

AGATE. Young man, are you sure that you're not confusing ' value ' with ' function ' ? For half a crown I can buy a pair of braces. I suggest that braces, considered functionally, are worth more than half a crown. Do you mind if we talk about the function of criticism ? It might make what we're discussing clearer.

Y. M. All right. Let's put it that way. What is your view of the function of dramatic criticism ?

AGATE. Dramatic criticism has three functions. The first is to let the world know what the previous night's new play has been about. There's no reason why a report of this kind should not be written by the same man who describes how in the afternoon he saw a man knocked down in Oxford Street trying to stop a runaway horse. The second function is to tell the public whether the new play is good, bad, or indifferent. This means that the critic must know his job. That is if you hold with my dictionary, which defines criticism as " the art of judging with knowledge and propriety of the beauties and faults of a work of art."

Y. M. But just how do critics know a good play from a bad ?

AGATE. A play is good when the playgoer wants to know what some character—let us call him A—is going to do next, what B will say to C, and what is C's come-back.

Y. M. But, surely, even a cheap melodrama can have this effect on a popular audience ?

AGATE. Then that cheap melodrama is a good play for that audience.

Y. M. This brings me to my next point. How would you tell a good play from a great play ?

AGATE. That fine critic William Archer settled this years ago. In the case of a good play the spectator leaves the theatre in very much the state of mind in which he entered it. In the case of a great play he goes home feeling that he has undergone an experience. That he has been spiritually enriched by, say, a performance of *Everyman,* emotionally enriched by *King Lear,* intellectually enriched by *St Joan.*

Y. M. Yes, I follow that, but what is your third function of criticism ?

AGATE. Reporting the theatre in terms of the art of writing. It is one hundred and fifteen years since Mrs Siddons died, and it still gives me exquisite pleasure to read that great passage in Hazlitt which runs : " She was Tragedy personified. She was the stateliest ornament of the public mind. She was not only the idol of the people, she not only hushed the tumultuous shouts of the pit in breathless expectation, and quenched the blaze of surrounding beauty in silent tears, but to the retired and lonely student, through long years of solitude, her face has shone as if an eye had appeared from heaven ; her name has been as if a voice had opened the chambers of the human heart, or as if a trumpet had awakened the sleeping and the dead."

It is fifty years almost to the day since I read Shaw on Mary Anderson, an extremely beautiful woman who wasn't a very good actress. Shaw wrote : " The position our Mary wanted to begin with, in her teens, was that of Mrs Siddons. It is useless to gasp at such presumption ; for she got what she demanded. She knew that it was childish to cry for the moon ; so she simply said, with quiet dignity, ' Be good enough to take that moon down from its nail and hand it to me.' Which was accordingly done. The world which once sent Mrs Siddons back to the provinces as a failure prostrated itself like a doormat to kiss the feet of Mary Anderson."

It is forty years since Walkley wrote about *The Doctor's Dilemma* : " A thoroughly ' Shavian ' play, this, stimulating and diverting, occasionally distressing, now and then bewildering. O philosopher ! O humorist ! you say with gratitude. And then you whisper, with a half-sigh, O Pierrot ! O Faun ! "

It is thirty-five years since I read C. E. Montague's estimate of Bernard Shaw : " Mr Shaw is one of the cyclonic kind of talents that charge through their time as an express train tears through country stations, and if your mind be only a piece of straw or an empty paper-bag, or is not pulled in any special direction by something else, it leaves all and follows the express until the express drops it a little farther on."

Y. M. Reading dramatic criticisms, I am sometimes inclined to think a great deal of it is destructive. Oughtn't criticism to be constructive ?

AGATE. Will you tell me how to write constructive criticism about a building after it has been erected ?

Y. M. Not of the finished play, perhaps. But shouldn't criticism of the production and the acting be constructive ?

AGATE. Neither producers nor actors take the slightest notice of critics. There is a famous scene in Ibsen's *A Doll's House*. The persons on the stage are Torvald Helmer, his wife Nora, and Dr Rank, their old friend, a dying man. Rank asks Torvald for a cigar, and Ibsen's stage direction is : " Nora hands match. Rank lights his cigar at it." Rank then makes his exit on the words " Thanks for the light " uttered to Nora, and obviously a reference to the solace and comfort which her friendship has brought him over the years. At a West End production some time ago it was the husband who gave the cigar and struck the light. And Rank, taking no notice of the wife, went out saying to the husband, " Thanks for the light," jauntily, as we should say to-day, " Ta, old man." I pointed out in my paper that this was all wrong. Was any notice taken ? No. A fortnight later I saw the performance again. No change had been made.

Y. M. But surely actors would benefit by constructive criticism ?

AGATE. Once a mumbler always a mumbler. That's all there is to be said about actors.

Y. M. Well, is criticism any use from the box-office point of view ?

AGATE. You mean : Does criticism help to drag the public in ? I could tell you an old story of how, many years ago, the then dramatic critic of the B.B.C. so taunted and goaded the public by telling them that to give it Sherriff's *Journey's End* was like casting pearls before swine—so enraged the public that, to prove the critic wrong, on the day the booking opened Maurice Browne had enough applications for seats to fill the theatre for three weeks.

Y. M. Ah, but that's a long time ago.

AGATE. Well, then, I'll tell you a story of to-day. The takings for *No Room at the Inn*, produced at the Winter Garden Theatre some six weeks ago, were £35 on the Monday night and £105 on the Saturday night. Then Alan Dent got busy and wrote a magnificent eulogy of the play in his paper. On the Sunday I did my little bit. On the following Monday the takings were £104 as against £35, and on the Saturday £350 as against £105. I have a letter from the management saying that the result of those two articles was to treble the play's takings.

Y. M. Do you think a young man can be a good dramatic critic ?

AGATE. There may be the makings of a good critic in a young man. But you would not say that a beginner who had ascended only Snowdon was as good a judge of a mountain as a more experienced climber who had tackled the Matterhorn and Mount Everest.

Y. M. Would it be wrong to say that one man's opinion is as good as another's ?

AGATE. Let's talk sense. Suppose you found a bit of shiny stuff in the gutter and wanted to know whether it was diamond or glass. Would you take it to Hatton Garden or Covent Garden ?

Y. M. Is there anything else that you can say to young playgoers ?

AGATE. Yes, a great deal. But nothing that can be *usefully* said. In my day young people knew they didn't know ; now they are certain they know. I was turned thirty before I wrote my first dramatic criticism, having spent twenty years getting to know about plays and acting. The modern young man has no notion of educating himself for his job, or that he needs educating. He leaves Oxford by the morning train, and goes straight from Paddington to get himself appointed dramatic critic to some highbrow weekly. And on the following Saturday he has a column telling me Irving was ham. Good night !

June 20   Yesterday was a busy day, even for me ! I tabulate :
Thursday.

9.0 A.M. Ring up all my acquaintance begging the loan of a pair of evening socks. Nobody has a pair, or else is wearing them. Finally succeed through the good offices of a cinema organist.

11.0 A.M. Rough-out first draft of article on last night's play.

Noon. Sally forth to Broadcasting House to record to-night's talk, a thing I insist on in case of asthma, hiccups or that unforeseeable migraine which virtually blinds me for twenty minutes, and always the wrong twenty.

1.0 P.M. Lunch with Gwen Chenhalls.

2.0 P.M. Preside at the Annual Meeting of the Hackney Horse Society and hand over the Presidency to my old, greatly esteemed friend Horace Smith, the first horse-dealer to be elected President in the history of the Society.

3.30 P.M. Back at the flat. Read and review three books until

7.30 P.M. Put on aforesaid socks with gear to correspond and

8.0 P.M. Take a snack at the Ivy. Sardines, cold salmon, asparagus, pint of champagne, coffee, brandy, and cigar. Bill, with tip, £2 16s. 0d., or rather more than I get for the broadcast after allowing for tax and service cars, taxis being unprocurable in this wet weather.

9.15 P.M. Broadcast.

10.0 P.M. Pick up my deplorable doctor and take him to the National Horse Show Ball at the Dorchester, where we make merry till

2.0 A.M. Bed.

So much for yesterday. My mail this morning contains this letter from a lady :

You state in your column this morning that you have always understood that angels were masculine ! ! Emanuel Swedenborg, who claimed to be acquainted with them, stated that an angel was a married couple, and that when talking to them you could see both, but that at a slight distance you only saw one. And the same thing applies to the black kind, which is quite understandable, don't you think ! To be always tied to some one you hate would be a quite sufficient hell !

Also this from Scott Goddard :

21 *Vanbrugh Fields*
Blackheath, S.E.3
June 18, 1946

DEAR AGATE,

It was a joy to have your letter ; the first ever, I think.

Before that night at the R. A. H. I'd been to one or two feasts when the old gasworks had been crowded with people who had come to hear or see a performer (which I suppose is what you want me to do when old Tossy and his La Scala Boys come to C. G.). Here, I said, is superb music, Handel at his most magical ; and the hall is a quarter filled. So much for musical taste.

What the hell has that got to do with Bartók (that lovely fiddle concerto) ? Or do you suggest that the young people, having had their attention directed to Bartók and Tippett, smile down on Handel from some Olympian height of their own scaling ? For the

377

life of me I can't see why the one desire (for B. or H.) must exclude the other for H. or B. As for Tippett's exploring mind . . . well, I guess the phrase is a silly one ; but when I'm moved watching a man's mind earnestly working at something huge, that is the sort of thing my pen does. Your Second Young Person has got hold of the cat by the wrong end.

Yours ever,
SCOTT GODDARD

To which I reply :

Of course *you* don't see why one can't like both Bartók and Handel. But the young people who form the bulk of concert-goers haven't your mind. If you will go on dinning into their budding intelligences that the thing to like is music without tune they will naturally, if illogically, draw the conclusion that music with tune is not the thing to like. If I were to laud and over-laud, and go on lauding and over-lauding, plays in which the characters take off hats they are not wearing, read invisible newspapers, and drink cups of tea which aren't there, I should expect our young playgoers to stay away from *The School for Scandal* on the ground that Lady Teazle hides behind a real screen. Now put that in your imaginary pipe and smoke it.

June 21   A young man sends me, anonymously, part of a letter he
Friday.   has written to a friend in America :

It is quite some time since I have recommended any books to you, so prepare yourself for a broadside : subject, the *Egos* of James Agate. His essays are chiefly noted for having *less* to do with their ostensible themes and *more* with almost every other subject in the galaxy, from horses to Hamlet, than those of any of his literary compeers—presuming it admissible that he has any ! Personally, I find they provide as stimulating a mental exercise, following the (at times almost untraceable) linkage of ideas, as, say, chess, or a chapter of Susan Stebbing. His other identifying features are a pedantic flow of quotations—usually, to give the devil his due, apt—and a regard for Sarah Bernhardt as idolatrous as mine for Yehudi Menuhin—and *you* have ploughed through sufficient pages of my ravings to know what a standard *that* sets up. . . .

The *Egos*—I have read up to 7 so far—are yearly-issued instal-ments of his Diary ; consisting of letters to and from the agate tower, reviews, personalia . . . definitely the most amusing, gossipy, callous, exhibitionistic, sentimental, florid, arrogant, pathetic, boring, Rabelaisian, aggravating, *readable* books ever published ! It must be slightly, if only subconsciously, worrying to his friends to know that they are writing to a man who auto-matically assesses every letter first on its literary and secondly on its personal value . . . rather like marrying a film actor and never being quite sure whether he is regarding you as his wife or the Flame of the Desert, episode six. . . . None of his correspondents ever seem to send him thoroughly dull letters on commonplace subjects like Junior's teething or the acquisition of some new goldfish for the pool in the back garden : even when they deal with ordinary subjects they are brilliantly witty and quotable—unless 'tis the touch of the Master transforms them ?

Physically he looks like a cross between a bailiff and a farmer ; granite-hard and strong; short, bulky build, bald, tiny porcine eyes, wide thin lips, Churchillian aggressiveness, wears ridiculous small round black bowler hat. . . .

Anyway, J. A. is a National Institution as much as tea, Sunday, and the Albert Memorial, and, in spite of his capacity for often arousing an almost homicidal fury in my breast, I thank God that there exists still one blatant egotist, one interesting individual in the spreading grey gloom of professed altruism in this " Century of the Common Man." . . .

June 22   " Still harping on my daughter." Meaning that when
Saturday.   I have got my teeth into a subject I never let go,
        though I may sometimes pretend to. Here is part of
my *Express* article to-day. I am reviewing H. L. Hitchins's *Chaucer for Present-day Readers* :

I have long had in mind a plan for shortening the classics. Let me take as an example Boswell's *Johnson,* of which I am a fanatical admirer, but which contains a colossal amount of dead wood. Who, for example, cares tuppence that in 1741 Johnson wrote for *The Gentleman's Magazine* one article entitled " Debate on the Proposal of Parliament to Cromwell, to assume the Title of King, abridged, modified, and digested," and four other contributions equally appetising ? Anybody opening Boswell at this point might well be excused for being frightened off this masterpiece for ever.

The foregoing is merely a preamble to what I have to say about Mr Hitchins's ' outrage,' which will make purists plunge razors and carving-knives into their gizzards. I will be frank with you, reader. I have tried to be a Chaucerian and failed. I can just make out what is meant by " Your eyen two wol slee me sodenly." But I have not the vaguest notion of what is meant by " The faire body, lat hit nat appere." Yet I have always wanted to read Chaucer, and now comes Mr Hitchins, who enables me to do so. Why shouldn't I, who haven't the time to study fourteenth-century English, be grateful ? Mr Hitchins begins with a blunt, straightforward, honest Foreword entitled " Where Angels Fear to Tread " :

" If you are already a reader of Chaucer, put this book down ! It is not meant for you. If you are a student of Middle English, take it with the tongs and put it on the back of the fire out of harm's way ! It might give you a nasty pain."

I have no notion what is meant by " ferne halwes " or a " bis-motored gypon." Mr Hitchins has made Chaucer readable to the ordinary man by substituting the modern word when absolutely necessary, printing " distant shrines " for " ferne halwes," and re-spelling, as in the case of " sweete breath " for " swete breeth." For my part, I thank him. I am now able to read about the Prioress :

> Full well she sung the servicé divine
> Intonéd in her nose full semély,
> And French she spake full fair and gracefully
> After the school of Stratford-atté-Bow,
> For French of Paris was to her unknowe.

Mr Hitchins says that this conglomeration of Middle and Modern English will be horrid to the learned etymologist. I don't care. Let the learned etymologist Morris-dance himself silly !

June 23   At last a critic who sees the point about my divagations.
Sunday.   The *Times Lit. Supp.* says of *Around Cinemas* :

When the cinema tickles or scratches Mr Agate's critical faculty he reacts readily enough to the challenge—indeed, Charlie Chaplin still awaits more comprehensive study than this critic gave him in 1921, but it would appear that of nine-tenths of the films that come up for notice week by week there is little or nothing to be said. Some weeks the proportion of dead matter is even higher. Mr Agate, on his devious way to dispose briskly and amusingly of the week's rubbish, has always something else to talk about. It may be as remote from Wardour Street as Prince's golf course, which the critic once holed in 75. " Everybody in his life plays one faultless round of golf," he begins fantastically ; but with " it has fallen to my lot to play two such rounds " he is on the hard and happy ground of fact. Moreover, he is in the saddle and away. In place of what might have been an unreadable analysis of a forgotten mediocrity a very entertaining essay remains. It is not, needless to say, about golf, but a discussion of whether the enjoyment of a thing and the enjoyment of its reproduction are separate and incompatible pleasures. It leads eventually into the cinema.

I think this is intelligent as well as mighty handsome.

June 24   Went this morning to a wee picture theatre in Dean Street
Monday.   to see the first of a series of films by which Marylebone
            Film Productions propose to bring Shakespeare to the
masses. I was horrified, confounded, not by the attempt, but by the deed. First let me get rid of the popular misconception that there is no need to take Shakespeare to the masses because the masses lose

no opportunity of flocking to Shakespeare of their own accord. Harold Hobson wrote in yesterday's *Sunday Times* :

> I am mildly puzzled by the notion that Shakespeare needs popularising with the general public. Few actors earned more from the general public than Irving did ; and he got most of his two millions out of Shakespeare. But that was a long time ago ? Very well then. Did Mr Richardson's Falstaff, did Mr Olivier's Richard III need popularising with the public, general or otherwise ? The only problem the Old Vic had when it was playing Shakespeare in its last two seasons at the New Theatre was that so many people came that many of them couldn't get into the house. But Mr Olivier and Mr Richardson gave superb performances ? Of course they did. Superb performances, not " popularising," are what Shakespeare needs. . . . Shakespeare is already beyond all dispute or cavil the world's most popular dramatist. Mr Rattigan and Mr Coward have golden fingers, but the money their admirable plays attract is a cabby's tip compared with what Shakespeare draws into the earth's box-offices. No, the proper way of tackling Shakespeare is not to begin his pieces half-way through, and then miss out half of what is left in the fear that audiences can't be expected to stand more than a bit of him. Play him magnificently and they will take it on the chin.

With all due respect to an old and valued friend and a brilliant writer, this is flat nonsense. The masses, always with the exception of the Old Vic faithfuls, do not flock to Shakespeare. What they flock to is Gielgud in something, and Richardson and Olivier in something else, and if it's Shakespeare it's just too bad. I quote from *Ego* 5 (entry for January 22, 1942) :

> It is owing to Wolfit that for four weeks in succession, *en pleine guerre,* there have been four revivals of plays by Shakespeare played to full or nearly full houses. But this is no reason why the London playgoer should lay flattering unction to his soul in the matter of improved taste. D. W.'s manager telephoned me this morning to say that at each and every performance Czechs, Poles, Norwegians, Belgians, and French had accounted for 50 per cent. of the audience and sometimes 75 per cent. " The rest have been Jews ; had we relied on the Christians we should have played to empty benches."

What happened, pray, when Wolfit announced his *Lear* at the Scala ? The theatre was empty until J. A. soundly berated what Shakespearian public there is. Hobson talks of the drawing power of Rattigan and Coward, as to which I have to say that their drawing power is real. Coward's *Blithe Spirit* ran for five years and suffered three or four changes of cast ; Heaven and John Parker alone know how long *Private Lives* ran. The original cast for the second of these was headed by Gertrude Lawrence and Coward himself; the piece is again running at the reopened little Fortune Theatre *without these artists*. Can Hobson really believe that the First and Second Parts of Shakespeare's *Henry IV* could run for five years with actors of diminishing fame ? As we used to say in Lancashire, " Have a bit of common ! "

But to return to this morning's picture. I was horrified to see that Othello's colour was glossed over and that there was no suggestion that Desdemona (*a*) married a blackamoor or (*b*) married against her father's will. Horrified to find that the play started with one of Iago's most difficult soliloquies, full of metaphysical straining. Horrified to see nothing of Cassio and Roderigo. Horrified when the business of the handkerchief was cut to an unintelligible two-thirds. Horrified that the audience was not told that the tragedy of Othello is that of a noble and simple soul undone by a subtle, scheming rascal. Horrified when they drowned Othello's closing speeches with the last movement of Tschaikowsky's Sixth Symphony. Horrified when Iago, instead of having the lean, sinister look which the *optique du théâtre* demands, was presented by an actor chubby of face, Falstaffianly stomached, and ready, one thought, at any moment to burst into an aria *à la Caruso*. Horrified when in enormous letters the screen announced " IAGGO," followed by the actor's name.

There was some talk of getting me to do the short version of *Macbeth*, and I confess that nothing would please me better. But I should have to be given a free hand. I hold that two things are essential in anybody who is going to film Shakespeare for the masses—reasonable understanding of Shakespeare and a thorough understanding of the masses. What is the little chit whom I overheard in the bus saying to her friend, " You wasn't taking us to the pictures Setterday, was you, 'Orace ? "—what is Camden Town going to make of :

> Will all great Neptune's ocean wash this blood
> Clean from my hand ? No ; this my hand will rather
> The multitudinous seas incarnadine,
> Making the green one red.

Wherefore I should insist upon making the plot as plain as if it was something enacted by Alan Ladd and Veronica Lake. I should make it clear, probably by a Reciter in the Obey manner, that *Macbeth* is a tragedy of retribution. Further, that the murder was not suggested by Lady Macbeth, but originated in Macbeth's mind

("What beast was't then That made you break this enterprise to me?") long before he encountered the Witches. Having established beyond any manner of doubt what was the core of the play —I should show the Witches as spirits abetting evil rather than instigating it—I should then trust to the poetry to get by, though I have almost no hope that it would. As the inventor of the law called the Non-increasability of Nothing I must believe in the Non-educability of the Masses, either by Shakespeare, Beethoven, or anybody else. But I am a firm believer in the Lost Cause, and as such can only hope my chit in the bus will be able to conceive that somebody can incarnadine something beyond her multitudinous toe and fingernails.

June 26   Luncheon party at the Ivy to celebrate my fifteen years
Wednesday.   on the *Daily Express*. Guests: E. J. Robertson,
               manager; Arthur Christiansen, editor; Percy Cudlipp,
editor of the *Daily Herald*; Tahu Hole, B.B.C.; and Bertie van Thal.
The Ivy in great form, with a magnum of Pommery 1928 and other vinous kickshaws.

Kay Hammond told me this. Her younger son, Timothy, aged eight, had been to see his brother, John, aged eleven, play in his first cricket match. "He didn't bat, because it was six o'clock. But he bowled two overs and took ten wickets for no runs."

The Gentle Art again. Letter to the *News Chronicle* Gossip Writer:

> Queen Alexandras Mansionses
> Grapes Streets
> *Junes 26th*, 1946

DEAR ELIZABETH FRANKSES,
   Who is this Georges Sands you tell us about this morning in your Shows Newses? Am looking forward to *Summers at Nohants*.
                              Ever,
                                   JAMES AGATES

June 27   Should *Dombey and Son* be filmed? I think I would
Thursday.   rather ask, Can Dickens be filmed? The point is what
               you mean by Dickens. I suppose if anybody were to
ask me how well I knew *Pickwick* I should answer, "By heart." Yet I haven't the vaguest notion, and I should have to turn up the book to see, whether Mr Pickwick went to Bath before the trial or after. It is the people he met at the trial and the people Sam Weller met at Bath who are the everlasting miracle and joy. When anybody

383

mentions this masterpiece to me I immediately think of the Pot-boy, the Muffin Youth, the Baked-potato Man, the large-headed Young Man in a black wig who brought with him to Bob Sawyer's party a Scorbutic Youth in a long stock. The Gentleman at the same party who wore a shirt emblazoned with pink anchors. The Pale Youth of the plated watchguard. The Prim Man in the cloth boots who had forgotten his anecdote, but hoped he should manage to recollect it in the course of half an hour or so. It is the same thing with *Our Mutual Friend.* I care nothing at all for the Riderhood-Rokesmith side of the business. On the other hand I am fascinated by the young gentleman with the lumpy forehead. I quote for the sheer pleasure of setting down the words :

> A youngish, sallowish gentleman in spectacles, with a lumpy forehead, seated in a supplementary chair, at a corner of the table, here caused a profound sensation by saying, in a raised voice, " ESKER," and then stopping dead.
> " Mais oui," said the foreign gentleman, turning towards him. " Est-ce que ? Quoi donc ? "
> But the gentleman with the lumpy forehead, having for the time delivered himself of all that he found behind his lumps, spake for the time no more.

Is that all we hear of him ? No. There is one more sentence :

> But the lumpy gentleman, unwilling to give it up, again madly said, " ESKER," and again spake no more.

It is this young gentleman and not who found whose corpse in what bend of what river that, for me, is the real Dickens.

Now consider the film or, for that matter, the stage. Neither medium is going to make anything of pale youths with plated watchguards or sallowish young gentlemen with lumpy foreheads. Both screen and stage want plot, and Dickens's plots are, to-day, a sheer downright nuisance. Some ten years ago I saw at the Palace Theatre the film which Metro-Goldwyn-Mayer had made of *David Copperfield.* This film ran for more than two hours, and still could not find time for the Michaelangelesque waiter, the gentleman who bred Suffolk Punches wholesale, the voiceless Mr Creakle, the lonely Mr Mell who, even before Browning recommended it, blew out his brains upon the flute. There was nothing of the volatile Miss Mowcher, or Mrs Crupp of the nankeen bosom, or even of Hamlet's Aunt. But these were only minor omissions. In the major matter we saw nothing of Mr Spenlow, Mrs Steerforth, Rosa Dartle, Julia Mills, Traddles, the elder Miss Larkins, or the butcher boy whom David defeated. What

did the film find to put in their place ?   A fine view of the shipwreck !
A great deal, too, about David.   In fact, far too much, because David
is not a character at all, whereas Master Freddie Bartholomew was at
that period a great Hollywood draw.

And then there was the great mistake of casting W. C. Fields as
Micawber.   Here is Dickens's description of this great character at
his first appearance : " ' This,' said the stranger, with a certain condescending roll in his voice, and a certain indescribable air of doing
something genteel, which impressed me very much, ' is Master
Copperfield.   I hope I see you well, sir ? ' "   What is wrong with Fields
is that he is about as genteel as a pork pie.   It is impossible for him
to condescend, because it is not conceivable that this jovial creature
would hold anybody to be beneath him in the social scale.   It is
impossible that this Micawber would use a word like ' peregrination '
or know the meaning of ' arcana.'   These high-sounding phrases
should roll off the tongue, whereas Fields gave one the impression of
having mastered them with difficulty.   Indeed, the only really first-
class impersonations were those of Edna May Oliver as Betsey Trotwood, who had that exact wooden appearance, as of an Aunt Sally,
with which Phiz has immortalised her.   The other first-rate performance was Lennox Pawle's Mr Dick.   All the rest were approximations.
The film was rattling good entertainment, but it just wasn't Dickens's
novel.

What do I want to see in a film of *Great Expectations*, upon which
novel some British company is now wreaking its best or worst ? First
of all Trabb's boy strutting along the pavement attended by his
delighted friends, " pulling up his shirt-collar, twining his side-hair,
sticking an arm akimbo, smirking extravagantly by, while wriggling
his elbows and body, and drawling to his attendants, ' Don't know
yah, don't know yah, 'pon my soul don't know yah ! ' "   Next a shot
of the outside of Wemmick's castle with the real flagstaff, the real
drawbridge and portcullis, and that piece of ordnance which was a
Stinger mounted in a lattice-work fortress and protected from the
weather by an ingenious tarpaulin contrivance of the nature of an
umbrella.   I want to see the owner of the castle, the Aged One, and
Wemmick's fiancée, that Miss Skiffins of wooden appearance who
washed up the tea-things " in a trifling ladylike amateur manner that
compromised none of us " !   And at least five minutes of Mr Wopsle's
Hamlet, preferably the scene in the churchyard " which had the
appearance of a primeval forest, with a kind of small ecclesiastical
wash-house on one side and a turnpike gate on the other."   And two

minutes of Mr Waldengarver saying, " You must have observed, gentlemen, an ignorant and a blatant ass, with a rasping throat and a countenance expressive of low malignity, who went through—I will not say sustained—the rôle (if I may use a French expression) of Claudius King of Denmark ! " And what do I think we shall get ? A terrific amount of plot. Plot in which Compeyson, Magwitch, and Miss Havisham play enormous parts. Then I am afraid we shall see a great deal too much of Pip. Now Pip, like David, doesn't exist. Or if he does it is by virtue of Herbert Pocket. Pip really wants a death scene to bring him to life, when, like Stevenson with Dumas's Raoul de Bragelonne, we could " congratulate him, who has so long pretended to be alive, on being at last suffered to pretend to be dead." Once again I am inclined to think that the essential Dickens must escape the camera even though the hand of genius turns it.

The people I am most attached to in *David Copperfield*, *Great Expectations*, and *Dombey and Son* are Traddles, Herbert Pocket, and Mr Toots. I have, for this trio, the same affection that, as a boy, I entertained for Athos, Porthos, and Aramis. Gossiping about Dumas's novel, Stevenson said :

> Madame enchants me ; I can forgive that royal minx her most serious offences ; I can thrill and soften with the King on that memorable occasion when he goes to upbraid and remains to flirt ; and when it comes to the " *Allons, aimez-moi donc*," it is my heart that melts in the bosom of de Guiche.

It is my heart that melts when Toots, told by Susan Nipper that Florence will never love him, has his immortal, " Thank'ee ! It's of no consequence. Good night. It's of no consequence, thank'ee ! " To think that George Gissing in his *Critical Study* makes no mention of Mr Toots ! Let me correct myself ; there is a mention :

> You lay down, for instance, Thackeray's *Pendennis*, and soon after you happen to take up *Dombey and Son*. Comparisons arise. Whilst reading of Major Bagstock, you find your thoughts wandering to Major Pendennis ; when occupied (rather disdainfully) with Mr Toots, you suddenly recall Foker. What can be the immediate outcome of such contrast ? It seems impossible to deny to Thackeray a great superiority in the drawing of character ; his aristocratic Major and his wealthy young jackass are so much more ' real,' that is to say, so much more familiar, than the promoted young vulgarian Bagstock and the enriched whipper-snapper Toots.

Whereupon I have great difficulty in not hurling the book across the room. Enriched whipper-snapper, forsooth ! Compare Chesterton :

Toots is what none of Dickens's dignified characters are, in the most serious sense, a true lover. He is the twin of Romeo. He has passion, humility, self-knowledge, a mind lifted into all magnanimous thoughts, everything that goes with the best kind of romantic love.

And again :

Dickens makes us not only like, but love, not only love but reverence this little dunce and cad. . . . We know Toots is not clever ; but we are not inclined to quarrel with Toots because he is not clever. We are more likely to quarrel with cleverness because it is not Toots. All the examinations he could not pass, all the schools he could not enter, all the temporary tests of brain and culture which surrounded him shall pass, and Toots shall remain like a mountain.

I turn again to Gissing, and I read about Mrs Skewton :

Her paralytic seizure, her death in life, are fine and grisly realism ; but we do not accept Mrs Skewton as a typical figure. Too obvious is the comparison with Thackeray's work ; Dickens is here at a grave disadvantage, and would have done better not to touch that ground at all.

And here the book is definitely flung away. But then I don't think that Gissing had much sense of fun or really understood Dickens.

Of fair women in drama and the novel Stevenson wrote :

Who doubts the loveliness of Rosalind ? Arden itself was not more lovely. Who ever questioned the perennial charm of Rose Jocelyn, Lucy Desborough, or Clara Middleton ? fair women with fair names, the daughters of George Meredith. Elizabeth Bennet has but to speak, and I am at her knees.

Dickens's Cleopatra has only to attempt her sketchiest *œillade* and I am all pulse.

I assure you, Mr Dombey, Nature intended me for an Arcadian. I am thrown away in society. Cows are my passion. What I have ever sighed for has been to retreat to a Swiss farm, and live entirely surrounded by cows—and china.

When I think of *Dombey and Son* I am immediately surrounded by Mr Toots and Cleopatra. Like those figures on that Grecian Urn, For ever will he love, and she be fair ! Pray, how can the screen hope to present these ? Instead we shall be given some tearing melodrama in the first half of which Little Paul takes an unconscionable time a-dying, and in the second an express train whirls through the night lit only by Carker's gleaming teeth.

June 28
Friday.
Lunch with George Harrap, and to show my gratitude for the really lovely production of *A Shorter Ego* make over to my godson, James William Harrap, a one-twentieth share in My Pretty. Say one hoof, one ear, and a bit of the tail.

In a letter from George Lyttelton :

> Were you at the Test Match ? I saw the last two days. It wasn't really nearly so easy a victory as it looked. The black men fielded superbly, their bowlers kept the batsmen playing all the time, and their batting was full of skill and spirit. P. F. W. told me that Charles Fry said they are the finest natural cricketers he has ever seen and that in ten years they will be beating England, Australia, and anyone else. I don't see the English bowlers troubling Hassett and Co. much. Bedser the Press with one accord compare with Tate. I shouldn't go higher than Kermode. Has there ever been a Test Match bowler with a *clumsy* action ?

And *The Times* has this :

PROPAGANDA AND THE NATIVE

Sir,

In the recent debate on the future of the B.B.C. you report Lord Morris as saying :

> " He would like to know what control the Postmaster-General exercised over the foreign broadcasts from this country. To talk about the Mufti was a digression, but these foreign broadcasts were important. Had the B.B.C. taken the opportunity to see that it was being poured, day and night, into the ears of Arabs, Jews, Levantines, and Syrians what a wicked old scoundrel the man was ? "

Is it permissible to suggest that the ear-pourers should have sufficient knowledge of native psychology to know what the ears are going to make of the stuff poured into them ? A friend of mine who is a trader on the Congo told me that British propaganda about Hitler's crimes staining the soul of Germany and offending the conscience of civilisation did the British cause infinite harm. The African native, said my friend, or, rather, the native of that part of Africa, knows nothing about souls, conscience, or stains ; when his boys heard about Rotterdam and the mass murders and the gas chambers they did whatever is the native equivalent of rubbing their hands. The African knows force and worships it, and their view of Hitler as put out by our broadcasts was that he must be the very devil of a fellow and a man they would go through fire for.

Yours faithfully,
JAMES AGATE

June 29   Letter from Lord Beaverbrook :
Saturday.

Cherkley
Leatherhead
Surrey

27th *June*, 1946

DEAR AGATE,

I send you my warmest congratulations on completing 15 years as Book Critic of the *Daily Express*.

It is a long record of fine service to the public and the newspaper.

And, as one of your steadiest readers, I send you my personal thanks for much pleasant reading.

Yours sincerely,
BEAVERBROOK

To which I reply :

Queen Alexandra Mansions
Grape Street, W.C.2

June 29th, 1946

DEAR LORD BEAVERBROOK,

Many thanks for your kind letter. Do you remember Hilary Jesson in Pinero's *His House in Order* ?

" Encouragement, sir. Don't we all need encouragement, in every department of life ? Did you never hunger for a word of praise, Sir Daniel—aye, and receive it—during your period of stress and struggle ; and, in memory of that time, have you never thrown a bone into the kennel of that promising young dog there ? "

I am an old dog now, but none the less one who is very grateful for the bone you have so charmingly thrown to him this morning. Thank you again.

Yours sincerely,
JAMES AGATE

Also letter from Bertie van Thal questioning the last sentence in my letter to *The Times*. My reply :

No, dear ass, the other way is pedantic. No African native says, " Hitler's the man for whom I would go through fire ! " What he says is " Wolla, wolla, wolla ! Hitler's the man I would go through fire for ! " Do you imagine, sweet idiot, that I didn't weigh this up ?

Your impeccable,
JAMES

June 30   Ivor Brown ends his article on Rodney Ackland's adapta-
Sunday.   tion of *Crime and Punishment,* at the New Theatre : " My
             interest (and respect) were continuous : but I never
could escape from the awareness of my address, which was neither
St Petersburg nor Parnassus, but the New Theatre, London." And
I compare something I wrote twenty-two years ago about the Yiddish
Art Theatre's production of *The Seven Who Were Hanged* : " If on
leaving the Scala you had asked me what the piece had been like I
could not have told you. If you had desired to know how I had
fared in Russia I should have made shift to reply." I remember the
remarkable figure of Isidor Cachier's Cabinet Minister. He is told by
the Chief of Police that the authorities have discovered a plot to
assassinate him next morning, but that his Excellency is in no danger
as the conspirators are known and will be arrested in front of his
house before the bomb is thrown. In spite of this assurance the
Minister is so terrified at the idea of death that he dies of apoplexy.
The second act gives the trial and sentencing of the five anarchists,
to whom are joined a half-witted, subnormal vagrant and a brigand.
The third act shows them all in prison ; the fourth depicts their
behaviour on the train that is to take them to the place of execution.
The last act gives the procession on the way to the scaffold. Never
have I forgotten the impression Cachier made on me. At the
beginning a figure of farce as the elder Guitry might conceive farce,
scenting his waistcoat, hands, and the tufts of hair surrounding his
little pig-like ears, then changing to a figment of Grand Guignol with
his horrible, stertorous death-agonies.

Ivor complains that Ustinov's Chief of Police lacks " the knock-
down veracity " that Charles Laughton put into a similar part in
J. B. Fagan's *The Greater Love* of nineteen years ago. As Jock in
the *News Chronicle* makes the same comparison I am all agog to see
what I wrote. I find :

Mr Laughton has played, to my knowledge, three parts in
London—Ephikhodof, the clerk in *The Cherry Orchard,* the
humorous wastrel in *Liliom,* and now this Russian Governor. To
my knowledge, I say, but only because of the programme. In each
part this actor has been at once superb and unrecognisable, achiev-
ing his differences not by inessential wiggery, but by seizing the
essence of the character and making his body conform. This is
character-acting as the great and not the little masters of that art
have always understood it. To watch this sleek, polite, overfed
tyrant wake from eupeptic slumber to smile a possible assassin to
Siberia — this was to be told something authentic about the

Tsarist terror. Pleasures too refined and cruelties too barbarous were in the flutter of those sleepy eyelids, the indolent, caressing voice, the slow-moving, velvet hands. Now I am not going to make a song about three performances and proclaim Mr Laughton a great actor on the strength of them. But I will say this, that whenever he has been on the stage my eyes have never left him, and that on Wednesday night his abstractions held more of Russia than all the talkers put together.

About Sybil Thorndike, who played the heroine, I find this :

Nadeshda, when once she got going, was obviously a part to tear a cat in, and Miss Thorndike split and rent whole tribes of *felidæ*, while managing to retain every appearance of rationality. But the swooning and the transports were not altogether convincing, and the part offered little scope for the actress's finer brand of spiritual magnetism. The exotic languors and molten grace, the purring and scratching of a Bernhardt are essential to these man-eating leopardesses who would induce Russian Chiefs of Police to change their spots. Miss Thorndike's art invites to serener raptures, and where orchidacity is the fashion homespun leaves one unsatisfied. The actress was magnificently reasonable throughout, but one would have preferred her to be less reasonable and more magnificent. What is the use of melodramatic Russia if you cannot sweep through it in tea-gowns of Babylonish allure ? Miss Thorndike wore a dress of modest drab and behaved like a woman of sense. But, again, is sense the wear for that femininity which braves a barrack-room at midnight ? Are not sables the only cloak for virtue in such case ? It is true that Miss Thorndike wore furs. But then again they were reasonable furs, whereas Sarah's, when she played Fédora, trailed behind her to the length of several versts. In this Russia of Sardou which Mr Fagan has tried to make his, governesses must look like princesses, and princesses like prima donnas. Miss Thorndike will forgive me if I say that she wasn't nearly scrumptious enough, that she was too much like life, that I prefer her Jane Clegg to her Ivanovna Cleggorovitch.

All that's a long time ago and, I am afraid, of no interest to to-day's young people, who seem to think that the art of acting began with Margaret Lockwood.

Took Gwen Chenhalls to lunch at the Savoy, after which we dropped in to Harold Holt's last of the season's Albert Hall concerts. Just in time for Ravel's *La Valse*, played by the L.S.O. conducted by Antal Dorati, who seems to have modelled his style half on Houdini and half on Joe Louis. Ravishing performance, during which I thought of Leo, who adored this piece. Gwen, whose wedding anniversary falls to-day, thought of Alfred ; it seems that he insisted on having an organ version of this played in place of the anthem, much to the astonishment of the congregation at the Marylebone Parish Church.

July 1   The B.B.C. ran true to form last night. Voice from
Monday.   America : " The Bomb will now be dropped half an hour
         earlier, at 9 P.M.—sorry, I mean 9 A.M., British double—
sorry, I mean British Summer Time." Then a quite good lecture by a professor. As the broadcast sounded like Donald Duck in a railway-siding during shunting operations and a thunderstorm it was suspended and replaced by records of Sousa. *Sousa!* " The operation is to decide whether Man is to become obsolete " had been the Professor's last words. And after it was all over ? Two dance-bands !

Letter from Stanley Rubinstein, to whom I had given a *de luxe* copy of *A Shorter Ego* inscribed, Vol. 1: " To Stanley Rubinstein, who has so often dragged me out of the quagmire . . ." Vol. 2: " . . . to plunge me into the morass ! "

24 *St Mary Abbot's Court*
*Kensington, W.*14

30.6.46

MY DEAR JIMMIE,
    I did not have an opportunity during the week of writing to thank you for the magnificent present which arrived so opportunely for the party we gave to celebrate the thirty-first anniversary of our wedding, Joan's success in becoming a solicitor, and Anthony's release from the Royal Marines. The books have been adopted as family heirlooms, and the inscriptions produced the quite inevitable rejoinder—" More ass you for permitting me to do so ! "
    Re-reading, I am reminded of a *Conte Scabreux* which I intended sending you long ago.
    Do you remember Moore's *Fudges in England* ? And Miss Betty Fudge—piety in petticoats—torn between Heaven and earth and mixing the carnal with the spiritual indiscriminately—in verse ? Her concern for the soul of a man—her hopes to save—and how the idea of marriage to him occurs to her :

> Not *this* world's wedlock—gross, gallant,
> But pure,—as when Amram married his aunt.

And this was published in 1835 !

Gratefully,
STANLEY RUBINSTEIN

Also this from Tahu Hole :

Oriental Club
29.6.46

DEAR MR AGATE,
The way in which, at your delightful luncheon party on
Wednesday, you appeared, with such a wealth of exhilarating
theatrical gesture, so soon after popping the cork of a magnum,
rapidly to tire of trying to open a mere *bottle* of champagne, struck
me—and, obviously, the other guests—so happily as a piece of
refreshing impishness, that it was easy to imagine that Miss Kay
Hammond and Mr John Clements, together with the rest of the
amused company watching from neighbouring tables, were, with
their smiles, saluting an established master who had nothing to
lose by the indulgence of a charming whim. I hope you will never
deny yourself indulgences of the kind ; and it must be the wish of
all your friends that you will see to it that any suggestion for
economy of effect is treated with the acrid contempt of a Cesare
Borgia, which, assuredly, it would merit.
Yours sincerely,
TAHU HOLE

In the meantime I am in terrible trouble with *Daily Express*
readers for saying that I don't believe a witty thing is ever said north
of Willesden. Scores of letters pointing out that Middlesbrough is
the backbone of the country. To which my answer is, Yes, but I
don't want my clothes made there. I have no doubt that Brighouse
has claims to vertebral consideration. But I don't see Gwen
Chenhalls buying a hat there. If I dared I would treat *Express*
readers to Balzac on the subject.

Quelque grande, quelque belle, quelque forte que soit à son
début une jeune fille née dans un département quelconque, si,
comme Dinah Piédefer, elle se marie en province et si elle y reste,
elle devient bientôt femme de province. Malgré ses projets arrêtés,
les lieux communs, la médiocrité des idées, l'insouciance de la
toilette, l'horticulture des vulgarités, envahissent l'être sublime
caché dans cette âme neuve, et tout est dit, la belle plante dépérit.
Comment en serait-il autrement ? Dès leur bas âge, les jeunes filles
de province ne voient que des gens de province autour d'elles, elles
n'inventent pas mieux, elles n'ont à choisir qu'entre des médiocrités ;
les pères de province ne marient leurs filles qu'à des garçons de
province ; personne n'a l'idée de croiser les races, l'esprit s'abâtardit
nécessairement ; aussi, dans beaucoup de villes, l'intelligence est-
elle devenue aussi rare que le sang y est laid. L'homme s'y
rabougrit sous les deux espèces, car la sinistre idée des convenances
de fortune y domine toutes les conventions matrimoniales. Les
gens de talent, les artistes, les hommes supérieurs, tout coq à plumes

éclatantes s'envole à Paris. Inférieure comme femme, une femme de province est encore inférieure par son mari. Vivez donc heureuse avec ces deux pensées écrasantes ! Mais l'infériorité conjugale et l'infériorité radicale de la femme de province sont aggravées d'une troisième et terrible infériorité qui contribue à rendre cette figure sèche et sombre, à la rétrécir, à l'amoindrir, à la grimer fatalement. L'une des plus agréables flatteries que les femmes s'adressent à elles-mêmes n'est-elle pas la certitude d'être pour quelque chose dans la vie d'un homme supérieur choisi par elles en connaissance de cause, comme pour prendre leur revanche du mariage où leurs goûts ont été peu consultés ? Or, en province, s'il n'y a point de supériorité chez les maris, il en existe encore moins chez les célibataires. Aussi, quand la femme de province commet sa petite faure, s'est-elle toujours éprise d'un prétendu bel homme ou d'un dandy indigène, d'un garçon qui porte des gants, qui passe pour savoir monter à cheval ; mais, au fond de son cœur, elle sait que ses vœux poursuivent un lieu commun plus ou moins bien vêtu.

I just can't see myself telling *Express* readers that the most gifted young woman who marries in the provinces and remains in the provinces becomes provincial. That to this inferiority is added the inferiority of her husband, since every cock with feathers to its tail has flown to London. Last indignity of all. That when she makes her little slip it is not with a man of talent, since there are none, but with somebody who wears gloves or thinks he looks well on a horse. No, I can't think Lord Beaverbrook would give me a pat on the back for this. So break, my heart, for I must hold my tongue.

July 2   The Secretary of the Hallé Concerts Society having asked
Tuesday. me for an article for their new magazine, I have sent
them the following :

ALBUM LEAF

The Pleasures of Listening. Yes, but why seek the opinion of a dramatic critic almost entirely preoccupied with the Pains of Looking, a book critic stifled with the Plagues of Skipping, a film critic asphyxiated with the Penalties of Technigazing ? Presumably because I am an old Hallé fan. I shudder at the last word, and could almost break off to write an essay on the Decline of Taste.

The joy of great music ? Too big a subject for an essaylet. Let me take refuge in reminiscence. I attended my first Hallé concert at the age of seven. Yes, the year was 1884. I was taken by my nurse to the Reform Club in King Street, and deposited in the hall to wait until my father had finished his dinner. Then in a yellow four-wheeled cab with red plush seats to the Free Trade Hall and a seat in the gallery with a view of Hallé's left profile and, when he was playing the piano, a full view of his back, the idea being that I, as a commencing student of that instrument, might observe the fingering. I thought Hallé a nice old gentleman, but a tame player, with less than half my mother's fire. It is only fair to say that she had studied under Madame Heinefetter, a pupil of Chopin.

Later on came the Christmas performance of Handel's *Messiah*. Edward Lloyd looked to me as though he wore a *toupet*—but nobody else has ever sung " Comfort Ye " so well. Santley's voice was gone even then (I don't believe there was ever a time when it wasn't gone !). He sounded like a lion in *delirium tremens*, and in " Why do the nations " his head and hands shook with something which was half dæmonism and half palsy. Albani was always tremendous in ruby velvet, which made me feel sorry for Ada Crossley, who, as became her inferior station as a contralto, gene-rally moped in black. I adored Norman-Neruda long before she became Lady Hallé. I thought her ugly but supremely elegant, and still can see that thin gold bangle slide up and down her bowing arm.

Enfin Richter vint. And I remember how, at the first perform-ance in Manchester of Tschaikowsky's Pathetic Symphony, Richter laid down his bâton in the second movement and let the orchestra conduct itself. Carreño in the Tschaikowsky Piano Concerto in B flat minor. There, if you like, was fire and force and a walloping pair of arms, and the proper atmosphere of a blacksmith's shop. Lots and lots of great pianists—Busoni, d'Albert, Rosenthal, Backhaus, Petri, Pachmann, whom I thought a charlatan, and one or two Englishmen I didn't think much of because (a) they were English and (b) I didn't think they could really play. Piano quartets, yes ; but the Concerto in the grand style, no. I remember crying when on one occasion the pianist turned out to be Leonard Borwick.

The meandering Delius. Was ever anything less like a fair ? Or less like Paris ? And I remember my Daudet :

> Maison Bénie ! Que de fois
> je suis venu là, me reprendre
> à la Nature, me guérir
> de Paris et de ses fièvres.

Did Daudet in very sooth desire to be cured of Paris and its fevers ? Did Delius ever have fevers of which to be cured ? My first Symphonic Poem, Strauss's *Don Juan*. My first Elgar. And, of course, lots of Wagner, conducted in the heavy, beer-and-tobacco-stained, German and proper manner.

But those were the days of *tune*, when, as likely as not, the season would open with the *Euryanthe* Overture of Weber, always provided it was not Cherubini's *Anacreon* or Nicolai's *Merry Wives*. And once at least during the season we should be given the *Oberon* and *Freischütz* Overtures, and some stout lady in yellow satin would sing " Ocean, thou mighty monster," and look as though she was prepared to swallow as well as apostrophise it. Or shriek a greeting to some Hall of Song, and later, after clapping on more tulle, send out an SOS in the shape of Senta's Ballad. But all this was the age before Bartók.

In those days the leader of the orchestra was Willy Hess. At the same desk sat Siegfried Jacoby, who taught the violin to two of my brothers, and was a great consumer of tea and buttered toast, and a mordant wit. I remember being called in to play the piano part in a *concertante* by somebody, and being in a state of terror the entire time and hardly reassured by his " Vell, ve finished together, und dat is something." Yes, mine is a musical family. It is not given to every young man to have got lost on Snowdon in company with the grandson of the great Manuel Garcia. Or to have met Carl Fuchs, the 'cellist, on the top of Helvellyn. Or even to have played the piano to Henry Wood two years before his first promenade concert.

But I must be getting back to Manchester and the Free Trade Hall. Of what did I think as my legs dangled and my cream socks fell over my black shoes, which fastened with a button and strap ? Well, I used to weave romances about the people in the gallery opposite. And I conceived a violent hatred of the man on my other side, who never spoke to me throughout eight years and sat stiff as a poker, rather like a male Betsey Trotwood.

With my dislike of him I connect certain distastes which have remained with me all my life. Nearly all slow movements, *because they go on too long.* Beethoven, in my early view, was a great offender, particularly in the Seventh Symphony, where I still think he should have wound up the Allegretto three minutes earlier. Anything called a recitative, nearly all Bach, vast quantities of that dry pedant Brahms. All the piano pieces of Schumann, and most of all that loathsome thing called " Grillen." As against this I had my special favourites. There was Adolph Brodsky, who didn't seem to me to be very good as soloist, leader, or conductor, but whom I liked for his genial expression and tummy. Singers, too. Marie Brema ; a lady who was always known as Miss Fillunger ; that great bass singer George Henschel, whose " Spring " is one of the most beautiful songs ever written ; a colossal Swede of the name of Lundquist.

With these goes the memory of the best musical criticism this country has ever seen :

" Mozart has done more to debauch the critical sense of musicians than any composer who ever lived ; practically no one ever mentions his name except in words of absolutely undiscriminating eulogy. . . . But those who do not lose their heads over Mozart are constrained to point out that no organism can have such qualities as his without having the correlative defects. If the stream of speech runs so easily and so unceasingly, it is bound at times to run a little thin ; and it is this thinness that wearies some people after a day or two spent in going not merely through the half-dozen masterpieces of Mozart but through a large quantity of his work of all kinds. One rather tires of seeing what is almost nothing at all said with such perfect grace and such formal impeccability . . . The Mozart fanatic rhapsodises about Mozart, but does not think enough about him."

That was written by the musical critic of the *Manchester Guardian* on the hundred and fiftieth anniversary of the birth of Mozart. It comes first in my first newspaper-cutting book, and the date is January 27, 1906. Is anybody writing stuff as good as this to-day, in London, Sydney, Kamchatka, Colwyn Bay ? No. The *Manchester Guardian* and the Hallé Concerts are the last remaining glories of a city which, when I last visited it, seemed entirely given over to motor salesmen.

And here I must stop. All that I have been writing about happened many years ago. And I am still listening to music. As the great poet so nearly wrote :

> The Child is Father of the Man ;
> And I could wish my days to be
> Bound each to each by natural melody.

And no Bartókery, if you please !

July 4   Ivor Brown laid it down recently that a critic who finds
Thursday.   himself allergic to any department of entertainment
            " ought to stay away from these, to him, foolish things." I agree, with the reservation that if he is allergic to too many things he should chuck his job and go in for something else. Fortunately I am not allergic to much. Modern British music, modern poetic drama, Shaw's plays, ballet, mime, musical comedy, Fred Astaire, skating films, and British film acting—this is very nearly the lot. Remains only Walt Disney. There is nothing on land or sea, nothing in the air or in the bowels of the earth, that bores me so abysmally as the later pictures of Walt Disney. Which goes for Donald Duck too. I would rather sit at the bottom of a coal-mine, in the dark, alone, and think of nothing, than go to see any of the successors to *Fantasia*. I would rather listen to Bloch's String Quartet played in a goods-yard, with shunting operations in full swing and all the Jews trying to get into or out of Palestine (I never remember which) wailing up against the walls—there is no noise known to me, including the road drill and the later compositions

of Béla Bartók, that I execrate so deeply as the squawking of that abominable fowl. Wherefore I have told the *Tatler* that I will not go near *Make Mine Music*.

July 5   Letter from Christopher Fry :
Friday.

Shipton-under-Wychwood
Oxfordshire
July 3, 1946

DEAR JAMES,

I haven't forgotten that I owe you a penny and all because that waiter of yours didn't look in the least like Valentino in *The Sheik*, or even as though he could fold a tent. He can have no sense of psycho-physico-fitness. Here's the penny.

I'm sorry not to have sent it before—I hope you haven't been needing it—but I have been trying to get hold of a script of my small-sized comedy which you said you would try to read ; and I've got hold of it, and this is it.

I enjoyed the Café Royal with you very much.

Ever sincerely,
CHRISTOPHER FRY

My answer :

No, my dear Christopher, I decline to let your *Phœnix* cheat me of a sigh or charm me to a tear. I get almost no pleasure from it, because it makes me work too hard. I know what Macbeth means when he says :

> Light thickens, and the crow
> Makes wing to the rooky wood.

The sense goes with the sound. But I don't understand what your Dynamene intends when she says :

> What a mad blacksmith creation is
> Who blows his furnaces until the stars fly upward
> And iron Time is hot and politicians glow
> And bulbs and roots sizzle into hyacinth
> And orchis, and the sand puts out the lion,
> Roaring yellow, and oceans bud with porpoises,
> Blenny, tunny and the almost unexisting
> Blindfish ; throats are cut, the masterpiece
> Looms out of labour ; nations and rebellions
> Are spat out to hang on the wind.

What does she mean by " the sand puts out the lion " ? That the sand is so yellow that the lion cannot be seen against it ? I fault this speech in three ways. It makes me think too hard ; the thoughts expressed are not feminine (the " blacksmith " metaphor

would not enter any woman's head); it has no music. Compare
Emily Dickinson's verse about our last bed :

> Be its mattress straight,
> Be its pillow round ;
> Let no sunrise' yellow noise
> Interrupt this ground.

How yellow is your lion now ? Can't you hear that this verse
sings, and that your

> You have the air of a natural-historian
> As though you were accustomed to handling birds' eggs,
> Or tadpoles, or putting labels on moths. You see ?
> The genius of dumb things, that they are nameless

just doesn't ? You get nearer with

> But insects meet and part
> And put the woods about them, fill the dusk
> And freckle the light and go and come without
> A name among them, without the wish of a name
> And very pleasant too. Did I interrupt you ?

But then there's that dreadful last line :

> And very pleasant too. Did I interrupt you ?

And you want me to slog out to some hole in some suburban
corner to listen to

DYNAMENE

> Stop, stop, I shall be dragged apart !
> Why should the fates do everything to keep me
> From dying honourably ? They must have got
> Tired of honour in Elysium. Chromis, it's terrible
> To be susceptible to two conflicting norths.
> I have the constitution of a whirlpool.
> Am I actually twirling, or is it just sensation ?

TEGEUS

> You're still ; still as the darkness.

DYNAMENE
>   What appears
> Is so unlike what is. And what is madness
> To those who only observe, is often wisdom
> To those to whom it happens.

TEGEUS
>   Are we compelled
> To go into all this ?

The answer is that I am not, and won't.

Ever your well-wishing,

JAMES AGATE

July 6   Sent this letter to *The Times*:
Saturday.

SIR,

Let us have a little less emotionalism and a little more logic. Dr Moody and Mr Horrabin must find means of proving that my friend's statement was untrue. [See entry for June 28.] That the British broadcasts did *not* make the natives of a certain specified part of Africa think Hitler a fine fellow.

Suppose some European monster who cut off his victims' heads, pickled them, and put them in a show-case. Would a broadcast of the monster's trial have the same effect on the head-hunters of Borneo and Assam that it would have on old ladies listening at, say, Buxton and Marlow? I can conceive that such a broadcast might be followed by an increase in our show-case trade. (Export, Malay Archipelago, North India.)

Chinese music affects the ear according as the ear is Chinese or European. May not a principle, a precept, a piece of propaganda change its colour according to the latitude and longitude of the receiving set?

Sentimentalists should keep in mind Hamlet's "There is nothing good or bad, but thinking makes it so." Are Dr Moody and Mr Horrabin quite certain that Upper Thames and Upper Congo think alike, or interpret thought in the same way? The point is not how nice it would be if they did, but whether they do.

Yours faithfully,

JAMES AGATE

July 7   *Toujours* the Gentle Art:
Sunday.

Queen Alexandra Mansions
Grape Street, W.C.2

7th July, 1946

DEAR BEVERLEY BAXTER,

A little learning, etc. "Who will forgive God?" does not occur in *For Services Rendered*. It is a line out of the second act of Somerset Maugham's *The Unknown*, produced at the Aldwych on August 9, 1920. It was spoken by Haidée Wright in the character of Mrs Littlewood. H. W. did not play in *For Services Rendered*.

By the way, there was no such person as "A. B. Walkeley."

Ever your,

JAMES

P.S. And what in hell's name do you mean by "Perhaps they could not cope with unsmiling Maugham"? Can you be one of the people who pronounce 'Maugham' as though it were spelled 'Maughan'? Like the chorus-girls who pronounce 'pantomime' as though it were spelled ' pantomi*ne* ' ? If you aren't, then what becomes of your joke ? In which cleft stick I leave you, my dear, muddle-headed friend.

P.P.S. And how can you call Shaw an *artist* ? Intellectual giant, innovator, wit, superb craftsman, yes. Artist, NO. He is no more an artist than he is a poet. Don't you know your Montague —I am writing this with *Rosenkavalier* in full spate on my newly restored E. M. G. gramophone ; you must come and hear it some time and I'll give you a first lesson in the rudiments of dramatic criticism, you chuckle-headed Big Ben-ite—who wrote " So when Mr Shaw makes his young poet talk ' softly and musically, but sadly and longingly ' of a ' tiny shallop to sail away in, far from the world, where the marble floors are washed by the rain and dried by the sun ; where the south wind dusts the beautiful green and purple carpets,' we salute an honest effort, but also we feel that, as Holofernes said of Biron's verses, ' Here are only numbers ratified ; but, for the elegancy, facility, and golden cadence of poesy, *caret* '. . . When Mr Shaw, the rationalist, the determinist, the literalist, the man who thinks, as Tybalt fenced, ' by the book of arithmetic,' essays the description of golden dreams, the result is a chill or a bewilderment." Artist my foot ! Everything else, but not that. Or only once. Where ? In *Androcles and the Lion.*

And again :

Queen Alexandra Mansions
*Grape Street, W.C.*2
July 7, 1946

Dear Caryl Brahms,
I read in your column yesterday :

" The scene of Antony Tudor's *Pillar of Fire* is set in a small town in 1900—so small that a searchlight of scandalised curiosity plays over Hagar. She is in love with a man whom she believes to be in love with her younger sister, and fears that she will share the fate of her elder sister—a spinster. These three sisters have not the slightest desire to go to Moscow, or its Middle West equivalent. They are in search of a moderate meed of happiness. Hagar gives herself to a man she does not love, only to have the man she does love given back to her. This is the story of the ballet—fit material for Du Maupassant. And Tudor has set it to the ineffable music of Schönberg's ' Verklaerte Nacht.' "

This is just to say that I have made a ballet out of Shakespeare's *Macbeth* set to the ineffable music of Mozart's " Eine Kleine Nachtmusik." Do you think you could get Covent Garden interested ?
Incidentally who is this " *Du* Maupassant " ?

Yours sincerely,
James Agate

The Gentle Art of Keeping Friends.

To Dilys Powell:

Queen Alexandra Mansions
Grape Street, W.C.2
July 7th, 1946

DEAR DILYS,

How scrumptiously good you are in to-day's *S.T.* You are absolutely right about *A Night in Casablanca*, though I haven't seen the film. That shows what a good reader of criticism I am! I hardly dare go to it. Somebody tells me that some young woman says, "I stop at this hotel," and Groucho Marx replies, "I stop at nothing!" It can't be as good as that all through, and that's what makes me hesitate. I put Groucho with the very great comics—Chaplin, Little Tich, and Grock.

Yes, my dear, you are a very great critic—until you start that nonsense about the visual effect of an undone bootlace while not caring two hoots if the owner of the boot is going upstairs when by all the laws of logic he should be coming downstairs. My other monitress said to me at *Boys' Ranch*—DON'T see that unless you adore freckles and Butch Jenkins—Lejeune said, "You must like Dilys if you like me. We're halves. I'm all heart, and Dilys is all brain." So bless your dear heart, dear brain!

Ever,

J. A.

And now arrives a charming letter :

I am a British working-man, acquaintance with journalism began 55 years ago by selling newspapers at the age of 9 on London's streets. Finished with school at 11½—St Andrew's Church School, Willesden Green. Am just finishing your Autobiography : *Ego, Ego* 2, 3, 4, and nearly read 5, and would like to tell you how thoroughly I have enjoyed all five volumes—the best treat after Arnold Bennett's *Journals*. Our £1000-a-year Lambeth Librarian has had all your volumes strongly bound, and they are in great demand. Some time back I presented the Library at Brixton with Voltaire's *La Pucelle*, which the librarian has also had bound—" variants " and all ! As he is so discriminating and appreciative, I purpose leaving the Library my copy of Diderot's *Les bijoux indiscrets* ! It is strange that in all your Diary you have never mentioned Denis Diderot ! ?

Did poor old Zola really die " with his nose in *le boudin*," as mentioned page 213, *Ego* 5 ? I thought I knew quite a lot about Emile. I had a handbill once, which was distributed on the Paris streets *circa* 1898 : on one side calling him all the " dirty Jewish bastards unhanged "; on the reverse side, in type three inches high, the one word : " *M E R D E* "! After this he came to live in a hotel near the Crystal Palace here for a time. Old Dreyfus, cold as ice, never as much as thanked Zola for his efforts and sacrifices on his behalf.

Mentioning Zola : I thought, Sir, the little bit of pure Gallic on page 4, col. 2 of the new Normandy weekly *Cité Nouvelle*, of 1/6/46 : " Des W. C. ! S. V. P. ! " might interest you ? You couldn't read such in the *Sunday Times* or the *Daily Express*. I like the " . . . les dockers doivent se ' *plier* ' . . . sur les quais, aux exigences de la nature." This (enclosed) is number 5 of the new Rouen Normandy Socialist weekly. It was at Barentin, near, that Zola staged his train smash in *La Bête Humaine*, which recently ran as a film at the Curzon here, but at such high price of admission, I couldn't afford to see it. The film has since disappeared from England !

Please forgive me if I'm a boor, and have written boorishly. You're a busy man, and so am I. But I felt impelled to let you know, although so late in the day (we can't afford to *buy* your tomes !), how very much a working-man has enjoyed *Ego* 1 to 5. Je tiens à ce que vous sachiez que je vous serai toujours reconnaissant pour l'aide remarquable que vous nous avez apportée.

The cutting :

Des W. C. ! S. V. P. !

L'homme a besoin, pour maintenir une vitalité indispensable, d'ingérer des substances connues sous le nom d'aliments.

Hélas ! tout ne peut être digéré ! Hélas ! le corps a besoin de se débarrasser de certain détritus, et voilà pourquoi, dans certains quartiers de la ville, on voit des " chalets de nécessité."

Mais, ce que l'on reconnaît utile aux promeneurs, ne pourrait-on le donner aussi à ceux qui travaillent et peinent dur ?

Un docker, voyons, c'est un homme, et ce docker, travaillant par exemple quai de la Garonne, doit aller jusqu'à la " General Motors " pour soulager sa personne de ce gênant fardeau.

Il n'y a pas toujours d'usine aux alentours et les dockers doivent se " plier " . . . sur les quais, aux exigences de la nature.

Un docker, messieurs les P. A. H., doit être considéré comme étant aussi digne d'intérêt qu'un rond de cuir quelconque.

Un peu d'hygiène, voyons.

I have replied :

Many thanks for your delightful letter. Diderot ? You will find an allusion in *Ego* 3, p. 56. *Re* Zola's death. George Moore writes in *Impressions and Opinions* :

" Zola has no love of money, he has squandered all he made on vulgar decoration and absurd architecture. . . . He wrote for four hours every morning at a novel, and every afternoon he wrote an article for a newspaper, and those who have felt the pressure of a weekly article, while engaged on a work of the imagination, will appreciate the severity of the ordeal that Zola bore for many years unflinchingly. . . . The influence of Manet and Flaubert and Goncourt persuaded him that he was interested in the external world, and we hailed *L'Assommoir* as a masterpiece, for we wished to group ourselves round some great writer. . . . We believed that he would cultivate refinement of thought, and refinement of literary expression. But Zola was not naturally an artist. Instead of the books becoming more and more beautiful, they have become larger, looser, and uglier, and they serve no purpose whatsoever, except to find money for the purchase of cock-eyed saints on gold backgrounds. Alas ! The ridiculous towers of Médan ! Alas ! the arrival of translators from Paraguay ! Alas, the blowing of trumpets before the Lord Mayor of London in honour of *La Terre*, *La Débâcle*, *L'Argent*, and *Docteur Pascal* ! And, three times, alas, for are we not now menaced by a novel on Lourdes, on Rome, and on Paris ? In these novels he will re-write everything that he has written before. His friends will drop away from him ; he will be left alone ; his excellent cigars will fail to attract us, and smoking bad ones in the café we shall regret his life and his works, and the mistake we made ; and when the café closes we shall stand on the pavement wondering what the end will be. One of us will say, it will probably be Huysmans : ' In *Le Ventre de Paris* there is a pork butcher who, after having worked ten hours a day all his life, is found dead sitting before a table *son nez dans le boudin*.' ' And you think,' I shall say, ' that he will just drop from sheer exhaustion over his writing-table *son nez dans le boudin* ? ' Huysmans will not answer, he will remember that Zola is the friend of his life."

Zola was found dead in the bedroom of his Paris house, having been accidentally asphyxiated by the fumes from a defective flue. The film showed this happening at his work-table in his study, which is nearer to Moore's conception. You are not quite fair to Dreyfus. Zola was given a public funeral, and Dreyfus was present at it. I send you a picture of myself looking up at the famous article in *L'Aurore*, one of my most treasured possessions.

I have published *Egos* 6 and 7. No. 8 is due this autumn, and I am half-way through No. 9. I hope nobody will refer to my work as *le boudin* !

Many thanks for the cutting. It is delicious.

With kindest regards,
Yours sincerely,
JAMES AGATE

July 8   The affair with the *Express* continues to repercuss.
Monday.   From a letter :

I would like to remind you that these dull, absurd, and un-cultured people form a formidable part of this country—in fact, they constitute the strength and character of this country. Which is more than can be said for some of the personalities who float like pathetic, comic images around London's West End—so full of " good theatre, good music, good food, good conversation " that a pick and shovel in their hands and a breath of God's clean air would do them a world of good. A bricklayer is important to the community. We can't do without bricklayers, but we can well do without the company of poseurs, epicures, and the rest of this small and, thank goodness, dwindling number of " stranded gentry " who still claim special privileges by virtue of a background and an upbringing fortuitously bestowed on them. These people didn't make this nation or any other nation ; they are merely the parasites which decorate it.

My reply :

I do and don't agree with you that a good bricklayer is better than a bad poet. I won't maintain that a great poet is worth ten thousand bricklayers, for the reason that ' worth ' connotes scales, and you cannot weigh sonnets against dwelling-houses. The point is that a novel about social riff-raff written by a Ronald Firbank amuses me more than a novel about a Dorsetshire bricklayer unless the novelist happens to be a Thomas Hardy. I am aware that Flaubert's best novel is about the wife of a provincial doctor. But the book was written from the outside, so to speak ; Flaubert doesn't want you to feel that the world would be a better place if all the women in it were Emma Bovarys. Whereas you, like Priestley, are obviously convinced that a human species composed of Yorkshire manufacturers would be ideal.

Of course we can't do without the people who build our houses, grow, bring and cook our food, dispose of our refuse, and keep the streets clean. But would you like to live in a palace, wear sumptuous clothes, stuff yourself with all imaginable delicacies, sleep on the softest of beds, and enjoy innumerable concubines if it meant having no books to read, no music to listen to, no pictures to look at, no reasonable conversation ? I should hate it. I could be bounded in a hovel, and very nearly am. My curtains are rotting, my carpets are in rags, and my bookcases are falling to pieces. I have worn the same white linen collar for six days, and it is filthy, and my food is mostly atrocious. Yet I still count myself king of infinite space. My subjects are social riff-raff who have drunk themselves into their graves, died of syphilis, or stupidly got themselves into gaol.

There is a modern craze for educating the lower classes. I don't believe in it. I should hate to think that the driver of my express train has any views on Jean-Paul Sartre's *Huis Clos*. What I want him to have views on is when to open and when to shut the throttle of his engine. If he knows how to do that, and does it, I don't care if, at the end of his day's work, he gets blind drunk, takes some trollop home, undresses her in front of his wife, and gives that poor wretch a couple of black eyes because she isn't amused.

July 9   Letter to a man accusing me of getting on my high moral
Tuesday.   horse :

> *Moral*, you idiot ? In all my seven, getting on for eight, million
> words you won't find a single word about morality in its sexual
> connotation. Do you remember the idiosyncrasies of Felix,
> Savarel, Pradon, and Saphius ? What, you don't know your
> *Venus and Tannhäuser*, Beardsley's original version of *Under the
> Hill* ? I still have my privately printed copy given me in 1910
> by George Mair and inscribed " To J. E. A. To be read once a
> year this thoroughly disgraceful book which, happily, he will not
> in the least understand. G. H. M." No, sir, I have no morals,
> nor is my criticism intended to be moral in the matter of the
> caprices of the body. My truck is with the minds of great men.
> George Moore used to laud to the skies a short story by Balzac
> entitled *Une Passion dans le Désert,* all about a pantheress " that
> met a soldier starving in the desert, and taken with a sudden
> fancy galloped off and brought him back the hind quarter of an
> antelope, and in such wise continued to feed the soldier for many
> months ; . . . Balzac tells the story of this strange caprice with
> rare intensity." But why do things laudable in deserts become
> impermissible in Regent's Park ? Why should I be shocked if a
> polar bear should offer a Chelsea pensioner a bun in exchange
> for a hug ? But the brain-pan of the English doesn't work that
> way. I don't know a single ratepayer who would not sacrifice *The
> Importance of Being Earnest* for the assurance that its author had
> led a life as blameless as that of the Rev. Robert Spalding.

Came across this in Hazlitt apropos of Charles Kean :

> We do not say no great actor improves, but no actor becomes
> great by improvement. Garrick fell as it were from the clouds ;
> Mr Kean's father rose at once from obscurity.

A hard saying for any young actor. But true. A great actor is
like a great harness horse. He is there or he isn't. I should know if
a really great horse entered the ring though I had my back turned to
him. I should recognise a great actor in my sleep.

Dined at Cherkley, Lord Beaverbrook's beautiful place at Leatherhead. Three other guests, including two lovely ladies. The Beaver
in great form. We began with a jeroboam . . .

July 10   *A Night in Casablanca* is frankly a disappointment.
Wednesday.   This film has suffered from one of two things—either
            Groucho has not been given a free hand, or his wit has
begun to fall off. I am tempted almost to embark on an essay
entitled *Grandeur et Décadence de Groucho Marx.* There is still the
old impishness, that lascivious leer in which only the whites of the

eyes are seen, that bland delight in enormity. There is even Tarquin's ravishing stride. But, alas! there is too little to be impish about or leer at, no dowager to be kicked in the stomach, and no Lucrece to rape. Groucho, in this film, is like a singer who has nothing left but his style. And yet how good he might have been, and what chances he might have had as a hotel manager whose three predecessors have been bumped off. The late A. B. Walkley said that if Grock had been a dramatic critic he would have blandly thrust his feet through the seat of his chair and with them written better criticism than Sainte-Beuve. If Groucho had only been allowed to manage that hotel in his own way he would, I feel sure, have put his feet through his desk and with them given demonstrations of hotel-management at which Ritz would have boggled and Carlton gaped.

And then whoever made this film made a first-class mistake in allowing Sig Ruman to have any share in it. I have for years admired this actor, the greatest master of controlled exasperation that I have ever seen. "Can anybody wonder, like him?" asked Lamb of Munden. And I ask, "Can anybody bottle wrath like Ruman, and with such extraordinary comic effect?" He has a scene with Harpo and Chico, and behold, the two more celebrated clowns disappear. I can bear this. What I cannot bear is that Groucho should fade into the light of common day.

July 11   From Christopher Fry :
Thursday.

Shipton-under-Wychwood
Oxfordshire
July 7, 1946

DEAR JAMES,

Bless you for reading and returning the *Phœnix* so speedily. I can only wish you'd found some amusement in it for your pains, but, alas, it seems to have been a very solemn affair to you and not a joke at all. I can't defend it, of course. If to you it isn't funny, to you it isn't funny : but I can answer one or two of your queries.

You're probably very right about Dynamene's "mad blacksmith" speech not being feminine, but you're wrong to think I wrote it for high poetry : It was meant to be mock heroics, to be laughing at a certain kind of verse, to be a joke (why else should I have said "oceans bud with porpoises, blenny, tunny"?): and all it means is that there are a hell of a lot of things in the world but they're all as good as nothing now that her husband is dead.— Yes : "the sand puts out the lion roaring yellow" is ambiguous,

I can see that. I meant " begets," as in " the branches put out shoots "—shouldn't it be clear following, as it does, the roots sizzling into hyacinth and orchis, and preceding the ocean budding with porpoises, etc. ?

As for the " dreadful " line : " And very pleasant too. Did I interrupt you ? " you can't pretend to me, Jimmy, that you didn't know it was meant to be comic bathos. You know it's a trick I have all the way through, following the flickers of poetry : as I prick the bubble of the love-scene with " Is your husband expecting you ? " And the laughs come and that's what I want.

No, you don't win your case by quoting passages which were never meant to be poetry in order to prove that I can't write it.

If it weren't my own play there's a good deal I should enjoy arguing about. Perhaps when I'm in London again we can ? Or perhaps we let the subject drop ? I'll try to give you some verse in the new play which will give us less to argue about.

Ever sincerely,

CHRISTOPHER FRY

I have replied :

Queen Alexandra Mansions
Grape Street, W.C.2

July 11th, 1946

DEAR CHRISTOPHER,
So that's what highbrows laugh at ? Well, well, well ! But I mistrust, and I think Beaumarchais would have mistrusted, the playwright who can be humorous only in verse. " What is un-funny in prose . . ." However, I confess that " blenny, tunny " made me think of " linnet ! chaffinch ! bullfinch ! goldfinch ! greenfinch ! " Perhaps you should have used Sheridan's exclama-tion marks, " connoting *espièglerie* "—to use my and Alan Dent's phrase. However, it's nice of you to take my non-appreciation so charmingly.

Ever,

J. A.

P.S. Is *This Way to the Tomb* meant to be funny too ? And what started all this wild hilarity—*Murder in the Cathedral* ?

The Gentle Art :

Queen Alexandra Mansions
Grape Street, W.C.2

July 11th, 1946

DEAR SCOTT GODDARD,
You write in the *News Chronicle* to-day :

" It would be easy to dismiss with a smart phrase the eight movements of the French composer Olivier Messiaen's ' Quatuor pour la fin de Temps ' for piano, violin, 'cello, and clarinet.

" Nevertheless, this is heartfelt music, having passages of much beauty.

" To me it seemed not only exasperating music but bad art ; the organist improvising ' meditations ' after the service."

Please tell a floundering dramatic critic, trying to find his way about the arts, how a heartfelt work containing much beauty can be exasperatingly bad art.

Yours sincerely,
JAMES AGATE

Vignette. Hermione Gingold at the Ivy wearing a hat like a Martello tower with cascades of veiling, putting a bunch of carnations in her mouth à la Carmen, and saying with an atrocious leer, " Any gentleman like to strip to the waist ? "

July 12
Friday.

If anybody likes to present Boadicea as a combination of George Eliot and Mrs Humphry Ward I am quite willing, since I have no views about the Queen of the Iceni. Nor do I mind if Messalina is presented as a combination of Jane Shore and Mae West ; I have no views about Messalina. Whereas I have views about George Sand. I am certain that there was more ' to ' this tremendous figure than a pair of trousers, a top-hat, and a cigar. To begin with, she had the power of making people take her at her own valuation ; did not her memorialist in the *Encyclopædia Britannica* as late as 1898 say of her that she was " the second, if not the greatest, of French novelists " ? She could, and did, pass herself off as a budding Rousseau-cum-Chateaubriand. She even gammoned a critic of her own nationality, no less a person than Sainte-Beuve, who, however, begins his essay in *Causeries du Lundi* with the words, " I have been for some time in arrears with Mme Sand." (I know a dramatic critic who intends always to be in arrears with Mme Sand.) History records that she was for a period on the staff of the *Figaro*, but that as she had neither wit nor piquancy her earnings at the end of the month did not amount to more than fifteen francs. Further, that she could be taciturnity itself, and would sit for hours together without a word, devouring her lovers with her sombre eyes. Now what is a playwright going to make of a woman who spends her time between moping in a corner and astonishing the Parisians with a new shape of top-hat ? And then her lovers, of whom she had as many as, according to Miss Mitford, the poet Cowley had mistresses ! Is the playwright to show us the novelist making herself ridiculous on the fond bosoms of Musset, Pagello, Heine, Liszt, Chopin, Sandeau, and Mérimée ? Or a selection of them ? Or none at all ? And then there is the actress to be considered. If she is a showy actress the character must show off. Wherefore Mrs Patrick Campbell, when she played the author of *Consuelo*, got herself up in a costume which would have been appropriate equally to Little Lord Fauntleroy and Archibald Grosvenor. Wherefore she took the stage like a Spanish galleon in full sail. Wherefore she would have an idea—something about sunburnt cathedrals or music wooing the stars—and strike an attitude and look for her tablets and find it meet that she should set the cliché down. Was Mrs Pat going to shed her personal glamour to impersonate a hard-bitten egocentric who burned up her lovers under the pretence of mothering them ? No. If I had to dish up George for popular entertainment I think I should use the film. My first shot would show this really frightening infant at the age of three crossing the Pyrenees to join her father, who was on Murat's staff, occupying with her parents a suite of rooms in the royal palace, adopted as the child of the regiment, nursed by rough old sergeants, and dressed in a complete suit of uniform to please the general. After the Shirley Temple stage I should show her falling into trances like Blake, and worshipping that deity of her own invention, the mysterious Corambé, half pagan and half Christian, and erecting to him a rustic altar made out of moss and ferns and pretty pebbles. Half-way through I would show her waking to find herself famous and, of course, donning the celebrated trousers. For pudicity's sake I should forget about her lovers, and end by showing the old girl in her garden at the age of seventy, surrounded by grandchildren, and writing the pants off Balzac. Why all this about G. S. ? Because to-night's play at Hammersmith, *Summer at Nohant*, bored me stiff.

July 13   The Gentle Art. To-day's bag includes all women, the
Saturday.   Editors of *Windmill*, and Macmillan's the publishers.
    First the women. From my review of Vachell's *Now Came Still Evening On*:

Mr Vachell understands women very nearly as well as Lord Dunsany understands them. There is a scene in Dunsany's *Alexander* in which the Queen of the Amazons tells Alexander that if he wants to conquer her people he must come up against them with elephants and battering-rams, which the Amazons can't withstand, and not with spears, which they can. " And then ? " says Alexander. " Well," says the Queen, smiling sweetly, " once you've destroyed my army and captured me, I shall be yours, shan't I ? "

Next to the Editors of *Windmill*:

It is the mark of the highbrow to do things less accurately than the lowbrow. Why, for example, does the author of an otherwise admirable article on Hubert Crackanthorpe talk about "*Le* Maison Tellier," when every schoolboy knows that it is "*La* Maison Tellier"? Why, further, does he make Henry James speak bad French? Why does the clever author of *August Diary* give us an entry about Paul Valéry and get his name wrong? Why are the most ordinary French accents omitted? This has nothing to do with the rule of the magazine, since accents are given elsewhere. Why does the brilliant author of *Letter from Cambridge* publish a French poem of eight lines in which there are four mistakes? Don't the Editors know that the word for ' in ' is *dans* and not *danse*, that adjectives should agree with their nouns? I am a very common, ordinary, lowbrow reader and reviewer, and this highbrow slovenliness annoys me. I am just as much annoyed as I should be if Henry Cotton at the first hole of a championship inadvertently turned his back on the hole and drove in the opposite direction. But then Cotton would be annoyed too, whereas our insufferable highbrows are so pleased with themselves that they wouldn't care if their editors printed them upside down, which they very nearly do.

Letter to Macmillan's:

> Queen Alexandra Mansions
> Grape Street, W.C.2
> *July 13th, 1946*

DEAR SIRS,

Why, in your new Book List, do you say " John Palmer succeeded Bernard Shaw as the dramatic critic of the *Saturday Review* "? He didn't. Unless, of course, you hold that Henry II succeeded Henry I. Max Beerbohm is the Stephen in this case. Can you have forgotten G. B. S.'s valedictory " The younger generation is knocking at the door ; and as I open it there steps spritely in the incomparable Max. For the rest, let Max speak for himself. I am off duty for ever, and am going to sleep "? Shaw's last article appeared on May 21, 1898 ; Max's first appeared on May 28, 1898. There was no interregnum. And Max reigned for twelve years.

> Your obedient servant,
>
> JAMES AGATE

Letter from a young gentleman at West Hampstead:

May I express the pious hope that ere long some Northern numbskull will seize you by the scruff of the neck, ram your hard little hat over your hard little head, thrust a cheap edition of *Madame Bovary* down your throat, and with cloddish contumely kick you off the end of Wigan Pier?

July 14   Beverley Baxter sends me this :
Sunday.

54 *Hamilton Terrace*
*N.W.*8

12*th July*, 1946

MY DEAR JAMES,

That was a bad *gaffe* of mine about Maugham's play. I could not wait to see the last act of the production at the Lindsey, and asked an actor friend of mine if this was the play in which Haidée Wright had uttered the words about not forgiving God. He said that it was, and very wrongly I let it go at that. As for the extra ' e ' in ' Walkley,' I am not responsible for the vagaries of compositors.

Now, my dear James, while I deeply appreciate your concern for my iniquities and your anxieties for my incompetence as a critic, I think perhaps you should recognise what you are yourself. You are that delightful creature, a café wit. You have no faith, no philosophy, and when you want real thought you summon the thinkers of the past. In fact, you are something between a resurrectionist and a cloakroom attendant for other men's thoughts. Your reverence for the past is almost as moving as that of Viscount Simon. He would rather quote the dullest platitude by an ancient Greek than quote the wit of a modern Scot. Therefore, when you find me writing that Shaw is a greater artist than he is a thinker you are horrified because it has not been said before. Your compass, your rudder are gone. The resurrectionist does not know which way to turn.

Then, wherein is your charm ? You have excellent moods which play like footlights upon other men's thoughts and enhance their attractiveness. This is a valuable work and adds greatly to our pleasure on Saturday and Sunday mornings. For example, what could be better than your recent articles on the Provinces ? It has all been said before, but you brought your own mood to it—and that is your supreme gift.

Now, my dear James, I do not give a damn what Hazlitt or Walkley said or anybody else. I do my own thinking, and if the result is terrible to you then remember that we do not come from the same womb. Go on quoting and I shall go on thinking.

With much affection,

BAX

July 15   *Men of Two Worlds*, at the Gaumont this morning, was
Monday.   all about a negro composer-pianist performing at the
                National Gallery in London the piano part of his own
Bagwash, or some such name, devised for piano, orchestra, and male choir. Well, I just don't believe in the negro pianist who, having tasted blood à la Myra Hess, feels himself compelled to fly to

Tanganyika to second Phyllis Calvert in her fight against the tsetse fly. My attention wandered, and when that happens I have very little control over where it wanders to. The negro pianist calling himself Kisenga, I found myself saying, " Kisenga—Gasenga—Gazingi. That's it, ' Miss Gazingi,' of course." And from that it was only a step to Miss Petowker, the only sylph Mr Crummles ever saw who could stand upon one leg and play the tambourine on the other knee, *like* a sylph. In Mr Crummles's opinion " The Blood Drinker " would die with that girl. Not that she was the original Blood Drinker. That honour belonged not to Petowker, but to Mrs Vincent Crummles, who was obliged to give it up. " Did it disagree with her ? " asked Nicholas. And Mr Crummles replied, " Not so much with her as with her audiences. Nobody could stand it. It was too tremendous."

At this point my thoughts returned to the screen, where the witch-doctor was imbibing something that looked like crimson treacle, and Robert Adams was saying in an awed tone, " He's drinking my blood. I can't stand it. It's too tremendous ! "

July 16   Some twelve or fifteen dramatic critics gave a luncheon
Tuesday.   at the Savoy to John Mason Brown, the New York critic.
    Darlington made a dignified and elegant speech ; my contribution was the recounting of a talk I had with J. M. B. at the time of the lease-lend bargaining :

  J. A. Tell me, Brown. Why do you Americans, delightful individually, taken collectively add up to a nation of twerps ?
  J. M. B. All right, Agate. Why, with you Britishers, is the converse the case ?

A jolly couple of hours with a good deal of wit and the best thing coming, as was right and proper, from our guest. The party took place in the Mikado Room. Somebody saying that Winston Churchill was lunching in the next room, J. M. B. said, " Ah, the Sorcerer Room, I feel sure ! "

July 17   *Vicious Circle*, the English version of *Huis Clos*, at the
Wednesday.   Arts Theatre to-night, gave one the chance to study
    Jean-Paul Sartre's new metaphysic for oneself. The notion I got from this excruciatingly boring play was that hell consists in what you look like to other people. As far as I am concerned this is nonsense. Hell for me is going to be how I appear to myself.

The play to-night was very well acted. There was even a moment of humour. This was when the Lesbian was asked how she came to be in hell. " Gas," replied the Lehmann, referring to a particular type of oven, but using the sepulchral tones in which, in the Dorothy Parker story, the celebrated, gin-soaked actress Lily Wynton alluded to another affliction.

July 18   Cochran ! The name comes o'er my ear like the sweet
Thursday.   South, breathing upon a bank of violets, stealing and
                giving odour. One hundred and twenty-four visions of colour and design, dreams of fair women and clever actresses. Delysia, Spinelly, Florence Mills. But for the time-factor it might have been with some memory of a Cochran revue that Kipling's exile sang to his banjo :

> In the twilight, on a bucket upside down,
>   Hear me babble what the weakest won't confess—
> I am Memory and Torment—I am Town !
>   I am all that ever went with evening dress !

But what has this magician to do with political satire ? " The word poltic surprises by himself," said Count Smorltork. Yes, but in the old days it was Cochran who surprised by himself, and there was nothing in to-night's *Big Ben* (A. P. Herbert and Vivian Ellis, Adelphi Theatre) to spring a surprise about. Shall suggest on Sunday that a part—say, of Lord Chancellor or Speaker—be instantly written in and Fred Emney sent for. Surely in a comic opera there should be one funny character ? Let the Prime Minister and the Leader of the Opposition doze off and give us their Cochranesque dreams. Let the lady members pirouette on the Terrace and give us twiddle instead of twaddle. Let Trefor Jones substitute songs of his own choosing— Handel, Rachmaninoff, Wolf, the stuff he sings at the Savage Club on Saturday nights. C. B., put on short commons in the matter of wit and beauty, is like a juggler denied his cigar, top-hat, and umbrella. A. P. H. was accorded a call and, what is more, took it !

July 19   Supper to-night to Lillian Gish, looking lovely in a cowl
Friday.   and opals. I had asked Jock, Wilfred Rouse, and Bertie
                van Thal, and we were like fervents at the shrine of a young and witty saint. An enchanting evening, in the course of which she gave me her handkerchief, now being put under glass, and

I told her that her fame rested not upon her art, but upon the lovely, *baby* contour of her forehead.

July 20   Found this note from Jock pushed under my door :·
Saturday.

33 *King Street*
Covent Garden, W.C.2
July 20*th*, 1946

DEAR JAMIE,
   The lady you had us to sup with last night was so like Lillian Gish that it took my breath away and left me an infatuated oaf— I dare say rather like Phiz's view of Mr Guppy in the theatre pit staring up at Esther Summerson in the circle, his hand on his heart. Now and again I managed to desist from my gaze at her to give a glance at you, and I must say you were pretty Guppyish yourself. I had a sharp pang of jealous rage when you claimed and were granted her dear, minute handkerchief. But I reckon I scored over you (for she gave me the sweetest smile out of her eyes) when you said you'd drive her back to the Savoy and I said Nonsense, I'd carry her back !
   But you won all the time in the talk, of course. You had that triumphant *aperçu* in comparing her to the Madonna herself—the ageless demure little mouth is exactly that of a Raphael or a Perugini Madonna, whereas the poise of the head is Botticellian— if it isn't just that of a primrose fretting at the dew. But, heavens, what clish-ma-claver between a couple of ageing men !

Your daft, grateful,

JOCK

   P.S. Her wistful smile haunts me still. She is an Unbroken Blossom—a flower that time has mysteriously overlooked. And I say, did you notice the respect amounting to awe with which she once or twice referred to " Mr Griffith " ?—when your normal piece of pretty film-mindlessness would say " Griffith " or " D. W. G. " Admirable !

July 22   Devas Jones, my C.O. in the last war, turned up at the
Monday.   Café Royal. He said, " Seventeen years ago you told me
             not to come back from Africa until I had acquired white hair and a thousand pounds. I've got both, and arthritis as well ! " All the old charm. He said, " There are things in East Africa that you couldn't do over here. Could you, my dear James, dine at the same table with the public hangman, a man under sentence of death afterwards reprieved, and a man who was later on hanged ? " Wants to get back. " Come to Kenya, where the Zoo looks at you, and not you at the Zoo ! "

July 23   Lunch at the Savoy with Lillian and Dorothy Gish, who
Tuesday.   give me champagne and wave at me the current number
          of *Theatre To-day*, in which I have two pages about George
Joan Nathan ! In this I find I am made to write, " Let's *calve* him
as a dish fit for the gods " ! ! ! !

July 24   From a letter : " Have you ever heard yourself read
Wednesday.   poetry (by recording, of course) on the wireless ? Like
          boiled lemonade, isn't it ? "

July 25   A sweltering night, and a play by Dryden ! I feel
Thursday.   inclined to say about *Marriage à la Mode* what Hazlitt
          said about one of Godwin's tragedies : " We can hardly
think it would have been possible for him to have failed, but on the
principle here stated : *viz.*, that it was impossible for him to succeed."
The moment we start on the play within the play the modern
spectator, or at least one modern spectator, is sunk. The story of the
Usurper of Sicily is flat, intolerable fudge, told in verse that is worse.
I don't believe that any interest now attaches, or ever attached, to
this story of Thermogene, Polygamous, Pabulum, and Uvula, or
whatever their wretched names are. Sixteen years ago I began my
notice of the Hammersmith revival with the sentence : " Nobody is
going to risk saying that Dryden is a dull dog." Well, I shall risk it
on Sunday. Not too well acted. John Clements and Robert Eddison
goodish, but Melantha a disappointment, principally because Kay
Hammond chose to be inaudible.

July 26   In the *Daily Express* :
Friday.

    When, in the 'nineties, the controversy over Ibsen was at its
height the late A. B. Walkley asked why people made so much fuss
over " a respectable, elderly Scandinavian who lives at Munich,
taking from time to time a few whiffs at a very short pipe. Why
cannot they make up their minds to like him or lump him ? "
Similarly with regard to to-day's respectable Irishman embarking
on his personal nineties in Hertfordshire without the aid of tobacco.
Surely we made up our minds about him years ago ? Why, then,
the fuss ? Because Shaw is a very great man, and it is fitting that
in the winter of old age . . . But this is nonsense. Shaw will
never be old.
    " Had I three ears, I'ld hear thee," said Shakespeare's Macbeth.
Had G. B. S. thirty mouths he would speak with all of them. Let
us see what mouths he has. Musical critic, literary critic, dramatic

critic, social critic, novelist, dramatist, polemist, economist, vestry-man, educationalist, scenarist, wit. Well, that's twelve of them. I propose, in the short space at my disposal, to discuss two aspects of Shaw—Shaw the dramatic critic and Shaw the dramatist.

Shaw is the greatest of English dramatic critics after Hazlitt and G. H. Lewes. Hear him on himself :

" I consider that Lewes in some respects anticipated me, especially in his free use of vulgarity and impudence whenever they happened to be the proper tools for his job."

And more seriously :

" The cardinal guarantee for a critic's integrity is simply the force of the critical instinct itself. If my own father were an actor-manager, and his life depended on his getting favourable notices of his performance, I should orphan myself without an instant's hesitation if he acted badly."

And this superb thing which goes to the very roots of criticism :

" Whoever has been through the experience of discussing criticism with a thorough, perfect, and entire Ass has been told that criticism should above all things be free from personal feeling."

I say " Amen " to this. " Amen " does *not* stick in my throat. Which brings me to Shaw the dramatist.

Of that popular opera Verdi's *Il Trovatore* G. B. S. wrote : " It is absolutely void of intellectual interest ; the appeal is to the instincts and to the senses all through." Shaw's drama is absolutely void of romanticism ; the appeal is to the intellect and to the reasoning powers throughout. What dramatist with a visual sense of the theatre would in *Saint Joan* have followed the pow-wow in the English tent with the pow-wow in the ambulatory, by-passing the coronation ? The truth about Shaw the dramatist is that he is a theorist passionately interested in humanity and caring nothing about people, an upholder of the Life Force who finds no fun in living. As Chesterton said : " Shaw has always had a secret ideal that has withered all the things of this world. He has all the time been silently comparing humanity with some-thing that was not human. . . ."

For the greater part of ninety years this Great Man has given himself, his energy, the vigour of his superb intellect, to the con-struction of a world in which not one per cent. of the human race would want to live. A world without red meat, beer, cigarettes, pipes, horse and dog races, cricket and football matches, saloon bars, darts. A world without flowers, which commit the sin of being decorative instead of functional. A world in which every-body argues interminably round a table, refreshing himself from time to time with a little grass and some cold water. Like that character in Dryden, G. B. S. has " made almost a sin of abstinence." A world without women in the feminine sense, but full of harpies pursuing the potential fathers of their children, viragoes screaming that they are the votaries of Creative Evolution. This is the world that Shaw's plays are about. A world conditioned by Pure Thought.

What sticks most in my playgoing throat ? Many years ago Shaw wrote of Shakespeare : " With the single exception of Homer, there is no eminent writer, not even Sir Walter Scott, whom I can despise so entirely as I despise Shakespeare when I measure my mind against his." Speaking for Shakespeare, I say that when Troilus has his " I am giddy ; expectation whirls me round," he is saying what every lover in the world has felt. And that when, in *Man and Superman*, Tanner has his " I love you. The Life Force enchants me," he is pretending to feel what no lover has ever felt, or will feel to the end of time.

Shaw is not an artist, because he knows and despises the kind. " The true artist will let his wife starve, his children go barefoot, his mother drudge for his living at seventy sooner than work at anything but his art. Perish the race and wither a thousand women if only the sacrifice of them enable him to act Hamlet better, to paint a finer picture, to write a deeper poem, a greater play, a profounder philosophy." That is why the plays of Shaw the sociologist are discussions about the nature of God, whereas the plays of Shakespeare the dramatist are about the nature of Man. The author of *Back to Methuselah* is concerned with As Far As Thought Can Reach ; the author of *Othello* with how far emotion can feel. Well, it is for the playgoer to choose. On the one hand, a mysterious female clasping He and She Ancients to her chilly breasts. On the other an unhappy man, perplex'd in the extreme, saying,

> " Here is my journey's end, here is my butt,
> And very sea-mark of my utmost sail."

Why, then, all the fuss ? Because of a " stream of mind " which, like that of another Irishman, Edmund Burke, has been perpetual. Because mind is mind, whether you agree with it or not. Because always, once in every play, some speech is unloosed in which you hear Shaw's thirteenth voice, which might be the voice of Isaiah. Some such speech as that in *Good King Charles's Golden Days*, in which Shaw, using Kneller as his mouthpiece, praises the Creator in that " He has seen fit nowhere to repeat Himself, since there are no two things—suns, moons, stars, men, fishes, birds, beasts, flowers, landscapes, consciences—alike and not to be differentiated in the entire created universe."

A world peopled by Shaws would be unthinkable ? I see no danger of this. One Shaw was unthinkable till he happened ; two is impossible. There have never been two Shakespeares, two Mozarts, two Leonardos, two Dan Lenos. There will not be two Shaws. For Shaw is a genius, and genius knows no duplication.

July 29   Supper last night at the Dorchester with Basil Cameron,
Monday.   always a magnificent host, and Gwen Chenhalls. Such a
            cold that an exquisite hock was wasted on me, and I
could tell salmon from Welsh rarebit only by the texture. What a
highbrow would call intellectual appreciation of good food. Afterwards Basil gave me a photograph of himself, which he said I might
use in *Ego* provided I gave his caption : " Shall I take my niblick ? "
He was. in great form and full of good stories. I liked one about
Beecham, who had been asked by some ass whether he did not
admire Beethoven. " Beethoven," said T. B., " is the Dogberry of
music." I told them how the management of the Proms had sent me
the season's programme and asked me to indicate which concerts I
should like to attend. And how I had replied, " Every concert in
which there is nothing by any living British composer." Basil
said, " As I am engaged to conduct some of these gentlemen's
works . . ." I then said that Bucalossi (*Grasshoppers' Dance*) and
Kern (*Showboat*) were better composers than Shostakovitch—a
remark which was met with a smile and half a wink. Basil is the
most conscientious of men. Told us that throughout the concert
season he never opens a newspaper. " I keep my eyes for score-
correcting."
    Lunched to-day with Leonard Russell, who said he thought that
August 4, 1914, marked the end of the age of culture and the beginning
of the age of frustration. " Young people to-day have not enough
talent to fill the old forms, and are driven to invent new forms to
conceal their lack of talent." Told me he had spent some time with
Dorothy and Lillian Gish. " They could talk of nothing and nobody
except you, James, and what a gentle, sensitive, gracious person
you are. I stood this for two hours, after which *I told them the
truth* ! "
    Two letters. The first from a masseuse who wants to know
if she should write a book about her experiences. " They begin
with a woman who suffered from flatulence. She mistook this
for an immaculate conception, and was very worried about
it." The second, from an ex-Captain in the Royal Artillery,
begins :

    I inherit, through study, small portions of the brains of Clerk-
    Maxwell, Einstein, Rutherford, and gigantic Newton. They are
    superior in wit, beauty of thought, and perception to your beloved
    Shakespeare, to Johnson and Lamb. I am a Welshman who also
    speaks and writes a nobler and grander language than the mongrel
    English.

July 30
Tuesday. Welsh preachers getting into their stride lash themselves into an emotional frenzy by the use of a singing cadence called, I believe, the *hwyl*. It is a kind of prolonged, controlled, and rational hysteria. Sybil Thorndike *hwyl'd* most effectively to-night at the G. B. S. Celebration organised by the International Arts Guild, at which I had been bullied into taking the chair. But then, in opening the proceedings, I had given dear Sybil something to *hwyl* about. Here is what I said :

We are met together to-night to honour a great man. A very great man. A great dramatist who has never wrung a tear from any playgoer. St Joan ? She argues like blazes, and one feels that blazes are her appropriate end. The author of a vast number of acclaimed masterpieces each of which loses by being transferred to the stage. A dramatist without any sense of the theatre. A playwright inferior, as a maker of plays, to Goldsmith, Sheridan, Pinero, Wilde, Galsworthy, but with more brains in his little finger than the others had in their entire bodies. The writer of deathless prefaces to plays which are now dying, if not dead. In other words, a very great master, who can afford to neglect the antipathies and allergies, if there is such a word, of lesser minds. It is here that the critical instinct asserts itself. The fact that I happen to dislike Sibelius will not make me declare that Sibelius is a puling composer. The fact that I do not happen to like the shape of a mountain does not make me deny its height. I hope never again to see any play by Shaw acted in a theatre ; I would brain any man who stole one from my shelves. Forty years ago I attended a meeting of the Manchester Playgoers' Club. The chairman was his Honour Judge Parry, an indifferent playwright who never got over the fact that he was supposed to be a wag. He said, " We are to discuss this evening "—and I will remind you that the year was 1906—" the tendencies of the modern drama. And I shall rule out of order any allusion to the plays of Mr Shaw." The whirligig of time brings in his revenges, and as your chairman to-night I shall rule out any allusion to the plays of Mr Shakespeare. Night and day, height and depth, plus and minus are not more opposite than these two geniuses. I am aware of the metaphysical difficulty, and expect Dr Joad to tell me that you cannot discuss black without reference to white. I don't care. It is my ruling that no mention shall be made this evening of Shakespeare, and I do this in the hope that it will give some rest to that spirit which Mr Shaw has so often, so wilfully, and so woefully perturbed.

Joad followed Sybil, and I itched to correct him but didn't. This was when he said that coming out of a Shaw play he felt pity for the people he saw coming out of a revue at the Ambassadors. I wanted to ask whether one may not like *La Fille de Madame Angot* as well as Wagner's *Ring*. Then came Professor Denis Saurat, who made a

I live in a world where taxi-drivers won't wait, bus-conductors are rude, and a collar takes six weeks to wash. A world in which there are no longer ladies and gentlemen, but merely people with more money and more leisure to spend it in. A world which has not realised that if you abolish distinctions you automatically do away with distinction. A world in which, as a returning soldier said to me the other day, " There's nothing to eat, nothing to drink, nothing to smoke, and you're damned lucky if you can find anywhere to sleep." A world in which the telephone doesn't work. A world in which nothing works. A world which has ceased to be fun.

Aug. 4   Letter received during the week from an unknown friend :
Sunday.

It was September 1902, one velvety black midnight in the Karroo, at a little railway station at De Aar, in the Cape, 500 miles from Capetown. My family were returning to the Transvaal, four months after the Peace at Vereeniging. We were all in a tiny little waiting-room, furnished with benches and a table on which was the usual massive Bible which the railways provided in South Africa. It was hot and oppressive, and I could not sleep, so I walked out on to the platform. In the Karroo desert the nights are wonderful—pitch black, with not a star to be seen, and you could not see your hand before your face. But it was cool and fresh. Far away, miles away, I thought I saw a little golden light, just a pinpoint. At first I thought it was a bush-fire, but it was too small and confined for that. It couldn't be a star; it was too low on the ground. Then I heard the noise of a train approaching, the golden light grew bigger and brighter, and presently the train came into the station, slowed down, and stopped. Most of the carriages were in darkness, the passengers were asleep. But one compartment was lit, and in it I saw what to me then was a fairy queen. And she was singing. Two men in evening dress were sitting in the compartment. I glued my nose to the window (I was ten), and the fairy queen, suddenly spotting me, ended her song with a gasp. One of the men opened the window. " It's only a little boy," he said. " Bring him in," she said. I was lifted into the compartment and stammered my explanation. I was enchanted and enthralled. She looked more like a fairy queen than ever, and wore a sort of silvery dress and what looked like a narrow crown in her dark hair. " Do you like singing ? " she asked. I nodded. " Would you like me to sing to you ? " Again I nodded ; my heart was too full for words. One of the men picked up a violin lying on the seat and began to play. Then she sang. I thought she was the divinest thing I had ever seen, and as for her voice, I couldn't find any words for it. It was golden, celestial, something that had come straight from heaven. My sisters sang, but it was nothing like this. I was transported. When she finished she asked me if I had liked it. I nodded, entirely bereft of words. " Do you know the name of that song ? " she asked. I shook my head. " Write it down for him," she commanded, and one of the men did so on the page of a notebook. She tore out the page and gave it to me. " When you grow up," she said, " you can tell people that Albani sang it specially for you." Then she kissed me (oh, rapture !), and I was put back on to the platform, clutching the paper tightly in my hand. A moment or two later the train moved out. I went back into the waiting-room. My people were all asleep, and presently I too became drowsy. When I awoke it was morning. Excitedly I told my sisters about my adventure. " You've been dreaming," they said. Triumphantly I showed them the piece of paper. On it was written, " Ah ! fors' è lui," from *La Traviata*. The strange thing about the story is that nobody on the station heard the train come in or depart or heard the singing. But it was Albani, who was touring South Africa, and it remains my most precious memory.

Aug. 5   In to-day's *Express* I write :
Monday.

How shall I spend bank holiday ? Pottering round the garden ? Alas ! I have no garden, and I do not potter. My staff being away enjoying itself, I shall rise at nine, make myself a cup of tea, and fail to reconstitute the mustard, which I mistake for egg-powder.

I shall then tackle the job of opening and reading the three hundred letters received by me last week in response to my STOP and GO ultimatum. [I had invited readers to send me a single sheet, not a whole manuscript.] Half a minute to decide whether the sender is a genius, an idiot, or something in between. Half a minute to settle his hash one way or the other. Three hundred minutes is five hours, meaning that it is two o'clock and I am peckish.

Since the buses are full I shall not be able to lunch out. Wherefore I mess about with a crust of bread I saved from last week, a bit of cheese nobody has wanted for a long time, and some pineapple jam which has just arrived from South Australia.

After lunch I shall play all my records of Strauss's *Rosenkavalier* and read Wordsworth at the same time. Does somebody think the two don't go together ? How about oil and vinegar ? I shall, with luck, drop off to sleep for an hour or two. On awakening I shall stagger, on foot, to my favourite grill-room, where I shall get solemnly sozzled, to the extent permitted by my doctor and the price of champagne. I shall listen to the bleating of Bloomsbury, and learn how the world is to be saved by young men with beards, corduroy trousers, and dirty finger nails. I shall nod, and they won't know whether it is approval or sleep.

Round about eleven the body will be carted back to its abode by a Hire Service Company specially retained six weeks ago at a fee of £50, with a £10 tip for the driver.

Well, this is exactly how I have spent to-day. Three hundred letters doesn't sound much, but after a time the mechanical job of opening and returning gets on one's nerves. Still, I wasn't going to say STOP to the author of :

Cousin Dorothy, who is a charmingly conventional person, told me not to be morbid. " Let's go and see the Picasso Exhibition," she said.

Or to the young man who wrote :

I was fourteen when my Aunt started to turn into a horse.

And I sense a feeling for words in :

The unsuccessful scribbler slit his throat decently and daintily.

On the other hand I signalled STOP to a budding poetess who submitted in all seriousness verses entitled *The Love Spasms of Gwendolen*.

Aug. 6   Reviewing Sir Lionel Lindsay's *Addled Art*, I wrote in
Tuesday.   the *Express* :

Some years ago I, who know nothing about art, and a young friend who knew less, put our heads together and produced the following piece of spoof art criticism :

" Marcel Tirelajambe conveys plasticity not by the laborious modelling of a Raphael, but by the juxtaposition of flat masses of colour, so nicely balanced and so perfectly related as to compel the sensation of recession. In the ideated picture space the planes circulate freely and rhythmically. Here, surely, the superb art of the Kan-kan Negroes of the pre-Jub-jub period finds its consummation."

This was submitted to an art magazine and accepted. I have before me a picture of a young woman sitting on a chair holding a cup to her mouth with her elbow resting on the floor. Can you do it ? If you can't, is the picture a joke ? No. At least it is not intended to be a joke. This nonsense pervades all the arts. The reason for it ? They tell me it is the state of the world. That the soul of the modern painter is so much moved by the fact that the Nazis murdered 12,000,000 Jews that when he draws a man he sees him with ears growing out of his knees and his eyes staring out of the back of his head. This is why a playwright with nothing to say tries to humbug you by making his characters draw off gloves they are not wearing, light pipes they are not smoking, and sit on chairs which are not there. Sir Lionel Lindsay's book magnificently debunks all this modern nonsense—Cubism, Purism, Constructionism, Neoplasticism, Vorticism, Expressionism, and Surrealism. He quotes with devastating effect a sentence from a Surrealist leader who is a combination of Mad Hatter and March Hare : " I demand that you consider anyone an idiot who still refuses to *see* a horse gallop upon a tomato."

To-day I receive this from Alfred Munnings :

Beldon House
96 *Chelsea Park Gardens, S.W.*3
Aug. 5, '46

DEAR MR AGATE,

Nobody could have handled these rascals as you've done. I never read anything approaching it, or half as funny. This morning artists were ringing me up full of it. So was a fellow outside painting the windows. He brought the *Express* in to me. At the races at Epsom lots of my friends had seen it.

You are the only critic who has dared to attack these people.

On behalf of myself and many others I thank you twenty times over.

Yours sincerely,
ALFRED MUNNINGS

Aug. 7   A letter :
Wednesday.

Chy-an-Garrack
St Ives
. *Cornwall*
August 3, 1946

ADMIRABLE MR AGATE,

To-day you have surpassed yourself in debunking the highbrow, in the *Daily Express* and on the radio. Though I admire, sir, your wit and naughty comments on all things highbrow, I do not admire your complete disregard of the good in some of the contemporary artists, poets, and musicians. It is no use condemning *all* modern paintings, poems, or symphonies with one sweeping Agatian gesture. Please be moderate with Matisse, affectionate towards Auden, and bounteous to Bartók.

Below, a poem I wrote with my pen in my cheek, for your secretary's and your delight—mainly for your secretary's. I think it is as praiseworthy as any of the so-called poems which are printed in periodicals with titles like *Fresh Letters* and *Nightlight* .

SUCKLE THE BREEZE WINTER

Suckle the breeze winter,
Fiddle and fold cocoa,
Put lukewarm in radiance
And pick the pleased cockroach.
Like conscious flesh tincture
And dank draughty cobwebs
Is smoky verisimilitude.
Push the tocsin belling to the fore,
Wipe the slow patella round,
Clavicle the stairs
And sing a ringing swing sneeze
To the innocuous nightsickness,
To smooth the supernacular narcissism.
O begone fantastic ungual picaroon !

Here's luck to you and your *Ego* biographies !
Yours impertinently,

PATRICK W. ROWE

P.S. *de résistance*—I have enclosed a stamped and addressed
envelope for a reply from you, however brief. I hope it'll be
worth 2½*d*.

Aug. 8   Shall have some fun on Sunday apropos of *Fear No*
Thursday.   *More* at the Lyric, Hammersmith, a dramatisation by
             Diana Hamilton and Conrad Aiken of a story by Aiken.
This well and truly led me up the highbrow path, the play being
nearly over before I realised that what I was seeing was not happening
at all, but passing through the mind of a man under an anæsthetic.
Shall begin by telling *S.T.* readers of a dream which has obsessed me
since the age of nine and dating back to the time when my parents
first took me to London. Entering a chemist's shop to inquire the
price of a piece of old brocade exhibited in the window, I left my
mother sitting on the doorstep. The dignified proprietor bowed and
said, " Good morning, young gentleman, I am Mr Hermann Vezin."
Abashed, I quitted his counter in haste and stumbled over my
mother, who rose and pointed to the street, where I beheld a procession of grooms in Lincoln green, with cockades in their hats,
leading a string of white and dappled palfreys. From wallets
slung at their sides they took handfuls of gay-coloured butterflies
and launched them into the air. " That," said my mother
composedly, " is the new way of advertising croquet on the
Thames Embankment ! " I shall then tell the story of the
Hammersmith play and end, " At which point, everybody on
the stage took off his rubber gloves and launched them into the
auditorium. ' That,' said my great-aunt, who had been sitting
on my knee throughout the entire performance without my
perceiving it, ' is the new way of advertising greyhound-racing
in Trafalgar Square ! ' The subconscious is a game that two can
play at."

Aug. 9   Bored G.I. at repertory performance of *The Cherry*
Friday.   *Orchard* : " Cripes, if I'd known there was going to be
             all this fuss about a bloody orchard I'd have bought it
myself in the first act."

Aug. 10   Letter from Jock :
Saturday.

Spooncreel
Maybole
Ayrshire

Dear Jamie,

I have come home for a week's holiday, and within an hour of my arrival went down, on a glistening summer morning, to the cemetery to see how the engraver had dealt with my father's tombstone. My heart was full of sorrow—and the fear of misprints.   I looked first at the quotation at the foot of the stone, fearing the worst, though I had printed the Spenser carefully in a letter full of minute instructions.   But there it was, all correct and touching :

Sleep after Toyle, Port after Stormie Seas,
Ease after Warre, Death after Life does Greatly Please—

archaic spelling and all.

But above it, to my horror, I then saw that the stone had been erected to the memory of JOHN DENT by TESS, JACK, and ALLAN (Allan—not Alan !).   What does one do about such things in such circumstances ?   Nothing, I suppose.

I am always happy here, where I was born and bred.   But this time I'm shocked to see that nearly all my schoolfellows have grey hairs.   And so have I !

Ever,
Jock

I have replied :

Queen Alexandra Mansions
Grape Street, W.C.2

Dear Jock,

You can't do anything about it.   No one can do anything about anything.   But it isn't as bad as being an officer of the Crown and winding up a peroration with a passage about the German character which you attribute to Goethe before the event (with a passing compliment to that sage for his prescience), when the passage really belongs to Thomas Mann, writing after the event. I can never quite make out who Gog and Magog were.   But I should take their statues down, always presuming they weren't bombed, and put up two to Slipshod and Sloven.

Yours ever,
Jamie

Aug. 12   Letter from Ernest Helme :
Monday.

Llangennith
Swansea
August 10th, 1946

Dear James,

I must trespass on your time to let you know how greatly I enjoyed your devastation of some youth in your best Johnsonian

style over the wireless. I actually burst into frenzied " Hear !
Hears " of sympathetic support ! You may like to know that
your voice came over splendidly ; I never heard it more plainly.

I have been confined to my bed for five weeks with a rather
serious attack of concussion resulting from a fall down a flight of
stone steps *after breakfast* (N.B.), when I struck my right temple
against a rock. I was picked up unconscious some thirty minutes
later, having lost a considerable amount of blood.

The week before last I was bitten by an adder on the ankle,
which has left my right foot very tender. And the third and
worst experience was having to open two fêtes this week ; one in
the village of Llanmadoc, where seventy-two years ago this month
I was put on shore from my father's yacht—beastly thing. I hate
yachting, and my father had four at different times. Nothing on
the sea for me under 20,000 tons, and yachts rarely attain a rating
of 200 tons.

I am struck by the number of fine pianists now before the
public : Clifford Curzon rendered the final movement of the
Emperor Concerto with greater virtuosity than any pianist I have
heard since Sophie Menter; to-night also a young Pole, Malcuzynski,
in Rachmaninoff No. 3 Pianoforte Concerto, electrified the Albert
Hall audience deservedly, and was brought back nine times according to the announcer. In comparison with this the vocalists are
not even mediocre ; there is not one who would have been allowed
to sing in my parents' house after dinner, with the possible exception of Elisabeth Schumann, if she sings what is suitable to her
light soprano.

What a damned nuisance the Jews are !

Yours aye,

ERNEST HELME

I replied :

Queen Alexandra Mansions
Grape Street, W.C.2

August 12th, 1946

DEAR DICKY,

Congratulations on your birthday. Bless me, how old we are
all getting ! I shall be sixty-nine next month. Did you see that
Albert Garcia, son of my father's old friend Gustave Garcia, grandson
of Manuel Garcia the centenarian, great-nephew of Malibran and
Pauline Viardot-Garcia, great-grandson of Manuel Garcia the
singer, died this week at the age of seventy-one ? Yes, Master
Dicky, we cannot choose but be old.

This afternoon I called on C. B. Cochran, who is seventy-four.
Told me that a day or two ago he received a letter from the son of
Jenny Lind, who regarded his mother as in every way superior to
Patti. What do you say ? J. L.'s last stage performance was in
1849. She did, however, make occasional appearances up to her
death, in 1887, so that it is just possible that you heard her as a
very small boy. If you didn't hear her, how would your parents

have compared the two ? In the matter of the son's letter I don't believe that family feeling enters into it at all. Brotherly affection has never interfered with my brother Mycroft's judgment of my work, or with my judgment of May's.

Est-ce que je voyage, moi? as the French station-master said. My doctor has gone to Cannes, my lawyer to Switzerland, Bertie van Thal to Sweden, Charles Smith to Hollywood, Jock to Scotland, George Mathew to Torquay, my understanding chemist to Clacton, my favourite waiter to Hove, and my pet photographer to Blackpool. I badly want to refer to a certain book, unobtainable in the shops, and find the publishers closed for a fortnight. Owing to summer holidays, bank holiday, the gas strike, and the soap and starch shortage I have not had a collar from my laundry for eight weeks. So roll on the Atom Bomb ! Apparently it is rolling all right without any encouragement from me. Here is something from to-night's paper which you may possibly have missed : " Within four years rockets will travel up to 6000 miles and be capable of delivering with considerable accuracy ' a telling tonnage of explosives,' says Maj.-Gen. Curtis May, head of the U.S. Army Air Force Development Staff. It is also possible, he told A. P., that by 1950 there will be jet-propelled aircraft which can carry atomic bombs." Seriously, I am glad this thing has fallen in my time. I should have hated to die without knowing the Supreme Joke of All—that Sentience, all there is of self-awareness in the Cosmos, should destroy itself. I wonder what Dr Johnson, Charles Lamb, and my brother Edward would have found to say about this jape so truly awful and so irresistibly comic.

What a damned nuisance the Russians are !

Ever,

J. A.

Aug. 13   One evening last week a personable and strangely clean
Tuesday.   ~~young man came up to me in the Café Royal and said,~~
" Where is Wiltshire ? " I said, " Next county to Hampshire. Why ? " He said, " That's odd ; I thought it was somewhere in the Fen District. The reason I ask is because I've just been posted to the Wiltshire Regiment. [Grunts from J. A.] My name is Peter Forster, Second Lieutenant. It seems that the cradle of civilisation—Egypt, you know—is rocking, and they want me to steady it."

J. A. Who's ' they ' ?
Y. M. The War Office.
J. A. (*waking up*). What the devil has all this to do with me ?
Y. M. Only that I'm going to succeed you on the *Sunday Times*.
J. A. The hell you are ! What are your qualifications ?
Y. M. That I'm a first-class dramatic critic.
J. A. How old are you ?

Y. M. Twenty.

J. A. Then what you mean is, you are a potentially first-class critic.

Y. M. I'm a jolly good writer.

J. A. When do you start for the Middle East ?

Y. M. Wednesday morning next.

J. A. Lunch with me here Tuesday next, and bring with you 3000 words establishing that you are not just a conceited young fool.

Devas Jones arriving at this point, I said, " Let me introduce a young man I don't know to my Commanding Officer in the First World War." Forster said, " I hope I am on speaking terms with my C.O. in thirty years' time. It's more than I am now ! " To-day he turned up on time with an essay of exactly 3000 words entitled *A Very Short View of the English Stage.* I cull :

I have never seen a great actor. Of course I have never seen a great actor. Nobody has since 14th October 1905. But then in these days we set genius at a discount and concentrate on the Lowest Common Denominator. O you reformers ! Is it not enough that a communal hand should rock the child in a communal crèche ; that individual lives should become no more than Vital Statistics ? Would you also take away my gilt and plush ? Would you abolish boxes ? Would you have me sit in some civic shed and listen to solemn tracts about the economic problems of plough-men in the Caucasus ? And must I consider this good drama because you consider it good politics ? O City Corporation Censor ! Dost thou think because thou art communist there shall be no more Somerset Maughams ? . . .

Ralph Richardson's portrait of the scruffy, frowzy stage of early middle age, the age when for the first time a man doesn't bother to put on a clean collar : that was wonderful acting. And the final realisation that " Vouloir ce que Dieu veut, est la seule science qui nous met en repos," as Vanya and Sonia began work again, was most moving. His Falstaff I thought a wonderful piece of bluff, all brilliant overtones, with every resort of comic technique . a spoiled-baby Falstaff, bigger, brighter, funnier than ever before He is the least extraordinary of actors in the front rank to-day. His performances are on view, with all credentials in order ; and all of the highest integrity ; " no offence i' the world," he seems to say ; hard-working, self-effacing interpreter of difficult rôles ; his face the face of Everyman—meeting him casually on a bus the last thing you would take him for would be a distinguished actor. . . .

By his Hamlet Gielgud will be best remembered. He played him not like Wolfit, as a private detective watching over the Danish Royal Family ; nor in the Clunes manner, like Young Woodley on the eve of expulsion ; nor yet in the style of Maurice Evans's new version, broadened and abridged for soldiers, as a

Yankee at the Court of King Claudius. With Gielgud it was the ruin of a noble nature. Exquisite in delivery, in action liquid grace, he sustained the excitement and tension right up to the sad heroics of the sword play, until finally the rest was silence, save for the heavy breathing of the dead.

Good enough for twenty years of age. We shook hands on the understanding that he is to save £150 before he comes out of the Army next spring. This will give him £3 a week to starve on for a year, during which time I undertake to find him a job as a fledgling critic.

Aug. 14
Wednesday.
Reply from Clive Brook to a message I sent him asking whether he would play Aubrey Tanqueray if we could find a good Paula. He said, " Tell Mr Agate I am too dull an actor to risk so dull a part." Charming !

Aug. 15
Thursday.
" The idea of criticism," said George Saintsbury,

as something positive and positively attainable and ascertainable, once for all—like the quotient of a sum, the conclusion of a syllogism, or the cast of a death-mask—is a mere delusion. Criticism is the result of the reaction of the processes of one mind on the products of another, or, to put it more popularly, it tells us how something looks to or ' strikes ' somebody.

Well, how did Jonquil Antony's adaptation of Jane Austen's *Sense and Sensibility* strike me to-night ? Which is only half the question. How am I struck by the novel itself ? Am worried about what I shall say on Sunday. I shall have to stoke up my courage, since your Janeites can be savage-wild, more fierce and more inexorable than empty tigers or the roaring sea. I am no more than half a Janeite. I care nothing which Jack gets which Jill ; as far as I am concerned Elizabeth Bennet can make a match with Knightley and Emma hit it off with Mr Collins. This perversity, blind spot, hoggish stupidity, makes me a wholly unreliable critic of any play made out of an Austen novel. That long speech between Willoughby and Elinor ? Well, I just don't see Pinero, Sudermann, Sardou, having their big third act with Paula, Magda, La Tosca upstairs in bed with a temperature. The play was still going on after three hours and a quarter, when I left. The acting ? I remember nothing except Marie Löhr's second-act headdress, a turban'd monstrosity which Kean might have worn in *Oroonoko.*

Aug. 16　　Letter from George Richards informing me that his new
Friday.　　Siamese kitten, Mount Pleasant Agate, is by Wansfell
　　　　　　Ajax by Job Bangkok, out of Mount Pleasant Bluebell,
whose sire and dam were called Fontmell Ali and Toddy Twinkletoes.
The letter goes on :

> Recently, during the interval of a concert held in a bleak,
> dilapidated, and spectral town-hall ballroom, I began to explore
> the dingy passages leading to the dens of the drivers of municipal
> pens, and all of a sudden found myself face to face—with the
> recitalist. On the platform : *Quelle belle tête!* And here before
> me stood merely an amiable, rather ordinary, egg-faced Jew. I
> came away from the unsought encounter wondering whence and
> what is the spark innate in the artist.

And ends :

> My undeniable poetic talents are evidenced by the fact that
> never a day passes without at least *one* line of pure serenest poetry
> coming unbidden into my head. Two days ago I swore a holy
> oath never to permit in future a single one of these gems to pass
> unrecorded into Oblivion's Great Abyss. Here, then, is the first
> fruits of this resolution so momentous for the future of English
> poetry. The title I have chosen after much thought is

> ### BEN NEVIS
> Sandy reed-patches mildewed snow
> There on the solemn summit
> In a tiny hat stuttering muttering
> Rock-bellied nonsense
> Sit
> Two dentists

No punctuation, please.

Aug. 17　　British Paramount News came along to Grape Street
Saturday.　with a demand that I should talk next week for two
　　　　　　minutes about H. G. Wells. People going out and
coming in. Of that part of the audience which is not on the move
half have never heard of H. G., while the other half have not heard
of me. However, I do my best, which isn't easy with a small
furnace blazing away at my left ear, a dangling mike, and the place
festooned with rubber piping as though Jack the Ripper had been
at work. I am not really a Wellsian. H. G. wanted to be more
than an artist, and I could never see why the great novelist, the
master of the Shape of Things as they Are, should bother about
the Shape of Things to Come. However, I keep quiet about this and
quote my favourite passage from *Mr Polly*, the bit about " sufficient
beauty."

Aug. 19　　Have been reading John Dover Wilson's new edition of
Monday.　　*King Henry IV, Parts I and II*, and find him a little
　　　　　　　less than sound on a point that is, to me, of intense
interest—the real character of Prince Hal :

If Hal be the cad and hypocrite that many modern readers imagine, or even if he seem merely " dimly wrought " by the side of his gross friend, then the whole grand scheme of the Lancastrian cycle miscarries, since it is the person and reign of King Henry V which gives the bright centre to that dark picture, a brightness that by contrast makes the chaos that follows all the more ghastly.

" Tellest thou me of ' ifs ' ? " In all English literature I do not know a more revolting passage than that in Part I, Act I, Scene 2, beginning : " Yet herein will I imitate the sun." The gorge of Pecksniff himself must have risen at the hypocrisy of :

> And like bright metal on a sullen ground,
> My reformation, glittering o'er my fault,
> Shall show more goodly and attract more eyes
> Than that which hath no foil to set it off.
> I'll so offend, to make offence a skill ;
> Redeeming time when men think least I will.

Quiller-Couch said that this speech, if we accept it, poisons all of Harry that follows :

Most of us can forgive youth, hot blood, riot : but a prig of a rake, rioting on a calculated scale, confessing that he does it coldly, intellectually, and that he proposes to desert his comrades at the right moment to better his own repute—*that* kind of rake surely all honest men abhor.

(" Q," whom this greatly bothered, tried to throw the responsibility upon Burbage, who, he half-heartedly suggested, came to the poet and said at a later date : " Look here, the audience aren't going to stand for a rapscallion turned Sunday-school teacher. You've got to get them right about him in the beginning ! " Whereupon Shakespeare went back and obediently inserted the miserable stuff.) The Professor says : " The anointed king who emerges from the Abbey is a different *man* from the prince who entered." Who, then, is right ? " Q," who condemned the anointed Henry as a cad, or J. D. W., who talks of spiritual change ?

When literary critics differ, who shall decide ? Obviously, a dramatic critic. In his earlier book *The Fortunes of Falstaff* J. D. W. put forward the theory that Shakespeare intended Falstaff to appear in *Henry V*, thus fulfilling the promise in the Epilogue to *Henry IV*. That Shakespeare made this promise in the belief that Kempe would be there to play Falstaff, and that, Kempe having left the company and no other Falstaff forthcoming, Shakespeare had to kill off the big fellow. I'm sorry, but I don't believe a word of it. I prefer " Q " 's manly, direct :

Shakespeare could not bring Falstaff upon the stage in *King Henry V*, because he dared not. . . . Henry must not be allowed to meet Falstaff. For Falstaff can kill him with a look. . . . It was Henry who wronged Falstaff and killed his heart ; Falstaff had never a thought of hurting Henry : and therefore, or ever you can present Henry of Agincourt as your *beau idéal* of a warrior king, you must kill Falstaff somehow and get his poor old body behind the arras : for, as Hazlitt said, he is the better man of the two.

Let me put it that J. D. W. is right in the study, and " Q " a hundred times right on the stage.

Aug. 21
Wednesday.
Letter from George Jean Nathan thanking me for *Around Cinemas*, telling me that the drawing of Lillian Gish which I used as frontispiece is by Tilly Losch, and making this highly Nathanish confession : " My interest in the cinema has lapsed since women began to talk."

Aug. 22
Thursday.
Am making one last effort to drive into the heads of *Express* readers that writing is an art. Nobody expects to be a county cricketer, League footballer, ballet dancer, without special aptitude. People recognise that you have to be an engineer before you can put a motor-car together, an architect before you can build a cathedral, an actor before you can play Hamlet. What most people fail to realise is that *you have to be a writer before you can write*. Let me deal with the last three letters in this morning's STOP and GO mail. The first offers a poem entitled *Boyhood*. This begins :

> Of noblest form, a boy's mould,
> His eye so clear and blue,
> His chestnut hair with ev'ry fold,
> Entrances all but few.

A young woman whose ear does not tell her what is wrong with the first line, and whose sense of humour lets her write the fourth line, is not going to be a poetess if she lives to three times the age of Methuselah.

The second letter offers another poem. This is called *Wild Symphony*. It ends :

> But most of all I love to hear
> That lovely voice of you, my dear,
> The way you speak, the way you sing,
> The way you let your laughter ring,
> The way you softly lullaby
> To soothe a pain ; to still a cry.

Will intending poets please realise that liking some young woman has nothing to do with the ability to write a sonnet to her eyebrow ? That it is easier for a poet to write a convincing sonnet to a woman he loathes than for a non-poet to write anything but drivel to a woman he adores.

The author of the third letter is nearer the mark :

After the children are in bed I hammer out, on an antiquated typewriter, articles on How to do This or That. In this way I earn several useful shillings, so naturally I shall continue to sell my quite worthless advice on every possible subject. But at the back of my mind there lives a group of people who only move and talk when I am alone ironing, or darning, or washing up the supper things. Some day I am going to write their story, but it will be the story of ordinary decent folk, living eventful but unspectacular lives. In other words, a novel which will be unutterably dull *unless I happen to possess the all-important talent.*

At last somebody who realises that to write well requires at least as much aptitude and practice as to cut out an appendix, walk a tight-rope, or stand up for ten seconds against Joe Louis ! In other words, writing is a conjuring trick, and the only person who can perform conjuring tricks is a conjurer.

Aug. 23   Letter from my little Irish friend :
Friday.

> 18 *Park View Avenue*
> *Harold's Cross*
> *Dublin*
> *August 21st, 1946*

DEAR JAMES,

My friend Miss Wood has written me of her visit to your flat :

" A little before noon a near-petrified young person crept up the stairs at Queen Alexandra Mansions and rang the bell with trembling hand. There was a short silence, then a discreet fluttering among some long curtains which could be glimpsed through the frosted-glass door. A hurried conference inside, then the door was opened by a quiet, shy, very gentle young man in a dark suit, and wearing an oddly tired, peaceful look. . . . At the end of the dark hall there hovers for an instant a Vision, some Sage of the Lower Ganges, wrapped in many a billowy shirt (none of which covers its dainty ankles), white hair standing straight up, large horn-rimmed spectacles terrifyingly directed towards me. The Vision disappears."

Mr Agate says will the boy please write to him. The boy would be very pleased to spend his nights and days writing to Mr A., if Mr A. ever replied. Indeed, the boy's admiration for Mr A. has been revivified by hearing him broadcast two or three times of late. The boy agrees that no poet living can write as Tennyson did *at his best*. The boy agrees that all modern composers, except Sibelius, can't hold a match to Beethoven, or for that matter poor, dear, unappreciated Haydn. The boy would give all modern music—always with the glorious, soul-ravishing exception of that tremendous genius Sibelius—for Beethoven's Violin Concerto, or, indeed Tschaikowsky's Symphony No. 5. (However much people sneer at T., the fact remains that his melodies are still lovely and infinitely better than anything done by contemporary composers.) The boy would give all books published by intellectuals to-day for one volume of Dickens or Jane. (He likes, however, Kate O'Brien and Elizabeth Bowen, Evelyn Waugh, Graham Greene, Seán O'Faoláin, and one or two others.) The boy still likes Mr A. better than any other critic, despite his lapses into nonsense, his jaundiced eye, his bourgeois complacency, and his rather boring vulgarity.

The boy signs himself Mr Agate's devoted servant,

J. E. JORDAN

Aug. 24 Saturday. I don't suppose there are six people left in England who would be interested in Lysiane Bernhardt's new life of her grandmother. Wherefore I shall keep my interest to myself. Lysiane gives at the end Sarah's contribution to Diderot's famous Paradox :

> On croit généralement dans le public que les comédiens lâchent leurs rôles après dix ou quinze représentations. Je les vis absolument. Sophie Croizette, après la scène d'empoisonnement dans *Le Sphinx*, restait quelques minutes pâle et claquant des dents ; parfois, elle perdait connaissance et cela, pendant les cent représentations. Le tragédien Beauvallet pleurait tous les soirs à chaudes larmes dans la scène de la forêt (*le roi Lear*). Mounet Sully était parfois réellement halluciné dans les fureurs d'Oreste. Morain avait de tels battements de cœur dans le quatrième acte de *La Dame aux Camélias* que souvent il ne pouvait plus parler, et, durant les cent cinquante représéntations de *Fédora*, j'ai cru cent cinquante fois que ma dernière minute était arrivée. Ipanoff, aveuglé par la colère, m'étranglait plus sérieusement que Pierre Berton ne l'eût voulu. Enfin je n'ai jamais joué *Phèdre* sans m'émouvoir ou cracher le sang ; après le quatrième tableau de *Théodora*, dans lequel je tue Marcellus, je suis dans un tel état nerveux que je remonte en sanglotant dans ma loge. Si je ne pleure pas, j'ai une crise nerveuse beaucoup plus désagréable pour ceux qui m'entourent et dangereuse pour les objets.

Well, Sarah wrote that and presumably meant it, though I don't see how she would square it with the fact that often before the last act of *La Dame aux Camélias* she would jump into bed with a ravishing smile, saying, " Allons mourir ! " I fail to see how an actor, having gone pretendedly mad, and feeling it, every night during a run of *King Lear,* could fail to go mad in earnest. I suspect the truth to be that the actor who thinks he feels his part is feeling some 90 per cent. of it, and that it is the 10 per cent. margin which enables him to go on committing suicide, slaying, and being slain. That if it were not for this margin our Romeos would die of grief and our Othellos of remorse, while our Lears would all be put into asylums.

Aug. 25   Always when human imbecility becomes too much for me
Sunday.   I turn to the stories of Villiers de l'Isle-Adam. This afternoon I rang up the Duty Officer at the B.B.C. and demanded that on behalf of the *Radio Times* the announcer of this afternoon's programme should apologise for printing the title of Poulenc's little piece as " Mouvements Perpétuelles " (*sic*). After which I took down the *Contes Cruels* and read *Le Secret de l'Ancienne Musique.* A German work was to be produced at the Paris Opera House ; la France ne saurait prendre sur elle de tronquer, par une exécution défectueuse, la pensée d'un compositeur *à quelque nation qu'il appartienne.* But there figured in the score an instrument known as *le Chapeau chinois,* fallen, alas ! into desuetude. Consternation ! And then Cymbals bethought him of an ancient professor of the forgotten instrument. To seek him out, to climb his nine flights of stairs, to implore his co-operation, was the work of a second. Dans les angles s'ébauchaient de vieux Chapeaux chinois ; çà et là gisaient plusieurs albums dont les titres commandaient l'attention. C'était d'abord : *Un premier amour !* mélodie pour Chapeau chinois seul, suivie de *Variations brillantes sur le Choral de Luther,* concerto pour trois Chapeaux chinois. Puis septuor de Chapeaux chinois (grand unisson) intitulé : *Le Calme.* Puis une œuvre de jeunesse (un peu entachée de romantisme): *Danse nocturne de jeunes Mauresques dans la campagne de Grenade, au plus fort de l'Inquisition* (grand boléro pour Chapeau chinois) ; enfin, l'œuvre capitale du maître : *Le Soir d'un beau jour,* ouverture pour cent cinquante Chapeaux chinois.

Cymbals spoke up on behalf of the National Academy. The old musician bowed his head. " Mon pays avant tout." Il leur tendait ses mains pâles, rompues aux difficultés d'un instrument ingrat. But mark what follows : Le maître allemand, par une jalousie tudesque, s'était complu, avec une âpreté germaine, une malignité rancunière, à hérisser la partie du Chapeau chinois de difficultés presque insur-

montables ! Elles s'y succédaient, pressées ! ingénieuses ! soudaines.
C'était un defi ! Qu'on juge : cette partie ne se composait, exclusive-
ment, que de *silences*. Or, même pour les personnes qui ne sont pas
du métier, qu'y a-t-il de plus difficile à exécuter que le *silence* pour le
Chapeau chinois ? . . . Et c'était un CRESCENDO de silences que
devait exécuter le vieil artiste !

Did the master go down in defeat ? Nenni ! The old player bent
all his energies to his task. Il joua. Sans broncher ! Avec une
lmaîtrise, une sureté, un *brio*, qui frappèrent d'admiration tout
'orchestre. Son exécution, toujours sobre, mais pleine de nuances,
était d'un style si châtié, d'un rendu si pur, que, chose étrange ! il
semblait, par moments, *qu'on l'entendait* ! The dedication of the
story ? " A Monsieur Richard Wagner."

Aug. 26   What do I remember about Marie Bashkirtseff ? I was
Monday.   eleven years old when the Diary was first published, but
              I was alive to the extraordinary stir it made. That
" noble foghorn " Mr Gladstone gave tongue about it. And I wasn't
allowed to read it. The world into which this Russian child was born
was a world in which wasp-waisted women must either sit bolt
upright or recline at full length. It was into this hingeless world,
this museum, that this astonishing little combustion engine was born.
She was bored by her family, and put down the fact in her Diary.
She admired the size of her own hips and put that down also. She
came to Paris and fell violently and hopelessly in love with the Duke
of Hamilton, of whose mistress she publicly proclaimed her envy.
With the politician Cassagnac. With an Italian count. With a
French steeplechase-rider whose neck she wished broken rather than
that he should marry any other woman.

Yes, I have always collected scraps of information about Marie.
She was a *nymphomane de tête*, if there is such an expression. Unless
I'm greatly mistaken her love affairs were all in her head. What
interests me most about her is her colossal egotism—greater than
mine and Napoleon's put together. If God would give her fame
as a painter she would " go to Jerusalem and do a tenth of the
journey on foot." Well, she was a goodish painter. But she realised
that she was not going to live long enough to win immortality by her
brush. What else had she ? Only the Diary, begun at the age of
twelve. And then she started a campaign which makes me boggle.
Boggle because of the extraordinary mixture of splendid audacity
and unbelievable lack of tact. The idea at the back of Marie's mind

was to get some celebrity to publish, edit, or lend his name to her Diary. She invited Dumas *fils* to meet her, and, receiving a reply from the great man saying that novel-reading had gone to her head and advising her to go to bed early, sent him back a snorter : " Sleep well yourself, Monsieur, and continue to be as *bourgeois* in small matters as you are an artist in great." Next she tackled Edmond de Goncourt, who had used her as model for his novel *Chérie*, which has been on my shelf for forty years. This begins with a dinner party given by Chérie, aged nine, to little friends some six and seven years old :

> L'amusant spectacle que la réunion autour de la table de ces petites Parisiennes, au minois futé, aux yeux éveillés de souris, à l'intelligence hâtive de la physionomie, à l'enfance menue, distinguée, rafinée, quintessenciée de l'enfant des capitales et des salons, gracieux petits êtres dont la pâleur intéressante avait été enjolivée par les mères avec tout le goût possible, bouts de femmes déjà montrés en les galants arrangements que la mode fashionable crée pour les petites filles des riches !

To return to Marie and her letter to Goncourt. This begins : " Monsieur, like every one else, I have read *Chérie*, and, between ourselves, it is full of platitudes." Naturally Goncourt did not answer. She wrote to Zola, and ended her letter : " I don't suppose you will answer this : I am told that in actual life you are a complete *bourgeois*." No answer from Zola. But her most formidable attack was made on Maupassant, with whom she exchanged half a dozen letters, all of which are to be read in Dormer Creston's *Fountains of Youth*. But all Marie's efforts were unavailing, Maupassant wittily but firmly declining to meet her.

The concernancy ? Only that this afternoon at the Carlton Cinema in Tottenham Court Road I saw a film entitled *Marie Bashkirtseff*, and described as " freely adapted from passages in the Journal." Half the picture is about Marie having her money stolen by a gang of thieves, and learning to roller-skate. The other half shows her and Maupassant in the throes of mutual passion, meeting surreptitiously in crowded *salons* and by moonlight. How, learning that her time is short, and wishing to spare the dramatist pain, she tells him that she has never loved him, and has merely used him as part of her scheme for winning the Academy's gold medal. Whereupon Maupassant goes and gets the gold medal and presents it to her on her deathbed. And Marie, opening her eyes for the last time, says, " Glory and Fame are nothing so long as I have you ! " How came the authors not to realise that the real woman and her real life are a thousand times more interesting than this tepid twaddle ? Hear Dormer Creston :

> The interior of the Russian church in the Rue Daru was illuminated as if to receive a monarch, and along the streets there slowly drew towards it a funeral procession. Bright autumn sunshine fell on the massed-up wreaths, on the six white horses, on their housings of silver. On the white velvet that covered the coffin itself had been laid one green palm leaf. All this emphasis of a young death, the white horses, their silver trappings, the palm leaf, the folds of white velvet, would have responded exactly to what Marie, with her romantic self-idealisation, would have considered appropriate. In all probability she had herself arranged these details. . . .

When will the makers of films realise that the truth about historical figures—and M. B. is an historical figure—is more exciting than any romantic fiction ? How much better a film of this utterly purposed chit, gloomily, savagely bent on immortality, throwing herself in her short twenty-four years at the heads of everybody likely to help her, unendingly snubbed, *and ending by getting what she wanted* !

Aug. 27   In a letter from the mother of the Arnhem boy :
Tuesday.

> I thought maybe you would be interested to hear that my husband, myself, and little family have just enjoyed a week's holiday at the seaside out of the prize money. It is the first time the kiddies had seen the sea, and only the second holiday my husband and myself have had in our 25 years of married life, so I think my son would be very pleased we had used it so. Also, my husband and myself go to Arnhem with members of 1st Airborne Div. on Sept. 15th. This again would have been out of the question.

Aug. 28   The new film, *London Town*, at the Leicester Square
Wednesday.   Theatre, is an extravaganza put together to hold the best five bits out of Sid Field's music-hall performance —the Cockney, the Musician, the Photographer, the Golfer, and the Man about Town. (Appalling when it's about anything else.) Field is in the great tradition. He cannot put hand, foot, eyebrow, or tongue-tip wrong, is immensely and unendingly funny, and as a great comedian he cannot escape the law which insists that performers in this kind shall be known for something outside their comedy. With Leno it was swell of soul, with Grock it is logic, and with Charlie Chaplin pathos. Field has a quality I have not seen on the stage since Hawtrey, of whom Henry Maxwell wrote :

> Whoever—man, woman, or child—has *pouted* to such effect as Hawtrey ? He would pout to indicate a certain type of displeasure.

Babies are often given to it, but Hawtrey—contriving to look more like a baby than any infant in its cradle—could yet impart something additional, piquant and pertinent ; he could impart to it just that element of pathos which it is the rare achievement of the lovable to command, even when they are being as difficult as only the lovable know how to be.

Sid Field is always a great baby, and never more than when he is being, as he thinks, sophisticated.

P.S. Fame at last ! My waiter at the Café Royal said, " I saw you last night on the News Reel. You was very good." I said, " Where was I very good ? " He said, " At the Classic, Balham ! "

Aug. 29   *The Windmill* having asked me for An Alphabet of
Thursday.   Literary Prejudice, I append an

INTAGLIO

ASYLUM. From the *Broadmoor Chronicle* for June 1946 : " What are our prospects for the cricket season ? There are a number of new players who, if they practise and listen to the good advice from the staff members who will take them in hand down at nets, will prove to be an asset. F. E. and W. G. P. are shaping well."

Suggested advertisement : " Wanted change bowler and fourth at bridge. Cut-throat not objected to."

BATOUALA. Balzac, Berlioz, Bernhardt—everything I have liked best in life has begun with a B, including the part-author of Shakespeare's plays. Nevertheless I choose this book by René Maran, who claimed that it was a " véritable roman nègre." " Une fois qu'il se fut frotté les yeux du revers de la main et mouché des doigts, il se leva en se grattant. Il se gratta sous les aisselles. Il se gratta les cuisses, la tête, les fesses, les bras. Se gratter est un exercise excellent. Il active la circulation du sang. C'est aussi un plaisir et un indice. On n'a qu'à regarder autour de soi. Tous les êtres animés se grattent, au sortir du sommeil. L'exemple est bon à suivre, puisque naturel. Est mal réveillé qui ne se gratte pas. Mais si se gratter est bien, bâiller vaut mieux. C'est une façon de chasser le sommeil par la bouche."

This seems to me to be nearer the real thing than van Vechten's gigolo burying his crimped hair in Harlem's most opulent bosom.
" ' Coty ? ' he queried.
' No. Body,' she lisped."

CORTEZ. " Silent, upon a peak in Darien." But of course. He was stout and out of breath. On the other hand Vasco da

Gama, according to Meyerbeer, was excessively vocal in similar circumstances.

DRAMATIC CRITICISM. Yes, I know most of the show-pieces by the big-wigs. But the lesser wigs have done well too. Here is Allan Monkhouse in the early years of this century :

" Mr Benson's Coriolanus strikes one as a splendid rough sketch. It is immensely spirited, and if he bellows like a bull, it is one of Mr Meredith's

Bulls that walk the pastures with kingly-flashing coats.

His movements tell more than his words, but Mr Benson makes the queer paradox of an imaginative actor who is careless of words."

" Happily *Love's Labour's Lost* has an essential sanity, though its surface is so riotous. The year's probation for the gay young people is an artful corrective to the cloying feast. To the audience unstinting praise may be given. When the play grew very dull and no ingenuities of the actors could save us from what might have been critical moments, there was no impatience, but only the nervous attention of agitated friends. We all breathed freely again when Mr Benson turned a somersault or made some other exhilarating diversion."

" Even in a jocular play we expect the dramatist to steady himself occasionally and say something about the Union Jack or the sanctity of home, and this austerity of art that never trifles with morals or realities, except in the sense that it is all trifling, is almost disturbing to respectable citizens. It is a little bewildering, too, to find that nothing is happening, for nothing of importance does happen, and Importance surely must have been to Wilde a word of purely comic significance."

ERCLES' VEIN. M'yes.

> . . . roasted in wrath and fire,
> And thus o'er-sized with coagulate gore,
> With eyes like carbuncles, the hellish Pyrrhus
> Old grandsire Priam seeks.

I fancy that Hamlet should speak this with good accent and good discretion, but that

> And never did the Cyclops' hammers fall
> On Mars's armour, forged for proof eterne,
> With less remorse than Pyrrhus' bleeding sword
> Now falls on Priam.

should be mouthed out of all reason by First Player, and that Hamlet has this in mind in his remarks about the robustious periwig-pated fellow who insists on tearing a passion to tatters.

FRANCE.   Yes, but what part ?   I choose Arles.

" Arles has no misgivings on the score of pedigree ; her line comes down unbroken.   The historian will tell you that through Arles Hannibal's Numidians marched to the sack of Italy, that within her walls a Roman Emperor had his palace, that during the governorship of Decimus Junius Brutus, a Greek designed and built the exquisite theatre, still to be seen.   He will go on to tell you of the Amphitheatre, of the thickness of its walls, its diameter, its seating capacity.   He will compare you the Coliseum at Rome. He will reconstruct you the Vénus d'Arles, and discuss whether she may not be a reproduction of the lost Aphrodite of Praxiteles. If your historian have imagination he will tell you of the seas of blood that have flowed within the walls of the arena and of horrors that belong more properly to the nightmare pages of a Huysmans than to sober history.   If he have sentimental leanings, he will talk of Petrarch and Laura, Aucassin and Nicolette, and others of the world's famous lovers.   Then will he grow lyrical over the famed Arlésienne beauty, and rhapsodical over the inability of alien blood to debase its coinage.   ' At Marseilles the Phocœans may have planted their arsenals, founded their markets, trained their sailors. But at Arles they loved and bred.   Here was the bosom upon which the weary seafarer reposed, and here paid back to posterity the debt he owed the woman of his choice.' "

Baedeker ?   No, Agate.   First book, written during the First World War.

GAFFES.   The greatest in my experience is George Moore's in *Impressions and Opinions*, the essay on Rimbaud and Laforgue.

" But Verlaine's hour of grace had not yet come, and he sought to dissuade the young disciple from his resolve to abandon the vain glory of art, and consecrate his life to the redemption of his soul. But Rimbaud closed his eyes and ears to allurements and temptations, bade Verlaine farewell, and left Europe to immure himself for ever in a Christian convent on the shores of the Red Sea ; and where it stands on a rocky promontory, he has been seen digging the soil for the grace of God."

The facts ?   Destroyed as many of his manuscripts as he could lay hands on, tramped half over Europe and entered the French Colonial Army, disembarking at Batavia.   Deserted after three weeks.   Spent eighteen years in North-east Africa, trading in incense and ivory, ostrich plumes and coffee.   Achieved a turnover of three million francs a year and made a moderate fortune.   Contracted synovitis during mad gallops among the African hills, neglected it, had a leg amputated, and died at Marseilles on November 10, 1891, denying he had ever been a poet.

Question for moralists : If Verlaine had never met the ugly boy

with the " huge red hands like a washerwoman's " would he have
made a more exquisite thing of " Pensionnaires " in *Parallèlement* ?

> L'une avait quinze ans, l'autre en avait seize ;
> Toutes deux dormaient dans la même chambre.
> C'était par un soir très lourd de septembre :
> Frêles, des yeux bleus, des rougeurs de fraise,
>
> Chacune a quitté, pour se mettre à l'aise,
> La fine chemise au frais parfum d'ambre.
> La plus jeune étend les bras, et se cambre,
> Et sa sœur, les mains sur ses seins, la baise,
>
> Puis tombe à genoux, puis devient farouche
> Et tumultueuse et folle, et sa bouche
> Plonge sous l'or blond, dans les ombres grises ;
>
> Et l'enfant, pendant ce temps-là, recense
> Sur ses doigts mignons des valses promises,
> Et, rose, sourit avec innocence.

HERMANT, Abel. For his brilliant novel in the form of a
play—*La Fameuse Comédienne*. A young man is addressing his
mother :

> LUCIEN. Maman . . . j'en ai assez ! . . . Elles sont toutes après
> moi. Ça m'a paru drôle jusqu'à dix-sept ans. Et j'en ai vingt-
> cinq ! Calcule . . . Tiens, la dernière fois que ça m'a paru drôle,
> c'est quand M. Bellême, pour se venger de don Ramire, s'est fait
> homme à bonnes fortunes et m'a soufflé Bibiche Morgan. Toi, tu
> te moquais qu'il te trompe ; mais, avec la maîtresse de ton fils, tu
> n'as pas avalé ça. Alors, tu as divorcé. Tu ne saurais croire
> comme j'étais fier d'occasionner un divorce . . . surtout le tien . . .
> Mais ces puérilités ne m'amusent plus . . . Je suis dans les tabacs,
> maman ! Ça ne m'embête pas d'être beau . . . Je regretterais
> de me faire horreur . . . Mais je voudrais bien qu'on me f . . . la
> paix . . . Maman . . . je veux me marier . . . en province . . . avec
> une jeune fille . . . qui est folle de moi, naturellement, et moi je
> sens que je l'aimerai un jour. Les parents ont des idées moins
> larges que moi . . . Alors, ils demandent que tu régularises ta
> situation.

To think that this was written before the clever young men of the
modern English theatre had stopped sucking their thumbs.

INQUISITION. It was not long after I had stopped sucking
the Agate thumb that I came across Foxe's *Book of Martyrs* sand-
wiched in the family bookcase between *Don Juan* and *Zimmer-
mann on Solitude*. I was strictly forbidden to read or look at the
pictures, and of course did both. I thought the latter woefully

lacking in imagination. I remember rewriting a nursery rhyme so that it ran

Froggie would a-flogging go.

And I thought I was the world's only flagellant. Which distressed me until, somewhere, somehow, at the age of sixteen I tumbled across a copy of Somebody's *The Rodiad*, ending as far as I remember

Say what you will, when other joys are past
Flog and be flogged—'tis no bad end at last.

J. My two favourite words—*jonquil* and *jadis*. What a title for a novel. *Jonquil and Jadis.*

KAFKA. Am thinking of starting a movement to be called " Kafka Is Balls," with a club of which I propose to make myself Perpetual President. Not on the strength of having read Kafka— indeed, I have never opened him—but because of what the high-brow magazines tell me about him. Am considering a button with the letters P.P.K.I.B.C. Perpetual President Kafka Is Balls Club.

LOVENJOUL. Gosse (blast him for a snob !) once said that every book-lover had a Lovenjoul on his shelves. Meaning that he was annoyed to find his copy wasn't unique. Meaning that he didn't want anybody else to know Albéric Second's piquant skit published in *Le Constitutionnel* in 1852—Balzac died in 1850—in which the characters in the *Comédie* come to life.

" Je me sentis pris d'un vif désir d'examiner de près cette artificieuse blonde qui fut tant aimée par le jeune baron Calyste du Guénic (voir *Béatrix*) et j'eus recours au binocle de M. de Rastignac. Madame de Rochegude, devenue osseuse et filandreuse, maigrie, flétrie, les yeux fermés, avait fleuri ses ruines prématurées par les conceptions les plus ingénieuses de l'article-Paris. Comme le soir mémorable où Calyste, marié à mademoiselle de Grandlieu, la retrouva au théâtre des Variétés, sa chevelure blonde enveloppait sa figure allongée par des flots de boucles où ruisselaient les clartés de la rampe, attirées par le luisant d'une huile parfumée. Son front pâle étincelait ; elle avait mis du rouge dont l'éclat trompait l'œil sur la blancheur fade de son teint refait à l'eau de son. Une écharpe de soie était tortillée autour de son cou, de manière à en diminuer la longueur. Sa taille était un chef-d'œuvre de composition. Ses bras maigres, durcis, paraissaient à peine sous les bouffants à effets calculés de ses larges manches. Elle offrait ce mélange de lueurs et de soieries brillantes, de gaze et de cheveux crêpés, de vivacité, de calme et de mouvement qu'on a nommé le *je ne sais quoi*. Conti fut aussi de ma part l'objet d'un minutieux

446

examen. Conti avait l'air maussade, distrait, ennuyé, il semblait méditer l'éternelle vérité de cet aphorisme profond et sombre comme un gouffre : ' Il en est des femmes abandonnées comme des cigares éteints ; il ne faut ni reprendre les unes ni rallumer les autres.' "

MAGRE, Maurice. Wrote *La Tristesse du Nain Chinois*, the story of a Chinese dwarf who refused to dance for his Western hirers.

> Le fouet tourbillona sur le nain impassible.
> Les mirlitons criaient et claquaient les drapeaux.
> Dans sa face immobile ainsi qu'en une cible
> La patronne planta son épingle à chapeau.
>
> Et le lutteur vint lui donner la bastonnade,
> Et la foire chanta son plaisir, ses amours. . . .
> Toujours le nain voyait parmi le bleu des jades
> Un Bouddha souriant au fond du demi-jour. . . .

N. A miserable letter. Nullity and Negation. No English writers except Nash, Newman, and Newton. No foreign writers except Charles Nodier and that ass Nietzsche. No composers except Nicolai. No painters that I can think of. A world of nincompoopery, neurasthenics, and necrophilism. Even so, the two great characters in history that I should like to have been belong to the " N " category—Nero and Nebuchadnezzar.

O. The sunflower of the alphabet. The usherer-in of some of the handsomest words in the language. Orchidaceous. Orgulous. Orgiastic. Orgasm. O is an organ with all the stops out, where I is a piddling little vowel which makes a noise like a hollyhock in a night breeze.

PARIS. "Et moi, couché dans l'herbe, malade de nostalgie, je crois voir, au bruit du tambour qui s'éloigne, tout mon Paris défiler entre les pins. . . . Ah ! Paris ! . . . Paris ! . . . Toujours, Paris ! " ALPHONSE DAUDET, *Lettres de mon Moulin*.

QUOTATION. My favourite passage in fiction :

"Tiens ! voilà Satin, murmura Fauchery en l'apercevant.
La Faloise le questionna. Oh ! une rouleuse du boulevard, rien du tout. Mais elle était si voyou, qu'on s'amusait à la faire causer. Et le journaliste, haussant la voix :
Que fais-tu donc là, Satin ?
Je m'emmerde, répondit Satin tranquillement, sans bouger.
Les quatre hommes, charmés, se mirent à rire."

ÉMILE ZOLA, *Nana*

RUSKIN.

" There is a mean wonder, as of a child who sees a juggler tossing golden balls ; and this is base, if you will. But do you think that the wonder is ignoble, or the sensation less, with which every human soul is called to watch the golden balls of heaven tossed through the night by the Hand that made them ? There is a mean curiosity, as of a child opening a forbidden door, or a servant prying into her master's business ;—and a noble curiosity, questioning, in the front of danger, the source of the great river beyond the sand,—the place of the great continents beyond the sea ;—a nobler curiosity still, which questions of the source of the River of Life, and of the space of the Continent of Heaven,— things which the angels desire to look into. So the anxiety is ignoble, with which you linger over the course and catastrophe of an idle tale ; but do you think the anxiety is less, or greater, with which you watch, or *ought* to watch, the dealings of fate and destiny with the life of an agonized nation ? Alas ! it is the narrowness, selfishness, minuteness, of your sensation that you have to deplore in England at this day ;—sensation which spends itself in bouquets and speeches : in revellings and junketings ; in sham fights and gay puppet shows, while you can look on and see noble nations murdered, man by man, without an effort or a tear."

Sesame and Lilies

Mighty fine stuff in 1871, 1971, 2071, or any old '71.

———————

STANYHURST'S, ALL NIGHT AT MR. I have never been able to get anybody to read this except my houseboy, who read it once, and Max Beerbohm, who read it twice.

———————

THESE I HAVE LOVED. With acknowledgments to Rupert Brooke for his " comfortable smell of friendly fingers." Stale aroma of Chelsea pensioners. Odour of warm, moist wicket-keeping gloves. New-laid straw in show-yards and the droppings thereon. Stale of horses. Fragrance of old ladies. Garlic-laden waftage of Provençal peasants. The ringside spume of boxers. Flit. The aftermath of asparagus.

———————

UDALL. I remember a professor of drama reading *Ralph Roister Doister* through inch-thick glasses during the intervals of John Gielgud's Old Vic *Lear*. During the play he held a Temple Shakespeare three inches from his nose, and followed the text through the same glasses. He did not see any actor at any time. I know because I sat immediately behind him.

———————

V. Ernest Dowson told Arthur Symons that his favourite line of verse was Poe's

The viol, the violet, and the vine.

W. It is not generally known that in its original form *The Importance of Being Earnest* had four acts. There are four in Teschenberg's German translation. The scene which was cut concerns Algernon and a warrant for his arrest in connection with an unpaid bill of £762 14*s.* 2*d.* for suppers consumed at the Savoy Hotel. There are some admirable lines. " Late supper is the only meal the dear fellow's doctor allows him." I like best the lawyer's " Time presses. We must present ourselves at Holloway Prison before four o'clock ; after that it is difficult to obtain admission. The rules are strict on that point."

X. That I am becoming, or have become, xanthodontous cannot be of interest to anybody. Nor am I likely to contract xenogamy. I admit a certain amount of xenomania.

YANN. This takes me back to Loti, who didn't realise, or didn't want to realise, that the genuine Icelandic fisherman stinks so fearsomely that you can't go within six yards of him.

ZORAÏDE TURC. Frédéric and Deslauriers, having learned to smoke a pipe, went to visit la Turque :

" On appelait ainsi une femme qui se nommait de son vrai nom Zoraïde Turc ; et beaucoup de personnes la croyaient une musulmane, une Turque, ce qui ajoutait à la poésie de son établissement, situé au bord de l'eau, derrière le rempart ; même en plein été, il y avait de l'ombre autour de sa maison, reconnaissable à un bocal de poissons rouges près d'un pot de réséda sur une fenêtre. Des demoiselles, en camisole blanche, avec du fard aux pommettes et de longues boucles d'oreilles, frappaient aux carreaux quand on passait, et, le soir, sur le pas de la porte, chantonnaient doucement d'une voix rauque."

And the story ends :

" ' C'est là ce que nous avons eu de meilleur ! ' dit Frédéric.
' Oui, peut-être bien ? C'est là ce que nous avons eu de meilleur ! ' dit Deslauriers."

FLAUBERT, *L'Éducation Sentimentale*

Aug. 30
Friday.
Am trying a lighter vein of literary criticism :

Pipe Night, by John O'Hara.

Thirty-one American short stories in the Dorothy Parker class. Full of pep and bite, and immensely readable provided you can read them at all. The lingo, I mean.

"So Quinn asked me to join them and I did and this mouse with them named Jean Benedict looks like 10,000 other dames on the line of some B'way show except when she opens her trap she has an accent that is so British even Sir Nevile Chamberlin would not be able to understand her."

I hold this to be ten times better English than James Joyce wrote towards the end of his life, and a hundred and fifty times better than Gertrude Stein wrote at any wrote wrote at wrote wrote wrote period any any at.

Sept. 2   It was a shock to open *The Times* this morning and read
Monday.   that Granville-Barker had died. I never met him. My
            estimate, for what it is worth, is something like this. A
man of near-genius who kept running away from one job to do
another. A, to me, intolerable actor, perhaps because *Man and
Superman* is, to me, an intolerable play, and I did not see him in
anything else. About G.-B. as dramatist I could never quite make
up my mind. Here is a piece of what I wrote about the revival of
The Voysey Inheritance at Sadler's Wells in 1934 :

Mr Granville-Barker obviously wrote this play on the assumption that a chip off the old block is as interesting as the old block
itself. It isn't, and won't be till it becomes an old block in its
turn. That is why nobody has ever really cared whether Edward
Voysey decides to throw up the sponge or carry to a successful
issue his father's malpractices. The first two acts, in which we see
the old buccaneer in full sail, are magnificent. In the third the
interest begins to fall away. In the fourth the play is over and
the talking has begun, until we finally get to the fifth, where the
Voysey family, with all its knees under the dining-room table,
waits for half-past eleven to strike before beginning to discuss the
place of the upper-middle-class in society. . . . At the beginning
of the evening Mr Felix Aylmer was first-class, and in the middle
of presumably the same evening Mr Maurice Evans was very good.
In the small hours Mr O. B. Clarence was capital, and towards
morning several ladies were excellent.

The *Manchester Guardian* says : " He could teach people how to
act." I don't believe this, and reject all evidence in support. Less
than a month ago Cedric Hardwicke said to Jack Priestley and me in
his room at the Savoy, " Nobody can teach anybody to act." I agree.
Nobody can teach anybody to be poet, dramatist, actor, critic. It
comes or it doesn't. Shall, therefore, pass over the producer side of
G.-B. and go on to regret the time he wasted over translating Spanish
and French plays when he might have been getting on with the thing
he will live by—the Prefaces to Shakespeare. The Vedrenne-Barker

Experiment and the subsequent managements, all associated with the intellectual theatre ? Yes, but these have vanished, whereas the Prefaces are tangible, living pieces of writing. And, alas ! only nine of them, and *Macbeth* ignored. Granville-Barker was the English theatre's great hope from 1904 to 1914, when, on the outbreak of war, he went to New York and, says the *M.G.*, " ceased directly to influence the English theatre, in whose development during the early years of the twentieth century he had played so considerable a part." The truth about Granville-Barker, always as I see it, is that there was not enough grindstone in his life.

Sept. 3   Letter from Ernest Helme :
Tuesday.

> *Llangennith*
> *Swansea*
> *September 1st, 1946*

MY DEAR JAMES,

The Garcias would naturally acclaim Jenny Lind, as she was their pupil and owed everything to old Manuel Garcia, who in 1841, after she had made her name in Sweden, ordered complete rest for twelve months, which were devoted to study of correct deep-breathing in an attempt to increase the power of her voice, in which, however, he was unsuccessful. Now Patti never had a lesson in voice production in her life, but studied her enormous répertoire of operatic rôles with her brother-in-law Strakosch. Jenny Lind scored a big success in only one operatic rôle, in Donizetti's Opéra Comique *La Fille du Régiment*, which also, fortunately for her, happened to be Queen Victoria's favourite opera. J. L. was at this time the only artist who sang in German, which was naturally very pleasing to the Prince Consort and therefore to the Queen.

Jenny Lind may, must, have been elated by her enormous success as Marie (*La Fille du Régiment*) and to a lesser degree in Meyerbeer's (a great admirer of her, who introduced her to Berlin) *Robert-le-Diable*, and she was then so ill-advised as to attempt the great dramatic rôles such as Donna Anna (*Don Giovanni*) and Norma, which were associated still with Grisi (the greatest dramatic soprano of all time) ; the consequence was complete failure, and J. L. retired for ever from the operatic stage (which she had only graced in London for two seasons) in 1849 when she sang in *Robert-le-Diable* at Her Majesty's. My grandmother, a fine musician, *abonnée* at the Opera all her life and a first-rate critic, heard her several times, and detested both her singing and acting, always alleging that her voice was thin and wiry and her intonation unreliable, as she was apt to sing sharp at times. My grandfather, who had worshipped at the shrine of Malibran, concurred in this criticism, and he could not tolerate any artist with such a stupid face. J. L., however, was by no means stupid, as she proved in her American tour, when she placed herself in Barnum's hands, who advertised her before she had landed to an extent greater than has ever attended a singer before or since; and she can claim to have originated *réclame*.

My grandmother knew her personally and as Mme Goldschmidt. J. L. had been to our Essex house, where, however, she was not very popular, as, I have been told, she gave herself great airs. I personally have seen her singing in the chorus of the Bach Choir, which her husband directed. J. L. was also astute enough to cloak her failure and end of her extremely short operatic career under the pretext of her religious convictions, which were a valuable asset throughout her career in this country, more especially to the Queen and the then huge and influential Exeter Hall public.

Jenny Lind's private life was *sans reproche*. Patti enjoyed life, and was divorced by the Marquis de Caux (practically she bribed him and allowed him £2000 a year for life to get rid of him), with Nicolini, whom she subsequently married, as co-respondent; there was considerable scandal at the time; the British Public will always interfere in artists' private lives.

J. L. made her name remembered through concert singing, and her career commenced in 1844 in Dresden and, with the exception of a charity concert in Malvern in 1883, ended in, I think, about 1856 after her marriage in Boston in 1852; though she made occasional appearances at the Big Festivals, as at Norwich, when in the St Andrew's Hall in a concert, whilst singing the Prayer in Agathe's Aria from Weber's *Der Freischütz*, she pretended to be so overcome with emotion that she fell on her knees. This vulgar exhibition was put on probably to please the large number of Norfolk Quakers amongst the audience; but she was accorded severe comment by the musicians present, and she did herself considerable harm.

In short. Patti natural and gifted. No musician. Jenny Lind. Studied. Handicapped by nature. A fine musician.

I don't suppose you'll wade through this.

Yours aye,

ERNEST HELME

Sept. 5
Thursday.
Was a whole hour late for Gwen Chenhalls's luncheon party. But Gwen is an understanding hostess and knows that journalists are not human. Found a great lady telling Basil Cameron he ought to think this and that about Beethoven, and Basil saying he ought indeed. Ivor Novello told us how in Bond Street he had met Lady X, almost bent double but as shimmeringly, jinglingly dressed as ever, and wearing a patch over one eye. " On the patch was pinned a bunch of violets." I said,

" So Cleopatra didn't die after all ! " But the sally was lost owing to the irruption of a charming, undulating gazelle, a lovely creature to whom Joey Bagstock must have paid instant court. We drank Constantia, a delicious South African wine, tasting of furniture polish and with a bouquet like Peau d'Espagne. After the other guests had gone Gwen, who is a good violinist, played as much of the Mendelssohn Concerto as I could manage the piano part of. Not a good sentence ? It has been a very good lunch.

Sept. 6
Friday.
Lonsdale's father and son in *But for the Grace of God* had not been on the St James's stage two minutes to-night before I realised that this was the theatre of the 'nineties. I found the first act exciting. Gerard, the son, began his career of villainy in a low key, tentatively. The cur was at the snivelling stage ; biting could come later. Would the cur's father lend him a thousand pounds ? No ? Then let him take what was coming to him, the father ; he, the son, proposed to go ' inside.' Old Dog asked inside where ? " Gaol ! " snapped the boy, impatient at having to explain what a man of the world should take in with his mother's milk. And now came a point which showed the Lonsdale weakness and strength. The father, shrugging his shoulders, said, " Will you be leaving us for long ? " Witty, but on the Wildean level, and not that of a purse-and-family-proud Scotch baronet. Compare that old play of Hankin's in which the elder brother setting up for Parliament forced his father to despatch the younger and prodigal brother to Australia. " I will allow you £250 a year and you may write once a month," said the father. " Make it £300," said Eustace, " and I won't write ! " Bless me, how little we have advanced since 1909— either in persiflage or probability. Nevertheless Lonsdale has a wit of his own, as when he didn't stress the tell-tale little point that the amount the boy had embezzled was *nine hundred* pounds, the odd hundred being his profit. Gerard is the authentic, real-life version of the scapegrace who, in the sentimental drama of the 'seventies and 'eighties, would come back from the outer darkness " in a soft hat and a cloak like Tennyson's with white hair and a moved voice, as a Gold, Silver, or Copper King, the lovable fellow who in exile had let practical wisdom burn with a hard, gem-like flame resulting in a very ecstasy of acquisitiveness. He is often quite ' nice,' and sometimes has a Virgil in his pocket." One credited Gerard with having a Verlaine in his pocket to-night ; the type often has. Michael Gough made an engrossing, Firbankian creature out of Gerard—one felt that

453

he had this laugh, this *ricanement*, in the cradle. Unfortunately at the end of the first act a slight case of blackmail ended in a slight case of murder, and we saw no more of Gerard. And I lost interest in the play.

Sept. 7　　　From this morning's paper :
Saturday.

> The dreaded bolo punch—the short right upward swing aimed below the heart—of Ike Williams, Georgian negro world light-weight champion, paralysed Ronnie James and 40,000 Welsh fans at Ninian Park, Cardiff, to-night. James was knocked out in the ninth round. The crowd was hushed into silence by the murderous punch. Ten days ago I warned James of Ike Williams's murderous bolo—so called because it is delivered with the action that Malayans use when hacking down the parasitic bolo plant with a long knife known as a bolo-knife. Williams saved this wonderful blow until the seventh round, and then swung it with terrifying power and accuracy so that it landed immediately below James's heart.

Going to lunch, I happened to see in the Charing Cross Road a copy of *Cashel Byron's Profession*. The preface to this shows how the young Shaw fell into the first infirmity of noble mind, the proneness to believe that what is non-intellectual must be dull :

> The sport of prizefighting was supposed to have died of its own blackguardism by the second quarter of the century ; but the connoisseur who approaches the subject without moral bias will, I think, agree with me that it must have lived by its blackguardism and died of its intolerable tediousness ; for all prizefighters are not Cashel Byrons, and in barren dreariness and futility no spectacle on earth can contend with that of two exhausted men trying for hours to tire one another out at fisticuffs for the sake of their backers.

Can G. B. S. really have thought that the fight between the Gas-man and Bill Neate was a dull thing ? Can he think to-day that to watch a couple of boloists in action is duller than, say, sitting at a repertory performance of *Back to Methuselah* ?

Sept. 8　　　Letter to George Lyttelton :
Sunday.

> *Queen Alexandra Mansions*
> *Grape Street, W.C.2*
>
> 10 P.M. *Sunday, Sept. 8, 1946*

Dear George Lyttelton,
　　This is a birthday letter—my birthday. In two hours' time I shall be sixty-nine. I grow old, Master Lyttelton, and my temper

454

is not what it was. I spent yesterday in a state of frenzy in comparison with which Lear was a baby banging his spoon. And here is the reason. I had written a goodish review of a book about boxing and singled out this passage :

" ' The Bomber ' is one of the great fighters of all time, and no one can deny that in and out of the ring Joe Louis has done everything to elevate the standard of life among his fellow-countrymen. His behaviour was pathetically summed up by poor, blind Sam Langford, the great negro heavyweight of yesteryear, who, visiting Louis in training, touched his face with his groping hand, and said : ' You've brought credit to your race, Joe boy. You'll beat Conn. It takes a million punches to get a referee's decision, but only one to score a knockout.' Langford, incidentally, sat at the ringside, in a twenty-five-pound seat bought for him by Louis, smelling the resin and listening to the thump of wet leather, and knowing that it was not the erudite men of learning, the lawyers, the doctors, or the writers who brought a new respect for the negro race, but the flailing fists of an illiterate cotton-picker from Alabama."

To which I appended this note :

" A good bit of writing which won't pass the test of examination. All it says is that no white man can stand up to this negro. Good. But can this negro stand up to a gorilla. No. And is the scale we are talking in ascending or descending ? I leave it to the reader."

Will you believe that some fool of a sub-editor cut the last sentence—from "Langford, incidentally" to "Alabama"—*but left the comment* ? I don't mind being cut ; no experienced journalist does. But why not cut to make sense ? Were there not six lines from Coleridge, stuck in to fill up, that I would gladly have dispensed with ? To go back to my opening simile, I am a King Lear sub-edited by Edward Lear. Crown me with flowers ! Dost thou squiny at me ? Sa, sa, sa, sa.

I have a sixth sense which tells me when in the theatre I am going to be bored. For example, I knew beyond any peradventure that I should have fled shrieking from Ronald Duncan's adaptation of Cocteau's *The Eagle has Two Heads*. Wherefore I sent Harold Hobson. And how right I was ! *The Times* talked next morning of " monstrous tirades " and repetitiveness which " becomes a little tiresome." Wilson had his doubts about the play's merits. The *Express* dismissed it as " annoying." Alan Dent wrote that it was obviously not intended to amuse or even perplex the multitude : " It is esoteric, intricate, subtle, intellectual, highly literary blethers." And Hobson writes in to-day's *Sunday Times* : " This is M. Cocteau's idea of an agreeable evening. But not mine, thank you very much. A performance of remarkable stamina by Miss Eileen Herlie, who talks and talks and talks. . . ."

But what about my stamina ? Why should I listen and listen and listen to a speech taking some say twenty-one, and some twenty-seven, minutes? (The famous Récit de Théramène cannot be dragged out to more than eight minutes by the Comédie's slowest actor.) I wouldn't take it from Sarah herself. If the Herlie wants the stamp of my approval she must present herself in a berlie I can sit through. Yes, it is entirely due to my sixth sense that I am not in an asylum.

Look out for my Alphabet in *The Windmill*. Some of it, particularly the letter ' T,' is " un peu shoking," and perhaps a bit more. The point is whether they will take in prose from a non-highbrow the kind of stuff Bloomsbury never stops writing sonnets to.

But enough. In ten minutes I shall have spent sixty-nine years on this planet, and not more than forty-four of them misspent. I promised my mother not to smoke or drink until I was twenty-one. And my father that I would leave sex alone until I was twenty-five. I kept both promises.

Ever,

J. A.

P.S. " The bell then beating one— " Shakespeare's master-stroke. The bell now beating twelve—sixty-nine ghosts file past.

Sept. 9 Sixty-nine. Lyons having asked me to write something
Monday. for the Golden Jubilee of the Troc, I have spent most of the day reconstructing the London of fifty years ago. Here are some bits :

Tennyson and Stevenson had died ; Gladstone and Beardsley were dying. The Maybrick case and the Baccarat scandal were things of the past, Dreyfus was safely on his island, " W. G." in the previous year had scored his hundredth century. In the womb of Time were still the Boer War, the defeat of Fitzsimmons by James J. Jeffries, the fifteen-stone boiler-maker, *The Belle of New York, Florodora, San Toy,* the drama of Shaw and Galsworthy.

So much for past and future. What about the present ? I take down my *Yellow Book*. Here I am ravished by a lady in full evening dress playing a piano in a field. There is no stool, and the musician must needs stand to her instrument. Alas, the Japanese lanterns of Beardsley's day are all out, and the yellow of the old book has faded ! What else happened in 1896 besides the antics of the æsthetes ? The public was greatly incensed by the German Emperor's message to President Kruger respecting the defeat of Dr Jameson. The Queen received congratulations at having reigned longer than any British sovereign. Persimmon won the Derby for the Prince of Wales, who was present. Lord Rosebery resigned the leadership of the Liberal party. Lord Leighton died and received a public funeral at St Paul's. Alfred Austin was appointed Poet Laureate. The *Drummond Castle* was wrecked. Alfred Harmsworth founded the *Daily Mail*. Charles T. Wood-ridge, the trooper in the Royal Horse Guards to whom Wilde dedicated *The Ballad of Reading Gaol*, was executed for the murder of his wife. [This was a real find.] An international peace demonstration in Hyde Park was stopped by a thunderstorm. The year's first-nights included *The Sign of the Cross* (Wilson Barrett), *Cymbeline* (Irving and Ellen Terry), *As You Like It* (George Alexander and Julia Neilson, Aubrey Smith), *Richard III* (Irving and Geneviève Ward), Henry Arthur Jones's *Michael and his Lost Angel* (Forbes-Robertson and Marion Terry), *Magda* (Mrs Patrick Campbell), *Under the Red Robe* (Herbert Waring, Cyril Maude, Holman Clark, Winifred Emery), *Little Eyolf* (Mrs Patrick Campbell, Elizabeth Robins, Florence Farr, Courtenay Thorpe), *The Geisha* (Marie Tempest). The popular songs of the day were " Ta-ra-ra-boom-de-ay " (Lottie Collins), " Twiggy voo, My Boys " (Marie Lloyd), " Two Little Girls in Blue " (Lily Burnand), " Down the Road " and " It's a Great Big Shame " (Gus Elen), " At Trinity Church " (Tom Costello). Thomas Hardy, annoyed at the reception given to *Jude the Obscure*, had packed up novel-writing. George Meredith was revising his works. Harold Frederick published *Illumination*, Flora Annie Steel *On the Face of the Waters*, Kipling *The Seven Seas*. Wells was preparing to follow up *The Time Machine*. W. W. Jacobs was being very, very funny, and Bennett and Conrad were preparing to be very, very serious. Max Beerbohm, an old man of twenty-four, issued his *Works*.

Sept. 10   Letter from Peter Forster, the young man who didn't
Tuesday.   know where Wiltshire is :

Cairo
3/9/46

DEAR MR AGATE,
    What do you think was the first thing to greet me on landing yesterday ? A native, boosting his sales of the *Egyptian Mail*, by yelling " Sheamus Act ! " which weird words turned out to be nothing less than a far-flung version of your name, over an article " Harry—Hero or Cad ? " illustrated by a portrait of " Mr Laurence Olivier," looking like a *jeune premier* of the period 1912 ! " That, Sir, is true fame," said Dr Johnson !
    Egypt is remarkable for three things : (1) the smell, (2) the national determination to keep death *on* the roads, (3) the Pyramids. In that order. I was taken this afternoon to see the Sphinx : a most unnecessary rock, I thought, standing out there in the middle of the desert. And the heat . . . I am melting, Egypt, melting. So much for the land of portentous gongs and Sydney Greenstreet ! But whiskey is as cheap as water, and laundry comes back in a day !
    I expect to move on almost immediately, though where to I have no idea ; I am beginning to think that my destination is the one real mystery of the East !

Yours,
PETER FORSTER

The newest—and most difficult—hat is Le Groux's Mang'betu turban. It's so called because it exactly follows the line of the headdress worn by this Central African tribe.

Daily paper

Sept. 11
Wednesday.
Brian Desmond Hurst turns out to have done an admirable job of work in the Arnhem film, the Press show of which I attended this morning. Very noble and very moving, with the saving grace of some occasional humour. Napoleon or somebody said that an army marches on its stomach. I think that Haig in the First World War and Montgomery in the Second would agree that the British soldier lives by and on his sense of humour. I have no doubt that many a man spent those eight days at Arnhem in a mortal funk ; I doubt whether a single man ceased to see the comic side of discomfort. This in the film ranges from the dry humour of the high-ups to the Rabelaisian lubricity of the low-downs. One of the Arnhem colonels is told by the Germans that if he doesn't evacuate his headquarters the German tanks will blast him out. " Surrender and let your men indicate same by waving white handkerchiefs." " Blimey," says a Tommy, " white 'ankerchers arter six days of this muck ? Wot does 'e take us for—a lot o' bloomin' pansies ? " And again, when a sergeant tumbles into a narrow trench and the occupant says, " I say, Sarge, don't you go taking off your boots in my boodwah. Wot would the neighbours . think ? " The picture confers upon the screen a dignity which one had thought to be the exclusive property of the flesh-and-blood stage. It is enormously helped by Guy Warwick's music. Now and again there are shots of great beauty, as when a snowstorm overtakes the summer sky and the flakes turn out to be parachutes, and the music tinkles as in Cyril Scott's *Rainbow Trout*. I had Devas Jones with me, and he sniffed and blew his nose more than a hard-bitten major should. One small criticism. I remember, when I was R.T.O. at Arles during the First World War, General Plumer coming through with a train-load of men. The train pulled up for ten minutes, and just as I started it off again a Tommy came running and holding his trousers up with both hands. I flagged the train to stop and the General said, " When the Last Trump sounds it will find some British Tommy on the latrines and refusing to budge." There was only one French accent in to-day's film, and they got it wrong. The Last Trump will find some British compositor insisting that a grave accent is an acute.

Sept. 12
Thursday.   The Gentle Art again.   Letter to Hugh Beaumont :

> *Queen Alexandra Mansions*
> *Grape Street, W.C.2*
> *September 12th, 1946*

DEAR BINKY,

I had a telephone message from your secretary asking me to go and see Miss Herlie. Will you bear with me for a few lines ?

I am highly sympathetic about the work being done at the Lyric, ᐧHammersmith ; I put the best of my thought and the utmost space at my disposal into *The Brothers Karamazov, Summer at Nohant,* and *Fear No More.* Whether I was right or wrong in my opinions about these plays isn't the point. I happen to hold that the modern poetic drama is pretentious nonsense. I was not gammoned by *Murder in the Cathedral,* and will not be gammoned by stuff of the *Turn Right for the Crematorium !* order. Work of this kind bores me to a point which at my age I can no longer stand. I get a kind of mental claustrophobia and feel that I shall cause a disturbance. I am utterly unable to sit through a speech which is one thousand words longer than the famous Récit de Théramène and the Inquisitor's jawbation in *St Joan* put together.

Now obviously it would be unfair for me to criticise productions to which I am completely allergic, and that is why I hand them over to Harold Hobson. On the other hand I can quite understand that Miss Herlie may want me to see her performance. It would be mock-modesty for me to pretend that the opinion of the senior critic of the *Sunday Times* carries no weight. Wherefore I make the following suggestion. Why not let me see Miss Herlie in something more seeable than the modern poetic drama ? Why not let me see her as Lady Macbeth, Mrs Alving, Paula Tanqueray ? My best suggestion is that the Council of Four should put on Strindberg's *Dance of Death* for her ; with a little contrivance both parts could go into one evening. The stage setting is nothing, and there are only three and a half characters that matter. Miss Herlie, judging from her performance in *The Trojan Women,* would be superb as Alice, and there would be a lot of kudos for everybody.

Yours sincerely,

JAMES AGATE

Hugh Beaumont, Esq.
H. M. Tennent, Ltd.
Globe Theatre, W.1

The Beaver gave a good party at the Savoy last night prior to his departure for Canada. " Business or pleasure ? " I asked. He said, " I'm going to talk to my old minister about my soul." I said, " You'll have a lot to talk about ! " He said, " James, I'm going to put you in charge of the paper while I'm away. Bully Robertson [managing director] and keep a tight hand on Chris [editor]. As for your own contributions, carry on as usual. The maximum of quotations and the minimum of original matter."

Sept. 13   The *Yorkshire Dalesman* publishes an article by Brother
Friday.   Harry giving an account of the summer holidays spent
             by the Agate family in Appletreewick fifty years ago.
Harry writes :

But there were wet days too, days when outdoor activities had to be restricted. For these days also the five boys provided. *Together they produced a Magazine.* As a family they had many friends, and the boys' father invited these friends in relays to join the family party at Low Hall. While, on these wet days, the elders read or played cards, the boys were busy writing their magazine for parental and guest consumption. No. 1 of this single-copy, hand-written, 16-foolscap-page journal, bearing the somewhat grandiloquent title of the *Craven Times*, appeared on the 13th August 1894. This lone copy has miraculously survived many removals, and, glancing through its pages, one is set to speculating whether modern city-born-and-bred young folk to-day, accustomed to ready-made amusement as they are, ever think of putting forward during a holiday so much effort as was necessitated by this production for the entertainment of parents and friends.

No. 1 of the *Craven Times* had fourteen sections, as follows :

1. Chronicle—a diary and comments on events at Low Hall.
2. English Parliament—a history by C. G. A.
3. Book review, *Dodo*, by J. E. A.
4. Notes on Low Hall cricket.
5. Musicalia, by E. A.
6. Weather diary.
7. Visitors' list—a record of arrivals and departures.
8. Accounts of excursions by wagonette.
9. Engagements.
10. Page of puzzles, by H. B. A.
11. Correspondence.
12. An essay on " Courage," by S. E. A.
13. Batting and bowling.
14. Editor's notes.

Here indeed was no ' gutter ' Press, with its stunts and catch headlines, but an attempt, albeit private and immature, at serious journalism.

This set me hunting, with the result that I found something I thought I had lost—an earlier paper entitled the *Appletreewick Journal*, edited by me (fourteen) and Brother Mycroft (thirteen), from which I quoted extracts in the Introduction to *Ego*. This begins :

Mr Agate, Mrs Agate, Miss Young [my aunt], and nurse [Lizzie Barson, happily still with us] journeyed down to Low Hall on the 8th in not very favourable weather. The ride from Skipton was charming. At the station we were warmly welcomed by our old friends Mr Ramsden and Tom; we came from Skipton in two wagonettes. Mr Ramsden with Mr and Mrs Agate, " Baby " [Brother Harry], Sydney, and nurse leading. The rest of us followed with Tom. It must, however, be remarked that Mr Ramsden's horse was by no means equal to Tom's, for several times Tom's was compelled to wait for them to go on. Mrs Holden was there to meet us, and we once more crossed the threshold of dear old Low Hall.

The " Hours of Regulation at Low Hall " will be found on the drawing-room mantel-shelf, so that anyone may refer to them.

The editors have great pleasure in announcing that the most celebrated Lady Cricketer, Miss Young, during her stay at Low Hall will make several appearances.

Mrs Agate looks for help and comfort from all the boys staying at Low Hall, as she has provided many things for all our comfort and has gone to great trouble about packing, etc. We sincerely hope due attention will be paid to this most important article.

I say nothing about a letter from Brother Edward pleading for revivals of *Semiramide* and *Zampa*, and a sentimental poem by Brother Mycroft, though this isn't bad for thirteen :

> The greenest leaves are sere and yellow laid,
> And barest branches everywhere I see,
> And memories crowd on me that time has made,
> Till death itself feels welcome now to me ! ! !

What I cannot resist is the following. It should be said that C. J. Agate was our father, then getting on for sixty, and that the only available cricket material was his gracious self and his four elder sons, Harry being too young. (My father played with us every day, and went solemnly through the formality of donning pads and gloves. He was a very good underhand bowler, and always kept a perfect length.) We played with a net for wicket-keeper, and as everybody took part all the time that gave us one batsman, one bowler, and three fielders. It fell to me to keep the record of every ball bowled. Here, then, is a page. The date is August 15, 1891 :

CRICKET

C. J. Agate Esq.'s team *v.* J. E. Agate's team. C. J. Agate's team commenced their innings sending S. Agate to the wicket to the bowling of C. G. Agate. In C. G. Agate's first over S. Agate was caught one-handed at cover-point by J. Agate, and E. Agate came in. He hit the bowling very much about, contrary to his usual custom, playing well, and making 14, all singles. He very foolishly ran himself out, just as he was getting set. C. J. Agate then went in. Their hopes were high, and they said

> We should not have done
> Hunting the leather till set of sun.

But it was not to be so. With one of C. G. Agate's balls he was out. He hit the ball ; it rolled toward his wicket. In attempting to stop it he hit his wicket. Their innings closed for 14. J. Agate's side commenced their innings after a short interval. J. Agate made two off the first ball, and one off the second. C. J. Agate's third ball he ran out to drive, missed it, and was bowled. C. G. Agate went in and played very well. At the call of time the score was 22 for 1 wicket, C. G. Agate (not out) 19.

Note the egotism even at that age. J. Agate makes a one-handed catch. J. Agate is not bowled, but runs out to drive and misses !

And here is a contribution by Harry himself :

DIARY OF A SMALL BOY
By H. B. Agate

6. 0. Arise myself.
6.30. Dresst and down if can or sooner.
6.30–7.30. Do nothing.
7. 0. Put strite my box.
7.30. Bref. [breakfast].
8. 0. Finish bref.
8.30. Rest on sofa.   Cork work.
9. 0. Chest [sketch].
10. 0. Go walk.
12.59. Come in and wash my face.
1. 0. Eat my dinner.
2. 0. If dirty wash my hands go out to burnsall go to mister dales buy 1 penny sweets each day.
5. 0. Have my tea.
6. 0. Play.
7.30. Go to bed if allowed to stop up 8.0.

The fact that these journals of sixteen foolscap pages, all of them fair-copied in one hand, came out weekly throughout the five weeks of our summer holidays and were resumed every summer that we spent at Appletreewick argues much for the principle of industry instilled into us by our beloved parents. The journals came to an end with the arrival of a baby sister (May), when Llanfairfechan took the place of Appletreewick, and we were all too busy doting and waiting on her to bother about journalism.

Friendly letter from "Binky" Beaumont removing all
shadow of trouble between us. Making new friends is
a change from losing old ones.

> Those friends thou hast, and their adoption tried,
> Grapple them to thy soul with hoops of steel . . .

is all very well. But suppose the man you thought to be your friend
turns out to be a Houdini ? I have come to the conclusion that there
is no such thing as modern friendship (*a*) between women and (*b*)
between men. Friendship between women is unthinkable ; a new
hat is enough to wreck it. In the Forest of Arden Rosalind made a
fuss of Celia merely in order to have some one to confide in ; woe
betide that little besom if Orlando had fallen for *her* ! A smattering
of the real thing between Diana of the Crossways and Lady Dunstane ?
Nonsense. That friendship existed merely to enable the parties to it
to loll in elegant equipages, hold parasols, and exchange epigrams.
Dickens's Sairey Gamp and Betsy Prig ? Even that partnership
foundered on the rock of Mrs Harris. Not here the true gold of
friendship, the gold as has passed the furnage !

But who can doubt Traddles's affection for David, or Pip's for
Joe Gargery ? Had Sam Weller friendship for Mr Pickwick ? Yes,
but that fathering of the great baby was not without a smack of
amiable contempt. Is it old-fogyish to like to read about East and
Arthur in *Tom Brown's Schooldays* ? I confess to greater pleasure in
Stalky and M'Turk and Beetle. Also Kipling's Soldiers Three—
Mulvaney, Learoyd, Ortheris. Magnificent fellows, though I think
my favourite is the Cockney, whose speech to the recruits I know by
heart : " Don't you think you've come into the H'army to drink
Heno, an' club your comp'ny, an' lie on your cots an' scratch your fat
heads. You can do that at 'ome sellin' matches, which is all you're
fit for, you keb-huntin', penny-toy, bootlace, baggage-tout, 'orse-
'oldin', sandwich-backed soors, you." This is better than Stevenson's
boasted Musketeers. There is another trio of whom I never tire :
Pooter, Cummings, and Gowing. As another in the same field I call
attention to one of the best sentences that was ever diarised : " The
parlour bell is broken, and the front door rings up in the servant's
bedroom, which is ridiculous." A really delightful trio is that of Harry
the Horse, Spanish John, and Little Isadore. The narrator of the
Damon Runyon stories does not know where these three live because
they don't live anywhere in particular. It is they who get Mr Jabez
Tuesday out of his breach-of-promise affair with Miss Amelia Bodkin.
It is they who put the snatch on Bookie Bob. Personally I do not

wish for any part of them. But I can see that they are very good friends, at that. What was there about Boswell that made Johnson, at an advanced age, go walking with him in the Hebrides? What affinity was it that made Hazlitt a lifelong friend of long-winded Coleridge? What bound Dickens to that boring Forster? Or Samuel Butler to that bone-dry Festing Jones? Did they all heed Johnson's " A man, Sir, should keep his friendship in constant repair "? But I grow to an essay and must stop.

Sept. 15
Sunday.
Sent my second contribution to the American *Go* magazine. To be able to write what I really think, unhampered by the susceptibilities of the people one is always running across—this is as good as a visit to the seaside. Here is part of what I am saying :

It needs an Ibsen to point out the evil that genius brings in its train. A Béla Bartók masterpiece—if there is such a thing, which I doubt—at once gives birth to twenty cacophonous scrapings calling themselves violin concertos. Picasso is immediately succeeded by pretentious nincompoops who, unlike the master, couldn't draw if they tried. In the film world a *Citizen Kane* is succeeded by phantasmagoria which would be hissed off the screen if the producer allowed one enough light to see them by. It is the same with the theatre. Let me take it that there is some merit in the dramatic works of T. S. Eliot and Maxwell Anderson. What happens? A number of young men too lazy to do a day's work and too unkempt to be tolerated in any office imagine that they have only to string some pretentious rubbish together, rubbish without action, sense of character, or wit, to achieve a masterpiece of the first order. *The Other Side* (Comedy) was an adaptation by Ronald Millar of Storm Jameson's book. The first act was all about what the French should do with the repentant Nazi, after which the play degenerated into a thriller about a Nazi who was not repentant at all. The first night was graced by the presence of Charles Morgan, looking as though he had taken the entire French genius under his wing . . .

Am off to Paris to-morrow, having been invited by the French Government to attend the Film Festival at Cannes. In view of the hazards of a Continental journey and some films I have recently seen about George M. Cohan, George Gershwin, Cole Porter, and others I think it advisable to bequeath to posterity the outline of any picture which may at some future date be made about me : The son of Henry Irving and Sarah Bernhardt, I was found in a bassinette on the sands at Deauville. Adopted by an English maiden lady of bizarre tastes, who arranged for my education at the Muswell Hill

Academy of Music. At the age of seven appeared at the St James's Hall, giving a rendering of Scriabin's Study for the Left Hand, which was acclaimed by the music critics of the day as second to everybody. The end of the film is tragic. During the second act of *Jam Tarts* I rise in my stall, stutter " In the name of Dame Madge Kendal," expire, and am received into a Technicolor Hereafter by Hazlitt, G. H. Lewes, George Jean Nathan (who has unhappily predeceased me), and the M.-.G.-M. choir of angels.

Sept. 16   Wilfred Rouse comes with me to Paris, and afterwards
Monday.   Cannes, for the Film Festival. Willie is the perfect courier, who realises that a ten-bob tip saves a pound's worth of discomfort. (The secret of foreign travel is to sit still and let somebody else do the running about.) Four hundred and seventy-two francs to the pound. Eightieth birthday of Tristan Bernard, and perfectly remember Coquelin as the Interpreter in *L'Anglais tel qu'on le parle*, who got his job on the strength of three English phrases— 'Ow do you do ? Little Tich, Vataire-closet. Dieppe, some time in the 'nineties. The old play accounts for my sudden outbreak, on seeing the sign " Messieurs," of French *tel que* Terry Rattigan's characters speak it : " Un demi-jiffy. Je vais popper dans ici." Perfect weather, with land and seascape decked out in primary colours as in a travel poster. Am the only person on board with a bowler, which is perhaps the reason the Captain invites us on to the bridge. From here we get a distant glimpse of the *Helena Modjeska,* the American steamer which broke her back on the Goodwin Sands last Thursday, and whose captain committed suicide in a Ramsgate hotel yesterday. The only passenger I recognise is the French boxer that Bruce Woodcock gave a drubbing to the other day. And now nostalgia has me in its grip. Meaning gulps at all the well-remembered things—the fields and trees, the groups of workmen who really work, the carts drawn by three horses abreast, willing slaves on whom no care is lavished, the coquetry of the villas, the magnificence of two châteaux glimpsed for a moment, the silly ornamental gates standing alone and with no walls or palings to keep them in countenance, Amiens, where in 1915 I had a wonderful shave, the mixture of per-emptoriness and ingratiation which characterises the French dining-car attendant, the food which the most unexacting could not mistake for English garbage. Hors-d'œuvres, veal, cream cheese, and grapes. The bill for two, including a bottle of rough Rhône wine, is Frs. 728·20. No taxis, so take an antiquated fiacre drawn by the oldest and

most melancholy horse I have ever set eyes on. Fare to the Hôtel Sainte-Anne Frs. 250, or rather more than ten shillings, whereas a London taxi-driver would have been delighted with, say, four bob. Dinner at the Café de la Paix—onion soup, eggs and bacon, beer, coffee, and brandy—cost Frs. 700. On the whole I think Paris is no dearer than London. What struck me most to-day was the appalling damage left by the Hun at Pont de Briques, the crowded suburban trains with passengers hanging half out of the windows and doors and perching precariously on the running-board, the emptiness of the cafés, the lack of gaiety, the flood-lit Opera. Add the Calais porter who took our luggage, six-foot seven and the strappingest, most Michaelangelesque ruffian I have ever set eyes on. A fist to fell beeves and span the better part of three octaves. Can't understand why some French Lady Wishfort hasn't snapped him up. Balzac's Diane de Maufrigneuse would have hung him at her girdle as a prelude to a ten-page lecture to Nathan on the maternal instinct. Bed at 12.30, very tired after a long day.

Sept. 17
Tuesday.
But I was too tired to sleep, just as this morning I am too tired to do anything except work. Sat up till 3 A.M. reading Montague's *The Right Place.* When, oh, when, will our young highbrows recognise this great master ?

The upshot of C. E. M.'s book is that to the man of full mind the right place is wherever he happens to be. How many right places have I known ? Giggleswick, where I learned self-reliance—not the Manchester Grammar School, where I merely imbibed knowledge. The mill at Nelson where I learned the art of weaving, and not the grimy Manchester office where I sold the disgusting, smelly stuff. The First World War, where I thought I was doing something if it was only bundling hay. And most of all Provence. I can still see those windswept terraces of stunted olive-trees and smell the thyme that grows between the pebbles of the Crau. Have conjured Wilfred to wake me to-morrow as the train nears Avignon. I want to have every sense alert as we pass through Arles.

In the meantime here are to-day's doings, which are precisely nothing. Took a tip from the French and walked about, not with any destination in view, but to and fro, like Lamb's Superannuated Man. Considered buying a dressing-gown in crimson velvet that would have vastly become the Prince Regent. Price Frs. 22,000. Refrained. Took our apéritifs at the Café de la Paix, and got great fun out of the half-hourly motor collisions. Lunch—omelette made of real eggs, liver pâté, salad, and grapes—Frs. 1350. After lunch sat about, sometimes sitting and thinking and sometimes just sitting. Have been in Paris the best part of two days and still not seen a man with my kind of hat. Why is there no Manet to paint my portrait and call it *L'Homme au Bowler* ?

Sept. 18
Wednesday. Nothing like a Government for making a muddle. They told us we were dining on the train, only to find that there was no restaurant car. Fortunately we arrived 1½ hours too soon, which enabled us once more to admire—for Willie concurred—that wonderful room whose bedaubed and bedizened ceiling shouts down on one with Sitwellian magniloquence. Was roused as we entered Avignon by Willie singing *Ah, fuyez, douce image ! !* at the top of his crazy voice. Found Provence just as I remembered it, down to the tethered goats. A trifle melancholy as far as Marseilles. " Que de fois je voudrais venir ici me guérir de Londres et de ses first-nights ! " And then I bethought me of the opening sentence to Montague's book : " You may wonder how it will feel, to find you are old, and able to travel no more." But I am able, and I say to that invalid-chair bogey, " Know thy betters ! " Flattering reception and all well, except that they had put me at the Carlton and Willie at the Martinez. On my inquiring the time of the next train for London this was at once put right. We are both at the Martinez, where the *luxe* is *insolent* without being *écrasant.*

Sept. 19
Thursday. Am writing this with almost nothing on by an open window at eight o'clock of what is obviously going to be a blazing hot day. There is a milk-white Tennysonian sail in the bay and another that is pure turquoise ; the hills on the farther side are beginning to come through the haze. Fortunately we are leaving in four days from now. Another day and I should have lost all interest in books, music, theatre, film ; will-power would be sapped, and I should laze about like everybody else. These Southern Frenchies have the fantastic notion that life is something to be enjoyed ; as an Englishman I am not used to this, and it disconcerts me. For twenty-four hours I have seen nothing but brown bodies ; I don't believe that there is a mind in Cannes or that, if there is, it is functioning. For my part I continue to be aggressively English. I will not wear an open shirt with half-sleeves, or shorts, or sandals. I stick to my collar, tie, and, of course, bowler.

Last night Willie and I tumbled across a *boîte* called the Zanzi-

Bar, or some such name, where the company consisted of the daughter of the house, witty and charming, her nondescript husband, two obvious tarts, an old flower-seller à la Marie Lloyd, an elderly gigolo, an American colonel, and a young man who might have been Yvonne Printemps' brother. Presently a row developed between the flower-seller and the gigolo. But a first-class row with horse, foot, artillery, and hand-grenades. Time and time again the flower-seller made tearful exit through the bead curtains only to come back with a fresh supply of insults, finally flinging the flowers at the head of the gigolo—who had more than held his own—so that some of them lodged in his toupet and he looked like a French King Lear. And all the time the proprietor, an enormously fat man, familiarly called La Poupée, sat behind his counter reading his paper and smoking the stump of a cigarette that never seemed to grow less. About midnight I found myself telling some of my best stories with a command of French slang I did not know I possessed. (I suspect it of being a good deal out of date and Zola-esque.) But it seemed to go down all right, and I haven't enjoyed myself so much since, at the party at the French Embassy, I showed the members of the Comédie Française how Sarah Bernhardt played Phèdre. Got home about two, and Willie came into my room to tell me that I had engaged Yvonne Printemps' brother as secretary at a salary of twenty pounds a week, and that he was coming round this morning to sign the contract! An entirely delightful evening. As I sit here on the fifth storey looking down on the Swedish, American, Belgian, French, English flags, and the pole from which the Russian emblem has been removed, I wonder whether Montague is right in saying that Leeds is just as much the "right place" as Athens if you look at it "with your mind and body decently fit, and your feelers well out and your retina burnished." Somehow or other I don't find Cannes a good advertisement for Colwyn Bay. Even the waiters, and I dare say the scullions, have more charm than our British *jeunes premiers*, and a taxi-driver who failed to keep his appointment with us last night has just telephoned to apologise!

Osbert Sitwell would have been the best writer to describe our experience of this afternoon—a visit to the Villa Sardou, in the Boulevard Carnot at Le Cannet, where Rachel died. The house is strictly closed to the public, and we were only allowed to inspect it on the representations of the Mayor that I have written a book about Rachel. For years I have dreamed of such a visit. The place was untouched. Here was the marble bed with its antique sculptures at the head and the figure of Tragedy at the foot. Here was the *salle-à-manger*, with the decanters and glasses Rachel used. The salon is a very dark, long, narrow room with a ceiling representing the firmament. Exquisite stained-glass windows everywhere. Rachel's piano. The fireplace, in the shape of the trunk of a marble tree whose branches enclose the whole room, still black with smoke. Ceremonial chairs. Statues in every corner. Hearing of our visit, the owner of the house next door, which was formerly part of the Villa, showed us round an extraordinary affair of terraces, balconies, stairs, and towers, from which a hundred years ago there was an uninterrupted view of the sea. A miniature and baroque version of Tower Bridge with a faint suggestion of Mr Wemmick's Castle. It was all extraordinarily impressive, like a last act of Victor Hugo. We were shown round by a remarkable old lady of great age, who said, with finality, " Voici le lit de mort de Rachel. N'y touchez pas ! " No plaque. Nothing to tell the passer-by that here, jealously guarded, are the last links with the world's greatest actress.

Sept. 20 This morning there arrives for me at the hotel a photo-
Friday. graph of Rachel's balcony, kindly sent by M. Marcel
Lenormand, the owner of the other half of the villa. I wonder whether the dying Rachel ever climbed this and said sepulchrally :

> Soleil, je te viens voir pour la dernière fois !

In the emotion yesterday I forgot to note another odd character-istic of the French—the idea that food is meant to be enjoyed. We took our lunch at a tiny restaurant called La Reine Pédauque, in the Rue du Maréchal Joffre. Ten kinds of hors-d'œuvres, deux œufs sur le plat, a mutton chop, French beans, Camembert, fruit, and a bottle of excellent Côtés du Rhône. Bill for the two of us, Frs. 870. Most amusing of all was an Englishwoman of quality who sat alone in the middle of the room, in yellow and with a purple parody of a hat, and looking as though at any moment she might turn into Henry Kendall's Duchess. In the evening a Battle of Flowers, charmingly carried out with a *camion* decorated to look like a Chariot of Victory by Cecil Beaton. Only one really vulgar exhibit—that offered by a film company whose name I don't propose to give. No drunkenness and no rowdyism. Some of the women were astonishingly beautiful, and the dresses were exquisite. After the flowers came the fireworks—a brilliant display which we saw perfectly from the hotel balcony. After that the Official Reception by the Mayor, to which we didn't go, partly because we were too tired and partly because we weren't asked. (Not even a British Government could have so muddled this festival !) Instead Willie and I bought champagne and gave a little party to Yvonne Printemps' brother and his aunt. (Willie has coped with the secretaryship affair.) Oddly enough the young man has a *copain* in Paris who is the grand-nephew of Victorien Sardou, a relative of the Sardou who owned the Villa in Rachel's day. It was to the family of Victorien's brother that the Villa eventually passed. It occurs to me at this point that I have received no letters and not opened a newspaper since I left London. I don't know, or care, which conferences have made peace and which war, which trades are on strike, whether Goering and Co. have been hanged, and whether Joe Louis is still world champion. As I write this the floor-waiter arrives and asks if I would like to see the afternoon paper, which, he says, is of the most surprising interest. I open and read :

> Neville Heath, qui soulève plus d'intérêt et d'émotion parmi les Londoniennes que n'importe quel chanteur de charme ou champion de cricket, est probablement un des fous les plus dangereux qui puissent exister : les deux crimes dont il paraît avoir été l'auteur ont été accomplis d'une façon particulièrement sadique. Tous deux semblaient absolument sans motif.

Later. The Festival is in a complete state of disorganisation. *There are no tickets.* Willie has this afternoon received a letter addressed to " Madame le Recteur Roussy," at the wrong hotel, containing invitations for last night's reception and an aviation meeting to be held after we have left. Six attempts to attend to-day's showing of *Cæsar and Cleopatra* have failed, and *The Times* is sitting in the corner with its head buried in its hands. In the meantime the aircraft carrier *Colossus* has arrived, and a plague of ants has broken out in my bedroom.

Still later. Attended a cocktail party given by the film producers in spite of not having received an invitation. Met the delicious Public Relations Officer, who, like Mrs Erlynne in Wilde's play, explained everything. And we agree that no woman can be expected to cope single-handed with twenty-four different Government Departments.

Sept. 21
Saturday.
Yesterday's opening day at the Film Festival was a fiasco. In the morning *Cæsar and Cleopatra* bored everybody stiff and sent British stock down to zero. The evening's principal film was the Mexican *Les Trois Mousquetaires*,

a travesty of Dumas's story in the Bob Hope manner. In Spanish, without sub-titles, and, as far as we could gather, totally unfunny. After two hours of this, in sweltering heat, the audience began to pour out in hundreds, preferring to stroll about in the open air till it was over. Willie and I went across to La Jetée, a charming café, where, under the lime-trees, we drank some cool beer and listened to an orchestra of eight deal with Liszt's *Les Préludes* and selections from Grieg, Wagner, and Sibelius. We returned an hour later to find the wretched film still going on to an almost empty hall! Some time after midnight they put on the new Hitchcock film, *Notorious*. At a quarter to one this was discontinued and re-started, as they had got the reels in the wrong order. Too much for us, and we left in search of supper, or anyhow a drink. We found this at the Zanzi-Bar, where a furious *bagarre* suddenly started, somebody saying that any Frenchman who allowed himself to submit to Buchenwald was *un lâche*. This was violently resented by two ex-Buchenwalders. Things were beginning to look ugly, when the barman rapped on the counter and said, " M'dames et M'sieurs, j'ai une triste nouvelle à vous annoncer. Raimu est mort ce soir." And at once the quarrel was submerged in the general grief.

This morning I attended a *conférence*, the idea being to set up an International Critics' Circle. On the adoption of the motion that delegates should not give their own personal views of films, but act as mouthpieces for the majority view, I left. Eric Dunstan motored us to lunch at his charming little estate, called Le Moulin de la Mourrachoux, about ten miles from Cannes. I cannot imagine a more lovely little house, situated on the banks of a stream and waterfall. " My nearest neighbour lives a mile and a half away," said Eric. " I have no idea who she is." Here we met Commander Tommy Thompson, personal attendant to Winston Churchill throughout the War, and Tommy Partington, whom somebody described as looking like a tame eagle accustomed to playing poker in church. What we ate and drank I don't remember, but it was exquisite. Everybody in very good form, the best remark being Eric's " I remember Sarah Bernhardt's funeral perfectly. I have never had so long to wait to cross the street." Still no letters and no English papers. But the French sheets are a joy. One of them, after noting the presence of Margaret Lockwood, Schiaparelli, and Duff Cooper, gets out of last night's fiasco with the headline : " Bing Crosby, Fred Astaire, et Erroll Flynn brillent par leur absence."

Sept. 22   Willie burst into my room at 8 A.M. to ask if we would
Sunday.   take to-day's two o'clock 'plane or wait for seats on the
             train some time in October.   Not sorry to leave Cannes,
in spite of its amenities.   The Festival has been the trouble.   To be
bored in Spanish and Russian was enough ; last night they added
Danish, with a film about some serious ass who bumped his head and
imagined he was in love with a drug-addict.   But I finished with all
that twenty years ago when Pirandello's Emperor got his skull kicked
in by a horse.   In the meantime we are sitting at the airport in the
taxi of our very good friend Lucien Gastaud, who has been charming
to us in every way.

Later.   After a wait of three hours we hear from the authorities
that in view of the Aviation Meeting to-day's civil 'planes must be
cancelled.   Whereupon I hear myself say in Lady Bracknell's best
tones, " Wilfred, we have already missed five, if not six, 'planes.
To miss any more might expose us to comment on the runway."
I now know the meaning of Existentialism.   This is to make endless
return to the hotel bedroom one has just vacated.   Can we have the
same rooms ?   Yes, we can.   We must !   That is the essence of Sartre.
How are we to get to Paris to-morrow ?   And will it be to-morrow ?
There is a fifty-fifty chance that the air line will be working again ;
and if not there is talk of a military 'plane.   (Railway accommodation
is out of the question.)   At this point I bitterly regret something I
wrote in an earlier *Ego* : " There is a degree at which exasperation
attains the ecstasy of the saints."   This was to strike twelve before
midnight.   Never have I been so worried.   Time-tables altered, hotels
substituted, letters not delivered—the result is that at the *reprise*
of *Auprès de ma Blonde* at the Michodière, with Yvonne Printemps
and Pierre Fresnay, our two stalls, most ingeniously reserved by a
French friend of mine who dotes on Yvonne, were the only two
unoccupied seats in the house since the beginning of a phenomenal
run !   They have been reserved again for Tuesday.   *But can we get
there ?*   In the meantime we resolve to take things easy, and in
pursuance of this go out to dine at our little restaurant and spend the
rest of the evening listening to the orchestra under the limes dis-
coursing Weber, Bizet, and Debussy, and recovering our tempers.
After all, the property of Governments is to be idiotic.   Does somebody have the pleasing idea that I should spend five days looking
at the French cinema and five looking at the French theatre ?
Excellent !   Is my grateful acceptance conveyed to the Departments
concerned ?   But of course !   Do the Departments correlate their

arrangements ? *That is not what Departments are for !* The result
is that the French Government will have spent a lot of money,
Willie and I will have got rid of £150, and I shall have no material
for any article worth writing.

Midnight. A note has just been sent up praying that we will not
present ourselves at the airport this afternoon, the service having
been suspended by superior orders. Well, I have lived into the Age
of the Atom Bomb. This week I have seen the perfecting of the
Ancient Game of Sixes and Sevens now for the first time reduced to a
science.

Sept. 23   I think that ' taste ' sums up the French character
Monday.   better than any other word. You see it everywhere—in
         their buildings, their table appointments, their manners,
their little attentions. They lay themselves out to charm, and
whether there is anything behind that charm doesn't seem to me to
matter. I am tired of your surly Briton, and am not compensated
by his heart of gold. The wardrobe in my bedroom is faced with
book-bindings in imitation calf splendiferously gilt. Balzac's *Père
Goriot*, George Sand's *La Petite Fadette*, Zola's *Le Rêve*, Loti's *Matelot*,
Flaubert's *Trois Contes*, Mérimée's *Colomba*, Willy's *Chéri*, Gide's
Isabelle. Daudet, Bourget, Stendhal, Pierre Louys. I know that
these are as little real as the books in a stage set. But they do what
they are meant to do—they put French culture in the van of one's
thoughts. One sense, the eye, has been satisfied, and to look farther
is not to know how to live. An exquisitely dressed woman is a woman
exquisitely dressed, whether she is faithful to her husband or not.
The same holds about manners and sincerity. Our little *boîte* has
provided us with more and better manners in one short week than
all London's grill-rooms and restaurants since the beginning of the
year. And then I am not at all sure that people don't get to resemble
their manners. In the meantime if I had to invent a motto for these
Southern Frenchmen, it would be, " Nothing is too small to give
pleasure." Which does not mean that they are not infuriating. No
news to-day about the promised 'plane ; Willie has been pestering
the authorities since nine o'clock, going without lunch. Taxi-avion
has offered us one seat on October 1 and another on October 14 ;
Air France won't answer. Dreyfus was not more firmly fixed on his
island than we are here. I dare hardly leave my room in case of a
message, and somebody has just presented me with a leaflet inscribed
" Taxis-Aëriens. Départs quotidiens de Paris et de Cannes dans

toutes les directions sur simple demande "!!!! Now I seem to remember when I was at school noting two lines in *Julius Cæsar* :

> Of your philosophy you make no use
> If you give place to accidental evils.

Wherefore I take an hour off and go to lunch at La Napoule while Willie sits on the authorities' tails. Heavenly little restaurant (Le Provençal) perched on the edge of the sea. Sun and glorious breeze. Œufs sur le plat, rougets, gigot, and a bottle of Châteauneuf du Pape. (Frs. 2058.25.) The chauffeur tells me all about his wife and little boy—for whose baby neck I promise a chain in the French manner—chatting the while in his soft *accent du Midi* of Martigues, Stes-Maries de la Mer, Istres, Fos-sur-Mer, Saint-Rémy, and lots of places that I have " loved long since and lost awhile."

Sept. 24 Voluntary lotus-eating, yes. Compulsory ditto, no.
Tuesday. Meaning that even the black market in transport has failed us. Everybody bribable has been approached without success ; even my best cigars have gone and nothing happens. I 'gin to be a-weary of the Provençal sun, of these ubiquitous red roofs and blue shutters, of all this charm that gets nothing done. Something of the Southern laziness has crept into my bones, or I should now be writing an essay on A Too, Too Distant Prospect of the Odeon Cinema. After all, what does it matter whether I get back this month, next month, next year ? And now I am at the end of my tether. There is nothing to do, and all day to do it in. I shall go and sit on the beach, always with my bowler, and pretend I like looking at the pale blue inanity of the sea, at the stomachs of wealthy *rentiers* and the *omoplates* of their womenfolk. That I find surf-riding, or whatever it is called, sensible. That I am not sick of piano-accordions. That my heart leaps up when I behold such signs as Liberty Plage, Les Dauphins, Waikiki, Les Flots Bleus. And there I shall sit until the Powers that Be have returned from that Festival Trip to Nice and Juan-les-Pins for which we shall doubtless receive the official invitation to-morrow morning. *En attendant* have wired my friend, asking him to make our excuses to the Théâtre de la Michodière.

Since writing the last sentence offers of transport have been pouring in. The Festival Authorities will fly us to Paris to-morrow if we pay a *supplément* of 5000 francs for two, the head-porter at the hotel offers two seats on a 'plane at 6000 francs each, while an enterprising firm at Nice offers to take us and any third person for an inclusive fee of 56,000 francs. We have accepted the Festival offer. Here ends my first and last experience of foreign travel at the expense of foreign Governments. In future I shall pay my own fare and hotel bills, with Boulogne as the butt and sea-mark of my utmost sail.

Sept. 25
Wednesday.
Merde! The arrangements yesterday morning were clear, definite, and precise. I took them down myself and repeated them twice. We were to present ourselves at the aerodrome at Mandelieu, Cannes, at 2.30 P.M. to-day, Willie to call on the Festival Transport Director at 9 A.M. with the cash. Good. We spent yesterday lounging and idling with a clear conscience, and in the evening threw a little party to Tommy Linden, the dancer, and one or two other London friends who had turned up. And went to bed with quiet minds. But this was to reckon without our hosts. The Transport Director, having gone over to Nice, and learned that the director of a travel agency there has two seats on a 'plane leaving at eight o'clock this morning, *books them and cancels the seats already arranged for this afternoon.* His telephonic message to this effect is taken down by a clerk and casually added to the papers on my dressing-table, where I find it when I wake this morning an hour after the 'plane has gone. Our cancelled seats have, of course, been snapped up.

So back to the treadmill again, since a beach is a treadmill to him who has not learned to idle. I am a poor nature-lover. I regard a field as a flat space on which to show off the paces of a horse, and a moor as something over which to drive a little white ball. I should not quarrel with the man who had no use for mountains apart from scrambling up and down them, or for streams except as they may be whipped for trout. Woods? I know of nothing one can do with a wood except picnic in it. What, then, am I expected to do with a beach? Comb it? I sat for two hours this morning burying my toes in sand and wriggling them, after which I paddled! Later, Willie and Tommy hired an odd contraption which is rowed by the feet, leaving me to read the Heath murder case in French. Turning to another page of the *Nice-Matin*, I find a photograph of Salford, my native town, showing a flooded street, and two lorry-drivers up to their waists in water. Would I were with them!

Sept. 26
Thursday.
To drink champagne in the pink and gold heat, in a décor by Emile Littler, ministered to by olive-skinned ingratiation is pleasant but demoralising. I cannot read, and no longer want to write. There is nothing I feel impelled

475

to do, and I hate it. I have never been lazy before in all my life. How right the fellow in Kingsley's book was to shoot the English sailors who insisted on remaining behind with their native concubines ! To put on a sozzled elegance at midday and spend a hoggish afternoon in an armchair and a darkened room—this cannot be right. *En attendant* I have made some concessions. I no longer wear a collar, but a scarf, though the bowler perches *toujours*, giving the impression of an elderly Sid Field astray in France. " Slasher Guitry " is Tommy Linden's name for me down here.

Sept. 27   Our last day, thank Heaven ! Why my disgusting doctor
Friday.   ever allowed me near this stoke-hole I can't understand ;
he knows that Torquay kills me. I loathe the heat, and will make no sartorial compromise. I will *not* wear sandals, even if the alternative is sun-stroke ! I *will* wear the proper complement of clothes. My light suit, which is as far as I will go, is now so besweated and begrimed that I look like Charles Laughton in some story of Otaheite. For me better a winter of fogs in Holborn than a week of sunshine here. My one satisfaction is that I have managed to steer clear of the film-stars ; I have enough with the silly stuff they babble on the screen without wanting to hear what they invent for themselves. Anyhow, this is our last day. Unless . . .

There is a wonderful medieval story by Villiers de l'Isle-Adam called *La Torture par l'Espérance*. In this a wretched man, imprisoned for heresy, is allowed to escape. He passes through door after door, and just as he is about to draw the breath of freedom he finds himself in the arms of the Grand Inquisitor murmuring dreadful consolation about the love of the Church and the garnering of the poor wretch's soul. I hope fervently that something of the sort is not going to happen to us.

Willie began to-day by throwing a morning party, which, since his wit and Dante-like mask have made him a great success here, overflowed into my room. However, I managed to clear them all out soon after eleven, when I sallied forth to buy all those little things one is expected to bring back from abroad. Then once more that impossible beach, which, however, has taught me one thing— why the Buddhist contemplates his navel. By the greatest good luck I had slipped Vol. II of my big Hazlitt into my luggage, and so whiled away the time reading Thomas Holcroft's admirable *Diary* begun in June 1798 and kept up till March 1799. Wonderful stuff

and, I suppose, as dead as mutton. It gives me a thrill to read
" After dinner, sat half an hour at Opie's. G. Dyer there." The
friend of Lamb cropping up in a diary preserved by Hazlitt ! And
again :

> Finished Boswell's *Life of Johnson* : the author still continuing
> a pompous egotist, servile and selfish and cunning. . . . As a piece
> of biography, it is a vile performance ; but as a collection of
> materials, it is a mine.

And what about this ?

> Went to Debrett's. Met B—— and Parry. Saw Emery and
> Mrs Mills in second and third acts of *The Road to Ruin*. Both have
> merit. Emery the most. Second illumination night for Nelson's
> victory. Passed through the mean streets leading to the Seven
> Dials. The poor did not illuminate. I was in a coach, being too
> weak to walk.

And last :

> Was in some danger of being run over by B—— D——, driving
> a kept woman furiously in a curricle.

La Torture par l'Espérance . . . Willie, returning at lunch-time,
brings the horrific news that our departure is postponed till Sunday.
The paper arriving at the same moment announces that Stromboli is
in action for the first time in forty-five years. Good ! It is time
something burst.

Was sitting at the Café de la Jetée to-night listening to the music,
when the pianist announced a piece I have not heard played for
sixty years and more—Weber's *Rondo Brillant*. This was part of my
mother's repertoire, the notes of which, when I was a kid, used to
come floating up to me in my bedroom at the top of the house together
with the aroma of my father's cigar. Always the same programme.
The " Moonlight Sonata," Chopin's *Fantaisie-Impromptu*, this *Rondo*,
Thalberg's Arrangement of *La Sonnambula*. When my aunt took
my mother's place the pieces were Beethoven's Funeral March
Sonata, Schumann's *Arabeske*, two of the Impromptus of Schubert,
two waltzes of Chopin, and Pauer's Arrangement of *Norma*. I have
never heard any of those pieces better played in my entire life. I
will go further : I never heard them so well played. They were not
taught for nothing in Heidelberg, by Heinefetter, on a piano that had
belonged to Chopin. I could teach them, with one finger, to most of
to-day's performers . . .

Sept. 28   " A blank, my lord."
Saturday.

Sept. 29   Paris. The drive to Nice was lovely, and the air trip
Sunday.   bearable, once I had got over my initial *frousse*. But
              there's many a slip between French cup and lip. *The
'plane had no licence to proceed farther than Paris !* So here we are
dumped in a little *hôtel* in the Rue Caumartin wondering what we
shall do, since our money is all gone except for what remains after
' liquidating ' my dress clothes and half of Willie's wardrobe.

Sept. 30   Still Paris. This is the ninth day of our attempt to get
Monday.   home. It is midday, and the representative of the air
              company which took our money for the complete journey
to London and then dumped us here has not yet returned from his
week-end. I have been sitting in the doorway of this hotel since eight
o'clock this morning watching the coal-man and what I call the Jean
Gabinerie of the French streets. As it is Monday no shops in this
maddening place are open ; one cannot get either a shave or a newspaper. At the moment I am watching an elderly Frenchman of
distinguished appearance pick up ends of cigarettes and stow them
away in what appears to be a silver box.

   Am I going, or have I gone, mad ? Twice seats have been reserved
for us at the Théâtre de la Michodière for the *reprise* of *Auprès de
ma Blonde.* The little paper called *Paris-presse* has just arrived, and
there is no mention of the revival *at any theatre* ! What is being
played at the Michodière is something announced as *Ars. et V.
dentelles.* At this point Eric Portman drives up in a car, says I never
looked saner, and what about a glass of champagne ? I thank him
kindly, and accept on the strict understanding that I don't offer him
one in return, Willie meanly declining to part with his wrist-watch,
and me determined to hang on to my cuff-links as long as possible.

   Later. Have just run into Harold Nicolson. Also very kind,
and makes me feel less like an orphan of the storm. And now Willie
arrives with the news that the air-company representative has
returned from his week-end, has created hell all round, and ordered
a 'plane from London which is to take us home to-morrow morning.
I shan't believe it till the wheels are off the ground. Propose, if we
can afford it, going to see Louis Jouvet in something or other at the
Athénée. Stroll across to ask price of cheapest seats and find the
melancholy word " Relâche." It is, of course, still Monday.

Oct. 1   Whether we leave to-day is still uncertain. We were
Tuesday. promised two seats on a big Pan-African liner leaving at
            noon to-day. The tickets would be at our *hôtel* in the
course of yesterday evening. Directors-in-chief swore this on the
heads of their infants. *No tickets arrived.* But then I didn't really
expect them to. The air-liner ? I don't suppose that has arrived
either. I have one piece of consolation. Even in this nightmare
country it can't be Monday again for another week.

10.0. News that the air-liner has arrived.

10.15. Tickets to hand.

10.30. The taxi appears on time, and while it loads I spend our
last remaining francs on a leather belt for the adorable and inde-
fatigable Cynthia, who types this.

11.30. We make Le Bourget after a hair-raising drive in which
157 pedestrians nearly lose their lives.

12.0. Willie produces a thousand francs I didn't know he had,
which means ham sandwiches and a bottle of champagne.

12.40. We're off, and the fever called waiting is ended at last.

1.15. " The wrinkled sea beneath him crawls."

1.50. Croydon. The first words I see breathe the spirit of
England, Home, Beauty, and Dr Johnson. They are " Barclay
Perkins, Ltd."

Oct. 2   Found this letter from George Lyttelton awaiting me :
Wednesday.

> *Finndale House*
> *Grundisburgh*
> *Suffolk*
> *September* 15, 1946

Dear James Agate,

I was delighted to hear from you again and to see that the
steady slide of civilisation into the abyss has in no way dimmed
" the fire that in your heart resides." (What a poor verb that is !)
I hope you had a good birthday. I would have sent you a present,
but I have a notion that unless something original turns up you
have no great taste for such. I sent you a book once, and it took
you some weeks to forgive me ! I cannot step into your brother
Edward's shoes, but it might give you a moment's pleasure to know
that in East Bergholt church there is a small memorial to one
John Mattinson, who in the eighteenth century was " for eleven
years a beloved schoolmaster in this parish, but was then unfortunately shott." And then, as Carlyle says, " impenetrable
Time-Curtains rush down," and no one will ever know what lay
behind that tantalising adverb.

How you must suffer under sub-editors—as under printers ! I
suppose they are always in a hurry. Once in an iron-hard summer
(were there ever such things ?) I wrote an account of a cricket

match and mentioned that the wicket took many of the batsmen by surprise. The sub-editor gave me the heading: " A sticky wicket at Lord's." There hadn't been a drop of rain for weeks. And now in one of the reputedly driest corners of England it rains at least every other day, and has done since June. We are all very harvest-minded these days, and do a lot of head-shaking over laid barley, etc. The silver lining to my personal cloud is that all the rain has made my garden a lovesome thing, God wot; which, I am sure you agree with me, is the most nauseating line in English poetry. In fact, I believe you added ' Godwottery ' to the language, didn't you? Why wasn't my old colleague of Clifton fortunately shott before writing it, and what *was* " Q " thinking of when he let it into the *Oxford Book*? By the way, I have to set a paper shortly on *Lear*, and I want some really original question. I am sure you could think of several, but am *not* sure they would be printable! Hazlitt doesn't help. Surely a good deal of his *Characters of S.'s Plays* is surprisingly commonplace. Where do you find the extremely subtle and pointed remarks of his that you quote? " The concluding events are sad, painfully sad, but their pathos is extreme," stirs neither heart nor mind, about *Lear*. Perhaps Miss Walker had been particularly standoffish that day. Are you quite fair in calling her a *slut*, as you do in *Ego* 6? Wasn't she rather flattered and frightened and very cold and made of rather cheap material? Hazlitt, unshaved, and looking, in a rage, " like one of M. Angelo's devils," would be too much for most landladies' daughters. I have just been reading in (no one could read through) *Born under Saturn*, by Miss Maclean. I expect you know it. Isn't it much too long and every episode overhandled? Some women write so *portentously*. That Keswick episode is led up to as if it was an exploit of some super-Jack-the-Ripper.

That selection of Fry's is very interesting. Ranji is always to him what Sarah B. is to you. But I always wonder on what grounds Hobbs is not put right at the top. He was a superb artist, could score at any pace on either side of any wicket against any bowling; he had the best average in every series of Test Matches he played in after 1909 except two, and then his average was 63 and 50. What more could anyone do or has anyone done? But the fact must be faced that C. B. F. knows more about the art of batting than I do. Do you know him well? He must be great fun.

This was all written yesterday, and this morning I opened *Ego* 6 in bed, and at once came on what you say of *Born under Saturn*. I ought to have known that you had read every word of it. How on earth could Hazlitt have said on his deathbed, " Well, I have had a happy life "? I suppose the hypersensitive have many compensations. They can forget debts, unpopularity, nagging wives, dyspepsia, and even sub-editors the moment that stellar and undiminishable something which is greatness comes their way.

This is true of you too, though you have more skins than H. Is your face ever wrenched and twisted and unrecognisable from rage ? Have you ever seen the Ivy emptying before your eyes ?

I must stop. Don't forget that on Wednesday you must drink twenty-seven memorial cups of tea. It is a grim thought that the other Bolt Court luxuries—veal pie and rice pudding—are in 1946 unprocurable.

Yours ever,
GEORGE LYTTELTON

Oct. 3
Thursday.

Sat next to Eddie Marsh at to-night's revival of *Our Betters*. Eddie now looks like some serene baby ; his eyebrows have lost their truculence, and he has that look—Plum Warner has it too—which I suspect comes to good men when they grow old. (I see no trace of it in the mirror when I shave !) Went into Willie Maugham's box in the second interval, and told him his play stood up perfectly to my recollection of it. He seemed pleased. Whether it will stand up to our young playgoers' expectations is another matter. The old piece, for all its wit, was a castigation, and who castigates what to-day ? In Maugham's theatre social enormity still existed and carried its penalties; it still exists, but the modern name for it is " rather fun," while non-transgressors are " drears." I remember that at the first performance the audience was almost as much shocked as the young girl at the goings on in the Grayston summer-house ; the young people of to-day think that goings on are what summer-houses are for. Cecil Beaton's scenery, as usual, reminded me of Pinero's French governess—" overgowned and over-hatted." The acting goodish, but not *right*. Turning up my notice of twenty-three years ago, I find :

The play stands or falls by the two women. As Lady George Grayston, Miss Margaret Bannerman is quite ravishingly good, continually calling to mind Woodley's remark in the Henry James story : " Here comes a great celebrity—Lady Beatrice Bellevue. She's awfully fast ; see what little steps she takes." Miss Bannerman has acquired a wonderful carriage of the head—half the drawings by Charles Dana Gibson, so popular a few years ago, and half Herkomer's idea of the *maintien* of great ladies. She exhibits a very perfect sense of well-bred comedy, and makes not the smallest concession to any kind of *bourgeois* decency. There is so much sparkle about her performance that whenever she appears it is as though the lights in the theatre have suddenly gone up. Constance Collier, as her *vis-à-vis*, was richly comic. She trailed behind her clouds of the pork-packing business, yet wore her clothes and her manners with an air. She was, you felt, vulgar only of

481

soul. Her archness, her fatuousness, the ridiculousness of the Duchess's passionate forties was a joy.

Dorothy Dickson to-night had none of that quality of pure stone which Margaret Bannerman achieved, and got no nearer to it than angelica, that pretty Christmas sweetmeat. Her famous curtain line in the second act—" You damned fool, I told you it was too risky ! " —fell quite flat. Nuna Davey did well, but the part needs Constance Collier's contralto preposterousness, rich, snuffling, and absurd, and there just aren't two Constance Colliers. Some little time ago I proposed a revival of this play to Coral Browne on condition that she could get Alfred Drayton for his old part of the befooled millionaire. George Woodbridge couldn't have done better, and he delivered the famous " Slut ! " with tremendous effect. But I longed for Drayton's bald cranium, and the way it used to glow first with doting and then with fury. But, again, there aren't two Draytons.

Oct. 4
Friday.

I shall be in trouble with Hamish Hamilton to-morrow when he reads my review of Bemelmans' *The Blue Danube*. Bemelmans is said to be a great wit. The *New Statesman* likens him to the Marx Brothers. The *Listener* is reminded of Tchehov. Jack Priestley finds him " engrossing and convincing." Ralph Straus holds him to be " Southwindish." *Sphere* and *Tatler* fall over each other in admiration, one finding the brilliance of O. Henry, while the other talks of " poetic majesty." My own view of Bemelmans' latest book is that it is humourless, jokeless, unwitty, and unfunny. On the other hand, the author's drawings are pure genius, and I shall recommend *D.E.* readers to retain these and throw away the letterpress.

Oct. 5
Saturday.

The Trocadero celebrations were charmingly carried out. Owing to illness, professional engagements, and jewel robberies my party dwindled considerably—from twenty guests to four. Let me say that the Countess of Dudley, Vesta Tilley, Bea Lillie, Hermione Gingold, Harry Kendall, George Robey and Charlie Cochran with their missuses, George Graves, Ivor Novello, Jack Hulbert and Cicely Courtneidge, Dorothy Ward, Noel Coward, and Gladys Calthrop " brillaient par leur absence." However, we managed to be gay, " we " being Dorothy Hyson, so pretty that one could eat her, Gwen Chenhalls in her best Molyneux, Michael Shepley, and Wally Crisham. Lovely food and lots of champagne—I hold three bottles among five persons to be ' lots.' The talk turning on titles and honours, I told them something George Mair once said : " People like us feel we can get the O.M. any old time. What you and I want, James, is a knighthood ! "

Oct. 6   Letter to George Lyttelton :
Sunday.

Queen Alexandra Mansions
Grape Street, W.C.2
October 6, 1946

DEAR GEORGE LYTTELTON,
    No, I haven't any good poser about *Lear*. Unless it is : Mention in the whole of dramatic literature a greater gumph than Cordelia. *Answer* : There isn't one. By the way, do you know the test for a great Lear ? It is this. Do you instantly recognise who it is that enters " fantastically dressed with wild flowers " ? We have not seen Lear since the " anatomize Regah " scene in the hovel (Act III, Sc. 6), and here we are (Act IV, Sc. 6) on the cliffs at Dover. In the interval we have had the putting out of Gloucester's eyes, the Grand Guignolism of which has for the moment taken me out of Lear's world so that I have to switch my mind back. And I am conscious of the switching ; it takes me at least the tenth part of a second before I recognise the strange old gentleman now coming on the stage. I have never yet seen a Lear who bridged the gap to perfection, making it seem that there has been no gap. Similarly all Macbeths have to begin again after the scene in England and Macduff's " All my pretty ones ? " Shakespeare doesn't make this mistake in *Hamlet* ; nobody has ever had to ask himself who the gentle figure is entering to the clowns in the graveyard.
    You ask me where in Hazlitt I find my good things. No, *not* in the *Characters*, which I find enormously overrated. The great mine is *A View of the English Stage*. But there is a lesser mine entitled *Essays on the Acted Drama in London*. The *View* runs from January 1814 to June 1817, beginning with the famous discovery of Kean and ending with the retirement of Kemble. The *Essays* are ten in number, one for each month in the year 1820. October is missing, and the November number, being by another hand, is not given. (All of this is to be found in Vol. VIII of Dent's complete edition.) Here is a bit out of the essay for June :

    " The passion in Othello pours along, so to speak, like a river, torments itself in restless eddies, or is hurled from its dizzy height, like a sounding cataract. That in Lear is more like a sea, swelling, chafing, raging, without bound, without hope, without beacon, or anchor. Torn from the hold of his affections and fixed purposes, he floats a mighty wreck in the wide world of sorrows. Othello's causes of complaint are more distinct and pointed, and he has a desperate, a maddening remedy for them in his revenge. But Lear's injuries are without provocation, and admit of no alleviation or atonement. They are strange, bewildering, overwhelming : they wrench asunder, and stun the whole frame : they ' accumulate horrors on horror's head,' and yet leave the mind impotent of resources, cut off, proscribed, anathematised from the common hope of good to itself, or ill to others,—amazed at its own situation, but unable to avert it, scarce daring to look at, or to weep over it. The action of the mind, however, under this load of disabling circumstances, is brought out in the play in the most masterly and triumphant manner : it staggers under them, but it does not yield. The character is cemented of human strength and human weaknesses (the firmer for the mixture) :—abandoned of fortune, of nature, of reason, and without any energy of purpose, or power of action left,—with the grounds of all hope and comfort failing under it,—but sustained, reared to a majestic height out of the yawning abyss, by the force of the affections, the imagination, and the cords of the human heart—it stands a proud monument, in the gap of nature, over barbarous cruelty and filial ingratitude."

The *Dramatic Essays* are all too few for me. The last page but one of the last essay contains my favourite bit in all W. H.

" Macready has talents and a magnificent voice, but he is, I fear, too improving an actor to be a man of genius. That little ill-looking vagabond Kean never improved in any thing. In some things he could not, and in others he would not."

Which shows what an ass Carlyle was with his stuff about genius and " transcendent capacity of taking trouble." Transcendent tosh ! I hope all this has not been too heavy going for you. Let me lighten it. Have you ever had dealings with a *conversational* dentist ? One who says, " Did you have fine [pyrotechnics with forceps] weather in the South of France ? "

Ever,

JAMES AGATE

Oct. 7   Letter to Kenneth P. Tynan, who asks me to explain to
Monday.   *Cherwell,* of which he is the Editor, why I detested
          Oxford :

Queen Alexandra Mansions
*Grape Street, W.C.*2

October 7, 1946

DEAR K. P. T.,

My E.P.T., plus my Lancashire upbringing, prevents me from doing owt for nowt. Besides, I didn't detest Oxford. I was prepared to adore it very much, as Jude was prepared to adore Christminster. (Was it ?) But I was too obscure for that city, which ignored me. For which I have not forgiven it, and shall not till the day it offers me that honorary degree. And then we'll see whether he snubs best who snubs last.

Ever,

J. A.

Oct. 8   Spent the morning writing an article on Principal Boys.
Tuesday.   The first principal boy I ever saw was Harriet Vernon. She wore black tights and had the air of a battleship. The date must have been round about the middle 'eighties, and I remember the low comedian in the pantomime turning a statue of Mr Gladstone round and round. Harriet said, " You can turn him round as often as you like, but you'll never make him Dizzy." Maggie Duggan was a very pretty woman. Pretty in the Victorian, ladylike sense. She was not common, or pert, or smart, and she had the one thing that the Wests, Grables, Bacalls, and all the modern breed of husky hyenas would give their larynxes to have—charm. Maggie belonged to the era of Mrs Langtry. She brought on to the stage an atmosphere of guilty splendour which included heirs apparent, racehorses, and bottled stout. The last of the great Principal Boys was Queenie Leighton. Queenie's best song was " The Automobile Honeymoon," with words and music by Harry B. Norris. And here is the refrain :

> Wedding bells with their ding, dong, dinging,
> Little birds with their sing, song, singing,
> Tell you 'tis the wedding day of Miranda and her fiancé !
> The wedding trip they will not take by boat or
> Train ; they mean to try a tour by motor ;
> They left this afternoon for an automobile honeymoon.

Fix the date when automobiles first became a feasible mode of locomotion and you get the date of Queenie's pantomime song. My guess is 1902, because it was in that summer, walking in the English Lakes, that I had to climb up a bank to avoid a snorting dragon coming round a bend of the road at the terrifying speed of some twelve miles an hour.

Lunch with Jock to celebrate the twentieth anniversary of his joining me. The other guest was Gerald Barry, now Jock's editor (*News Chronicle*), and for whom, when he was editor of the *Saturday Review*, Jock wrote his first article. Naturally a lot of the talk was about the past. Gerald recalled how my first serving-man, counsellor, and friend, Freddie Webster, brought a bottle of port to table saying, " I 'aven't shook it because of the sentiment." G. B. also told us about a Dutch journalist who had asked Clemenceau his opinion of Pétain.

Clemenceau replied, " He is an immortal. He has no heart, no brain, and no guts. How can a man like that die ? " Went with Jock to the Curzon afterwards to see a revival of *La Femme du Boulanger* with Raimu. Equally amused and touched.

In the meantime here is *Winged Words, No.* 18 :

> To enjoy Rossini one needs only youth ; to know Chopin one must have suffered either an incomplete schoolboy love-affair or a bad bout of toothache. . . .
>
> <div align="right">Henry Treece, " <i>How I See Apocalypse</i> "</div>

Oct. 9
Wednesday. The editor of a theatrical magazine having asked which I consider the better actor, Olivier or Gielgud, I sent him this letter :

Queen Alexandra Mansions
Grape Street, W.C.2

October 9th, 1946

DEAR SIR,
Many years ago I asked my ancient caddie at St Andrews which was the better golfer, young Tom Morris or Bobby Jones. He looked at me distastefully and said, " Baith o' them played pairfect gowf ! "

Yours faithfully,

JAMES AGATE

Lunched with Bertie van Thal, who asked whether he should publish a translation of Marcel Boulestin's *A Londres, naguère.* 'Phoned him later in the afternoon, " Yes, if the translator can reproduce M. B.'s style, which is amusing, often *chichi,* and always *très snob* " :

> J'ai dit que les nègres étaient fort recherchés dans le privé. Naturellement, on les invita à ces fameuses *parties* ; on se les disputa. Je conduisais une nuit Mrs L. d'une soirée à une autre. Sur le trottoir elle aperçut un nègre ; elle se pencha par la portière, les bras tendus, criant : *Oh ! boy !* . . . C'est à elle qu'arriva une aventure qui fit quelque bruit dans Chelsea et Bloomsbury. Elle avait à un moment une " affaire de cœur," comme l'on dit, avec un des acteurs nègres des *Black Birds* ; la femme de celui-ci, danseuse dans la troupe, le sut et, une après-midi, les surprit dans l'appartement de Mrs L. D'où explication violente, cris, coups, tandis que les passants contemplaient avec étonnement, sur le balcon un nègre terrifié qui cherchait à s'enfuir. Il était vêtu d'une chemise et d'un chapeau melon.

Some delightful misprints : Evelyn Waugk ; J. K. Chesterton, Olive Bell (the art critic), Winifred Holtly, Damon Rumyon, *The*

Jorsyte Saga, Hounddisch. Poor Marcel ! " The Gestapo got him," said Bertie, " but fortunately he managed to commit suicide."

Two tea-time callers. Edgar Lustgarten, to say that he submitted his first book to Curtis Brown, the agent, five days ago and signed the contract with Eyre and Spottiswoode yesterday. The other visitor was my young friend John Compton, who has neglected me somewhat lately, scoring 500 runs up and down the country in 25 innings, of which he is inordinately proud, and taking 102 wickets at a cost of 10 runs apiece, which he thinks is poor.

Oct. 10   The wind of inspiration has blown my way but once.
Thursday.   This was when I set down Ellen Terry for Gertrude in an
ideal casting of *Hamlet.* This game of imaginary casts grows upon one ; it is habit-forming, and one should beware of it. But there are times when it is useful and helps one to get through an evening. It helped me through to-night. How would one ideally cast *Dombey and Son* ? For Dombey I think first of John. But has Mr G. quite the weight and his voice the sonority ? Wherefore I pass him over in favour of Cedric Hardwicke, who would be required to convey Dombey's Macreadyisms in his best Wimpole Street manner. Major Bagstock ? I suggest Frederick Lloyd, so good an actor that he would have no trouble with this monstrous sycophant and toad-eater. Solomon Gills ? Anybody. Mr Carker ? Anybody with teeth. Walter Gay ? Any one of our colourless young leading actors. Mr Toots ? Here comes a piece of casting about which there is no inspiration because it is obvious to anyone with two eyes in his head. Or even one eye.

> Toots is what none of Dickens's dignified characters are, in the most serious sense, a true lover. He is the twin of Romeo. He has passion, humility, self-knowledge, a mind lifted into all magnanimous thoughts, everything that goes with the best kind of romantic love.

Thus Chesterton. Well, and who is the actor for this " holy fool " ? Alec Guinness. For Mrs Chick I would have Marian Spencer. For Miss Tox, Gillian Lind, who did wonders with Miss Bates. For Susan Nipper, Megs Jenkins. Mrs Skewton presents something of a difficulty ; the actress must not be old, but able to suggest infinite eld. Edith Evans would have enormous fun with the part, but she is to play another Cleopatra presently, and one is enough. What about Cathleen Nesbitt to protest that Nature intended her for an Arcadian ? Florence doesn't matter, and Edith obviously calls for Eileen Herlie. The reason I have left Captain Cuttle for the end ? Because his enactor to-night couldn't have been bettered, and I should have no hesitation in keeping him in my ideal cast. His name is Frederick Ross, and he is, if not an old actor, then an actor of the old school. In other words, he is *an actor*. If I have not cast Paul, or Mrs Pipchin, or Dr Blimber it is because they did not occur in to-night's play, which was hardly a play at all. But for my little game I don't think I could have got through the evening.

Oct. 11
Friday. John Mason Brown has a passage in his new book, *Seeing Things*, which unquiets me :

> I doubt if in the whole history of the stage any of its more distinguished critical servitors have written about it for so many years with such sustained high spirits and intelligence as Mr Nathan has done. Shaw, who as a reviewer was responsible for the best dramatic criticism ever to have provoked the stage or to have been provoked by it, rebelled at the end of three and a half years at being the theatre's slave. " It has tethered me," he groaned in his valedictory, " to the mile radius of foul and sooty air which has its centre in the Strand, as a goat is tethered in the little circle of cropped and trampled grass that makes the meadow ashamed." Lessing's *Hamburgische Dramaturgie* consumed less than two years of his life. Beerbohm, " the incomparable Max," could tolerate only twelve years lived in the dread of those Thursdays, ever blackened as they were by the preparation of his critical copy. William Archer sat in judgment for more than thirty years. But he was a solemn judge—and a tired one towards the end. Woollcott's enchanted aisles lost their nightly enchantment for him after fourteen seasons. Clement Scott in England and William Winter and J. Ranken Towse in this country may have thundered about the stage for fifty or sixty years, but they were men who had died long before death overtook them.

Have I died without knowing it ? Seven years with the *Manchester Guardian*, two with the *Saturday Review*, and twenty-three with the *Sunday Times*—thirty-two years in all. Or am I just tired ? There must be some reason why I didn't find Sid Field very funny last night in *Piccadilly Hayride*. Can it be that he wasn't very funny ? In his first scene he appeared as Shakespeare's King John, modern style, asking why the Malmsey tastes queer and being told that it comes from the butt his brother Clarence was drowned in three weeks ago. As bad joking as it is history. There was a Frenchman with a duck and three women contortionists who contorted first and sang afterwards. And, of course, a ballet, which to me was boring, and, as Wilde's Lady Stutfield would say, quite, quite meaningless. But then

I shouldn't understand the plot of any ballet if it were explained to me in letters a foot high on the backs of sandwich-men.

Oct. 12
Saturday.

Bertie van Thal and I have invented a jargon which is entirely crazy. Here is this morning's telephone conversation :

BERTIE. Bon jour, jeune homme. Lunchen Sie ?
J. A. Danke sehr. Beaucoup plaisir. Où ?
BERTIE. Au Lierre.
J. A. Entendu. Um wieviel heure ?
BERTIE. Two sharp !

Oct. 13
Sunday.

Letter to George Harrap :

Queen Alexandra Mansions
Grape Street, W.C.2
October 13, 1946

DEAR GEORGE,
Will I write something for the *House Notes* you are thinking of reviving ? Of course I will. But first let me tell you a little story about a dry old stick of my acquaintance who was asked whether he played contract bridge. He replied, " I do not, but I know more about the game than most of the people who do." That is exactly my attitude to publishing. Here are some of the things I would insist on if I were a publisher :

1. I should employ a clever young man with seventeen degrees and a knowledge of at least six languages, including English, to proof-read my firm's books *after they had been published,* and keep a file reference to see that the mistakes did not occur in subsequent editions. Yesterday in the umpteenth reprinting of Wells's *Mr Polly* I found " Ain't the old woman meau nt ? " Work that one out !

2. I would divide my output into three categories : Good Books, Sentimental Slop, Sheer Muck. And I would separate the departments which produced them and wall them off with ship's bulkheads.

3. I should abolish the Art Department, or at most let it play about with the Slop and the Muck. The words " Art Department " mean " beautifying " the books, which even old Polonius knew to be an abomination. No sane man wants to see anything on a jacket except the title of the book and the name of the author, with perhaps the name of the publisher at the bottom *in very small print.* In my life I have had some forty battles about this with my nineteen publishers, all of which, with one exception, I have won. In the odd case the result was a brown glazed mess which looked as though somebody had been wrapping up inferior chocolate creams in acanthus leaves. I sent the usual twenty copies to friends, and

before doing so destroyed the wrapper. After which the W.C. wouldn't work for a month.

4. I should not allow advertisements of a book by B to disfigure the dust-cover of a book by A. I should hate to find any jacket of mine advertising *Tales of the Crimea* by some old walrus everybody thought had got himself sunk in the Black Sea way back in '55.

5. In the case of novels, I would have no synopsis of the plot printed on the jacket. Let the reviewers read the bloody thing!

6. I would abolish the preposterous habit of making accounts up to Lammastide, payable on the next Shrove Tuesday but one. This doesn't apply to you, my dear George, who have fed me as Elijah fed the ravens. Or was it the other way round, and did you and Walter come hopping with cheques in your eleemosynary beaks?

7. I would publish no novels of passion by frustrated spinsters angrily cluttering up Bath, Buxton, and Budleigh Salterton.

8. And seriously, I would bring out a library of masterpieces that had no luck at their first appearance. To be called " The Misfire Library." I could give you a dozen titles. *Si editorem requiris*, have a look round Queen Alexandra Mansions.

9. Lastly, I would hamstring anybody who suggested an illustrated edition of Jane Austen. Disembowel anybody who proposed a Dickens with any except the original illustrations. As for the fiend who suggested an *Alice* with drawings other than Tenniel's, my dear George, I would have his brains taken out, buttered, and given to the dog.

That's all, my dear fellow, except my love to you, Walter, and the staff.

Ever your

JAMES

Oct. 14   George Lyttelton writes :
Monday.

Finndale House
Grundisburgh
Suffolk

October 13, 1946

DEAR JAMES AGATE,
    Your delightful letter found me in bed with jaundice, and was as good a medicine as anything the chemist has since produced. Have you ever had the complaint? Don't. It has nothing to recommend it and lets go with the utmost reluctance while tingeing all one's thoughts with sourness. Shakespeare must have had it when he wrote *Timon*, and almost any contemporary poet when he writes anything.

What you say of Lear is immensely interesting, part and parcel as it is of one of your main theses—*viz.*, that physique and voice and personality (tho' I doubt if you use that loathsome word) must all be right, and if they aren't no amount of cleverness and thought and prayer and fasting can bridge the gap. It is sickening that you were off duty when Olivier's Lear appeared. Have you seen it? I have never seen anyone get such ecstatic notices from the good critics. But most of us will not be satisfied that it is the biggest thing ever till the right voice has told us so. I am going to see it in about a month.

I am glad to be fortified by your opinion that Hazlitt's *Characters* is poor stuff. Almost anybody might have written it. I am fulfilling a vow I once made that if I was laid up I would again tackle *War and Peace*, which had baffled me a good many times. I believe it is to you one of those " books that are no books," as Lamb said. I don't wonder. I never see why any of the characters says or does what he or she does say or do, and the great battle scenes have, of course, been made pretty commonplace by events. The second part may perhaps revise my notions, but I still suspect it to be one of those mammoth books the labour of reading which is so enormous that the reader is convinced he has had a tremendous experience. A trivial and cynical view no doubt. That old genius definition of Carlyle's has always puzzled me, because the old man was very far from being a fool, yet the definition as applied to Napoleon or Shelley or Kean or Ranji is so obviously beside the mark. Does it perhaps apply only to the art of government? Wasn't it about Frederick he said it? Even so it is inadequate. Emerson's " that stellar and undiminishable something," though no definition, throws a shaft of light, and that I suspect is all we shall ever get.

A friend sends me the following which I hand on to you with confidence. From a girl's school story : " Sara's fourth ball was quite unlike its predecessors ; it had a funny break-back which seemed to puzzle Joan. She cut at it a little uncertainly. It broke again in mid-air and skimmed her off-stump. The bails flew. Joan was out fourth ball. ' Well done, Sara,' Mrs Maxwell said, as though she could not help it." I think Bedser and Co. will need a tip or two from Sara. I suppose West Australia bat about as well as Hants. Did you see that the last four Australian batsmen are likely to be McCoo, Trade, Lindwa, and Toshak? Rather like the list of names on the screen before Hollywood does its worst. Forgive all this. But I had to answer yours.

Yours ever,
GEORGE LYTTELTON

I have replied :

Queen Alexandra Mansions
Grape Street, W.C.2

October 14th, 1946

DEAR GEORGE LYTTELTON,

Very sorry to hear about your jaundice. Yes, I had it some forty years ago, and sometimes think I have never quite recovered.

If you want a definition of genius you have come to the right shop for it. But before I tell you, hear a little story. Many years ago at the Free Trade Hall, Manchester, Joynson Hicks was debating with Victor Grayson, the Socialist M.P. Grayson told his audience that he could not only define the meaning of every word he used, but derive it from its original sources. Whereupon a man at the back of the hall shouted, "Derive the word gramophone." "That's easy," said V. G. "Gramophone comes from two Greek words: *gramos*—'I speak'; *phonos*—'through a tin tube.'" And now for my definition. Genius is the ability to achieve masterpieces without trying.

You ask me about Olivier's Lear. The answer is: m'yes and m'no. First let me say that I gave it every chance, that I knocked off work at four o'clock to allow myself a rest. I thought Olivier began extraordinarily well, with just the right amount of testiness. A magnificent head, and everything royal about him. The whole subsequent performance brilliantly imagined and achieved. Mind working all the time and making one see things one had not previously noticed. For example, in the "loop'd and window'd raggedness" speech, at the line "O, I have ta'en too little care of this!" one sensed an unclouding of the mind and a return to the responsibilities of kingship. Yes, any amount of subtlety and intellectual appeal. But was I moved? Not so much as I ought to have been. Was it because of the echoes of the same actor's Justice Shallow? And shouldn't Olivier, knowing he was going to tackle the big thing, have let the lesser one alone? Couldn't he see that there were bound to be repercussions and overtones? Wouldn't a stupider actor have done better? Wasn't it a mistake, when Lear entered "crown'd with flowers," to make him run on and put us in mind of one of Jean Cadell's old maids in a nightgown? I have no doubt that mad old men do behave like that. But I think the *optique du théâtre* demands here not a skipping folly, but a loss of wit which is almost happy. That we ought to be reminded of Dowson's *To One in Bedlam*:

With delicate, mad hands, behind his sordid bars,
Surely he hath his posies, which they tear and twine;
Those scentless wisps of straw, that miserably line
His strait, caged universe, whereat the dull world stares,

Pedant and pitiful. O, how his rapt gaze wars
With their stupidity! Know they what dreams divine
Lift his long, laughing reveries like enchanted wine,
And make his melancholy germane to the stars?

And then I thougnt the voice too high-pitched. Lear is a bass that pipes treble in his old age; Olivier is a natural tenor verging upon alto. The actor chipped off every bit of the character—but took me out of my critical self not more than three times—in the "Terrors of the earth" speech, in the second half of the mad scene, and from the entrance with the body of Cordelia to the end. Here the handling of the limp bundle as though it were the dummy certain dancers tie themselves to for a partner, the attempts at artificial respiration, the quiet at the end so that death took place without one's knowing the exact moment of passing—all this was masterly. Do you want it in a nutshell? Wolfit's Lear is a ruined piece of nature; Olivier's is a picture of ruins most cunningly presented.

Then there's another matter. I have the conviction that Olivier is a comedian by instinct and a tragedian by art. He keeps his sense of fun under control in his tragic parts, but I can see him controlling it. Of his Coriolanus in 1938 I wrote: " I think, too, that he must resolve to discard that clowning which he probably adjudges to be mordancy. There is not much of it in the present performance, but what there is is wholly bad. For where it is used it turns into a naughty boy a figure whose dignity should be pauseless." And then I don't surrender to him as I did to Irving. (That there should be any coupling of the two names is in itself significant.) Olivier challenges me, and I take up the challenge. He bids me observe how well he is doing this bit of pathos, whereupon I consider and agree. I never stopped to consider whether, and to what extent, Irving was being pathetic. When I look at a watch it is to see the time, and not to admire the mechanism. I want an actor to tell me Lear's time of day, and Olivier doesn't. He bids me watch the wheels go round.

The rest of the cast was disappointing—all very clever and well meaning, but just not big enough. I was immensely disappointed with the Fool, for whom they had got the one actor I should have chosen in fifty years. The one player able to convey the dumb capacity for being hurt. And to babble while his heart is breaking. I should have said that there were two characters that Alec Guinness was born to play—Mr Toots and the Fool in *Lear*. So what do they do but chalk his face and make him stick on a putty nose, like Noni, the music-hall clown. The result was that he was forced to play throughout with the same unvarying mask, like an Edwardian beauty afraid that her enamel will crack. And why not Ralph Richardson for Kent?

And now to other things. I have decided that *Ego* 9 shall be the last. My publishers say that if I deliver now what stuff I have got ready and the balance at the end of the year there's a chance that they may be able to publish on my seventieth birthday. E. V. Lucas said that one of the marks of a gentleman is never to show that he is tired. That's as may be. I am sure that one of the marks of an artist is not to let his work show signs of fatigue. I am very weary. Yesterday afternoon Gwen Chenhalls took me to Harold Holt's box at the Albert Hall. We arrived in time for my favourite piano concerto, Beethoven's C minor. This begins, as you know, with a long exposition by the orchestra. Half-way through this I fell asleep to wake only with the applause at the end, and not having heard a note of Pouishnoff. And this after a lunch of monastic simplicity—meaning two double whiskies and an omelette. Now here's the point. In this state of tiredness some of my work must necessarily suffer. I am determined that it shan't be *Ego*, and by any code of fairness it mustn't be my papers. I am not overlooking the possibility of a postscript, to be published if and when my literary executors—horrid phrase—think fit. I might even call it *Postscript to Ego*, or *Letters from Grundisburgh*.

I hear that the latest cure for jaundice is a trip to town. Why not try it ? Now, not in a month's time.

Ever,

JAMES AGATE

P.S. I have just come across this in Clifton Fadiman's *Reading I've Liked* :

" When Somerset Maugham prepares tripe, he practically puts a label on it stating its high percentage of adulteration. I find this a virtue. It makes his work so much more agreeable than the novels, for example, of Charles Morgan, which are not only tripe, but are rendered doubly unpalatable by the fact that Mr Morgan doesn't seem to know it."

What nonsense ! Our Charles is magnificently unreadable, but he doesn't write tripe. If I had to use a culinary metaphor it would be the funeral baked meats served up to the sorrowing relatives of a dead duke. In the meantime I have started an anthology called *Reading I Haven't Liked*.

Oct. 15   On this matter of work and overwork. Yesterday I
Tuesday.   brought up the total of words written by me since I joined
            the *Saturday Review* in 1921 to the staggering figure of seven millions. In figures, 7,000,000. Or just about double the number of words in Balzac's *La Comédie Humaine*. Now I am aware that the average reader has no idea of how much, say, 10,000 words is. Any more than I know how much 10,000 acres amounts to, whether it is a big estate or a small. Does Lord's cricket ground constitute one acre or six ? I have no idea. Wherefore let the world know that seven million words is the length of one hundred average-sized novels. Twenty-one from forty-six leaves twenty-five. Meaning that for twenty-five years I have written at the length of four novels per year. Whaur's your Arnold Bennett noo ?

When the cat's away . . . From the *Tatler* for October 9, D. B. Wyndham Lewis's article :

It is not generally known that Livingstone used a pseudonym for emergency purposes, such as being suddenly discovered by a bouncing chap like Stanley. Casting round for an alternative name suggestive of great, true, violet-like, illustrious modesty, Livingstone had just hit on the ideal one when Stanley burst through the Bush.

"Dr Livingstone, I presume?"
"My name is Agate. Good morning."

This put Stanley in a nice quandary, requiring two elephants and sixteen native bearers to pull him out.

Oct. 16   I have received the following from Neville Cardus :
Wednesday.

Sydney

July 28, 1946

MY DEAR JAMES,

During the last twelve months I have sent you cables and/or letters of commiseration, of congratulation, of supplication. I have even sent you a book on cricket. But not a sign from you. There is the evidence of the *Sunday Times* that you are still in being, unless (and you are capable of it) you have arranged for a post-humous reign and dictatorship. Please put an end to a silence which is becoming dramatic. And tell dear old George Lyttelton that very few things in my life have given me more pleasure than to be called by him (p. 107, *Ego* 7) "the well-beloved Cardus."

You may be interested to hear that an American teacher of music has written to me from Fort Worth Conservatory of Music (Texas) saying of my *Ten Composers* that "I have read it through twice, and cannot honestly alter my opinion that it is *pure hogwash* in the worst possible tradition." . . . I have replied thanking him for his refreshing candour, and have concluded thus :

"*Ten Composers* is at present being translated into Swedish. Perhaps some day an American translation will be made of it, and then possibly you'll arrive at a more favourable opinion of my essays."

I hope you are well, and more than half-way through *Ego* for 1946. There was no falling off in *Ego* 7 ; and it is a preposterous notion that any committee or council of candid friends should be given executive power over the future of the best bed-book since Boswell. I talk of you every week for hours amongst civilised people in Sydney ; they all of them, the whole three of them, send you affectionate greetings. I send you, as ever, my love, which, in spite of your indifference to it, will not be proticipated or deniged.

NEVILLE

I have replied :

Queen Alexandra Mansions
Grape Street, W.C.2

October 16*th*, 1946

DEAR NEVILLE,

There's only one lunatic outside Bedlam, and that's me. I have —let me count them on my fingers—five books on the stocks at the moment. *Ego* 8, which is to appear shortly ; *Ego* 9, which is five-sixths finished ; *The Contemporary Theatre, 1944 and 1945* ; *Around Cinemas, Second Series* ; and *Thus to Revisit . . .*, a collection of essays. I have three papers to keep going. I have to read the bloody books, see the bloody plays, and sit through the bloody films. I know no passage in the works of Shakespeare which moves me so much as this from *The Importance of Being Earnest* :

ALGERNON. What shall we do after dinner ? Go to a theatre ?
JACK. Oh, no ! I loathe listening.
ALGERNON. Well, let us go to the Club ?
JACK. Oh, no ! I hate talking.
ALGERNON. Well, we might trot round to the Empire at ten ?
JACK. Oh, no ! I can't bear looking at things.

And you would make a letter-writer of me ! Don't you realise that my books are my letters to my friends ? Also, that if I had a beard it would be snow-white ? That I propel myself on my two legs only because bath-chairs are even more difficult to come by than perambulators ?

Besides, I have nothing to tell you, except that I love hearing from you and that I think Alban Berg's Violin Concerto is filth. If this reaches you in time for the Test Matches give our side a little chirp for me.

> Ever,
>
> JIMMIE

Oct. 17   Jolly party last night at Lady Juliet Duff's. Lady
Thursday.   Birkenhead, Willie Maugham, Arthur Macrae, Simon
              Carnes. Willie was in as good form as my chattering would allow him to be. He said of Kipling, " To the end he had the mind of a fifth-form boy at a second-rate school. He dined with me on the day after Gene Tunney beat Jack Dempsey : ' Gene is a white man.' I made a bet with myself that his next two words would be ' pukka sahib.' They were." I was a fool to talk so much. A wise man would have been stimulated to listen, not to jabber.

The post brings this :

DEAR MR AGATE,
     It was with a sense of despair that I read your criticism of *Dombey and Son* in the *Sunday Times* this morning.
     I am sorry you were so bored with the play. I too was very bored with the lengthy column you devoted to showing off your doubtless brilliant powers as a casting director. Can you honestly say that you gave an intelligent, constructive criticism, which the ordinary theatre-going public look for in the *Sunday Times* ? Surely, when so much is said these days about the encouragement of Art in Britain, and when we are so often treated to so many

meaningless plays in the West End, an unpretentious attempt to present *Scenes from Dombey and Son* should at least be given a helpful criticism, and not merely ridiculed and dismissed with contempt.

Would it not have been to every one's advantage if you had used your great knowledge of the theatre to give us at least an intelligent account of the play, with its good and bad points, instead of using your column for a display of West End snobbery? If, as you say, you find your work so tedious at times that you have to invent a " little game " to help you through, I suggest you have spent too long in the atmosphere of the theatre, and I think it might be a good idea if you made way for a younger, keener mind, who will give us some sound constructive criticisms, to help us in our choice of plays, and our judgment of them.

I am not an actress : I work in a big London hospital. Therefore I am not speaking from a professional, but a reader's point of view. Neither have I seen the play, so I am not defending the cast or the author. I am merely very disappointed in you as a critic. However tedious the work of an ordinary citizen, boredom is not an excuse for making it a game.

I shall be interested to see whether you will have this letter printed, and what your reply will be.

To which I answered :

Queen Alexandra Mansions
Grape Street, W.C.2

October 17, 1946

DEAR MADAM,

Your letter raises a point of considerable interest.

I must ask you to realise that nothing can be done, constructively, about a play that is already written. What is done cannot be undone, as a lady in one of Shakespeare's plays remarks. Hints which will prove helpful to the author in his or her next attempt ? *I do not want to help anybody to dramatise Dickens's novels.* The thing cannot be done and should not be attempted, even with an ideal cast.

To help you to choose your plays ? Dear lady, you have the daily papers. If you are an intelligent reader, as, of course, you are, you will have said to yourself, " Why does a conscientious critic like James Agate go out of his way to say nothing about this production ? " And then, if you are very intelligent, you have said to yourself, " Because anything he could honestly say must be so damaging and hurtful that he preferred not to say it." And at once you knew whether to book for this play or not.

A dramatic critic has another function besides handing out tips about what to see and what to miss. This is to entertain his circle of readers. Some of my little circle have written to tell me that they were greatly amused by my " ideal " casting of *Dombey and Son* (though I still maintain it should never happen), and all of them gathered that the venture in question was something to be kept away from.

Lastly I am going to take the trouble to copy out for you something a very great man wrote many years ago. This is it :

" You must love these people [writers and critics] if you are to be among them. No ambition is of any use. They scorn your ambition. You must love them, and show your love in these two following ways. First, by a true desire to be taught by them, and to enter into their thoughts. To enter into theirs, observe ; not to find your own expressed by them. If the person who wrote the book is not wiser than you, you need not read it ; if he be, he will think differently from you in many respects. Very ready we are to say of a book, ' How good this is—that's exactly what I think ! ' But the right feeling is ' How strange that is ! I never thought of that before, and yet I see it is true ; or if I do not now, I hope I shall, some day.' But whether thus submissively or not, at least be sure that you go to the author to get at *his* meaning, not to find yours."

In other words when you read a dramatic critic that you think is worth reading look to see what he wants to tell you, and not what you want to be told.

Yours faithfully,

JAMES AGATE

Oct. 18   Audrey did not know what ' poetical ' is, and I should
Friday.   have no hesitation in telling her modern counterpart that
             poetical is what the fashioners of the modern verse drama
are not. I know that there are poorish lines in Shakespeare. I am not greatly moved by such doggerel as, for example,

> Hopeless and helpless doth Ægeon wend,
> But to procrastinate his lifeless end.

On the other hand I feel pretty certain that I shan't see or hear any more of the old bore till the time comes to dive for my hat. Whereas when the soldier in Peter Yates's *The Assassin* says,

> I somehow feel that he will speak again,

I know, by gosh, that John Wilkes Booth is only just getting steam up. Surely, prose and not verse is the proper medium for such sentiments as

> You take a mean advantage of my leg

and

> It's near Port Royal in Virginia.

I don't know that I am particularly interested in the reasons which made Booth do what he did. But if I am, then the interest is factual and not poetical. I want to hear the evidence of the actors who played with him as to whether, in their opinion, he was sane or mad. I want to hear a summary of the great mass of evidence tending to show that Booth was the tool of those early racketeers who disapproved of Lincoln's cleaning-up operations. What I do not want to hear are this third-rate actor's speculations on the nature of death and the hereafter. Booth may have been sane. He may have been acting out of his own will and disposition. He may have thought himself the avenger of the martyred South. All well and good. But he committed one of the foulest crimes in history, and was rightly shot for it. To which I say Amen. We already have one play about Brutus and another about Hamlet, and as far as I am concerned there is no room for another play about Lincoln even if it pretends to be about Booth. Nor for any highbrow tosh in which young men in unison exhort the statue and spirit of Lincoln to fulfil and animate what follows. And when that statue which one had supposed to be marble, or at least plaster, nods its head—why, then, as the poet says, I " to nothingness do sink." And I dissent absolutely and *in toto* from the view that Lincoln owes his immortality to a crazy actor, and that if he had not been murdered he would have declined to a nonentity. Last night's play began and ended when the old negro said to Booth, " You gets shot, you'se dead. When Mr Lincoln gets shot he ain't dead at all."

Oct. 19
Saturday.

" Bring forth men-children only." Yes, but suppose the actress doesn't look as though she could produce any kind of child. Say, one of our modern teeny-weenies. Lady Macbeths should be like brood mares—' wealthy,' in horse language, with room to carry a foal. " I have given suck." Then take Beatrice. I shall never forget Ellen Terry's entrance at the words

For look where Beatrice, like a lapwing, runs
Close by the ground.

I can see her now in a full, wide, and, I think, green silk skirt sewn with pearls. How she filled the whole stage and sailed to the bower in part like a bird, but in part, too, like a modern aeroplane making a perfect landing. This Beatrice was a great lady ; the character is not to be essayed by actresses who at best are little ladies. A pert Rosalind is an abomination ; a Viola about whom there is a smack of the teashop is a horror ! The same with the men. What I am trying to say is that when I know that a player cannot fill a great rôle I do my best to avoid seeing him fail. It is my duty to attend the performance and point out the faults that the player may mend them ? But I am talking of faults that are ineradicable and shortcomings that can never be made up. If an actor is common he cannot play Hamlet, and if he lacks virility he will not be Othello. And twenty columns in the *Sunday Times* won't help him. Commonness cannot be put off, or virility put on. My duty to the public ? The public can't be taught and won't believe. Why should I bother to tell readers that Ellen Terry could play Beatrice and little Miss Periwinkle can't ? All that happens is an avalanche of letters informing me that I am a foolish, fond old man. It is the public who are the fools. Did my recollections of George Robey prevent me from acclaiming Sid Field ? When another Ellen Terry happens—another actress whose talent is as great in to-morrow's way as Ellen's was in yesterday's— I shall know her.

Oct. 20
Sunday.
Delayed nerves ? The result of not panicking in France is two nightmares. In the first I am back again in Cannes, without Willie, penniless and having lost my luggage. I wake up from this in a cold sweat. In the other I am sitting on the top of an aeroplane, holding on with both hands, and nothing to hold on to. Suddenly the mass of Mont Blanc rises in front, less than a hundred feet away, and we must crash. At this moment the delectable Cynthia, who is my pilot, turns round and with a dazzling smile says, " It's the first time I've driven one of these things ! " I wake up screaming.

Lady Alexander, who died to-day, was a remarkable figure. She had great charm, and at the age of eighty looked like a white French poodle. There was not an inch of her that did not gleam or shake or tinkle. She wore powder and patches to the last.

Oct. 21
Monday.
This week being the centenary of the birth of C. P. Scott, my thoughts naturally turn to the *Manchester Guardian*. I like to think that I joined the *M.G.* in its high and palmy days, and sometimes, when I'm feeling very vain, to believe that I made part of them. They were a wonderful team in 1906—C. E. Montague, Allan Monkhouse, Herbert Sidebotham, Ernest Newman, and, in London, James Bone. George Mair came a little later. Forty years ago Manchester had three theatres, the Royal, the Princes, and the just opening Gaiety. I was called in to help Montague and Monkhouse, and there we were in our splendour every Tuesday morning with the best part of a column each. Montague would write

me a little note saying that he was selfish enough to want to see Jane Hading at the Princes, and that he had asked Monkhouse to deal with the new Galsworthy at the Gaiety. Would I mind covering the Benson company in *The Merchant of Venice*? Yes, I spent two or three years covering this and that. Then Montague became a little tired, and Monkhouse was ill, and at the beginning of the First World War most of the dramatic criticism devolved upon me, with Mair as second string.

I have a great collection of unreprinted Montague in a buckram-bound newspaper-cutting book that has accompanied me in my peregrinations throughout forty years. And I want to ask: Why is not Montague republished? Shaw, Max, Walkley, Grein in their fullness, and too much of J. A. But, apart from the tiny *Dramatic Values*, no Montague. I would put him together myself except that a labour of love requires time, and I just can't go trotting off to Hendon, or wherever the *M.G.* keeps its files. Perhaps when I am eighty. . . .

Oct. 22
Tuesday.
It is a commonplace that women bear pain better than men. What has not been decided is whether, as a lower organism, they feel pain less or have more courage to meet it. Moral courage, of course, women have; otherwise they would not be seen at the Ivy in hats that would make chimpanzees gibber and giraffes stampede. At this point Gwen Chenhalls rings me up:

J. A. Do women bear pain better than men?
Gwen. But of course.
J. A. Why?
Gwen. They have to. No man would put up with a woman who let out the screams a man does when he pricks his thumb.

But women possess another kind of courage—you can call it artistic intrepidity—meaning the quality of rushing in where the more stupid male would hesitate. Your woman novelist who has resided all her life in Bournemouth has no hesitation in describing the love-life of a horse-slaughterer in Chicago or the adolescent dreamings of a bull-fighter's apprentice. Men are not like this; I have been a novelist and I know. When I wrote about a shop-girl it was because I once kept a shop and there was a girl in it. Nothing would have induced me to say what that girl thought; I was content to set down what she did. But women writers will describe and differentiate between the agonies of an Alpine climber whose boot has come off, an air-pilot who suspects the damn' thing to be on fire, and a boxer hit below the belt. Whereas I, a mere male, would hesitate to describe what it feels like to have purled two instead of plained three, and would not dare to hazard what goes on at Dorcas Meetings and Spelling Bees.

Our Dilys has been telling us that *Le Grand Jeu*, the new French film at the Academy, " has its share of Foreign Legion and other boloney." But what does Dilys know about the life of Foreign Légionnaires in Morocco ? What can any woman, or any man who has not served in the Legion, know what does and what doesn't go on ? The camels may have an inkling, but they won't tell. There is a line in Kipling's old poem that I'm very fond of, the line which tells me that " single men in barricks don't grow into plaster saints." I am perfectly certain that what road-makers in Morocco want after three months of road-making and occasional sniping is not a rock-bun and a reading of Edith Sitwell's poems. The maker of this film knows perfectly well what they want—plenty to drink and women with some go about them. This film has a scene in which the brothel-keeper in this wretched imitation of a town complains to the local trader about the non-arrival of the new batch of girls. He has paid Frs. 2000 a head, the troops are expected hourly, and why hasn't the Barcelona bunch arrived ? I see no boloney about this ; it seems to me that the brothel-keeper's attitude is strictly reasonable.

Dilys finds in this picture " passages of poetic realism." It is these which seem to me, as a mere man, to be boloney. Indeed, so strong in my mind is the association of modern poetry with boloney that in future I propose to talk of " boletic realism," just as, in another place, I shall write of " the Boletic Drama." What is sheer bunk in this film is the suggestion that a young crook who made away with over a million francs to keep his expensive doxy in a good temper should imagine, on the strength of a physical likeness, that the pathetic drab who has somehow got mixed up with the Barcelona consignment is the same woman. She has let her gold hair go back to brown. Good. She doesn't remember him ? Yes, but that is explained by the bullet mark on her temple acquired in a moment of remorse when she sought to become shot. Embezzlers should have enough brains to know that doxies don't shoot, and if they do don't miss. But worse remains behind. The audience is led to believe what the young man believes. Jacques Feyder should know that while you may fool your characters to the top of your boletic bent you must never, never mislead your audience. I don't think I am ever going to take a wild fancy to Marie Bell, though she slogs through her dual rôle conscientiously enough. But to Françoise Rosay, who has a very large and important secondary rôle, I surrender entirely. I should surrender if they showed the film the other way up. Which, if it had been given at the Film Festival at Cannes, is doubtless what would have happened.

Oct. 23   " I thowt a said whot a owt to a' said an' I coom'd
Wednesday.   awaäy." But dramatic critics are not Northern
                  Farmers, old style or new.   They may think a play-
wright is saying what he ought to say, and they may even think he finished saying it a couple of hours ago—but they cannot come away. Hugo Bastin, a fading film-star, having decided in 1938 that the post-War world was not fit to live in, bought an island in the Pacific and retired to it with his claret, cigars, first editions, and three other *fainéants*—a thug, a professor, and a terrified Jew. He also took with him his wife, and what I believe is technically called a ' lovely,' the wife observing that he would want a fresh face to look at occasionally.   Quantities of gowns and dressing-gowns, and a Chinese staff big enough to keep the place as spick as any villa at Cannes.   The author of *Away from it All* at the Embassy last night asked us to presume that in 1946 none of the party knew of the Second World War, and that all heard of it first from an airman and his girl, who, having run out of petrol, had made a forced landing on Bastin's beach.   During the hours that followed I thought of those amusing times in the Pacific at the close of that eighteenth century about which Bastin was always babbling.   How Fletcher Christian and his eight men of the *Bounty* sailed away from Otaheite to Pitcairn Island, taking with them nine Otaheite wives and seven men to act as their servants.   How after a time the natives became jealous of the white sailors and murdered them all except one—John Adams.   How the Otaheite widows rose up, drugged the Otaheite men and killed the lot, with the result that John Adams became husband to the entire female population.   One wondered at what point Val Gielgud's thug would liquidate the males on the island and become monarch of all he surveyed.   Alas that nothing of the sort happened !   Nor was there any word about the hell of having nothing to do for eight years except drink claret and read Richardson's interminable novels.   The airman and his girl talked faintly of finding means of departure.   This was negatived by Bastin, who said that the publicity attendant on his still being alive would be repugnant to his ex-film-star's sense of delicacy.   How did Bastin propose that they should all spend the rest of Time ?   Just talking.   What is to be remembered is that five-sixths of any theatre audience has never indulged in abstract specula-

tion, six-sevenths has never thought at all, and seven-eighths only goes to a theatre once in a blue moon. Obviously to such an agglomeration philosophisings on the nature of war and peace will be wildly exciting when conducted in luxurious surroundings by smartly dinner-jacketed men and sumptuously dressed women. Whereas they can only be a crashing bore to the professional playgoer who spends nine-tenths of his time in the theatre and has had this play's conclusions rammed down his throat by every highbrow playwright ever since they made the wretched peace. Nice acting if you think talking is acting. But then before you can act you must have a play to act in, and I regard this as far better material for the radio than the stage.

Oct. 24 Suppose a poetry recital at which the reciter said, " The
Thursday. rainbow goes and comes, and the rose is lovely ; the
  moon likes looking round an empty sky ; water under
the stars is a sight for sore eyes ; sunshine is a good beginning ; yet somehow I feel that things aren't as jolly as they used to be. That, ladies and gentlemen, is Wordsworth." Whereupon you would be justified, I think, in rising in your seat and saying in a loud voice, " No, it isn't ! " There was not a moment during to-night's performance of *Cyrano de Bergerac* at the New Theatre when I was not conscious of saying to myself in a small, silent voice, " This is not Rostand."

Montague has pointed out the special quality of Rostand's verse, the " accented artificiality," the " triumphant click of the French rhymes into their place," the " mannered daintiness," the " porcelain fragility," the " intimate preciosity of diction, which seems to co-opt the playgoer into a rather choice set of co-heirs of French literary and dramatic tradition and co-possessors of a kind of elegant bookishness." Another way of putting it might be that Rostand delights to create difficulties for himself, funambulist-wise.

The translation by Brian Hooker used at the Old Vic to-night is in lumbering blank verse, and if the translator never falls it is because he has given himself nothing to fall off. Anybody with an ear for French will realise the fun of

Que Montfleury s'en aille,
Ou bien je l'essorille et le désentripaille !

Whereas nobody with an ear for English will find much fun in

Fly, goose ! Shoo ! Take to your wings,
Before I pluck your plumes, and draw your gorge !

If Cyrano's blood runs cold at the thought of an amputated comma it is because *virgule* is a jolly rhyme to *coagule*. " My blood curdles at the thought of altering a comma " is not the same thing.

But any translation stands or falls by the famous first-act speech about the Nose :

> Par exemple, tenez :
> Agressif : " Moi, monsieur, si j'avais un tel nez,
> Il faudrait sur le champ que je me l'amputasse ! "
> Amical : " Mais il doit tremper dans votre tasse :
> Pour boire, faites-vous fabriquer un hanap ! "
> Descriptif : " C'est un roc ! . . . c'est un pic . . . c'est un cap !
> Que dis-je, c'est un cap ? . . . C'est une péninsule ! "
> Curieux : " De quoi sert cette oblongue capsule ?
> D'écritoire, monsieur, ou de boîte à ciseaux ? "
> Gracieux : " Aimez-vous à ce point les oiseaux
> Que paternellement vous vous préoccupâtes
> De tendre ce perchoir à leurs petites pattes ? "

Now compare to-night's translation :

> For example, thus :—
> Aggressive : I, sir, if that nose were mine,
> I'd have it amputated—on the spot !
> Friendly : How do you drink with such a nose ?
> You ought to have a cup made specially.
> Descriptive : 'Tis a rock—a crag—a cape—
> A cape ? say rather, a peninsula !
> Inquisitive : What is that receptacle—
> A razor-case or a portfolio ?
> Kindly : Ah, do you love the little birds
> So much that when they come and sing to you,
> You give them this to perch on ?

Even when the translator essays rhyme he does poorly. Think of the wonderful rhymes Cyrano found for *Gascogne—vergogne, bastogne, cigogne, vigogne, ivrogne, carogne, renfrogne*. The English translator, unable to find rhymes for " Gascoyne," substitutes " defenders," and then goes on to talk of " spenders," " contenders," " lenders," " sword-benders," " befrienders," " engenders," " pretenders." Not a patch on the original ! And so throughout the whole of the evening. Wordsworth's sense without Wordsworth's sound may be worth while. Rostand's isn't. Deprive him of his tinkle and he is nothing.

Is the play untranslatable then ? Well, that highly accomplished poet Humbert Wolfe failed, and the authors of the version used by Robert Loraine were so conscious of impossibility that they left out the Nose speech ! Cannot the thing, then, be done ? Yes, but perhaps not by any living poet. I think Austin Dobson might have achieved it on the lines of

> With the coming of the crow's feet
> Goes the backward turn of beaux'-feet.

But for a Casabianca-like sense of duty Thursday night would have seen the backward turn of critics' feet.

Is the production good in an English way ? I just wouldn't know, any more than I should know whether a claret made at Stoke Newington is a good claret. Or whether a Chopin Ballade *with different notes* is still a good Chopin Ballade. The acting ? A lady was heard to say as we were going in, " The play must have *sabretache*. No actor who has not got *sabretache* can play Cyrano." Ralph Richardson has any amount of *sabretache*, but I doubt whether, even given a better equivalent of Rostand's words, he would have that for which the lady was fumbling—*panache*.

Oct. 25   Letter to George Lyttelton :
Friday.

> *Queen Alexandra Mansions*
> *Grape Street, W.C.*2
>
> *October 25th,* 1946

DEAR GEORGE LYTTELTON,
    I shan't have my full say about *Cyrano* on Sunday owing to lack of space. Five Hazlitts would not be able to cram Rostand's play and an importantish political thing at the Embassy into one column which has also to accommodate Harold Hobson on Henry James at the Arts and something else at the Westminster, plus next week's Theatre Diary. *C'est gigantesque !* And there were so many things I wanted to say. Brian Hooker, who made his translation in 1923, appears to have had no feeling whatever for the original French. Listen to Rostand :

> Eh bien ! toute ma vie est là :
> Pendant que je restais en bas, dans l'ombre noire,
> D'autres montaient cueillir le baiser de la gloire !
> C'est justice, et j'approuve au seuil de mon tombeau :
> Molière a du génie et Christian était beau !

Now read Hooker :

> It was always so !
> While I stood in the darkness underneath,
> Others climbed up to win the applause—the kiss !—
> Well—that seems only justice—I still say,
> Even now, on the threshold of my tomb—
> " Molière has genius—Christian had good looks—"

Note how beautifully after the word *tombeau* Rostand's last line clicks into place, whereas in the English there is no clicking. And then I am conscious of a faint commonness about " Christian had good looks." It's the sort of thing one says about a young man behind a glove counter !

Then, again, compare

> C'est vrai ! je n'avais pas terminé ma gazette :
> . . . Et samedi, vingt-six, une heure avant dîné,
> Monsieur de Bergerac est mort assassiné.

with

> I did not finish my Gazette—
> Saturday, twenty-sixth : An hour or so
> Before dinner, Monsieur de Bergerac
> Died, foully murdered.

And then the ending :

> Ah ! te voilà, toi, la Sottise !
> —Je sais bien qu'à la fin vous me mettrez à bas ;

Hooker renders this :

> Ah, you too, Vanity !
> I knew you would overthrow me in the end—

What the hell has *Vanity* got to do with it ! It goes without saying that half of the cast pronounced Cyrano properly while the other half called him Cyrahno. But then, as somebody remarked, " It's no use trying to teach French to actors who can't speak English." That somebody is a rather important body, and I won't give away who it was. He also said, " I agree with you, my dear Agate. The difference between Rostand and Hooker is the difference between pinking a man with a rapier and hitting him over the head with a shovel." And I said, " *Missing* him with the shovel."

Yours ever,

JAMES AGATE

P.S. I reopen this because of a poem entitled *Of Silence* I have just come across in a highbrow magazine. Here is a stanza :

> Silence loves rhythm ; and of wind walking on heather
> The pause : the intermissions of the sea ;
> And, I have found, lovers can make together
> A better silence than the solitary.

I wonder whether the poet—one Hal Summers, by the way—knows the story of the two drummer-boys, waiters, or grooms who, at a queerish party in the 'nineties, sat by the door twiddling their caps and not saying a word. Presently Reggie Turner, who was a wit in his own right as well as a friend of Wilde, said, " I suppose when you two cherubs are alone together neither of you can get in a silence edgeways ! "

P.P.S. And again to say that the American *Go* magazine makes me write of Jean-Paul Sartre's *Huit Clos* ! ! ! ! Also it chops my stuff up into tiny paragraphs, thus doing away with any question of continuity. Have cabled the editor that I am not Romeo, and will not be cut out in little stars to please the New York Juliets.

507

Queen Alexandra Mansions
Grape Street, W.C.2
October 26th, 1946

DEAR JOCK,

I am going to break a lance with you over your notice of *Cyrano.*
Not the whole of the notice, but that part in which you say :
" *Cyrano de Bergerac*, indeed, is no more like true poetry than a
quarter-pound of jujubes is like a bottle of vintage Burgundy."
What do you mean by " true poetry " ? Is Rostand not a true
poet because he does not write like, say, Ronsard ? Was Herrick
not a poet because he didn't write like Milton ? Lovelace because
he was not another Marvell ? Or Suckling because he didn't
imitate Spenser ? You are right, of course, in saying that Rostand's
play is not true to life. It isn't meant to be, which does not justify
your use of the word " rubbish." No, not even if you add the
words " alluring " and " betinselled."

Here is a sentence from Montague on another of this great little
master's plays : " This week in *Les Romanesques* (translated, with
relish and vivacity, by ' George Fleming ') we are given about as
much of engaging artifice as even M. Rostand can embroider on the
very minimum of study from the life." The point here is the little
word " even." And again : " The performance showed the real
Rostand, the extreme living example, in letters, of one of the two
classes into which most artists can be divided—those who seem to
be always fighting down the resistance of their medium, crushing
its intractability, driving its special difficulties out of sight, and
those who seem to hug these very terms of bondage, to parade and
salute and play round them. Rostand, you feel more than ever
when seeing him acted, is one with the poets who crib and cabin
themselves by choice in rondels and triolets and the designers whose
special joy is to have a queer-shaped space to fill on some convex
surface." I don't see Montague going to all that trouble about a
writer of " rubbish."

Your idol, Max, was not easily humbugged. In his article
on *Cyrano*—incidentally the first criticism he contributed to the
Saturday—occurs this : " I like the Byzantine manner in literature
better than any other, and M. Rostand is nothing if not Byzantine :
his lines are loaded and encrusted with elaborate phrases and curious
conceits, which are most fascinating to anyone who, like me, cares
for such things."

Two years later, writing about Wyndham's production, Max
had this : " Cyrano is the fantastically idealised creation of a poet.
In M. Rostand's poetry, under the conditions which that poetry
evokes, he is a real and solid figure, certainly. But put him into
French prose, and what would remain of him but a sorry, disjointed
puppet ? " I do not find any suggestion here that Rostand was not
a poet, and that what he wrote was " rubbish." And again :

" Cyrano, in the original version, is the showiest part of modern times—of any times, maybe. Innumerable limelights, all marvellously brilliant, converge on him. And as he moves he flashes their obsequious radiance into the uttermost corners of the theatre. The very footlights, as he passes them, burn with a pale, embarrassed flame, useless to him as stars to the sun. The English critic, not less than the English actor, is dazzled by him. But, though he shut his eyes, his brain still works, and he knows well that an English version of Cyrano would be absurd."

I feel, my dear Gemel, that in your article you were barking up the wrong tree. That you should have told your readers, not that Rostand was no poet, but where and how the English version failed to do justice to a dazzling playwright with a gift for something that the French themselves have allowed to be poetry.

About Ralph's performance. I cannot believe that the ideal representative of Horatio, Enobarbus, Kent, and, of course, Thackeray's Dobbin, can be the ideal Cyrano. There is gold and silver in this actor, but not quicksilver. " Though you can guess what temperance should be, you know not what it is." Substitute " temperament," and you have R. R. It's no good telling me I don't know about temperament. I was brought up on it ; my father and Gustave Garcia were not lifelong buddies for nothing. I thought R. was magnificent in the death scene which had real pathos, and just a good, hard-working actor everywhere else. The exact opposite of Coquelin, who—I have a most vivid recollection of the performance—was superb in the first four acts and failed in the last. " All the paraphernalia of emotion were in that memorable passage of acting—were there most beautifully and authentically ; but emotion itself wasn't there ; and many a duffer could have moved us far more than Coquelin did." Max again, of course. Can't you hear, can't you feel that there is always something of the schoolmaster in Ralph ? And an English schoolmaster, at that ? Did you believe for one moment the other evening that this was a Frenchman revelling in French absurdity ? Loraine, as I remember, played the part as he played every other part, like a policeman on point duty. And Wyndham made Max look forward to the actor's next production.

It is possible, of course, that I am the wrong critic for this production. The right one ? William Archer, of course.

Ever,

JAMIE

P.S. I shall be lamentably inadequate on Sunday, owing to my space being reduced to 14 inches. " O rage, ô désespoir, ô vieillesse ennemie ! " as somebody in Corneille remarks. Old age is not so hostile to me that I have lost my power of fury. Can you imagine me sitting up in bed this morning, opening my proof and finding the request to cut seventy-six lines ! I hurled my salts into one corner of the room, and my cup of tea into the other ! I could have cried with disgust.

P.P.S. Have just decided to tackle the thing again next Sunday. What a bore we old men are who cannot leave a subject until we have finished with it ! How much more amusing to be young and pull a face at a masterpiece or toss it a posy !

Having posted the letter to Jock, I set about and produced the following :

There is a story of Irving looking on at a rehearsal of the Montague-Capulet fray and saying, " Very good, gentlemen. But don't fuss ! " There is a lot of inescapable and tedious fussing in *Cyrano*, tedious because during the fifty years since it was written the film has come about, and crowd scenes are ten for ninepence— in the West End one-and-ninepence. Let it be said that Mr Guthrie has inspired or perhaps dragooned his gallants, *précieux*, buffoons so that they skitter and scamble, leap and bounce and leg-twiddle with an agility and a *désinvolture* proper to another stage.

But the thing, after all, is a poem and not a mindless hop, skip, and jumpery. I thought the scenery designed by Miss Tanya Moiseiwitsch very delightful, always with the reservation that two minutes finds the most glittering landscape fading on my sight. Is Mr Menges's music a trifle low in key ? But let that pass. The poetry's the thing. Or would be if there were any. Whether Mr Brian Hooker is a good poet it is not for me to say. What I will, and must, maintain is that he is not a good poet in Rostand's kind, which, as was said last week, is the tight-rope-walker's kind. Now the essence of tight-rope-walking is that a slip shall have consequences. Scores of times Rostand wilfully gets himself into difficulties so that you say to yourself : " Surely he can't get out of that one ? Surely he must slip now ? " But he always gets out, and he never slips. The rhyme is there pat, and you realise that he had it up his sleeve all the time. Mr Hooker refuses to rhyme and takes refuge in blank verse, like a tight-rope-walker whose wire is stretched along the floor.

If scenery and music don't matter, and there is no poetry, what remains ? The story ? But is *Cyrano* so very much of a story ? Sir Max Beerbohm has written : " Put Cyrano into French prose, and what would remain of him but a sorry, disjointed puppet ? . . . An English version of Cyrano would be absurd." No, the story by itself is no great shakes. The thing was to find an actor to translate unmagical blank verse into terms of rockets and fizgigs, or, if you prefer, the bits of coloured glass which hold the secret of the kaleidoscope. In other words to find a second Lewis Waller. " Cyrano is kept up with half-Bacchic, half-chivalrous exuberance and depends for its success on a heroic pitch of madness in the interpretation," wrote Oliver Elton. Waller was a master of the heroic pitch. If he could not do much else he could do this, and while Mr Richardson can do many other things he just cannot exuberate vocally, though you can hear him trying. This is a grand actor when the part is honest; he would be my first choice for Mr Valiant-for-truth with his " I fought till my sword did cleave to my hand." But Cyrano is a Mr Valiant-for-embroidery, his sword no Jerusalem blade, but a tavern impertinence. Here then we had a super-Bunyanesque actor harnessed to a poem which, as Lemaître reminds us, owes a debt to d'Urfé, Corneille, Gautier, Banville, Scarron, Regnard, Marivaux, Hugo, and Dumas *père*, all of them worlds away from everything that Richardson stands for.

How then did our well-liked actor get through ? Admirably, within the limits of his personality. He had to be, in turn, " arrogant, gorgeous, mad, magnanimous, jovial, tender, subtle, ironic, heroic, melancholy," and Lemaître knew not what else. Well, the new Cyrano was all these things in turn. Everything, in fact, except that he lacked that Puss-in-Boots air which the part demands, for the play is not a tragedy, but a tragic nursery tale. The actor was best, I thought, in the death scene, where he achieved pathos and so was better than Coquelin, who did not. I remember my disappointment of fifty years ago when the great comedian who had enthralled us all with his *fougue* proceeded to die a well-calculated death which turned out to be as unemotional as the bark of the tree which held him up. I remember that the house that afternoon in Manchester was as dry-eyed for Cyrano as it was to be for M. Jourdain in the evening ; at the New Theatre many eyes were wet. But I think Cyrano should die on his feet ; there is a chance that the audience may miss that last word—the famous *panache*—when it is uttered by a man on his back with his face upside-down. Or isn't Mr Richardson too keen on having it heard ?

Oct. 27   In a letter from a young actor :
Sunday.

The prolonged and unnatural void in the Sunday paper (Nature, they say, abhors a vacuum) has made me fear you may be ill. I hope not, but if so, that you are recovered and will soon be writing again. It is rumoured that you have been in Paris. I wonder if you managed to enjoy yourself ; there is certainly plenty to eat and drink if you can afford it. I had a rather hot and hectic week there some little time ago, but did not really like it much. The *puanteurs* of the Black Market were a little blatant even for my torpid social conscience.

After that I had about six weeks of sunshine, food, and wine in Switzerland—very salubrious. The people I met were mostly not at all the worthy, stolid Swiss I had been led to expect. Zürich has the highest rate of suicide and insanity in Europe, and is full of the most fascinating neurotics and broken-down grandees. I was put up for a time by a Mme X, who has purple teeth, and wears good clothes, but of the 'twenties—" C'était un Patou, mon cher "—and if you look close enough you can see that it might have been once. She is said to have married young to avoid unhappy home life, and to have found wedlock not much happier. She never liked her husband much, but when he started coming to meals in dark glasses so as not to see her she decided This is Enough, sold her *bourgeois* furniture and bought a cinema in Zürich, and later a café, which is hung with Picassos, Klees, etc. She also paints *des abstraits*, and says, " Moi, je déteste les italiens, mais comme gigolos ils sont *parfaits*." After I left she was prosecuted by the *Sittlichkeitspolizei*, and I was cited as one of her gigolos—alas! unjustly. I came home without even a watch!

I know you don't like the society of young actors, but when I am in London (which is rare) I shall venture to ring you up in the hope of your receiving me and buying me a supper.

Oct. 29   I think I have found a cure for that testiness which has *Tuesday.*   been growing upon me. And why shouldn't it ? This afternoon's post brings three letters. The first is from an ass at High Wycombe who wants to know why in my book reviews I indulge in so much quotation. " You are getting money for words you haven't written." The second is from some cretin who asks why I attribute " You are old, Father William " to Southey, when all the world knows that it's Lewis Carroll. I get this bunged at me three times a year ; the last complaint came from Rugby. Third letter : Will I tell a lady in Colchester the name of a good book she can take out to New Zealand as a present to a man of forty-five ?

The cure ? I sit in my armchair and let Joseph Azzopardi, my assistant houseboy, play me an hour of records. I leave the choice entirely to him. Here is to-day's programme :

Beatrice and Benedict Overture. Berlioz.
Airs from *Pagliacci* and *La Tosca.*
Second and third movements of Beethoven's C minor Piano Concerto.
Trio from *Rosenkavalier.*
" Baiser de la Fée." Stravinsky.
" Variations on a Nursery Tune." Dohnányi

After which, being somewhat comforted, I sally forth to watch somebody scamper about as the heroine of a whale of a novel turned into a shrimp of a stage-play.

Oct. 30   This morning's mail is an improvement on yesterday *Wednesday.*   afternoon's. The first letter, from St Osyth, in Essex, informs me that " good poets like Shelley can write nonsense, and nonsense-writers like Wordsworth can occasionally rise to real poetry."

The second letter was accompanied by a copy of Lysiane Bernhardt's book on her grandmother :

Magdalen College
Oxford

26.10.46

DEAR MR AGATE,

While holidaying in Paris I chanced on the enclosed biography, and, like all good *Ego* readers, there chugged into my mind the train of thought: Pepper and salt; knife and fork; Bernhardt and Agate.

Anyway, I thought you might like to have the book. Yet, for all I know, you may have read the book. For all I know you may have written the bloody thing! As for me, although I could cope with reading it in French, to have to slit open the pages—'tis too much. One might move a mountain, but to have to climb it as well . . .

Please accept this gift, then, from a slave who bows before the tank-like irresistibleness of the *Ego* books. And the slave is an English Literature student into the bargain!

Best wishes,
RONALD CAMERON

Have answered :

Queen Alexandra Mansions
Grape Street, W.C.2

October 30th, 1946

DEAR MR CAMERON,

No, this is one of the books I have *not* written about S. B. Many thanks all the same. Your gracious present and graceful note accompanying it are now enshrined—or, anyhow, ensconced —in my 9th and last *Ego*.[1]

I quite agree about cutting pages. That was part of a more leisured age.

Again many thanks.
Yours sincerely,
JAMES AGATE

[1] In eight weeks' time I finish the thing. Nobody will ever begin to guess what a labour it has been. And this generation won't know what a work it is!

Third letter was from George Lyttelton :

Finndale House
Grundisburgh
Suffolk

October 29, 1946

DEAR J. A.,

How I wish I had your knowledge of French! Mine is a very humdrum affair, and I never really *feel* the language. You seem to possess it as Dr Johnson did Latin. But I can see the holes in B. Hooker. " Christian had good looks " is housemaid's English. Pronunciation is going the same way as spelling. In that spectacular rubbish *Cæsar and Cleopatra* most of the cast said " Brittanus " for " Britannus," and do you think any stockbroker's or solicitor's clerk ever spells my name right first go ? I always take an acid pleasure in stressing the fact that the *only* function of clerks is to be accurate about details, rather on the lines of Johnson's explanation of a vaguely malevolent line in the *Dunciad,* " Sir, he hoped it would vex somebody."

Here is a small point which may bore you, though it is fundamentally your fault, as it occurred to me while reading *Around Cinemas* (which is quite fascinating—like Shaw's *Dramatic Opinions and Essays,* in that it doesn't in the least matter whether one has seen the play criticised). It is the old question of Holmes's university. Well, in *The Two Students* one of the clues is a small lump of *black clay* left on the chair where the young man had put his running-shoes. He had been practising the long jump. Well, in those days, whatever it may be now, it was *only* at Fenner's, Cambridge, where he could have jumped into black clay. The normal long-jump bed was of loose brown loam, but old Watts, the Fenner's groundsman, produced this stuff—probably from the fens —claiming (quite rightly) that, as there was no crumbling at the edges of a footprint, measurement of the jump was far more accurate. Surely this is proof positive. There is no doubt about the fact, because when I was in the C.U.A.C. I often went to Oxford and saw their long-jump arrangements.

And here is a cutting from an Eton housemaster which I am confident cannot fail. I wish he had boldly gone ahead with the passage. Boys' attention at House Prayers is such that I believe he would have got away with it, though it is an undeniably arresting sentence.

I am still a horrid colour, though perhaps it is now primrose rather than buttercup. But they won't let me leave the house, and in any case I should hate to appear in public with this leprous façade.

Yours ever,

GEORGE LYTTELTON

Cutting alluded to above :

Well, I thought of you a week or so ago. For Prayers I use a dark blue book called *A Chain of Prayer through the Ages.* Last Thursday, after I had read my bit of St Luke, we all knelt down and I opened the *Chain* to utter a choice piece of Jeremy Taylor or Cardinal Newman. What met my eyes was " Bout of wind at the Savage Club after luncheon to C. B." As you will surmise, I had in error brought down *A Shorter Ego : vol. I* ! Like a Scotch Meenister I had to extemporise brilliantly, and we got through somehow.

Oct. 31
Thursday.   Postcard from Lyttelton :

Grundisburgh
October 30, 1946

Mental decay goes *pari passu* with bodily. I think I omitted to mention that in *The Three (not Two ?) Students* there is a strong indication that Holmes was visiting his old university, but I cannot lay hands on my Sherlock omnibus, so cannot prove it. Rather a down-at-heel little episode. Forget it. The doctor told me yesterday I ought to be still in bed. I refused to go, so he compromised by saying I must behave as if I was in bed. How does one do that ?

G. W. L.

Letter from Jock :

33 *King Street*
*Covent Garden, W.C.*2
30*th October,* 1946

DEAR JAMIE,

Hoots and havers ! Rostand is no more a true poet than W. S. Gilbert was a true poet. And, similarly, *Cyrano de Bergerac* is no more translatable into English than, say, *Iolanthe* is translatable into French. That is all there is to be said about that pair of pyrotechnicians.

Incidentally I looked up A. B. Walkley on Loraine's first production in 1919. Heed him : " *Cyrano* is audaciously, triumphantly, flamboyantly romantic. Yes, we know it is rhetoric, not poetry. Yes, we know it is high artifice rather than high art. Artifice its passion, artifice its pathos—the whole thing as artificial as Cyrano's duel in rhyme. But it remains supremely romantic . . . romantic to the tip of Cyrano's nose. Romantic love, romantic self-sacrifice, romantic courage, romantic clothes, romantic noses, romantic highfalutin', and romantic death. . . ."

About Ralph's performance. My piece had to be written *before I saw the performance.* I should explain the circumstances. Many weeks ago Richard Winnington was asked to move his film stuff back to Friday because the *News Chronicle's* Saturday Page was too congested. He refused to budge. Whereupon they asked me to move to Friday in his stead. I moved—and have been sorry and uneasy ever since. It means that my stuff has to be delivered and printed on Thursday morning—and that if there is a Thursday-night *première* I have to write about the thing without seeing it and add a word at ten at night (if the printers are in a good temper). The result is that—*Cyrano* being done on Thursday night—my piece was written before the production. I am well aware of it. It has the air of having been written a day before—just as your *Sunday Times* piece has the air of being written thirty or forty years ago !

In a Radio-News-Reel (overseas) broadcast *next day* I could say of Ralph's performance—having seen the play (for the first time !) :

" This first-night was naturally one of those occasions when what I may call the Ah !-you-should-have-seen people were very much to be heard during the intervals. Aged playgoers were around to tell us we should have seen the great Coquelin, for whom the part was originally written away back in the 'nineties. Elderly playgoers even more volubly told us that we should have seen Charles Wyndham in the first English translation in the year 1900. People of middle age or rather over informed us that we should have seen Robert Loraine when he made his name in the part in 1919, and again when he revived the play in 1927.

" Well, we younger playgoers can now say that we have seen Ralph Richardson as the poetical swashbuckler with the unhappy nose, and that we are fairly satisfied. Richardson plays this superb part probably as well as any Englishman can ever play that intensely French Gascon. He is without the Gallic temperament, of course, the quality that the French themselves call *fougue*. But he has almost everything else that is needed—great vocal range and speed, colour, variety, and pace, animation when needed and tenderness when called for, a convincing expertness in fencing both with swords and words (and in both at the same time—as in the famous rhyming duel scene in the first act). One of the minor characters calls Cyrano ' the three musketeers rolled into one.' Richardson's Cyrano is at least two of them—probably as much as is possible for an actor who is an Anglo-Saxon actor."

I should have said much the same in the *News Chronicle if* I had seen the damned thing—except that, since I was writing for an English penny paper instead of talking to the rest of the habitable globe, I should have concluded : " Probably as much as is possible for an actor who is as Anglo-Saxon as Portland Bill."

Ever,

JOCK

To which I replied :

Nonsense, dear Jock. Wait till I've finished this bloody Diary, after which my next two jobs will be to translate *Cyrano* into English and *Iolanthe* into French ! So sucks to you ! in the language of my boyhood.

JAMIE

Nov. 1   Again to George Lyttelton :
Friday.

> *Queen Alexandra Mansions*
> *Grape Street, W.C.2*
> *November 1, 1946*

DEAR GEORGE LYTTELTON,
Have you seen *The Times* on the revival of T. S. Eliot's piece of super-bosh, *The Family Reunion* ?

" It is good to see this play again less for its own sake than for the sake of the verse. No verse written by any other modern poet approaches more nearly to the condition of drama. Its idiom has no archaic inflections ; it is consistently precise and lucid ; it can carry a joke which Mr Wodehouse would not disdain and, without breaking its own texture, pass to a delicate transfiguration of religious and poetic experience."

And I will maintain against the entire body of critics that the poetry is not poetry at all, and that the whole thing is pretentious rot. I remember writing my *S.T.* criticism in the form of a pastiche, and laughing my head off while I was doing it. Some bits of it might help to tickle away your jaundice :

I do not expect modern art to sound nice,
Or even to look nice.
I am not alarmed because a horse by Chirico bears no resemblance to
    one by Solario.
Or perturbed when Hindemith sounds like somebody shooting coals.
Or distressed when a block of luxury flats looks like a ship or a warehouse.
That the pretty-pretty should give place to the ferro-concrete
Is just the age expressing itself.
What does worry me about this play is something altogether different—
The sneaking suspicion that I may not be intellectually up to it.
" Il est si facile," said Balzac, " de nier ce que l'on ne comprend pas."

These highbrows will be the death of me yet. Do you know the story of the naval officer who was heard to say, " What with the grog and the fog it appears that I picked up an old aunt of mine " ? Read Arturo Barea on Lorca and you will pick up

Soledad Montoya, the impassioned woman—
        yellow copper, her flesh
        smells of horse and of shadow—

In the same book—*Writers of To-day*—there is an essay on James Joyce by somebody called Stuart Gilbert. S. G. recounts a meeting between Frank Budgen and James Joyce in Zürich at the time when *Ulysses* was in the making. Joyce told Budgen that he had been working hard all day on two sentences : " Perfume of embraces all him assailed. With hungered flesh obscurely, he mutely craved to adore." Joyce said to Budgen, " You can see for yourself in how many different ways the words might be arranged." S. G. is terrifically impressed. Doesn't he realise that long before Joyce was born schoolboys had great fun in seeing in how many different ways they could arrange " The ploughman homeward plods his weary way " ? And is it too much to ask of clever people that they should get their French right ? Then there's Jack Lindsay on Jack Priestley. But I should be more impressed with Lindsay on what constitutes a Dickensian if he could spell the names of Dickens's novels correctly !

Under another cover I send a book which you may like, *The Happy Cricketer,* by somebody who calls himself " A Country

Vicar." Do you know who this is ? Probably you know that in 1902 Ranji's scores in three Test Matches were 13, 0, 2, 0. And that C. B. Fry's figures for three Test Matches in the same year were 0, 0, 1, 4. Which should teach our Edriches and Comptons not to be downhearted when they strike a bad patch. Keep the book, or give it to some youngster. I am in generous mood to-day owing to the arrival from New York of two exciting-looking books sent by Tom Curtiss, and four pounds of chocolates, of which I suspect Dorothy and Lillian. Have just written what I regard as a model letter : " Dear Gishes, Yours more succulently than ever. J. A." Which goes for you too.

JAMES AGATE

P.S. Your friend's letter. Delicious ! The bouts still go on, aggravated, possibly, by my having only one tooth left in my upper jaw. (If ever you have a denture don't tread on it in the bath-room. The new one has been ready these eight weeks, but I haven't had time to collect it. My dentist lives in Hackney, excusable because he is a great artist. But for me he's un-get-atable. Three hours at least, and I haven't got three hours.) The bouts are now followed by palpitation, to which succeeds panic, for which there is no rational cure. Hamlet was in the best of health and spirits in his " defy augury " speech. I take my comfort in recollection of a Manchester pantomime of forty years ago—*Sinbad the Sailor*. Harry Tate played a negro sea-cook, and at the sight of his black face and rolling eyes—Montague called them " emergent and convolving "—some other clown said, " You make my heart palpitate." Harry said, " Let it palp ! " And I do.

P.P.S. A kind friend sends me the cheap edition of *Playgoing*, a little book, in a series edited by Priestley, that I wrote in 1927. The lettering on the back reads

PLAYGOING

J. B. Priestley

What a lot of fun one could have with this sort of thing. *The Sorrows of Satan*, by Edith Sitwell; *Jude the Obscure*, by Ursula Bloom ; *Gentlemen Prefer Blondes*, by Dean Inge ; *No Orchids for Miss Blandish*, by Charles Morgan.

Nov. 2
Saturday.
There are times when I wish I had been born with the gift of insincerity. I wasn't, alas ! Some little time ago an old Yorkshire friend took me over his stables and carefully explained how each animal in turn would prove to be, if it wasn't now, the wonder and the marvel of the Hackney world. " What do you think of them ? " he asked. I said, " You've got one first-rate and one promising animal. The rest of the thirty-six aren't worth a damn." Yes, I am a blurter out of truth. And now I am

faced with having to tell the *Tatler* what I think about last night's
Royal Command Film Performance at the Empire. A cleverer man
than I am would realise that just as there are horses for courses so
there are different kinds of critical truth for different occasions. He
would recognise that this was a National ' do,' that the nation concerned was Great Britain, and that all the idiotic newspaper fuss
about what frock this film-star would wear and what that film-star's
jewels were worth was entirely right and proper. Opening this
morning's paper, he would have agreed that last night's mass hysteria,
the casualties which resulted in the foyer being turned into a first-aid
station, and the inability of the police to do more than prevent things
from being worse were only to be expected. A critic of this calibre
would proceed to ask himself what kind of film would be correct to
show on such an occasion. A work of art ? Hang it, he would say
to himself, this is a national occasion, and nobody wants the thing
to be a flop. Wherefore he would refrain from saying that Michael
Powell and Emeric Pressburger's *A Matter of Life and Death*, which I
had seen at the Press Show a few hours previously, was the worst big
film he had ever seen. Or, if he must say it, it would be in support of
the view that the worst big film was exactly right for the occasion.
According to the preliminary literature the picture is a " stratospheric
joke told against the background of Two Worlds, photographed in
Technicolor and monochrome." Well, why not ? Don't jokes and
jamborees go together ? And then the diplomatic fellow would, I
think, take refuge in divagation, and launch into an essay on the
difference between the earthbound joke and the joke stratospheric.
Whereas I, clumsy fool, cannot help pointing out that (*a*) matters of
life and death are not jokes, stratospheric or otherwise, and that
(*b*) the function of any kind of joke is to be funny. And this film was
deadly serious. All about an air-pilot who, simultaneously meeting
with an accident and a pretty girl, finds himself between life and
death, and thinking, as Damon Runyon would say, of this and that,
and one thing and another, especially things that have proved most
confusing to many citizens. In other words, it is all a dream. Whereupon I blunderingly suggest that the function of dreams is to be
poetic. But the Powells and Pressburgers of this world know better.
Remembering *Cabin in the Sky*, they realise what must be the fate
of any film about the Hereafter which should leave the safe ground
of flat thinking and even flatter imagination. Doubtless it was for
this reason that they caused their hero to dream after the manner of
cinema addicts. To postulate heaven as a *palais de danse* swollen to

the size of Wembley Stadium with New York's Grand Central Station thrown in. (I shouldn't have been in the least surprised if at any moment Fred Astaire had come twinklingly on.) How does one get to this Paradise ? Obviously by means of an escalator about five hundred times the size of those in use at London's Tube stations. And what does this Elysium look like when you get there ? The answer is a speculative builder's ecstasy of lath and plaster with an odd suggestion of Hollywood's Bowl. What happens to the pilot in his dream ? He becomes the subject of legal proceedings. Is he, an Englishman, a fit mate for an American girl ? Here the film becomes a welter of singularly ill-timed Anglo-American bickerings. America taunts this country with the Crimean War, the Zulu War, the Boer War, our treatment of India, the Boxer riots, and the troubles with Ireland after the 1914–18 war; we reply by throwing in America's face the things of which we have disapproved. (Did P. and P. conveniently forget about lynching ?) Now I hold that this cannot possibly do good and may easily do harm. Why show at a Command Performance a film which is, on balance, anti-British ? Is the production good ? I have no opinion. The highbrows may talk about ' visual narrative ' and ' cinematic sense '; I just don't and won't associate the Hereafter with something that would have ravished the soul of Madame Tussaud.

Nov. 4   Letter from Jock :
Monday.

> 33 *King Street*
> *Covent Garden, W.C.*2
> *3rd November,* 1946

DEAR JAMIE,
   I fear I'll never be penny-paper-minded. Here is the piece about Becky Sharp which the *News Chronicle* cut out of me o' Friday— *not* for reasons of space, *but* because it was a quotation !

   " Here is a glimpse of Becky's real-life prototype—not at all a well-known passage—from the memoirs of Lady Ritchie, Thackeray's daughter :

   " ' One morning a hansom drove up to the door, and out of it emerged a most charming, dazzling little lady dressed in black, who greeted my father with great affection and brilliancy, and who, departing presently, gave him a large bunch of fresh violets. This was the only time I ever saw the fascinating little person who was by many supposed to be the original of Becky ; my father only laughed when people asked him, but he never quite owned to it.'

   " The lady's name was never divulged."

I showed this excised but surely interesting thing to Lady Colefax, whom I was visiting in hospital the other day. She said, " Oh, yes, I remember meeting Anne Ritchie when I was quite a girl, and she told me an exceedingly interesting thing. She told me that when *she* was a very young girl, ten or eleven in fact, she was taken to a great gaunt house in Paris where in a singularly tall room a pale, thin, dark-haired, sick-looking man was playing the piano beautifully. One of the ladies turned to little Anne Thackeray and said to her, ' Always remember, my dear, that when you were very young you came here to-day and heard Chopin play ! ' "

Jamie, I hope, this thrills you as it does me. Sybil Colefax, by the way, seems to rate me as importantly as Boswell. For you, on the other hand, her regard is very much of the sort that *Mrs* Boswell had for Dr Johnson !

Ever,

Jock

Winged Words. No. 19 : Nowhere, unless it be in *Ein Helden-leben*, does his [Strauss's] clever blatancy achieve such a measure of triumphant vulgarity as in *Tod und Verklärung*. If the awakening to eternity is like this (the tune on the brass), any man of taste would prefer death.

Music critic, " The Times "

I take leave of my *Winged Words* with what Kipling's Beetle would have called " a final exhibition, a last attack, a giddy parergon." Here, then, is No. 20, culled from an " In Memoriam " tribute to a former Official Receiver in Bankruptcy. Then follows the line :

" I thank my God upon every remembrance of you."

Nov. 8 Friday. My secretary having resigned, I thought of advertising for a young man whose first qualifications should be that he did not wear corduroy trousers or hold any views about anything. And then I had a bit of luck. The Canadian boy who used to write to me from Iceland (see *Ego* 5, p. 140) walked in yesterday and asked for a job. Incidentally he was a sailor and not a soldier. Age thirty-one, has had secretarial experience, can take down in shorthand, type, spell, and speak a little French. I asked him when he could start. He said, " Not before to-morrow afternoon." He started at 3.30 to-day. Name, Michael Russell-Smith.

In the meantime here is a charming story from Hélène Vacaresco's *Mémorial sur le Mode Mineur*. The author is talking about Calvé :

J'ai d'elle bien des souvenirs encore. En voici un qui me semble significatif. Nous parlions ensemble de notre auguste et si généreux ami le roi Édouard VII. C'était lors de notre dernière entrevue avenue Kléber à Paris.

"Oh ! " me dit Calvé, " il était sublime alors qu'il voulait simplement être drôle. Figurez-vous que la reine Victoria, admiratrice passionnée de *Carmen*, avait commandé mon buste à je ne sais quel sculpteur anglais en renom. Je fus représentée avec des œillets dans les cheveux et une mantille. Enfin je devenais, en marbre, s'il vous plaît, c'est-à-dire presque pour l'éternité, l'héroïne même de Bizet.

" La reine fit placer ce buste à Windsor parmi d'autres objets d'art. Lorsque après son avènement je revis le roi Édouard, incidemment il me parla de ce buste. ' Oh sire ! ' lui répondis-je, ' je pense que la pauvre Carmen doit être mise de côté, car je sais que tout a changé dans la salle où elle avait été placée.' ' En effet,' me répondit le roi, ' plus d'un changement a eu lieu au château après la mort de ma mère, mais je dois vous avouer que j'ai eu soin de votre buste. J'ai ordonné qu'on le place à côté de celui du duc de Wellington. Vous pourrez ainsi lui répéter le mot de Cambronne pendant toute l'éternité . . .' "

Nov. 9   A lady writes :
Saturday.

I don't agree with you that Coquelin " did not achieve pathos." I was only seventeen at the time, it is true, but I shall never forget how much I was moved by his death scene in *Cyrano.* Even now, when the leaves fall in the dusk I think of him. I think one often forgets that the great furore caused by the play in those days was its absolute break with the tradition of the then French stage. I have read it three times in the original, and nothing would induce me to see it in English however well done.

Let me try to settle this question once and for all. I was twenty-two and my brother Edward was twenty, and we were both terribly disappointed. Now hear Max Beerbohm on the subject :

On the stage it was always with his brain alone that he made his effects. He had observed, and studied, and thought, and had thought out the exact means of expression. He never let emotion come between himself and his part—never trusted to imagination or inspiration. These, indeed, are qualities which he did not possess. They are incompatible with absence of " nerves." And it was, I suppose, because he could never surrender himself to a part, was always conscious master of it, that Sarah Bernhardt wrote of him in her memoirs that he was " plutôt grand acteur que grand artiste." Certainly, great emotional acting does demand the power of self-surrender—is a passive rather than an active business. Coquelin, in his writings and in his talk, was a sturdy champion of Diderot's paradox. And Coquelin, in the last act of

Cyrano de Bergerac, was a shining refutation of the truth of that paradox. All the paraphernalia of emotion were in that memorable passage of acting—were there most beautifully and authentically ; but emotion itself wasn't there ; and many a duffer could have moved us far more than Coquelin did. If Coquelin had been capable of the necessary self-surrender, he would not have been the unapproachable comedian that we loved and revered. It was because his fine brain was absolutely his master that he stood absolutely alone in his mastery of comedic art.

" Plutôt grand acteur que grand artiste." But Sarah told May that she herself, on the stage with Coquelin, had been enormously moved by his pathos at the end. (How did Sarah come to play such a bad part as Roxane ? Quite simply. She wanted Coquelin for Flambeau (*L'Aiglon*) in her American tour, and held out her Roxane as a bait. I have a photograph of her in the rôle.) There are three possibilities : (1) Sarah drew something out of Coquelin that was not in him at other times. (2) With any other Roxane he had no pathos even when he was trying (Max). (3) When I saw him at Manchester he was just not trying. On the whole I pin my faith to Max, and believe him to have been right both in the matter of fact and the reason why it must have been so. Except that that fine and fastidious critic does not make allowance for the physical factor. All the surrender in the world won't help if the actor hasn't got " les larmes dans la voix."

Nov. 10   A letter :
Sunday.

Queen Alexandra Mansions
*Grape Street, W.C.*2
November 10, 1946

Dear D. B. Wyndham Lewis,
    It is so long since I was in the Savage Club that I have forgotten what is our brotherly name for you.
    This is to tell you that last night round about eleven-thirty I took up *The Hooded Hawk*—why the devil didn't you just call it *The Real Boswell* ?—and until nearly four in the morning boiled over with admiration and rage. Perhaps I was drunk, but certainly last night I would have given all I have written for that one introductory chapter. (I am not quite so certain this morning.) The whole book breathes the very air and spirit of the time. How you do this I don't know ; it has nothing to do with the wealth of detail proceeding from your immense erudition. To put the matter shortly, I live in your book as I do in Boswell's. (By the way, I have never *read* the *Life* ; what I have done is to dip into it on an average of twice a week throughout fifty years.) It was a

stroke of genius to begin with Boswell's deathbed. And what enchanting phraseology! " All his life Boswell was teetering on the verge of complete sanity." And I like very much, too, your " Boswell had as good a right to the infinite mercy of God as Lord Macaulay himself."

There is just one point I want to make. You write (p. 78) of Boswell dying to cut into the conversation and distinguish himself " like Mr Kipps in the Imperial Grand." And again, on the same page, of Boswell retiring after that first interview " bloody but unbowed." To what extent is one justified in illustrating an eighteenth-century happening by a nineteenth-century reference? Suppose a playwright who tells us his action is happening in the 'nineties should make one of his characters say, " My dear, how very sick-making! " Would not the switch from Pinero's idiom to Waugh's jerk the spectator momentarily out of the period? Suppose I am writing a play about Hannibal. Can I safely make a Captain of the Guard say that he saw his master standing silent on a peak in the Pyrenees? I think you have seen the difficulty, because on the next page (p. 79) you write, " The Doctor, in modern idiom, was in the bag." Resolve me about this.

I have two odd Boswellian snippets for you. One is about a laundry-boy at Barnet whose name turned out to be James Boswell Crummy. His birthplace? Lichfield! The other is a correspondence I had some years ago with a seventeen-year-old schoolboy named James Boswell, the great-great-grandson of Boswell's daughter Elizabeth, who married her cousin William Boswell. You can read about this last in *Ego* 5, pp. 89 and 93.

By the way, I have decided to wind up my Diary at the end of this year. " Superfluous lags the vet'ran on the stage." I wonder who wrote that?

Ever your devoted and abashed

JAMES AGATE

Nov. 11   Another letter to George Lyttelton:
Monday.

Queen Alexandra Mansions
Grape Street, W.C. 2

November 11, 1946

DEAR GEORGE LYTTELTON,

My delighted reading of your letter was interrupted by a policeman at my elbow. (" An' I sez to my flutterin' 'eart-strings, I sez to 'em, ' Peace, be still! ' ") Bow Street wanted to know whether I would go bail in a hundred pounds for somebody with a name I had never heard of. Rang up the station. Age? Thirty-eight. Walk in life? Gentleman. Charge? Larceny. Stealing a motor-car. No. J. A. won't go bail for total strangers.

You ask me what I thought of Alexander Woollcott. I met

him once only, and perhaps it isn't fair. . . . Nonsense, of course it's fair. He impressed me as being a ready but not fine-witted vulgarian. It was at a luncheon party given, I think, by Cochran, and he never said a single pleasant, or even unpleasant, memorable thing. I can no more explain why America's millions listened to him on the wireless than George Jean Nathan could have explained the English passion for Mr Middleton. I seem to be writing a lot of rubbish to-day. Of course Nathan could have explained that. He knows that the English are Middleton-minded.

Have got a difficult job on hand. Am to tell Light Programme listeners what I think of the Film Censorship. But what do I think of any censorship ? In the theatre good, because it prevents raids by old ladies with umbrellas, and asinine police. But where draw the line ? Ninety per cent. of Hollywood's films lay it down that for a girl to stick to her commonplace lover, marry him, and bear him commonplace brats is to fail in life, while to get more mink than the girl next door is to succeed. You and I laugh at such twaddle ; the withers of every typist in the audience are horribly wrung. What must I, as censor, do about a well-made picture which sticks to the truth ? Say the life of Emma Crouch, who as Cora Pearl did far better for herself than the sixteenth child of an ex-seaman had any right to expect. She died at the age of forty-four ? Yes, but for twenty years she had a magnificent run for fifteen million pounds of other people's money, and I don't see how you can make cancer retributive. Or take Zola's Nana. Where's the moral in smallpox ? What about the penniless Miss Rebecca Sharp, who, after a rattling good time, ended up hanging about Bath and Cheltenham " and never without a footman " ? If I ban films about successful gold-diggers on moral grounds I must ban good pictures about the Cora Pearls, the Nanas, and the Becky Sharps. If I let these through on artistic grounds I am setting up the doctrine of one moral law for the uneducated many and another moral law for the cultured few. The which I fervently believe, but am not going to make confession of in the Light Programme. I think I shall approve the Censorship as a principle, but lay down one law only. This is that if sniggering films on the subject of, say, prostitutes and ' pansies ' are permitted, then the same licence must be granted to films dealing seriously with the tragedy of these unhappy wretches.

To change the subject. I have been having the oddest experiences lately—a kind of *Intimations of Immortality* in reverse. It is as though the glory and the freshness were coming back. I have been finding myself gay for no reason. Recapturing all sorts of early delights—my first summer holidays, what walking in the Lake District used to be like, the feel of a really good crack to leg. Is this the beginning of second childhood ? If so it's going to be delicious.

By the way, I've just discovered or invented a new limbo, which I take to be something superior to a dimension. In this, anything that you want to happen, happens and goes on happening, always.

For ever Sir Toby has his " *Pourquoi, my dear knight ? " And longer than any figure on a Grecian urn Traddles looks forward to union with his dearest Sophy.

Yes, it's second childhood all right.

Ever,

JAMES AGATE

Nov. 12   In a letter from George Richards :
Tuesday.

Some weeks ago, unable to sit through any more, I wandered out of the auditorium of the Bournemouth Pavilion toward the end of the first act of a more than usually lame and impudently incompetent domestic comedy-farce and, encountering two Little Men emerging from a door marked Private, I was overcome by an eruption of pent-up righteous indignation. Giving way to impulse, I said, in the politest tones I could command, " Excuse me, gentlemen, are you by any chance connected with the show now being performed in this theatre ? " Beamingly they signified an affirmative, being, as I afterwards discovered, the Press Representative and the Assistant Stage Manager. " Well," I said, " perhaps you will permit me to inform you that never in all my theatregoing experience have I encountered such an imbroglio of unadulterated rubbish or such an unimaginably tedious farrago of dreary, demoralising drivel. If its excuse is that it is intended merely as a vehicle for the leading performer, I can only say, gentlemen, that a self-respecting vehicle should have more than one wheel. The play has not a wisp of talent, merit, novelty, or inspiration of any kind and in plot, dialogue, and acting is an insult to the British race."

Pausing a moment to gauge the effect of this, I for the first time took a real look at the Little Men. And beheld in their eyes a vast, unquenchable contentment, and read on their countenances the outward and visible sign of inward and spiritual happiness.

Nov. 13   " The measure of choosing well," wrote Sir William
Wednesday.   Temple, " is whether a man likes what he has chosen."

This applies particularly to one's friends. It is twenty years since I chose George Mathew, and I have been amply repaid. At least four nights a week, and often five and six, he looks in for an hour's chat on his way to Regent's Park. In that hour we discuss practically everything, though the subject which most crops up is the exact meaning and use of words. Fowler is our Bible here, though a Bible of which one can be critical. Said George to-night, " Why doesn't he come down heavily on those people who say ' infer ' when they mean ' imply ' ? " I said, " What about Shakespeare, who uses the two indifferently ? " " Oh, Shakespeare," said George. " He was an ignorant b——, anyway ! "

Nov. 14
Thursday.

Waking early and unable to get to sleep again, I made a list of my Likes and Dislikes.

Dislikes :

Inaccuracy. Beards. Anglo-Catholics. Jews (most). Bartókery. Surrealism. Imagist poetry. My pictures in the *Daily Express*. Choral singing. Curry. Walking. Women who make up in public. Young men who carry combs. Shaw's plays. Radio comedians. Musicals. Crooning. Dance bands. War books. Heat waves. Walt Disney. Cats. Plays about Schubert. British films. British opera. Cold spells. Crowds. Cinema organs. Dog-racing. English phlegm. Scotch humour. Welsh *hwyl*.

Likes :

Irish blarney. Jews (some). Americans. French films. Shaw's prefaces. Groucho Marx. Making a speech. Actresses at the Ivy. Berlioz. Dogs. Babies. Acrobats. Seaside bands. Renoir. Damon Runyon. Wordsworth. Test Matches. Fire-engines. Flood-lighting. Walking-sticks. Asparagus. Work.

Nov. 15
Friday.

The post brought this note from D. B. Wyndham Lewis :

31 *Pembroke Road, W*.8
November 13, 1946

MY DEAR JAMES,

I needn't tell you what pleasure your letter gave me. And as you are one of the very, very few people whose judgment I respect, especially in literary matters, you may take me as being in a very pleasant glow at this moment, bless you.

You're quite right about lapses into modern idiom. It's slip-shod and silly, and I don't know how it happened, except that there are times when one's attention slips a cog. I wish now I'd asked you to look over the proofs, but I know you have enough to do without that. My only excuse is that I got them in a nursing-home, recovering from an almost fatal nephritis last March, and dizzy with morphia.

No, don't give up *Ego*, James ! It's the perfect bedside book (except that it keeps one awake), and it's a classic exercise in the difficult art of not boring. I can't think of any reason for your not going on till the gong rings, and I mean it, as a fan of long standing. Moreover, I doubt if I could ever think of anything even faintly malicious to say to you, even in fun. I keep that sort of thing for what Barbey d'A. called the richly antlered herd. Do change your mind, I implore you.

Thanks for the Boswell items.

I wish I could afford the set of the Boswell Papers (Isham's). It's a beautiful piece of work, and I don't grudge the time I spent at the London Library. Incidentally, do you know what the Doctor really said to Garrick about his going behind the scenes at Drury Lane : " I'll come no more behind your scenes, David ; the white bosoms of your actresses excite my genital organs." Compare the discreet version in the *Life*. The Papers are full of meat.

Yours ever, and with warm thanks for a letter I shall treasure,

BEVAN

P.S. I had meant to quote, *en passant*, something about that Boswell descendant you mention in *Ego 5*, but like many other things it slipped my memory. I was feeling ill all last year. " James Boswell Crummy " is an admirable name for a laundry-boy. Here's another—I met a chap called Jorian Jenks. Wouldn't you swear he was out of a G. K. C. story ?

Nov. 16   A letter to Jock :
Saturday.

As from Queen Alexandra Mansions
Grape Street, W.C.2

November 16th, 1946

JOCK, MA LADDIE,

I am writing this sitting in Charles Smith's front room in his high flat on Marine Parade, Brighton. A gentle day, and I look down on a fisherman " diminished to his cock," if you know what I mean. At this moment I am asking myself : Do seagulls have asthma ? And if so, do they stop for breath, and, stopping, do they stall like aeroplanes ? I ask because last night it took me five minutes, and perhaps a bit more, to cover thirty yards ! I had a dreadful experience the other evening at the theatre, where I had to climb four flights of stairs to get to the what-d'you-call-it.

In future my criterion for any play is : Are the foyer, stalls, bar, and so forth all on the same level ? (I don't care where they put the stage.) Similarly the acting will be judged according as to whether my stall is an end one and on the same side as the Gents.

Am down here for a couple of days' rest, which it seems I need. (I find it humiliating to be dictated to by one's body.) Charles is a perfect host. George Mathew came down with me, and we sat up till 2 A.M. settling the affairs of Europe—nay, of the globe. This morning at nine Charles gets up, cooks, and serves three breakfasts—bacon, sausage, toast, real butter, strawberry jam, tea. He brings one tray in to me, takes another in to George, and retires to bed with his own. His housekeeper comes in about eleven, when we are supposed to think about getting up. One of the things which distresses me in this matter of increasing infirmity is the nuisance one is to one's friends. This week-end I am embarking on the finer tact of not apologising. It should be presumed that people who invite old buffers to stay with them know what they are in for. They must know that you may die on their hands. The time was, Jock, when I wanted this to happen when I was driving off the third tee, into the purple hills, on the old Chapel-en-le-Frith golf course. But since that cannot now happen the armchair in Charles's bow-window will do very nicely.

But to come to the point of this letter, which is you and not me. (If grammar says the last word should be ' I ' then grammar is wrong.) I have before me the *Tatler*, in which Clifford Bax has an article. He asks who is our best dramatic critic, and answers " Alan Dent." Next I hear that you are to be one of the six judges in the Embassy Theatre's award of " Oscars " for the year's best playwright, actor, and actress. Finally Gerald Barry told me two nights ago that you have been appointed film critic to the *Illus-trated London News*. I could, of course, just pat you on the back with a few well-chosen words of congratulation. Let me do it more elegantly. Let me remind you of somebody—de Marsay, I think— who in *Le Père Goriot*, if I mistake not, said about Rastignac, " Décidément, ce jeune homme commence à percer."

It is the duty of the elderly to say nice things about the youngish ; this time duty puts on her pleasantest face. In other words, I'm happy about you, and Paul Dehn, who has suddenly started to write very much better, and Lionel Hale, whom I met in Regent Street recently almost recovered from his accident.

I have drooled a little too much on old age in this letter. But the springs of emotion are not entirely dried up. When the porter at the Grand Hotel welcomed me and remembered my name I wept. Eight years and an intervening war ! But between sobs I managed to tip him two shillings. It would have been half a crown if Stanley Rubinstein hadn't telephoned me just as I was leaving to say that he must have £300 for income tax on Monday morning, and where is it coming from ?

Ever,

JAMIE

Nov. 17   A seventy-m.p.h. gale. " Lines of white on a sullen sea,'
Sunday.   make me feel Tosti-ish. To shake this off sit down to
                    compose my broadcast :

Films are fun. But the funniest thing of all about them is, I am persuaded, the Film Censorship. In this country censorship of the theatre was originally a device to prevent the Government of the day from being attacked by playwrights holding contrary political views. It was a political muzzle. Censorship as a means of supervising morals came later. How about America ? Well, I happened to be in New York when the movement to ban strip-tease and fan dancers started. Now note this. As long as these exhibitions confined themselves to the vaudeville theatres of Greenwich Village and that part of New York which corresponds to our East End American morality was not disturbed. It was only when these shows began to invade Broadway and draw the public away from the legitimate theatres that the public conscience was stirred. And who stirred it ? The owners of the legitimate theatres.

I am in favour of censorship for one reason, and one reason only. Without it any play or film would be at the mercy of some old woman of either sex marching down the gangway brandishing an umbrella and protesting that she is being outraged and insulted. Or at the mercy of some ignorant policeman or asinine Watch Committee. The censorship saves us from that.

But for whom are we to censor films ? Adults or juveniles, the educated or the illiterate ? I have been studying Raymond Moley's book entitled *The Hays Office*, published last year. Here are some items from the list of " Don'ts and Be Carefuls " adopted by the California Association for the Guidance of Producers. The Association resolves that none of the things mentioned in the first half of its list shall appear in pictures " irrespective of the manner in which they are treated." I will take four points only.

One. The words ' hell ' and ' damn.' I see. A soldier who has his hand blown off is to wave the stump and say, " Bless my soul. Look at this ! " Such an embargo would put an end to the filming of half of Eugene O'Neill's plays, and, of course, to Shaw's *Pygmalion*.

Two. Miscegenation, or sex relationship between the white and black races. I see. White girls may make friendships with coloured soldiers—our English girls did in the War—but they must not be allowed to know to what such attachments may lead.

Three. Sex hygiene and venereal diseases. Again I see. Prevention and cure are to be put beyond the pale. By this edict Brieux's *Damaged Goods* and Ibsen's *Ghosts*, two of the world's most moral plays, are out.

Four. Any inference of sex perversion. But the walk, accent, mannerisms, and phraseology of what are known as ' pansies ' are part of the stock-in-trade of nine-tenths of our music-hall and film comedians. I see no objection. To what, then, do I object ? To the fact that a serious play or film dealing with the tragedy of those unhappy persons, male and female, whose sex instincts are not normal would be rigidly banned. What about the film called *Children in Uniform* ? That film was possible because the audience could pretend that the attachment which was its subject matter was romantic and abstract. The same with gold-digging. If Betty Grable and Rita Hayworth are allowed to show nitwits the glamorous side of that profession, then sanity demands that some serious actress should be allowed to show us the real side !

The second half of the Association's list deals with subjects about which special care is to be exercised. These include, to mention again only four, the use of firearms, brutality, third-degree methods, a woman's sale of her virtue. Let us take these in their order. In the matter of firearms I seem to have made acquaintance with a good many sawn-off shotguns. Brutality ? We have all seen some pretty hefty fights. Third-degree methods ? I think you and I could recall one or two pictures in which these have been fully exploited. The sale of a woman's virtue ? What do the film-makers imagine that the opulent charmer so brilliantly portrayed by Mae West offers her customers when they come up to see her ? Rock buns ? No. Hollywood still contrives to evade its own laws. In spite of its Hays Office it has succeeded in making the world's dirtiest pictures.

In my view America has a right to say what shall or shall not be shown on her screens. Therefore I have no sympathy with the maker of British pictures who complains that they are censored when they get to the other side. He should use his brains, and learn to be dirty in the manner which America approves. I am not attacking Hollywood. I have no doubt that the frantic nonsense which besets the Hays Office has its counterpart in English censor-ship. But English censorship is clever enough not to publish its guiding principles. At least, I have never seen a copy of them.

The Hays Office insists that in every picture virtue shall be rewarded and vice punished. And it lays further stress on this, that evil shall not be presented so attractively that when the audience emerges into the street it forgets the ultimate fate of the sinner and remembers only the delights of sinning. But consider this. I, a grown man, will not easily be turned into a gangster ; the idea that I could be a ' big shot ' does not appeal to me. But what about the grocer's boy ? You, madam, listening to me—take your case. You are happily married, adore your husband and children, and are adored by them. The idea of being a gangster's moll may not be your idea of fun. But what about the little missie who cleaned your doorstep this morning ? Dangle mink and diamond bracelets before her, and is she going to be deterred by the thought that twenty years hence she will die a miserable death in gutter or hospital ? Remember that by the Hays Code she has not been allowed to know that such a death impends.

The censorship can do what it likes in the way of embargoes and warnings. *It cannot censor the minds of the young, and particularly of the uneducated young.* The grocer's boy may well elect for a short life and a merry one. He may think getting bumped off at forty a fair price to pay for twenty years of high-powered cars and expensive women. The little maid who keeps your house clean may not grumble at the prospect of having to chuck herself into the river at some distant date provided that for the next twenty years she is the envy of every other woman in town. In other words, both grocer's boy and hired help may think the game worth the candle.

And now I make my last point. As I said, I approve of the censorship only because non-censorship can be a greater nuisance.

But I would have a super-censor who would be a man of culture, a man who knows a work of art when he sees one, and not somebody who might just as well be in the Post Office. There is a famous French film entitled *Le Rosier de Madame Husson*. In this a young man wins a prize for possessing more of innocence than any other lad in the village. He spends the money on getting drunk, and for the rest of his life is never sober. My super-censor would say to his subordinate, " Hands off ! This picture is a masterpiece of irony. It is adapted from a story by Guy de Maupassant, one of the world's great writers, and recognised as such in a country at least as intelligent as this one. Therefore I say, ' Hands off ! ' But if you like to ban *Getting Gertie's Garter* or *Up in Mabel's Room* on the ground not of morality but of sheer, stark, staring imbecility, that is O.K. by me."

Nov. 18   " The bright day is done, and we are for the dark." But
Monday.   it's the twilight I object to and not the blackness. What
             must it be like to retire from the prize ring a world-beater
at forty, and know forty years of oblivion ? I think perhaps it doesn't matter with boxers ; it takes brains to be bored. But what about actors who can no longer remember their words ? Or actresses carried into the Ivy on litters ? Old Age—I do detest, abhor, execrate, and give thee to sixscore thousand devils.

Nov. 19   Like every other young Canadian who goes to a university,
Tuesday.   Russell-Smith when he was at McGill filled in the holidays
             by doing odd jobs for pocket money. At one time he was
a waiter, at another a grave-digger. This morning, my houseboy being in bed with flu, R.-S. kindly deputised by bringing in my breakfast, which he did with the poise of experience. Dusting the table with an imaginary napkin, he said, " I wonder whether my other job will come in as handy ? " Now we defy augury, and all that. All the same, it was just as well that I had got up in good spirits.

Nov. 20   A letter from Arthur Rose :
Wednesday.

30 *Old Queen Street*
*Westminster, S.W.*1
November 19*th*, 1946

DEAR JAMES,
    I always whoop with joy when you tell them that plays must have skeletons ; but I groan when you slip up and say it is a defect of Mr Bates's play, *The Day of Glory*, that its action can be foreseen.

You know as well as I do that drama can't begin until the play's action is foreseen. What masterpiece omits the foreshadowing of its action ? Look at the bluntness with which Master Will always foretells his action. Take *Othello* as example. See how Iago acts as his author's chorus to foretell crisis after crisis. The fact is, adult suspense in the theatre lies not in the audience wondering what is going to happen next, but in their foreknowing, and waiting in dread or hope for some one in the play to learn what they foreknow. I know I am teaching grandpa the ancient art of sucking eggs, but didn't he ask for it ?

Yours,

ARTHUR ROSE

I write :

Queen Alexandra Mansions
Grape Street, W.C.2

November 20th, 1946

DEAR ARTHUR,

You would be right if you said that the highest kind of drama cannot begin, etc., etc. Obviously we know that Lear's children are going to make it hell for the old boy. But who at the first performance knew that Friar Laurence's letter was going to miscarry ? Which just puts *R. and J.* on a lower level than *K. L.* Whoever in *La Dame aux Camélias* foresaw the visit of old Duval or what that visit portended ? Who knew what was going to happen in *A Doll's House* ? The audience on that first night was as much surprised as Nora when Thorvald called her a bloody little fool.

Bates's play is all talk, and as the talk isn't quite good enough we want something to turn up to relieve the monotony of regurgitated leading articles. And you'll agree that the property of things turning up is unexpectedness. Consider those three superb *coups de théâtre*—the discovery that the man in *La Parisienne* is the lover and not the husband, John Worthing's entry in mourning in Wilde's play, and Lady Frederick's appearance *en déshabillé*. Where would the fun be if one expected these ? And what is a *coup de théâtre* if there is no *coup* ? Think it over.

Always,

JAMES

Nov. 21   Letter to George Lyttelton :
Thursday.

Queen Alexandra Mansions
Grape Street, W.C.2

November 21, 1946

DEAR GEORGE LYTTELTON,

In spite of all efforts to get rid of my obsession about misprints, not only in my own work but in other people's, the damned thing continues. Here is the latest crop. In his *Time Was* Graham

Robertson is made to write of Alexandre Dumas *file*, and this in the book's seventh impression ! *Stalky and Co.* Stalky continues the conversation in a loud and cheerful *noice*. This, if you please, in the twentieth reprinting of the pocket edition. One of our high-brow musical critics gives the title of Debussy's piece as *L'Aprés Midi D'Un Faune*. One wrong accent, one hyphen omitted, and four capital letters which should be lower case. The American paper *Go*, whose London correspondent I have just become, makes me add an extra ' l ' to Dame Madge Kendal. This particu-larly infuriates me, since I must have written twenty letters to thumb-sucking critics misspelling the name of the old rhinoceros.

Apropos, I hear from Bertie van Thal that you are cross with me for calling Milton " a monumental and boring old buffer." Some geniuses are set so high that the stones you throw at them never get there, and perhaps I thought that " monumental " made it safe. Of course, I realise that *Lycidas* is the greatest long-short poem in the language, with Wordsworth's *Intimations* as its only rival. Similarly, I realise that Prospero's " cloud-capp'd towers " speech is one of the greatest things in Shakespeare. But if you turn to my first article in *Brief Chronicles* you will see that I call Prospero " that endless chunnerer " and " an old josser." Yet if I had to choose any one article of mine suggesting that delicacy of perception was not utterly beyond me, I think it would be that one. Wherefore I stick to " old rhinoceros " as a proper term to apply to Madge K., the third or fourth greatest actress I have seen.

And now I have to plead really guilty to something. Some-where in *Ego* 8 I allude to the extraordinary influence that *Macbeth* had on the mind of Charles Dickens, citing three references in the novels—two in *David Copperfield* and one in *Dombey and Son*. Yesterday, if you please, I found a reference in *Little Dorrit*. The guests at the great Physician's have assembled, all but Mr Merdle : " Mr Merdle's default left a Banquo's chair at the table ; but if he had been there, he would have merely made the difference of Banquo in it, and consequently he was no loss." The point ? Simply that there may be lots more allusions to Shakespeare's play, and unless I am prepared to come forward with all of them I ought not to have broached the subject. Paris gave my mother her light-ness of touch and Heidelberg her thoroughness. I have inherited the latter, which with me has become mania. I respect the com-petent thug more than I do the bungling knight-at-arms. There's a lot to be said for Germans, even Nazis. And now I suppose you're shocked.

To change the tune. Here is something I jotted down this morning that I shall use when some highbrow ass provokes me sufficiently : " To me a poet is somebody who writes something that is going to make me happier, in the way that the sweep of some Handelian air or haunting melody of Chopin makes me happy, for the rest of my life. Something about magic casements, glimmering squares, mantles blue, incense-breathing morns, sprays the bird clung to, thoughts that lie too deep for tears. T. S. Eliot is not a poet in the sense that Keats, Tennyson, Milton, Gray, Browning, Wordsworth were poets. He is a philosopher-cook bent on frying metaphysical fish in free verse."

However, I don't suppose my views on poetry matter. As for the misprints, things without all remedy should be without regard. So don't bother to answer this. I only trouble you with it because it helps to get one's mind straight. Friendship with an egoist has its drawbacks !

Ever,

JAMES AGATE

P.S. As I am about to post this I see that in Whymper's book on the Matterhorn the Deity is represented as in trouble with His French accents. On the tomb of Édouard Goehrs, the young Strasbourg climber, appear the words : " Mes pensèes ne sont pas vos pensèes . . . a dit l'Eternel."

Nov. 22 Spend the morning over a notice of *Caste*. Call attention
Friday.   to the fact that dramatic critics who reprint their notices
             in book form do something more than satisfy their vanity
—to wit, compile stage history. The value of this is realised only when one comes across a gap. In the matter of Tom Robertson's play there is not a line to show the reaction of contemporary criticism. (I have not the time to go trotting off to Hendon or wherever the newspapers buried their files when the bombing started.) Henry Morley stops his *Journal of a London Playgoer* twelve months all but a day before *Caste's* first night. And Dutton Cook begins his *Nights at the Play* four months and a few odd days after that first night. Maddening ! In despair I turn up *The Journal of the Bancrofts*, and find nothing except a long story of how on the first night somebody played a practical joke with George d'Alroy's wig. As I can't find anything I have to do some hard work of my own. Incidentally, I point out that if it hadn't been for J. A. and eight devoted publishers there would not be a single line in book form from which any future student could glean anything about the English theatre in the last quarter of a century. Why shouldn't I indulge in a tootle on the trumpet when it's justified ?

Having finished the *S.T.* article, rushed down to Grosvenor Square and delivered a wireless talk to soldiers left behind in Burma and Japan. I find that the old mind still gets about fairly easily ; the nuisance is carting the old body around.

Nov. 23   Note to Jock :
Saturday.

Queen Alexandra Mansions
*Grape Street, W.C.*2
November 23rd, 1946

Dear Jock,

Do you really think that Hare played Eccles at the age of twenty-three ? He was a fine character actor, but not as fine as all that. The original Eccles was George Honey. Hare played Sam Gerridge. Sizeable bloomers like this deserve showing up in *Ego.* But this eternal blazon shall not be on condition that you send me a letter dulcet and excusatory.

But who am I to talk ? I, who in the *D.E.* describe the eighteenth century as " the age of lace ruffles and lack of brains." Shades of Johnson, Garrick, Goldsmith, Reynolds, Fielding, Pope, and all our friends ! I had, of course, written " drains."

By the way, I had a charming letter this morning from a man wanting to know whether I will settle a dispute his sixteen-year-old daughter is having with some of her school friends. " Is, or is not, Macbeth a butcher ? " Cheque for one guinea enclosed. I know what this means. Sending back the cheque and with it a fifty-guinea essay on S.'s butchers and the differences between them.

Ever,

Jamie

P.S. Have decided that the blazon is on after all. This will give you the chance to do something better than the old " Ignorance, madam, pure ignorance."

Nov. 24   Supper at the Café Royal with George Mathew :
Sunday.

G. M. How comes it that a person so obviously devoted to things of the mind as you are should be so scornful about the intellectuals ?

J. A. I'm not !

G. M. The highbrows, then.

J. A. That's the point. Your intellectual and my highbrow are not the same thing.

G. M. What's the difference ?

J. A. A highbrow is a pseudo-intellectual. A mind thinking above its class. A mind in corduroy trousers.

G. M. You mean a braying ass who doesn't know how long his ears are ?

J. A. Exactly. It all boils down to something Basil Macdonald Hastings said years ago. Do you know it ?

G. M. I ought to. You've told me a hundred and fifty times. " There's nothing like consulting a highbrow if you want to hear something that's funny as well as daft."

Nov. 25   Note from Jock : " You are right, of course, about the
Monday.   original Eccles. Shall sleep this week, alone, in sackcloth.
       And eat ashes."

Nov. 26   To Liverpool yesterday afternoon with Bertie van Thal·
Tuesday.   Re-read Gerald Kersh's *Night and the City*, reissued by
       Heinemann. I would sooner have created Harry Fabian,
the ponce, than any character in modern fiction since Mr Polly.
Train forty minutes late. Our rooms on the sixth floor (I loathe
heights) and a hundred yards from the lifts (I nauseate walking).
Scramble into some clothes and arrive out of breath just in time for
lecture. Gaunt, hideous, Wesleyan-Methodistical building. Huge
auditorium. Not a soul in the circle ; handful of people on the
ground floor. Chairman sends apologies for absence. Choir practice
in adjacent building. In circumstances I am not at my best, though
Bertie says I warm up after the first ten minutes. Routine stuff
about the theatre, and stay on my feet for an hour. Bright spot of
the evening is the supper afterwards, where I drink a bottle of
champagne and kiss Ivy St Helier's hand. Sleep well, thanks to
sleeping tablets and plentiful bedroom provision of whiskey.

Lovely morning, and not too many people on the train. Autumn
sunshine, which makes me think of Leo. Shake off melancholy and
bury myself in a book Bertie lends me, Ada M. Ingpen's *Women as
Letter-writers*. Thoroughly interested in Fanny Kemble's account of
Macready :

> Macready is not pleasant to act with, as he keeps no specific
> time for his exits or entrances, comes on while one is in the middle
> of a soliloquy, and goes off while one is in the middle of a speech to
> him. He growls and prowls, and roams and foams, about the stage
> in every direction, like a tiger in his cage, so that I never know on
> what side of me he means to be ; and keeps up a perpetual snarling
> and grumbling like the aforesaid tiger, so that I never feel quite
> sure that he *has done*, and that it is my turn to speak. I do not
> think fifty pounds a night would hire me to play another engage-
> ment with him ; but I only say, I don't think—fifty pounds a night
> is a consideration, four times a week, and I have not forgotten the
> French proverb, " *Il ne faut pas dire : fontaine, jamais de ton eau
> je ne boirai.*"

All of which reinforces my opinion of Macready as a great actor and
cad, and Fanny Kemble as a poor actress and a delightful woman.

> I do not know how Desdemona might have affected me under
> other circumstances, but my only feeling about acting it with Mr
> Macready is dread of his personal violence. I quail at the idea of

his laying hold of me in those terrible, passionate scenes; for in *Macbeth* he pinched me black and blue, and almost tore the point lace from my head. I am sure my little finger will be rebroken, and as for that smothering in bed, "Heaven have mercy upon me!" as poor Desdemona says. If that foolish creature wouldn't persist in *talking* long after she has been smothered and stabbed to death, one might escape by the off side of the bed, and leave the bolster to be questioned by Emilia, and apostrophised by Othello; but she will uplift her testimony after death to her husband's amiable treatment of her, and even the bolster wouldn't be stupid enough for that.

Yes, I feel I should have liked Fanny.

Get back to my desk this morning and find forty dull letters and two bottles of Pol Roger, 1928, the gift of some unknown benefactor.

Nov. 27   Speech at the Foyle Luncheon, Arthur Rank in the
Wednesday.   chair :

Ladies and gentlemen :
    The first thing I said to my secretary this morning was, " Ring up Christina Foyle. Ask her where the lunch is, what time, who's in the chair, will there be any drink, how long I am to speak for, and what about ? " He came back with six businesslike answers to these six businesslike questions. Five of them highly satisfactory. I didn't much care for the reply to the sixth question, telling me that I was to speak on the " Function of Criticism." Many years ago, when I was a young man, I asked a doctor something about the function of medicine. He said, " Damn it, young man, I don't know anything about it! I'm a physician and a surgeon. If you've a cold I'll cure it. If your leg wants cutting off I'll cut it off. But don't bother me with theories." Well, I'm a practising critic, not a theorist. Mr Rank produces a picture. That's his job. I say, " This is a damned good picture," or " This picture's bloody awful." That's my job. And there I stop. I know nothing about the " Function of Criticism."
    Now this, my dear friends, doesn't make a speech. At least not a speech that is going to satisfy that Foyle woman. If I sit down now she will think her luncheon wasted. Christina has asked for a talk on the function of criticism. Well, she shall have one, but she mustn't be surprised if it sounds like a talk on film censorship. Astonishingly like a talk I broadcast last Wednesday. And I say boldly : Anybody who heard that talk will want to hear it again, and anybody who missed it ought to be damn' well pleased to be given a second chance.
                    [Repeat broadcast talk.]

The speech went off better than I could have hoped. The room was full and the audience highly intelligent, so that I managed to be as much above my usual form as I was below it at Liverpool. This in

spite of the fact that just as I rose to speak the toast-master whispered
—I didn't know they could—" You've got ten minutes, sir." And my
speech was timed to last fifteen. However, I managed.

Nov. 28   Letter from Roger Machell :
Thursday.

90 *Great Russell St.*
*London, W.C.*1

Nov. 27, '46

Dear Mr Agate,
   Discussing your broadcast about the Hays Office and film
censorship, a Hollywood magnate who is now in London told me,
quite casually, that the use of the word ' behind,' whether as a noun
or a preposition, is banned in American films. As a preposition,
the phrase ' in back of ' is substituted. He instanced " the garden
is in back of the house." When I asked whether in its next Biblical
epic Hollywood would make our Lord remark, " Get thee in back
of me, Satan," he nodded gravely and said he thought so.

Yours ever,

Roger Machell

Nov. 29   Letter to George Lyttelton :
Friday.

Queen Alexandra Mansions
*Grape Street, W.C.*2

November 29, 1946

Dear George Lyttelton,
   This is an SOS.
   As you know, I have announced *Ego* 9 as the last of the series.
And now I'm beginning to be worried. I feel that I shall be in the
position of the man who, having burned his boats, looks round for
wood to build another fleet. I feel that on the second or third day
of the new year I shall clutch at a piece of paper and begin to
scribble. Where shall I be able to record some such saying as one
I overheard at a theatre last week—" The play I am dying to see is
Scenario de Bergerac " ? Must I let the rampancy of current error
go unchecked ? Must I let publishers announcing *Pilgrim's Progress*
and *Cousine Bette* without the article go unrebuked ? What am
I to do about the measureless ass who tells me that Tchehov in
his groupings " had one eye on ballet " ? Of what other " philistine
with the conscience and equipment of an intellectual "—see the
Times Lit. Supp. on my first *Ego*—will Bloomsbury go in fear ?
What do I do about some delicious letter from you ?
   And yet I must stop. I just can't go on working from nine in
the morning till three next morning. If I do, something is going to
suffer, and there is an implied clause in my newspaper contracts
that it shan't be the work I do for them. But I am not going to
find giving up easy. I feel that instead of writing new books I shall

begin to chunner and mumble about those that I have written. That I shall become a bore to my friends and a laughing-stock to my enemies. I have tried telling myself that I shall now have time to live. But I have the idea that no writer lives absolutely, for the sheer joy of living. That when he stops writing life becomes practically meaningless. There is probably some tremendous error here, and I wish you would put your finger on it for me. There was a time when meadow, grove, and stream . . . But was there ever a time when for Wordsworth Nature was not just something to write poetry about ? And yet . . . The rainbow comes and goes, and lovely is the rose. Well, the rainbow isn't going to stop coming and going or the rose cease to be lovely because J. A. no longer puts on paper his piddling views about them. You see, I have some rudiments of sanity left.

The matter has been brought to a head by a letter from a Naval captain which I received this morning. The writer tells me of his grandfather's diary, which he kept for thirty-four years, beginning in 1854. There is, it seems, a great deal about the theatre in it, with accounts of what the old gentleman thought of G. V. Brook's Othello, Irving's Hamlet, and Sarah Bernhardt's Lady Macbeth ! ! ! You know my passion for rescuing things from oblivion. If the whole diary is publishable I shall get Bertie van Thal to do it. But suppose there are half a dozen lucky shots, sentences of miraculous felicity, what do I do about these ?

Of course I know the real remedy. This is that people who write and tell me how enraptured they are with my diary should show their rapture in a tangible way. That old ladies in Tunbridge Wells doting on me should stop leaving their property to cats' homes and leave it to J. A. I don't insist on their dying ; let them hand over the cash and go on doting. Endow me and I will never enter another English theatre. Endow me handsomely and I will never again look at a British film. Make the endowment handsome enough and I will never open a new book in any language. I lunched yesterday with Fred Dehn, father of my godson Paul. He has just sold his business for a figure with an incredible number of noughts after it. Why can't I sell my newspaper connections ? Given the leisure, I could Egotise for a long time yet.

No, I don't think there is anything to be done about it. What is the Latin for ' diarist ' ? I am not at all sure that instead of printing " The End " I shan't put :

" *Qualis* something-or-other *pereo* ! "

Ever,

JAMES AGATE

Nov. 30   I get so annoyed when people talk about talent that
Saturday.   cannot get an opening. I don't believe a word of it. I
don't believe there is one scrap of genuine talent that doesn't find its way, provided the owner of the talent is ready to do

his part. I have no use whatever for the creator of masterpieces who sits at home waiting for the world to come to him when he should be putting on his coat and sallying forth to ram his masterpieces down the public's throat. Some six weeks ago I saw in the manager's office of the Lyric Theatre, Hammersmith, a delightful painting by a boy of fourteen, one Gerald Grimes, son of the caricaturist. I doubt whether Dufy, who seems to be the boy's master, did as well at this age. I commissioned a painting on the spot, if you can call a fiver a commission. I collected it on Monday, and have now got three more commissions for him. Jock wants him to paint a bit of Covent Garden market, Jack de Leon would like a picture of the " Q " Theatre, and Stanley Rubinstein leaves the subject to the artist. I will have nothing to do with the argument that the boy was lucky in that his work caught my attention. The point is that he managed to interest Lovat Fraser, who liked a picture of his well enough to hang it in his office, where, if I hadn't seen it, somebody else would have done.

My experience of life tells me that any man of talent who is a failure deserves to be a failure. Leo ? Whoever tried to help Leo was instantly and wittily destroyed.

Dec. 1   Motored with Michael Russell-Smith to Haywards Heath,
Sunday.   the occasion being the birthday of my old friend Helen
             Dehn, Paul's mother. Lovely day of autumn, not winter,
sunshine, with a gentle wind in which a few russet leaves fluttered bravely, like old actresses. Michael told us how when he was sixteen he met Mrs Patrick Campbell in Montreal. She said, " Oh, my dear boy, why do you take dope ? " He said, " But I don't." Whereupon she intoned, " Then what tragedy you must have known to have eyes like that ! "

Dec. 2   A letter from Jock :
Monday.

                                33 *King Street*
                                    *Covent Garden, W.C.*2
                                            1*st December* 1946
DEAR JAMIE,
        You flatter me—a most unusual thing for you to do. I think I prefer your more usual critical praise !
        I can't agree that I *commence à percer* so very much. 'Tis true that since last May I have been doing a monthly talk on the London theatre, which is translated into ten different European languages and sent out in those languages (but not by me !).
        'Tis also true that I have just been appointed English corre-

541

spondent to *La Revue Théâtrale,* a lofty-browed Paris quarterly whose *Comité Fondateur* of fourteen contains Gaston Baty, Jean-Jacques Bernard, Jean Cocteau, Fernand Crommelynck, Charles Dullin, Louis Jouvet, Stève Passeur, Michel Saint-Denis, Armand Salacrou, and Charles Vildrac, and whose second issue contains the text of a new play by André Obey.

'Tis still more true that an incomparably less lofty-browed English publication called *The London Annual* has just appeared containing a full-dress review of the year by me (but only a *réchauffé* of my *News Chronicle* stuff)—a full-dress attack on you (muddled and insufficiently witty for such a target)—and a page of Notes on Contributors which embarrassingly opines of me as a dramatic critic that I am " the best in the business." It goes on : " He is a Scotsman, and was at one time secretary to James Agate, another critic." (!)

This is, of course, havers—and rude havers—and silly havers. Only last Friday I was giving an hour's talk to fifty Service officers (men and women) on a Leave Course ; and one of them got up and asked me who were the tip-top dramatic critics. I replied, " That's easy. Agate of the *Sunday Times*, Brown of the *Observer*, and Cookman of *The Times*. There you have them—the A, B, and C of dramatic criticism." A twinkling-eyed Marine sprang up thereon, and said, " And whom would you call the D, sir ? " Whereupon, in less time than it takes to twinkle back, I said, " Desmond MacCarthy of course ! Any more questions ? "

By the way, don't try to be in two rendezvous at once, the way you were last night at supper. Bad for anybody. I've given it up now I've turned forty, and you should be giving it up now you're turning seventy.

Ever,

Jock

I reply :

Queen Alexandra Mansions
Grape Street, W.C.2
December 2, 1946

Dear Jock,

Some forty years ago one of the music-hall comedians—either Albert Chevalier or Leo Dryden,—had a song about A Fallen Star. If mine has not fallen, it is falling. Let me now a tale unfold to harrow up thy soul, freeze thy young blood, and do something or other to thy knotted and combined locks. That excellent French paper *Spectateur* commissioned an article from me on the subject of Olivier's Lear, the publishing date to coincide with Larry's visit to Paris. This morning the paper's London representative bunged the article back at me with a note from the French editor :

" J'ai bien reçu l'article de M. Agate. Je me vois dans l'obliga-tion de vous le retourner, celui-ci n'étant pas utilisable. En effet, il ne peut intéresser qu'un public anglais, et me semble même pour celui-ci d'une qualité discutable."

Well, Jock, I've had a pretty long run. It will be forty years next month since I was taken on by the *Manchester Guardian*, having served a year's apprenticeship with the *Daily Dispatch*. May it be forty years before any editor, French, Turkish, or Chinese, uses the word *discutable* about an article of yours.

More in anger than in sorrow,

JAMIE

Dec. 3
Tuesday. The *Daily Express* rang up to ask if I could give them a quotation which should be at the same time one of my favourites and also unhackneyed. Sent them this:

> Gawd bless this world! Whatever she 'ath done—
> Excep' when awful long—I've found it good.
> So write, before I die, " 'E liked it all! "

Dec. 4
Wednesday. The diaries of the Naval captain's grandfather—Henry Spencer Ashbee—have arrived, and I permit myself an

INTAGLIO

February 18, 1874. George Cruikshank came to me to-day to inspect the frontispiece of a book which I have, *The Cherub, or Guardian of Female Innocence*, drawn and etched by his father, Isaac Cruikshank. The book was published in the same year (1792) in which George C. was born. What a wonderful man is this George Cruikshank, taking to account his age, 84 years, and the immense quantity of work which he has done. I was prepared to see a decrepit old man, but it was quite the contrary. The great artist is still a young man in the possession of all his powers, both physical and mental, upright in carriage, quick in movement, ready and sprightly in conversation. His face, indeed, retains still its beauty, for the features are regular and well formed and not at all warped by age. But the most striking thing is his wonderful bright and keen blue eyes, which are as clear and piercing as of a young man in the prime of life. Mr Cruikshank seems to observe and grasp everything by his wonderful eyes. His conversation is not refined, but is most interesting as long as he can be kept upon his art and upon the recollections of the great literary men with whom he has had to do during his lengthy career. Of all these, Charles Dickens is he of whom he has least good to say. To him, indeed, he scarcely accords any originality, and seems to look on him as a sorry rascal. In the praise of Charles Lamb he was very warm.

George Cruikshank is the great prophet of teetotalism. This is his weak point, from which it is difficult to keep him away, and to which he slips back at any and every moment during the most interesting part of a conversation. His experiences of the effects of the bottle, it must be confessed, are sad enough. His father and brother Robert shortened their lives by drink, and the list of literary men whose great talents have been paralysed and their careers prematurely closed through intemperance, which Mr Cruikshank has at his finger-ends, is quite appalling. He is a strict teetotaller himself, not having drunk any alcoholic drinks for many years. Is the retention of his faculties in their almost pristine freshness to be attributed to this determined teetotalism ?

March 3, 1874. Mr George Cruikshank was to have dined with us to-day, but could not come till eight o'clock, when he brought a book with him for our children. He saw for the first time the charming child's book *Springinsfeld* von Oscar Pletsch, with which he was much delighted, looked every plate through from first to last, and exclaimed, " I should like to have done this book." How fond he is of children ! He seems to be wanting always to be doing something for them, something to promote their happiness. What a fund of information there is in the old man, and how delightfully he imparts his gossip ! What a checkered life his has been ! He wanted, as a youth, to go to sea. Then he had nearly become an actor, tried to get into Drury Lane Theatre as a scene painter in order that he might be able, as he says, " to creep on to the stage." He says he never had any proper instruction in his art, which, considering the wonderous proficiency to which he has attained, seems almost incredible. What a host of celebrated people he has known—John Kemble, Mrs Siddons, Barham, Grimaldi, Greenwood of Sadler's Wells notoriety, Dickens—Dickens, yes, of him he cannot speak well, but considers him mad. The fact is he is intimate with Mrs Dickens, who was undoubtedly badly treated by her husband. A most entertaining old man truly, and endowed with great dramatic power. To see him imitate Grimaldi and John Kemble brings one back to palmy days of the stage. Had he been an actor he would certainly have been a great one. He firmly believes (as every truly great man must) in himself, and this without one spark of egotism. " Had I gone to sea," he exclaimed, " I should either have gone down or become an admiral ! "

December 13, 1874. I went with Elizabeth Collins and wife to the Lyceum to see *Hamlet*. Irving took Hamlet, Chippendale Polonius, and Compston 1st Gravedigger. The two latter were not to be surpassed, but Irving, well as he undoubtedly sustains the part, came far short of my *beau idéal*. He avoids points,[1] and has succeeded wonderfully in doing away with his mannerisms, but altogether his performance, in spite of the excitement which it is causing, can not be ranked higher than a good average one. Miss Bateman as Ophelia was simply villainous.

[1] *Cf.* Clement Scott's notice in the *Daily Telegraph* the morning after the first performance : " Those who have seen other Hamlets are aghast. Mr Irving is missing his point, he is neglecting his opportunities."

April 21, 1875. Went with Elizabeth and Charles to see the Italian actor Salvini in *Othello*. A finer performance as far as Salvini was concerned I do not recollect ever having seen. S. is most easy and graceful, even in his movements, has a full, rich, melodious voice, is calm and subdued in his play until passion is really required, and then he is terrible. His countenance is most flexible. Every feature, but more particularly the eyes, is expressive, and the ease and force with which he depicts on his countenance the thoughts which Iago's insinuations suggest to him are simply inimitable. His ability to portray love is as great as it is to show forth hate, and in the early scenes he was as charming as in the later ones he was terrible. He certainly is a great artist, and it is not to be wondered at that our own actors have been anxious to see him. The way in which they have received him does them great credit, both as men and as artists. Desdemona was fairly interpreted, but Iago and Roderigo were as badly acted as they could possibly be.

February 25, 1880. Just returned from the Théâtre Français, where I assisted, as the French say, at the crowning of the bust of Victor Hugo. At the conclusion of *Hernani*, a drama which I do not like, the curtain again rose after a short pause. In the centre of the stage was the bust of Victor Hugo, and around it were grouped the company of the Comédie Française, with Sarah Bernhardt in front of it. She recited some verses written by François Coppée for the occasion, and then placed the palm branch which she held in her left hand upon the statue. The enthusiasm did not seem to me to be very great. In a box to the right of the stage, looking towards it from the auditorium, were the daughter-in-law of Hugo and his grandchildren. Victor Hugo, although demanded, did not appear. The whole ceremony was very French.

April 25, 1882. Went with Elizabeth and Charley to the Lyceum to see *Romeo and Juliet*. H. Irving as Romeo was abominable, not a redeeming feature in his whole performance, which frequently made me laugh ; Ellen Terry a good Juliet, better than I expected. She is an actress of the head, not of the heart, and yet she performed Juliet admirably. Terriss very good as Mercutio, perhaps a little too boisterous. The *mise en scène* was too beautiful, and, to my mind, the action was hampered by the superabundance of accessories.

July 13, 1883. On Friday took Elizabeth and Frances to the Lyceum to see *Hamlet*, which I have seen before with the same cast. Ellen Terry as ever charming. A more perfect and more pleasant Ophelia (the part in my estimation is not a pleasant one) I do not think possible. Howe's Polonius, if not marked by originality or distinctiveness, is straightforward, clear, unassuming, and pithy. Irving more objectionable than ever, indistinct, stilted, angular, incorrect in conception, full of mannerism, no spontaneity, no *abandon*. The *man* is never there, the *actor* for ever present. It is inconceivable to me how the British public, high and low, can so worship Henry Irving, whom I cannot but consider a very bad actor.

February 14, 1884. Took Elizabeth and Frances to the Savoy Theatre to see the *Princess Ida*, by far the weakest comic opera of Gilbert and Sullivan which has yet appeared. Much more might have been made out of the Princess, and of the music scarcely a bar struck me as original. Barrington's part did not suit him. The same may be said of Miss Braham. Grossmith was as usual admirable, in spite of his want of voice, but he had not enough to do. The *mise en scène* as usual most beautiful.

March 29, 1884. *The Scrap of Paper* at St James's is a clever adaptation of a very clever piece, very well acted. Hare is inimitable both in get-up and rendering of his part. Kendal is as good as I have ever seen him. Mrs Kendal good of course, although she lacks *abandon*. She is always acting and hoping that you are admiring her.

September 17, 1884. To the Porte St Martin with Arnold and his wife to see *Macbeth*—Sarah Bernhardt and Marais. The costumes were horrible—as ugly and tasteless as they were untrue, and the *mise en scène* poor in the extreme ; the translation literal and frequently trivial and with modern slang. But the play, barring the long *entr'actes*, went briskly and the supernatural scenes not ludicrous. Marais was a very fair Macbeth, and, although nearly all the English points were missed, rendered the part in a very satisfactory manner. Sarah lacked the stiffness and coldness of the great Scotch lady, and was entirely deficient in dignity as the queen. Indeed, she never threw off the *demi-monde* impression for a moment. Her costume was that of an acrobat. She was subtle and serpentine, had the lure of the harlot more than the influence of the strong-minded consort, was indeed Fédora or Froufrou, never Lady Macbeth. Yet, with all this utterly un-English bearing, her performance was most powerful, and she held me completely every moment she was on the stage. Her sleep-walking scene was one of the finest things I have seen. The masculine vigour which one looks for in Lady Macbeth was never attained, but on the other hand a subtlety all her own, and certainly not to be found in any living English actress, lent to her performance a charm and an originality which made one overlook all the other drawbacks. The last act— the arrival of Birnam wood, etc., where some stage accessories are needed—was feeble, and I cannot believe that the French audience unfamiliar with the plot of the play could have understood the realisation of the Witches' prediction. Altogether I was most agreeably surprised, and apart from the long waits I spent a most enjoyable evening. The theatre itself is one of the most comfortless and inconvenient in Paris, and were a panic to arise no one could be saved.

Dec. 5
Thursday.
Letter to Neville Cardus :

Queen Alexandra Mansions
*Grape Street, W.C.*2
December 5, 1946

DEAR NEVILLE,

" From Our Special Correspondent." But neither you nor *The Times* can fool me. I read your column on the first and second days' play at Brisbane and wasn't quite sure. To-day comes your account of England's first knock, and *I know*. If there were a cricket reporter of this calibre in this country I should have heard of him. Which means that *The Times* has not sent out a man to report the Tests. Therefore he must be in Australia. Now I just don't believe that that land of half-wits and whole cricketers has any writer of this class except you. Therefore YOU are " Our Special Correspondent." *Q.E.D.*

Besides, the stuff is full of fingerprints. (Know what I mean ?) Of Hammond : " Using his bat like an old Roman centurion's shield." Of Compton : " He played with a lovely gallantry." Of the weather : " Darkness covered the earth, then a storm of awful grandeur flooded and submerged deep the field. To describe it would tax the language of the Old Testament and Joseph Conrad." You didn't really think to diddle me, did you ?

But might you not have dropped a hint ? Why not a sentence for your James's private eye ? Something about Bedser's action reminding you of Brahms's melodic line ? In the meantime know that your articles are tremendously appreciated here, and that I am continually being asked if I know who is writing them. My reply is " a headshake and the pronouncing of some doubtful phrase." But to you, old mole, my warmest felicitations.

Ever,

JAMES

Dec. 6
Friday.
To-night at 7.45 Alexis Kligerman ' made ' the Albert Hall. This is a long trek from the " Q " Theatre. (See *Ego* 6, p. 15.) " The Emperor," with Malcolm Sargent and the L.S.O. Played very well, with a *cantabile* he did not have before, acquiring which, however, he seems to have lost some of his fire. Perhaps the size of the hall and the occasion were a trifle on the big side. He told me when I went round afterwards that this was his first performance of the concerto. Said that he was playing in Derby to-morrow, Pontefract on Sunday, and Sunderland on Tuesday.

Which suggests that he will be able to pay his laundry bill, which is more than I can do.

Dec. 7   Note from Jock :
Saturday.

33 *King Street*
Covent Garden, W.C.2
5th December, 1946

Dear Jamie Gummidge,
   Don't be daft.
   'Tis true, too, that I have just been asked for the first Christmas in twenty Christmases to the luncheon party at the Olympia Circus.
   'Tis true, moreover, that by the same post I am invited to write an article on Theatre (Great Britain) in the last Ten Years for the next edition of the ENCYCLOPÆDIA BRITANNICA.
   But, on the other hand, hark at what happened last night as ever was. I was supping alone Au Petit Savoyard in a practically empty room, when, from the other corner, I heard a snatch of conversation between a Polish officer and his girl-friend. The Pole had obviously been declaring that our theatre criticism was in a bad way, for what the girl said was exactly this (I wrote it down there and then) : " Oh, no, but you must except James Agate of the *Sunday Times*. Now he just can't be overlooked—by far the best of them—and, what's more, he's the only one of them with any chance of immortality, you know, ranking with Hazlitt and those few . . ." Wherewith I paid my bill and came out into the black wet night !
   So, you see, *ce vieillard commence à s'immortaliser !*

Ever,
Jock

To which I reply :

Queen Alexandra Mansions
Grape Street, W.C.2
December 7, 1946

But Jock dear,
   I am like a child who, given one toy, clamours for another. I am not in the running with Hazlitt. In the spectrum of dramacology I approximate to mauve, and you remember Whistler's " Mauve is only pink trying to be purple." Compared with Hazlitt my purplest passages are a sickly puce. And then I haven't Shaw's knowledge, Max's wit, Walkley's urbanity, Montague's style. Besides, I don't particularly want the stuff to live. I might have wanted if there had been an Irving to write about, but there hasn't. I tell you, Jock, that I would give the whole of Olivier, Richardson, Wolfit, and Gielgud for the smile the Old Man gave the little serving maid at his first entry in *The Bells*. All the same, I am sending with this note a copy of *The Contemporary Theatre*, 1944 *and* 1945.

548

Nicely printed, I think, but with two gratuitous commas on pages 23 and 33 which you will ignore.

Besides, my dear boy, in a sense dramatic criticism must always be parasitic. The writer of it is working over and recasting the stuff of other people's brains. *Ego* is the result of my own brain. Alone I did it, reckoning as nothing, in the Ellistonian sense, the help I got from Edward, Leo, George Lyttelton, Jock. I would like a hundred years hence to be put on the same shelf with Pepys and Evelyn. Your *Enc. Brit.* says of the latter, " Written with no thought of publication, it embodies the frankest expression of its author's opinions, and affords much curious and interesting information which the historian would have probably passed over, but which throws a strong light upon the customs and feelings of the age." Substitute " With every eye to publication," and doesn't this passage hold equally well of me ? In some respects I am a better diarist than either P. or E. I have had no Plague and no Fire to help me. The 1939–45 war ? It is hardly mentioned. There is no reference to politics. *Ego* is as non-political as the Savage Club, about which I said to those poor fellows from East Grinstead when they dined with us : " We are entirely non-political. There is not a single Savage who would object to sitting at table next to some unwashed Communist ruffian or even a member of the present Government." *Ego* is a gold brick made from no straw. It may live or it may not. It would be nice if it did. If it doesn't, the nine volumes will make an excellent trouser-press.

Now that I am finishing the damned thing I realise that diary-writing isn't wholly good for one, that too much of it leads to living for one's diary instead of living for the fun of living as ordinary people do. There was a time when to watch my little horse win a class put me on the highest point of being. But I seem to have lost this. They are to revive the International Horse Show at Olympia next year, and in the ordinary way of things I should be looking forward to having something for the Novice Class. I shan't have anything because my filly is only two. But if she were three and won the class I should not be greatly excited. What is the good of anything if you have nowhere to write about it ?

To be less serious, did you see the announcement in to-day's *Telegraph* that some French chemist has found a way to split the atom into four ? About which some ass at the Sorbonne said, " These discoveries—tri-fission and quadri-fission of the atom of uranium—would permit of important progress in the field of research into the use of atomic energy *for peaceful ends*." To which, of course, the only answer is Beachcomber's " Tra-la-la ! "

Ever,

JAMIE

P.S. Did you see that Richard Capell calls Kligerman " an exceptionally fine pianist " ?

Dec. 8
Sunday.

Took tea with Lady Reid, Maurice Baring's sister, the occasion being the presentation to me of the big Littré which Maurice wanted me to have. She also gave me one of his treasured possessions, a photograph taken in 1879 of Sarah as Doña Sol in *Hernani*, wearing her little silver crown. When I got home I turned up Maurice on Sarah. Yes, I know I'm a bore. " I will not sink without a struggle into that period when a man begins to bore young people by raving to them about mimes whom they never saw " (Max Beerbohm). But I don't pretend to write for young people. What have I to do with youth ? Therefore, for my own pleasure, and because Maurice would like it, I set down here the unforgettable ending to the essay on Sarah in *Punch and Judy*. It is twenty years since this was published, and I cannot believe that many people do as I do, walk about their flats murmuring chunks of it by heart :

When in the future people will say, " But you should have heard Sarah Bernhardt in the part ! " the newcomers will probably shrug their shoulders and say, " Oh, we know all about that ! "
But they will not know, nor will anybody be able to tell them or explain to them what Sarah Bernhardt could do with a modulated inflexion, a *trait de voix*, a look, a gesture, a cry, a smile, a sigh, nor what majesty, poetry and music she could suggest by the rhythm of her movements and her attitudes, what it was like to hear her speak verse, to say words such as :

Songe, songe, Céphise, à cette nuit cruelle,

or,

Si tu veux faisons un rêve.

Nobody will be able to tell them, because, in spite of the gramophone and the cinematograph, the actor's art dies almost wholly with the actor. It is short-lived, but only relatively short-lived ; and nobody understood that better than Sarah Bernhardt, one of whose mottoes was " Tout passe, tout casse, tout lasse."
(It was tempered by another : " Quand même.")
On the loom of things the poems of Homer are only a little less ephemeral than a leading article, and the art of a Phidias is, after all, as perishable as the sketches of a ' lightning ' music-hall artist.

Le temps passe. Tout meurt. Le marbre même s'use.
Agrigente n'est plus qu'une ombre, et Syracuse
Dort sous le bleu linceul de son ciel indulgent.

The most enduring monuments, the most astounding miracles of beauty achieved by the art and craft of man, are but as flotsam, drifting for a little while upon the stream of Time ; and with it now there is a strange russet leaf, the name of Sarah Bernhardt.

Dec. 9   Have decided to have one last fling at all I hate in modern
Monday.   art. Am unloading the following on the *S.T.* :

Somebody having sent me Walkley's *Dramatic Criticism*, being
three lectures delivered by him at the Royal Institution in 1903, I
open the book and read :
"A picture, whatever else it does, must first please the eye ;
music, whatever else it does, must first please the ear. And pleasure
of the senses—this is the important point—is only to be had at the
price of perpetual change ; for it is an elementary physiological law
that the mere repetition of the same stimulus will not be followed
by the same pleasurable reaction. Contrast art, in this respect,
with *pure* science or with *fundamental* morals. Pure science does
not change, and cannot, so long as man remains as we know him.
Have not two and two always made four, two sides of a triangle
always been greater than the third, two bodies in space always
attracted one another inversely as the square of the distance
between them ? And, so long as man remains in society as we
know it, the first principles of conduct cannot change : Thou shalt
not kill, steal, bear false witness against thy neighbour. Not so
with art. Our pleasure-sense becomes sharpened by use, more
subtle, more exacting. In order to procure the same thrill we are
driven to vary and to intensify the exciting cause ; or, as Mr
Arthur Balfour has pithily expressed it in one of those amiable
digressions with which he has enlivened his *Foundations of Belief*—
he is actually speaking of music, but the statement may be general-
ised—' A steady level of æsthetic sensation can only be maintained
by increasing doses of æsthetic stimulant.' "
So far, so good. But suppose stimulation has reached saturation-
point—a vile phrase, but let it go. Does this justify the resort to
false stimulants ? Are the makers, I sometimes feel inclined to say
fakers, of modern art, music, and poetry in the position of the man
who, no longer getting a kick out of brandy, has resort to methy-
lated spirits ? Suppose one of two things. Suppose (*a*) that everything that can be drawn, sung, or said in the old way has been
drawn, sung, said. In parenthesis let me insist with some firmness
that I do not believe this. Now suppose (*b*) that while some
humdrum clods still contrive to find sufficing stimulant along the
old lines there exists a type of progressive artist whom the old lines
no longer excite. (I shall ignore the humbugs who try to disguise
poverty of talent by dressing it up in new clothes.) Is an artist
belonging to type (*b*), having exhausted the pleasing, entitled to
embrace the unpleasing ? And does the unpleasing, by virtue of
that embrace, take on acceptability ? In Walkley's day the artist's
job was to provide pleasure. If he wanted to play the artistic fool
he could do it in's own house. What pleasure, what delight is the
shade of A. B. W. discovering in the new and lying anatomies, ear-
splitting atonalities, untunable assonances ? Can it be that that
great critic was wrong to confine himself to two senses ? Is it

possible that Picasso tickles the palate, Bartók reeks of odious savours sweet, and imagist poetry, printed in Braille, enchants the finger-tips ? Last, can it be that the arts have said good-bye to the senses ? That we are to recognise them as handmaids of the First Cause, and as such part of that mathematical conception of the universe which has nothing to do with pleasing or displeasing ?

On Christmas Day I received from my favourite photographer a self-picture showing him to be possessed of three eyes, two noses, and four beards. Far be it from me to say that this eccentricity, while not pleasing in the accepted sense, failed to achieve some other of the qualities which Walkley conceded to a picture. It was ' amusing ' ; it tacitly recognised one as a modernist who can laugh at the right things in the right way ; in one's immediate circle it excited comment. Now if I make the full allowance in the case of the photographic art must I not in logic make it for all the others ? In the theatre must I not look sympathetically on the playwright who finds his " increasing stimulant " in the subconscious, and writes a verse drama about it for intellectuals who can't act and never will ? Councils of Five, Groups of Art, and all the Little Theatres in Town would tumble over themselves to secure a piece of pretentious nonsense that I should hate but must in logic praise.

This brings me to the old question of the function of the critic. Here I am in 100 per cent. agreement with A. B. W. " It is not the dramatic critic's trade to make plays, or to teach the way to make plays. It is the function of criticism not to inculcate methods, but to appraise results ; to examine the thing done, not the way to do it. It is, in short, the evaluation of pleasurable impressions." (Still harping on that demoded matter of pleasure !) But pleasurable to whom ? To the critic, of course, who is the only person in the audience for whom he can speak. Many people have complained about dramatic notices that they are too much concerned with the writer and too little with the play ; they do not realise that what they are looking for is not a dramatic critic but a theatrical plumber ! [1] It is of this that Anatole France was thinking when he said, " In order to be frank the critic ought to say, ' Gentlemen, I am about to speak of myself *apropos* of Shakespeare, or Racine, or Pascal, or Goethe—by no means a bad opportunity.' " Criticism is not an exact science like algebra or chemistry. Criticism is the knack of communicating to others the kind and amount of delight the critic has received from a work of art, or one of skilful and popular contrivance. The knack, too, of spotting and slaying the bogus and pretentious, even if all the world's pseudo-intellectuals are on their knees before it, high brow to low floor.

[1] The *Irish Times*, reviewing *The Contemporary Theatre, 1944 and 1945*, says, " After watching Mr Agate capering heavily round the London theatre, mumbling of Duse and Bernhardt, scattering extracts from Walkley and Montague, gabbling involved witticisms and generally doing everything except theatrical criticism, one begins to wonder whether the British drama is worse served by its playwrights or by its critics. . . . Writes like a decrepit Sainte-Beuve."

> *Grundisburgh*
> *Suffolk*
> *December 8, 1946*

Dear James,

At last that ill-bred and dilatory germ seems to be definitely in retreat, and I am sitting up and taking the bleak nourishment with which a rebellious liver is cajoled into a sulky resumption of its duties. I hope you didn't think I was in the grip of :

> Convulsions, epilepsies, fierce catarrhs,
> Intestine stone and ulcer, colic pangs,
> Demoniac frenzy, moping melancholy,
> And moonstruck madness, pining atrophy, etc.

By the way, to drop for a moment into blasphemy, I have discovered the two worst lines in *Paradise Lost*—*viz.*, apropos of Noah and Sodom and Gomorrah :

> At length a reverend sire among them came
> And of their doings great dislike declared.

But, excluding the occasional puns and flops (*e.g.*, " No fear lest dinner cool "), what an extraordinary level of majesty and rhythm the grim old man maintains in his " slow planetary wheelings." The best short summary of *P.L.* was made by a Russian soldier who, according to Maurice Baring, loved it " because it makes you laugh and cry."

With regard to your SOS, I am afraid, my dear James, I have no comfort to bring you. Of course you work far too hard, and equally of course you always will. How can you stop writing ? It isn't merely something you do, it *is* you or, at least, an inalienable part of you. Your writing has many qualities, as your admirers (and enemies) have often said, but, in the ultimate analysis, what stands out above, behind, beneath all the rest is your *integrity*—by which I mean that every word you write has all of J. A. in it and nothing, for all your quotations, of anybody else. All the care you take is to put down with vivid exactness what you think at the moment. You never tone down or dress up in order to placate, or disarm, or please anyone but yourself. And that, besides making you one of a small and select company, means two things—continuous cerebration (which is exhausting) and continual delight (which outweighs all else) when, as you know quite well you often do, you hit the bull's-eye. And when this urge to express is backed by your other leading characteristic—an intense savour of the quality of all that you come across in literature and drama and music and life—well, the case is hopeless ! Your proposal to stop commenting is on all fours with Lamb and some friend resolving one evening to give up snuff, and then each finding the other early next morning searching for their respective snuff-boxes in the bushes where they had thrown them. The day after you have burnt your pens and sold your typewriter you will be writing with a piece of coal. What happened before when the doctor told you to stop writing ? What is the alternative ? To cultivate a Wordsworthian " wise passiveness " ? I can't see it. Haydon, being insane, could picture the Duke of Wellington " musing " on the field of Waterloo. But even he could not have conceived of J. A. musing in Grape Street. It is hard that you can't doff any of your harness and that there is no comfortable loose box well supplied with hay awaiting you. After all, you have served the stage more diligently than many have served the State who end up with some fat sinecure or pension.

Meanwhile the seed sown by J. A. sprouts. Isn't it your godson whose play is being broadcast this evening ? About a schoolboy " who loved beauty and hated pedants " ?—two of the main points of his godfather's creed (though astonishingly patient with pedagogues !).

I have had a more concentrated dose of the wireless lately than ever before. What a lot of Saharas there are with no oasis, long periods when there is really nothing to listen to that helps one, in Johnson's words, " to enjoy or to endure life." There is, of course, that Frenchman who, literally, never stops talking day or night. I think he must be doing it for a bet, except that he must have won it years ago. And I listened twice to the whole of *Itma*. I remember in one of the *Egos* an impressive posse of your friends who told you you were wrong in not thinking *Itma* very funny. Well, put this to them now. The readiness of a Colonel Blimp to have a drink and to mishear any remark as an invitation to do so may be funny enough once or twice, but half a dozen times *every* Thursday for literally years ? ? Again the audience splits its sides when A asks B if he will have a sninch of puff. So did I—in 1892. Has the common man (to whose tastes and standards we must to-day all bow down or be considered highbrow or hidebound) in his ascent of Parnassus only just reached the modest height of " Kinquering Kongs " ? I think Dan Leno and Little Tich and Pélissier did better.

I must stop. On re-reading I have misgivings about my dogmatics about your personality (repulsive word). Sich imperence, you may well think. But you are a forgiving man except to those who talk nonsense, and if I have done that I'll eat my head with more than grimwiggian conviction !

Yours ever,

George Lyttelton

P.S. A friend tells me that in an obituary of J. K. Mosley the printer gave the title of one of his books as *The Impossibility of God*. As my friend says, it is really the theologians' fault for inventing such a word as ' impassibility,' of which none but they knows the meaning.

Queen Alexandra Mansions
*Grape Street, W.C.*2
December 11, 1946

DEAR GEORGE,

Opus operatum est. I am utterly determined to wind up the thing. Your letter, giving me that Nunc Dimittissy feeling, has done the trick. But the book had been ending for some time and of its own accord. Like the last movement of a Concerto, it has *finis* written all over it.

Besides, I have a horror of people who won't stop when they've finished. Like the guest who can't make up his mind to go. Do you know that wonderful passage in the story of Jack Sheppard in the *Newgate Calendar* ? He had got out of gaol and lowered himself on to the turner's leads, a house adjoining the prison. Fortunately the garret door was open. The boy stole down two pair of stairs and heard company talking in a room, the door being open. Here is Jack's own account : " My irons gave a small clink, which made a woman cry, ' Lord ! what noise is that ? ' A man replied, ' Perhaps the dog or cat,' and so it went off." Jack returned to the garret, and being terribly fatigued laid himself down for two hours. Then once more he crept down to where the company were, " and heard a gentleman taking his leave, being very importunate to be gone, saying he had disappointed some friends by not going home sooner. In about three-quarters more, the gentleman took leave and went." I intend to take leave and go at once, though the manner of the exit is not yet settled. The organ close ? The nonchalant touch ? Prospero or Eulenspiegel ? I shall leave that to to-morrow's inspiration.

The future stretches before me like a desert. No more the juice of Holborn's Grape Street . . . I shall, of course, have leisure for private quarrels. But what I like is public ones. Glancing through one of last week's novels, I came across a description of Réjane as possessing " a wide-awake little mug." But that's *my* phrase, *my* rendering of Sarcey's " petite frimousse éveillée." The authors go on to quote the French, and *get it wrong*. They print the last word " eveiller." Of course, I can and shall cane them in the *Express*. But what's the good of that ? When I pillory anybody or anything I want it to be not for a day, but for an age. Wherefore I have started to toy seriously with the idea of a Postscript. (Suppose the King of Spain makes me a Knight of the Golden Fleece ? And why shouldn't he ?) Yes, a Postscript's the thing. Perhaps on the lines of " Walt Whitman's Last " in which, you remember, the old boy likened himself to Lear. So if you read of my being arrested for going up to citizens in Piccadilly Circus and saying, " Ha ! Goneril with a white beard ! " you will know that Bedlam is henceforth the address of   Your old friend,

JAMES AGATE

P.S. Have just had a brain-wave. This is to lock the stable door *now* by getting Harrap's to announce *Ego* 8 as "the penultimate instalment of Agate's Diary." With the implication, of course, of *Ego* 9 as the last instalment. This will be effective in two ways. First, the horse won't be able to get out. Second, it will stop the mouths of reviewers yapping about this tedious old fool going on for ever.

P.P.S. I may not have the courage to wind up with the end of the year. I may go on yapping until the spring. The first entry in *Ego* is dated June 2, 1932. I seem to see the date June 1, 1947, hanging in the air. Very much as Macbeth saw the dagger. They marshal me the way that I am going, since they complete the fifteen years' cycle. Even if I finish a shade earlier I feel that I shall cheat a little and tell the printer to date the last entry June 1, 1947.

Dec. 12   Letter to Edgar Lustgarten :
Thursday.

> *Queen Alexandra Mansions*
> *Grape Street, W.C.2*
> *December 12, 1946*

DEAR EDGAR,

As you are the only person of my acquaintance who really knows his Damon Runyon, I have a proposition for you. This is that you should do what Cerfberr and Christophe did for Balzac—compile a Repertory of all the characters in the stories. There are times when I must *at once* renew acquaintance with Angie the Ox, Sam the Gonoph, Dave the Dude, The Lemon Drop Kid, Milk Ear Willie, Joe the Joker, and Big Nig, not to mention Mesdames Beulah Beauregard, Cutie Singleton, Billy Perry, Missouri Martin, Lola Sapola, and so on. I can generally put my hand on them, but not always. Now if there were a Repertory one would be in no trouble.

Here is the model :

HARRY THE HORSE. A character from Brooklyn who is mobbed up with other characters such as Spanish John and Little Isadore. With these two and Educated Edmund, and at the request of Mr Jabez Tuesday, makes a personal call on Miss Amelia Bodkin with the object of recovering certain letters which would be very embarrassing to Mr Tuesday if Miss Valerie Scarwater, to whom he is affianced, should get a wrong notion of their nature (*Breach of Promise*). In the spring of 1931 and in company with Spanish John and Little Isadore kidnaps a rich bookmaker (*The Snatching of Bookie Bob*). Hires Big Butch to open a safe in an office in West Eighteenth Street containing money deposited by a personal friend who is the paymaster for the company (*Butch Minds the Baby*).

Or

THE BRAIN. Right name, Armand Rosenthal. A large operator in gambling and a collector of dolls, which include Doris Clare, Cynthia Harris, and Bobby Baker, in addition to his ever-loving wife, Charlotte. Okays Feet Samuels with Dr Bodeeker, to whom Feet wishes to sell his body (*A Very Honourable Guy*). Presses Homer Swing for payment and is carved up more than somewhat by Daffy Jack. Dies in the basement room of a brick-layer's widow with five children to whom he leaves his money (*The Brain Goes Home*).

What about it ?

Ever,

JIMMIE

Dec. 14
Saturday.
In a letter from Delhi : " In Lahore last week I found a copy of *Ego* 7. Does it ever give you a curious feeling to think that at this moment you may be being read in Clapham, New Orleans, Lima, and Saidu, the capital of Swat ? "

Dec. 16
Monday.
Letter from Neville Cardus :

Sydney
December 11, 1946

MY DEAR JAMES,

From your review of Warner's book, *Lord's* : " Ranji waved a conjurer's wand, and a small boy picked the magic up and threw it back." I have never said anything so lovely ! But you mustn't *again* refer back to that Richardson piece of mine, written in my greeny-flowery period. I have modulated to observation and irony in my cricket stuff ; for example : (of Wright's bowling) " Possibly there was some want of variation, but it was good to watch. A certain defect in it was that Hammond at first slip was as free as most of us to watch and admire it with some detachment."

" As he put himself to the ball, receiving many blows and bruises, there was a very distinguished melancholy in his demeanour, as though he were saying, ' We Edriches suffer no pain.' "

I'm afraid the rubber is being lost because the England team doesn't contain enough Edriches.

Blessings on you,

Ever,

NEVILLE

P.S. I'll drink to you on Christmas Day at 8.30 P.M. (10.30 A.M. English time).

Dec. 17   Letter from the young man who wanted to know the
Tuesday.   whereabouts of Wiltshire :

661 *Company*
TAHAG, Egypt
M.E.L.F.

10/12/46

DEAR MR AGATE,

It is so hard to imagine that anything written here can ever reach London, that I dare make so bold as to remind you of my existence, with the added excuse of sending Greetings for the New Year when it arrives.

Alas ! It seems so long since I set forth from home, a silver shoe-horn in my breast pocket to ward off infidel bullets, and a typewriter in my hand to write back of the Wonders of the World ! And where am I now ? RIGHT in the middle of the desert. You will have seen sand before, of course, but never, I think, as much as this unless you have been here yourself. My diet is desert rat, my relaxation spade and bucket on the unending beach, there are Pharaohs at the bottom of my garden, and the nearest small town is thirty-five miles away down one of Mr Priestley's Highways. (Our position, I believe, is " strategically vital.") I and five other officers sleep in tents, eat and live in a tiny two-room mess, which is just as you might expect it to be : battle-splintered furniture, wheezy gramophone, old *Punches* . . . The sole decoration a huge Pin-up Girl, reclining all over one wall.

My work is to look after three-ton lorries. Now, I know as much about three-ton lorries as I do about Venezuelan bird-life (on second thoughts I know more about Venezuelan bird-life), so I spend the days desperately trying to delegate efficiently the incomprehensible jobs thrust upon me ! As for the Wonders of the World . . . I have seen the Valley of the Nile, and it is very dirty ; Cairo, and it smells. And the Pyramids also : a practical joke played on History.

Ego 8, which you gave me in proof before I left, has been a constant pleasure, and is, I think, in many ways, the best of all. It and the *S.T.*, which I have sent weekly, are my constant reminders that there is " a world elsewhere," while the encouragement you gave me has been my main comfort and stay amidst all this nonsense. I hope you are in good health, Sir, and send my Very Best Wishes for the coming year.

Yours sincerely,

PETER FORSTER

Dec. 20   *Antony and Cleopatra* at the Piccadilly. Godfrey Tearle
Friday.   and Edith Evans both miscast. Antony is winding up a
                lifetime of gormandizing, wine-bibbing, and running after
women ; Tearle no more suggests this than Evans can suggest
Cleopatra's essential sluttishness. " Think on me, That am with

Phœbus' amorous pinches black." And at once one remembers Millamant's " I nauseate walking." Obviously this Cleopatra nauseated pinching. Why will Evans insist on a part she can't play even in Dryden's tamer version? *All for Love* was produced a year or so before I joined the *Sunday Times.* Here is what St John Ervine had to say about Edith in the *Observer* :

> I do not know who had the bright idea of using Restoration costumes for a play about Romans and Egyptians, but I suggest to the Council of the Phœnix Society that if this genius has any more bright ideas he should be persuaded to keep them to himself. The effect of this particular idea was to strip all the sincerity from the play and turn it into a piece of artifice. We could not believe in a Cleopatra so bedizened with petticoats that any period of residence on the banks of the Nile must have been a clammy one. Miss Edith Evans seemed to share our disbelief, for this remarkably able actress misinterpreted the part so completely that she appeared to be miscast. She began by telling her love for Antony as if she were the Princess Victoria telling her governess, the " dear Lehzen," that she *would* be good, and ended up with an excellent imitation of Mrs Gummidge, " the lone, lorn creetur," thinking of the old 'un.

Dec. 21   The Lord send me not too good a conceit of myself !
Saturday. This morning comes a letter from a rubber planter in
             Malaya saying he has bought *A Shorter Ego* on the
advice of a Chinese bookseller.

Dec. 22   Lunched with Gwen Chenhalls, after which I slept
Sunday.   through the greater part of a dull B.B.C. concert from
             Liverpool, at the end of which they had the impertinence
to perform Hamilton Harty's setting of Keats's *Ode to a Nightingale.*
Why couldn't Harty, if he must maunder, get somebody to write
words apt for maundering ? If this sort of thing is to be condoned
Bliss or somebody will be laying hands on Wordsworth's *Intimations,*
and Bax or somebody will make an oratorio out of Boswell's *Johnson.*
I will have nothing to do with this game of musical paws.

Dec. 23   *Between Ourselves.* The new revue at the Playhouse.
Monday.   First- and tenth-rate in equal parts. Brilliant sketches
             by Eric Maschwitz, including one in which a greengrocer's
offspring have gone all Picasso, Bartók, modern poetry, and coterie
theatre. Sister confides to brother that she has grown out of

Beethoven. Brother says, " Oh, but you will grow back into him again. Promise me you will grow back ! " Bill Fraser's Bloomsbury queer had the audience rocking. Elsewhere several young women piping ditties of little or no tone, and a lot of graceless gawks with bony knees skittering about in ill-fitting tights. One dreadful song beginning " I have heard the mavis *swinging*." Only the sex of the singer prevented her from getting my walking-stick in her chest, javelin-wise.

Dec. 24
Tuesday.
Worked all day at my *Antony and Cleopatra* notice. In the middle of it an odd little waif walked in with a cake she had baked as a Christmas present for me. Why ? Because in July I had written her a kind letter about some well-meaning wisps of poems. This promptly set Russell-Smith, who is a sentimentalist, blubbing. Whereupon I cuffed him, and all very merry. In the evening to the pantomime at the Adelphi. Nervo and Knox—in spite of whom I slept almost solidly throughout. No, not drink, since nobody can call one double whiskey drink. Just fatigue. Afterwards to supper with Claire Luce and Peter Page. Claire told us that when she played Cleopatra at Stratford—Jock says she played it oddly well, with a puce navel!—Robert Atkins went up to her as she was waiting in the wings ready to face the audience, and growled, " Remember that the part hasn't been played properly for forty years." And shoved her on. Claire said, " I had the greatest difficulty in preventing myself from beginning :

' If it be love indeed, tell me who played it ! ' "

Claire is possessed of as pretty a wit as any actress I know.

Christmas Day. Lunch at Louis Sterling's. Beecham with an eye more rolling and mischievous than ever, Lady B., Trefor Jones, Bobby Howes, Heather Thatcher, and a lot of people on the fringe of music and drama. I sat almost all of the time in a corner with Godfrey Tearle, and listened to him on the subject of *A. and C.* I had expounded my theory of Antony as a spent amorist and showing it in his face. Tearle said, " I agree. But how am I to look ravaged ? " (He leaped at my suggestion that the ideal Antony would have been John Barrymore.) Wonderful charm and no hint of the actor's vanity. Told me how on the preliminary tour his Aberdeen dresser said, " If it's Rob Roy ye're playin' ye'll be needin' a kilt."

Boxing Day.   **In my mail this morning :**

Date ....

1. I *have/have not
   received your last three letters

2. I have not replied owing to my
   *Absence from home⎤
    Change of address⎟
    Indifference⎟
    Forgetfulness⎟
    Laziness⎬
    Rudeness⎟
    Illness⎟
    Imprisonment⎟
    Insanity⎟
    Death⎦

3. I *Apologise for
    Commiserate with you over⎤
    Laugh at⎟
    Gloat over⎬
    Regard with indifference⎟
    Intend to continue⎟
    Intend to discontinue⎦

the inconvenience caused to
you by para. 2 above

Signed..........................

* Strike out words not required.

The sender is a Naval captain who has never allowed charm to
undermine authority.

Dec. 28   **In *The Times* :**
Saturday.

> Queen Alexandra Mansions
> Grape Street, W.C.2
> December 27, 1946

To the Editor of " The Times " :

Sir,
    Your obituarist says of W. C. Fields that he was " an almost
ideal Mr Micawber in the film of *David Copperfield*." Sir, you will
permit me to say that he was not, and demonstrably not, and could
not be. Consider Micawber's first appearance in the novel.
" ' This,' said the stranger, with a certain condescending roll in his

voice, and a certain indescribable air of doing something genteel, which impressed me very much, ' is Master Copperfield. I hope I see you well, sir ? ' " There was nothing remotely genteel about Fields's Micawber, who in the film made his first appearance by a highly ungenteel fall through the roof of his own house.

Consider again. " ' Under the impression that your peregrinations in this metropolis have not as yet been extensive, and that you might have some difficulty in penetrating the arcana of the Modern Babylon in the direction of the City Road—in short, that you might lose yourself—I shall be happy to call this evening, and install you in the knowledge of the nearest way.' " Fields's Micawber would not have used the word " peregrination " or known the meaning of " arcana."

Mr Micawber's manners which " peculiarly qualify him for the Banking business " ? Not even Mrs Micawber at her most doting could have said this of Fields. Micawber is a gentleman who keeps his fallen day about him, and if he is not played like this is not played at all. Fields was a glorious buffoon. But being possessed of no more gentility than a pork pie he could do no other with Micawber than turn him into an obese Ally Sloper, with very much the same nose and hat. And that, I submit, is not Dickens's character.

I am, Sir,
Your obedient servant,
JAMES AGATE

Dec. 30   An anonymous letter :
Monday.

W. C. FIELDS AS MICAWBER

De Mortuis nil nisi bonum
You
Self-advertising
Flamboyant
Swollen-headed
&
Utterly bloody
Bastard.
God wither your right hand !

To James Agate,
Queen Alexandra Mansions,
Sour Grape Street,
W.C.2.

Dec. 31   My year's work :
Tuesday.

Sunday Times	57,000	words
Daily Express	42,000	,,
Tatler	55,000	,,
Ego 8	100,000	,,
Odd articles	10,000	,,
	264,000	words

Now let me repeat a little sum which fascinates me. Turning up *Ego* 4 (page 152), I find that between September 1921 and December 1939 I had written a total of 5,000,000 words. Again I do the little sum :

December	1939	5,000,000	words
,,	1940	350,000	,,
,,	1941	250,000	,,
,,	1942	265,000	,,
,,	1943	300,000	,,
,,	1944	316,000	,,
,,	1945	311,000	,,
,,	1946	264,000	,,
		7,056,000	words

Whaur's your Balzac and your Bennett noo ? In the scales of quantity, not quality, idiot !

1947

Jan. 1
Wednesday.
I am convinced that this country, as I knew it, is finished. What next? Am just not interested. It may be that society has no right to buy elegance and comfort at the cost of miners crawling on their bellies three miles to their stations and then standing all day up to their waists in water. It may be that elegance and comfort should go if the result is an additional penny an hour on the collier's pay. *I am just not interested in the working conditions of coal-mines.* What I am interested in is a first-class performance of *Rosenkavalier* with a bottle of champagne at the Savoy afterwards. To me inequality always has been, and always will be, the spice of life. I think, however, that this country could pull through if the difficulties were purely economic. But they are not. There is a new spirit abroad. I was brought up to believe that the main thing in life was work, and that all pleasure was in the nature of a treat. This spirit is not in the world of to-day; the only connection the modern nose has with the grindstone is to snub it. Modern youth regards life as one unending round of football matches, dog races, crooning, and the pictures, to the last of which it must go four times a week or die. "Après nous le déluge." How right the Pompadour was! After us the deluge. And now it is here. Will it cease? And when the flood subsides what will the new land be like? *Je m'en fous!*

Jan. 2
Thursday.
The first thing I demand of a dramatic critic is that he should be able to use words. A man who can use words tells me something about his mind; he who can't use words doesn't. If I know why a man thinks a Hamlet good and a Macbeth bad I can make my own corrections; he gives me the evidence, so to speak. Ken Peacock Tynan (see *Ego* 8) sends me to-day his views upon Wolfit's production of *Othello* with Valk as the Moor and himself as Iago. I append a few extracts:

> I have seen a public event of enormous, constellated magnitude and radiance; I have watched and become part of a transfusion of bubbling hot blood into the invalid frame of our drama. Some, I am told, brag of having seen the Chicago fire; others, more preciously, boast of having escaped the Quetta earthquake by the merest pebble's-breadth; and I have known men swell visibly as

564

they recalled the tremendous and bloody exploits at Krakatoa. My vaunt is more assuming; I have lived for three hours on the red brink of a volcano, and the crust of lava crumbles still from my feet. I have witnessed a performance of Shakespeare's *Othello*, in which Frederick Valk played Othello and Donald Wolfit Iago. How hushed I was! And how chastened! So much so that for days afterwards, long after I had sent my final, particular roar of " Bravo ! " coursing and resounding about the theatre, I could speak of little but the names of these twin giants and the authentic ring of their titles to greatness. In the mind's middle distance I do think I perceive that other players flickered intermittently across that bare, memorable stage, that flat scene of astounding war ; I can, if I screw up my memory, hear them now, grunting and twittering and shrilling and crying out. Who they were I have not the smallest notion. They it was, as I think, who buzzed and rattled and railed when the big gladiators fell fatigued or retired for momentary refreshment. I should, if there are no strong passions about the matter, prefer to ignore them thus dismissively . . .

Shakespeare, perhaps for fear of too much alarming his audiences, has dealt very unfairly with Othello. Up to the crucial temptation scene (III, 3) he utters only 240 lines of verse, to Iago's 574. And Wolfit took full advantage of this early ascendancy. What a muscular actor he is! Yet how oddly his ponderous gait contrasts with his rasping whine of a voice ! I need not celebrate again the parts and virtues of his Iago ; its stout craft, its unhurried, terrifying certainty and precision. I would only append a tiny animadversion—upon his treatment of spoken poetry. Wolfit speaking high verse is an experience (for me, at least) analogous to watching a rebellious rogue elephant walking a tight-rope. It is enjoyable only because it is very, very odd. Like a prize-fighter nursing a young flower, like John Steinbeck's Lenny petting a puppy, so is Wolfit when a line of poetry is delivered into his hands. He has doubtless fostered in himself a love of poetry ; but I trace hints of an unwilling courtship that went badly against the grain. This quibble settled, I salute a performance which laid quite bare that " diseased intellectual activity " of which Hazlitt spoke ; a performance worthy the seeing, if only to hear Wolfit giving the hapless word " Nature " its full eight or nine syllables . . .

But this was Valk's private adventure, no other near, and we were soon made to acknowledge it. In appearance he was quintessential teddy-bear ; " not " (I hear Coleridge grumbling) " thorough-bred gentleman enough to play Othello." No aristocracy of gait or bearing; no regularity of profile ; in short, no leg. Yet, temperamentally (and here, I am persuaded to think, is the secret), there is no other such tragic player on our stage. In all honesty, I cannot believe that there is blood in the man's veins ; it must be some vile compound of corrosive venoms, explosive and nameless ; some crazy river having its dayspring in spleen, and adulterated with black bile. Why, he was to be touched into mad, lambent flame in a very instant ! He broke every rule of our stage-craft, this berserk Colossus. Following the imperious laws of his agony, his voice would crack and pause, minute-long, in mid-line ; and there would be crazy signallings the while, and rushes as of a wild bull. Then the voice would rise and swoop again into unknown pastures of word-meaning, scooping up huge, vasty syllables of grief as though carving some ancient bed of clay. He seemed, at times, almost to sing, so unlike our custom was his elocution ; a bully's song, a bludgeoner's song, yet its strains moved to pity, as great verse should. I shall see him always, in the latter end of time, singing impious, villainous lullabies to soothe his own congenital disquiet. You could almost hear thin skins splitting and half-shut minds banging and locking themselves about you ; the audience was perturbed, yet pin-still . . . Under Valk, I discovered, verse collapses. I have heard it plausibly objected to him that he loses all the music in words. Now I hold that words are neither harmoni-ous nor discordant ; the verse is either smooth and end-stopped or it is not. But that kind of minuteness is blankly impertinent when Valk is acting, piercing to the core of elemental, wordless things, willing to tear a heart from sheer granite. There was no time for R.A.D.A. modulations and exquisiteness ; a man was hacking a horrid path for himself, and it was neither pretty nor fanciful ; it was inviolable rage, and there were gulfs awash with tears opening all round him. He stood, as if petrifact, bellowing in their dreadful midst . . . The play, the words, all plays, all words were too small for the immensity of this passion. It transcended the prescribed limits of acted drama, the sublunary business of stage-trafficking, and strode boldly through Hell-lake and bade the white-clad recording imps take notice of foul disorders and malevolent conceits ; of the dilapidation of a sturdy tower ; of the climax of a great anguish ; of the disintegration and molten intoxication of a warrior and demigod.

We who saw these things passing were caught up with Valk to his own impossible pinnacles, and when the curtain fell it was as if an end had been put to the tales of mortal suffering ; after this single, enormous catastrophe there could come no more, no further refinement of woe. The sense of relief preceded the permanent sense of awe ; the full tragic action was communicated like the hot breath of the ferocious antique gods. . . .

Anybody reading this in a hundred years' time should know what these two actors had been like in these two great rôles. And that, and nothing else, in my view is dramatic criticism. In other words, here is a great dramatic critic in the making.

Jan. 7   Spent the day jotting down notes for article on *The*
Tuesday.   *Master Builder.*

Jan. 8 *Wednesday.*	Tore up yesterday's notes. Too much like 'prentice-work—allusions to Shaw, Arnold, Montague. Wrote a new article and delivered it at *S.T.* offices.
Jan. 9 *Thursday.*	Retrieved article and destroyed it. Wrote another and, I hope, final one.
Jan. 10 *Friday.*	It wasn't final.
Jan. 11 *Saturday.*	Letter from Neville Cardus :

January 5, 1947

MY DEAR JAMES,

Your letter about my articles has given me a lasting pleasure. To retain your good opinion of my work is an aim always before me, consciously or subconsciously. Of course, I have my ups-and-downs. My song, you see, is compounded like music ; it hath high and low, sharp and flat . . . Sorrow and joy, trouble and peace, sour and sweet, come by vicissitude (especially into an Australian press-box during a Test Match). But this discord in our music, I hope, hurts not, but graceth the song. . . .

It is extremely kind of you, James, to tell me that my articles are " tremendously " appreciated. I only hope George Lyttelton is reading me too. It is a strenuous job ; I have never before watched so closely, and worked so hard. And to-night, after four days of this fluctuating game at Melbourne, I have to broadcast for an hour on the second symphony of Elgar . . . I had nearly written Bradman ! A slip of the pen in such a context which proves how much B. can still get on one's brain. There is no explanation for the England team's troubles as a whole except one : they are just not good, and on the whole not young, enough. Bless you. And now truepenny must soon work i' the earth his way to Adelaide.

Affectionate wishes for 1947 and always,

NEVILLE

Jan. 15 *Wednesday.*	Three Arts Ball at the Dorchester. President H.H. Marie-Louise. Judged the costumes with Gladys Calthrop, Hermione Gingold, and Harold Holt. Felt

like death throughout the evening, but put a smiling face on it.

Jan. 17 *Friday.*	Godfrey Tearle told me at the Ivy that on Wednesday we awarded one of the first prizes to Philip Guard, the young

actor who is so extraordinarily moving as Eros in *Antony and Cleopatra*. I did not recognise him.

Jan. 18   Spent the day at the Queen Victoria Hospital at East
Saturday.   Grinstead. Plastic cases. Nerve-racking but reward-
               ing. McIndoe is a wonderful fellow. In the evening
took Gwen Chenhalls and Tahu Hole to the magician Dante's last
performance. As he made pointed reference to me, had to stand up
in the box and do some bowing. Felt gratified and an ass in equal
proportions.

Jan. 20   At the invitation of Sydney Box lectured to some Society
Monday.   at Beckenham—I never found out what or which. Three
               hundred people and the best audience I have ever had.
Bertie van Thal in the chair. Was told a good story by the Head-
master of the County School. Being asked at some Brains Trust to
say what, in his opinion, had been the invention most beneficial to
mankind, he replied, " The water-closet." Whereupon an elderly professor on the other side of the Question Master leaned across and said,
" And would you, sir, include with that the chain ? "

Jan. 23   An anonymous note sent to me at the Ivy : " Please
Thursday.   don't look quite so angry. In Stockholm people rose
               when Ibsen entered a restaurant. The accompanying
brandy is my way of rising."

Jan. 30   A correction :
Thursday.

                                              10 *St John's Wood Road*
                                                   *London, N.W.*8
                                                   29 *January,* 1947

DEAR JAMES AGATE,
     I gather from the *Egos, passim,* that it causes you neither
surprise nor embarrassment to be thus addressed by total strangers ;
but, in case I seem to be taking too much for granted, let me say
that Gwen Chenhalls (who has just lent me *Ego* 5 to cure the
bronchitis) is a very old friend of mine—so I hope we are as good
as introduced.
     It is about an entry in *Ego* 5 that I write. On p. 227 you print
a letter from Osbert Sitwell in which he quotes Robert Ross as
saying that Marie Lloyd, when a girl of about sixteen with lovely
red hair, sat to D. G. Rossetti. Stop me if you've already heard this
one in the five years that have since elapsed, but the fact is that
D. G. R. died in 1882, when Marie Lloyd was twelve years old.
This was two years before she appeared at the Grecian Music Hall
under the name of Bella Delmare. It is possible that by 1882 she
had already formed her troupe of little girls, " The Fairy Minstrels,"
who sang in schoolrooms and mission halls, but it seems a very

remote possibility indeed that these activities could have brought her into contact with Rossetti.

I think the explanation is fairly evident. Ross, having heard this apocryphal story, goes to her and says in an awed voice, " So *you* knew Rossetti. . . . Do you remember him well ? " What *could* a warm-hearted creature like Marie Lloyd reply to such an appeal ? To have said " No " would have been like snatching the sweet out of a child's mouth : naturally she rose to the occasion at once and replied, " Of *course* I remember him. . . . I've often wondered what happened to the young chap afterwards . . ." ; and Ross went away happy. But that reply proclaims itself to all the world as an amiable tarradiddle : for can anyone conceive that a worn-out and prematurely aged man of fifty-four would impress himself on the memory of a girl of twelve as a " young chap " ?

I can only hope that your passion for accuracy will deaden any disappointment you may feel at having this pretty legend blown upon. If I thought otherwise I should hesitate to risk such an unhandsome return for all the curious pleasures I have got (and hope long to continue to get) from the *Ego* series.

Yours sincerely,

HAMILTON TEMPLE SMITH

Feb. 12
Wednesday. The worst cold snap for a hundred years joining hands with my asthma, and all-fours being an undignified way of mounting stairs, my disgusting doctor has given me the choice between a nursing home and three weeks in bed at Grape Street. Have compromised on a fortnight.

Feb. 14
Friday. Male nurse arrives :

M. N. You'll be easy !
J. A. What's that ?
M. N. I've just finished a job in a lunatic asylum. Refractory ward. You'll be the first patient in five years I've been able to turn my back on.
J. A. Don't be too sure !

Feb. 25
Tuesday. Had written to George Lyttelton *re* my calling Milton " a monumental and boring old buffer." Now comes this letter :

> *Finndale House*
> *Grundisburgh*
> *Suffolk*
> *February 24, 1947*

DEAR JAMES,

I was just about to write to you, having heard from B. van Thal that you were ill, and having again missed you in the *S.T.*

I am glad to see from your letter that you really are on the mend.

I hope you are faring better in what B. v. T. aptly called these disgraceful times. I see some kindly Yank says Britain is " an old run-down country." How one would like to call him a liar ! But can one, while we are governed by shop-stewards behind a façade of ministers who behave like angry hens ? Enough ! I know you hate political jaw, though that again is hard to avoid. Let us talk of other things. Milton ! The shock was to find one whose taste in big things is, as Keats said of Hazlitt's, a recurrent cause for gratitude in being alive, apparently on the side of the stockbrokers in the matter of Milton. I see your point about " monumental " counter-acting " boring," but I submit that your *Tatler* readers will rejoice to find J. A.'s taste the same as theirs. Philistia will take your half-truth (for of course the old man could be boring) for the whole, and be glad of you.

Exactly at this point the post arrived, with exactly the right parcel to put the Government, the weather, and the pipes in their proper unimportant places. I am, as I told you, childishly pleased to see my name on the title-page of *Ego* 8, and as, temporarily, your chief " stooge," as Ivor Brown on p. 228 calls your chief correspondents in *Ego* 7. Ungrateful man !

How utterly *monstrous* that your party on August 28 with two votes apiece didn't give one of them to Dickens—who could have put Barry Pain and Dornford Yates in his ticket pocket without noticing. *Alice*, of course, is in the right place. But have you ever seen a child reading *Alice* ? Intense *interest* but not a smile, it being, of course, his or her world. I am glad to see the *Irish R.M.* got a vote. I should have put in one for Burnand's *Happy Thoughts*. Do you know it ? Long out of print !

Later. *Ego* 8 and indeed all the *Egos* are *hopeless* bedside books ! —veritable Macbeths ! One cannot stop reading, and that pleasant slide into drowsiness never happens. I have far exceeded my ration, and shall have finished dreadfully soon. I shall write again. So far the only lapse from bliss was in reading of your shearing the previous *Ego* by thousands of words. I don't like Agates " very vilely cut." And I will end with this : " For Britain . . . as it is a land fruitful enough of men stout and courageous in war, so it is naturally not over-fertile of men able to govern justly and prudently in peace, trusting only in their mother-wit . . . valiant, indeed, and prosperous to win afield, but to know the end and reason of winning, unjudicious and unwise ; in good or bad success alike, unteachable."

The author ? That monumental . . . old josser. He seems very up to date on this occasion.

May you long continue to contribute, though sore set and hindered by stooges and small fry, to the gaiety of nations !

Yours ever,

G. W. L.

Feb. 26   From George Richards :
Wednesday.

Some one—I am not sure it wasn't myself—stated in a letter to the Press some time ago that there was no *real* reason why, if only the will were present, the City Fathers of Bournequay should not, by wise investment of their municipal funds and the engagement of a first-rate conductor, use their nucleus of a local orchestra to turn their native seaside city into a Salzburg in England's green and pleasant land. The said Fathers have now got to the point of putting a selected number of candidates for the post of permanent conductor through their paces, and one of these guest-conducted concerts was held at the Pavilion this afternoon. So far so good— ONLY, as this was Great Britain, not little Austria, things in practice work out rather differently. To cope with the weather, to begin with, I put on cape, goggles, sou'wester, and leggings. In one pocket of my overcoat, underneath, I put a flask of brandy, and in the other . . . a good novel.

Other equipment needed and (providentially as it turned out) also taken along included (*a*) an ear-trumpet (the orchestra numbers less than fifty all told, including the staggering total of twelve violins, with the result that the British municipal concert-goer's first difficulty in that vast arena is to hear anything at all), (*b*) a set of ear-*plugs* (to blot out from audition what *should* be those passages of pure serene in the heavenly second movement of Grieg's piano concerto (played by Miss Dorothy Spottikins aged twelve) which absolutely and uncompromisingly require and unconditionally desiderate horn-players capable of using their instrument for more than two bars running otherwise than for the purpose of giving an involuntary representation of a crapulous, crippled, and constipated tortoise wobbling on a mud-bank on the way home from a lost week-end, and likewise to blanket the inevitable murder of that jaunty little passage for the horns in the first movement of the inevitable Dvořák *New World*).

These minor blemishes, however, are only a few ways in which national characteristics affect the musical enterprises of different countries. That, when the concert is over and the audience finds itself back in the dripping Sunday streets, there is not even a cup of tea anywhere to be had goes of course without saying. I am told that later in the year there is to be a Grand Inaugural Concert with which the new conductor will open a Musical Festival To End All Musical Festivals. The opening item on the programme of this concert will be Beethoven's Leonora Overture No. 3, and to mark the occasion fittingly a new musical precedent will be created. The cornet player, when he leaves his stool to play his famous solo, will not retire to the wings to do so, but descend to the auditorium and play it there in the centre gangway *fortissimo*, the rest of the orchestra playing muted throughout.

Feb. 27
Thursday.
One of the panic acts of our Socialist Government during the past fortnight has been to economise electric current by stopping publication of all the weeklies ! I had done an article on Ellen Terry for *Picture Post*, and am delighted to find this morning that the *Daily Graphic*, acting as host, has offered *P.P.* a whole page, and that the article chosen to fill that page is mine. Thus I have been able to pay my last respects to Ellen.

March 1
Saturday.
This book would not be complete without a portrait of " Brother Mycroft," who has never failed to live up to that letter written to me at Giggleswick when he was twelve :

Please tell me whether there are any violin-playing boys in the school, *and whether the violin master knows anything at all about it.*

Mycroft knows more about engine-driving than any engine-driver, and about steeplechasing than any winner of the Grand National, this without ever having mounted a footplate or thrown his leg over a horse. He is perfectly prepared to give Cotton a lesson in golf, and his advice to anybody taking to his bed would be not " Get a doctor," but " See if there is a doctor in your street, and find out whether he knows anything about medicine." The annoying thing about it is that these pretensions are perfectly founded. Give him a subject about which he knows nothing—if there be such a subject—and Mycroft will know instinctively the way to set about getting to the heart of it. Does so much perfection become a little wearing ? As a family we have got used to it. I know before I start on any of my books that my approach to it, Gustavianly considered, will be wrong, and that even along my lines I shall make a mess of it. However, we are all very fond of the dear fellow, whose leading characteristic is modesty. *He just can't help being right.*

March 2
Sunday.
Centenary of the birth of Ellen Terry, and not a single word about her in any of the papers. It appears that she is no longer news. But let nobody mention her name within earshot of any tomb of mine. My dust would hear it and beat, had I lain for a century dead.

March 3
Monday.
In a letter from a lady :

I have just come back from Paris—an absorbingly interesting fortnight. Among other things, eight plays and two operas. *Don*

Giovanni was *not* good, though Leporello worked hard to pierce the gloom ; I ventured to chuckle once, but my neighbour looked as if I'd committed an act of irreverence.

Two queer things occurred. The first was a violent, personal, and quite irrational dislike taken by me to Marie Bell in Bernstein's *Le Secret*. And why on earth is Pierre Dux wasting that lovely concave dial of his in that particular *galère* ?

The second was—watching a modern French audience watching *Ruy Blas* ! Yonnel was grand, and young Deiber most affecting, but even that had hardly prepared one for the terrific applause that greeted the tirades of *Ruy Blas*. It was absolutely a revelation. The audience was vast and the play far, far more 'living' than any of the modern ones I saw, which were disappointing. It was just that they seemed to have little relation with live people of any age.

L'École des Femmes was lovely, and I hope Molière enjoyed seeing himself, over the bar of heaven, in Christian Bérard's settings. Bless the French, anyway, and may they soon be more prosperous and able to find many playwrights, other than M. J.-P. Sartre.

March 4   Wonderful misprints in Eric Partridge's *Usage and*
Tuesday.   *Abusage* :

> To die—to sleep
> No more ; and by a sleep we say we end
> The heart-ache. . . .

To sleep no more ? Hamlet hath murdered sleep. And who is " we " to say we end the heartache ?

Who is going to ' take care of ' nonsense when I have stopped diarising ? Here is Geoffrey Grigson in the current *Windmill* : " No man can retain any scrap of the God within him if he stays in the latrine of daily journalism a month beyond reaching thirty." Shades of Montague, Monkhouse, Sidebotham, Mair, Bone, and a score of London journalists who would not have sold one ounce of their souls for all the wealth of Fleet Street !

March 8   In their delightful history cum treatise cum anthology
Saturday.   entitled *The Bed* Cecil and Margery Gray have forgotten, or anyhow left out, the delicious conclusion to Maupassant's *Bel Ami*—my favourite ending after Zola's *L'Assommoir* and Flaubert's *L'Éducation Sentimentale*. Here is the Maupassant—the point being that Georges Duroy, having married Suzanne Walter, daughter of his ex-mistress, descends the steps of the Madeleine

with his bride on his arm and his thoughts bent on another
enchantress :

> Il descendit avec lenteur les marches du haut perron entre deux
> haies de spectateurs. Mais il ne les voyait point ; sa pensée main-
> tenant revenait en arrière, et devant ses yeux éblouis par l'éclatant
> soleil flottait l'image de Mme de Marelle rajustant en face de la
> glace les petits cheveux frisés de ses tempes, toujours défaits au
> sortir du lit.

March 11
Tuesday.
"No scandal about Queen Elizabeth, I hope." Sydney
Carroll's *The Imperial Votaress* is all about Elizabeth's
love affair with the Earl of Leicester. Sydney indicates
his views about his heroine by showing her at the age of fourteen
engaging in fun and games with Sir Thomas Seymour, the Lord High
Admiral. This old fribble, half Balzac's Hulot and half Nucingen,
being arrested for the aforesaid fun and games, Elizabeth protests
against beheading as a punishment for " a harmless bit of slap and
tickle." But then Sydney's Elizabeth is nothing if not modern. She
tells Leicester that as a lady-killer he is " worse than my old Dad
was." And when warned that Drake, Hawkins, and the others are
out for loot, she says, " Out for loot I grant, but if they get any I
shall have my whack." However, there are some unsuspected good
things, though I am not quite sure whether Sydney has suspected
them. I like the royal lover who can come to his Queen and say,
" Let us be practical, Elizabeth. There are things more important to
you at this moment than my miserable wife." And I dote on the
executioner who says to a victim, " Why should I flinch at grey hair
or shudder for the lovely and the young ? It's my profession. I am
paid well and it's dignified. It makes folk like you realise your
unimportance. You must excuse me now. I like a chat—but duty
calls."

March 12
Wednesday.
Ego 8 published.

March 19
Wednesday.
Brighton disagreeing with me—I have not closed an eye
for three nights—I returned to Grape Street to-day,
where I intend to stay put till some kind of strength
returns to me. Not too pleased to discover that the drug my d.d.
is giving me is paraldehyde, the stuff they gave the dipsomaniac in
The Lost Week-end. Delirium tremens, emphatically no. Delirium
minimens, possibly !

March 20
Thursday.
My nurse has left. He was extremely kind and efficient, and gave me all the comfort that comes from reliability. Name of John Southern. He leaves because on arriving home yesterday he found a letter offering him and his wife the joint secretaryship of a nursing institute. With the offer goes a large flat; this has a playroom for the two-and-a-half-year-old kiddie they have adopted. Selfish I may be, but not a monster. So I pack him off at once. Which isn't very brave of me, as I know that in this sort of emergency my luck always holds. I fully expect that in about ten minutes it will be raining male Sarah Gamps and Betsey Prigs.

March 21
Friday.
This morning two ex-Sick Bay Attendants presented themselves, and can I use them ? They appear to know all about high explosives and what to do with a man who has been six hours in the water, so I shall let them take on my job in turns. There was a third alternative, also a sailor, who fell from a mast forty feet high some months ago and is still suffering from concussion. I advised him to go on the pictures, on the principle that every film actor is as concussed as he.

March 22
Saturday.
In a letter :

These are the books I have carried in my kitbag throughout the war : Hesketh Pearson's *Bernard Shaw* ; Boswell's *Johnson* ; Shakespeare ; Kingsmill and Pearson's *This Blessed Plot* ; T. E. Lawrence's *Letters* ; Shaw's *Pen Portraits and Reviews* ; Agate's *Brief Chronicles*. These seven books were more to me than the sailor's seven necessities : lifebelt, electric iron, " private " bucket (for dobeying), tiddley suit, Post Office Savings Bank book, pillow, Burberry. And, if Shakespeare was my lifebelt, *Brief Chronicles* was the little red light on it one switched on, when struggling in the water, to attract the attention of passing ships. I have carried this book with me to Liverpool, Belfast, Glasgow, Devonport, Gibraltar, Malta, Alex, Bombay, Trincomali, Colombo, Fremantle, Sydney, and, finally, to a Japanese surrender at Rabaul. . . .

March 24
Monday.
Second printing of *Ego* 8 put in hand.

March 25
Tuesday.
Allowed out and about. Not very far out and not very much about. A sort of bath-chair existence on foot. But it's better than nothing. What a good and understanding doctor Norman Newman is ! A tower of strength to his patients,

because he persuades them that they are towers in their own right. Gwen Chenhalls called for me in the car and gave me one of her kill-or-cure luncheons. Bill of fare: anchovies, lobster salad, treacle tart, coffee laced with brandy. Bringing two glass ornaments out of her dining-room, she planked them on the kitchen table—we were lunching in the kitchen—and said " Claridge's ! " And Claridge's it seemed. After lunch more coffee, more brandy, a rug over my knees, and an hour's snooze. After which she drove me back to Grape Street. Gwen is my ideal of a ministering angel—not too sympathetic, and therefore bracing. I have been astonished at the amount of kindness showered on me since I have been ill. My papers have vied with each other in consideration and generosity. George Harrap has been a fountain of champagne ; Larry Sullivan, when he called, bulged in every pocket ; grapes galore and dozens of anonymous eggs. Gwen has called every day with a lunch she has prepared with her own hands. My good friends Alfred and Dolly Burger have sent me a hot meal every night from their little club. And, of course, all my particular cronies rallied round me. Most touching of all was a bunch of flowers sent by that dear actress Elliot Mason, who has been ill in a flat above mine since before Christmas and whom I am not yet allowed to visit.

March 26   In a letter from my, and Leo's, little Dublin friend,
Wednesday.   J. E. Jordan, now official play-reader to the Gate
            Theatre :

I sometimes wish I'd never read a line of you, that I'd never, out of curiosity, taken down from the library shelves the bulky first two volumes of *Ego* ; then I should never have acquired, perhaps, a taste for the past, its people and its art, far exceeding in intensity my taste for the present and the future. I should then have developed in the normal fashion of the modern youth, and cultivated a passion for poetry about lavatories and copulation, and novels about lavatories and copulation and (dare I say it ?) music about lavatories and copulation. I should then have acquired a healthy contempt for doddering dramatic critics dribbling about an old barn-stormer called Irving and a French cow called Bernhardt. I suppose it's possible to retire into one's own intellectual and spiritual planet and gaze only occasionally and with complacency on the worlds of one's fellows. But it comes with age, I imagine. At fifty it may be that I shall be able to write in perfect sincerity, like Edward Agate : " What do I care for anything that can happen to me at Thompson's Cross so long as I have the surge and surf of the great Pandemonium in my ears ? " But not at seventeen.

March 27   From Elizabeth Bowen's review of *Ego* 8 in the *Tatler* :
Thursday.

> I think Mr Agate should stand out as the prominent man who has talked least nonsense about the atomic bomb.

March 28   I can live without food, but not without wit, a commodity
Friday.   that doesn't easily find its way into a sick-room. I was
delighted, therefore, when I undid a parcel this morning and found that Tommy Earp had sent me three volumes of Henry Becque. I open *Querelles Littéraires* and read how a M. Abraham Dreyfus had written to a number of authors—Augier, Dumas, Sardou, Gondinet, Legouvé, Doucet, Dennery, Pailleron, Zola—asking them how they set about writing a play. He was inundated with replies, the best of which, says Becque, came from Halévy, who didn't answer at all ! And then this follows :

> Quant à l'auteur du *Voyage de M. Perrichon*, il faut lui rendre cette justice, l'esthétique n'a jamais été son fort et il y est visible-ment embarrassé ; mais il a esquivé la difficulté avec un mot d'une drôlerie irrésistible. " Pour faire une pièce," a dit M. Labiche, " je cherche d'abord un collaborateur."

March 29   Even the pin-pricked get tired of it. In a letter from
Saturday.   Park Lane :

> On p. 64 of *Ego* 8 you write : " My obsession about misprints continues." But on the book's very first page you will find the word " kingdoms " misspelt.

Have duly returned thanks. " Indeed, unusual thanks, since I now realise that some Park Lane millionaires can spell."

March 30   Ivor Brown's review of *Ego* 8 suggests that he has at last
Sunday.   cottoned on to the fact that *Ego* is my diary, and not
Adam Smith's or Mr Attlee's. I am very pleased with :

> Mr Agate has certain fields and the sight of a fence does not tempt him to jump out of them. Politics, economics, ethics, religion, or its secular substitute—all the great foundations of living he mainly chooses to pass by, at least in these chronicles. To the trimmings, bedizenments, and decorations of life he brings a reading, an experience, a memory and a gusto without parallel in our time.

March 31   I am always mindful of that passage in Max's *Around*
Monday.   *Theatres* about " that period when a man begins to bore
            young people by raving to them about the mimes whom
they never saw." (My copy has a note in Jock's handwriting :
" Must tell J. A. this.") I have made it a rule never to talk about
Irving unless some playgoing chit tells me that some nincompoop at
Gunnersbury playing the lead in *The Donkey Has Two Tails* is a great
actor. Then I let fly. This train of thought has been suggested to me
by the fact that in my mail this morning an unknown friend sends me
Henry Arthur Jones's *The Shadow of Henry Irving.* This has the
wonderful last sentence " To the remotest corners of time and
humanity we will not part from him." For forty years I have felt
about H. I. what Iago pretended to feel about Othello : " I am
your own for ever." It has not been within the power of Time to
weaken this.

April 1   There is, I hope and pray, nothing of Chadband in my
Tuesday.   make-up. As an a-moralist I have all my life studiously
            avoided claptrap about behaviour. Wherefore, being
invited by the B.B.C. to give a talk on " How to Live," I have gone
to work circumspectly, I might almost say gingerly. Here is a bit of
the MS., which I have arranged to record, as I am not quite up to the
excitement of doing it ' live.'

    The first condition of learning how to live is to avoid doing that
which will stop you from living at all. For example, there is no
point in finding out how to conduct your life if you are busy
drinking yourself to death. Even so, I have respected some men
who have drunk themselves into their graves more than others
who, as Pinero's Dick Phenyl said, have trembled at gravy and
lived to the age of ninety. On the 15th of May, 1933, I attended a
ceremony to see Sir Frank Benson and Dame Madge Kendal do
honour to the memory of a man who on that date one hundred
years before had died of drink. Now there must, you will agree, be
something extraordinary about a drunken vagabond to whom two
noble spirits of our own time went to do honour. Well, there was.
The place was the foyer of Drury Lane Theatre ; the honour was
the placing of a wreath at the base of a statue ; the statue was that
of Edmund Kean, England's greatest tragedian. I do not say to
anybody listening to me, " Don't abuse Nature so much that at the
age of forty-six Nature has had enough of you." That is outside
the scope of this talk, and would be an impertinence. What I do
say is that if you must abuse Nature, abuse her to some purpose.
If you must die of drink, then leave behind something that men are
going to talk about. If you must end your life selling matches on

the kerb-stone, see to it that you have done something that has enriched the world. And if you have no talent, then I implore you not to indulge in those follies and exuberances which are the prerogative of genius. This is my advice to the ordinary man. Live your life so that when you pass on people will say, " He was a decent sort."

This is a reconstruction of something I said to 1000 Boy Scouts in a field at Uxbridge three days after the Kean centenary. I remember that there was a disapproving bishop in the chair. Or let me say a faintly approving one.

April 2
Wednesday.
Letter from Gerard Bell, a brilliant, modest young man, reminding me of a benevolent eaglet, engaged in the editorial department of Harrap's :

> 46 *Museum Street*
> *W.C.*1
> *April* 1, 1947

DEAR MR AGATE,

When you invited me last week-end to be your guest for lunch on Monday I was very much afraid, I must confess, of boring you to distraction with my feeble prattle during our first ten minutes together. But you gave no sign of being bored ; and it is for this exercise in self-control that I am writing to thank you now, as well as for the excellence of your hospitality. Mr Mathew is a charming man ; it was nice of you to let me meet him. The way you described him—as looking rather like " a bemused St Bernard "—delighted me very much. At any rate, the " St Bernard " part of it hits him off exactly ; he struck me as particularly wide-awake.

During the past twelve months I haven't seen you in better health or spirits than just before your illness ; and I was shocked to find such a great change in you when you came back from Brighton. But you have recovered now so well that my greatest pleasure yesterday was not in sitting at table with you, but in knowing that you were back to form.

You always consider your friends in everything else ; please now consider them in the thing that matters to them most : please don't overwork again. You will only distress us. If you knew how much you upset us all, from the heads of the firm down to me, a month or two ago I do not think you would take risks with your health as you have been doing for so long.

You will not be annoyed with me for writing to you in this strain, because I am sincerely, dear Mr Agate, and, may I say, most affectionately, yours,

G. F. BELL

April 4	Any port in a storm, and any joke in a period of depres-
Friday.	sion. In my mail a day or two ago a Belgian refugee from
	the First World War asked me if I would kindly forward

a letter. On the envelope was written :

> Winston Churchill
> c/o James Agate, Esq.
> *Daily Express*

I duly forwarded the letter, and had a charming acknowledgment in
Winston's handwriting.

April 12	Some people after an illness resume their job with a
Saturday.	whimper ; I prefer the bang. Here is my *rentrée* for
	to-morrow. If the essential Rachel is not here, com-

pressed into a miserable seven hundred words, let my brains be taken
out, buttered, and given to a dog :

THE GREATEST ACTRESS

Miss March Cost's novel, *Rachel*, is like a palatial mansion,
exquisitely decorated and handsomely appointed. Not a period
piece is missing. Alas, the rightful owner is from home ! Somebody
who might be a French Helen Faucit or Fanny Kemble, a nice-
minded daughter of the arts who has absent-mindedly come by two
children and a rabble of lovers without acquiring a husband, is the
châtelaine.

Take that extraordinary *liaison* with Véron, pill-maker and
theatrical patron, stout, bald, baby-faced baboon, with a thin ring
of yellow beard and a scrofulous neck hidden in so many neck-
cloths that wits addressed their letters to him : " Monsieur Véron,
dans sa cravate, à Paris." This was the scurvy rascal to whom
Rachel, knowing well what she did, gave herself at the age of
sixteen. Miss Cost, making her heroine say, " This experience was
to remain the most revolting of my life," seeks to excuse the pecca-
dillo on the score that the great public, prompted by Jules Janin,
had not yet discovered the new genius, and that she sacrificed her
virtue to her art. But what nonsense to attempt condonation of
the subsequent life of luxury and riot on the ground that " every
capitulation on my part inevitably rendered the first less important."
And how explain away the fact that Rachel was Véron's mistress
for three years after all Paris had declared itself prostrate at her
feet ? How explain that she broke off relations with this acclaimed
grotesque because of the public scandal, and later on resumed those
relations privately ? The explanation is that both Rachel and

Véron were of the gutter, fellow-adventurers revelling in the *nostalgie de la boue.*

A few days before her death Rachel wrote, " If the scandal-mongers busy themselves with my life, let them tell the truth in all its simplicity." Well, what is the truth ? The truth is that Rachel was the greatest actress the world has ever seen, the panther to Kean's lion. That she was in her private life a close-fisted, avaricious, rapacious cheat. That she had a mania for cadging, and never left a house without begging some gewgaw. That she would put her name down for a charity concert knowing she would not appear, and then demand twenty tickets, sell them to her lover of the moment, beg them back and sell them again to the lover next in favour. That she and her father blackmailed the Comédie Française into subsidising the entire Félix brood. That she would feign illness, obtain leave of absence, and undertake a whirlwind, money-making tour. That she richly earned the quip of Judith Bernat : " Je suis juive, moi, mais Rachel est un juif."

She acted by intuition. She could not spell. She did not read the plays in which she appeared, and in *Les Horaces* never knew who said " Qu'il mourût ! " or why. Age-long paradox ! Rachel alone of all actresses had the voice and stomach for

> On ne voit point deux fois le rivage des morts.

The world has agreed with our own G. H. Lewes, who said, " Whoever saw Rachel play Phèdre may be pardoned if he doubt whether he will ever see such acting again."

Rachel died at the age of thirty-seven fingering a bedspread covered with gold pieces. The mourners at the graveside included Déjazet, Jane Essler, Scribe, the older and the younger Dumas, Sandeau, Sainte-Beuve, Alfred de Vigny, Mérimée, Augier, Halévy, Gautier, Murger, and Michel and Calmann Lévy, Balzac's publishers. Alone the Comédie was not represented. Why ? Because, years before, Samson, thinking that the *père* Félix was coming it a bit too strong, had kicked the old man downstairs. Papa Félix, remembering this, objected to Samson's presence at the graveside. To compensate, Matthew Arnold wrote some inspired nonsense.

Less than six months ago I stood by the bed on which Rachel died. The room, whose furniture had not been touched, still breathed the spirit of the virago, drab, harpy, *grande amoureuse*, great artist, tormented, unhappy soul. Of Miss Cost's equable heroine not a trace.

April 13   Much touched by this telegram :
Sunday.

SO HAPPY TO FIND YOU BACK ON SUNDAY TIMES WARMEST WISHES—DOLLY AND MARK HAMBOURG.

April 14   Criticism is not what it was either in this country or in
Monday.   France. Esmé Percy called to-day and gave me a copy
             of Léonard de Géréon's *La Rampe et les Coulisses*, being a
volume of thumbnail sketches of the directors, actors, and actresses
of the principal theatres in Paris in 1832. The first sketch, if you
please, is one of my and Rachel's adored Véron. " Industriel, artiste,
amateur-homme-de-lettres, la nature, en créant M. Véron, semble
avoir voulu essayer tout ce qu'elle pouvait faire pour un directeur
d'Opéra."

The book fills me with a curious sort of envy. What would I not
give to be able to write of a well-known actor what was written here
of Monval : " Les succès obtenus par ses camarades lui font mal ; il
étouffe d'envie, il mourra d'amour-propre."

I know at least a dozen actresses about whom it would be a joy
to write as the author wrote about Mlle Théodorine :

> M. Poirson peut dire comme Napoléon : *c'est une de mes erreurs !*
> mauvaise à l'Ambigu et plus mauvaise encore au Gymnase, made-
> moiselle Théodorine n'a pas même l'avantage d'une figure agréable.
> Laide, mais laide à plaisir, elle est sans aucune espèce de grâce, ne
> se doute pas des premiers éléments de l'art dramatique. On dit
> qu'elle cherche un mari, probablement parce qu'elle ne peut pas
> trouver un amant.

April 15   There is a story about a nobleman who was buying his
Tuesday.   ticket for Paris when his valet touched him on the sleeve
             and said, " M'lord, the man behind me in the queue has
just fallen down dead." " Nonsense," said his lordship. " Fetch a
policeman." The notion that you can cure abnormality by sending
for the police or dispatching its victims to work in the coal-mines is
on the same level of imbecility. Douglas Home's *Now Barabbas* swims
in homosexuality, treated in comic and sentimental but never in
realistic vein. I hold that this highly specialised subject is not one
to which the stage should be much beholden, but that if there is to
be treatment at all that treatment should be adult. Why doesn't the
prison governor send for the chaplain or the medical officer or both
and ask to be told what Housman meant by that poem about the
young man doomed to oakum and the treadmill because of " the
nameless and abominable colour of his hair " ? Will the Law never
realise what psychologists have been shouting in its ear for forty years
—that the born homosexual is one of Nature's carefully arranged
vagaries, that for one of this type contact with the opposite sex is as

repugnant as homosexuality is to the normal man ? Let the Law take the strictest measures against proselytism, acts of public indecency, the violation of, or any lesser offence towards, young boys—let it come down with the greatest severity upon peccant schoolmasters, scout-masters, choirmasters doing harm to children placed in their care. But let the Law realise that at twenty-one a young man should know what sex he belongs to, and that it is nonsense to send a Walt Whitman to gaol for two years because he likes holding hands with a beard-enamoured bus-conductor. What the governor in this play does is to shelve his problem by sending the young man to another gaol, in the hope that the change of air will turn his tresses into a crop of manly stubble like the Manassa Mauler's. I do not believe in placating the Censor by throwing a sop to Colonel Blimp.

This play has a further fault. It is nearly an hour too long for its intellectual content. If ever a playwright missed his chance for a fine ending it was this author in this piece. The murderer has been told that a reprieve will not be granted. It is next morning, and the prisoners have been ordered to their cells. The warder is exhibiting traces of something which may be nerves or even compassion. It is nearing eight o'clock, and the doomed man has heard the steeple " sprinkle the quarters on the morning town." And into the minds of some in the audience to-night must have come recollection of Housman's great lines :

> Strapped, noosed, nighing his hour,
> He stood and counted them and cursed his luck ;
> And then the clock collected in the tower
> Its strength, and struck.

The gaoler removes his cap. Was ever opportunity so missed ?

April 18   Sentimental objection being taken to my view of Rachel,
Friday.   I have sent this further letter to the *Sunday Times* :

Rachel not of the gutter ? Legouvé said that at her most tragic she had " un fond de titi gouailleur," meaning that she could never quite get away from being a nose-thumbing street-arab. Con-temporary opinion ? Hear Mlle George talking to Victor Hugo : " Being horribly hard up, I took my courage in both hands and went to see Rachel to ask her to play in *Rodogune* with me at my benefit. She would not see me, and sent word that I was to write to her. No, thank you ! Low though I may have sunk, I have not sunk as low as that ! I have been as great an actress as Rachel and as big a slut . . ."

Jules Janin wrote : " Sometimes superb, sometimes mediocre, to-day she will ride the clouds, to-morrow she will be in the abyss. There is no praise and no censure that she has not deserved. Statue . . . spectre . . . a projection of the human will . . . a shadow." My theory of acting sees no reason why the paramour of a vulgar *coureur de filles* like Véron should not have constituted herself the full orchestra of human passion, just as it sees no reason why some blameless incarnation of all the female virtues should do justice to a hurdy-gurdy. I am not astonished when I read Rachel's letter to her flighty sister Sarah : " Je suis décidée à rentrer grosse en France, dont le chagrin doit être exclu." This and twenty-four similar letters, all addressed to Sarah, the *soupeuse vaillante*, were part of the collection of M. Félix Drouin, to whom Sarah originally sold them. What was Sarah's income at the time of the re-sale ? Six thousand francs. Left her by whom ? By Rachel. How much did the letters fetch at the re-sale ? Two hundred and twenty-seven francs. Two hundred and twenty-seven francs to save the reputa-tion of a dead sister and a great artist ! But Rachel, *de son vivant*, would not have parted with the odd twenty-seven, and Sarah was not Rachel's sister for nothing.

In all that is known to me as Rachel's biographer I find nothing that I should not expect in the daughter of an Alsatian pedlar and a Bohemian dealer in second-hand clothes. Except, of course, the genius. Matthew Arnold, writing a lot of nonsense at her death, had the sense to wind up with the superbly under-standing " Her genius and her glory are her own." I am not incommoded when a woman whose genius and glory have become legend turns out to have had avarice, meanness, and cupidity written on her brow, and to have spent her life getting to know the torments of hell. What, pray, has genius ever had to do with non-hell ?

April 23   On a Saturday in December 1899 Benson in *Richard II*
Wednesday. gave the finest Shakespearean performance I have ever
             seen, and on the following Monday morning Montague
came out with his famous two-column notice about Richard as artist getting exquisite pleasure out of muffing the royal job and paying the medieval penalty for royal failure. Was C. E. M. upset because Benson omitted " Yet I'll hammer it out "—" it " being the comparison between Richard's prison and the world—five words which set the seal on the actor's interpretation and gave C. E. M. his cue ? No. He was content to call the omission " a strange mischance."

Being twenty-two at the time, I thought that any young man had the right to ask any actor why he had missed this point or that. Forcing my way into Benson's dressing-room at the next performance,

I demanded to know why he had omitted those five vital words. Benson said he *didn't think they mattered*. Further, that the notion of Richard as artist was quite new to him. I then pulled Montague's notice out of my pocket and read :

> Mr Benson made amends with a beautiful little piece of insight at the close, where, after the lines
>
> > Mount, mount, my soul ! Thy seat is up on high,
> > Whilst my gross flesh sinks downward, here to die,
>
> uttered much as any other man might utter them under the first shock of the imminence of death, he half rises from the ground with a brightened face and repeats the two last words with a sudden return of animation and interest, the eager spirit leaping up, with a last flicker before it goes quite out, to seize on this new ' idea of ' the death of the body. Greater love of art could no man have than this, and, if we understood him rightly, it was a brilliant thought of Mr Benson's to end on such a note.

Benson listened courteously to the provincial hobbledehoy and said, " That is a brilliant thought on the part of your friend. But I confess the idea has never entered my head. To me it has just seemed that to rise on my elbow would be theatrically effective."

A paradox ? If you like. Sixty years of intensive playgoing have taught me that the great actor knows *what* he must do, but never *why*, and that when an actor knows why he must do a thing the doing of it by him just isn't worth watching.

Now comes Alec Guinness, who does well in the matter of verbal *panache*. His performance is finely calculated, yet, to me, remains inescapably only semi-Richard. This is because of this actor's Herbert Pocket, that miraculous glove-fit of player and part. But then if Edward Terry had ever essayed, say, Enobarbus, my ear must have caught the echo of Dick Phenyl's " Last time, Clemmy, my boy ! " These things cannot be helped. What schoolboy, then, does this Richard suggest to me ? Steerforth. But a schizophrenic Steerforth, half peeved at being no longer head of the school, half smacking his lips with Henry James's Mrs Highmore at the discovery that " a failure in the market is something that a success somehow isn't." The result to-night was, for me, not an overwhelming Richard, but a sincere one trying to get away from Pocket, Steerforth, and, yes, Mr Toots, and never quite succeeding. " Will majesty give Richard leave to live till Richard die ? It's of no consequence, thank you." Guinness's genius is for the rueful comic, a note which this play never strikes. He received a tremendous ovation. But then so did everybody else. And, as all the other characters are insufferable dullards, I can only conclude that much of the applause was a tribute to the skill with which the company threaded its way in and out of a décor consisting entirely of the unremoved supports and stanchions of the old, reinforced, war-time shelter.

April 24   Letter to Tom Curtiss :
Thursday.

Queen Alexandra Mansions
Grape Street, W.C.2
April 24, 1947

DEAR TOM,

I have received a wonderful package from you containing butter, ham, pheasant, rice, and candy. I am sending this to Gwen Chenhalls for her to cook for me, with some idea of getting a teaspoonful or so of it down. I have completely lost my appetite and am getting steadily weaker. Stairs now give me as much trouble down as up, and ten yards is an adventure. It may well be, then, that this is the last letter you will receive from me. Which is why it should be a jolly one. Every moment of our friendship has been a delight ; I remember most of them, and I don't think we could have quarrelled if we had tried. If necessary, give two messages for me. The first, of course, is to the adorable Gishes ; they will know what is in my mind. The second is to Nathan, to whom you are to say that George and James put together would have made a damned fine dramatic critic.

On the other hand, my dear boy, I may go on being a public nuisance for another ten years, though, judging by the way I am feeling at the moment, if this isn't dying I am inclined to say what Barrie's Cinderella said about her policeman's effusion : " In my poor opinion if it's not a love-letter, it's a very near thing."

Let's hope this isn't good-bye.

Ever,

JIMMIE

P.S. I am just going out to stand George Harrap lunch and a bottle of champagne. At 5.30 I'm engaged to drink champagne with C. B. Cochran before the dress-rehearsal of *Bless the Bride*. And, damn it, if I can't find somebody to buy me champagne for supper I shall buy some for myself. With mirth and laughter let death-rattles come !

FICTION, 1837

" How old is that horse, my friend ? " inquired Mr Pickwick, rubbing his nose with the shilling he had reserved for the fare.

" Forty-two," replied the driver, eyeing him askant.

" What ! " ejaculated Mr Pickwick, laying his hand upon his note-book. The driver reiterated his former statement. Mr Pickwick looked very hard at the man's face, but his features were immovable, so he noted down the fact forthwith.

" And how long do you keep him out at a time ? " inquired Mr Pickwick, searching for further information.

" Two or three veeks," replied the man.

" Weeks ! " said Mr Pickwick in astonishment—and out came the note-book again.

" He lives at Pentonwil when he's at home," observed the driver, coolly, " but we seldom takes him home, on account of his veakness."

" On account of his weakness ! " reiterated the perplexed Mr Pickwick.

" He always falls down when he's took out o' the cab," continued the driver, " but when he's in it, we bears him up werry tight, and takes him in werry short, so as he can't werry well fall down ; and we've got a pair o' precious large wheels on, so ven he *does* move, they run after him, and he must go on—he can't help it."

Pickwick Papers

FACT, 1947

<small>MARE ' PROPPED UP '</small>
Owner Fined £25

When John Newman, of South Farm-road, Worthing, was fined £25 at Brighton to-day for causing a mare to be worked while in an unfit state, it was stated that four men had to support the mare to prevent it from falling after it was removed from the shafts. Mr S. Balfour-Jones, veterinary surgeon, said that the mare was in such a deplorable condition that he ordered it to be shot on the spot.

The " Evening News "

May 2   For the delectation of readers who insist that a diary shall
Friday.   be personal. As the result of a paroxysm of coughing I
            am now encumbered with more harness than Achilles's
horse when it dragged the body of Hector round the walls of Troy.
Spent to-night whimpering with pain in a box at Ivor Novello's new
comedy, *We Proudly Present*. Supper consisted of a bowl of warm
water with some bits of dejected macaroni floating in it—why do
they cut it so short ?—and a square inch or so of escalope of pork or
perhaps venison, looking and tasting exactly like linoleum. Home
early and jotted down the following, still in pain :

"And are etceteras nothing ? " Let Ancient Pistol be told that
they may constitute the entire evening. Mr Novello will not insist
too strongly on the credibility of his plot, which is that you can
make a rip-roaring success of some highbrow nonsense with a title
like *The Mock Turtle has Two Shells* by playing it as farce.

The author, I think, was out less to write a play than to give
a witty, malicious peep behind repertory scenes. His principal
character is an easily recognisable type. Sandra Mars is your
repertory leading lady *par excellence*, the kind which can play every
West End actress off the stage and is never going to get on that
stage herself. The sort which brings to mind something written
about Bernhardt by the great Rumanian actor de Max :

"Acteur, je connus l'actrice Sarah. Je connus aussi à son
Théâtre une petite fille, qui s'appelait, par hasard, Sarah. Ai-je
détesté, ai-je aimé cette insupportable petite fille ? Je ne sais
plus. C'est si loin. J'ai vieilli. Pas elle. C'est toujours une petite
fille, une insupportable petite fille, qui a des caprices, des cris, des
crises. Ah ! les crises de cette petite fille ! "

To translate this would be to spoil its cadences. Wherefore I
refrain, but offer as glossary : *Acteur*, actor ; *Actrice*, actress ;
Théâtre, theatre ; *Caprices*, caprices ; *Crises*, crises.

Miss Ena Burrill gives a wonderful performance. Opposite her
is Phyl Perriman, the old trouper who can play anything from
Gertrude to Mrs Bouncer. Lovely playing by Miss Phyllis Monkman. Then there is Franzi Mahler, the Viennese opera-singer,
whose gusto and jargon throughout the War made life at Swiss
Cottage a joy. " But, Madame," says the highbrow producer,
"there's no part for you in my play. The *Turtle* is not a musical."
Replies the Viennese star, " But in the second act there should be a
drawing-room mit piano. Vell, at dat piano I sink five sonks. It
is qvite simple ! " I stopped counting the number of times that
Miss Irene Handl snatched the play from Miss Monkman, Miss
Monkman from Miss Burrill, and Miss Burrill from Miss Handl.

The men are not so well served. The producer who is prepared
to gamble his all on a play that shall be unusual, vital and significant—" Rather a lot for one playwright, don't you think ? " says
Miss Monkman acidly—should be a short, bespectacled, spotty,
Bloomsbury ass. The solemn idiocies of the type entirely escaping

elegant Mr Peter Graves, I found myself hoping that the second act would contain a drawing-room mit piano, silk hat, walking-stick, and a nineteen-tennish ditty about Full Moon in Half Moon Street. It didn't, alas. But it's never too late to mend.

For a man in pain I don't think this too bad. In other words, I feel that some of the plugs still spark, though the ironmongery as a whole is falling to pieces.

May 10
Saturday.   Letter to a highbrow in Rugeley, Staffordshire, who asks what are the chances for a dramatic poem whose characters are called Yesterday, To-day, To-morrow, Infinity, and Mother Time :

Who do you think is going to pay money to listen to a pow-wow between Shrove Tuesday and Ash Wednesday ?

May 12
Monday.   An exchange of letters. From Neville Cardus :

> *Sydney*
> *Australia*
> 5th *May*, 1947

My dear James,
    Blessings for the latest *Ego*. I agree with Ivor Brown (p. 228). When *you* are writing the book is as good as ever. I miss Pavia. He was not happy with *Saccharissa*—if, indeed, it was by essential Leo. But Alan Dent is back to form. The trouble with both of you, though, is that you *will* be ' funny ' and play upon words. You, with your " Cheops and Tomato Sauce," and Alan with his " rose-red city half as old as Denham." You can see them coming ; one bows before them. I'm sure that when I return to London (in June) you'll both make me feel tongue-tied and simple—and very wise. But I am not attempting root-and-branch belittlement. I merely note mannerisms.
    I have come to the conclusion that you are the best critic of acting since Lewes. Whether you are as good about a play I daren't say, because usually you agree with my own feeling about plays ; and I'm not an expert. I'd rather see a Forbes-Robertson in, say, *Mice and Men* than never mind who in something by Pirandello. When you write about the theatre I see it all—from Crummles to Jean Yonnel—Naphtha to ' modern ' lighting ! Montague hadn't the sense of the vital vulgarity of the stage. And Ivor Brown is able to write of the theatre as felicitously as about Ricardo on Rent. Best of all, you are, on all matters, stimulating, alive, honest—and a writer born.
    My *Autobiography* has been chosen by the Book Society as the " Book of the Month " for September. I hadn't the nerve to ask you again to correct proofs for me. Besides, I wanted you to come

to the book fresh. In my most depressingly self-critical moods I think it is first-rate. When I have taken two glasses of Australian Burgundy I think it is a masterpiece.

Lay in some chicken and champagne against my descent on you in June. And give my love to Gwen Chenhalls.

With deepening affection,
NEVILLE

Have replied :

Queen Alexandra Mansions
Grape Street, W.C.2

12th May, 1947

DEAR NEVILLE,

Thanks for letter. Harold Hobson picked out *Saccharissa* as the best thing in the book. Of course, it can only succeed with people who know, as Leo and I knew, the full idiocy of nineteen-year-old highbrows. But if it fails it fails. It is the perfect thing in collaboration. Neither of us could remember who wrote what, with the exception of the phrase " Looking round, Raoul was surprised to find Messalina Oldcock in tears." That was pure Leo. About " Cheops " and " rose-red Denham," I don't believe anybody in Australia would see these things after they had come, let alone when they were on the way.

It is quite possible that I am not a good judge of plays. For example, I regard the whole of the later Sean O'Casey as pretentious twaddle. On the other hand, I not only think, I *know*, that I am the best critic of acting during the last hundred years.

I am sick of the reviewers who complain of the absence in *Ego* of the ' real ' me. Well, the foregoing is as much essential me as Shylock's pound of flesh would have been the essential Antonio. And I wish them joy of it !

I am enormously looking forward to your return in June, and promise you not only chicken and champagne, but a visit to Lord's, when I will expound to you the finer points of the game. That is, if they allow bath-chairs at the ringside. I am in the middle of a long and serious illness, peevishly borne. The other day I said to Gwen Chenhalls, " Have you noticed on my face any of that strange spiritual beauty which novelists tell us is the result of prolonged physical suffering ? " Gwen said, " No, dear."

Ever,
JIMMIE

May 18   My oldest and best friend, Fred Dehn, died to-day. Have
Sunday.   sent this to the *Manchester Guardian* :

Round about the turn of the century I met a young German who possessed a quality not shared by the hundreds of other young Germans invading the great shipping houses in Manchester. This was the quality of being light in hand, engaging in personality, and witty in talk, an enormous change from the serious young men of Hamburg who came over to Manchester to worm themselves into the city's trade on a pittance on which only a German worm could live. But Frederick Edward Dehn—Fritz to his friends—was Manchester-born, being the son of the extremely cultivated and highly musical Gustav Dehn, to whom and to whose kind the Hallé Concerts owed their existence and then their pre-eminence. Dehn's mother was a woman of wide culture whose uncle had been Bismarck's doctor. The young man grew up in an atmosphere of thoroughness and discipline, absorbing all the best principles of German life yet entirely lacking that overseriousness which is the Teuton's bugbear.

We became buddies, not without causing concern to our two families, each lot of parents wanting their son to find his bosom friend in the noblest of his kind. I do not think I struck Fritz's parents in that light, and my parents thought that my friend's peremptoriness—the one German thing about him—was not in the best English tradition. But we stuck together : his home was mine, and conversely. Together we saw Bernhardt and all the great players of the day. We saved our pocket money and went abroad for holidays together.

Then came the time when, for his firm, he travelled to South America and would write me wonderful letters about adventures in Buenos Aires and Rosario, where, to impress the wealthy traders, he wore clothes tailored in Albemarle Street and drove about in a carriage and four. And while he was making a great name and profits for his firm I sat in my dingy little Manchester office sticking tickets on to samples of flannelette and awaiting his return six months later. The idea that I could make another friend never occurred to me.

I was best man at his wedding and godfather to his first-born, now the witty film and drama critic for the *Sunday Chronicle*. In an excess of pro-British fervour at the beginning of the First World War Fritz had changed his name to Fred. Well, it is not for me to say anything of Fred's married life, except that he and his adorable partner always seemed to me to live it as Darby and Joan must have lived theirs. For his family there was no sacrifice he would not make. There were times when money was made hand over fist, and it was during these periods that my old friend renewed a foible, that of making on any pretext political speeches of the die-hard, last-ditch variety. Bazaars, sales of work, were all the same to him. I remember an agricultural show at Great Harwood where he used the toast of " The Society " as the pretext for a long and impassioned protest against increased taxation on Indian dhooties.

And then came that dreadful slump in which so many good Manchester businesses went under. But Dehn made a meal of difficulties, and the greater the difficulties the nearer that meal approached a feast. Great banking houses surrendered to his personal integrity, which preceded him into their council chambers. He was a gay and witty man, and never gayer and wittier than when things were at their worst. He wore, like my brother Edward, without being conscious of wearing, Cyrano's *panache*.

Whit Monday. A week to-day this Diary will be fifteen years old. When I began it I knew that it would not be concerned with politics, because I am not a politician. No war clouds loomed, but I knew also that no diary of mine would ever be a war diary, because I am no soldier ; I am not interested in war except as a means to end tyranny and filth. I knew that it would not mirror the gay London round, because I am not in Society ; yachts and grouse moors bore me. But I did feel that Chance or Fate or perhaps something in my own make-up had enabled me to touch life at more points than falls to the lot of the average journalist. I had worked in a mill and sold millions of yards of dingy, sour-smelling calico. I had been thrown among the best spirits of Cross Street, Manchester, and was then (1932) in daily contact with the best of Fleet Street. I had spent some forty-five years looking at great acting, listening to great music, and being instructed in both by parents of unusual culture, who had made me very nearly as free of the French language as of the English. I had read every word of Balzac and Maupassant and most of Zola. I was about to make acquaintance with my hundredth golf-course, and had exhibited harness ponies at half the horse-shows in Great Britain. I had had a quarter of a century's experience of making a little money go a long way. I was ready for adventure, and at the age of fifty-five was still a young man. I had the power to work fourteen hours a day, week in week out, if necessary without holidays. I had published some twenty books. It occurred to me that the foregoing constituted a plurality of things not to be looked for in the diaries of specialists, and so I set to work. And work it has been. Four hours a day for fifteen years is the equivalent of two and a half years working all round the clock. If the motive has been vanity, so be it. If not vanity but the desire to repay some of the delight the world has given me, so be it too. Anyhow, between now and June 2 the work will be finished. No man at all can be diarising for ever, and we must be satisfied.

May 27   It is easy to misread what the eminent have written
Tuesday.   about Shakespeare's contemporaries. Lamb writes
         about Webster :

    To move a horror skilfully, to touch a soul to the quick, to lay upon fear as much as it can bear, to wean and weary a life till it is ready to drop, and then step in with mortal instruments to take its last forfeit : this only a Webster can do. Inferior geniuses . . . know not how a soul is to be moved. Their terrors want dignity, their affrightments are without decorum.

Yet nine out of ten critics will quote Lamb as saying that " Webster's terrors, etc." Whereas, of course, the charge is against Webster's inferiors.

" This only a Webster can do." In my view there is one quality in which the author of *The White Devil* exceeds Shakespeare. This is the *deadness* of dead men, which in this play is absolute, probably owing to the fact that the author was the lesser poet. Othello's " If 'twere now to die " bespeaks other-world felicity. Romeo's " Here will I set up my everlasting rest " is full of the drugged enchantment of all death-pacts. Antony's " Where souls do couch on flowers, we'll hand in hand " connotes the bliss of eternal honeymoons. One feels that if these things can be said about Death, Death cannot be as dusty as the pessimists have tried to make out. That there is a penitential limbo for the Macbeths and Richards, and a poetic one for all hired murderers, all these limbos to start the moment the breath is out of the body. Nobody in Shakespeare, except Mercutio, and he would have meant it as a joke, could have said

> I have caught
> An everlasting cold ; I have lost my voice
> Most irrecoverably.

The cutting of this play is always a perilous matter, and the present management has done well to retain that passage in which the murders of Isabella and Camillo are revealed in dumb show to Brachiano by a conjurer, Isabella being made to kiss her husband's portrait, which has been previously poisoned, and Camillo having his neck broken during a vaulting match. This dumb show is exactly in the vein of the dead hand, the Masque of Madmen, and Bosola's coffin, cords, and bell in *The Duchess of Malfi*. One suggests that the attempt to bring Webster by omission into touch with sweet and Shakespearean reason is to diminish him. Probably the best way to enjoy this gloomy dramatist is to put the greater man out of mind and concentrate on the things that are Webster's and Webster's alone. Once in the play and once only Webster comes out of his dimension and trespasses into Shakespeare's. This is when Flamineo says :

> I have a strange thing in me, to the which
> I cannot give a name, without it be
> Compassion.

This is the only touch of heartbreak in a play compact of horrors. Bobbie Helpmann said the lines finely to-night. But then his whole performance was marked by a virtuosity, a virility, and a rare quality of sheer verbal passion. I shall tell the reader whose only interest in criticism is the answer to the question " Shall I enjoy this play ? " that the answer is simple. If he gets a pleasurable shudder at lines like

> Millions are now in graves, which at last day
> Like mandrakes shall rise shrieking,

he will. If he thinks the Last Trump should sound to the strain of " Oh, What a Beautiful Mornin'," he won't.

May 28
Wednesday.
Brother Mycroft sends me a letter he has received from Stanley Rigby, with whom I went on my first walking tour exactly fifty years ago. What days those were ! I remember a broiling Bank Holiday on which, starting from Rosthwaite, the charming hamlet at the head (or is it foot ?) of Derwentwater, we conquered Great Gable, Scafell, and Scafell Pike, legging it wearily to Seascale. Wearily because of my camera, the case of which Stanley, dear, unselfish fellow, insisted on carrying, leaving me only the legs. A beautiful 'cellist, and possessed even as a boy of a dry wit, deriving from the same fount as Mr Bennet's. Here is a bit out of his letter to Mycroft :

Snatching a seat in the London-Bournemouth train the other day landed me in an encounter with a sort of Miss Flite. She was a gentle creature with a weak top storey and a passion for asking the most searching personal questions. Where was I going ? Was I married ? Would my wife be pleased to see me home ? Where did I live ? Above all, she was interested in my book—I was reading Jimmie. Was I reading for pleasure or for study ? I couldn't resist admitting it was the latter. What did *Ego* mean ? It meant " himself," I told her ; that the writer found it the most interesting subject in the world and expected the rest of us to do the same. I had reached page 164 and she wanted to know whether the picture of Tartuffe was the author. I resisted that one and showed her the frontispiece, which impressed her as *The Soul's Awakening* used to move our young generation. . . .

May 31
Saturday.
Letter to Brother Mycroft :

> *Queen Alexandra Mansions*
> *Grape Street, W.C.2*
> *May 31, 1947*

Dear Whiskers,
I was getting quite nicely through or over or around all the illnesses which end in " -itis," when yesterday I discovered that a humiliating complaint, dropsy—not to be elegantised by the fact

that Johnson was a great sufferer from and Balzac died of it—had set in. How would you feel if you suddenly discovered that your feet were podgier than Queen Victoria's, and that from what used to be the ankles upwards you were the same size and shape as Daniel Lambert? However, my two doctors—yes, two—tell me there is nothing to worry about, that I must believe them and not use up energy in worrying. So I don't.

I have always had an itch towards philosophy, the riches of old age, and I am not going to throw away those riches when I need them most. I recall Bacon's "For strength of nature in youth passeth over many excesses, which are owing a man till his age." Well, the time has come to pay the debt, and I am not going to grouse about it. Incidentally, it has given me great pleasure to read my two doctors the ending to *Of Regiment of Health*, which fits them perfectly :

" Physicians are some of them so pleasing and conformable to the humour of the patient, as they press not the true cure of the disease ; and some other are so regular in proceeding according to art for the disease, as they respect not sufficiently the condition of the patient. Take one of a middle temper ; or if it may not be found in one man, combine two of either sort ; and forget not to call as well the best acquainted with your body, as the best reputed of for his faculty."

One thing, my dear Whiskers, that irks me is the extraordinary combination of fatigue and insomnia. Owing to the pain all my body cries out for sleep, and I just can't catch it—probably something to do with the asthma. Fortunately, however, my flat faces two ways, so that I put an extremely comfortable, high-backed, well-pillowed chair in the windows of two rooms with different aspects. Both windows have ledges which will take a cushion. I go to what I call bed at eleven o'clock, sit in the dark, and get amusement out of Holborn's cats and other late *noceurs*. Quite frequently, round about four, I put my head on the cushion and drop off for a couple of hours, after which there is the delight of seeing Holborn wake up. To get the best of this entertainment I go into the room which has a view of a lot of little shops, including a tyre-dealer's, and it is fun to watch dust-carts jostling Rolls-Royces for priority. And when the doctor comes in the morning and asks what sort of night I have had, I say, " Splendid ! "

I can't read new books because of the fatigue, but I can still quote Micawber in chunks. I don't play the gramophone much, as I find the noise hurts, but I can sit and nurse the records and play them in my head. When friends come round I like them to be more or less silent, while I recall the witty things they have said in the past. I have an immense amount to be thankful for, and never cease marvelling that a contentious and truculent fellow like me can have acquired, without angling for it, so much that gives old age its value. To-day I have had telephone messages from Lilian

Braithwaite and Helen Haye ; Abel of the Ivy sent me a dozen peaches ; Gwen Chenhalls's kindness is not to be believed ; my room is almost as full of flowers as Sarah Bernhardt's *loge* on a first-night. I could have cars here every hour of the day, but the doctors say I am not strong enough to go for drives. So I sit and muse and am thankful that, so far as I can perceive, my intellectual vigour has not abated. It shows itself best in this, I think—the realisation that it is not within the power of present pain to lay a finger on past ecstasy. I thank God that He has made this world more perdurable than any but a poet's view of it—that a thousand poets could fall off a mountain without doing anything except add to its grandeur. What does it matter if my spirits droop a little now and then so long as the butcher-boy can whistle, or how many aches and pains I groan under so long as the cherry blossoms in the Park ?

So don't worry about me. I have had enough happiness and excitement and joy of work to fill ten lifetimes. Don't come up to London to see me ; so long as you stay put I shall feel that " There's sap in't yet."

My best love to yourself, Lizzie, and Mary.

Ever,

JIMMIE

June 1
Sunday.
There was a time when I planned to end this Diary on my seventieth birthday—a project no longer feasible. I think I should have finished with something like this :

I thank Thee, God, for all the things life has meant to me. For the seaside and cricket on the sands which made up my childhood. For the golf-courses and show-yards of my youth and middle age. For the books, acting, and music, recollection of which makes my old age rich and enviable. For the stone walls of Derbyshire, the dales of Yorkshire, Welsh mountains, and English lakes. For fun, good talk, and enjoyment of the minds of others. For Brother Edward's wit and courage. For Brother Harry, who has taught me what unselfishness may be. For Leo Pavia. For those great spirits —Montague, Monkhouse, Mair. For the loyalty and devotion of my friends everywhere. For the humble friends and helpers who have made my work possible. For any talent I may have possessed, and the gift of energy to prosecute it. For never having utterly lost the sense of the glory and the freshness of a dream. For never having for one instant believed that there hath pass'd away a glory from the earth. For the power of being two persons.

I loved the garish day, and, spite of fears,
Pride ruled my will : remember not past years.

June 2
Monday.
On the first page of *Ego* there is a cutting from an evening paper which, first with the news, was overjoyed to tell its readers how James Agate, " described as a dramatic critic," at some police-court in Essex had been committed to prison

for a debt of twenty pounds. Well, history repeats itself; or at least mine does. Received this morning a curt communication from the Revenue saying that unless I find £940 within a week everything in my flat except the bed I lie on will be taken away. The fact that since the War, despite reduced income and increased tax, I have paid off some £6000 of arrears appears not to weigh with these gentry, who do not rise above a twopenny bus-ride view of existence. And why should they? It takes one Balzac to write, and another to comprehend, " La dette est une œuvre d'imagination que les créanciers ne comprennent jamais." It would be absurd to expect tax-collectors to think on these levels. Or on any level. One of these paper-cuffed, inky-fingered gentry said to me the other day, " Mr Agate, with all the money you have made you ought to leave nine rows of houses." I said, " Mr Inspector, with all the money I have spent I am going to leave nine volumes of *Ego*." But it was lost on him, just as the Revenue threat is lost on me. I am not unduly perturbed because in three months' time they are going to demand another £940, plus £300 for Amusement Tax or something. I am just not worrying. Something has always turned up, and something will turn up now. I have lived for so long on the edge of so many precipices that for me *terra firma* has become *terra incognita*. In the meantime I cannot think of a better note on which to end my Diary. " The deadest deaths are the best," said old Montaigne, and I hold the same about quick endings. So, with a friendly nod to the readers who have kept me company during the last fifteen years, I set about my final sentences. As I pen them I see Brother Edward rubbing his long nose as though wondering how a man who has written so much can have said so little. While over my shoulder comes the voice of Leo, saying, " Tell me, James; will your *Ego* 9 be Choral?"

Footnote to " Ego 9 "

by

Alan Dent

James had definitely and finally decided to make this volume the last of the *Ego* series. We therefore have here the strange and, I should think, unprecedented spectacle of a man coming to the virtual conclusion of his autobiographical diary at the moment when Death's hand—without his knowing it—was upon him. He terminated his autobiography even as his life was ending.

The end came suddenly, just before eleven o'clock on the evening of Friday, June the 6th. He had a heart-attack, collapsed, and died beside his bed. I last set eyes on him on the previous Monday evening, when I called to see him and found him sitting up in his study, in some pain and discomfort, yet zealously correcting the early galley proofs of this same volume. He was by no means pessimistic, and did not mention death.

Exactly a fortnight earlier there had been a very remarkable incident in the lives of both of us. Newspapers have to be unsentimental, and to envisage possibilities of the dissolution of any and every celebrity. One of my editors had asked me to prepare an obituary notice of James. In spite of his being so obviously ill, it had never occurred to me that he was going to die in my own lifetime, and I was therefore a shade alarmed at the request. I telephoned him to ask how he was, and he insisted on my breaking a previous appointment and lunching with him. " The Ivy at one, and not a minute later. I have to see a film at two," he said. I was in his favourite restaurant at one o'clock sharp, and sitting at the corner table on the right as one enters. No James ! So there and then, alone at the table, and with most of the theatrical celebrities that matter in full view, I took out my tablets, and then and there, and full of the subject, wrote my obituary of James—straight on to the page, as is my wont, modelling each sentence in my mind before committing it to writing.

This article appeared, eventually, in *The Manchester Guardian* on the Monday after James's death. I was setting down the last words of its last sentence—this is plain and simple truth—when he looked round the door and, grey of face but smiling, said, with a flash of his uncanny percipiency, " Fifty minutes late, I know, but it takes me a time to dress. What are you writing there, Jock—*my obituary, I suppose* ? " I did not deny the fact, but put my papers away. We ordered food and drink, and when I was beginning my soup he startled me by saying, " Come, boy—as one journalist to another— let me read what you really think of me ! " I think anyone in my shoes must have found this an agitating experience—indeed, a distressing one. With his great horror of death he might there and then have had his fatal heart-seizure. He might, at the least, have taken violent exception. I therefore hesitated—but he very firmly insisted. I thereupon gave him the article to read and continued to eat my soup, though with a trembling hand.

Never have I felt so foolishly like James Boswell, and never in his life did James so resemble Dr Johnson. He read the piece through with a kind of beaming solemnity, paused only when he came to the list of his enthusiasms to entreat me—yes, entreat me—to make mention of " golf," and then handed me back my manuscript with a single observation : " I'm proud, Jock, to have that written about me, and you've written it well ! " Thereupon he changed the subject, and never again throughout the hurried luncheon—or in the remaining three weeks—made any mention of the following obituary, which I wrote in those circumstances, which he read in those circumstances, and which duly appeared in that great newspaper to which, to our pride, we have both belonged :

" Death hath this also, that it openeth the gate to good fame and extinguisheth envy. *Extinctus amabitur idem.*" (How James would have chuckled over an appreciation that begins with a quotation involving both Bacon and Horace !)

Now that he is dead, few will deny that he was the leading dramatic critic of our time. He was the chief of our craft, and a warrior chief, and a working chief right up to the end. As a critic he was cogent, never smooth, often belligerent, often capricious too, but always forthright, and sound and consistent in his standards ; angrily impatient of the slipshod, the gimcrack, the pretentious, full of words and notions and allusions and audacities, full of sound and fury too, but always signifying something. And he used everything he had to write about or around—even the most trivial and unpromising play, book, film, or essay-topic—as an occasion for spilling the words and ideas with which his large mind so generously overflowed.

For fifteen years, which seemed like five, I served my apprenticeship with him in the craft of criticism, and never once in that time did I see him, when well and working, ' dry up ' for lack of anything to say. He was extravagant in all ways, and did not pretend to be anything else. He had a large amount of that self-knowledge which the Greeks called ultimate wisdom. He loved praise even more than most of us do, and would let you call him all the things he was—witty, immensely readable, discriminating, irresistible, provocative, Pepysian, Johnsonian, Hazlittean, and even Shavian—till the sun went down (or rose) and the wine-bottle was empty. But if any commentator, or any mere flatterer, praised his writing style the critic in him invariably ousted the inordinate vanity. His prose was lively and prickly, but not that of a great stylist. He knew this and admitted it honestly. He slaved all his life to express himself in a style comparable to that of his lofty models and ideals—Hazlitt, C. E. Montague, and the critic Shaw. He was genuinely satisfied with his writing only when it seemed to him a passable approximation to any one of these.

In his later life he turned to diary-making—writing, naturally, far more loosely than in his criticism—and produced nine big volumes of the celebrated autobiography *Ego*—a kind of huge vat to catch all that overflow of the verbal energy that was in him or which he occasioned in his followers, friends, and enemies. Like Falstaff in more ways than one, he was not only witty in himself, but the direct occasion of wit in his inferiors.

In his person as in his work he could be overbearing, browbeating, blunt, and then " incalculably he could do the nicest things," as some one once phrased it to me in a letter. In my secretarial time I have called him many things to his face—a monster, a ton of saturated self, a " bletherin' blusterin' blellum " (just to tease and just to be Scots), but he easily forgave and was easy to forgive. He had, beside true and unexpected kindness, a formidable amount of charm (a valuable gift even when one trades on it), was full of delightful surprises, and was never a bore (except about personal health, a subject on which Dr Johnson himself was probably a bore).

In fine, we are mourning a great character, undeniably a great dramatic critic, and possibly a great diarist. Only time can determine his status in the last faculty. How he would have beamed at my triple and considered application of the word ' great '—a word he wisely taught me to use with the most critical discretion !

He was at his consummate best—either writing or talking—on the subject of great acting, and was almost unique in his profession in having seen some ! The ruling passions of his life were for the stage, for informed and witty conversation, for the language and literature of France, for golf and Hackney ponies, and for all that goes with urbane living. He loved life dearly, and " the vasty hall of death " can seldom have had a more unwilling visitant.

NOTES ON PERSONS IN *THE LATER EGO*

The reader of this volume will have found that Agate generally introduces with great skill the host of persons, alive or dead, whom he has occasion to mention. He either tags them as they come or places them by context. But since this book contains only the last two installments of the diary, some persons met in earlier volumes required identification here. An entry has accordingly been made whenever the first mention of a name in either *Ego 8* or *Ego 9* did not sufficiently identify it. Dates have been added where it seemed useful to indicate the span of a person's activity, or the fact that Agate is not speaking of a contemporary. A special effort has been made to distinguish between pairs of names—Arnold and Clifford Bax, Lucien and Sacha Guitry— and to indicate family relationships. If the information given occasionally seems needless, its presence may be generally ascribed to the desire for clarity: a comment or witticism gains in force when the reader knows the background or profession of the person speaking or spoken of. Again, certain names in the diary are incompletely given: is the Mrs. Campbell on page 234 of *Ego 8* Mrs. Patrick Campbell? Of all the possible Moores, who is the one mentioned on page 392 of *Ego 9*? In answering these or kindred questions, I have received the generous help of two learned Agatians, Mr. Alan Dent and Mr. Roland Gelatt, to whom I here express my thanks. Names outside the specified categories, and not listed here for reasons other than the fallibility of the annotator, will be found in great works of drama and fiction, and chiefly in the novels of Dickens.

J.B.

GLOSSARY

Campbell, Mrs. Patrick. English actress, creator of Shaw and Pinero parts. Died 1940.

Charlot. French nickname of Charlie Chaplin, sometimes used by Agate.

Charlot, André. Parisian Theatre manager, in England since 1912, producer of Charlot's revues.

Chenhalls, Gwen. Widow of Alfred Chenhalls, accountant killed in wartime aircrash with the actor Leslie Howard.

Christiansen, Arthur. Editor of the *Daily Express*.

Clements, John. English Shakespearean and film actor, as well as manager and producer.

Clunes, Alec. English Shakespearean actor, manager and producer; associated with Old Vic; now Director of London Arts Theatre Club.

Cochran, Sir C. B. English theatre manager and producer. Died 1951.

Cohen, Harriet. English pianist and writer on music.

Cooper, Sir Alfred Duff. English statesman and author, biographer of Talleyrand.

Cooper, Gladys. English actress and film star, author of *Gladys Cooper, 1931,* her memoirs.

DARWIN, BERNARD. English critic, writer on literature and sports, especially golf.

Daudet, Alphonse (1840–1897). French dramatist and novelist.

Daudet, Léon (1867–1942). Son of the preceding; journalist, critic, and leader of royalist *Action Française.*

Day, Frances. English actress and vocalist, film star and friend of Agate's.

Dehn family. Old Manchester friends of Agate family. See *Ego 1,* pp. 78–79.

De Leon, Jack. Panamanian-English theatre manager, founder of the Q Theatre for new plays.

Dent, Alan. See "Jock."

Dyall, Franklin. Actor and producer contemporary with Shaw's drama-reviewing days. Died 1950.

EARP, THOMAS W. English antiquarian and art critic, biographer of Van Gogh.

Eckersley, Roger. English civil servant. Chief censor of BBC since 1940.

Ego. Agate's favorite hackney horse.

FARJEON, HERBERT. English playwright and dramatic critic, brother of Eleanor and Jefferson Farjeon. Died 1945.

Field, Sid. English music-hall comedian. Died 1950.

Fitzgerald, Edward (p. 209; p. 350) (1809–1883). English poet and critic, translator of Omar Khayyam.

Fogerty, Elsie. Teacher of acting. Died 1945.

Forster, John (1812–1876). Dickens' friend and first biographer. Also a dramatic critic.

Frith, W. P. (1819–1909). English genre painter.

Fry, C. B. Famous English cricketer and writer on sports; friend of Agate's.

Fry, Christopher. English poet and playwright, friend of Agate's.

"G.", MR. = John Gielgud. English Shakespearean actor.

García family. Famous musicians of 19th and 20th centuries. For relationships and careers, see p. 132.

Gautier, Théophile (1811–1872). French poet, novelist and critic.

Gemmell, Alexander. Hackney-pony exhibitor and judge.

Gillett, Eric. English writer and lecturer.

Gingold, Hermione. English comedienne.

Gosse, Sir Edmund (1849–1928). Eminent English critic. See Introduction to this book.

Grace, W. G. (1848–1915). Famous long-bearded English cricketer. *See* pp. 300–1.

Graham, Winifred (Mrs. Theodore Cory). English novelist and authority on Mormonism.

Grantham, Wilfrid. Husband of Agate's sister May; actor, producer and playwright.

Gray, Cecil. English musicologist and critic.

Green, Harry. American comedian.

Griffith, Tibby (Hubert). English playwright and critic of dance and drama for the *Sunday Graphic*.

Guitry, Lucien (1860–1925). French actor of the then "new" theatre.

Guitry, Sacha (b. 1885). Son of preceding; actor, dramatist, film producer.

HALLÉ, SIR CHARLES (1819–1895). Born Karl Halle, pianist who lived in France, then in England, where he founded at Manchester the present Hallé Orchestra.

Hambourg, Mark. Russian-English pianist, composer and author of memoirs. Friend of Agate's.

Hamilton, Hamish. British publisher.

Hammond, Kay. English comedienne, friend of Agate's.

Hardwicke, Sir Cedric. English actor on stage and screen, friend of Agate's.

Hardwicke, Lady. Wife of the preceding.

Harmsworth, Alfred, Viscount Northcliffe (1865–1922). Newspaper potentate, owner of *Daily Mail,* etc.

Harrap, George. English publisher of most of the *Ego* volumes.

Haye, Helen. English actress and friend of Agate's.

Helme, Dicky (Ernest), Colonel. Friend of Agate's. Authority on nineteenth-century opera. Died 1949.

Henley, H. J. (1882–1937). English writer on sports, critic of music and plays for *Daily Mail*.

Heredia, José Maria de (1842–1905). French poet of Parnassian school, chiefly a sonneteer.

Hirst, George. English cricketer.

Hobbs, Jack. English cricketer.

Holmes, Richard. Friend of Agate's and of Monty Shearman's.

Holt, Harold. English concert manager and impresario.

Horniman, Miss A. E. (1860–1937). Suffragette and founder of theatres in

London, Manchester and Dublin (Abbey Theatre). See *Ego 1*, pp. 60–3.
Horsnell, Horace. English novelist, drama critic for *Tatler*. Died 1949.

IDEN, ROSALIND. English actress of Shakespearean roles; wife of Donald Wolfit.

Irving, Sir Henry (1838–1905). Famous Shakespearean actor-manager.

Irving, H. B. (1870–1919). Son of the preceding, actor too, and manager of the Savoy Theatre until his death.

JACOBS, W. W. English writer of humorous sea tales, ghost stories, etc. Died 1943.

Janin, Jules (1804–1874). French dramatic critic, whose collected reviews fill six volumes.

Jerrold, Douglas. English novelist, political writer and publisher.

Jerrold, Mary. Cousin of the preceding, actress on stage and film.

Joad, C. E. M. English philosopher, critic and radio chairman of discussion programs.

Jock = Alan Dent, Agate's one-time secretary, collaborator and friend. Now dramatic critic of London *News-Chronicle* and film critic of *Illustrated London News*.

Jowett, Benjamin (1817–1893). Famous English theologian, classical scholar, translator of Plato and master of Balliol College.

KEAN, CHARLES (1811–1868). English actor and manager, son of Edmund Kean.

Kean, Edmund (1787–1833). Great tragedian who died of intemperance; subject of essays by Hazlitt and Leigh Hunt.

Kendall, Henry. English light comedian.

Kingsmill, Hugh (1889–1948). English journalist and popular biographer.

LEGOUVÉ, ERNEST (1807–1903). French author of plays and memoirs, co-author with Scribe of *Adrienne Lecouvreur*.

Leighton, Frederick, Baron (1830–1896). Painter of historical and mythological scenes. President of the Royal Academy.

Leo = Leo Pavia, musician, dilettante, part-time secretary and permanent guest of Agate's.

Lewes, George Henry (1817–1878). English actor, critic and philosophical writer, "husband" of George Eliot.

Lewis, D. B. Wyndham. English critic and satirist, biographer of Villon and Boswell. No connection with American-born painter and satirist Wyndham Lewis.

Lishman, Tom. English pianist.

Littré, Emile (1801–1881). French positivist and lexicographer, whose name is equivalent to the American "Webster."

Lockwood, Margaret. English stage and film actress.

Loti, Pierre. Julien Viaud (1850–1923). French novelist, author of *Iceland Fisherman*.

Lucas, E. V. (1868–1938). English essayist, contributor to *Punch* and the *Sunday Times;* writer of travel books and bibliographer of Charles Lamb.

Lustgarten, Edgar. English lawyer, writer of crime stories, etc., friend of Agate's.

Lynd, Robert (1879–1949). Irish journalist and critic, literary editor of the *News-Chronicle,* "Y.Y." of *The New Statesman.*

Lyttelton, George. Brother of Viscount Cobham, former master at Eton, close friend of Agate's.

MACRAE, ARTHUR. English playwright, author of *Under the Counter,* etc.

Machell, Roger. Publishing partner of Hamish Hamilton.

Mair, George. Writer on *Manchester Guardian* before First World War.

Marquis, The (p. 263) = Count Donatien de Sade (1740–1814). Known as Marquis. French novelist, first delineator of sadism.

Marsh, Sir Edward. British civil servant, author and translator, president of Contemporary Art Society.

Mathew, George Felton. English editor and writer on architecture, close friend of Agate's. See *Ego 1, passim.*

Matthews, Denis. English pianist.

Maugham, Willie = W. Somerset Maugham, English novelist and playwright.

Max = Sir Max Beerbohm. English essayist and dramatic critic, author of *Zuleika Dobson, The Happy Hypocrite,* etc.

Melford, Austin. English playwright, actor and producer.

Messel, Oliver. English stage designer.

Mills, John. English actor, in films since 1932.

Mitford, Mary Russell (1787–1855). English essayist, author of *Our Village.*

Monkhouse, Allan (1858–1936). English critic, novelist and playwright, on staff of *Manchester Guardian.*

Montague, C. E. (1867–1928). English dramatic critic and novelist, on staff of *Manchester Guardian.*

Moore, Thomas. (p. 392) (1779–1852). Irish poet, musician and wit, biographer of Byron.

Morley, Henry (1822–1894). English critic, anthologist and editor.

Morley, John, Viscount (1838–1923). English historian and Liberal statesman.

Mortimer, Raymond. English critic, former literary editor of *New Statesman and Nation,* now critic for the *Sunday Times.*

Morton, J. B. English critic and miscellaneous writer; "Beachcomber" of *Daily Express.*

Moult, Thomas. English critic of music and drama, writer on *Manchester Guardian.*

Munnings, Sir Alfred. British painter, President of Royal Academy since 1944.

NEVEU, GINETTE. French violinist, killed in airplane crash in 1949.

Newman, Ernest. Music critic of the *Sunday Times,* biographer of Wagner.

Newman, Norman. One of Agate's physicians.

"Norman Neruda" = Lady Hallé (1839–1911). Famous woman violinist, daughter of Josef Neruda, widow of Ludwig Norman, became wife of Sir Charles Hallé [*q.v.*] in 1888.

Novello, Ivor. English playwright, actor and film star, as well as composer and theatre manager.

OLLENDORFF (PAUL). Paris publisher of language texts and grammars, synonym for the style of such books.

Oxford, Lady. Margot Asquith, Countess of Oxford and Asquith, widow of the Liberal Prime Minister, Herbert Asquith (1852–1928), first Earl of the name.

"PALINURUS." Cyril Connolly, British essayist and editor, author of *Enemies of Promise, The Unquiet Grave,* etc.

Page, Peter = Philip Page. Former drama critic, friend of Agate's.

Pavia. See "Leo."

Percy, S. Esmé. English actor and producer, pupil of Sarah Bernhardt, friend of Agate's.

Pomeroy, Jay. Russian-English musical director and impresario.

Portman, Eric. English stage and film actor.

Potter, Gillie. Music-hall and radio comedian.

"Q" = Sir Arthur Quiller-Couch (1863–1944). English critic, novelist and teacher. Compiler of *Oxford Book of English Verse.*

RANJI = Prince Kumar Shri Ranjitsinhji. Famous Hindu cricketer and theorist of the game.

Richards, George. Art connoisseur, close friend of Agate's.

Richardson, Sir Ralph. English actor of Ibsen, Chekhov and Shakespeare.

Richardson, Tom. English cricketer of giant stature.

Ricketts, Betty (Mrs. Arthur). Née Betty Wertheimer, close friend of Agate's.

Robey, George. Famous music-hall comedian and producer.

Robey, Blanche. Wife of the preceding, both friends of Agate's.

Ros, Amanda (M'Kittrick). Untutored woman writer, whose novels are enjoyed as unwitting parodies of the grandiloquent. Thomas Beer said of her *Irene Iddesleigh,* "Her style has the final merit of concealing thought and plot."

Ross, Robert. Friend and correspondent of Oscar Wilde, one of the very few who remained loyal and helpful to the end.

Rouse, Wilfred. Friend of Agate's, accompanied him on his last holiday in France.

Rubinstein, Stanley. Agate's friend and man of business; lawyer by profession.

Rubinstein, Vera. Wife of the preceding.

Russell, Leonard. Literary editor of the *Sunday Times;* edits *The Saturday Book* annual.

"saki" = H. H. Munro (1870–1916). English satirist and short-story writer.

St. Helier, Ivy. English actress and vocalist.

Santley, Sir Charles (1834–1922). English baritone, pupil of García.

Sargent, Sir Malcolm. English orchestra conductor; leader of Hallé Orchestra since 1939.

Scott, C. P. (1846–1932). Reorganizer and editor of the *Manchester Guardian* from 1872 to 1929.

Shearman, Monty (Montague) (1846–1932). English barrister, art patron and dilettante. Close friend of Agate's.

Shephard, Firth. English playwright and producing manager. Died 1949.

Shepley, Michael. English actor and film star.

Short, Ernest. Australian writer and publisher in London, student of the fine arts, railroading and the theatre.

Slaughter, Tod (N. Carter). Actor and manager, friend of Agate's.

Smith, Sir Charles. English film actor and cricketer.

Squire, Sir John. English critic, poet and editor.

Sterling, Sir Louis. British company director.

Sullivan, Larry (Francis L.). English stage and film actor, friend of Agate's.

Sutro, John. Film director.

tatham, eddie. Wine merchant and friend of Agate's.

Thatcher, Heather. English actress.

Throup, Albert. Trainer and manager at Agate's stables at Sutton Coldfield, near Birmingham.

Tooke, John Horne (1736–1812). English philologist and radical pamphleteer.

ustinov, peter. English actor and playwright, of French and Russian parentage, author of *House of Regrets* and other plays. In films since 1940.

van thal, herbert. London publisher.

Viardot, Pauline, née García (1821–1910). Famous singer, sister of Malibran. *See* García Family.

walbrook, anton. Austrian-English actor. In films since 1931.

Walkley, A. B. (1855–1926). Drama critic of the London *Times* from 1902 until his death.

Warner, Sir Pelham ("Plum"). English cricketer and sports writer, editor of *The Cricketer.*

Wood, Sir Henry (1869–1944). English orchestra conductor; founder of Queen's Hall Promenade Concerts.

Index

A

A *Londres, naguère*, 486
Achurch, Janet, 26, 55–56
Ackland, Rodney, 309, 390
Actors, 26–27, 76, 110, 119, 172, 381, 359, 580
Actors, Actresses, and Goldfish, 311
Addled Art, 425
Aesthetic Adventure, The, 22
After October, 309
Agate, Ann, 148, 151, 152, 153, 155, 157, 158
Agate, Charles Gustave ("Brother Mycroft"), 7, 74, 230, 265, 278, 326, 336, 345, 430, 460, 461–462, 572, 594–596
Agate, Charles James, 461–462
Agate, Edward, 23, 181, 221, 233, 330, 331, 332, 341, 460, 461, 522, 576, 596, 597
Agate, Eulalie Julia, 461
Agate, Harry B., 148, 151, 152, 153, 155–156, 157, 158, 191, 335, 336–338, 460, 461, 462, 596
Agate, James, death of, 598
Agate, Lizzie (Mrs. Gustave Agate), 596
Agate, Mary, (daughter of Charles Gustave Agate), 596
Agate, May, 47, 158, 277–278, 301, 302, 370, 462, 523
Agate, Sydney, 460, 461
Aiken, Conrad, 427
Ainley, Henry, 25, 244–245
Albani, Dame Emma, 390, 423–424
Alexander, Lady, 216, 500
Alexander, Sir George, 457
All Night at Mr. Stanyhurst's, 356
Allegory of "Othello", An, 318
Also Sprach Zarathustra, 61
Ame en Peine, L', 119
American Language, The, 348
Anatomy of Courage, 35
And Even Now, 267
Anderson, Mary, 374–375
Andreyev, Leonid, 77
Androcles and the Lion, 54, 258

Antony and Cleopatra, 48, 310, 558, 560, 567
Appointment in Samarra, 59
Archer, William, 28, 109, 374, 488, 509
Ardrey, Robert, 78
Arlésienne Suite, L', 86
Arletty, 328, 329
Arnold, Julian B., 79–80
Arnold, Matthew, 79–80, 581, 584
Arnold, W. T., 129, 156–157
Around Cinemas, 64, 273, 335, 345, 346, 347, 357, 365, 367, 372, 380, 435, 496, 514
Around Theatres, 64, 578
Arthur, Jean, 293
Artist's Model, An, 119
Asche, Oscar, 134, 145
Ashbee, Henry Spencer, 543–547
Ashcroft, Peggy, 92, 159–160, 207
Asquith, Anthony, 259–260
Asquith, Herbert, 97
Assommoir, L', 320
Atkins, Robert, 25, 560
Atom Bomb, 213
Attlee, Clement R., 214–215
Auchmountain Glen, 92
Auprès de ma Blonde, 472
Austen, Jane, 21, 34, 36, 41, 432
Austin, Alfred, 456
Away from it All, 503

B

Babes on Broadway, 366
Bacall, Lauren, 133
Back to Methuselah, 54
Bacon, Francis, 286–291, 304, 317–318, 360–361
Baiser de la Fée, 60
Ballet criticism, 172, 401
Balzac, 44, 204, 230, 331, 393–394, 406
Bankhead, Tallulah, 107, 108
Bannerman, Margaret, 481, 482
Banville, Théodore de, 257–258, 266, 267
Bard, Wilkie, 342
Baring, Maurice, 9–10, 47, 256, 258, 266, 292, 293, 311, 358, 550, 553
Barrault, Jean-Louis, 296

H

Wright Morris - real losses
Byron   vol. 5